The Literary Essays
of
THOMAS MERTON

By Thomas Merton

THE ASIAN JOURNAL

COLLECTED POEMS

EIGHTEEN POEMS

GANDHI ON NON-VIOLENCE

THE GEOGRAPHY OF LOGRAIRE

THE LITERARY ESSAYS

MY ARGUMENT WITH THE GESTAPO

NEW SEEDS OF CONTEMPLATION

RAIDS ON THE UNSPEAKABLE

SEEDS OF CONTEMPLATION

SELECTED POEMS

THE WAY OF CHUANG TZU

THE WISDOM OF THE DESERT

THOMAS MERTON IN ALASKA

ZEN AND THE BIRDS OF APPETITE

About Thomas Merton

WORDS AND SILENCE: ON THE POETRY OF THOMAS MERTON
by Sister Thérèse Lentfoehr

Published by
New Directions

The
Literary
Essays
of
THOMAS
MERTON

EDITED BY

BROTHER PATRICK HART

A New Directions Book

Manufactured in the United States of America
New Directions books are printed on acid-free paper.
First published clothbound by New Directions in 1981 and as New Directions Paperbook 587 in 1985
Published simultaneously in Canada by Penguin Books Limited Canada

Library of Congress Cataloging in Publication Data
Merton, Thomas, 1915–1968.
   The literary essays of Thomas Merton.
   (A New Directions Book)
   1. Literature, Modern—History and criticism—
Collected works. I. Hart, Patrick. II. Title.
PN 710.M338 1984   809'.03   84–20561
ISBN 0-8112-0931-8 (pbk.)

New Directions Books are published for James Laughlin
by New Directions Publishing Corporation,
80 Eighth Avenue, New York 10011

SECOND PRINTING

CONTENTS

ACKNOWLEDGMENTS

Grateful acknowledgment is made to the editors and publishers of the following journals and magazines where some of these essays and reviews first appeared, but in considerably different form: *The American Benedictine Review, American Pax, The Catholic Worker, The Catholic World, Charlatan, The Columbia Review, Commonweal, Continuum, The Critic, Jubilee, Katallagete, Motive, New Lazarus Review, The New York Herald Tribune Book Review, The New York Times Book Review, Saturday Review, The Sewanee Review, Thought, Unicorn Journal,* and *Worship*.

The publisher and editor would also like to extend grateful acknowledgment to all those who gave permission to reprint from previously published sources:

The following essays are reprinted by permission of Farrar, Straus and Giroux, Inc.: "The Pasternak Affair" from *Disputed Questions* by Thomas Merton (Copyright © 1953, 1959, 1960 by The Abbey of Our Lady of Gethsemani); "Peace and Revolution: A Footnote from *Ulysses*" and "The Answer of Minerva," from *The Nonviolent Alternative* by Thomas Merton (Copyright © 1971, 1980 by the Trustees of the Merton Legacy Trust); "The Legend of Tucker Caliban" from *Seeds of Destruction* by Thomas Merton (Copyright © 1961, 1962, 1963, 1964 by The Abbey of Gethsemani).

"Baptism in the Forest: Wisdom and Initiation in William Faulkner" was originally used as an introduction to *Mansions of the Spirit*, ed. George A. Panichas (Copyright © 1967 by the University of Maryland) published by Hawthorn Books; it is reprinted here by permission of Elsevier/Nelson Books.

"J. F. Powers—*Morte D'Urban:* Two Celebrations" was originally published in *J. F. Powers,* compiled by Fallon Evans and published by Herder Book Company; it is reprinted here by permission of Tan Books and Publishers, Inc.

"Albert Camus' *The Plague:* Introduction and Commentary" by Thomas Merton (Copyright © 1968 by The Seabury Press, Inc.) is reprinted by permission of The Seabury Press, Inc.

"Camus and the Church" is reprinted by permission of Macmillan Publishing Co., Inc., from *A Penny a Copy,* ed. by Thomas C. Cornell and James H. Forest (Copyright © 1968 by Macmillan Publishing Co., Inc.).

"Agnes Addison—Love of Change for Its Own Sake," "William Nelson—John Skelton, Scholar, Poet, and Satirist," "E. M. W. Tillyard and C. S. Lewis—A Spirited Debate on Poetry," "G. Wilson Knight—That Old Dilemma of Good and Evil," and "William York Tindall—D. H. Lawrence: Who Saw Himself as a Messiah" first appeared as book reviews in *The New York Times* (© 1939, 1940 by The New York Times Company) and are reprinted by permission.

Quotations from *Collected Poems* by Edwin Muir (Copyright © 1960 by Willa Muir) in Merton's essay on Muir are reprinted by permission of Oxford University Press, Inc.

Excerpts from *Dr. Zhivago* by Boris Pasternak, translated by Max Hayward and Manya Harari (Copyright © 1958 by Pantheon Books, Inc.), as quoted in "The Pasternak Affair," are reprinted by permission of the publisher.

Quotations from *All: The Collected Short Poems, 1956–1964* by Louis Zukofsky (Copyright © 1966 by Louis Zukofsky), cited in "Louis Zukofsky—The Paradise Ear," are reprinted by permission of W. W. Norton & Company, Inc.

The excerpts from William Faulkner's *The Sound and the Fury* (Copyright 1929; renewed 1957 by William Faulkner) and *The Wild Palms* (Copyright 1939; renewed 1967 by Mrs. William Faulkner and Mrs. Paul D. Summers), quoted in Merton's talks on Faulkner, are reprinted by permission of Random House, Inc.

Many persons have been helpful with suggestions and encouragement during the progress of this work, notably James Laughlin of New Directions, Naomi Burton Stone and Tommie O'Callaghan, Trustees of the Merton Legacy Trust. Others have provided valuable assistance and helpful advice: Abbot Timothy Kelly, Monsignor William Shannon, Fathers Thomas Nelson, Paul E. Dinter, Gerald Twomey, and George Kilcourse, Brothers Columban (Richard) Weber and Daniel Carrere, James Y. Holloway, Robert Lax, Michael Higgins, Victor A. Kramer, Robert E. Daggy, Anne McCormick, Deba P. Patnaik, Else Abrecht-Carrié, Peggy Fox, Peter Glassgold, Marquita Breit, and Michael Mott. To these, and all whom I may have omitted, my deepest gratitude.

Finally, I wish to express my appreciation to The Trustees of the Merton Legacy Trust for permission to include four hitherto unpublished essays: Thomas Merton's critique of Rolf Hochhuth's play *The Deputy*, "Why Alienation Is for Everybody," a short piece on the poetry of Fernando Pessoa, as well as Merton's Master of Arts thesis, "Nature and Art in William Blake."

INTRODUCTION

Following the death of Thomas Merton by accidental electrocution in Bangkok over a decade ago, there has been an enormous upsurge of interest in his life and writings. His own early books are being reissued in new editions, and collections of his essays and letters are beginning to appear both in America and abroad. However, Merton's true stature as a literary critic has yet to be fully appreciated. One reason for this is perhaps due to the fact that a collection of his distinctly literary and critical essays has not up to this time been collected and published in book form. Written for the most part during the last years of his life, these essays were first published in a variety of journals, some well-known, others much less well-known—all nearly inaccessible now. To these there has been added a number of hitherto unpublished pieces. With the publication of this volume it is hoped that a deeper appreciation of Merton's literary talent and critical judgment may be advanced.

Born of artist parents (an American mother and a New Zealander father) in southern France near the Spanish border on January 31, 1915, Merton's early education in France, England, and America was often interrupted by travel with his father after his mother's death. Merton's first inclinations to a literary career can be traced to his juvenile novels while attending the lycée in France and later in his school days at Oakham in Rutland, England, when in 1931 he became editor of the school magazine, *The Oakhamian* (he was sixteen at the time). Witty drawings and poems contributed by Merton, as well as his short stories on a wide variety of subjects, made *The Oakhamian* take on a cosmopolitan air under his editorship. He wrote an article describing New York as "The City Without a Soul"; others about Strasbourg Cathedral, an incident on a French train, and a strangely prophetic piece on Hitler and the German presidential elections of 1932.

Following a turbulent year at Cambridge after his father's death, Merton left England for good and came to America to live with his mother's relatives. In 1935, he entered Columbia University and soon became a part of the literary group on campus, serving as art editor of *The Jester of Columbia* in 1936 (he was editor of *The Columbia Yearbook* in 1937), with Robert Lax as editor and Ralph Toledano as managing editor. During his undergraduate years at Columbia, there is record of his publishing numerous cartoons, poems, and editorials in *The Jester, The Columbia Review,* and *The Columbia Spectator*. Two review articles from *The Review* are included in Appendix II: "Huxley and the Ethics of Peace" and "The Art of Richard Hughes." Merton is likewise responsible for an untitled story about "Observation Roofs" which was included in a column "What Goes On" in the now defunct *Rockefeller Center Weekly* of September 4, 1936. Throughout these years there was the profound influence of such professors as Mark Van Doren, Joseph Wood Krutch, and Daniel C. Walsh, as well as the stimulating companionship of fellow students, who included Robert Lax, Edward Rice, Seymour Freedgood, Robert Gibney, John Slate, Robert Giroux, John Berryman, Robert Gerdy, and Ad Reinhardt.

After graduation in 1938, Merton continued his studies on William Blake and finally wrote his Master's thesis, "Nature and Art in William Blake," which is included in this volume as Appendix I. During this same time, Merton began writing book reviews for *The New York Herald Tribune Book Review* and *The New York Times Book Review*. The earliest of these were on *The World's Body* by John Crowe Ransom and *Laughter in the Dark* by Vladimir Nabokov, both of which were published in *A Thomas Merton Reader* (edited by Thomas P. McDonnell; Doubleday Image Books, 1974). Merton continued to write reviews for both *The New York Times Book Review* and *The New York Herald Tribune Book Review* during 1939 and 1940. Finally, a critical essay entitled "Huxley's Pantheon" appeared in *The Catholic World* in the November issue of 1940, which apparently was Merton's last review article before entering the Abbey of Gethsemani in 1941. (See Appendix II.) These early reviews demonstrate Merton's critical faculties at work; they were to mature in the years that followed.

Shortly before he left New York for Gethsemani, Merton destroyed most of his early fiction. Only one novel, written in the summer of 1941, entitled *Journal of My Escape from the Nazis* (it was eventually published under the title of *My Argument with the Gestapo*), escaped the flames. The contract for this volume was signed shortly before Merton left for Asia on his final pilgrimage, but was not published until the year after his death. His other early novels, *The Labyrinth, The Man in the Sycamore Tree,* and *The Straits of Dover,* which became *The Night Be-*

fore the Battle (an autobiographical novel), were written in the summers of 1939 and 1940 when Merton lived with Bob Lax and Ed Rice in a cottage belonging to Lax's brother-in-law in upstate New York.

Merton was also faithfully keeping a journal during these post-Columbia years, one section of which he typed out before entering the monastery as a gift to Baroness Catherine de Hueck Doherty. Originally called *The Cuban Journal,* it was not published until 1959, under the title *The Secular Journal of Thomas Merton,* and covers the period of 1940 and 1941, the years he was teaching at Columbia University Extension and then at St. Bonaventure College and trying to enter the Franciscans. *The Secular Journal* makes it clear that Merton was seeking a way to combine a life devoted to God with his writing. There are notes about artists, poets, and prose writers, and the opening and closing entries are, significantly, about Blake. Other sections include commentaries and critiques on Dante, Graham Greene, Lorca, Rilke, Kierkegaard, Bloy, George Elliot, Joyce, and Huxley, to name only a few. Fra Angelico and Brueghel are singled out for comment as he attended the art exhibit of the New York World's Fair. *The Secular Journal* says a great deal about Merton the artist, as well as the man who seriously considered dedicating himself to the contemplative life.

Although there was little time for essay writing during Merton's first years in the monastery, it was to become his most popular mode of expression in his later years. He published over two hundred fifty essays during his lifetime, many of which were later collected and published in book form, such as *Seeds of Destruction, Disputed Questions, Seasons of Celebration, Mystics and Zen Masters,* and *Faith and Violence (Contemplation in a World of Action* was partially collected by Merton himself but was edited and published posthumously). *Disputed Questions* (1964), in particular, is of interest to us here, because this volume contained Merton's early essays on Boris Pasternak. It was decided to include these Pasternak essays in the present book along with Merton's later essay on "Pasternak's Letters to Georgian Friends," written in 1968, which was found among Merton's unpublished manuscripts following his death. "The Answer of Minerva: Pacifism and Resistance in Simone Weil" is also included as an example of Merton's social concern expressed in the literary essay.

Thomas Merton worked with ease (and not a little speed!) within the framework of the essay, especially during the years when he was Master of Novices (1955–65), since there was little time for the sustained writing a full-length book would require. Doubtless another reason why he chose the review article or essay as a literary form was the constant demands made upon him by editors of magazines and journals. At first, these requests were for pieces on racial justice (his essays on peace and nuclear warfare came later). A good example of this was his review article of *A Different Drummer,* a first novel by a Negro writer, William Melvin Kelley, which is included here under the title "The Legend of Tucker Caliban." Merton found it difficult to refuse such requests.

There is a strong personal appeal in the tone of these essays. His approach is usually conversational, tentative, and provisional rather than didactic, dictatorial, or authoritative. His gifts as an essayist are notably his lucidity, fluidity, and an engaging personal style. It may be recalled that Merton did his Master of Arts thesis on nature and art in Blake and had begun his doctoral research on the English Jesuit poet Gerard Manley Hopkins. His interest in the nature of art flowed from his consciousness of the artist's role in society, which he saw as having an intimate connection with morality. As Ross Labrie has rightly pointed out in his sensitive study of Merton (*The Art of Thomas Merton,* Texas Christian University Press, 1979): "He [Merton] came to feel that in a technocracy such as that evolved by twentieth-century man some form of religious idealism was necessary to sustain art. He sympathized with contemporary artists who fled from the sterility and vulgarity of their civilization, but he felt that, in the absence of any alternative value system, these artists were destined to vanish in the dead world of subjective abstraction."

Thomas Merton was not a literary critic in the usual sense of the term, and his ability as an essayist has only recently begun to be seen for its true greatness and versatility, thanks in large measure to the recent studies by Ross Labrie and George Woodcock (*Thomas Merton: Monk and Poet,* Farrar Straus and Giroux, 1979), as well as the comprehensive study of Merton as a poet by Sister Thérèse Lentfoehr (*Words and Silence: On the Poetry of Thomas Merton,* New Directions, 1979). Merton's essays tended to coincide with his usual Sunday afternoon conferences to the community at the Abbey of Gethsemani during these last years of his life. Whatever he happened to be engaged in at the moment turned out to be the subject of his talks to his fellow monks. This was especially true of his lectures on Albert Camus and William Faulkner. Two of the essays on Faulkner which appear in this volume were actually written for publication by Merton himself, while the other two were transcriptions from his taped conferences and edited for publication in *Katallagete* by James Holloway, its editor. The latter have been included as Appendix III to distinguish them from the essays which Merton wrote precisely for publication. They are significant in showing how easily Merton could relate literary themes to the basic values of monastic and contemplative life.

Both Camus and Faulkner were considered by Merton as genuinely prophetic in their writing, taking over the function of the monk, which was seen by Merton as prophetic witness. This vision led Merton in the mid-sixties to shift his attention from formally religious writings to literary models. After a visit from Jacques Maritain to Gethsemani in the fall of 1966, Merton wrote to his publisher and friend, James Laughlin of New Directions, that both Maritain and he agreed that perhaps the most living way to approach theological and philosophical problems in our day was in the form of "creative writing and literary criticism." (Letter to James Laughlin, October 8, 1966)

Merton wrote in "Day of a Stranger"[1] (*The Hudson Review* XX, 1967) a paragraph on the voices he chose for his solitude. It provides the reader with a rather accurate picture of his select hermitage library:

There is a mental ecology, too, in living balance of spirits in this corner of the woods. There is room here for many other songs besides those of birds. Of Vallejo for instance. Or Rilke, or Rene Char, Montale, Zukofsky, Ungaretti, Edwin Muir, Quasimodo or some Greeks. Or the dry, disconcerting voice of Nicanor Parra, the poet of the sneeze. Here is also Chuang Tzu whose climate is perhaps most the climate of this silent corner of woods. A climate in which there is no need for explanations. Here is the reassuring companionship of many silent Tzu's and Fu's; King Tzu, Lao Tzu, Meng Tzu, Tu Fu. And Nui Neng. And Chao-Chu. And the drawings of Sengai. And a big graceful scroll from Suzuki. Here also is a Syrian hermit called Philoxenus. And an Algerian cenobite called Camus. Here is heard the clanging prose of Tertullian, with the dry catarrh of Sartre. Here the voluble dissonances of Auden, with the golden sounds of John of Salisbury. Here is the deep vegetation of that more ancient forest in which the angry

[1] Peregrine Smith, Inc., is publishing "Day of a Stranger" as a book illustrated by photographs taken by Merton at this time.

birds, Isaias and Jeremias, sing. Here should be, and are, feminine voices from Angela of Foligno to Flannery O'Connor, Theresa of Avila, Juliana of Norwich, and, more personally and warmly still, Raissa Maritain. It is good to choose the voices that will be heard in these woods, but they also choose themselves, and send themselves here to be present in this silence. In any case there is no lack of voices.

Many of these voices are heard in this volume, but there are other voices as well, beginning with William Blake and James Joyce, Boris Pasternak and William Faulkner, Simone Weil and Julien Green, Roland Barthes and William Styron. Part II is comprised of seven essays on the prophetic witness of Albert Camus. The third section of the book is devoted to Merton's introductions to some of his favorite poets—mostly Latin Americans, whose work he frankly admitted he preferred to many of the North American poets. He admired these poets especially because their roots were in touch with the native Latin American people and their struggles for peace and justice. There are short essays on Ernesto Cardenal (he was once a novice at Gethsemani when Merton was Novice Master), Alfonso Cortes, Pablo Antonio Cuadra, César Vallejo, and Jorge Carrera Andrade, as well as the contemplative poet Raissa Maritain, certainly one of his favorites. "Rafael Alberti and His Angels" came afterward, along with Fernando Pessoa and Rubén Darío. Merton's translations of all these poets have been included in *The Collected Poems of Thomas Merton* (New Directions, 1977).

Finally, there is a fourth section of related literary essays which address such questions as "Poetry, Symbolism and Typology," "Poetry and Contemplation: A Reappraisal," "Theology of Creativity," and "Why Alienation Is for Everybody"—the latter was written for a local Louisville literary group but for some unknown reason has remained unpublished until now. To round out the volume, it was decided to include two essays from an earlier volume (*Raids on the Unspeakable*) entitled "Message to Poets" and "Answers on Art and Freedom," which discuss once again the problem of the responsibility of the artist, the question of art and morality. With the availability of these literary essays in one volume, it is hoped that the reader will be in a better position to evaluate Thomas Merton's literary gifts and critical acumen and thus come to a fuller understanding of his message for our times.

BROTHER PATRICK HART

I
LITERARY ESSAYS
(1959–68)

BLAKE AND THE NEW THEOLOGY

Thirty years ago when I was doing Blake in graduate school there were few people who thought the prophetic books could possibly mean anything to ordinary men. One might, of course, become initiated into their esoteric world, get the cosmic *dramatis personae* sorted out, discover why Los and Urizen did not agree, and become familiar with Beulah, Albion, Enitharmon, and even Luvah. But this had little to do with life itself. It was a purely subjective world belonging to Blake only and relevant only to a handful of Blake students. So if, at that time, Milton O. Percival worked out Blake's "system" and produced a book called *William Blake's Circle of Destiny,* the book was received without comment, put on the shelf with Foster Damon and the other Blake books, and more or less forgotten. It was as if someone had produced an obscure but useful reference book on alchemy.

Since that time Blake has fared better. People have given up the idea that he was a madman who wrote a few good short poems and many bad long ones. They have shown themselves more and more inclined to recognize him as a prophet and apocalyptic visionary who had a very real insight into the world of his time and of ours. This, of course, has been made somewhat easier to accept by two world wars, the atom bomb, the gradual disruption of Western civilization, and the emergence of a troubled and revolutionary Third World. In this situation Blake can be read as a "prophet" not of course in the sense of one who exactly predicts future events, but in the more traditional sense of one who "utters" and "announces" news about man's own deepest trouble—news that emerges from the very ground of that trouble in man himself. And of course the intensity of Blake's prophetic fervor was increased by the anger with which he viewed the blind complacencies of rationalism, of Enlightenment deism, and of the established Churches. Mark Schorer has well said of Blake: "most of the men of his time, certainly most of the poets, had no sense whatever of [the] conflicts . . . in the historical situation to which Blake's intuition immediately led him."

Written in April 1968, this review article first appeared in *The Sewanee Review, 76,* Autumn 1968. See Appendix I for Thomas Merton's Master of Arts thesis at Columbia University, "Nature and Art in William Blake," presented in February 1939.

The growing enthusiasm for Blake has finally erupted full force in the latest book of Thomas Altizer, the radical American God-is-dead theologian whose Blakean tract, *The New Apocalypse*,[1] drafts Blake with all his works into the militant ranks of the new antireligious Christians. And of course this is not hard to do, since in fact the so-called Christian atheism and radical Christianity stem via Nietzsche, Hegel, and Kierkegaard from roots in the Romantic era in literature and philosophy. The revolutionary energy of Blake and his impassioned fight for charism and vision against dogma and institution make him an obvious saint for radical Christians. Dr. Altizer's book therefore abounds in declarations that Blake is "the most . . ." and "the only . . ." in all categories about which a radical Christian would be likely to get excited. Blake is, then, "the most original prophet and seer in the history of Christendom, . . . he created a whole new form of vision"; "he is the only Christian visionary who has envisioned the universal role of the female as both a redemptive and a destructive power"; "the first visionary who chose the kenotic or self-emptying path of immersing himself in the profane reality of experience as the way to the God who is all in all in Jesus." But despite this kenotic and visionary "way to God" we are also told repeatedly that Blake is "the first Christian atheist" as well as "the most Christocentric of Christian seers." All this is now the familiar stock in trade of radical Christian theology, and we must keep in mind the language of that theology: for here "Christocentric" has nothing to do with what it means, for instance, to Evelyn Underhill. It means just about the exact opposite. The "death of God" moves the radical Christian to put Christ in the place of the dead God; but the kenotic Christ has so completely emptied himself that in fact he cannot be found anywhere except in "the individual" and in a generally "fallen humanity": the more fallen, the more Christlike, for fallenness itself is redemptive, and we even hear quite a bit about the "redemptive work of Satan." This is not sheer jocosity, and there are grounds for all this in the energetic and creative visions of Blake himself, "the sole creator of a post-Biblical Christian apocalypse," in which we find "the only Christian vision of the total kenotic movement of God or the Godhead."

Without pausing to dispute these statements, one is brought up short by such a profusion of *"only"* and one is tempted to muse on a lot of names, some of which Dr. Altizer mentions, others of which he perhaps overlooks: Soloviev, Berdyaev, and the Russian Sophianists; Boehme

---

[1] Thomas J. J. Altizer, *The New Apocalypse: The Radical Christian Vision of William Blake* (Ann Arbor: Michigan State University Press, 1967).

and Eckhart; Paracelsus; Nicholas of Cusa; Joachim of Flora; Scotus Erigena; a host of medieval visionaries, Beghards, Beguines, Hesychasts, Cathars. . . . One feels that Blake in his apocalyptic prophecy and protest has rather more company than Altizer suggests, in his zeal to proclaim Blake "a major prophet for the contemporary radical Christian." But that zeal is not misguided. Radical theology could hardly find a better and more persuasive prophet. Blake is ideal for its purposes and, as a matter of fact, it is not Blake who gains in stature by the association, but radical theology. Dr. Altizer's new book is the first one of his that shows, at least to my satisfaction, that the new theology is to be taken seriously.

One can certainly agree with Altizer that Blake cannot be explained either by those who seek to reduce him entirely to orthodox Christian mysticism or by those who show him purely as a heterodox and anti-Christian seer. If Blake is a Christian—and he certainly is—his Christianity has to be accounted for in some very special way. And if he is a mystic, then he is a very peculiar kind of mystic. There is some truth to Altizer's contention that "Blake's vision both transcends and inverts the Western mystical tradition . . . there is a clear parallel between the Buddhist path of self-dissolution and the apocalyptic form of Blake's vision." At the same time Blake's apocalyptic theology is basically Christian. Blake's kenoticism seems anti-Christian, Altizer thinks, only because it is so true to the "original" apocalyptic Christianity which (supposedly) vanished after Constantine and Augustine's *City of God.* Judged in the light of this later institutional and un-dialectical Christianity with God in His heaven and the City of God made visible on earth by the hierarchical Church, Blake's marriage of heaven and hell is nothing but a blasphemous and antinomian attack on established order. But for Altizer the attack is much more true to the New Testament and to the Gospel message of the "freedom of the sons of God" than is orthodox, traditional Church Christianity. Without arguing for or against this point, theologically, we can certainly agree that Blake was a radical Christian in his belief that Churches had perverted Christian truth and that the God of the Christian Churches was really Urizen, Nobodaddy, and even Satan—not the lover of man who empties himself to become identified with Man, but a specter whom man sets up against himself, investing him with the trappings of power which are not "the things of God" but really "the things that are Caesar's." There is indeed much in Blake that anticipates—with far more powerful poetic effect and human authenticity—the ideas of religious alienation in Feuerbach, Marx, and Freud.

Blake's vision is then—and here we can agree perfectly with Dr.

5

Altizer—a total integration of mysticism and prophecy, a return to apocalyptic faith which arises from an intuitive protest against Christianity's estrangement from its own eschatological ground. Blake saw official Christendom as a *narrowing* of vision, a foreclosure of experience and of future expansion, a locking up and securing of the doors of perception. He substituted for it a Christianity of openness, of total vision, a faith which dialectically embraces both extremes, not seeking to establish order in life by shutting off a little corner of chaos and subjecting it to laws and to police, but moving freely between dialectical poles in a wild chaos, integrating sacred vision, in and through the experience of fallenness, as the only locus of creativity and redemption. Blake, in other words, calls for "a whole new form of theological understanding."

Altizer seeks that new form in Hegelian dialectic. But this raises problems. Is there really anything that is more than superficially common to both Blake and Hegel? Dr. Altizer confesses a certain awareness that Blake would have responded to Hegel "with apocalyptic fury." And he develops the thought: "No doubt Blake like Kierkegaard would have condemned a thinker *whose very method makes impossible* the act of faith or vision [my italics]." Certainly Blake, like Hegel, is engrossed in a *coincidentia oppositorum;* but what for Hegel would be "coincidence"— the shock of billiard balls against one another in an historical process (which might no doubt have discernible mathematical laws)—is for Blake something totally different, the fourfold creative and prophetic vision in which opposites do not merely come together and fuse in synthesis, but are restored to a higher unity, an alchemical wedding of loving and fiery elements made all the more ardent by separation.

Dr. Altizer justifies his Hegelian approach, however, saying: "Just as Kierkegaard employed Hegel's dialectical method to establish the existential reality of faith, we must employ that method as a mode of entry into the mystery of Blake's apocalyptic vision." *"Must?"* At best we may try it, as Altizer has. I am not so sure he found the right key. But in any case there is a ground of dialectic in Blake which, though not Hegelian, is nevertheless fully concerned with man's predicament in the world and deals with history not with a simple "yes" or a simple "no" but with a "total acceptance, if ultimate reversal, of the full reality of a fallen history."

Needless to say, the conclusion is anything but Hegelian or Marxist. The fact that Hegel ends up with the deification of the state shows the danger of comparing him and Blake too glibly, and Dr. Altizer's final embrace of Satan and Antichrist has a carefree facility about it that makes one wonder if he has lost Blake and ended up with Hegel only.

Blake, like Marcuse after him, recognized the two-dimensional character of Western logic and also the endemic temptation to reduce this tension to a one-dimensional and authoritarian system. The ideological tension between "what is" and "what ought to be" is at the heart of the experience of fallenness, which should, in Gospel terms, open out in need for redemption. But it is also characteristic of fallenness that it evades this need and this tension by substituting an artificial and rigid one-dimensional "order." This falsification can be canonized and perpetuated by the "laws" of a frozen, authoritarian system, and the "god" who presides over such a system is at once a "nothing" and an absolute power, Urizen, the Negation, the "Abstract objecting power that Negatives everything/ . . . the Spectre of Man . . . /And in its Holiness is closed the Abomination of Desolation" ("Jerusalem"). True holiness and redemption, for Blake, lie in the energy that springs from the reunion of Contraries. But the Negation stands between the Contraries and prevents their "marriage." Holding heaven and hell apart, Urizen infects them both with his own sickness and nothingness. True holiness, faith, vision, Christianity, must therefore subvert his power to Negate and "redeem the contraries" in mercy, pity, peace. The work of this reversal is the epiphany of God in Man. The God that "is dead" is therefore the Negation set up in solitary and absolute authority as an idol and Spectre. But this God is endowed with life in proportion as men invest him with (earthly) power and adore him in his separateness and isolation—even putting one another to death in his honor. The beginning of faith must obviously be a "no" to this idol, this Negation of life and of love. But the negation of the Negation and the restoration of Contraries is not just the work of the intelligence. In Blake it was, and had to be, a mystical and prophetic experience involving the whole man.

Because the Hegelian dialectic is a purely intellectual operation and does not involve the whole man, it results, finally, in a return to the idol in a worse and more inexorable form. Or at least so Blake would have said. Blake here describes his own liberation in a letter (October 23, 1804): "I have entirely reduced that spectrous fiend to his station, whose annoyance has been the ruin of my labour for the past twenty years. . . . He is the enemy of conjugal love and the Jupiter of the Greeks. . . . Suddenly on the day after visiting the Truchsessian Gallery of Pictures, I was again enlightened with the light I enjoyed in my youth. . . ."

Now since this Nobodaddy-Urizen-Jupiter-of-the-Greeks is also Satan, the Negation, I think we have to be a little suspicious of the glibness with which Altizer's Hegelianism prompts him to embrace Satan at the end of the book. "If the Antichrist has appeared on our horizon, and is destined to become yet more fully incarnate in our world, then we can learn through Blake to greet His epiphany not only with horror but also with joy. For the Antichrist is the final kenotic manifestation of Christ." Well, that's just fine. But it only works when there has been a little occult shuffling of cards up the sleeve, in which the Antichrist of Church establishment (altogether bad, villainous, hateful, etc.) is transformed into the good, happymaking Antichrist of the "purely secular." I am afraid this offers one no way of not succumbing with sacred enthusiasm to the power of a totalitarian state on the Hegelian (or Marxian—or capitalist for that matter) pattern. We might paraphrase and slightly expand. "If Antichrist has appeared on our horizon at Auschwitz and is destined to become yet more fully incarnate in future camps and prisons, then we can learn . . . to greet His epiphany . . . with joy." Learn it you can, perhaps, from Hegel, not from Blake. He vigorously repudiated the Antichrist of inhuman authority whether ecclesiastical or secular: for this had been cursed by Christ—"The Abomination which maketh desolate, i.e. State Religion which is the source of all cruelty."

When Blake wrote, on the flyleaf of Bacon's *Essays,* "Good Advice for Satan's Kingdom," he was not greeting this reasoned epiphany with joy. The Kingdom of Satan is the kingdom of division, which puts the "truth of theology and the truth of civil business" into separate compartments. Then the Prince of Darkness sets himself up as Lord Chancellor and preaches War as virtue. "What do those Knaves mean by Virtue?" Exclaims Blake, reading Bacon, "Do they mean War and its horrors & its Heroic Villains?" And so, on a page of Bacon, we find Blake drawing "a presentation of hinder parts labeled 'the devil's arse' and depending from it a chain of excrement ending in: A King," by way of comment on Bacon's belief that a King is a "mortal god on earth." When Bacon claims to reason in favor of religion, Blake calls him "An Atheist pretending to talk against Atheism," and when Bacon praises social rituals Blake comments: "Bacon supposes that the Dragon Beast & Harlot are worthy of a place in the New Jerusalem. Excellent Traveller, Go on and be damned!" Blake's conclusion is that "a Lord Chancellor's opinions [are] as different from those of Christ as those of Caiaphas or Pilate or Herod." I think this should be kept in mind by anyone who wants to praise Blake as a "Christian atheist" or an apostle or purely secular Christianity, in the sense in which this is understood by some popular theologians.

Another characteristic ambiguity of the new theology is that which sees the "Godhead as living process"—i.e., as *historical* process. "Christian mysticism," says Altizer, "must know the Godhead as a living and forward-moving process." And note he says God*head,* not just God. God is *by nature* historical process.

This of course goes hand in hand with the other idea that God is "dead." He has now to be seen, apprehended, understood as dead in his transcendence in order that he may manifest himself immanently in historical process and there only. This means that the static God must die in order to live as dynamic. But it all depends on what you mean by dynamic.

Afflicted as I am with an incurable case of metaphysics, I cannot see where the idea of Godhead *as process* is more dynamic than that of Godhead as *pure act.* To one who has been exposed to scholastic ontology and has not recovered, it remains evident that the *activity of becoming* is considerably less alive and dynamic than the *act of Being.* Far from regarding "pure Being" as static quiescence, traditional metaphysics is in accord with Blake in regarding it as the source and ground of all life:

> The pride of the peacock is the glory of God.
> The lust of the goat is the bounty of God.
> The wrath of the lion is the wisdom of God.
> The nakedness of woman is the work of God . . .

Surely Blake's God is Creator who is present and immanent in his creation, not remote from it and solitary. But he is still the Creator and not the creation process—the ground of being, not the process of becoming. Nor can we confuse the "Godhead" and the "Kingdom of God." Traditional theology clearly distinguishes between God in himself and the work of God the Holy Spirit, but without separating them and dividing them. Maritain's expression *distinguer pour unir* may no longer be fashionable, but it still serves to avoid such ambiguities as a Godhead-process-in-history. The dynamism of eschatology is not a dynamism of the divine nature *ad intra* but a work of God in the world, "in the Spirit" and "in Christ." It is of course true that the elaborate Trinitarian theology of the Fathers has sometimes been misused and made to justify churchly and worldly power by certain mystifications. Nevertheless the idea of the Word "coming into the world" and of the Spirit possessing and transforming the world does adequately cover the idea of God in history without reducing the "Godhead" to a historical process.

The "forward-moving process" is the Kingdom and work of the Spirit, and it is not an attempt on the part of the Godhead to complete and perfect itself. It is God's self-manifestation and self-expression in man. The Kingdom of God is not "a dynamic epiphany of a Godhead in process of realizing itself" but rather an epiphany of God in process of *communicating and sharing himself.* The revelation of God as life-giving Spirit is surely a revelation of him as *not* solitary and remote but as completely "given," "poured out" in the world and man, and so, if you will, kenotic. But Altizer completely ignores all this and hence has to try to reach this same end by the fuzzy romanticism of a Godhead-process, immanent within history.

However, these subtleties and complaints may be set aside, and Altizer can be complimented on the frankly eschatological vision which is the most important thing about this book. He has certainly not toned down the apocalyptic and prophetic character of Blake's vision, but has sought to do it full justice. In so doing, he has also frankly faced the central importance of that most odious and unpopular of Christian doctrines: the fall. Without the fall not only is Christianity itself emptied of meaning, but Blake too becomes incomprehensible. Eschatology is the vision of a totally new and final reality, a cosmic reversal that brings ultimate meaning and salvation to the fallen world. That reality is, in effect, the total integration of God and Man in Christ—that is to say, in concrete and communal Mankind united not by politics but by mercy. At this point, instead of vague optimism about an abstract reconciliation of ideological opposites, let us give the last word to Blake himself and see what he thinks about a purely "secular Christianity."

> Man must & will have some Religion: if he has not the Religion of Jesus, he will have the Religion of Satan & will erect the Synagogue of Satan, calling the Prince of this World, God, & destroying all who do not worship Satan under the name of God. Will any one say, "Where are those who worship Satan under the Name of God?" Where are they? Listen! Every Religion that Preaches Vengeance for Sin is the Religion of the Enemy & Avenger & not of the Forgiver of Sin & their God is Satan, Named by the Divine Name.

The context of this is one of Blake's attacks on Deists from whose inadequate humanism follow wars, persecutions, and cruelties of all kinds. Altizer has some interesting observations on this kind of "enlightened" thinking. Western individualism, he says,

> has wholly isolated the individual from both God and the cosmos, an isolation which has produced the most secular culture in history, resulted in an unparalleled form of society in which individuals are hopelessly alienated from one another, and created a unique interior experience revolving around a solitary subjectivity.

This is a good analysis of the kind of predicament Blake saw fallen man to be in. It is the reign of Urizen. Yet at the same time, identifying the "individual" and the "person" (or, rather, confusing them), Altizer might make us miss the intense Christian personalism of Blake's thought. Altizer also shows the crucial importance of the fact that Christianity does not refuse history nor seek to escape from it like so many other religions. But the Christian acceptance of history must not be confused, he says, with a disease of the contemporary West—"a radically profane historicism that in granting ultimate value to historical events has abolished any meaning lying beyond them." It is necessary to keep this distinction in mind when Altizer says that only the radical Christian can successfully meet the gnostic temptation to evade history "with the faith that a totally fallen history is finally the redemptive Epiphany of Christ."

This book is one of the better productions of the new radical school of theology precisely because the substance and the vitality of Blake are called upon to give it serious meaning. There is unquestionable truth in Dr. Altizer's contention that Blake is talking a language similar to that of the radical theologians—and making their own points perhaps better than they do. Whether or not this book is a fully adequate interpretation of Blake's theology, it is certainly helpful in understanding that theology. One puts the book down, however, with the sense that Hegel has not made the decisive contribution that Altizer hoped he would, and that there is much more left in Blake that this key has failed to open.

NEWS OF THE JOYCE INDUSTRY

As early as 1932 Joyce wrote to Budgen: "Nine persons seem to be doing books on me at present." Today Joyce has the largest and most flourishing Ph.D. industry of any modern author in English. Twenty dissertations on him appeared in the United States between 1960 and 1963. On an average, five books on Joyce have been published annually since 1960, not to mention some eighty articles each year. There are two magazines entirely dedicated to Joyce studies, one in Oklahoma and one in New South Wales. And there is a special "newslitter" devoted to *Finnegans Wake*.

It is well known that Joyce himself anticipated all this and ironically entered into the game even before it began. He is known deliberately to have planted special puzzles for scholars and arranged for them to discover the solutions, hiding clues here and there in an academic treasure hunt which he took far less seriously than they. This is all very well for graduate English departments where, it is said, "Joyce's works are highly privileged touchstones of a literary student's or professor's competence. Joycean expertise is a well-known trademark of scholarly industry." In plain words, Joyce is "in," and an ambitious graduate student can hope to better his status in a highly competitive field if he picks Joyce rather than, say, Galsworthy or Arnold Bennett. This is unfortunate, because it means that people who would do well with Galsworthy are writing about Joyce, and as a result others may be deterred from reading Joyce, convinced, first, that he is stuffy and inscrutable and, second, that he is the exclusive property of humorless gnostics and mandarins.

Of course there is the special case of *Finnegans Wake*, certainly the most difficult book ever written in "English" and just as certainly a literary and linguistic dead end. Quite apart from the brilliance and versatility of its writing, it is a highly complicated fabric of themes—enough to keep Ph.D.'s going full speed until the crack of doom. Unfortunately, as Clive Hart points out, in *James Joyce Today,* one who dares to tackle *Finnegans Wake* can have the satisfaction of getting away with anything he likes.

The manuscript for this article is dated July 1968 and was published in *The Sewanee Review,* 77, Summer 1969.

An independent study . . . is difficult to challenge, and therefore easy to offer as a doctoral dissertation or barrier-hopping publication. Few people will be prepared to gainsay it. . . . No book, perhaps, has ever been more conducive to supposititious criticism. [Hence] . . . the publication of a mass of critical opinion which is uninformed, speculative, or absurd to a degree unthinkable in the case of books familiar to a wider audience.

We must admit that what is said here about *Finnegans Wake* is also true to some extent of *Ulysses* and indeed of the entire Joyce canon. And while Joyceans are busily revealing Joyce to us, we must soberly take account of the fact that they are also distorting and concealing him.

To parody the words of Stephen Dedalus on the artist, who "converts the bread of everyday life into something that has a permanent life of its own," some Joyce scholars want to transubstantiate the bread of *Ulysses* and *Portrait* into the unearthly and arbitrary substance of their own fantasies. Everything becomes something else that nobody ever before suspected it might be, and the more bizarre the assumption, the better thesis it will make, especially if it ends up by contradicting everything that Joyce himself ever said he intended. For instance, where Joyce made an emphatic point of renouncing Irish Catholicism, some scholars are having none of that; and it is not unusual to prove that Joyce was more Irish than Parnell and more Catholic than St. Pius X.

One of the more useful and engaging of the recent books on Joyce[1] is one which is not stamped with the industry's trademark. The author is neither a professor nor an American. He is an English novelist, Anthony Burgess, who modestly disclaims pretensions to scholarship but who obviously must acknowledge his debt to the scholars. It is unfortunate that he omits some of the best—for we have to give their due to the real professionals like Tindall, Kenner, Goldberg, and others, who are absolutely necessary for a full appreciation of Joyce. Burgess, one of the relatively few English commentators on Joyce, wants us to be quite clear about his amateur standing. He writes on Joyce for the nonspecialist and nonmandarin who wants to understand and enjoy *Ulysses*. The book was begun on the twenty-fifth anniversary of Joyce's death and appeared in England under the title *Here Comes Everybody* (better than the coy American title, *Re Joyce*). The emphasis is on the healthy catholicity of Joyce rather than on his allegedly sick Catholicism. Burgess's book is clear, independent, urbane, and plausible even where it does not succeed in convincing. At any rate, Burgess achieves his end:

[1] Anthony Burgess, *Re Joyce* (New York: W. W. Norton, 1968).

he has written in a readable book that makes Joyce more accessible to nonspecialists, without at any time claiming to initiate them, through a secret and ritual system of its own, into a Joyce that nobody ever before thought possible.

Another anniversary volume, *James Joyce Today*,[2] edited by Thomas F. Staley, presents a useful selection of essays by recognized Joyce scholars in England, the United States, Canada, and Australia. Richard M. Kain, Father William Noon, James S. Atherton, and Clive Hart are among them. The essays tend to be retrospective surveys with titles like "The Position of *Ulysses* Today" and *"Finegans Wake* in Perspective." Perhaps the most provocative is the study in which William Blissett claims a Wagnerian element in Joyce (acquired via Mallarmé). It raises a vexed question: just how much sense can you make out of a novel by treating it as if it were a musical composition? Apart from that and from the use of *Leitmotifs* (which does not have to be as "Wagnerian" as is claimed), there are certainly plenty of allusions to Wagner in Joyce. Stephen's ash-plant is "the ash-spear of Wotan, the 'augur's rod of ash,' and the sword of Siegmund reforged by Siegfried," but we must not forget this is irony.

The artistic experience of reading Joyce and enjoying his comedy is quite different in quality from the kinetic seriousness of Wagnerian opera. Professor Blissett himself admits that "the pseudo-heroics of the Cyclops episode [in *Ulysses*] blare out as an uproarious parody of the sort of heroic mythology often called 'Wagnerian.'" The treatment of the Tristan and Isolde theme in *Finnegans Wake* is of course also parody of Wagnerian romance in terms of Dublin bourgeois sentiment.

Professor Blissett's real point is not so much that *Finnegans Wake* is Wagnerian opera, as that the art of both Joyce and Wagner is "total" and "despotic"—an art that ravages all that went before it with a kind of scorched-earth tactic, or like a plague of locusts. An art that is at once *Götterdämmerung* and "final solution." Such art "lends itself to . . . demands, a cult." This is perhaps an overstatement. Joyce and Wagner did not end the world, but in both cases the cult and the industry are surely there.

The essays in *James Joyce Today* generally display the kind of discretion and openness one hopes for in good criticism. The mature critic recognizes that, in a work of such richness and complexity as Joyce's, one must not try to pin everything down, categorize, label, define, explain, classify, and prescribe. The art of Joyce is always rich in suggestion and

[2] *James Joyce Today: Essays on the Major Works,* edited by Thomas F. Staley (Bloomington: Indiana University Press, 1966).

in open possibilities, in delicate tensions, contrasts, unresolved problems that are meant to be left in the air, questions and polarities that are not meant to be reduced to definitive certainties. The stasis of the Joycean aesthetic is not a full stop in inertia, an end of living contradictions, but a delicate balance between them. The comic characters in Joyce are often comic precisely because they insist on judging and solving, on giving absolute and definitive answers to questions that must remain more or less open if our lives are to preserve a living and human measure. It is in this sense, for instance, that Stephen Dedalus, with his arbitrary and premature answers, is a comic character—and woe to the critic who is unequivocal in identifying Stephen with Joyce himself!

The very essence of comic art—the stasis of comic "joy," as Joyce himself might have said—is found in the living balance, the poise between vital uncertainties and unanswered questions which constitute, for a classic temper, the authentic mystery of life. The moral and cultural death which Joyce found so stifling in the Dublin of 1904 consisted precisely in this mania for prescription and foreclosure, this fanatic closing of doors and throwing away of keys, this craze for decreeing that all problems are hereby solved and all the questions answered. Consider the soliloquy of Father Conmee, S.J., in the "wandering rocks" section of *Ulysses*. Consider Bloom himself, whom critics tend more and more to treat as a real hero rather than a mock heroic figure: one of his comic features is that he has at least a provisional answer for everything. He finds an instant name for everything, locates it, pigeonholes it in an alienated experience that is one huge inexhaustible cliché. (And critics pore over these pathetic thrusts as if they were keys to all philosophy and all history!)

Now the main problem of the Joyce industry is that it tends to reward scholars for ignoring and destroying this delicate balance. They are encouraged, by the rules of their game, to espouse one contradiction against the other, to choose between polarized energies, to decree that the "real Joyce" must be situated on one pole or the other, not in the tension between them. In order to "prove" this, it is apparently enough to accumulate every scrap of material in Joyce—and in the industry—which says anything whatever about one's chosen aspect of his work. The job to be done is not one of qualitative judgment, but of quantitative accumulation. You pile up a mountain of evidence and set your chosen theme on top of it in splendid isolation. You select a small part of Joyce, remove it from its context, sterilize it, sedulously cleanse it from every trace of living and dynamic relationship with other organic parts of the whole. Then, having declared this to be the "real Joyce" or the "main theme" or the "central mystery" of his work, you proceed to bring all the rest of the work back into an artificial relationship with it, thereby re-defining Joyce in your own terms. Thus in an act of priestly and scholarly transubstantiation you have extracted a living organ from the whole body and given it "a permanent life of its own." If in order to do so you have to stand Joyce on his head, so much the better. Evidently the academic eye finds him more intriguing in that position.

Darcy O'Brien's study of *The Conscience of James Joyce*[3] is a typical exercise in one-sided reductionism. Identifying Joyce unequivocally with Stephen, crediting Joyce with all Stephen's romantic idealism—and indeed with the neo-platonic ideas of AE which Stephen himself derides in *Ulysses*—O'Brien imagines Joyce to be "an idealist tortured by the persistent intrusions of reality," "anachronistic enough to believe that matter and spirit were forever separate," "an idealist and a moralist"—indeed a preacher of morality, with a perpetually troubled conscience ("he seems to have writhed in perpetual guilt"), because he was obsessed with "a neo-platonic ideal of chaste love and beauty." These initial accusations are due to a misreading of the Joyce-Dedalus aesthetic, with gross overemphasis on that aesthetic in its earlier and less mature form. The later development of it in the "Scylla and Charybdis" episode of *Ulysses* (where Stephen attacks the neo-platonic idealism of AE and emphasizes the "now and the here") is completely ignored.

What is most intriguing about O'Brien's highly simplified view of Joyce's conscience is that, whereas Joyce used to be considered the very paragon of lustiness and abandonment to the flesh, he is now damned by O'Brien as a sex-hating puritan, a manichee, a Jansenist, a guilt-ridden and monastic mind afflicted with prudish inhibitions and moral prejudices. (O'Brien has an ax to grind about marital fidelity, which he considers romantic, obsolete, and impractical.) The most intriguing thing of all is that the same passages that were once cited with livid outrage in courts of law as evidence of Joyce's unrestrained animality are here brought out as evidence of his prudery and "hatred of sex"—Molly Bloom's soliloquy, for example!

A few quotations from O'Brien's book will give the reader a good view of this unique position.

"His [Joyce's] puritanism ran deep enough for him to associate sex with bestiality." (This in spite of letters to Nora in which Joyce rather outspokenly admits enjoying some of the more versatile approaches to

[3] Darcy O'Brien, *The Conscience of James Joyce* (Princeton: Princeton University Press, 1968).

16

erotic pleasure.) It had not occurred to most of us to regard Molly Bloom's soliloquy as "cheerless"—only as funny in its bawdy way. But for O'Brien it is a clear manifestation of "the peculiar, stringent, idealistic conscience of Joyce." For Joyce was "ever an idealist, ever a man bitten by the most stringent of moral consciences." O'Brien proceeds to elaborate this fantasy image of Joyce as the relentless enemy of joyous living who "devoted his artistic life to setting down our sins and his own sins in his enormous books, like some tireless medieval monk." One gets the impression that Joyce's real heroes were the Jesuits at Clongowes with their pandy bats, and that all his life he was a monk in disguise. ". . . Like those of a monk, his ideals were supernal, mythical, exalted, impossible." Like the most untutored and prejudiced of Irish Catholics, Joyce identified morality with sex.

O'Brien pays no attention to Joyce's evident repugnance for pride, self-complacency, hypocrisy, greed, cruelty, avarice, vanity, selfishness, and the rest. No, Joyce "fixes upon sexuality as . . . perhaps the most important moral issue."

But this is just a special aspect of a general Joycean hatred of mankind and of life itself, "the unpleasant Joycean belief that life originates from the womb of sin."

"He retained from Irish Catholicism . . . an essential mistrust of human nature and, most significantly, a mistrust of sex . . . as the most powerful element in man's moral degeneracy." "Sex predominates" in all Joyce's writings, "even as Molly Bloom predominates in *Ulysses*." (It is not difficult to see why O'Brien thinks Molly "predominates" in *Ulysses*. His argument is a perfect self-justifying circle.) Joyce is dominated by the "conviction that the sexual act is itself sinful." And man, born of sexual union, is therefore "at worst morally loathsome, a two-sided creature at best." It is true that O'Brien admits a certain growth and maturing of the Joycean conscience. Bloom is more mellow than Stephen. The humor of *Ulysses* has softened something of the stark hatred of life which O'Brien detects everywhere in Joyce. But do not be misled: the humor is only a mask! It helped Joyce to find his miserable worldview more tolerable, and it was also a ruse by which he made his moral preachments "more palatable to the reader." In *Ulysses* "his rage and rancor are controlled by elaborate jokes. . . . The Joycean snarl has been succeeded by a smirk."

No one who has read Joyce needs an argument against such an arbitrary thesis as this. It is a pure caricature, just as one-sided, just as wrong-headed and distorted, just as prejudiced, and just as Irish as all the criticisms directed against Joyce by his fellow-Dubliners, whether Catholics or not. We recall with O'Brien that Stanislaus, Joyce's brother, thought *Ulysses* represented a "monstrous vision of life."

Certainly Joyce was full of conflicts. He never fully recovered from the traumatic wounds of his childhood and adolescence. It is true those wounds were inflicted on him by a perversely rigid, insensitive, and cruel debasement of Catholicism. Joyce freed himself from his past in the best way he could; but he knew that he had not entirely escaped its after-effects, and never could. He broke with his Church and with his parents' subculture, but he could not renounce the conflicts and ambiguities built into the very civilization of the West. The conscience of James Joyce was not that of a provincial bigot or of a willful puritan. It was the conscience of a European of the post-Victorian era, of a man in a sophisticated, complex, self-contradictory culture about to fall apart in World War I. Though O'Brien tries, in a footnote, to contrast Joyce with Freud, it must be said that the consciences of Joyce and Freud were very similar indeed (though their characters were certainly quite different). One has only to read *Civilization and Its Discontents* to understand what lay behind the comic judgment of society and its repressions in *A Portrait of the Artist* and *Ulysses*. There is all the difference in the world between a conscience that seeks security in rigid and puritanical repression of sex and a civilized experience of ambivalence in sex, in a society where ideals are one thing and realities another. Joyce accepted that ambivalence and lived with it. One wonders if Lawrence, who insisted on breaking through it altogether and making a religion of sex, was not in some sense the greater idealist and the greater puritan. As to those who imagine that sex can exist in modern life without any ambivalence at all—as if there were no inner tension between *eros* and *thanatos*—one wonders if they are happier than the rest or just more thick-skinned.

Virginia Moseley's study of *Joyce and the Bible*,[4] while taking an entirely positive view of Joyce, has one thing in common with O'Brien: a firm conviction that Joyce was a religious man and that his view of life was entirely theological, Biblical, Christ-centered, and Jesuit. The difference is that Virginia Moseley is Christian and reads all these qualities as light and fair, while O'Brien is anti-Christian and sees them all as dark and foul.

It is true that Messianic themes are central to Joyce's work and that the Christ-image tends to appear everywhere, together with manifold

[4] Virginia Moseley, *Joyce and the Bible* (DeKalb, Illinois: Northern Illinois University Press, 1967).

other Biblical figures, types, symbols, and allusions. A study of Biblical themes in Joyce is therefore essential. But these themes have to be seen in the larger context of Joyce's work with all its other essential elements. Miss Moseley seems to respond to the importance of Biblical themes *in themselves* rather than to their importance *in Joyce.* The fact that Christian symbols have top priority for a Christian does not necessarily mean they have top priority in *Ulysses,* still less that they are the key to everything in Joyce and the final triumphant justification of all he ever wrote. Consequently, though Miss Moseley has made a diligent and useful study of Biblical allusions in Joyce, the result of her work is not so much a valid Christian interpretation of Joyce, as a Christian Biblical meditation, arbitrarily suspended on the Joycean hook. Lest the accusation of arbitrariness seem unfair, here are a few random examples of supposed Biblical allusions in Joyce.

The title of *Chamber Music* suggests, we are told, the bridegroom coming forth from his chamber (Psalm 19:5) and "not in chambering and wantonness" (Romans 13:13).

Molly Bloom's ejaculation "O, rocks" contains a veiled allusion to St. Peter as the rock on which Christ will build his Church (Matthew 16:18). (I had always been under the impression that the "rocks" in this text were more secular than sacred.)

Another Biblical allusion which involves Molly: as her arm reaches into the window of 7 Eccles Street to remove the sign "Unfurnished Apartments" (it is about 4 p.m. on Bloomsday), we are reminded, says Miss Moseley, of John 14:2: "In my Father's house are many mansions."

When Bloom says "this funeral affair" is a bore, Miss Moseley points to a New Testament confirmation: ". . . let the dead bury their dead" (Matthew 8:22). And this brings us to her contention that Bloom is a Christ-figure and Messiah.

There can be no question that Joyce ironically uses Biblical and specifically Messianic allusions in his treatment of Bloom. We can agree that Bloom is in some sense Stephen's "savior." But that does not mean that everything Bloom says or does must be ingeniously connected with the words and acts of Jesus in the Bible. For instance, the fact that he eats in the Ormond Bar can be thoroughly understood without reference to Matthew 9:9–13, where Jesus "eats with publicans and sinners." Nor does it throw any light on Bloom to say: "Like Jesus the missionary, Bloom is an advertising canvasser" or to contend that because he seeks to get an ad renewed, "the episode focuses on spiritual renewal." Still less is it relevant to say that Bloom's "looking at his nails" (when the men in the funeral carriage catch sight of Blazes Boylan) is a "suggestion of Jesus' nail prints." This kind of allegorizing, instead of adding valid critical insight, distracts from the real intentions of the author and weakens the impact of his work. It substitutes mechanical and verbal equations for direct epiphanies—and does so in exactly the same way that the allegorizing of medieval exegetes substituted fantasy for the revealed message of Scripture.

A case in point is Miss Moseley's elaboration of the "Martha, Mary and Lazarus" theme in *Ulysses*. Of course Joyce makes several allusions to this theme and it has its place in *Ulysses,* but it becomes for Miss Moseley the *"central biblical analogy"* and indeed the *key to Ulysses*. Bloom is Jesus, Stephen is Lazarus, Martha Clifford is Martha ("the active life"), and Molly is Mary the contemplative! When we reflect that there could hardly be a more "kinetic" character in the whole of Joyce than Molly Bloom, and when we consider the fact that her soliloquy and her whole behavior hardly suggest contemplative admiration for her husband, we must affirm that this analogy stands as *central* and *essential* only when Joyce is turned upside down. Yet Miss Moseley develops her idea with incredible equanimity. For her, Bloom and Molly lying in bed wrong way round are simply a tableau of contemplative peace and mystical union in the household of Bethany. "Why does Bloom lie with his head at Molly's feet and Molly with her head at his? Probably because Mary sat at the feet of Jesus in the biblical account."

More of the same, this time in *Dubliners*. Gabriel Conroy, in "The Dead," is, we learn, not only a Biblical figure (Christ), but he is also Dante. So we come to the part where he carves the goose at supper. Obviously, the supper has to be "the Last Supper." (We have a Judas—Freddy Malins—and a Satan—Mr. Browne, because he is "brown all over"!) Why does Gabriel have to carve a goose (instead of a turkey)? Because "he has been made a goose of." But then, that is a proof that he is Dante who "must have been considered a goose by his countrymen; and Christ appeared a 'goose' to many." The point is not simply that such wild shots are easy to make fun of, but that they completely miss the real aims of literary criticism. The food on the table in this story has no allegorical function whatever—any more than the food in a minute description of a supper in Flaubert. To say Gabriel "feels like a goose" is not allegory and fits the context. But it is the realism of the passage that counts, not labored and farfetched correspondences out of tune with the artist's expressed intention. One might say, perhaps impudently, that a more Joycean key to the text can be found in a Delphic remark of Aunt

Kate, who "said that plain roast goose without any applesauce had always been good enough for her."

O'Brien's treatment of Joyce is arrogant and negative, so one does not mind criticizing him. One hates to be hard on Miss Moseley, who is positive, friendly, and well intentioned. More than that, the basic ideas of her study are solid and plausible. The Biblical themes in Joyce are of evident importance. But what is plausible is made to seem questionable when there are so many ingenious guesses which, besides being arbitrary in themselves, ignore the obvious purpose of the author and the very nature of the work of art itself.

So much for some recent examples of scholarly criticism. Fortunately, there are always the works of Joyce. One can turn back to them and breathe freely again. The year 1968 has seen the somewhat elaborate publication in book form of a Joyce notebook (text, facsimile, and comment) under the title *Giacomo Joyce.*[5] Reviewers on the whole have slighted this document, but it has very real value for students of Joyce, and is in fact a little work of art in itself.

The notebook is of unique interest. It is autobiographical and shows us Joyce in Trieste, Vercelli, and Padua, just before World War I. *A Portrait of the Artist* is half done. *Ulysses* is on the way. *Giacomo Joyce,* an abandoned project, has been mined for both. It is a collection of prose epiphanies, mere essentials and jotted "quiddities" of experience that are nowhere elaborated, nowhere developed. As such they have a kind of freshness and contemporaneousness which make the publication more than timely. *Giacomo Joyce* can be read as a prose poem, and as such it is in many ways more beautiful, because more sober, simpler, more tolerant of ambiguity than the highly elaborated and "artistic" chiselings of *Chamber Music* and *Pomes Penyeach*. The unique interest of *Giacomo Joyce* lies in its imperfection, its total lack of any "finish."

Its significance from the point of view of Joyce studies is cardinal. The *Giacomo* notebook represents a pivotal development in Joyce's ideas about love, from the erotic idealism of *A Portrait of the Artist* to the more ironic and mature realism of *Ulysses*. It deals specifically with the theme of spiritual seduction—and with the curious ambiguities involved in it. The charming Jewish girl whom Joyce is tutoring in English is halfway between the idealized "wading girl" of *Portrait* and Gerty MacDowell on Sandymount Beach. Joyce in *Giacomo* is clearly both Stephen and Bloom and, as Ellmann remarks in his introduction, the sardonic

[5] James Joyce, *Giacomo Joyce,* with introduction and notes by Richard Ellmann (New York: Viking Press, 1968).

influence of Svevo is not unlikely. What comes clear in *Giacomo* is that Joyce, now middle-aged, has acquired the necessary ironic distance simultaneously to be in love and to see himself faking—or "forging"—his love. *Giacomo Joyce* is a lucid, ironic description of the involvement of art, eros, and social custom, of life, literature, and manners, of race, culture, history, in an essentially comic experience of love. It marks the crucial point at which the comic genius of Joyce emerges to full maturity and self-awareness. As such, I submit that its importance is not to be measured simply by its few pages or by the fact that Joyce threw it aside (though he did take the trouble to copy it out on sheets of drawing paper). It is an essential item in the Joyce canon and something that every interested reader of Joyce will surely enjoy.

At the conclusion of his essay on Wagnerism in Joyce, William Blissett has two significant quotes: one from E. M. Forster on Joyce and the other from Nietzsche on Wagner. Forster remarked that "even the police are said not to comprehend [*Ulysses*] fully" (which comment still applies to those who take upon themselves the office of morally or politically "policing" Joyce's work). But he added that when one had gone to the trouble to read one of Joyce's big books, one will naturally tend to be pleased with his own achievement and call it "a great book, the book of the age. He really means that he himself is a great reader." And Nietzsche said the same of Wagnerians. Lured into the mystery of Wagner, the hide-and-seek of symbols, "in the midst of Wagner's multiplicity, fullness, and arbitrariness, they are justified, as it were, in their own eyes—they are 'saved.'" This, I think, does a great deal to explain the Joyce industry. Joyce scholarship can be a kind of heresy, a justification by works, a way of salvation, a mystic communion and ingestion of Joyce into one's own card file, followed by the ritual *confessio,* the solemn gnostic witness of one's attainment in diligently footnoted research. It almost seems that what matters is not what you say but the ritual of saying it; not what you prove, but the fact that you made the effort to prove it. As long as you have put in enough time, accumulated enough cards, strung out a long enough bibliography, quoted a few unlikely sources, and paid homage to the Joyce establishment, nobody cares very much what you have to say about Joyce. You can get away with anything.

A FOOTNOTE FROM *ULYSSES:* PEACE AND REVOLUTION

> "How can people point guns at each other? Sometimes they go off."
>
> —Bloom, in *Ulysses*

> *"Love, says Bloom, I mean the opposite of hatred."*

In the "Cyclops episode" of *Ulysses,* Bloom, a peaceful Odysseus, confronts the Irish revolutionary Cyclops, the violent "Citizen" who is at once a Sinn Feiner and an anti-Semite. This meeting takes place in a Dublin pub where the Citizen, accompanied by his ferocious dog, is drinking with others like himself. They are a typical group of toughs: aggressive, foul-mouthed, suspicious of anyone outside their own group, truculently xenophobic, united in a hatred of the English oppressor and in a desire to get rid of him by violence. Bloom, though uncircumcised, thrice baptized, and a loyal Dubliner, is not acceptable to them as "Irish." He is an outsider and a Jew. And he has "funny ideas." Furthermore, they suspect him of having slyly placed a hundred-to-five bet on the dark horse, the winner of the day's Gold Cup Race. They think he has gone to collect his bet, and that he is keeping quiet in order not to have to buy drinks all round.

Bloom tries to pacify them with conciliatory speeches about civilized life and love of neighbor, but the Citizen is not having any of that. When the party gets rough, Bloom is hurried out of the pub into a waiting vehicle. As a parting shot he taunts the Citizen with a reminder that Christ was a Jew. For this "blasphemy" the Citizen threatens to kill him and hurls a big tin biscuit box after the open jaunting car as it drives away. Parodying the style of Celtic epic and legend, Joyce brings to mind not only the heroes of Irish past but also Cyclops, blinded and enraged, hurling a huge stone after escaping Odysseus.

Written in 1968 and first published in *American Pax,* it later appeared in *Thomas Merton on Peace* (New York: McCall, 1971) and the revised edition, *The Nonviolent Alternative,* in 1980 (New York: Farrar Straus and Giroux; edited with an introduction by Gordon Zahn). See Merton's Letter to the Editor of *The Sewanee Review,* 76, Autumn 1968, p. 694, for a clarification of Joyce's reference to the antiphon, *Vidi aquam,* in *Ulysses.*

You may think me facetious for bringing this up, but the episode may be instructive as we consider Peace and Revolution! We are not used to considering moral and political issues in the light of contemporary literature, but perhaps we would be wise if we did so more often. Whatever we may think of Joyce's philosophy of life and of his art, there is no question that *Ulysses* is, among other things, an ironic moral cosmology, a literary commentary on the decay of Western civilization as exemplified by Dublin before World War I. The genius of James Joyce observes and describes the forces at work in that decaying society, looking back from the experience of World War I, which was in progress at the time when he wrote. Bloom is the central character in *Ulysses*. He is to a great extent an embodiment of the alienated, confused, money-minded, respectable middle-class Western man of the early twentieth century. He is a jumble of ineffective drives, confused ideas, mental clichés, frustrations, petty fears, and more or less expedient strategies for meeting the problems and challenges of life. It is in this that Bloom re-lives, in his own very humble way, the adventures of the resourceful Odysseus. The mock-heroic style of Joyce's great comedy shows us, in Bloom, the decline of the classic, Greco-Roman, and Christian civilization that first flowered in Homer. The nobility, the idealism, the chivalry, the humanity that we encounter in our cultural tradition have become, in Bloom, a pile of nondescript linguistic rubbish, sentimental jargon without any real force, based on no deep experience of life, but rather devised to justify alienation and evasion. And yet we note in passing that Bloom, when compared to the other characters in the book, not excluding Stephen, gives the impression of being more mature, more civilized, more experienced, even more humane, than they. Stephen of course is much more "cultured" than Bloom, but he is still somewhat callow and negative in his revolt against Dublin life. Bloom is the type who accepts modern life fully and adjusts to it willingly, because for him there is really no other. But his adjustment is seen to be equivocal and riddled with bad faith, in the full sense given to it by Sartre.

Now the importance of all this for our consideration of Peace and Revolution becomes clear when we note that some of the more important Joyce critics have given a positive and favorable reading of Bloom as *pacifist*. Yes, we learn that Bloom is really a reasonable man who sees the futility of force and conflict, and who lives by the conviction that "kindness overcomes power." And indeed all through the book we find Bloom accepting many hard knocks without protest. He is even a victim of real injustice, but he does not assert his rights. For instance, he knows that his wife is unfaithful to him that very afternoon and does nothing to stop it. He just ignores the whole thing. He pays no attention to implied or to explicit insults, and accepts the rather general contempt of others in good part. The climax of his "pacifism" is in his encounter with the Citizen and his expression of sentiments about civilization and love.

Now it must be said at once that these critics seem to underestimate the force of Joyce's irony. Joyce obviously does not accept Bloom's truisms about love at their face value—any more than the Citizen does. In fact Joyce inserts a famous and sardonic little aside about everybody loving somebody and God loving everybody: "Nurse loves the new chemist. Constable 14A loves Mary Kelly. Gerty MacDowell loves the boy that has the bicycle . . ." We have to consider the context. There has been an argument going on, the Citizen and his friends advocating that the English be thrown out of Ireland by force, Bloom protesting, defending the values of Western civilization and deploring the fact that violence merely perpetuates hatred among nations. "And what's your nation?" asks the Citizen with heavy sarcasm. All right, so Bloom will defend his *race,* too! A race that is "plundered, insulted and persecuted." He protests vehemently, and his protest meets with some sympathy, if not from the Citizen, at least from one of the others. "Right," says this other, but adds: "Stand up to it with force like men." As far as they are concerned, this is a challenge that Bloom simply cannot meet. His plea for love is nothing but a "collapse," "like a wet rag."

Hatred and force, he says, are no use. They are "the opposite of what is really life." Joyce himself emphasizes the fact that Bloom's argument is all weakness, sentimentality, confusion. And Bloom runs out of the bar at once, only to return later and face real trouble.

Now it must be said first of all that whatever some Joyce critics may think of his intentions, Joyce has not portrayed, in Bloom, an authentic pacifist. Far from it. This "pacifism" is in line with everything else in Bloom. It is the expression of pathetic weakness, confusion, frustration, and ambivalence. It is not the product of any serious moral conviction. It is not even one of his more significant velleities. It may indeed indicate a desire to be left in peace, a desire not to be rejected and injured. Surely that is not "pacifism" or "love of peace." Indeed Bloom himself later admits it. He wants to score as much as "they" do. He tells himself that with the jibe about Christ being a Jew he really did come out on top after all. "Got my own back there. What I said about his God made him wince!"

To say that Bloom is a pacifist and even to commend him for it certainly does no service whatever to pacifism or to the cause of peace. But the point I would like to make—and this I think fits in with Joyce's real intention—is that the Cyclops episode does in fact spell out the whole issue of Peace and Revolution in terms of popular contemporary cliché. Whatever may be the truth of the case, this is in fact the way the majority of people today continue to see the question of nonviolence and force. This is the way all violent revolutionaries look at it, and it is also the way American public opinion and the established mass media of capitalism still generally regard it. If they are favorable, they see it more or less as the critics who "like" Bloom see it. There is a kind of heroism and nobility in *expressing these noble sentiments* and in *saying* that love is better than hatred. There is also something praiseworthy about refraining from violence in word or in act. This is an attitude which they feel to be nicer than its contrary. It appeals to them more than its contrary. They respond to it more than they do to its contrary. This reassures and pleases them—to hear a man affirm the priority of love! But to hear him affirm (with a few choice oaths) the prior efficacy of force is disturbing and unpleasant. Very well. And yet they have no alternative to force. They prefer love as an idea, but when confronted with force, they have only two ways out: to run away or else to call the police. In the end they fall back on force to defend and to affirm love.

As to those who, like the Citizen, have an open contempt for the civilization that Bloom does not want to see overthrown, they are in no doubt about what is really wrong with people who can't stand the idea of force. Such people are simply cowards, and they must be swept out of the way. They are slated for destruction with the structures they defend and justify with their humane inanities.

It is instructive to read the Cyclops episode again in a time that has become much more violent and much more revolutionary than the days before World War I. In fact, if we look back to Joyce's Dublin in 1904, we find an almost unbelievable era of peace, order, and stability. The Citizen was of course a normal part of that culture: but there are many more like him today, whether in the Klan or in Black Power; in the CIA or in the guerilla band; voting for Wallace or waving the Vietcong flag in demonstrations. It is therefore useful to spell out what Bloom's brand of "pacifism" means in the mind of the Citizen.

First of all, it is a lie. The pacifist, the nonviolent resister, in spite of subjective sincerity (even this is doubtful) is at once a crafty and ineffectual person. Ineffectual by definition, because his very ideas about love and peace mark him as cut off from reality. Ineffectual, too, because he is doubtless masochistic, fear-ridden, passive, pathetic; he invites beatings. He exercises that sort of appeal on the sadism of the man of force. The Citizen is looking for an excuse, any excuse, to pick a fight with Bloom and mop up the floor with him. Bloom's defense of love is in fact a defense of himself, a pathetic appeal to be considered and accepted as a human being. But the Citizen does not want to waste any time considering a member of an out-group as a human being. In fact he simply wants to prove that Bloom's glorification of love is a mask of dishonesty and fear. Thus the man of force is intent above all on discrediting and unmasking the presumed bad faith of the pacifist, the nonviolent resister.

To do this, he assumes a secret dishonesty and a hook-up of some sort that presumably give the pacifist a sinister undercover advantage, a quasi-superiority which, in spite of his surface innocuousness, makes him a real threat. So the Citizen assumes that Bloom is being both unjust and greedy in keeping his gains to himself. The modern man of force is convinced that the pacifist or the nonviolent resister is really allied with some hidden power group—generally the "Communists." In any case, it becomes not only possible but indeed honorable to unmask and destroy them.

One of the main themes of *Ulysses* is the breakdown of language and of communication as part of the disruption of Western culture. The extraordinary linguistic richness of the book—which, however, comes out mostly in parody—only reminds us more forcefully how much further the breakdown has gone in the last fifty years. Pacifism and nonviolence are fully and consciously involved in this question of language. Nonviolence, as Gandhi conceived it, is in fact a kind of language. The real dynamic of nonviolence can be considered as a purification of language, a restoration of true communication on a human level, when language has been emptied of meaning by misuse and corruption. Nonviolence is meant to communicate love not in word but in act. Above all, nonviolence is meant to convey and to defend truth which has been obscured and defiled by political double talk.

The real lesson of all this for us is this: we must clearly understand the function of nonviolence against the background of the collapse of language. It is no accident that Noam Chomsky, a leader in the Draft Resistance movement, is also an expert in the study of language. The special force of the Cyclops episode in *Ulysses* is that it shows how the language of pacifism and the language of force can both fit with equal readiness into a context of linguistic corruption. We have to be terribly aware of the fact that our pacifism and nonviolence can easily be nothing more than parodies of themselves. We must recognize the temptation to be quite content with this—to be content to express our weak convictions in weak and provisional terms, meanwhile waiting for an opportunity to abandon nonviolence altogether and go over to the side of force, on the ground that we have tried nonviolence and found it wanting.

Has nonviolence been found wanting? Yes and no. It has been found wanting wherever it has been the nonviolence of the weak. It has not been found wanting when it has been the nonviolence of the strong. What is the difference? It is a difference of language. The language of spurious nonviolence is merely another, more equivocal form of the language of power. It is used and conceived pragmatically, in reference to the seizure of power. But that is not what nonviolence is about. Nonviolence is not for power but for truth. It is not pragmatic but prophetic. It is not aimed at immediate political results, but at the manifestation of fundamental and crucially important truth. Nonviolence is not primarily the language of efficacy, but the language of *kairos*. It does not say "We shall overcome" so much as "This is the day of the Lord, and whatever may happen to us, *He* shall overcome."

And this, of course, is the dimension that is entirely absent from the Cyclops episode in *Ulysses*. Unhappily, it is too often absent from our world and our practice today. As a result people begin to imagine that to say "only force works" is to discredit nonviolence. This half-truth—that only force is efficacious—may turn out to be one of the most dangerous illusions of our time. It may do more than anything else to promote an irresponsible and meaningless use of force in a pseudo-revolution that will only consolidate the power of the police state. Never was it more necessary to understand the importance of genuine nonviolence as a power for real change because it is aimed not so much at revolution as at conversion. Unfortunately, mere words about peace, love, and civilization have completely lost all power to change anything.

THE TRUE LEGENDARY SOUND:
THE POETRY AND CRITICISM OF EDWIN MUIR

A recent popular survey of English philosophy since 1900 gives us a useful appraisal of the respectable grammarians of our day. It also includes, as an afterthought, a chapter on metaphysics. The chief purpose of this chapter is, of course, to remind us that there are no metaphysicians in England. At the same time the author gives us to understand that there is no justification for metaphysics anyway. Of such an attitude Edwin Muir would have said that it was a "denial of the roots"—and he would have added that such a denial cannot be made without cost.

Muir is one of those who intuitively realize that the giving of names is a primordial metaphysical act of the human intelligence—the Edenic office of the poet who follows Adam and reverifies the names given to creatures by his first father. Sartre (who has not much else in common with Muir!) brings this out clearly in writing of Francis Ponge. "The thing awaits its name. The giving of a name is a metaphysical act of absolute value; it is the solid and definitive union of man and thing because the *raison d'être* of the thing is to require a name and the function of man is to speak and give it one." Beneath the surface of this statement one can guess an existentialist fluidity which has nothing to do with the Biblical and epic solidity of Muir's grasp of the act of being. Whether or not Muir ever read *La Nausée* he would surely have been repelled by the meditation of Roquentin on the root in the park!

The poetry of Edwin Muir gives evidence of profound metaphysical concern: concern for the roots of being, for being in act, manifested by numinous and symbolic qualities. He does not seek these roots out of curiosity, nor does he find them in speculative and dialectical discussion. As a poet, Muir felt himself compelled to "divine and persuade"—to divine in the sense of a water-diviner finding hidden springs; to persuade, not by demonstration but by sharing the water with others.

It would of course be misleading to call Muir a "metaphysical poet." Intellectual irony, wit, and "conceits" are absent from his verse. But we must not forget the metaphysical preoccupations of Wordsworth, Cole-

---

The manuscript for this essay is dated September 1966 and was first published in *The Sewanee Review*, 75, Spring 1967.

ridge, and even more of Blake. Muir as critic more than once quotes the lines of "Tintern Abbey" about the "eye made quiet by the power of harmony" seeing into "the deep life of things." The business of the poet is to reach the intimate, that is ontological, sources of life which cannot be clearly apprehended in themselves by any concept, but which, once intuited, can be made accessible to all in symbolic and imaginative celebration. The poetic experience of Muir, rich and varied and reaching out on various levels of depth, sometimes seeks out the ground itself of being:

> It is not any thing
> And yet all being it is;
> Being, being, being
> Its burden and its bliss.
> > How can I ever prove
> > What it is I love?

At other times (and here he is more articulate) he shows that he could equal Rilke's power of "inseeing" (*Einsehen*) by which the poet "lets himself into the very center" of the particular existent that he sees. In Rilke's words, he becomes able to see the thing from the very point where it springs from the creative power of God, and is "approved" by God.

I think that we can find the best examples of Muir's "inseeing" in some of his poems about horses. Horses awed and fascinated him, and consequently some of his most inspired imaginative writing is about them: they were to him splendid and numinous archetypes, because of the extraordinary innocence of his vision of them as a child on a farm in the Orkney Islands.

We must remember that Muir's poetry rests on a substratum of authentically primitive experience. He was an Orkney islander, a peasant's child in one of the last primitive communities of Europe.

Muir speaks in his *Autobiography* of looking up at his father's huge plough horses with "a combination of emotions which added up to worship in the Old Testament sense."

> Everything about them, the steam rising from their soft, leathery nostrils, the sweat staining their hides, their ponderous irresistible motion, the distant rolling of their eyes which was like the revolution of rock-crystal suns, the waterfall sweep of their manes . . . the plunge of their iron-shod hoofs striking fire from the flagstones filled me with a stationary terror and delight for which I could get no relief.

His reference to the Old Testament, and this quoted passage, suggest that he was thinking of the cosmic praise of the Creator in Job or the Psalms.

Muir, who had left the Orkneys in his teens to work under abominable conditions in Glasgow, always resented the industrial society in which he had to live. He never adjusted to it and retained a thoroughly romantic contempt for it. He could thus say, typically, that it is possible to write poems about horses and not about cars because horses have "a life of their own." The horse becomes for him a symbol of the primitive and natural world as opposed to the artificial and unnatural world of modern technology. This artificial world is one in which he thinks there is no real place for poetry at all: it is essentially antipoetic and Muir's estimate of the possibility of poetry's surviving in it is to say the least "depressed." His half-admitted hope for poetry lies rather in the guess that technology will prove self-destructive. In his private and sometimes curiously striking eschatology Muir has a poem about the sudden spontaneous return of "the horses" to the wreckage of a world that has finally smashed itself by its own machines. T. S. Eliot, a great admirer of Muir, singled this poem out for special mention in his preface to the *Collected Poems*.[1] Actually, one of Muir's very first poems about horses is even more typical of his imaginative insight. It is the same vision of childhood referred to above, now embodied in a poem of Blakian power and intensity:

> Their conquering hooves which trod the stubble down
> Were ritual that turned the field to brown,
> And their great hulks were seraphim of gold,
> Or mute ecstatic monsters on the mould.

> And oh! the rapture, when, one furrow done,
> They marched broad breasted to the sinking sun!
> The light flowed off their bossy sides in flakes;
> The furrows rolled behind like struggling snakes.

> But when at dusk with steaming nostrils home
> They came, they seemed gigantic in the gloom,
> And warm and glowing with mysterious fire
> That lit their smouldering bodies in the mire.

> Their eyes as brilliant and as wide as night
> Gleamed with a cruel apocalyptic light,
> Their manes the leaping ire of the wind
> Lifted with rage invisible and blind.

[1] Edwin Muir, *Collected Poems,* second edition, with a preface by T. S. Eliot (New York: Oxford University Press, 1965).

Muir did not completely agree with Rilke's explanation of "inseeing." He thought it "Platonic." He was the enemy of all abstractions. His imagination, like his metaphysic, was Biblical and Homeric as well as Celtic. It was never Platonic (and the question arises: was the object of Rilke's inseeing merely the "Platonic idea"? Possibly this was a misjudgment on Muir's part). Still, Muir writes of animals as Rilke did, guessing at their vision of the world as uninfluenced by any self-consciousness, any introspection, any reflective memory, any language: purely looking outward and not knowing what their own names are.

> But these have never trod
> Twice the familiar track,
> Never never turned back
> Into the memoried day.
> All is new and near
> In the unchanging Here. . . .

Muir's metaphysical insight into the numinous and sacred, which does not underlie but actually *is* the ordinary reality of our world, was not an otherworldly mysticism. On the contrary, it was the ground of a deep and humane sympathy which expressed itself, for instance, in praise of Rabelais (in a remarkable essay on Panurge and Falstaff). On this metaphysical insight rests the sound sense of his critical essays; particularly about the novel.

Some of his poems treat love in a way that shows deep insight into the metaphysic of the person. The sweep of his vision, which is constantly aware of the beginning and the end of all things, naturally demands of him poems of theological scope, in which he rejects the austere Calvinism to which he was temporarily converted in adolescence. Later he turns, as we see in his *Autobiography,* to a warmer and more "Mediterranean" theology of the Incarnation and the Cross. Still he responds to Milton in a magnificent visionary poem (the first of his most important book), "One Foot in Eden."

> Milton, his face set fair for Paradise,
> And knowing that he and Paradise were lost
> In separate desolation, bravely crossed
> Into his second night and paid his price.
> There towards the end he to the dark tower came
> Set square in the gate, a mass of blackened stone
> Crowned with vermilion fiends like streamers blown
> From a great funnel filled with roaring flame.

The strong contrasting colors are those of the Italian primitives. Sometimes his eschatology almost suggests that of Hieronymus Bosch. Here he describes a city reflected in a river, seeming to fall apart in anticipation of Judgment Day.

> In its mirror
> Great oes and capitals and flourishes
> Pillars and towers and fans and gathered sheaves
> Hold harvest home and Judgment Day of fire.
> The houses stir and pluck their roofs and walls
> Apart as if in play and fling their stones
> Against the sky to make a common arc
> And fall again. The conflagrations raise
> Their mountainous precipices. Living eyes
> Glaze instantly in crystal change.

These few examples, sufficient to give at least a fair idea of Muir's poetic imagination, also show him to be a writer with little or no technical sophistication. Muir began writing poetry, almost under compulsion, in early middle-age. It was a psychological and spiritual necessity for him. He did not imitate Eliot or Pound or anyone else then in fashion: he wrote as he felt, in the ballad tradition that had still been alive in the community into which he was born, and in the tradition of Wordsworth and the Romantics he had read in his youth. He was never able to become deeply concerned with technical problems in poetry, whether as a poet or as a critic. As a poet he struggled to get the archetypes under control by means of the most obvious and familiar forms. He wanted to get the big symbols out and make them clear.

"I began to write poetry," he tells us in the *Autobiography,* "simply because what I wanted to say could not have gone properly into prose. I wanted so much to say it that I had no thought left to study the form in which alone it could be said."

Muir's poetry seeks the reconciliation of the inner and outer man, of the world of the present with its roots in the past. It aims at unity, and the power which restores this living unity is imagination. In the poetic imagination the heroes of Homer and the Biblical patriarchs not only manifest themselves and make themselves comprehensible to the poet and reader, but they "coexist" with him. Their typological experience is seen as realized in the crises of the poet's own life. Psychoanalysis played a very important part in Muir's life of inner struggle and seems to have liberated in him an altogether unusual creative power. (Contrast Rilke who, probably with equally good reasons, refused to be analyzed fearing that analysis, in "healing" his wounds, might relax fruitful tensions on which his creative power depended.)

The two books of critical lectures and essays which concern us here show Muir to be a reader of sound and catholic judgment, profoundly humane and careful not to do violence to authors or characters in the interests of any pet theory of his own. *The Estate of Poetry*,[2] containing his Norton Lectures, is preoccupied with the relation of the poet to his audience. His *Essays on Literature and Society*[3] range widely over poetry, the novel, and drama, and even include an essay on Spengler. In both these books Muir, as critic, returns again and again to what, for him, is the most important question: imagination. Imagination is for him at once poetic and metaphysical: "By imagination I mean that power by which we apprehend living beings and living creatures in their individuality as they live and move and not in their ideas and categories." The power of the poet's imaginative vision (in which of course the reader can participate) is that it directs our eye to beings in such a way as to *"feel the full weight and uniqueness* of their lives." Here as a matter of fact the poet has a prerogative which the speculative and abstract metaphysician might be tempted to deny him out of envy: the power to see being *in the concrete* and not by pure abstraction; to see it in its *individual actualization*—and even to express it as its concreteness. Both the vision and the expression of the individual evade technical and discursive ontology. Hence Muir's sense of mission in constantly reaffirming the vital necessity of poetic imagination in our age. Without it, we can have no real participation in the rich experience of the past. But the hubris of the present consists precisely in dismissing the past as irrelevant except to the prying and classifying eye of the specialist who studies it without ever realizing its relationship, and consequently its relevance, to ourselves. "When outward change becomes too rapid and the world around us alters from year to year, the ancestral image grows indistinct and the imagination cannot pierce to it as easily as it once could. . . ." A tragic loss, for then we no longer realize what it means that "our life is a rehearsal of lives that have been lived over and over." Not that we are meant to repeat, for repetition's sake, a series of futile and obsolete patterns: but there are in us inherited meanings and symbols which never come to life, never "connect" in our own existence, if we cannot identify with others

[2] Edwin Muir, *The Estate of Poetry*, with a foreword by Archibald MacLeish (Cambridge, Harvard University Press, 1962).

[3] Edwin Muir, *Essays on Literature and Society*, revised and enlarged edition (Cambridge, Harvard University Press, 1965).

in the present and in the past. Muir is concerned with imagination not only in order that there may be good poetry, but in order that man himself may survive.

Muir was distrustful of strictly technical and professional critical disciplines. He thought our refined modern criticism too esoteric, and felt that it was only a symptom of a generally bad condition in literature. This is the main theme of *The Estate of Poetry*. The "natural estate" of poetry is that in which the poet is in direct contact with an audience to which he speaks or sings his own poems. He needs no interpreter and no mediator. Poetry is then a general possession—the author himself may be forgotten, or may be a collective person. For Muir, then, the natural estate of poetry was already deranged by printing, which put the book definitely between the poet and the reader. (Readers of manuscripts in Rome and the Middle Ages usually read *aloud*. Monastic texts are punctuated for *singing*.) With the printed book poetry is not "heard." It becomes visual, mental, abstract. In his deep gloom about the modern world, Muir saw only more and more hopelessness ahead as technology came more and more to intervene between man and nature, man and the reality and immediacy of his own being. Poetry is now, he thought, in a "depressed state." Muir was in fact in despair about the modern world and felt that the poet was in a hopeless predicament, completely cut off from a popular audience, with no one to talk to, still less to sing to. Muir apparently had no inkling of the possibilities that have since surprised us: the influence of young Soviet poets reading their works in the parks, or the power exercised by an admittedly unruly poet like Bob Dylan making use of modern media. Dylan may certainly have more in common with *Mad* comics than with Shakespeare but he is nevertheless definitely conscious of a poetic vocation and has communicated an authentic fervor to an audience that is deeply involved. For Muir, the poet has become the helpless and passive prey of the critic. Poetry having now become not an experience but a problem, it is necessary to write problematical poems that critics will be interested in discussing. If the critics ignore you, you are no poet.

Indeed, what really matters is not so much the poem as the crowning brilliancy of its critical analysis. The poem is only an occasion. Thus poetry is only a humble, ordinary, rather useless tree which justifies its existence by allowing criticisms to bloom all over its branches like orchids. So, Muir says, the poet having lost contact with a living and popular audience has turned in despair to the consolations of an imprisoned and "kept" existence. Poets have locked "themselves into a hygienic prison in which they speak only to one another and to the critic their stern warder." Such a situation gives Muir claustrophobia.

Doubtless Muir is too pessimistic. His romantic allergies incline him to some exaggeration and he is perhaps too negative in his estimate of critical methods. Yet it is true that they may become, as he says, machines into which the poem is put in order to achieve a result already in the teacher's mind. As a result poetry itself tends to become artificial, unnatural, unimaginative, a formalistic exercise without interest except for those who have a private code they like to play games with.

Muir's own poems are, then, deliberately left in a state which many readers might consider crude and naïve. He could easily be neglected, except for the fact that poets now seem to be reading him with considerable interest, not for the way he says things but for what he actually says; not for the sophistication of his technique but for his imaginative power and his concern for "the creation of a true image of life." Muir is no doubt a poet who wrote to be read aloud. He wrote with his ear attuned to his own inflections and some of his poems scan with difficulty when skimmed over with the eye. I do not know if he was a good reader himself, but perhaps these poems should be given the benefit that he demanded for all poetry: and then they would reveal to us their "true legendary sound." This is perhaps essential to poetry, which is "the communication of something for which no other kind of speech can serve." Muir himself was not a technical but a charismatic poet, and he was faithful to his special grace: his keen awareness that "The first allegiance of any poet is to imaginative truth."

THE PASTERNAK AFFAIR

1. *In Memoriam*

On the night of Monday, May 30, 1960, the Pasternak Affair was finally closed. The lonely Russian poet's mysterious life of seventy years came to a peaceful end in the *dacha* at the writer's colony which he had made famous—Peredelkino, twenty miles outside of Moscow.

A year and a half had passed since the brief orgy of political animosity and righteous indignation which had celebrated the award of the Nobel Prize for Literature in the fall of 1958. The prize had been offered to Pasternak, not for his novel *Dr. Zhivago* (New York: Pantheon, 1958) alone but for his whole life work in poetry, for his other prose works, and presumably also for his translations. Under Soviet pressure Pasternak refused the prize. He also refused a proffered opportunity to "escape" from Soviet Russia, pointing out that he did not want to "get away" from his native country because he did not feel that he could be happy anywere else.

There was a great deal of excitement everywhere. The press made much of the Pasternak case, with the usual gesticulations on both sides of the iron curtain. While the smoke was still thick, and the excitement over the explosion still general, all one could do was to hope and pray that Pasternak would survive. There seems to have been every expectation, both in the West and in Russia, that Pasternak was about to become a "nonperson." The Russian writers fell all over one another in their eagerness to become as disassociated from him as they possibly could. Western writers, in appeals that were probably more effective than anyone expected them to be, asked that Pasternak's case be examined with the cool objectivity of nonpartisan fairness. Although the poet was menaced in every way, especially when his case was front-page news, after the excitement died down he was left alone. The visits of foreign newsmen, the "pilgrimages" of Western men of letters to Peredelkino, were suffered to continue. Pasternak's immense correspondence was apparently

---

The second section of this essay, "The People with Watch Chains," appeared first in *Jubilee*, July 1959, and the longer third part, "Spiritual Implication," was published in *Thought*, Winter 1959, under the title "The Pasternak Affair in Perspective." An introduction was added to these two parts when it was brought out in book form as a part of *Disputed Questions* in 1960 by Farrar Straus and Cudahy.

not much interfered with, and things went on "as usual" except that the poet could not write poetry or work on the historical play or on the new novel which he had planned. He was kept too busy with visitors and the writing of letters. The last phase of his extraordinary life was the most active of all. The whole world (including many of the younger writers in the Soviet Union) had turned to him as to a prophetic figure, a man whose ascendency was primarily spiritual. The impact of this great and sympathetic figure has been almost religious, if we take that term in a broad and more or less unqualified sense.

It is true that there are striking and genuinely Christian elements in the outlook of Pasternak, in the philosophy that underlies his writing. But of course to claim him as an apologist for Christianity would be an exaggeration. His "religious" character is something more general, more mysterious, more existential. He has made his mark in the world not so much by what he said as by what he was: the sign of a genuinely spiritual man. Although his work is certainly very great, we must first of all take account of what is usually called his personal "witness." He embodied in himself so many of the things modern man pathetically claims he still believes in, or wants to believe in. He became a kind of "sign" of that honesty, integrity, sincerity which we tend to associate with the free and creative personality. He was also an embodiment of that personal warmth and generosity which we seek more and more vainly among the alienated mass-men of our too organized world. In one word, Pasternak emerged as a genuine human being stranded in a mad world. He immediately became a symbol, and all those who felt it was important not to be mad attached themselves in some way to him. Those who had given up, or sold out, or in one way or another ceased to believe in this kind of human quality turned away from him, and found appropriate slogans or catchwords to dismiss him from their thoughts.

This does not mean, of course, that everyone who was "for" Pasternak was a real human being and all the rest were squares. On the contrary, one of the most salient characteristics of the Pasternak Affair in its most heated moments was the way Pasternak got himself surrounded by squares coming at him from all directions with contradictory opinions. Naturally, those who "believed" in Pasternak were not thereby justified, sanctified, or reborn. But the fact remains that he stirred up the unsatisfied spiritual appetites of men for ideals a little more personal, a little less abstract, than modern society seems to offer them.

But what, after all, has been the precise importance of Pasternak? Is this the last, vivid flareup of the light of liberal and Christian humanism?

Does he belong purely to the past? Or is he in some way the link between Russia's Christian past and a possibly Christian future? Perhaps one dare not ask such questions, and the following two studies are not by any means attempts to do so.

The first essay is the more literary of the two. The second examines, in detail, the development of the "Pasternak Affair" and tries to assess its significance for the spiritual and intellectual life of our time. In neither do I try to appropriate Pasternak for any special cultural or religious movement, to line him up with any religious position that may be familiar in the West, or to claim that he stands four-square for culture and democracy as against barbarism and dictatorship.

I might as well admit that, looking at the divisions of the modern world, I find it hard to avoid seeing somewhat the same hypocrisies, the same betrayals of man, the same denials of God, the same evils in different degrees and under different forms on either side. Indeed, I find all these things in myself. Therefore I cannot find it in myself to put on a mentality that spells war. These studies of Pasternak are by no means to be interpreted as my contribution to the Cold War, because I don't want any part of the war, whether it is cold or hot. I seek only to do what Pasternak himself did: to speak my mind out of love for man, the image of God—not to speak a set piece dictated by my social situation.

I am happy to record the fact that Pasternak himself read the first of these two studies, and accepted it with kind approval.[1] The second was not sent to him, being to a great extent "political." Because of my own warm personal admiration for this great poet, and because of the debt of gratitude I owe him for many things, this book is dedicated to his memory. I am persuaded that Russia will one day be as proud of Pasternak as she is of all her other great writers, and that *Dr. Zhivago* will be studied in Russian schools among the great classics of the language. I can think of no better and more succinct comment upon the life and death of Pasternak than these words of his own which express his belief in immortality and which I have quoted again in the second study. Because of the coming of Christ, says Zhivago, speaking the mind of Pasternak himself: "Man does not die in a ditch like a dog—but at home in history, while the work toward the conquest of death is in full swing; *he dies sharing in this work.*"

---

[1] See pages 81–82 for the text of his last letter to the author. Merton dedicated *Disputed Questions* to Pasternak.

2. *The People with Watch Chains*

> My sister-called-life, like a tidal wave breaking
> Swamps the bright world in a wall of spring rain:
> But people with watch-chains grumble and frown
> With poisoned politeness, like snakes in the corn.
>   From *My Sister Life.*

It is perhaps not quite fair to start a discussion of Pasternak with lines from an early poem. He repudiated his earlier style, together with much that was written by the Futurists and Symbolists who were his friends forty years ago. (He did not, of course, repudiate his friends. For someone like Pasternak, friends cannot become "nonpersons.") He may or may not have pardoned us for enjoying the freshness of this early verse, but in any case it is clear that Life who was his "sister" in 1917 became his bride and his very self in *Dr. Zhivago* ("Doctor Life"). Life is at once the hero and the heroine (Lara) of this strange, seemingly pessimistic but victorious tragedy: not, however, Life in the abstract, certainly not the illusory, frozen-faced *imago* of Life upon which Communism constructs its spiritless fantasies of the future. Life for Pasternak is the painful, ambivalent, yet inexhaustibly fecund reality that is the very soul of Russia. A reality which, with all its paradoxes, has certainly manifested itself in the Russian revolution and all that followed, but which overflows all the possible limits of recorded history. Hundreds of pages of turbulent and exquisite prose give us some insight into the vastness of that reality as it was experienced, quite providentially, by one of the few sensitive and original spirits that survived the storm. And since Life cannot be confined within the boundaries of one nation, what Pasternak has to say about it overflows symbolism, into every corner of the world. It is the mystery of history as passion and resurrection that we glimpse obscurely in the story of the obscure Doctor who gives his name to the novel. This frustrated, confused, and yet somehow triumphant protagonist is not only Pasternak himself and even Russia, but mankind—not "twentieth-century man" but man who is perhaps too existential and mysterious for any label to convey his meaning and his identity. We, of course, are that man.

That is the mark of a really great book: it is in some way about everybody and everybody is involved in it. Nothing could be done to stop the drab epic of Zhivago, like the downpour in the 1917 poem, from bursting on the heads of all and swamping them whether they liked it or not. For that is exactly what Life cannot refrain from doing.

The appearance of *Dr. Zhivago,* and all the confused and largely absurd reactions which followed upon it, form a very meaningful incident at the close of an apparently meaningless decade. Certainly the surprise publication and instant success of the novel everywhere (including Russia, where it has been avidly read in manuscript by all the young intellectuals who could get hold of it) has more to say in retrospect than all the noise and empty oratory of the Soviet fortieth anniversary. This significance will of course be missed by all those who insist on taking a purely partisan and *simpliste* view of events, and who therefore interpret the book as all black or all white, all good or all bad, all left or all right. The dimensions of Pasternak's worldview are more existential and spiritual and are decidedly beyond left and right.

In bursting upon the heads of all, Zhivago inevitably deluged first of all those simple and pontifical souls whose Gospel is passive conformity with the politicians and bigshots, with the high priests of journalism and the doctors of propaganda: upon those who though they no longer decorate their paunches with cheap watch chains, still thrive on conformity with the status quo, on either side of the iron curtain.

Zhivago is one of those immensely "popular" books that has not really been popular. It has been bought by more people than were able to read it with full understanding. No doubt many of those who have had Pasternak's heavy volume in their hands have approved of it only vaguely and for the wrong reasons. And others who have read it have put it down with the unquiet feeling that it was somehow not sufficiently businesslike. For such as these, "life" has ceased to mean what it means to Pasternak. For the people with watch chains, a life that gets along independently of the plans of politicians and economists is nothing but a reactionary illusion. This has been brought home to Pasternak in no uncertain terms by his devoted confrères in the Soviet Writers' Union. But the same judgment has finally worked its way out in the West also, where Isaac Deutscher, the biographer of Stalin, has accused *Zhivago* of being another Oblomov and scolded him for considering the revolution "an atrocity." Let us face it, the people with watch chains can easily reconcile themselves with any atrocity that serves their own opportunism, whether it be in the form of a revolution or of an atomic bomb. Life (claimed as a sister by escapists and cosmopolitan mad dogs) had better learn to get along in these new circumstances. The atrocities are here to stay.

All great writing is in some sense revolutionary. Life itself is revolutionary, because it constantly strives to surpass itself. And if history is to be something more than the record of society's bogging down in meaningless formalities to justify the crimes of men, then a book that is at the same time great in its own right, and moreover lands with a tremendous impact on the world of its time, deserves an important place in history. The reason why *Dr. Zhivago* is significant is precisely that it stands so far above politics. This, among other things, places it in an entirely different category from Dudintsev's *Not by Bread Alone*. Attempts to involve Pasternak in the Cold War have been remarkable above all by their futility. The cloud of misunderstandings and accusations that surrounded the affair did not engulf Pasternak: the confusion served principally to emphasize the distance which separated him from his accusers and his admirers alike.

Both as a writer and as a man, Pasternak stands out as a sign of contradiction in our age of materialism, collectivism, and power politics. His spiritual genius is essentially and powerfully solitary. Yet his significance does not lie precisely in this. Rather it lies in the fact that his very solitude made him capable of extraordinarily intimate and understanding contacts with men all over the face of the earth. The thing that attracted people to Pasternak was not a social or political theory, it was not a formula for the unification of mankind, not a collectivist panacea for all the evils in the world: it was the man himself, the truth that was in him, his simplicity, his direct contact with life, and the fact that he was full of the only revolutionary force that is capable of producing anything new: he is full of love.

Pasternak is then not just a man who refuses to conform (that is to say, a rebel). The fact is, he is not a rebel, for a rebel is one who wants to substitute his own authority for the authority of somebody else. Pasternak is one who *cannot* conform to an artificial and stereotyped pattern because, by the grace of God, he is too much alive to be capable of such treason to himself and to life. He is not a rebel but a revolutionary, in the same way that Gandhi was a revolutionary. And in fact those who have said: "Passive resistance is all right against the English but it would never work against Russia" must stop and consider that in Pasternak it did, to some extent, work even in Russia. Pasternak is certainly a man to be compared with Gandhi. Though different in so many accidental ways, his protest is ultimately the same: the protest of life itself, of humanity itself, of love, speaking not with theories and programs but simply affirming itself and asking to be judged on its own merits.

Like Gandhi, Pasternak stands out as a gigantic paradox in a world of servile and mercenary conformities. His presence in such a world has had an inescapable effect: it has struck fear into the hearts of everyone else, whether in Russia or in America. The reaction to Pasternak, the alternate waves of love, fear, hate and adulation that have rushed toward him from every part of the world, were all set in motion by the *guilt* of a society that has consciously and knowingly betrayed life, and sold itself out to falsity, formalism, and spiritual degradation. In some (for instance, the pundits of Soviet literature) this guilt has produced hatred and rage against Pasternak. The fear he aroused was intolerable. His colleagues in the Soviet Writers' Union began to yell for his blood, and yelled all the more loudly in proportion as they were themselves servile and second rate. There were a few notable exceptions, rare writers of integrity and even talent, like Ilya Ehrenburg.

The politicians of the Kremlin, on the other hand, not being writers, not thoroughly understanding what it was all about anyway, were less moved to guilt, felt less fear, and were slow to do much about the case at first.

In the West the reaction was different. We felt the same guilt, the same fear, but in a different mode and degree. On the whole our reaction was to run to Pasternak with fervent accolades: to admire in him the courage and integrity we lack in ourselves. Perhaps we can taste a little vicarious revolutionary joy without doing anything to change our own lives. To justify our own condition of servility and spiritual prostitution we think it sufficient to admire another man's integrity.

I think that later pages of this study will show that Pasternak's witness is essentially Christian. That is the trouble: the problematical quality of Pasternak's "Christianity" lies in the fact that it is reduced to the barest and most elementary essentials: intense awareness of all cosmic and human reality as "life in Christ," and the consequent plunge into love as the only dynamic and creative force which really honors this "Life" by creating itself anew in Life's—Christ's—image.

As soon as *Dr. Zhivago* appeared everybody began comparing Pasternak with Tolstoy and Dostoevsky. The comparisons were obvious, sometimes trite, but basically legitimate. However, they run the risk of creating misconceptions. Pasternak does not merely work on an enormous canvas, like the classical novelists of the nineteenth century. Sholokhov also has done that, and Pasternak is immensely more important than Sholokhov, competent as the latter may be. But to be a twentieth-century Tolstoy is in fact to disqualify oneself for comparison with one who was an original and unique genius of his own age. The thing that makes Pasternak a new Tolstoy is precisely the fact that he is *not* Tolstoy, he is Pasternak. He is, that is to say, a writer of great power, a man of new and original vision, whose work takes in an enormous area, creates a whole new world. But it is not the world of *War and Peace* and it is not constructed in the same way. In fact, Pasternak has as much in common with Joyce and Proust as he has with Tolstoy. He is a poet and a musician, which Tolstoy was not, and the structure of *Zhivago* is symphonic, thematic, almost liturgical. Both writers are "spiritual" in a very deep way, but the spirituality of Tolstoy is always more ethical and pedestrian.

Like Dostoevsky, Pasternak sees life as a mystic, but without the hieratic kenoticism of the *Brothers Karamazov*. The mysticism of Pasternak is more latent, more cosmic, more pagan, if you like. It is more primitive, less sophisticated, free and untouched by any hieratic forms. There is therefore a "newness" and freshness in his spirituality that contrasts strikingly with the worn and mature sanctity of Staretz Zossima purified of self-consciousness by the weariness of much suffering. Pasternak's simple and moving poem on "Holy Week" illustrates this point. It is the death and resurrection of Christ seen in and through nature. Only discreetly and for a brief moment do ritual forms present themselves, as when we see a procession emerge from a country church. The birch tree "stands aside" to let the worshippers come forth but the procession soon returns into the church.

> And March scoops up the snow on the porch
> And scatters it like alms among the halt and lame—
> As though a man had carried out the Ark
> And opened it and distributed all it held.

All the reality of Holy Week is there, but in a very simple, elementary shape—a shape given to it by Pasternak's humility and contact with the "sacred" earth.

The very scarce and slight expressions of explicit spirituality in *Dr. Zhivago* are uttered by people who might have qualified for a place in the *Brothers Karamazov* (Uncle Nikolai and the seamstress of Yuriatin), but they have about them the ingenuousness of a spirituality that has never yet become quite conscious of itself and has therefore never needed to be purified.

If Pasternak's view of the universe is liturgical, it is the cosmic liturgy of Genesis, not the churchly and hierarchal liturgy of the Apocalypse, of pseudo-Dionysius, and of the Orthodox Church. And yet Pasternak loves that liturgy, and belongs to that Church. It even occurs to him to quote from the liturgy frequently and in strange places: for instance, these words which he declared indicate a basic liturgical inspiration in the poets Blok and Mayakovsky:

"Let all human flesh be silent and let it remain in terror, and in trembling, and let no living being think within itself. For behold, there cometh the King of Kings and the Lord of Lords to offer Himself in immolation and to become the food of the faithful."

Notice, though, in what a subdued and apologetic manner Pasternak himself makes use of this powerful text. In the last stanza of the poem on "Holy Week," we read his lines on the Easter Vigil:

> And when midnight comes
> All creatures and all flesh will fall silent
> On hearing Spring put forth its rumor
> That just as soon as there is better weather
> Death itself can be overcome
> Through the power of the Resurrection.

To say then that *Zhivago* has a liturgical character is not to accuse it of hieratic ceremoniousness. On the contrary, it is to praise the spontaneity with which cries of joy and reverence spring up on every page to hymn the sanctity of Life and of that Love which is the image of the Creator.

And so, though Pasternak is deeply and purely Christian, his simplicity, untainted by ritualistic routine, unstrained by formal or hieratic rigidities of any sort, has a kind of *pre-Christian* character. In him we find the ingenuous Christianity of an *anima naturaliter Christiana* that has discovered Christianity all by itself. It is a Christianity that is not perfectly at home with dogmatic formulas, but gropes after revealed truth in its own clumsy way. And so in his Christianity and in all his spirituality Pasternak is exceedingly primitive. This is one of his most wonderful qualities and we owe it no doubt to the persecution of Christianity by the State in Russia. Where the Church was free we got the complex, tormented Christianity of Dostoevsky. Where the Church is confined and limited we get the rudimentary, "primitive" Christianity of Pasternak.

What *Zhivago* opposes to Communism is therefore not a defense of Western democracy, not a political platform for some kind of liberalism, and still less a tract in favor of formal religion. *Zhivago* confronts Communism with life itself and leaves us in the presence of inevitable conclusions. Communism has proposed to control life with a rigid system and with the tyranny of artificial forms. Those who have believed in this delusion and yielded themselves up to it as to a "superior force" have paid the penalty by ceasing to be complete human beings, by ceasing to live in the full sense of the word, by ceasing to be men. Even the idealistic and devoted Strelnikov becomes the victim of his own ideals, and Lara can say of him:

> It was as if something abstract had crept into his face and made it colorless. As if a living human face had become the embodiment of a principle, the image of an idea. . . . I realized that this had happened to him because he had handed himself over to a superior force that is deadening and pitiless and will not spare him in the end. It seemed to me that he was a marked man and that this was the seal of his doom.

The fact that this judgment is so closely akin to Freudianism and is yet explicitly Christian gives one much food for reflection. The Christian note is sounded in a strong and definite way at the very beginning of the book, as one of the themes which will recur most strongly in all its various parts. The "beast in man" is not to be tamed by threats, but must be brought into harmony with life and made to serve creativeness and love by the influence of inner and spiritual music.

> What has for centuries raised man above the beast is not the cudgel but an inward music; the irresistible power of unarmed truth, the powerful attraction of its example. It has always been assumed that the most important things in the Gospels are the ethical maxims and commandments. But for me the most important thing is that Christ speaks in parables taken from life, that He explains the truth in terms of everyday reality. The idea that underlies this is that communion between mortals is immortal, and that the whole of life is symbolic because it is meaningful.

The words about the "irresistible power of unarmed truth" are pure Gandhi. The rest, about the inextricable union of symbolism and communion, in life itself, is what gives Pasternak's vision of the world its liturgical and sacramental character (always remembering that his "liturgy" is entirely nonhieratic and that in him sacrament implies not so much established ritual form as living mystery).

Everyone has been struck, not to mention embarrassed, by the overpowering symbolic richness of *Dr. Zhivago*. In fact, Pasternak, whether he knows it or not, is plunged fully into midstream of the lost tradition of "natural contemplation" which flowed among the Greek Fathers after it had been set in motion by Origen. Of course the tradition has not been altogether lost, and Pasternak has come upon it in the Orthodox Church. The fact is clear in any case: he reads the Scriptures with the avidity and the spiritual imagination of Origen and he looks on the world with the illuminated eyes of the Cappadocian Fathers—but without their dogmatic and ascetic preoccupations.

However, it is not with scriptual images that Pasternak is primarily concerned. The Fathers of the Church declared that the Scriptures are a recreated world, a Paradise restored to man after Adam had disturbed the cosmic liturgy by his fall. Pasternak is not the prophet of this regained Paradise, as were Origen and Gregory of Nyssa. Rather he is a prophet of the original, cosmic revelation: one who sees symbols and figures of the inward, spiritual world, working themselves out in the mystery of the universe around him and above all in the history of men. Not so much in the formal, and illusory, history of states and empires that is written down in books, but in the living, transcendental and mysterious history of individual human beings and in the indescribable interweaving of their destinies.

It is as artist, symbolist, and prophet that *Zhivago* stands most radically in opposition to Soviet society. He himself is a man of Eden, of Paradise. He is Adam, and therefore also, in some sense, Christ. Lara is Eve and Sophia (the Cosmic Bride of God) and Russia. One should examine, for instance, the description of the Edenlike garden at Duplyanka in the very beginning of the book. The fragrant fields, the heat, the flowerbeds, the lonely coppice where Yurii speaks with his angel or his mother whose presence (again a sophianic presence) seems to surround him here. Here too Lara, as a girl, is shown to us in the beginning of the book (in one of those innumerable coincidences which Pasternak himself regards as of supreme significance in his novel):

> Lara walked along the tracks following a path worn by pilgrims and then turned into the fields. Here she stopped and, closing her eyes, took a deep breath of the flower-scented air of the broad expanse around her. It was dearer to her than her kin, better than a lover, wiser than a book. For a moment she rediscovered the purpose of her life. She was here on earth to grasp the meaning of its wild enchantment, to call each thing by its right name, or, if this were not in her power, to give birth out of love for life to successors who would do it in her place.

The allusion to that primeval, Edenic existence in which Adam gave the animals their names is transparently obvious. And Eve is the "Mother of all the living."

Yurii and Lara will be united in another Eden, at Varykino, but a strange Eden of snow and silence, lost in a vast landscape wasted by armies. There Yurii will give himself, in the night, to his most fruitful work of poetic creation.

In contrast to the Eden image which symbolizes the sophianic world of Yurii and Lara, of Adam, of Christ, stands the House of the Sculptures in Yuriatin. One of the most significant chapters of the book is called "Opposite the House of the Sculptures." It is the one where the seamstress develops the typological figures of the Old Testament, speaking by lamplight in the same enchanted atmosphere of warmth that pervaded the fields of Duplyanka. The opposition is obvious.

> (Lara) Antopova lived at the corner of Merchant Street opposite the dark, blue-grey house with sculptures. . . . It did indeed live up to its name and there was something strange and disturbing about it. Its entire top floor was surrounded by female mythological figures half as big again as human beings. Between two gusts of the dust storm it seemed to him as if all the women in the house had come out on the balcony and were looking down at him over the balustrade. . . .
>
> At the corner there was a dark grey house with sculptures. The huge square stones of the lower part of its façade were covered with freshly posted sheets of government newspapers and proclamations. Small groups of people stood on the sidewalk, reading in silence. . . .

With uncanny insight, the poet has portrayed the bourgeois world of the nineteenth century, a grey façade covered with "sculptures"—enormous and meaningless figures of nothingness, figures for the sake of figures. Yet a dust storm gives them an illusory life. Decorations with no inner reference: advertisements of a culture that has lost its head and has run soberly raving through its own backyards and factories with a handful of rubles. All that remained was for the house itself behind the façade to be gutted and emptied of its semihuman content: then everything was set for the Posters and Proclamations of the Red state. If the editors of *Novy Mir* read *Dr. Zhivago* with understanding they would have found in this passage a much more profound condemnation of Communism than in the description of the Partisan battle which they picked out for special reproof.

On the one hand we have the revolution: "what they mean by ideas is nothing but words, claptrap in praise of the revolution and the regime. . . ." Against this pseudo-scientific array of propaganda clichés, stands the doctor and poet, the diagnostician. One of his greatest sins (the term is chosen advisedly) is his belief in intuition. By his intuition, he is able to get "an immediate grasp of a situation as a whole" which the Marxists vainly hope to achieve by pseudo-science. But what does he seek most of all? What is his real work? As poet, his function is not merely to express his own state of mind, and not merely to exercise his own artistic power. Pasternak's concept of the poet's vocation is at once dynamic and contemplative: two terms which can only be synthesized in the heat of a prophetic ardor.

Language is not merely the material or the instrument which the poet uses. This is the sin of the Soviet ideologist for whom language is simply a mine of terms and formulas which can be pragmatically exploited. When in the moment of inspiration the poet's creative intelligence is married with the inborn wisdom of human language (the Word of God and Human Nature—Divinity and Sophia) then in the very flow of new and individual intuitions, the poet utters the voice of that wonderful and mysterious world of God-manhood—it is the transfigured, spiritualized, and divinized cosmos that speaks through him, and through him utters its praise of the Creator.

> Language, the home and receptacle of beauty and meaning, itself begins to think and speak for man and turns wholly into music, not in terms of sonority but in terms of the impetuousness and power of its inward flow. Then, like the current of a mighty river polishing stones and turning wheels by its very movement, the flow of speech creates in passing, by virtue of its own laws, meter and rhythm and countless other relationships, which are even more important, but which are as yet unexplored, insufficiently recognized, and unnamed. At such moments, Yurii Adreievitch felt that the main part of the work was being done not by him but by a superior power that was above him and directed him, namely the movement of universal thought and poetry in its present historical stage and in the one to come. And he felt himself to be only the occasion, the fulcrum, needed to make this movement possible.

This is the very key to Pasternak's "religious philosophy." He is a complete existentialist (in the most favorable and religious sense of the word). One might ask, in the light of this passage, if his Christian images were nothing more than secondary symbols, subordinated to this great, dynamic worldview. The answer is no. What we have here is a Christian existentialism like that of Berdyaev, and of course far less articulate and less developed than that of Berdyaev. The Christian cosmology of Dante, for example, was static and centripetal. But Christianity is not bound up with Ptolemaic astronomy. Pasternak is absorbed in his vision of a fluid, ever-moving, ever-developing cosmos. It is a vision appropriate to a contemporary of Einstein and Bergson: but let us not forget that it is also akin to the vision of St. Gregory of Nyssa.

It is not necessary at this point to investigate further the depth and genuineness of the Christian elements in Pasternak. They are clearly present, but their presence should not delude us into any oversimplifications in his regard. There are many differences between his Christianity and the Protestant, or even the Catholic Christianity of the West. To what extent are these differences fundamental? We may perhaps return to this question elsewhere. Sufficient to remember that if in the first pages of the book Christ becomes a kind of ideological or symbolic center for the whole structure, this does not alter the fact that Uncle Nikolai propounds his belief in the following terms, which cannot help but perplex the average believer:

> One must be true to Christ. . . . What you don't understand is that it is possible to be an atheist, it is possible not to know whether God exists or why, and yet believe that man does not live in a state of nature but in history, and that history as we know it now began with Christ, and that Christ's Gospel is its foundation.

Without commenting on this passage, let us simply remark that it is typical of the "religious statements" made here and there in the book which very frequently are much tamer and more simple than they appear to be at first sight. Here the difficulty arises largely from a misuse of the word "atheist." What Pasternak really means, in our terminology, is "agnostic," as is clear from his own explanation. Note that Pasternak does not necessarily make himself personally answerable for the theology of Uncle Nikolai, and that he records with full approval the remarkable discourse of Sima on the miracles of the Old Testament as "types" of the greatest miracle, the Incarnation. It is clear that Christ, for Pasternak, is a transcendent and Personal Being in the sense generally understood by such orthodox theologians as Soloviev or the Russian existentialist Berdyaev. The Christ of Pasternak is the Christ of Soloviev's "God-manhood." His view of the cosmos is, like Berdyaev's, "sophianic" and his "sister Life" has, in fact, all the characteristics of the Sancta Sophia who appeared to Soloviev in Egypt. His protestations that for him "believing in God" or in "the Resurrection" is not quite the same thing as it might be to the popular anthropomorphic mind is, after all, quite legitimate self-defense for one who has no pretension of talking like a professional theologian. So much for his terms. But as for his intentions and his spirit, of these there can be no doubt: they are genuinely religious, authentically Christian, and all the more so for their spontaneous unconventionality.

But the important thing to realize is that here, as with all deeply spiritual thinkers, to concentrate on a strict analysis of concepts and formulas is to lose contact with the man's basic intuitions. The great error, the error into which the Communists themselves plunge headlong at the first opportunity, is to try to peg genius down and make it fit into some ready-made classification. Pasternak is not a man for whom there is a plain and definite category. And we must not try to tag him with easy names: Christian, Communist; anti-Christian, anti-Communist; liberal, reactionary; personalist, romanticist, etc.

As Lara says, in one of her most "sophianic" moods: "It's only in mediocre books that people are divided into two camps and have nothing to do with each other. In real life, everything gets mixed up! Don't you think you'd have to be a hopeless nonentity to play only one role all your life, to have only one place in society, always to stand for the same thing?" Both the admirers and the enemies of Pasternak have tried to do him this great dishonor: to write him into one of their own "mediocre books," and to make of him a stereotype to fit and to excuse their own lamentable prejudices. Thus do the "people with watch chains" complain—and not too politely—"like snakes in the corn."

It is true that some names fit Pasternak better than others, and that he is certainly very much of a Christian and not very much of a Communist. Nevertheless his Christianity is first of all quite personal, then quite Russian. His politics are personal first of all and then again Russian, though it might be a lot safer to say that he is antipolitical rather than political. But it would be utterly false to say (as his accusers said) that he had rejected the Russian revolution as a whole.

Where precisely does he stand? The answer is that like life itself he stands nowhere, but *moves*. He moves in a definite direction, however, and this is what must be taken into account if he is to be properly understood. From the very first we must realize that this direction does not lie, simply, west of Russia. Pasternak's tendencies are neither geographical nor political. His movement is into the new dimension of the future which we cannot yet estimate because it is not yet with us. He looks beyond the rigid, frozen monolith of Soviet society; he looks beyond the more confused, shifting, and colliding forms that make up the world of the West. What does he see? Freedom. Not the freedom of Soviet man after the mythical "withering away of the state." Not the chaotic irresponsibility that leaves Western man the captive of economic, social, and psychological forces. Not even that vision which has been irreverently described as "pie in the sky," but really the freedom of the sons of God, on earth, in which "individual life becomes the life story of God and its contents fill the vast expanses of the universe."

3. *Spiritual Implication*

Boris Pasternak established himself in 1958 as one of the very few un-questionably great writers of our century. For forty years this deeply sensitive and original poet had remained hidden and practically unknown in a Russia that seemed entirely alien to his genius. It would be an under-statement to say that Soviet official criticism relegated him to oblivion, scorning him as a bourgeois individualist and an internal émigré. But the events of October and November 1958 were to bring out the fact that Pasternak had remained one of the most admired and loved Russian poets, even in Russia itself. It is true, both in Russia and outside it he was a poet's poet. But that was precisely his importance. He was a rare, almost miraculous being, who had survived the Stalin purges not only with his life but with his full spiritual independence: a kind of symbol of free-dom and creativity in the midst of an alienated society—an alienated world.

The fact that the prize award followed closely on the publication and the world-wide success of *Dr. Zhivago* made it easy for politicians to say that the whole thing was a plot, a new gambit in the Cold War. This popular oversimplification obscured the literary importance of the novel which represented the final maturing of a great talent that had been waiting in silence for many years, unable to express itself. A long disci-pline of sorrowful gestation had given the book a kind of unruly, explo-sive sincerity that demanded to be heard. And it was heard, in spite of the fact that critics took occasion to complain of many things in it. Was the story too involved? Were the characters really characters? Did the book really have a structure? Was it absurd to compare such a writer to Tolstoy? And above all, why so many curious and arbitrary coinci-dences? When all these things were said, it was still evident that the people who said them were wasting their time in doing so. It was some-how clear to anyone who had really penetrated the meaning of *Dr. Zhivago* that all these questions were really irrelevant. The book was much too big and too vital a creation for such criticisms to have much meaning. It swept them all away by its own overwhelming strength and conviction. The story was involved because life is involved: and what mattered was that the book was alive. You could not only forgive the complexity of the plot, but you were drawn to lose yourself in it, and to retrace with untiring interest the crossing paths of the different characters. *Dr. Zhivago* is one of those books which are greater than the rules by which critics seek to condemn them: and we must remember that it is precisely with such books as this that literature advances.

In the end, when everyone had had his say, and the first pronouncements on the book could be evaluated and summed up, it was clear that the deeper and more original critical minds were sold on it. They were obviously preparing to undertake a deeper and more detailed study of the work. This was the case with Edmund Wilson, for example, who came out with one of the most serious and favorable studies of the novel (*The New Yorker,* November 15, 1958) and who later plunged more deeply into what he believed to be the book's symbolism (*The Nation,* April 25, 1959). It is interesting that Wilson's enthusiasm led him into a kind of Joycean labyrinth of allegory which he imagined he had discovered in the book, and this evoked an immediate protest on the part of the author. Pasternak emphatically denied any intention of creating the allegorical structure Wilson had "discovered." But the effect of this protest was to increase one's respect for *Dr. Zhivago*. It is not by any means another *Ulysses* or *Finnegans Wake*. The genius of Pasternak is quite other than the genius of Joyce, and to imagine him plotting out and landscaping his symbolism is to miss what he is really doing.

In any case, it is quite clear that the publication of *Zhivago* was one of the most significant literary events of the century. This is confirmed by the fact that every scrap of poetry or prose Pasternak ever published is being dug up, translated, and printed in every language and that his great novel is already beginning to be the object of exhaustive study. We shall now undoubtedly have a lush crop of doctoral dissertations on every aspect of Pasternak's life and work, and this is certainly no cause for rejoicing. The perfectionistic critics, the group who have been turning over and over the least relics of Melville and Henry James will probably leave Pasternak alone, which is fortunate for everyone concerned. But a great many sensitive and alert writers are going to dive into Pasternak and come up with wonderful things for the rest of us, because Pasternak is a great sea full of sunken treasures and in him we have, for once, riches that are not fully expended in a column and a half of the Sunday Book Section.

It is not out of place to start by this affirmation that the award of the 1958 Nobel Prize for Literature was a *literary* event. Last year it was treated almost exclusively, both in Russia and out of it, as political event.

It was to be expected that Soviet officialdom would react a little hysterically to the prize award. Since Marxists think entirely in political categories, their hysteria was necessarily political. The publication of the book was a vile and sweeping attack on the revolution. The prize award was a direct blow at the Soviet Union. The whole thing was a reactionary plot cooked up on Wall Street. Pasternak was an unregenerate relic of the bourgeois past who had somehow been suffered to survive and to pollute the pure air of a new Soviet world. The capitalist wolves had taken advantage of this occasion to howl for Soviet blood. One mixed metaphor after another denounced the shameless author.

No one was or should have been surprised at this mechanical routine. It was inevitable, and so familiar as to have been supremely boring to everyone except the author and to those who appreciated his talent and personality enough to fear for his life. Nor was it entirely surprising that our side picked up the ball and got into the same game without a moment's delay. To the Western journalists, Pasternak at once became a martyr, a symbol of democracy fighting for recognition under Red tyranny, another proof of the arbitrary perversity of Soviet dictatorship. And of course all this was partly true. But it was slanted and given a political emphasis that was not really there, because *Dr. Zhivago* is in no sense a defense of Western democracy or of the political and economic systems that prevail here. The liberty that Pasternak defends is a liberty of the spirit which is almost as dead in the West as it is behind the Iron Curtain. Perhaps, in a certain way, it is *more* dead in those situations where men fondly believe that the spirit can continue to live in an atmosphere of crass materialism. Let us remember that the vilest character in *Dr. Zhivago* is not one of the Communist automatons but the shrewd, lecherous businessman, Komarovsky.

The fact that Christ is mentioned with sympathetic approval in all parts of the book and that there are quotations from the Bible and from the liturgy was perhaps overstressed by those who were too eager to find in *Dr. Zhivago* an apologia for a vague and superficial Christianity. Here too, Pasternak does not lend himself so easily to exploitation in favor of a cause. This is not a book that can be used to prove something or to sell something, even if that something happens to be the Christian faith. The dogmatic ambiguity of Pasternak's religious statements takes good care of that. Pasternak himself denies that there is an explicitly religious "message" in his book. But this does not mean that the book is not deeply religious and even definitely Christian. The sincerity of the author's own religious feeling is overpoweringly evident, even though it is not always easy to see how that feeling is to be translated into clear theological propositions. But can we not believe that this too is not only understandable, but much to be desired? Who would think of asking a citizen of the Soviet Union today to burst out periodically with a little homily, couched in the exact technical language of a manual of Catholic moral or dogma? Is it not perhaps all too evident that to demand such a thing would be to put ourselves unconsciously on the same footing as the Soviet Writers' Union, who insisted that Pasternak must have secret connections in the West, and must be engaged in an ideological plot?

To me, on the contrary, one of the most persuasive and moving aspects of Pasternak's religious mood is its slightly off-beat spontaneity. It is precisely because he says practically nothing that he has not discovered on his own that he convinces me of the authenticity of his religious experience. When one is immersed in a wide and free-flowing stream of articulate tradition, he can easily say more than he knows and more than he means, and get away with it. One can be content to tell his brethren in Christ what they devoutly desire and expect, no more and no less. But *Dr. Zhivago,* and the deeply religious poems printed in its final section, is the work of a man who, in a society belligerently hostile to religion, has discovered for himself the marvels of the Byzantine liturgy, the great mystery of the Church, and the revelation of God in His word, the Sacred Scriptures. The newspapermen who interviewed Pasternak in his *dacha* were all struck by the big Russian Bible that lay on his desk and gave evidence of constant use.

Pasternak's Christianity is, then, something very simple, very rudimentary, deeply sincere, utterly personal and yet for all its questionable expressions, obviously impregnated with the true spirit of the Gospels and the liturgy. Pasternak has no Christian message. He is not enough of a Christian "officially" to pretend to such a thing. And this is the secret to the peculiar religious strength that is in his book. This strength may not be at all evident to most of us who are formally and "officially" members of the visible Church. But it is certainly calculated to make a very profound impression on those who think themselves unable to believe because they are frightened at the forbiddingly "official" aspects our faith sometimes assumes. *Dr. Zhivago* is, then, a deeply spiritual event, a kind of miracle, a humble but inescapable portent.

It is my purpose to bring out and to emphasize the essentially spiritual character of the Pasternak affair. That is precisely its greatest importance for it is one of the few headline-making incidents of our day that has a clearly spiritual bearing. The literary significance of *Dr. Zhivago* and of Pasternak's verse would never have accounted for the effect they have had on our world. On the other hand, the real political content of Pasternak's work is negligible, and the brief political upheaval that accompanied his prominence in the news was quite accidental, except insofar as it was a tacit recognition of Pasternak as a *spiritual* influence in the world. Those who have been struck by the religious content of his work have been responding, consciously or otherwise, not so much to a formal Christian witness as to a deep and uncompromising *spirituality*.

Pasternak stands first of all for the great spiritual values that are under attack in our materialistic world. He stands for the freedom and nobility of the individual person, for man the image of God, for man in whom God dwells. For Pasternak, the person is and must always remain prior to the collectivity. He stands for courageous, independent loyalty to his own conscience, and for the refusal to compromise with slogans and rationalizations imposed by compulsion. Pasternak is fighting for man's true freedom, his true creativity, against the false and empty humanism of the Marxists—for whom man does not yet truly exist. Over against the technological jargon and the empty scientism of modern man, Pasternak sets creative symbolism, the power of imagination and of intuition, the glory of liturgy, and the fire of contemplation. But he does so in new words, in a new way. He speaks for all that is sanest and most permanently vital in religious and cultural tradition, but with the voice of a man of our own time.

This is precisely what makes him dangerous to the Marxists, and this is why the more intelligent and damning pro-Soviet critics (for instance Isaac Deutscher) have done all they could to prove that *Dr. Zhivago* is nothing but a final, despairing outburst of romantic individualism—a voice from the dead past.

On the contrary, however, the fervor with which writers and thinkers everywhere, both in the West and in Russia, have praised the work and the person of Pasternak, quickly made him the center of a kind of spontaneous spiritual movement. This has not received much publicity in the press, but it still goes on. Pasternak became the friend of scores of men still capable of sharing his hopes and fighting for the same ideal. The beauty of this "movement" is that it has been perfectly spontaneous and has had nothing to do with any form of organized endeavor: it has simply been a matter of admiration and friendship for Pasternak. In a word, it is not a "movement" at all. There were none of the "secret connections" the Soviet Police are always hopefully looking for. There was no planned attempt to make a systematic fuss about anything. The protests of Western writers like Camus, T. S. Eliot, Bertrand Russell, and so on were perfectly spontaneous. And at the same time, it is not generally known that in Moscow several of the leading members of the Writers' Union conspicuously refused to take part in the moral lynching of Pasternak. The most important of these was Ilya Ehrenburg.

The peculiar strength of Pasternak lies then not only in his own literary genius and in his superb moral courage, but in the depth and genuineness of his spirituality. He is a witness to the spirituality of man, the image of God. He is a defender of everything that can be called a spiritual value, but especially in the aesthetic and religious spheres. He is a thinker, an artist, a contemplative. If at times he seems to underestimate the organized ethical aspect of man's spiritual life it is for two reasons: first because he is portraying a world that has become an ethical chaos, and secondly because in that chaos ethics have been perverted into a nonsensically puritanical system of arbitrary prohibitions and commands. There are moments when *Dr. Zhivago* seems so much a creature of impulse as to have lost his ethical orientation. But this is deliberate: and we shall see that it is part of a protest against the synthetically false "moralism" that is inseparable from the totalitarian mentality today.

In order to understand the events of 1958, it is necessary to review briefly Pasternak's own career and the part played by him in the literary history of twentieth-century Russia. In particular we must examine his real attitude toward the Russian revolution which has been by no means simple. For Pasternak was one of those poets who, in 1917, received the revolution with hopeful, though perhaps not unmixed, enthusiasm and who, though he never succeeded in confining his genius within the paralyzing limitations of the Communist literary formulary, at times attempted to write in praise of the revolution. There are in fact many passages in *Dr. Zhivago* itself which favor the revolution in its early stages. In a word, Pasternak was one of that legion of writers, artists, and intellectuals who, though they began by a more or less fervent acceptance of the revolution, were forced sooner or later to reject it as a criminal perversion of man's ideals—when they did not pay with life itself for their fidelity to it. The special importance of Pasternak lies in the symbolic greatness of the protest of one who, having survived the worst of the purges conducted under Stalin, emerged after Stalin's death to say exactly what he thought of Stalinism and to say it not in France, or in England, or in America, but in the heart of Soviet Russia.

Everyone is familiar by now with the salient facts of Pasternak's life. He was born in 1890, in Moscow, the son of a painter, Leonid Pasternak, who was the friend and illustrator of Tolstoy. His mother was a concert pianist. In his early years, young Pasternak conceived a great admiration for two friends of his father—the poet Rilke and the musician Scriabin, and at first the boy planned to become a musician. He wrote: "I love music more than anything else, and I loved Scriabin more than anyone else in the world of music. I began to lisp in music not long before my first acquaintance with him. . . ." In other words, he had already begun to compose, and he soon played some of his compositions for Scriabin, who "immediately began to assure me that it was clumsy to speak of talent for music when something incomparably bigger was on hand and it was open to me to say my word in music" (*Safe Conduct*).

In 1912 Pasternak studied Kantian philosophy under Cohen at the University of Marburg in Germany, and returning to Russia became involved in the Futurist movement, publishing poems in the review *Tsentrifuga*. He had already long since been under the spell of the Symbolist Alexander Blok, and Blok plays an important, though hardly noticeable part, in the symbolic structure of *Dr. Zhivago*. The crucial symbol of the candle in the window, which flashes out to illuminate a kind of knot in the crossing paths of the book's main characters, sets Zhivago to thinking about Blok. The connection of ideas is important, because the candle in the window is a kind of eye of God, or of the Logos (call it if you like *Tao*), but since it is the light in the window of the sophianic figure, Lara, and since Blok in those days (1905) was absorbed in the cult of Sophia he had inherited from Soloviev, the candle in the window suggests, among other things, the Personal and Feminine Wisdom Principle whose vision has inspired the most original Oriental Christian theologians of our day.

Among the Futurists, the one who seems to have made the greatest impression on Pasternak is Mayakovsky. In the early autobiographical sketch, *Safe Conduct,* Pasternak speaks of admiring Mayakovsky with all the burning fervor which he had devoted to Scriabin. Later, however, in his more recent memoir, *I Remember,* he has corrected the impressions created by his earlier sketch. "There was never any intimacy between us. His opinion of me has been exaggerated." The two had "quarreled" and Pasternak says that he found Mayakovsky's propagandist activities for the Communists "incomprehensible." Mayakovsky devoted a turbulent and powerful talent to the Bolshevist cause and turned out innumerable *agitkas* (political playlets) and a long propaganda poem in honor of Lenin. But Pasternak himself wrote a fine poem about the bleak days of the revolution, in which he traces a vigorous and sympathetic portrait of Lenin.

I remember his voice which pierced
The nape of my neck with flames
Like the rustle of *globe*-lightning.
Everyone stood. Everyone was vainly
Ransacking that distant table with his eyes:
And then he emerged on the tribune,
Emerged even before he entered the room,
And came sliding, leaving no wake
Through the barriers of helping hands and obstacles,
Like the leaping ball of a storm
Flying into a room without smoke.

(From *The High Malady,* trans. by Robert Payne)

This, however, is no propaganda poem. Nowhere in it does Pasternak betray the truth in order to conform to some preconceived idea about the revolution. His vision is direct and sincere: he says what he sees. He describes not what he thinks he feels or "ought to feel," but what he actually feels.

These facts are important since Pasternak, who has been accused, by the Communists, of having always been an inveterate reactionary, obviously felt sympathy and admiration for Lenin and for the October revolution. As for the 1905 revolution, his position is unequivocal. Lara, for instance, walks down the street listening to the guns in the distance and saying to herself, "How splendid. Blessed are the down trodden. Blessed are the deceived. God speed you, bullets, You and I are of one mind." Her exultation is symbolic. The revolution means that she is temporarily delivered from her captivity to Komarovsky, the smart lawyer, the opportunist and man of business who, all in all, is the most sinister figure in the whole book and who typifies the wealthy ruling class. It is significant of course that after the revolution Komarovsky remains a powerful, influential figure: he is the type that revolutions do not get rid of but only strengthen.

All that Pasternak has to say both for and against the Bolshevik revolution—and there is very much of it—is summed up in a paragraph spoken by Sima, in Yuriatin (a very minor character who nevertheless expresses the clear ideological substance of the whole book). She says:

With respect to the care of the workers, the protection of the mother, the struggle against the power of money, our revolutionary era is a wonderful, unforgettable era of new, permanent achievements. But as regards the interpretation of life and the philosophy of happiness that is being propagated, it is simply impossible to believe that it is meant to be taken seriously, it's such a comic survival of the past. If all this rhetoric about leaders and peoples had the power to reverse history it would set us back thousands of years to the Biblical times of shepherd tribes and patriarchs. But fortunately this is impossible.

Pasternak's writing in the twenties is by no means purely an evasion of contemporary reality. It is true that in the collection of stories by him printed in 1925 there is only one, "Aerial Ways," which has anything to do with the revolution and this is by no means a glorification of the new order. That is in fact the thing that Pasternak has never really been able to do. He has not been able to believe in Communism as any kind of an "order." He has not been able to accept the myth of its dialectical advance toward an ever saner and better world. Even in his most sanguine moments he always viewed the revolution as a chaotic surging of blind forces out of which, he hoped, something new and real might perhaps evolve. *Dr. Zhivago* by and large represents his judgment that the whole thing was a mountain that gave birth to a mouse. No new truth has been born, only a greater and more sinister falsity. It is this that the Communists cannot forgive him. They do not seem to realize that this very fact confirms his judgment. If Communism had really achieved what it claims to have achieved, surely by now it could tolerate the expression of such opinions as are to be found in *Dr. Zhivago*.

In 1926 Pasternak published a poem on the 1905 revolution and in 1927 he followed with another revolutionary poem, "Lieutenant Schmidt." The former of these received a lengthy and favorable exegesis from Prince Dimitry Mirsky, who had at that time returned to Russia and was temporarily in favor as a Marxist critic—prior to his exile and death in one of the far north camps of Siberia.

Pasternak's writings about the revolution never quite succeeded with the Party because he was always interested too much in man and not enough in policies and the party line. It cannot really be said that he ever seriously attempted to write about the revolution from a Communist viewpoint and it is certainly false to think that he ever sacrificed any of his integrity in order to "be a success." The fact remains that he has been consistently criticized for "individualism," "departure from reality" and "formalist refinement." In other words he remained an artist and refused to prostitute his writing to politics.

No original work from Pasternak's pen was to appear from 1930 until 1943, when "Aboard the Early Trains" appeared and was condemned by Zhdanov as "alien to socialism." During the rest of these years he worked at translations.

That Pasternak fell silent was not a matter of isolated significance. Blok had died in 1921, disillusioned by the revolution. The Party's literary authorities were discussing whether or not "The Twelve" was really a Communist poem. Gumilyov had been executed in 1922. Esenin had written his last poem in his own blood and killed himself in 1925. Mayakovsky, at the height of fame and success as a "proletarian poet," committed suicide at the precise moment when, in the words of a historian, he was considered "the embodiment of socialist optimism." The last remaining representatives of the poetic ferment of the war years and the early twenties disappeared into the background, and remained silent, if they were not liquidated in the thirties. Pasternak was one of the few to survive. He was able to find support and expression for his genius by publishing remarkable translations of Shakespeare, Rilke, Verlaine, Goethe, and other poets of the West.

One of the most mysterious aspects of the Pasternak story is his survival during the great purges of the 1930s. The current guesses as to how he escaped death are barely satisfactory. Some allege that since Pasternak was supposed to have been Mayakovsky's "best friend," and Mayakovsky was now canonized, Stalin allowed Pasternak to live. But anyone who knows anything of Stalin and the purges knows perfectly well that the fact of being the "best friend" of someone who had died might just as well have meant a one-way ticket to the far north camps. Others believe that because Pasternak had translated the Georgian poets so brilliantly, Stalin could not kill him. But Stalin found it no hardship to kill the Georgian poets themselves—like Pasternak's friend Tabidze. Why then should he spare a translator?

By all the laws of political logic, or lack of logic, Pasternak should have died in the thirties and in fact he nearly did so, for the strain of living through those times undermined his health. Not only was he obviously suspect as a nonpolitical, antipolitical, and therefore automatically reactionary poet, but also he distinguished himself by openly defying official literary dogmas in meetings and conferences. Not only that, but he refused to sign several official "petitions" for the death of "traitors," and his friends barely saved him by covering up his defection. The general opinion is that Pasternak could not possibly have survived the purges unless Stalin himself had given explicit orders that he was to be spared. Why?

There has been much speculation, and an article by Mr. Mikhail Koryakov, published in Russian in the *Novy Zhurnal* (in America) and quoted by Edmund Wilson (*The Nation, loc. cit.*) seriously lines up some of the quasi-legendary possibilities. What they add up to is that because of some cryptic statement made by Pasternak in reference to the mysterious death of Stalin's wife, Alliluyeva, Stalin conceived a superstitious fear of the poet. The Georgian dictator is said to have imagined that Pasternak was endowed with prophetic gifts, was a kind of dervish, and had some kind of unearthly insight into the cause of Alliluyeva's death. Since Stalin himself has been credited with the murder of his wife, this does not make the mystery of Pasternak's survival any less mysterious.

The intolerably dreary history of art and literature under Stalin might have seemed hopeful to those who firmly believed that the Leader could really make Russia over and create a new, mass-produced Soviet man in his own image and likeness. But the death of Stalin and the "thaw" that followed showed on all sides that the need for originality, creative freedom, and spontaneity had not died. Even men like Ehrenburg and Simonov, successful Communist writers who could be relied upon to do exactly what the Party leaders wanted, discreetly began to suggest the possibility of a rebirth of initiative and even a certain frankness on the part of the writer. As if socialist realism might soon be replaced with something remotely related to real life!

The history of the "thaw" is well known. A few months proved that the slightest relaxation in favor of individual liberty and self-determination, in any field whatever, would bring about the collapse of everything that had been built up by Stalin. The events in Poland and Hungary in the fall of 1956 make this abundantly clear. In both these countries, outspoken writers had led the resistance against Moscow. There was no choice but a hasty and devout return to the principles used so effectively by Stalin. While notable ex-members of the Praesidium began to wend their way to places like Outer Mongolia, the millionaire novelist and editor, Simonov, became overnight a leading literary figure of Uzbekistan.

Yet no show of official severity has yet been able to discourage the determined resistance of a younger generation of writers. This resistance is in no sense overtly political; it takes the form of a dogged, largely passive protest against the dreariness and falsity of Communist life. It is a silent, indirect refusal to seek any further meaning in copybook formulas and in norms handed down from above by politicians. A young poet of today, Yevgeny Yevtushenko, has been publicly scolded by Khrushchev in person. Yevtushenko, as a kind of prophet of the New Generation, defies the limitations imposed on his spiritual and artistic freedom. He describes a friend returning from a forced labor camp bursting with interest in everything new, listening to the radio, and seeking out all kinds of information: "everything in him breathes character." Yevtushenko himself cries out in protest at not being able to fraternize and speak with the people of Buenos Aires, New York, London, or Paris. He wants art, but not socialist realism. He wants to defy the directives of a dying generation and "speak new words." He actively resents the attempts of the Party to regiment his talent, and replies to official criticism with startling lines:

> Many do not like me
> Blaming me for many things
> And cast thunder and lightning at me.
> Sullen and tense they pour scorn on me
> And I feel their glares on my back.
> But I like all this
> I am proud that they cannot handle me,
> Can do nothing about me.[1]

One cannot help but admire the courage of this young poet—it is a fact of deep significance. It shows that the boots of the MVD have never succeeded in stamping out the fires of independent thought in Russia: and that these fires can, at any time, blaze out more brightly than ever.

We are reminded of the revolutionists of a century ago. But there is one significant difference: the resistance of Russian youth so far has been largely nonpolitical. It is not revolutionary in the nineteenth-century sense. It is moral and personal. Even when there is protest against the pharisaism and obscurantism of Soviet propaganda and censorship, it is not the protest of men who want to overthrow the regime. It is singularly free from attempts to exercise political pressure. It is this special innocence from political bias that strikes us most forcibly, for this is a resistance of people who have become *utterly fed up with everything that savors of politics.* This is the most significant thing about the protest, and it is the key to the Pasternak affair.

To try to place in a well-defined political category the moral rebellion of Russian youth against Communism is not only to misunderstand that rebellion: it is the very way by which the Communists themselves would try to frustrate it. Communism is not at home with nonpolitical categories, and it cannot deal with a phenomenon which is not in some way political. It is characteristic of the singular logic of Stalinist-Marxism that

[1] See "The Young Generation of Soviet Writers," by A. Gaev, in *Bulletin of the Institute for Study of the U.S.S.R.,* Munich, September 1958, pp. 38 ff.

when it incorrectly diagnoses some phenomenon as "political," it corrects the error by forcing the thing to *become* political. Hence the incessant cries of treachery and attack on all sides. Everything that happens that is unforeseen by Russia, or somehow does not fit in with Soviet plans, is an act of capitalist aggression on the Soviet Union. If a late frost ruins the fruit trees of the Ukraine, this is a political event, fomented by Wall Street. When Pasternak writes a great novel, which for political reasons cannot be printed in the USSR; and when this novel is hailed as a masterpiece outside the USSR—even though the novel is obviously not a political tract against the Soviet system, its success becomes an act of political betrayal on the part of the author. Reasons: for propaganda purposes, the USSR has to appear to be the home of all true literature and the only sound judge of what is and what is not a masterpiece. To produce a book that is hailed as a masterpiece after it has been rejected by the Soviet publishers is therefore an act of treachery, for which Pasternak was publicly and officially called "a pig who dirties the place where he sleeps and eats." No one thinks of admitting that it was a sign of weakness and impotency on the part of the Soviet publishers not to be able to print this great work themselves!

Dr. Zhivago was written in the early fifties and finished shortly after Stalin's death in 1953. In 1954, the Second Congress of Soviet writers, with its rehabilitation of condemned writers living and dead, seemed to offer hope for the future. *Dr. Zhivago* was offered for publication to *Novy Mir*. In 1954 some of the poems from *Dr. Zhivago* appeared in a literary magazine and the prospects for the publication of the entire book really seemed to be good. Ilya Ehrenburg had read it, apparently with enthusiasm, as had many other writers. Meanwhile the manuscript had been given personally by Pasternak to the publisher Feltrinelli, of Milan.

In 1956, *Dr. Zhivago* was rejected by *Novy Mir* with a long explanation which we shall discuss in a moment. But Feltrinelli refused to give up the manuscript and manifested his intention to go ahead and publish it. From that time on, guarded attacks on Pasternak were frequent in the Soviet literary magazines. He was reminded that though he might have talent he "had strayed from the true path" and one critic, Pertsov, accused him of a happy acceptance of "chaos" and of being in his element in confusion. Nevertheless in June 1958, a sympathetic discussion of *Dr. Zhivago* was held over Radio Warsaw. Meanwhile of course the book had appeared in Italy, France, and Germany and had taken Europe by storm. The English edition came out in late summer of 1958 and the Nobel Prize was awarded to Pasternak on October 23.

This was hailed by an immediate uproar in the Russian press. The decision was regarded as an act of open hostility, a new maneuver in the Cold War. The award was "steeped in lies and hypocrisy" and *Dr. Zhivago* was a "squalid" work in which Pasternak manifested his "open hatred of the Russian people. He does not have one kind word to say about our workers." *Pravda* discussed the whole thing under the delightfully confusing headline: "A Reactionary Hue and Cry about a Literary Weed."

On October 27 Pasternak was solemnly expelled from the Soviet Writers' Union. This automatically made it impossible for him to be published or to make any kind of a living by his pen. On October 30 Pasternak, seeing the political storm that had been raised about the award, communicated to Stockholm his regretful decision not to accept the prize. Nothing had been said officially one way or another by the Kremlin. Of all the attacks on Pasternak, the most concentrated and bitter were those which came from his colleagues in the Union of Soviet Writers. The day after his refusal of the prize, eight hundred members of the Union which had already expelled him now passed a resolution demanding that he be deprived of Soviet citizenship.

At the same time, the issue continued to be discussed with a certain amount of frankness in Moscow. Pasternak was visited by newspapermen and friends. Poems and parts of *Zhivago* continued to circulate from hand to hand in typewritten or mimeographed editions.

The reports in the Western press tended, by and large, to miss the nuances and gradations of the Pasternak Affair in Russia. Everything was presented as either black or white. The Russians were *all* against Pasternak. The Kremlin was completely opposed to him, and would have done away with him if the protest of the West had not been so strong. In the West, on the contrary, everything was white, everyone was *for* Pasternak.

It is true that the protest of Western thinkers and intellectuals was decisive in arresting the all-out campaign against Pasternak in Russia, and in helping to keep him free. Nevertheless, his friends inside Russia were by no means idle. Efforts to organize a positive movement in his behalf were not very successful. But several of the most influential members of the Writers' Union refused to participate in the meetings where Pasternak was condemned. Ilya Ehrenburg sent word that he was "absent from Moscow" when everyone knew he was in his Gorky Street apartment. Leonid Leonov remained conspicuously aloof. Another writer tried actively to bring about Pasternak's rehabilitation and used his influence with Khrushchev for this end. A well-informed Western observer in

Moscow reported that the Kremlin in general was disturbed by the fact that the Moscow intelligentsia remained at least passively pro-Pasternak, and that the campaign was met with deep anxiety and even mute protest on the part of the young writers who admired him. Mute protest is not much, of course. But in Russia, any protest at all is significant.

It is said that Pasternak received a fair number of letters from people in the USSR who deplored the attacks on him. Later, many of the Soviet writers who had participated in the voting at the Writers' Union privately expressed their regrets to him. All this is true. But at the same time it must not be forgotten that a real wave of indignation and hostility toward Pasternak swept the Soviet Union, incited by the speeches and articles against him, and one night a resentful crowd put on a demonstration outside his *dacha* and even threatened to burn it down.

The political noise that has surrounded *Dr. Zhivago* both in the East and in the West does nothing whatever to make the book or its author better or worse. As far as politics are concerned, Pasternak takes the position of a "nonparticipant," or *obyvatel,* and as *Life* comments, "Pasternak's detachment sounds a little like the faraway voice of a monk in a beleaguered Dark Age monastery, a mood with which Americans cannot easily sympathize." For my own part, being not only an American, but also a monk, I do not find sympathy so terribly hard. On the contrary, it would seem that Pasternak's ability to rise above political dichotomies may very well be his greatest strength. This transcendence is the power and the essence of *Dr. Zhivago.* One of the more important judgments made by this book is a condemnation of the chaotic meaninglessness of all twentieth-century political life, and the assertion that politics has practically ceased to be a really vital and significant force in man's society. This judgment is pronounced upon the political confusion of the nineteen-twenties in Soviet Russia, but it also falls by implication, and with proper modifications, on the West as well as on the East. What Pasternak says about Russia goes, in a different way, for the Western Europe of Hitler and Mussolini, and for the whole world of the last war—not to mention the America of the '50s.

The protest of *Dr. Zhivago* is spiritual, not political, not sociological, not pragmatic. It is religious, aesthetic, and mystical. We cannot fully understand the author's view of the modern world if we insist on interpreting him by standards which have nothing to do with his work and his thought. We cannot fit into simple political categories one for whom the whole political chaos of our world is a kind of enormous spiritual cancer, running wild with a strange, admirable, and disastrous life of its own and feeding on the spiritual substance of man. The deep interest of *Dr. Zhivago* is precisely its diagnosis of man's spiritual situation as a struggle for freedom *in spite of* and *against* the virulence of this enormous political disease. For, to be more accurate, since man's spiritual substance is his freedom itself, it is precisely this freedom which is devoured by politics and transmuted into a huge growth of uncontrollable precocity. Hope of attaining true freedom by purely political means has become an insane delusion.

The great success of *Dr. Zhivago* is by no means attributable to the mere fact that it happens to contain sentences which level devastating blows against the Communist mentality. Anyone with any perception can see that these blows fall, with equal power, on every form of materialistic society. They fall upon most of the gross, pervasive and accepted structures of thought and life which go to make up our changing world. The book is successful not because these blows are dealt, but because, as they land, we gradually begin to realize that Pasternak seems to know what is wrong. He seems to know what has happened to our spiritual freedom. He seems to realize why it is that most of the world's talk about freedom, peace, happiness, hope for the future is just talk and nothing more. He knows all too well that such talk is only a palliative for despair. But at the same time he has a true and solid hope to offer.

The author who most reminds me of Pasternak in this respect is Ignazio Silone. His heroes too, perhaps on a smaller scale and in a more restricted area, travel the same road as *Dr. Zhivago,* but with a more explicitly political orientation. Silone's men, with all the pathetic yet admirable smallness of genuinely human heroes, are true to man, true to his real history, true to man's vocation to "be Christ."

Zhivago of course is not a saint or a perfect hero. He is weak-willed, and his life is a confused and unsatisfactory mess. He himself knows that he has not been able to make a success of it. But the point is, he sees that in the circumstances in which he lives it is not possible to make a real success out of life—that the only honest thing is to face meaninglessness and failure with humility, and make out of it the best one can. Under such conditions his tragic life is lived "successfully" under the sign of wisdom.

It seems that the main difference between Pasternak and Western authors who have sensed the same futility is that he is not defeated by it as they are. Nowhere in Pasternak does one get the impression that his heroes are up a blind alley, beating their heads against a wall. In the

West one sees very little else. For a great majority of Western writers, though in varying degrees, man finds himself as he does in Sartre, with "No Exit"—*Huis Clos*—that is to say, in hell. The Communists would explain this as a feature of capitalist decay. Yet their own society is up the same blind alley, pretending that the wall at the end is not there, and that the business of beating your head against it is proof of optimism and progress. Pasternak sees the blind alley and sees the wall, but knows that the way out is not through the wall, and not back out by the way we came in. The exit is into an entirely new dimension—finding ourselves in others, discovering the inward sources of freedom and love which God has put in our nature, discovering Christ in the midst of us, as "one we know not."

This exit is not a mere theoretical possibility. Nor is it even a mere escape. It is a real and creative solution to man's problems: a solution that can bring meaning out of confusion and good out of evil. It is something that has been sought after with hope and conviction by the greatest Russian minds of the past century: Dostoevsky, Tolstoy, Soloviev, and by Russians of our own time like Nicholas Berdyaev.

The solution is *love* as the highest expression of man's spirituality and freedom. Love and Life (reduced to one and the same thing) form the great theme of *Dr. Zhivago*. In proportion as one is alive he has a greater capacity and a greater obligation to love. Every degree of true and false love makes its appearance in the book—from the self-assured and bestial selfishness of Komarovsky, the businessman, to the different shades of compulsive and authoritarian falsity in the various revolutionaries. There are all aspects of parental and conjugal love (Zhivago really loves his wife Tonia, for example). Lara though seduced by Komarovsky in her girlhood remains the embodiment of a love that is simple, unadulterated spontaneity, a love that does not know how to be untrue to itself or to life. Her love is perfectly aware of the difference between sin and goodness, but her repentance (the Magdalen theme) has a creative power to transcend limitations and to emerge into a new world. Lara is thus the embodiment of the goodness and love of God immanent in His creation, immanent in man and in Russia, and there left at the mercy of every evil. Far from being a trite and prissy concept, this is both deep and original. One can see in Pasternak a strong influence from Soloviev's *Meaning of Love* and his theory of man's vocation to regenerate the world by the spiritualization of human love raised to the sophianic level of perfect conscious participation in the mystery of the divine wisdom of which the earthly sacrament is love.

At the same time we must remember that Zhivago's victory is tragic. Lara vanishes "without a trace," to die, probably, in a concentration camp. Nothing has been "transformed." It is the victory that shines forth in apparent defeat—the victory of death and resurrection. We notice too, that resurrection remains curiously implicit in the strange, impoverished death of the unsuccessful doctor who falls to the pavement with a heart attack while getting out of a Moscow streetcar. There is a strange parallel between the double death rite of Marina and Lara for Zhivago and the terribly impressive scene of lamentation at the end of *Safe Conduct* in which Mayakovsky's sister raves with Oriental passion over the body of the suicide. There is a gleam of hope in the Epilogue where Tania, the child of Zhivago and Lara, the "child of the terrible years," is seen for a moment in her own simplicity. The things she has had to go through have not ruined her. And we realize that the strange mystical figure of Evgraf, the "guardian angel," "will take care of her." She is the Russia of the future.

One of the singularly striking things about *Dr. Zhivago* is its quality of tragedy without frustration. Here everything is clean and free from ambivalence. Love is love and hate is hate. Zhivago says and does what he means, and when he is uncertain he is not dishonest about it. It is this spiritual cleanliness, this direct vision and fidelity to life here and now which Pasternak opposes to the grandiose and systematic ravings of politicians who turn all life into casuistry and bind man hand and foot in the meticulous service of unrealities.

It is time to quote. These are the thoughts of Zhivago, half starved and faint from hardships and exposure, as he reads a political proclamation pasted on a wall:

Had (these words) been composed last year, the year before? Only once in his life had this uncompromising language and single-mindedness filled him with enthusiasm. Was it possible that he must pay for that rash enthusiasm all his life by never hearing year after year, anything but these unchanging, shrill, crazy exclamations and demands which became progressively more impractical, meaningless and unfulfillable as time went by? . . . What an enviable blindness, to be able to talk of bread when it has long since vanished from the face of the earth! Of propertied classes and speculators when they have long since been abolished by earlier decrees! Of peasants and villages that no longer exist! Don't they remember their own plans and measures, which long since turned life upside down? What kind of people are they, to go on raving with this never cooling feverish ardor, year in, year out, on non-existent, long-vanished subjects, and to know nothing, to see nothing around them.

Pasternak was morally compelled to refuse the Nobel Prize in order to remain in Russia. Writers in England, France, and the United States protested against Russia's flat rejection of her only great writer since the Revolution. *Pravda* devoted eighteen columns to an unprecedented publication of the "original letter" which had been sent to Pasternak by the magazine *Novy Mir* refusing to serialize the novel in Russian. The letter was signed, curiously enough, by a poet, A. T. Tvardovsky, who, since writing it, had himself fallen under an official ban. The document is notable for its surprising lack of abusiveness and its relatively sympathetic effort to reason with the author. Pasternak was evidently respected in this case by a devoted colleague. The chief objection is not made against the passages in which Marxism is explicitly condemned, for these are relatively few and could have been expunged. The whole fault of the book, from the Soviet point of view, is something "which neither the editors nor the author can alter by cuts or revision . . . the spirit of the novel, its general tenor, *the author's view of life."*

This view of life, as we have indicated above, is that the individual is more important than the collectivity. His spirit, his freedom, his ability to love, raise him above the state. The state exists for man, not man for the state. No man has the right to hand himself over to any superior force other than God Himself. Man has no right to alienate his own liberty to become a cog in a machine. Man is of no use to man if he ceases to be a person and lets himself be reduced to the status of a "thing." A collectivity that reduces the members to the level of alienated objects is dooming both itself and its members to a sterile and futile existence to which no amount of speeches and parades can ever give a meaning. The great tragedy of the revolution, for Pasternak, was the fact that the best men in Russia submitted to mass insanity and yielded up their own judgment to the authority of Juggernaut.

It was then that untruth came down on our land of Russia. The main misfortune, the root of evil to come, was the loss of confidence in the value of one's own opinion. People imagined that it was out of date to follow their own moral sense, that they must all sing in chorus, and live by other people's notions, notions that were being crammed down everybody's throat. . . . The social evil became an epidemic. It was catching, and it affected everything, nothing was left untouched by it. Our home too became infected. . . . Instead of being natural and spontaneous as we had always been, we began to be idiotically pompous with each other. Something showy, artificial, forced, crept into our conversation—you felt you had to be clever in a certain way about certain world-important themes. . . .

Like Dostoevsky, Pasternak holds that man's future depends on his ability to work his way out from under a continuous succession of authoritarian rulers who promise him happiness at the cost of his freedom. Like Dostoevsky, also, Pasternak insists that the fruit of Christ's Incarnation, Death and Resurrection, is that true freedom has at least become possible: but that man, ignoring the real meaning of the New Testament, prefers to evade the responsibility of his vocation and continues to live "under the law." This is not a new complaint: it goes back to St. Paul.

Ironically enough, one of the most brilliant analyses of man's alienation came from the pen of Marx. Modern Russia, while paying lip service to Marx's theory on this point, has forgotten his full meaning. Yet in so doing, the Soviets have brought out the inner contradiction of Marx's thought: for the complete spiritual alienation of man which Marx ascribed in part to religion has been brought about by militant atheism, as well as by the economic system which claims to be built on an orthodox Marxian foundation. It is of course not fair to blame Stalin's police state directly on Marx, though Marx cannot be absolved from indirect responsibility.

At any event, Pasternak's "view of life" is what has brought upon him the outraged and unanimous condemnation of Soviet officialdom. While the letter from *Novy Mir* reproves Pasternak as immoral, the Soviet critics after the Nobel Prize award did not hesitate to find in *Dr. Zhivago* and in its author every possible kind of moral depravity. Pasternak, the lowest of the low, could not even be compared to a pig. He could no longer claim a right to breathe the pure air of Soviet Russia.

It would be a great mistake to think that for the Communists such accusations are taken as mere words without specific reference, to be used with cynical opportunism. The curious fact is that Communism today has forged its own rigid and authoritarian code of morals, which can be called "an ethic" only by doing violence to the meaning of words, but which nevertheless claims with puritanical self-assurance to show men how to "live."

The ideal Communist is a combination of a beaver and a wolf. He unites machinelike industry with utter insensitiveness to deep human values whenever they come into conflict with political duty. He either knows at all times the course of history and "the one correct thing" to do at the moment, or, if he does not know it, he obeys someone else who claims to know it. In either case, he "acts" with all the complacent self-assurance of a well-adjusted machine, and grinds to pieces anything that comes in his way, whether it be his own idea of truth, his most cherished

71

hopes for this world or the next, or the person of a wife, friend, or parent.

All through *Dr. Zhivago* we find an extraordinary and subtle range of such characters portrayed: some of them pure Communist types, others much more complicated and hard to label. The hero himself, Yurii Zhivago, *is in all respects the exact opposite to the New Soviet Man.* This, of course, is what constitutes, in Soviet eyes, the depth of moral degradation. To have human feelings, to follow the lead of spontaneous inner inspiration, to be moved by love and pity, to let oneself be swayed by appreciation of what is *human* in man—all this is nothing but bourgeois depravity and shameless individualism.

It almost seems that Pasternak has gone out of his way to make Zhivago act on impulse in a way that would seem utterly foolish to Communists. It always remains clear that this yielding to impulse is not presented (as it sometimes is in Western novels) as the ideal of freedom. No, freedom is something higher and more spiritual than that. But Pasternak makes the point that if one does at times follow a crazy urge and do something completely pointless, it is not an act to be ashamed of. Must one always be reasonable? Must one always have a ponderous ethical justification for every action he performs? Must one fear spontaneity and never do anything that is not decreed by some program, some form or other of duty? On the contrary, it is compulsiveness that warps life and makes it pointless. The apparent pointlessness of man's impulses may perhaps show the way to what he is really seeking.

This, for a Marxist, is deadly heresy: everyone knows that for a Marxist everything has to fit in with his fantasies of omniscience. Everything has to have a point, everything has to be guided toward some specific purpose. To this, Zhivago replies:

> You find in practice that what they mean by ideas is nothing but words—claptrap in praise of the revolution and the regime. . . . One of my sins is a belief in intuition. And yet see how ridiculous. They all shout that I am a marvelous diagnostician, and as a matter of fact it's true that I don't often make mistakes in diagnosing a disease. Well, what is this immediate grasp of the situation as a whole supposed to be if not this intuition they find so detestable?

It is therefore understandable that *Novy Mir* should have singled out with horror the passage where Yurii Zhivago finds himself accidentally in the middle of a battle between Red Partisans and White Russian volunteers. There can be no question that such a passage would make any good Communist squirm in his chair with acute moral discomfort. It would repel and horrify him in much the same way as a chapter of Sartre or Moravia might horrify a nun. It is the kind of thing he would take not only as alien and unpleasant, but as a threat to the whole foundation of his moral security and peace of mind. I do not doubt that Pasternak wrote this section deliberately with his tongue in his cheek. The Reds have responded admirably. The *Novy Mir* letter as reprinted in *Pravda* contains the whole passage quoted *in extenso,* in order to let each loyal Communist taste the full deliciousness of scandalized horror.

What happens? Zhivago, as a doctor, is not supposed to fight. But he is caught in this battle which like all battles is a silly and tragic mess. Zhivago impulsively takes the gun of a fallen comrade, but deliberately aims at a dead tree trunk, and only hits one of the enemy by accident. After the skirmish, he finds that his fallen Red comrade and the White soldier he has wounded each wear a locket containing the text of Psalm 90, which was devoutly believed to be a protection against death. The Red soldier, with a corrupt text of the Psalm, is dead. The White, with a correct text, is alive. Taking pity on him, Zhivago clothes him in the uniform of the fallen Red Partisan and looks after him among the Communist fighters, until he escapes, threatening that he will continue to fight the Reds.

This scene, which is essentially comical, contains just about every mortal sin in the Communist code. I leave the reader to discover them for himself.

The situation being what it was, the Soviet leaders were faced with the problem of blackening Pasternak in the eyes of East and West at the same time. He had to be regarded not only as a dangerous criminal by Russia, but as a hypocrite and coward by the West. Realistic politicians knew well enough that denunciations would not be enough to ruin Pasternak in the eyes of the young writers who undoubtedly looked up to him as a model and a hero. Soviet attacks on Pasternak could only add to his prestige in the West. For this reason, far from categorically forbidding him to accept the prize, they left the door wide open and urged him to leave Russia as long as he did not try to return. It would have been admirable, from their viewpoint, to have "proof" that Pasternak was a traitor to his country. At the same time their benevolence would remain to "prove" that "Pasternak has been left perfectly free to accept the Nobel Prize." Pasternak refused to abandon Russia, not out of political astuteness but merely because he loved his own country and did not feel that he would be able to write anywhere else.

Once again, he was acting with perfect consistency as one who is the exact opposite of a Communist. His staying in Russia was another victory for his personal integrity as an artist and as a human being. But perhaps there was some advantage to be gained here by the Reds. Perhaps Pasternak could be pressed a little further, and so diminish in the eyes of the West. Pasternak came out in *Pravda* with a letter of "apology," declared that he had made a "mistake" in accepting the Nobel Prize, and that his subsequent refusal of it had been "entirely voluntary." He stated that he had not been threatened and that his life had not been imperiled. This letter, which saddened and shocked readers in the West, but which could have been regarded as inevitable, was probably extracted from him in order to save face for the Soviet government and pay the price of his moral victory.

If one reads the letter carefully, he can detect the difference between passages written by Pasternak and those inserted by others to "make his meaning clear." The passages obviously written by Pasternak are clear and consistent with his position. He asks to be dissociated from the "political campaign around my novel" which he regrets and did not intend. "I never had the intention of causing harm to my state and my people." That is only a reaffirmation of the obvious fact that the book is not a political tract. In regard to the "political errors" of which he "might be accused," he declares that they are not to be found in the novel. This passage is interesting and entirely true. Here is what Pasternak writes: "*It would appear* that I am *allegedly maintaining* the following erroneous principles. *I am supposed to have alleged* that any revolution is an historically illegal phenomenon, that the October Revolution was such, and that it brought unhappiness to Russia and the downfall of the Russian intelligentsia." It is quite obvious that Pasternak nowhere holds that all revolution is "historically illegal"—nor does anybody else. Nor does he maintain that the October Revolution was "illegal." The texts we have quoted certainly show that Russia after the revolution is not portrayed in *Dr. Zhivago* as a bed of roses and that Pasternak plainly ascribes many bad effects to Communism. At the same time we have seen clearly that he accepted the necessity of the revolution, first of all in 1905, then in 1917. No one in his right senses could imagine that Pasternak was trying in *Dr. Zhivago* to lead Russia back to capitalism or to the old regime. But it is equally clear that he has maintained a perfect independence and objectivity with regard to the revolution, and after living through Stalin's five-year plans and the purges, he has concluded (with the vast majority of intellectuals everywhere in the world) that the Bolshevik revolution was a failure and that Marxism had nothing to offer man but a gospel of delusions. His apology as it stands does nothing to alter the substance of this belief. All that he regrets, about *Zhivago,* is the manner in which it was published and the way it was exploited by anti-Communist journalism. These two things were obviously not the fault of the author.

Pasternak's letter ends with a pious sigh which is utterly alien to his thought and his style and was almost certainly inserted by somebody else: "I firmly believe that I shall find the strength to redeem my good name and restore the confidence of my comrades."

The mystery of this letter has not fully been cleared up, but after its publication and the publication of other similar statements Pasternak cautioned a friend against believing any statement that was supposed to have emanated from him.

Meanwhile, November and December 1958 were months of bitterness and conflict. We have already considered the open explosions of hostility which occurred at the time of the prize award, when the Soviet authorities were trying to get Pasternak out of Russia. These explosions soon ceased, and the case vanished from the pages of *Pravda.* It ceased to be front-page news in the West and soon disappeared altogether but for a few sporadic flare-ups.

Meanwhile, Pasternak was exhausted and ill. In order to forget his troubles, he kept himself busy on a translation of a Polish play, a job that had been deliberately steered his way by sympathetic friends in the Polish Writers' Union. Letters continued to arrive from the West. Friends and even reporters continued to visit the *dacha*—where the presence of newspapermen did nothing to improve the peace of the household. Mrs. Pasternak strenuously objected to them, and uttered vigorous protests, all of which were dutifully reported in the Western newspapers.

December came, and with it the distribution of the Nobel prizes. Western journalists gloated over the possibility that it might turn into a good show—with an empty chair in evidence for Pasternak. No such thing was done, fortunately. It would have been very entertaining for minds that rejoice in devious forms of moral aggression, but it would not have made life any more comfortable for Pasternak.

At the end of the year a story broke in the Western press, stating that a Spanish exile in London, José Vilallonga, had arranged to tour free Europe and America with Pasternak, giving lectures. It was alleged that

Pasternak's life had been insured for three million dollars. The Russians seem to have taken this story seriously and *Pravda* reported a telegram in which Pasternak was supposed to have rejected the offer. In reality, as Pasternak himself made clear, he had never been in contact with Vilallonga and everything about the story was "pure invention," including the supposed telegram.

Early in the new year, Pasternak was again featured in a disturbing story. A reporter of the London *Daily Mail* printed a poem in which Pasternak complained bitterly at being rejected by his own countrymen. Pasternak did not deny having written the poem but protested against its publication as a breach of confidence. Once again it was felt that his life might be in danger. When in February Pasternak suddenly disappeared from his *dacha,* many came to the conclusion that he had been imprisoned and that the game was now up. The explanation given by the Soviet Press was that he had gone away for a "vacation" and in order "to avoid the newspapermen who were coming from London to Moscow with Prime Minister Macmillan." As it turned out, this explanation may have been substantially true.

Actually, Pasternak had left Peredelkino of his own free will and had gone to spend a few weeks at Tiflis, Georgia, as the guest of Mrs. Tabidze, the widow of the Georgian poet shot by Stalin's police. He returned home in good health, and gradually, as the affair ceased to appear in the press and began to be forgotten in the West, prospects began to look good for the harassed writer. In May, for example, a shake-up in the Soviet Writers' Union led to the replacement of Pasternak's enemy, Surkov, as head of the Union, by Fedin, who is friendly to Pasternak.

This was not a mere coincidence. The removal of Surkov was certainly a consequence of the Pasternak Affair, and those who interpreted this change in the Writer's Union as evidence that Pasternak's friends had won over the favor of Khrushchev are perhaps not too far wrong. Whatever may be the real facts, which remain to be discovered and made public, we can agree with the writer of *The New York Times* who said: "It was apparent that there were profound second thoughts about the persecution of Mr. Pasternak. All of the leading literary and party figures who participated in the verbal lynching were downgraded or demoted." And this is highly significant. It shows at least that the qualities of freedom and integrity for which Pasternak stood in the eyes of West and East alike were able in some measure to get themselves recognized in Soviet Russia.

This is no small achievement. It is quite clear that Pasternak emerged from the whole affair as the moral and spiritual conqueror of Stalinism, and that he conquered not for himself alone but even for those of his compatriots who were able to share to some degree in his outlook. And if he did this, it was not only because of his natural and human qualities but, I might venture to say, because of the depth and clarity of his Christian faith. Not that Pasternak is an explicit witness for the Christian message, in the face of Communism: his faith was never directly involved in the debate at all. And yet his resistance was spiritual and his spirit was essentially Christian not only because of his belief in "Christ as the center of history" but because of his existential dedication to the supreme inner value of personalism, which is one of the characteristic Christian contributions to Western humanistic thought.

Let us now draw a few conclusions.

Pasternak's book was offered for publication in Russia after the death of Stalin, during the "thaw" when, at the Twentieth Party Congress, Khrushchev openly admitted the "crimes and errors" of Stalin, implicitly showing that Russia needed to move back from extreme dictatorial authoritarianism to a freer and more flexible way of life. Pasternak obviously thought that his book could claim to represent the thought and aspirations of the intelligentsia, including many Communists, at that time. No doubt there would have to be changes, but the *substance* of his book was, it seemed, just what Russia was waiting for. As far as the young intellectuals are concerned, this may have been true.

Unfortunately, as regards the Party, he was premature! The fact that *Dr. Zhivago* could never be made acceptable by editing showed that Soviet Russia could never accept so fundamental an idea of freedom. The end of the thaw soon made this very plain.

A providential accident led to the publication of the novel outside the USSR by an Italian publisher who refused obedience to Moscow when the edition was condemned. When Pasternak was awarded the Nobel Prize, it showed that the whole world was glad that at last a great book had come out of Russia. The acclaim of critics and readers was certainly not primarily a political matter. Unquestionably, Western readers have not studied Pasternak's estimate of Communism without satisfaction. And of course the newspapers have turned the book into a political weapon, which was not the intention of the author. But the Nobel Prize was awarded on nonpolitical grounds to a book great in its own right.

The fact remains that if Soviet Russia had been strong enough to absorb the powerful contents of this book in the first place, and had been able to publish it, even in a somewhat edited version, the prestige achieved by this act would have been tremendous. One Nobel Prize winner in literature is of more value to Russia than a thousand winners in physics, no matter how set the Soviet government is on science. It is one thing to produce atomic counters or to win the pentathlon, and another to be recognized as a leader in the field of literature. If Russia wins the Nobel award in science it is because she has good scientists. If her athletes excel, it is because they are good. But her scientists and athletes are good because dialectical materialism cannot directly interfere in their specialty. (The attempt to do so in biology has been given up.) What remains but the conclusion that if Russian writers were not forced to sabotage their talent and their integrity and grind out political clichés, they too might win Nobel prizes? Here is one who has done it: but without benefit of a blessing from the Kremlin. The implications are so plain that even the Kremlin can see them, and, like the Hungarian revolution, the spectacle has proved disconcerting.

So much for Russia. But what does Pasternak have to say to the Western intellectual? The first thing, of course, is said by the triumphant artistic achievement of his novel and the poetry which accompanies it. *Dr. Zhivago* itself is greater than any "message" that might be distilled out of it. It is a superb novel which recovers the full creative fecundity that seems to have vanished from our cramped and worried literature; a book with a sense of orientation and meaning in strong contrast with our Western frustration and despair.

Pasternak has become a best seller and a widely read author in the West, but he will always be a writer's writer. His greatest impact has been on the *writers* of the West. He has received letters from all kinds of people, but especially from other writers, in many different countries, not the least being Camus and Mauriac. Pasternak answered all these letters with profound warmth of understanding, and those who were privileged to be in contact with him felt that he had given them much more than they expected—an inspiration and sense of direction which they had ceased to hope for from any other writer!

We have learned from Pasternak that we must never yield to the great temptation offered by Communism to the writer. I do not mean the temptation to be a member of a privileged and respected class, but the far more insidious one of becoming a "writer for the future." Surely there is something apocalyptic about the sinister complacency with which Communism, which has hitherto proved effective only in killing writers or ruining them, proposes itself as Master of the future of literature. "Write for us, you will be remembered forever in the Kingdom of the Messias who has now come! Refuse our offer, and you will be buried with the world that we are about to bury."

It is against such insinuations of the Beast that Pasternak replies with his doctrine of life and resurrection. This is a doctrine with a strongly Christian basis, using exclusively Christian symbolism. Needless to say, not all of Pasternak's expressions can be fully reconciled with those to be found in a manual of dogma. The Christ of Pasternak is the Christ Who has liberated man from death and Who lives in man, waiting for man's liberty to give Him a chance to transform the world by love. Love is the work not of states, not of organizations, not of institutions, but of persons. Hence:

> Gregariousness is always the refuge of mediocrities. . . . Only individuals seek the truth, and they shun those whose whole concern is not the truth. How many things in this world deserve our loyalty? Very few indeed. I think one should be loyal to immortality, which is another word for life, a stronger word for it. One must be true to immortality—true to Christ.

Pasternak looks at our world, dismembered by its obsessions and its factions, each one claiming to be on the side of the angels and calling everyone else a devil. Egged on by journalists, politicians, and propagandists, we cling with mad hope to fanatical creeds whose only function is to foment violence, hatred, and division. Will we never begin to understand that the "differences" between these factions are often so superficial as to be illusory and that all of them are equally stupid? Will we never grow up, and get down to the business of living productively on this earth, in unity and peace?

History is not a matter of inexorable scientific laws, it is a new creation, a work of God in and through man: but this theandric work is unthinkable not only without man's desire but also without his *initiative*. Christ has planted in the world the seeds of something altogether new, but they do not grow by themselves. Hence history has never yet really had a chance to become a Christian creation. For the world to be changed, man himself must begin to change it, he must take the initiative, he must step forth and make a new kind of history. The change begins within himself.

> You can't advance in this direction without a certain faith. You can't make such discoveries without a spiritual equipment. And the basic elements of this equipment are in the Gospels. What are they? To begin with a certain love of one's neighbor, which is the supreme form of vital energy. Once it

fills the heart of man it has to overflow and expend itself. And then the two basic ideals of modern man—without them he is unthinkable—the idea of free personality and the idea of life as sacrifice. . . . There is no history in this sense among the ancients. They had blood and beastliness and cruelty and pockmarked Caligulas who had no idea how inferior the system of slavery is. They had the boastful dead eternity of bronze monuments and marble columns. It was not until after the coming of Christ that time and man could breathe freely. Man does not die in a ditch like a dog—but at home in history, while the work toward the conquest of death is in full swing; he dies sharing in this work.

Here is the deep meaning of Pasternak's critique of Communism. It is blindness and sin to seek immortality in the bronze and stone which are already stamped with lifelessness and twice dead when they are frozen into an art without inspiration. "Why seek ye the living among the dead?" Communism, like all characteristically modern political movements, far from opening the door to the future is only a regression into the past, the ancient past, the time of slavery before Christ. Following these movements, mankind falls backward into an abyss of ancient, magical laws; man comes under the authority of numbers and astrological systems and loses all hope of freedom. But with the coming of Christ:

> The reign of numbers was at an end. The duty, imposed by armed force to live unanimously as a people, a whole nation, was abolished. Leaders and nations were relegated to the past. They were replaced by the doctrine of individuality and freedom. *Individual human life became the life story of God and its contents filled the vast expanses of the universe.*

These words occur on page 413, far into the book, in an apparently colorless, "unexciting" chapter which is in reality very important to Pasternak's great work—one of the nerve centers where all his meaning is fully experienced.

If we stop to think about what it says, we will realize that if Pasternak is ever fully studied, he is just as likely to be regarded as a dangerous writer in the West as he is in the East. He is saying that political and social structures as we understand them are things of the past, and that the crisis through which we are now passing is nothing but the full and inescapable manifestation of their falsity. For twenty centuries we have called ourselves Christians, without even beginning to understand one tenth of the Gospel. We have been taking Caesar for God and God for Caesar. Now that "charity is growing cold" and we stand facing the smoky dawn of an apocalyptic era, Pasternak reminds us that there is only one source of truth, but that it is not sufficient to know the source is there—we must go and drink from it, as he has done.

Do we have the courage to do so? For obviously, if we consider what Pasternak is saying, doing, and undergoing, to read the Gospel with eyes wide open may be a perilous thing!

Postscript

I had begun to correspond with Pasternak before the appearance of *Dr. Zhivago* in 1958, and exchanged two letters with him before the Nobel Prize affair. After that I received messages from him either through a correspondent of his in England, or through mutual friends with whom he corresponded in German. (It was through these friends that Pasternak made known his satisfaction with the article on "The People with Watch Chains.") I continued, however, to reach him directly with three or four letters and some books. I am not sure that all of my communications got through to him, and I believe at least one letter of his did not reach me. The last letter he wrote, in February 1960, was an acknowledgment of a privately printed Christmas book, *A Nativity Kerygma,* which I had sent him in late November. *Kerygma* is a Greek word meaning "proclamation" or "solemn announcement." Hence the Greek sentence at the beginning of the letter: "I acknowledge your *Kerygma* as soon as possible."

The letter, deeply moving in its hastily composed, improvised English, reflects the titanic inner struggle which the poet was waging to keep his head above water—no longer because of political pressure but because of the almost infinite complications of his life itself, as a result of his celebrity. I reproduce the letter here in witness of the generosity, courage, and boundless warmth of Christian charity which constitute the most eminent greatness of this great man, and which made him the friend of all.[2]

Febr. 7, 1960

My highly dear Merton,

Το κερυγμα ὑμέτερον ἀναγνώσομαι ὡς τάχιστα. I thank you immensely for giving me such inexhaustible marvelous reading for the next future. I shall regain myself from this long and continuing period of letter writing, boring trouble, endless thrusting rhyme translations, time robbing and useless, and of the perpetual selfreproof because of the impossibility to ad-

[2] In 1973, the University of Kentucky King Library Press published the correspondence between Thomas Merton and Boris Pasternak, *Pasternak/Merton: Six Letters,* with an introduction by Lydia Pasternak Slater, Boris Pasternak's sister.

vance the longed for, half begun, many times interrupted, almost inaccessible new manuscript [his historical drama of the 1860s in Russia].

I thank you still more for your having pardoned my long silence, the faint-heartedness and remissness that are underlying in this sad state of mind, where being mortally overbusy and suffering constantly from lack of leisure and time privation. I am perishing of the forced unproductiveness that is worse than pure idleness.

But I shall rise, you will see it. I finally will snatch myself and suddenly deserve and recover again your wonderful confidence and condescension.

Yours affectionately,

B. PASTERNAK

Don't write me, don't abash me with your boundless bounty. The next turn to renew the correspondence will be mine.

Although much has been said and written about Pasternak's death, there remain perhaps many unpublished facts about his illness. Here is one. Although his health was not good, and had obviously suffered to some extent as a result of his tribulations, Pasternak's "sudden" death in May came as a surprise to everyone, even those closest to him. And yet as early as November 1959 Pasternak himself was aware that he was gravely ill and was expecting to die. However, he kept this secret from his family and from all those near him "in order to avoid the slavery of compassion." He struggled on, supported by the hope that he might be able to finish the work in which he was engaged.

This information, which was kept hidden from his family, was revealed by Pasternak to one of his many correspondents: and here we gain new insight into the extraordinary character of these epistolary friendships the poet had contracted with people all over the world. In this case, it was a woman who, with her husband, runs a gas station in a small German city. Deeply impressed by the warmth and intelligence of her letters, Pasternak responded with characteristic generosity, not only replying to her letters with frank and open friendship but even arranging for some friends to get her a golden bracelet, on his behalf, as a present.

Everywhere in the world, even the readers of *Zhivago* who had never actually written to Pasternak, felt that with his death they had lost a close personal friend. The pictures and reports of his funeral evoked in a startling, almost awe-inspiring fashion, the funeral of Zhivago himself, even down to the grief of one of the women mourners. It is the lament of Lara, not in fiction but in reality.

But when the unknown doctor was buried, there were now the thousands of silent, deeply grieving mourners who filed in quiet procession through the trees of the valley at Peredelkino where Pasternak loved to walk alone. This was a witness to the love and respect of the Russian people for their greatest modern poet.

The parish priest was not present when the mortal remains of Boris Pasternak were laid to rest in the churchyard. But the religious rites of the Orthodox Church had been performed quietly, the evening before, in the *dacha*. The simple prayers ended with these words, repeated three times, by the priest and the people: *"May the memory of Boris Leonidovitch, who is worthy of praise, remain with us forever."*

PASTERNAK'S LETTERS TO GEORGIAN FRIENDS

The private letters of another are always difficult, even when they happen to be written to well-known people. Few in the West have ever heard of the obscure Georgian poets who were Pasternak's warmest friends. True, Pasternak became well known—perhaps *too* well known —during the Nobel Prize affair in 1958. Also the introduction and biographical notes help us to identify the strange names ending in -shvili and to become familiar with the people who bore them. Yet we must not expect the Pasternak of these letters to fit the stereotype fashioned for him by the mass media of the West. It is certainly true that he fought a quiet and independent battle for his own beliefs and his own integrity as an artist and a Russian. But he continued to believe in the Russian revolution in spite of the Stalinist terror, and for his exemplars of freedom he did not look West, to Europe and America, but within the Soviet Union itself—to Georgia.

Perhaps no one can fully appreciate these letters who has not lived under some kind of censorship. Only some analogous experience can fill in the immense gaps and help us read between the lines. Those who have had some taste of life under absolute authority can perhaps understand the conflict and its resolution. They can be aware of what Pasternak suffered but above all of the fact that he could also be happy. For one of the things that comes clear at least in some of these letters is a triumphant and almost scandalous happiness: scandalous, that is, to those who are completely convinced that any life under Communism must be one long uniform and excruciating misery, worse even than death.

On the other hand, it is to these letters and other documents like them that we must look for an explanation of Pasternak's capacity to be happy in a life which doubtless would have destroyed or dehumanized a weaker spirit. Georgia and the Georgian poets were for Pasternak an unfailing source of light and strength, a providential refuge and reassurance whose full significance we can perhaps begin to guess from these letters. Pasternak's visits to Georgia and his friendships with Georgian poets,

---

This essay on "Pasternak's Letters to Georgian Friends" was found among Merton's unpublished manuscripts and papers following his death. It was written in early 1968, but only published in the first issue of *The New Lazarus Review* in 1978.

his exposure to the Georgian language and culture, were of decisive importance in his own life and work. Indeed, they bore in them the secret of his survival.

Much more than Italy for Goethe or the Algerian beaches for Camus, Georgia for Pasternak was the living and indestructible witness of a reality that was beyond the reach of abstractness, that could not be reduced to banality—a light that could not be extinguished by the inhumanity of political or literary cliché. Georgia was the living expression of the victory of life over death and of freedom over bureaucratic regimentation upon which Pasternak himself consistently gambled. Georgia was the triumph of poetry, nature, humanity, and the future over political and literary entropy. The mountains, the sun, the city of Tiflis and the people in it, especially its poets and artists, were a miracle and a rarity, a unique victory of wholeness, "a country which has most astonishingly never experienced a break in its existence, a country which has remained down to earth even now and has not been carried off into a sphere of abstraction, a country of amaranthine colour and of everyday reality, however great its present hardships may be."

These words are taken almost from the first pages of the selection. And in the last letter of all, returning from his final visit to Georgia, and knowing he was about to die, Pasternak once again testified to the quasi-miraculous "indigenous and elusive quality in Georgian life" which had helped him survive through so many years of struggle. He felt that this peculiar quality had never fully been expressed even by the Georgian poets themselves, and hoped perhaps he might live to do so himself. He left us nothing but a last faint intuition of this beautiful and mysterious complexity.

Georgia was (Pasternak thought) so constructed that it could not be leveled by any kind of cultural bulldozer. Tiflis is and will remain a city where wandering lanes end up against the side of a mountain and where the rugged vigor of nature and primitive culture is at once "festively victorious" yet tempted to frivolity. However, the apparent surface frivolity hides a fathomless and tragic silence which is not inert but filled with unspeakable power.

The dialectic of joy and tragedy was not something Pasternak merely imagined. In 1936 one of his best friends, the poet Tabidze, was arrested and disappeared from view. Another, Yashvili, committed suicide. For almost twenty years thereafter Pasternak sustained by his love and loyalty Tabidze's wife, Nina, sensing in his heart that Tabidze was already dead. Yet he could not bring himself to admit that Tabidze would not finally return, as others had done, from some distant Siberian camp. It was part of his faith in Georgia that somehow the innocence and integrity of his friend would survive the cruel injustice of the Stalinist police state. Meanwhile, Pasternak's open support of Nina Tabidze and other friends demanded considerable courage on his own part. All around him other writers were being arrested or driven to suicide, and he himself was always suspect. His original work was banned and he was silenced, making his living only by translations.

Official news of Tabidze's death in 1937 did not reach his widow until 1955. When this news finally came, Pasternak only affirmed all the more strongly the innocence and loyalty of the Georgian poet.

Meanwhile, one can see from these letters that one of the great sources of strength in Pasternak's own sufferings was his power to respond to the sufferings of others. In supporting Nina Tabidze he also sustained his own life and his own courage. One who is not attuned to the full realities of the situation might not be able to respond rightly to the vibrant affection of these letters. We are trained to look for anger, bitterness, rebellion against tyranny: instead we discover a resistance that finds expression not in politics but in creativity, in life-affirming love for a few friends, in faith that the future will turn out right in spite of everything. This is the last and strongest kind of resistance left for those who have been pushed to the wall, for whom political activism and open rebellion are no longer rational options, and who have nothing left but to celebrate life itself not in ideology but in poetry, work, and friendship. So they stick together loyally and share the good things to which one may still have access: a party, a poem, a letter, a bottle of wine. If they are to be destroyed, let it be for this last loyalty to a human measure!

One thing must be kept clear about Pasternak and his friends: the accusation that he was disloyal to the Russian revolution was certainly false—except of course in the sense that disagreement with the arbitrary convolutions of the party line could be called a betrayal of the revolution. But it must be admitted that Pasternak's aesthetic is certainly not the kind of thing that is acceptable to official Marxism. It is completely incompatible with the kind of "socialist realism" dictated by political considerations—and in fact by higher authority—which substitutes abstract and doctrinaire routines for the personal inspiration and integrity of the artist formed by fidelity to life. The point is that Pasternak was never able to equate fidelity to the party line with fidelity to life itself. Hence, the revolution being rooted not in doctrine but in life, to prefer abstract doctrine to concrete life was to betray the revolution. This, in the eyes of Marxist orthodoxy, is arrant bourgeois subjectivism.

Just as Pasternak maintained Tabidze was loyal to the original revolutionary ideal, so he himself believed that he and his poetry, together with his translations of the Georgian poets—and of Shakespeare or Faust for that matter—represented the true spirit of the Russian revolution. He felt that the Stalinist literary establishment had in fact betrayed the revolution. He spoke out against the pretense that revolution could be found in "that ridiculous *Literary Gazette*" or in the writers' union or the pretentious stupidity of official competitions and prizes. For Pasternak, the true voice of revolution was not to be heard in the arrogant and doctrinaire pronouncements of the police state but in the "chemistry of thought" that produced the living ferment of poetry like Tabidze's. But the false revolution sought to destroy the true one. Which would win? To the end, Pasternak believed in the victory of the Georgian miracle and of his "sister life." And he intuitively placed his trust in the young poets who would come after him. He was right. The most effective voices of protest against authoritarian rigidity in Russia are those of poets inspired and in some sense formed by Pasternak (like Yevtushenko and Voznesensky).

(It is curious, by the way, that Stalin himself was Georgian: and some have said that Pasternak's survival under Stalin—when he should certainly have followed his friends to death in prison or to the labor camps, was somehow due to his enthusiastic love for Georgia. Perhaps this is myth.)

In any event, the strange and fully authentic happiness of Pasternak in the years after the war—the years when he was writing *Dr. Zhivago*—were in no sense due to his being a "success." It is true that his translations were highly appreciated, but he was never an establishment man. As he wryly remarked, "no one made big contracts" with him. He lived always on the margin of the Moscow literary establishment and one of the firmest components in his happiness was precisely this realization that he was not a phony success. His alienation from the circle of "wingless and unimaginative" bores in which we sense his great loneliness demanded strength and patience. His solitude in its turn called forth from him what it demanded. But he did not exist in total isolation: his communion with his distant friends in the south sustained him in his moral exile from Soviet society. The fervor of his friendship in his letters to them is the measure of the frustration he felt when he found no one to talk to in Moscow.

Pasternak did not altogether escape open conflict with the establishment: it was impossible. But the crisis came late, with the Nobel Prize and *Dr. Zhivago*. Then the full weight of official and inhuman censure descended on him—but only in words and demonstrations. Twenty years earlier he would have been put through the mill and perhaps have "re-canted" in the set fantastic formulas of the time, before being shot.

The very banality of the establishment, from which he was to a great extent excluded, forced him back upon inner resources which made him happy. And this is not a new formula. It is a good one for us to remember when we find ourselves in a similar position.

After all, who can guarantee to escape such things in our time? Total-ism and massive conformism are not restricted to police states. Nor is the police state itself confined to overt Communism and Nazism. Any power structure thriving on militarism and crisis is bound to silence dis-sent sooner or later. It is quite conceivable that even in America writers may one day find themselves in a position like Pasternak's: in which their silence says more than a vocal protest that might prove ambiguous, use-less—or fatal. Trained as we are to think that we have to keep shouting until we are either jailed or exiled, we are not used to the kind of solution Pasternak himself arrived at. He refused exile when he could have been lionized as a Nobel Prize winner in the West. He stayed in Russia, which he loved as his country, while refusing to agree with everything that went on there, and offering a silent resistance that was moral rather than political.

It is therefore instructive to study the scattered allusions in these letters which, added together, provide us with a strikingly coherent formula, a kind of ascesis for survival under totalism. In this, Pasternak falls into a long traditional line of sapiential thought which goes all the way back to the court literature of ancient Egypt, is reflected in such books of the Old Testament as Proverbs and Ecclesiastes, and echoes other wisdoms in India and China.

It is an ascesis of honesty, of work, of loyalty to one's friends, to one's task, and to oneself. It is above all an ascesis of fidelity to life itself and to the human measure. Therefore an ascesis not of rigor and restraint but of openness and response: not of solipsism but of self-forgetfulness, cele-bration, and love. It is an ascesis of generosity. As such it is fully conso-nant with the doctrine we find on one hand in *Prison Letters* of Dietrich Bonhoeffer and on the other in the essays of Albert Camus. (Camus' ideas of revolution and revolt in *L'Homme révolté* are very much like those which underlie *Dr. Zhivago.*) It is the kind of ascesis we find Karl Rahner suggesting for a "diaspora Christianity" and which is not only preached but practiced behind the iron curtain by people like Dr. Kro-madka. It is above all an ascesis of resistance and refusal that rejects the gross and vulgar inhumanity of political or cultural triumphalism. An ascesis that affirms quality and measure in the orgy of quantity which it sees to be a sign of death rather than an affirmation of life. "Women give birth to people, not to cyclopses," says Pasternak in an allusion to the crass stupidities of Soviet art. "Only the inorganic is gigantic, the cosmic spaces of nonexistence, the emptiness of death, the deadening principles of ugliness and humiliation." He is speaking of Russia, but we are reminded of Lewis Mumford's pertinent remarks on the architecture of the Pentagon.

Pasternak kept his sanity under Stalin by virtue of his quiet and dedicated work. Intuitively he found something that was at once a perfect outlet for his creative energies and a contribution to the intellectual life and aesthetic life of his society: translations of poetry from English, German, Georgian, and other languages. In the arid desert of political and aesthetic ultimatums, Pasternak fell back on the joy of silently *making* worthwhile translations. And like the writer of Ecclesiastes, he knew that "when a man eats and drinks and finds happiness in his work, this is a gift from God" (Ecclesiastes 3:13) and "I see there is no happiness for man but to be happy in his work, for this is the lot assigned to him" (*idem* 22).

Pasternak echoes this in one of his letters:

It seems to me that all a man's efforts must be concentrated on his activity—successful, bold and productive, and that life should be allowed to do the rest. Happiness in all sorts of higher spheres of existence, such as love (not only love of a woman, but love of one's country or love of one's contemporaries) creative work and so on, is either given or not given at all, in which case there is nothing to worry about because one could do nothing about it however hard one tried. To me unfaked failure is still more acceptable than faked success.

This is a remarkable piece of wisdom, for most of the delusions and conflicts of modern life are generated by the myth that happiness comes with power over what is essentially a gift and therefore beyond our control. We are happy, as Pasternak says, when we live within the measure of our true possibilities, do what we can, and allow the rest to be added as pure gift and "grace."

Therefore he can say:

"One must write wonderful things, make discoveries, and see to it that wonderful things happen to you. That is life. The rest is rubbish."

Certainly, this reflects a greater enthusiasm than the disillusioned old

Preacher ever managed to summon up in the dour lines of Ecclesiastes. But it is not a matter of art for art's sake or a mere cult of kicks. It springs from a depth and wholeness, an integrity and maturity that are not won without long experience and painful sacrifice. It springs from the kind of lucidity that Camus called for, and this lucidity is itself the fruit of unambiguous choice. Dedication to absolute sincerity in his work (a dedication which he was able to maintain as translator when all other avenues were closed to him) gave Pasternak's whole life a clarity which made everything else—as he said—"easy." As long as he was faithful to the task which had been carved out to his own measure by life itself, he knew he could be ready for anything else.

Here is the core of what we have been calling, for want of a better expression, his ascesis. Sacrifice is central to art, not just because art requires discipline, but because sacrifice is the price of living growth. For Pasternak, work is the way into the future, and sacrifice is what opens that way for the artist, because by devoting himself honestly and entirely to his work he grows insensibly into the future. By his work, man is integrated into a growing and evolving present, a world that is real and fully engaged in organic development. By his work man grows with that world into what it is going to be: there is no other way for man to find himself. What is to be sacrificed is then the idiosyncracy or the banal and dead conformity that bind him instead to what is dying, to what is being left behind.

This ascesis is remarkably like that which Teilhard de Chardin developed in *The Divine Milieu*. Without sacrifice, says Pasternak, art may be "covered outside with a sprinkling of superficial talent"—one may add "pseudomodernity"—while being inwardly rooted in what man has long ago outgrown. This of course is true of all establishment art, especially in totalist regimes.

This program of sacrifice is not one of masochistic niggling, but of positive abandonment to the dynamism of life. To give oneself up to serious work is for Pasternak identical with giving oneself up "into the hands of life itself." In the end, one must also take the further step and give oneself up "into the hands of death."

Surely one of the most arresting and beautiful pages in all Pasternak is in the letter where he describes how after a heart attack he is taken to a crowded Moscow hospital and bedded down in the hall. He lies in bed and gazes down the long corridor at the distant window, the dim lamp of the night nurse. He realizes the obscure presence of death and sees it all as "such an unfathomable, such a superhuman poem." In pure joy and gratitude he thanks God for having made him an artist! "I wanted more than ever to talk to God, to glorify everything I saw, to catch and imprint it on my memory. 'Lord,' I whispered, 'I thank you for having laid on the paints so thickly' . . ." The expression surprises us, and then we realize once again the peculiar meaning of the Georgian miracle in Pasternak's life. This intensity, this joy, this fervor, this innocence which might seem to us like so much impasto at times—our own enthusiasms have worn so thin—are all part of the richness of his Georgian friendships.

There was one expression of Tabidze, *gadavarda,* which Pasternak treasured and incorporated into his own life-view. *Gadavarda* means "to throw oneself headlong," to dive right into the life-stream without afterthought and without care.

That may have romantic overtones, but in the end Pasternak himself not only saw the full meaning of it but lived that meaning. To throw oneself headlong into life does not, unfortunately, mean being carried away in rivers of ecstasy. *Gadavarda* sounds like an enrichment and indeed it is: but it is the terrible enrichment of poverty and nakedness, solitude and abandon. In Pasternak's austere but inspiring words:

"Everywhere in the world one has to pay for the right to live on one's own naked spiritual reserves."

It was Pasternak's Georgian friendships that enabled him to pay for that grim right; and the Georgian miracle of celebration and silence, fully integrated into Pasternak's own life, became the living core of his own "naked spiritual reserve."

"BAPTISM IN THE FOREST":
WISDOM AND INITIATION IN WILLIAM FAULKNER

Perhaps the best way to approach the rather troublesome question of
literature and religion today is to begin with a typical case, an example
not of "religious literature" but rather of the confusions surrounding it.
When Camus undertook to adapt Faulkner's *Requiem for a Nun* for the
French stage, there was a certain amount of gossip in the press: "Camus
has been converted!" Why? Because the work of Faulkner was "religious." (Anything with the word "nun" in the title has to be Roman
Catholic, you know.) In an interview published in *Le Monde*[1] Camus
had to go through the usual tiresome business of explaining the fairly
obvious. He was fascinated by Faulkner, "the greatest American novelist."
To Camus, Faulkner was one of the few modern writers who possessed
the "keys of ancient tragedy" and who was able to discover in the back
pages of the newspapers myths embodying the essential tragedy of our
time. Faulkner could place modern characters in conflict with their destiny and could resolve that conflict in the way classic tragedy had done.
In a word, Faulkner made it possible to hope that the "tragique de notre
histoire" would one day be made credible on the stage.[2] In Faulkner the
theme of suffering was treated in a tragic, therefore (Camus thought) in
a basically religious manner. Faulkner combined and concentrated in himself the "universe of Dostoevski and, besides that, Protestant rigorism."
This was not at all a question of conventional moral sermons, which
(Camus admitted) bored him to death, but of the mystery of suffering as
a dark abyss into which Faulkner saw a possibility of a little light sometimes filtering. Without being "converted," Camus was certainly fascinated by the "étrange religion de Faulkner," readily suggesting that it
contained the secret of Faulkner's tragic power.

This essay was written as an introduction to *Mansions of the Spirit*, edited by
George A. Panichas (New York: Hawthorn, 1967).

[1] See the texts assembled by Roger Quilliot in Camus' *Théâtre, récits, nouvelles*
(Paris: 1963), pp. 1855ff.

[2] In his hope for a return of true tragedy Camus was influenced by the ideas of
Antonin Artaud's manifestoes on "Le Théâtre de la cruauté." See Artaud, *Oeuvres
complètes*, Tome IV (Paris: 1964), pp. 101ff. A reading of these helps us to appreciate what Camus saw in Faulkner.

In a preface to the regular French edition of *Requiem,* translated by Maurice-Edgar Coindreau, Camus roundly asserted that the paradoxical religious outlook of Faulkner, which made a saint of the prostitute Nancy and "invested brothels and prisons with the dignity of the cloister," could not be dispensed with in an adaptation. "Ce paradoxe essentiel il fallait le conserver." Nonetheless, Camus admitted that he had shortened the meditative passages on God and faith.

Camus added sardonically, "If I translated and staged a Greek tragedy, no one would ask me if I believed in Zeus." At the same time, in the aforementioned interview, Camus repudiated a superficial "godlessness" which he considered "vulgar and threadbare." "I do not believe in God," he said, "but I am not for all that an atheist."

The purpose of these quotations is not to approve or to disapprove of Camus' evaluation of Faulkner or of "Faulkner's religion." The case is adduced as evidence of two facts: namely, that there does exist a consensus which admits the existence even today of "religious literature" and that there is also a disquieting, even annoying, popular tendency to look for "conversions" in connection with this literature. I do not say that these popular beliefs substantiate all that critics sometimes say about literature and religion. I am merely showing what seems to me to be the source of the problem with which the present book attempts to deal. Far from taking these popular opinions as proof of "Faulkner's religion," I will merely use them as a starting point for a more pedestrian investigation of themes in Faulkner which might conceivably be called "religious" but which, I think, can better be classified by another term.

Meanwhile, let us firmly repudiate those vices which make this whole question of "religious literature" so distasteful and so confusing. First, there is the often morbid curiosity about conversions and apostasies associated with the writing or the reading of this or that literary work. This curiosity is every bit as vulgar and tiresome as the aggressive religion and irreligion which often go with it. In large part the blame may well lie with the prevalence of another critical vice, that of "claiming for the faith" (see, in this connection, the essay by Hyatt Waggoner). This is the habit of searching authors for symptoms of belief—whether Christian, Marxist, or any other—and of forthwith enrolling them in one's own sect. John Cruickshank would call this "intellectual imperialism," and we can join him in finding it repugnant, especially when it claims to be "Christian." Unfortunately, the embattled inferiority complex of much nineteenth-century thought made this tendency almost second nature in some quarters. The dead, whose hash was definitely settled and who could not be discovered to have been deathbed converts, were nevertheless shown to have been secret believers in one way or another. The living were always rumored to be about to bow their heads over the font. Aldous Huxley, for instance, was repeatedly rumored to be on the verge of becoming a Catholic, perhaps because (as Milton Birnbaum shows) he once said that he disliked Catholics less than Puritans! Nor is there any need to recall the fury of conversions and apostasies which thirty years ago kept a ceaseless procession of intellectuals moving in and out of the Communist Party.

Further refinements in these matters can be left to the very competent treatment of the essayists in the first part of this volume. Is there such a thing as religious literature at all? What is meant here by "religious"? Does "religious literature" imply the author's orthodoxy, his belonging to a Church, or his commitment to a recognizable set of beliefs? The writers in this volume do not agree in their terminology, although they do in fact come to pretty much the same conclusions. "Literary" and "religious" values must not be confused. Obviously, religious orthodoxy or sincerity is no guarantee that a work is artistically valid. If, on the other hand, an understanding of the work implies some awareness of religious values, then one must be able to identify oneself to some extent with the author in holding these values to be "real." Otherwise, it becomes impossible to enjoy the work in question. But, again, what are "religious values"? Father Blehl, for instance, says that Graham Greene's whisky priest displays religious values, whereas in Faulkner's "The Bear" "the experiences have almost no intrinsic religious significance at all." Here, by "religious" Father Blehl evidently means "Christian" and "theological." The "religious" is "sacerdotal and spiritually redemptive" and "shows the operation of God in a world of sin." I would like to suggest later that Faulkner (at least in "The Bear") does have a "spiritually redemptive" view of the world, though it is not necessarily the orthodox Christian view.

Thomas L. Hanna would also like the range of "religion" in this regard severely restricted. For Hanna, a work is religious only if God is in the cast of characters. The fact that an author happens to have a coherent view of the world and of man's struggle with destiny in the world does not mean that he is giving "religious" answers. Perhaps, Hanna suggests, we should call his outlook a "metaphysic" rather than "religion." In such a case Camus' statement about the "étrange religion de Faulkner" should be emended to read "l'étrange métaphysique de Faulkner." I submit that the idea is subtly transformed as soon as it gets into French. Hanna is undoubtedly right in protesting against the naïveté of disoriented Christians who, having no metaphysic and needing one badly, assume that when they find a few ingredients for one, they have rediscovered "Christianity." Still, this deficiency and this naïveté are perhaps more apparent in America than in Europe. When in the very next essay Edwin M. Moseley can speak calmly of "the essentially religious content of serious drama in every age," he seems to be contradicting Hanna; yet he is not. Moseley's statement is much more plausible in his own context, since he starts out from Greek tragedy and talks the language of people like F. M. Cornford. Here again our allusions to Camus come in handy. Everyone can still respond to the great religious and mythical motifs of Greek tragedy without being converted to a belief in Zeus. As a matter of fact, Greek tragedy could imply a very definite ambiguity toward the gods. Faith in the Olympians did not necessarily imply a personal commitment to their service, and devotion to one of them might bring the devotee into strained relations with another (as Homer brings out). Aeschylus was not at all convinced that Zeus' rule was beneficial or even fully justified. And the Zeus of *Prometheus* is regarded as a usurper against whom Prometheus has a very plausible case.

Nevertheless, there is no getting around the facts that Greek tragedy deals religiously with the great basic problems of human destiny and that one can accept this without committing oneself to a particular dogmatic faith. The "religious" elements in Greek tragedy are of the same nature as the "essential paradox" which Camus found in Faulkner's *Requiem*. They lie embedded in different ground from that in which the revealed truths of Christianity are found. They are embedded in human nature itself, or, if that expression is no longer acceptable to some readers, then in the very constitution of man's psyche, whether his collective unconscious or his individual character structure.

In this connection we can readily understand why the neopositivism of Alain Robbe-Grillet rejects all tragedy as sentimental and false because it inevitably implies certain basic religious postulates about the value of life. But he assumes that these religious postulates are something *added* to reality, not inherent in it. In his suppression of values he suppresses something of reality itself. Hence his people are, as Father Jarrett-Kerr says, like insects. Such is the fruit of a method which has triumphantly "made tragedy impossible" and has, at the same time, rejected as irrelevant the idea of human nature and, even more, that of the human person. But Father Jarrett-Kerr also raises the question whether there can be "Christian tragedy" in any context where the resurrection of the dead is taken for granted. "Theology," in I. A. Richards' words, "is fatal to tragedy."

But redemption is not automatic. "Salvation" can never be taken for granted. All the good potentialities in man can be irretrievably wasted and destroyed through his own fault. The Christian concept of damnation, whether one believes in it or not, is supremely tragic. When Camus (out of the bitterness of his experience under the Nazis and during the Algerian war) spoke of our time as "tragic," he was aware of the aspect of its *destruction of man*. And Camus excels in portraying the damned.

Greek tragedy is comprehensible irrespective of whether we "believe in" the Greek gods. It is so because it is not in fact concerned with truth about the gods but with truths about man. It is concerned with them in such a "classical," such a universal way that we, too, find ourselves involved in them without passing through the medium of a doctrinal explanation. This immediacy of Attic tragedy may be more obvious to us in the West because our whole culture is built on the basis of Greek and Hebrew literature and thought. But I think that with a very little initiation the Nō drama of Japan, for instance, or the religious drama of Bali[3] can have the same awe-inspiring and cathartic impact on a Western audience. In other words, once the ritual and symbolic language of gesture is grasped, one can participate in Oriental drama almost as well as in Greek tragedy. In either case, what is happening is not just that we are spelling out for ourselves a religious or a metaphysical message. Rather, the drama is having a direct impact on the deepest center of our human nature, at a level beyond language, where our most fundamental human conflicts find themselves not *explained,* not *analyzed,* but *enacted* in the artistic way which Aristotle tried to account for in his theory of catharsis, of pity and terror in tragedy.

In this way tragedy does not merely convince us that we ought to be resigned. Above all, it does not merely propose suitable reasons for resignation. Through its therapeutic effect it enables us to rise above evil, to liberate ourselves from it by a return to a more real evaluation of ourselves, a change of heart analogous to Christian "repentance." As we know, the mechanism of Greek tragedy is centered on *hubris,* that fundamentally false and arrogant estimate of one's self and of its capacities. The catharsis of pity and terror delivers the participant from *hubris* and restores him to an awareness of his place in the scheme of things—of his limitations as well as of his true nobility. It enables him to realize that "Puny Man," as Father Jarrett-Kerr says, "is still valuable for his freedom."

Now it is quite obvious that both Greek tragedy and Oriental ritual

---

[3] See Artaud, "Sur le théâtre balinais," *op. cit.,* 64ff.

dance-drama were not merely presentations which an audience sat and watched. They were religious celebrations, liturgies, in which the audience participated. Thus, although we can still be immediately stirred by the impact of these archaic dramas even when we read them in translation, it does not take much imagination for us to represent to ourselves what would be the effect of our being present *then,* in those days, for instance in the theater at Delphi during the festival of Apollo. (Note what Father Jarrett-Kerr says about a recent performance of *Medea* before an African audience in Johannesburg.) We—our twentieth-century selves—might possibly have found the experience too powerful to bear. Or perhaps we would have undergone the sort of thing that happens now to the people who take LSD, which is presumably why they take it and why the taking of it has been invested with a quasi-religious ritual atmosphere.

The point is, I think, to realize that something of the same excitement and discovery remains accessible to us today in reading not only ancient tragedies but works of our own time. Faulkner is certainly one of those writers who possess this power to *evoke* in us an experience of meaning and of direction or a catharsis of pity and terror which can be called "religious" in the same sense as Greek tragedy was religious.

Unfortunately, as we have seen, the term "religious" is also very ambiguous, insofar as it is associated with many other things that have nothing to do with this basic experience. For example, the idea of religion today is mixed up with confessionalism, with belonging to this or that religious institution, with making and advertising a particular kind of religious commitment, with a special style in devotion or piety, or even with a certain exclusiveness in the quest for an experience which has to be sacred and not secular. In spite of all the talk of believers about breaking down the limits between the sacred and the secular, one still feels that there is a very obsessive insistence that one's whole experience of life has to be dominated *from without* by a system of acquired beliefs and attitudes and that every other experience (for instance, that of reading a novel) has first to be tested by this system of beliefs. Thus one has to read Faulkner with suspicion and enjoy only what conforms to one's own moral and religious code.

In order to make this simple and easy, one just proceeds to codify the novelists themselves. What did they believe? What was the preferred system of each? What in fact were "their messages"? But I submit that if you sit down to codify the "strange religion of Faulkner" and if you do so in terms of some other no doubt less strange religion of your own, you are likely to miss the real "religious" impact of Faulkner. His impact has all the directness of Greek tragedy because, although he works in words, he produces an effect that is somehow not explicable by an investigation of the words alone. He has a power of "enactment" which, if you are open to it, brings you into living participation with an experience of basic and universal human values on a level which words can *point* to but cannot fully attain. Faulkner is typical of the creative genius who can associate his reader in the same experience of creation which brought forth his book. Such a book is filled with efficacious sign-situations, symbols, and myths which release in the reader the imaginative power to experience what the author really means to convey. And what he means to convey is not a system of truths which explain life but a certain depth of awareness in which life itself is lived more intensely and with a more meaningful direction. The "symbolic" in this sense is not a matter of contrived signification in which things point arbitrarily to something else. Symbols are signs which release the power of imaginative communion.

The power of symbols is, I think, fully explicable only if you accept the theory that symbols are something more than mere artifacts of a few human minds. They are basic archetypal forms anterior to any operation of the mind, forms which have risen spontaneously with awareness in all religions and which have everywhere provided patterns for the myths in which man has striven to express his search for ultimate meaning and for union with God. Needless to say, these myths retain their power and their seminal creativity in the unconscious even after conscious minds have agreed that "God is dead." The myth of the death of God and of the void consequent upon it springs from the same archaic source as other myths. The conscious determination to deny that there is any void and to suppress all anxiety about it is another matter.

At the same time it must be quite clear that this imaginative and symbol-making capacity in man must not be confused with theological faith. But, because faith implies communication and language, the language of symbols is most appropriate in activating the deepest centers of decision which faith calls into play.

I would submit that the term "religious" no longer conveys the idea of an imaginative awareness of basic meaning. As D. H. Lawrence asserted, "It's not religious to be religious." And I would also say that the word "metaphysical" is not quite adequate to convey these values. There are other possibilities. One of them is the term *sapiential*.

Sapientia is the Latin word for "wisdom." And wisdom in the classic, as well as the Biblical, tradition is something quite definite. It is the highest level of cognition. It goes beyond *scientia,* which is systematic knowledge, beyond *intellectus,* which is intuitive understanding. It has deeper penetration and wider range than either of these. It embraces the entire scope of man's life and all its meaning. It grasps the ultimate truths to which science and intuition only point. In ancient terms, it seeks the "ultimate causes," not simply efficient causes which make things happen, but the ultimate reasons why they happen and the ultimate values which their happening reveals to us. Wisdom is not only speculative, but also practical: that is to say, it is "lived." And unless one "lives" it, one cannot "have" it. It is not only speculative but creative. It is expressed in living signs and symbols. It proceeds, then, not merely from knowledge *about* ultimate values, but from an actual possession and awareness of these values as incorporated in one's own existence.

But *sapientia* is not inborn. True, the seeds of it are there, but they must be cultivated. Hence wisdom develops not by itself but in a hard discipline of traditional training, under the expert guidance of one who himself possesses it and who therefore is qualified to teach it. For wisdom cannot be learned from a book. It is acquired only in a living formation; and it is tested by the master himself in certain critical situations.

I might say at once that creative writing and imaginative criticism provide a privileged area for wisdom in the modern world. At times one feels they do so even more than current philosophy and theology. The literary and creative current of thought that has been enriched and stimulated by depth psychology, comparative religion, social anthropology, existentialism, and the renewal of classical, patristic, Biblical, and mystical studies has brought in a sapiential harvest which is not to be despised. Let me mention some of the more obvious examples: T. S. Eliot both as critic and as poet, Boris Pasternak, St.-John Perse, D. H. Lawrence,[4] and William Butler Yeats. Jacques Maritain's *Creative Intuition in Art and Poetry* illustrates what I mean, as do D. T. Suzuki's *Zen and Japanese Culture* and William Carlos Williams's *In the American Grain.* A great deal of what I call "sapiential" thinking has come out in studies of Melville and of the American novel in general, as well as in some of the recent Milton and Shakespeare criticism. I was fortunate to study in college under "sapiential" teachers like Mark Van Doren and Joseph Wood Krutch. In the classics Jane Harrison, Werner Jaeger, and F. M. Cornford have left us "sapiential" material.

The "wisdom" approach to man seeks to apprehend man's value and

---

[4] Vivian de Sola Pinto's essay in *Mansions of the Spirit* brings this out well.

destiny in their global and even ultimate significance. Since fragmentation and objectivity do not suffice for this and since quantitative analysis will not serve, either, sapiential thought resorts to poetic myth and to religious or archetypal symbol. These must not be mistaken for *scientific* propositions. Symbols are not, here, ciphers pointing to hidden sources of information. They are not directed so much at the understanding and control of things as at man's own understanding of himself. They seek to help man liberate in himself life forces which are inhibited by dead social routine, by the ordinary involvement of the mind in trivial objects, by the conflicts of needs and of material interests on a limited level. Obviously, we do live in a world of things and institutions. We need to eat and to manage our everyday lives. But we also need an overall perspective to liberate us from enslavement to the immediate without taking us altogether outside the "real world." Sapiential awareness deepens our communion with the concrete: It is not an initiation into a world of abstractions and ideals. The poetic and contemplative awareness is sapiential—and it used to be, normally, religious. In fact, there is a relation between all "wisdoms." Greek wisdom was not out of harmony with that of the Bible. "Pythagoras and his disciples, and also Plato, followed that inward vision of theirs which was aimed at the truth, and this they did not without the help of God; and so in certain things they were in agreement with the words of the prophets."[5] So said Clement of Alexandria, hinting that all wisdom opened out upon true religion.

Wisdom, in any case, has two aspects. One is metaphysical and speculative, an apprehension of the radical structure of human life, an intellectual appreciation of man in his human potentialities and in their fruition. The other is moral, practical, and religious, an awareness of man's life as a task to be undertaken at great risk, in which tragic failure and creative transcendence are both possible. Another aspect of this moral and religious wisdom is a peculiar understanding of conflict, of the drama of human existence, and especially of the typical causes and signs of moral disaster. I might add that one of the characteristic qualities of this wisdom is that it goes beyond the conscious and systematic moral principles which may be embodied in an ethical doctrine and which guide our conscious activity. Wisdom also supposes a certain intuitive grasp of *unconscious motivations,* at least insofar as these are embodied in archetypes and symbolic configurations of the psyche.

Sapiential thinking has, as another of its characteristics, the capacity to

[5] *Stromata* V. 14. 116. 1.

bridge the cognitive gap between our minds and the realm of the transcendent and the unknown, so that without "understanding" what lies beyond the limit of human vision, we nevertheless enter into an intuitive affinity with it, or seem to experience some such affinity. At any rate, religious wisdoms often claim not only to teach us truths that are beyond rational knowledge but also to *initiate* us into higher states of awareness. Such forms of wisdom are called mystical. I do not pause here to discuss the validity of various claims to mystical wisdom. It is sufficient to say that certain types of wisdom do in fact lay claim to an awareness that goes beyond the aesthetic, moral, and liturgical levels and penetrates so far as to give the initiate a direct, though perhaps incommunicable, intuition of the ultimate values of life, of the Absolute Ground of life, or even of the invisible Godhead. Christian wisdom is essentially theological, Christological, and mystical. It implies a deepening of Christian faith to the point where faith becomes an experiential awareness of the realities and values of man's life in Christ and "in the Spirit" when he has been raised to divine sonship.

In this collection of essays only the last two raise the question of Christian wisdom in modern life. Robert Detweiler's study of Flannery O'Connor introduces us to the radically new character of a wisdom that is "from above" and is based on a Word which is an offense, breaking through the hierarchical orders of cosmic sapience and overturning every other form of knowledge in order to bring man into confrontation with a whole new kind of destiny, a destiny to freedom in Christ. (Flannery O'Connor well knew how to exploit the ironies of this shocking situation!) The essay by George A. Panichas, on the other hand, brings us into contact with the ancient contemplative tradition of the Eastern Church, which represents a much more peaceful approach to a Christian wisdom from which Hellenic elements have not been driven out. The story of the Russian Pilgrim that so impressed Salinger's Franny informs us of a sapiential technique first devised by the monks of Sinai and transmitted from there to Mount Athos and then to Rumania and Russia. The purpose of this elementary technique was to dispose the contemplative to a possibility of direct illumination by God in the *theoria* described by the Greek Fathers and further developed by Athonite hesychasm in the fourteenth century.

For my part, I am not concerned in this essay with specifically Christian wisdom. I want to discuss two examples of what I would call the natural sapiential outlook in Faulkner: in other words, two examples of a conscious and deliberate construction of myth in order to convey a sense of initiatory awakening into the deeper meaning of life in terms of a tradition of natural wisdom. In the two works I take as examples, *Go Down, Moses* and *The Wild Palms,* it seems to me that this sapiential use of myth and of symbolic narrative, culminating in a new awareness of the meaning of life in a historical situation, has to be appreciated and accepted if one is to understand what the author is trying to say.

Let me be clear about what I mean by "myth." A myth is a tale with an archetypal pattern capable of suggesting and of implying that man's life in the cosmos has a hidden meaning which can be sought and found by one who somehow religiously identifies his own life with that of the hero in the story. For example, the *Odyssey* shows life as a journey with many trials and perils typified by symbolic test situations, a journey of return to one's home and one's place in the scheme of things. The ironic epic journey of the tall convict on the flooded river in *The Wild Palms* is a mystical *navigation* of this kind, but other important mythical elements enter into it. The flood is indeed seen as an eschatological deluge. It is not only a mystical journey for the tall convict (whose name we never know and who is a kind of archetypal man), but also a parable of judgment and a revelation of the meaning or un-meaning of human destiny. But the journey of the convict is a spiritual one, and its goal is a deeper sense of his own identity and his own "vocation." What he finds is a more definite, and more ironic, certitude of his own measure and of his place in the world which, in this story, is absurd and void.

The part of *Go Down, Moses* that interests me most is, of course, "The Bear." There has been a great deal of exciting criticism written about this exploitation of the "Paradise theme" and the "Lost Wilderness,"[6] but I would add that the story of Ike McCaslin's novitiate and initiation in the wilderness life has to be seen in the context of the whole book, *Go*

---

[6] For example, R. W. B. Lewis, "The Hero in the New World: William Faulkner's 'The Bear,'" *The Kenyon Review,* XIII, 1951, pp. 458–74. This essay was reprinted in *Interpretations of American Literature,* ed. Charles Feidelson, Jr., and Paul Brodtkorb, Jr. (New York: 1959), pp. 332–48. For Lewis, "The Bear" is "Faulkner's first sustained venture towards the more hopeful liberated world after the Incarnation," a canticle celebrating the new life "not lacking in dimly seen miraculous events." He sees in Ike McCaslin's renunciation an intimation of "conscious Christ-likeness," and the wisdom of "The Bear" is "the transmutation of power into charity." It is true that there is a definite and perhaps intended Christ-likeness in Ike McCaslin; but it seems to me that the forces of "redemption" and "renewal" in "The Bear" are more on the order of a wilderness cult and identification with cosmic spirits than explicit Christianity.

Down, Moses, since in fact Part IV of "The Bear" does not reveal its full meaning when "The Bear" is printed and read apart from the rest of the McCaslin story. The violation of the wilderness, symbolic of a certain predatory and ferocious attitude toward the natural world, is for Faulkner an especially Southern phenomenon here, because it is connected with slavery. Ike McCaslin's initiation, his "baptism in the forest,"[7] culminating in a "revelatory vision" followed by the death of the Bear and of Ike's spiritual "Father" and "Guru," Sam Fathers, leads to a religious decision, a monastic act of renunciation, by which Ike attempts to cleanse himself of the guilt that he believes to have become associated, like a classic "miasma," with the Southern earth. He renounces his ownership of land which, as he sees it, belongs to God and cannot be "owned" by anyone. But he finds that monastic poverty alone is not enough (note that he remains on his land but works as a carpenter, "like the Nazarene").

Poverty without chastity remains in some sense ambiguous and ineffective, as Ike's wife intuitively senses in the scene where she tries to bind him again, by erotic ecstasy and the generation of a child, to the earth he has tried to renounce. It is almost as if she has instinctively sensed the power of a countermysticism, another more elemental "wisdom," to cancel out the spiritual vision in the wilderness. And perhaps she succeeds, for after this Ike McCaslin remains an ambiguous personage. At the end of *Go Down, Moses* (in "Delta Autumn") he reveals the almost total loss of any prophetic charisma that might once have been supposed his. We must not then forget that in spite of his initiation and vision Ike McCaslin remains a failed saint and only half a monk. (Speaking after twenty-five years in a monastery, I would like to add that it is extraordinarily difficult for *anyone* to be more than that, and most of us are not even that far along.)

However, it is the account of the spiritual initiation that seems to me to be a particularly good, because evidently deliberate, use of the sapiential in Faulkner. It is clearly the story of a disciple being taught and formed in a traditional and archaic wisdom by a charismatic spiritual Father who is especially qualified for the task and who hands on not only a set of skills or a body of knowledge, but a *mastery of life,* a certain way of being aware, of being in touch not just with natural objects, with liv-

---

[7] The words are those of an interviewer who admired Ike "because he underwent the baptism in the forest, because he rejected his inheritance." Faulkner replied that rejecting one's inheritance was not enough: "He should have been more affirmative instead of just shunning people." Quoted in Michael Millgate, *The Achievement of William Faulkner* (London: 1966), p. 208.

ing things, but with the cosmic spirit, with the wilderness itself regarded almost as a supernatural being, a "person." Indeed, the Bear, Old Ben, is treated as a quasi-transcendent being, like Sam Fathers and like Lion, the fabulous brute of a hound that finally (when Old Ben has himself more or less consented) brings the Bear down into death. It is as if the wilderness spirit were somehow incarnated in Old Ben—as if he were a wilderness god. The annual autumn hunting party of Major de Spain becomes a more or less ritual performance in which Old Ben is ceremoniously hunted; it is "the yearly pageant of Old Ben's furious immortality." He is never seen and never expected to be caught, until the end comes for the whole wilderness and Old Ben, we are led to believe, is ready to surrender himself and the woods to the portentous ritual of desecration that awaits them. This desecration signals the beginning of a new age, not of gold or silver but of iron.

Thus the initiation of Ike McCaslin takes place precisely at a crucial moment of religious history, a turning point when all that he has learned and seen is to become obsolete. He will learn to be not only a wonderful hunter but a contemplative and prophet, a wise man who has beheld the real ground of mystery and value which is concealed in the Edenic wilderness and which others can only guess at. But his skill and his vision remain useless aristocratic luxuries. They are anachronisms in the modern world, and he is helpless when, as an old man, he sees a young relative getting involved in the ancient tragedy of miscegenation and injustice. He has seen the inner meaning of the wilderness as an epiphany of the cosmic mystery. He has encountered the Bear and had his "illumination." In the light of this he has seen into the religious and historic mystery of the South which lies under judgment and under a curse. Yet there is nothing he can do about it apart from his monastic gesture, which remains ambiguous and abortive.

Worst of all, Ike McCaslin seems to have become oblivious of the one vital, indestructible force that remains in the world—the force of human love. "Old man," says the Negro mistress of Ike's nephew, "have you lived so long and forgotten so much that you don't remember anything you knew or felt or even heard about love?" The failure is typically monastic. Ike is concerned exclusively with the ritual handing on of General Compson's hunting horn, which belongs by right to the illegitimate son. Thus, there is after all a fruitful ambiguity in Faulkner's treatment of this wilderness-paradise wisdom which no longer has any real application in the world of our time, any more than the romantic gallantry of the Sartoris family has.

Nevertheless, the story of the boy's formation by Sam Fathers, his growing awareness of the Bear as spiritual reality and as "presence," his experience of the numinous mystery of the Bear as quasi-transcendent being, his decision to make the sacrifice which is necessary to see the Bear, and his consequent entering into a quasi-mystical relationship with the Bear: all this is told with an inspired mastery that betrays Faulkner's own enthusiasm, another evidence of "his strange religion." The story has Old Testament resonances characteristic of Faulkner everywhere, and the gradual ascent of the disciple to vision suggests the mystery cults of Greece; but what Faulkner actually celebrates is the primitive wisdom of the American Indian, the man who was *par excellence* the wilderness hunter and the free wanderer in the unspoiled garden of Paradise.

Countless mythical themes have been discovered in "The Bear." Everything is said to be there, from the Great Mother to the Holy Grail. There is no need to go into all that. I am primarily interested in Ike McCaslin's introduction to the wisdom of the wilderness and his initiation into it as spiritual mystery. This has the deepest possible resonances. It is not just a matter of knowledge or even of maturity. It is a question of *salvation*. This is not, of course, salvation and redemption in any Christian or theological sense, but rather a natural analogue of supernatural salvation: a man justifying his existence and liberating his soul from blindness and captivity by acquiring a deep and definitive understanding of his life's purpose and deciding to live in accordance with this understanding. This is not mere solipsism, but an illuminating and mysterious communion with cosmic reality explicated in mythical and symbolic terms. Though Ike becomes in the end ambiguous as a charismatic figure (and this is perhaps necessary because the wilderness itself, which would be the very ground and source of his charism, has all but vanished), there is no question, at least in my mind, that Faulkner intended him to be one of "the saved."

This limited concept of salvation is not new, though it may seem so to most of us who have forgotten the classic tradition. It is a humanistic as well as basically a religious concept with an essentially ethical component, the same "old verities" which Faulkner said in his Nobel Prize acceptance speech he had always been writing about: "The old verities and truths of the heart, the universal truths lacking which any story is ephemeral and doomed—love and honor and pity and pride and compassion and sacrifice." These Ike learns from Sam Fathers in the wilderness, along with humility and courage ("Be scared but don't be afraid. . . . A bear or a deer has got to be scared of a coward the same as a brave man has to

be"). His wilderness life is essentially an education and a spiritual formation: "The wilderness the old bear ran was his college, and the old male
bear himself . . . was his alma mater." The term "alma mater" is not a
mere cliché. It is to be taken seriously enough here (with all its irony),
for Ike is *regenerated*, twice born; he enters into a new life because of
the death of the Bear and of Sam Fathers. He becomes the "child" and
"heir" of the wilderness spirit which was in them and which is passed
on to him. (Note that there is another, less profound way of participating
in the wilderness spirit. To hunters, whisky—not women—is a "condensa-
tion of the wild immortal spirit." This magic elixir is also well known
to have played a part in Faulkner's "étrange religion.") This experience
makes up not only an education but a spiritual and religious formation—
Ike's "novitiate to the true wilderness."

To understand fully this novitiate, we need to read "The Old People,"
another section of *Go Down, Moses,* in which Sam Fathers is shown
introducing him into a kind of timeless contemporaneousness with a
largely vanished race. "Gradually to the boy those old times would cease
to be old times and would become a part of the boy's present, not only as
if they had happened yesterday but as if they were still happening and
more—as if some of them had not come into existence yet." This extraordinary shift in consciousness makes Ike McCaslin aware that there is
a whole new dimension of being which is obscured by civilized assumptions and that in order to find himself truly he has to make an existential
leap into this mysterious other order, into the dimension of a primitive
wilderness experience. He will do so by "seeing" the Bear, an act of initiation in which his own identity will be fully established.

The successive experiences of closer and closer awareness of the Bear
are described almost like degrees of mystical elevation in which the Bear
(acting not without a certain suggestion of spiritual initiative of his own)
becomes more and more a real and finally almost a personal presence.
The Bear is first experienced as an insurmountable void and absence,
apprehended negatively in relation to the curious barking of the hysterically frightened hounds and then again in the silence created when a
woodpecker suddenly stops drumming and then starts again. "There had
been nothing except the solitude. . . ." The Bear has passed invisibly.
Then Ike realizes that he is *seen* by the Bear without seeing anything
himself. The Bear, he feels, now knows and recognizes him. In the end
he resolves to go out into the woods without a gun and "prove" to the
Bear that he is not an ordinary hunter. When this is not enough, he
leaves his watch and compass hanging on a branch and lets himself get

lost in the virgin forest. It is then that he finally sees the Bear in an instant of peaceful and Edenic revelation in which the Bear, incidentally, also brings him back to the place where his watch and compass are waiting. It is a description of the kind of "existential leap" which Kierkegaard demanded for any passage to a higher level of awareness or of existence. But what makes it possible for some critics to see the Bear as a symbol of Christ is the fact that in becoming *visible,* then *personal,* in manifesting himself to men, the Bear yields to a kind of weakness in his "supernatural" being, a kind of divine and *kenotic* flaw which will eventually make him vulnerable, destructible, mortal, and which will ultimately bring about his destruction. Hence I have no doubt that some will want to read "The Bear" as a fable of the death of God. Certainly there is good reason to see how Faulkner's myth *does* tell us something of the critical change in intellectual and spiritual climate, the irreversible mental revolution that has apparently made religious faith an impossibility for so many people. This could have been part of Faulkner's intention.

The wilderness-paradise in which Ike McCaslin receives his "baptism in the forest" is the archaic world of religious myth and traditional wisdom. Wisdom is perfectly at home in such a world. Initiation leads to a definite enlightenment which sets the seal of authenticity upon the communion of the initiate with the "gods" and "spirits" of the cosmic order which he now knows as a privileged and conscious participant. He has found his place in the hierarchy of being as a hunter who is worthy, who has earned his position by proving his respect and love for the other living beings in the forest, even those he must kill. In other words, the wisdom to which Ike McCaslin is initiated presupposes a traditional metaphysic, a structure which man can intuitively understand, which he can lovingly accept, and which is basically reasonable and right, with its own inner laws. The "wise man" knows these laws, knows the penalties for violating them, and knows how to avoid violating them. He lives in harmony with the world around him because he is in harmony with its spirits and with the Providence of God Who rules over it all. That Ike could pay homage to this underlying "will" by renouncing his property is, to him, a perfectly logical consequence of his enlightenment and a basically religious act of worship, though precisely *how* it has this religious character is not fully explained. Nor need it be. We know it to be more or less in the natural order, akin to the religious wisdom of primitive peoples and to classic stoicism. There may be Biblical allusions here and there, but it is essentially a pre-Christian type of wisdom in an archaic and classic scheme of things which is supplanted as soon as Ike is initiated.

In *The Wild Palms* we are in a totally different world: the world of Pascal with its vast emptiness, its terrifying void, the world in which, in the words of Nietzsche's madman, someone has provided us with a sponge that has wiped away the horizon. This, in fact, is precisely the image we get in Faulkner's masterly description of the convicts arriving on the levee and seeing for the first time the vast expanse of the flooded Mississippi on which one of their number is about to be carried away on a helpless and fantastic odyssey. As J. Hillis Miller points out in the present volume, it is the world where God is not merely dead but murdered, and murdered not so much by willful malice as by a new code of consciousness. The specific characteristic of this new consciousness, which if not *the* scientific consciousness is nonetheless a scientific consciousness, is that it excludes the kind of wisdom and initiation we have discovered in "The Bear." The wisdom of the Indian in the wilderness is a kind of knowledge by identification, an intersubjective knowledge, a communion in cosmic awareness and in nature. Faulkner has described it as a wisdom based on love: love for the wilderness and for its secret laws; love for the paradise mystery apprehended almost unconsciously in the forest; love for the "spirits" of the wilderness and of the cosmic parent (both Mother and Father) conceived as symbolically incarnate in the great Old Bear. But there is nothing of the kind in the new world. "This Anno Domini 1938," says Wilbourne in "The Wild Palms," "has no place in it for love." "If Jesus returned today we would have to crucify him quick in our own defense to justify and preserve the civilization we have worked and suffered and died shrieking and cursing in rage and impotence and terror for two thousand years to create and perfect in man's own image: if Venus returned she would be a soiled man in a subway lavatory with a palm full of French post-cards."

The new consciousness which isolates man in his own knowing mind and separates him from the world around him (which he does not know as it is in itself but only as it is in his mind) makes wisdom impossible because it severs the communion between subject and object, man and nature, upon which wisdom depends. In the new consciousness man is as radically cut off from the ground of his own being, which is also the ground of all being, as the struggling convict is cut off from a foothold on the solid earth of cottonfields by ten or fifteen feet of raging flood water.

Space does not premit us here to go fully into the problem of the person and society which is central in *The Wild Palms*. Faulkner faces a radical dilemma in modern life. Speaking of Sam Fathers and his wisdom in *Go Down, Moses*, Cass Edmonds says: "His blood . . . knew things that had been tamed out of our blood so long ago that we have not only forgotten them, *we have to live together in herds to protect ourselves from our own sources*" (my italics). But this does not imply that in order to return to vital contact with our own sources we need merely leave society. If people who have had the wisdom "tamed out of their blood" by civilization simply relinquish civilized society without being trained in the difficult work of recovering another wisdom, they will be as helpless as the convict in the flood and will be destroyed, in spite of themselves, like Charlotte and her lover.

But if the characters in *The Wild Palms* find themselves blind, help-less, and without wisdom, Faulkner, their creator, wants us to see them still from the point of view of classic tragedy and of an implicit wisdom. *The Wild Palms* is a mysterious pattern of fateful ironies which the char-acters themselves never see, or do not see until it is too late. Hence these characters remain starkly lonely and forlorn, struggling pitiably, full of determination and even of outrage, in a world they see to be absurd and against forces they cannot comprehend or manage in any way whatever, no matter how hard they try. The two "heroes," the lover Wilbourne and the tall convict, do end with a kind of dim and partially adequate illumi-nation. But can we say that they have been initiated into wisdom, or that they have been reborn, or that they understand and fully accept their destinies? They do the best they can in their circumstances. Their best is not much. In one case it is a kind of comic return to a beginning which the convict never wanted to leave anyway—with an absurd bonus of ten more years of prison for "attempting to escape." In the other story the lover goes without resistance and without comment to the same prison, in a resignation that is not without nobility. In either case, the prison is the last refuge of provisional meaning in an otherwise meaningless world. And prison itself means little more than a place in which to "do time." The one thing this book has in common with "The Bear" is that the solution is ironically "monastic." The tall convict likes the peace and order of his secluded existence, and Wilbourne is determined at least to con-tinue to exist and to grieve, rather than simply to let go and fall into total nothingness. To grieve, be it remembered, is the traditional function of the monk.

It is true that the saga of the tall convict, the story sometimes printed by itself as "Old Man," is able to stand apart from the other half of the novel, "The Wild Palms." But in actual fact the author's intention to play one against the other in counterpoint is not to be lightly dismissed. On the contrary, each section gains immensely in power when this counterpoint is perceived and appreciated. And it is precisely in the counterpoint of the two sections that the sapiential structure of the book is revealed.

It is true that the cosmos itself in *The Wild Palms* does not reveal a mysterious inner meaning. It remains a terrifying and inscrutable void speaking through its elements of water and air with no message that man can interpret. Yet man himself is still capable of giving his own life a meaning if he can grasp "the old verities" and be faithful to them. These "verities" are not arbitrary. One cannot simply select a value one feels to be appropriate and neglect everything else. Life is a balance of values and verities, and the true secret is in achieving wholeness and integrity. The two parts of *The Wild Palms* complete each other in a diptych which gives us the whole picture of man. Neither half is complete in itself. The wholeness of man is in the paradisal and integral union of man and woman, and in each half of the book *one* aspect of that union is sketched out. Charlotte and Wilbourne have erotic fulfillment, a passionately reciprocated love. The convict and the woman have no emotional relationship at all; in fact, they behave completely impersonally toward each other. They are pure archetypes. But what they do have is the complete moral responsibility toward each other and toward a basic truth of their relationship which is almost entirely lacking in Charlotte and Wilbourne. It is almost as if the convict and the woman were the mystical embodiment of what was morally lacking in the two lovers, acting itself out on a mysterious transcendent plane. But there is a positive conclusion: Man does not necessarily have to be overwhelmed by the tragic forces which are let loose within him. There is an authentic and saving balance, an order and an integrity which he can discover and live by, in his right relation with woman; and this integrity is sapiential, in a sense salvific. It is centered on life, not on death. It is an affirmation of life, but an affirmation of a peculiar kind: "He that would save his life must lose it."

The saga of the convict with the nameless woman on the flooded river is a mythical and symbolic counterpart of the moral and psychological disaster of the lovers in "The Wild Palms." All the peril and evil are external to the man and the woman in the boat. Here we have an archetypal, larger than life, eschatological myth—the Deluge in fact—as commentary on the Judgment under which the lovers stand without knowing it at all because it is taking place within themselves. An explicit correspondence is suggested between the immanent will of Charlotte to seek an "absolute" love and the blind exterior force of the river that sweeps away the convict and the woman. As Wilbourne meets Charlotte on the train, which carries them away together, he is struck by her poise and by "that instinctive proficiency in and *rapport* for the mechanics of co-habitation even of innocent and unpractised women—that serene confidence in their amorous destinies like that of birds in their wings—that tranquil ruthless belief in an imminent deserved personal happiness which fledges them instantaneous and full-winged from the haven of respectability *into untried and supportive space where no shore is visible*" (my italics). Here, of course, the "supportive" element is air, not water. Maurice-Edgar Coindreau, the French translator and critic of Faulkner, has pointed out the evident balancing of mythical functions between "air" and "wind" in "The Wild Palms" and "water" in "Old Man."[8] But the sea as the mythical element of death plays an important part in "The Wild Palms" too. The lovers end like driftwood cast up on an evil-smelling, low-tide beach, helpless, exhausted, one of them about to die. They have been destroyed, in contrast with the completely unsinkable and indestructible pair in their rowboat, without oars on the worst flood in Mississippi history, who bounce off every danger unharmed and return to "normal life" with a healthy new-born baby.

In each story a man and a woman are more or less completely isolated from the rest of the world in situations that still somehow explicitly recall the paradise myth, though only in tragic or comic irony. For the convict, it is a daydream situation come true, and yet everything prevents him from taking advantage of it. First of all, the woman is pregnant. Besides, she repels him. Second, he has an obsessive sense of responsibility for her and for the boat which has been entrusted to him, and he still thinks he can rescue a man stranded on the roof of a cotton house and get back to the group of convicts with whom he belongs. As far as the woman is concerned, he wants only to get rid of her and the baby as soon as he decently and humanly can.

For the two lovers, Charlotte Rittenmeyer and Harry Wilbourne, there is also a daydream situation which has been made to come true by her determination (that determination which ultimately destroys her). Their love comes before everything else. Wilbourne cannot be persuaded to leave her even to save his own life. They live in order to make love together, alone, away from everyone else. They work only as much as is necessary to keep themselves alive and capable of making love. They intend explicitly to be *lovers* and not married people; hence they flee from any situation in which they find themselves settling down and living like

---

[8] Maurice-Edgar Coindreau, "Préface aux *Palmiers sauvages*," *Les Temps modernes*, VII, January 1952, pp. 1187–96.

secure and comfortable spouses. They accept absurd hardships in order to be left alone to their ritual erotic dream. Their life is consciously planned and patterned according to what one might call a certain level of wisdom, a certain understanding of man and of human destiny, in which sexual fulfillment is seen as the only real value worth living for. An erotic relationship between two passionately devoted partners then becomes an absolute, an end for which everything else can and should be sacrificed. There is nothing very esoteric about this "wisdom." It would probably be accepted as more or less axiomatic by a rather large proportion of Americans and Europeans today. You have one life to live; you might as well get as much out of it as you can. The best way to do this is to find someone with whom you really get on nicely in bed. And many would accept, in theory, the conclusion which these two carried out together in practice: you then spend as much time as humanly possible in bed together.

Wilbourne and Charlotte were able to do this because of her unwavering determination to sacrifice respectability, security, comfort, and all that is socially acceptable in order that they might give themselves with complete single-mindedness to their love. What remains a daydream for others became their life. Yet the blind force of cosmic tragedy bore down on them as the flood bore down on the convict and the woman in the drifting rowboat. Only here the force of tragedy was the destructive power of their own myth, or rather the inscrutable polarization set up between their personal myth and the trivial dreams which society has substituted for wisdom. Though they withdraw to a marginal life and try to construct for themselves a world of values which cannot be found in society, they do not succeed because it is not possible for man to get along without society. What is destructive is not their eros, but their determination to ignore an insoluble dilemma.

The judgment of Faulkner goes a little deeper than the general erotic daydream. "The Wild Palms" is neither homily nor casuistry. It is not a lesson in ethics. It is tragedy and myth, in a highly sophisticated artistic and sapiential pattern. The tragic death of Charlotte, as the result of an abortion which she forced her own lover to perform on her, is seen to be a consequence of the same passionate forces which drove her to run away and live with him. The seed of tragedy was present in the very nature of their love, in its psychology, in the strange disordered relationship between this willful, deeply erotic woman and the passive male she drew into a destructive and symbiotic relationship with herself.

Faulkner everywhere plays the deep, archaic, archetypal sapiential myths against the shallow and trifling mythology of modern society. This is explicit in "Old Man," where the convict realizes that he is in jail because he let himself be seduced and deceived by cheap crime stories. Wilbourne, at one point in his liaison with Charlotte, works by writing *True Confession* stories. He feeds daydreams to others and is aware of his bad faith in doing so. Yet he and Charlotte are dominated by the popular myth that when man and woman satisfy each other sexually, they have no problems. Everything is taken care of. This, as any analyst knows, is a gross oversimplification. But, for a vast number of people in the so-called civilized world, it is the most basic of all articles of faith. It is easy to confuse this superficial notion with the more profound mystique of sexuality which Vivian de Sola Pinto analyzes in his essay on D. H. Lawrence. But even in Lawrence's terms Charlotte, for all her sexual freedom, is "fallen" through willfulness and through the modern consciousness "into herself alone . . . a god-lost creature turning upon herself."

In "The Wild Palms" the love of Charlotte and Wilbourne is perfectly gratifying and in a sense happy. Yet their relationship is essentially destructive and death-oriented. From the beginning we are disturbed by the "bad smell," the classic miasma, which plays such an important symbolic part in their story and which is much more than unconscious guilt. It is the willfulness which is the direct result of that new consciousness which has isolated modern man from the world around him and from other human beings as an atom in the great void. The utter moral isolation of the modern character—Tillich and others would stress it as alienation, estrangement—leaves it no other way than to assert itself by pure will. In the void where there are no standards left (once one has broken away from the purely external and artificial ones imposed by society and which the characters of Victorian fiction could still take seriously) what is there left but to try to "get what you want"? But what do you want? How do you know what you want? You simply follow the incline down which you are already rolling. In other days one called it the "dominant passion," which you could accept or resist. But now who knows? Maybe it is your very identity which speaks, not just a tendency in you. When a person arbitrarily decides that a part of himself or herself is henceforth, for all practical purposes, *the whole self,* life will necessarily be lived destructively because of its radical bad faith. The power at work in Charlotte becomes as capricious, as arbitrary, and finally as devastating in its own order as the cosmic power of the flooding river. The tall convict saves himself and the woman by pitting all his strength against this power and by having miraculously good luck from beginning to end.

Wilbourne has no strength to pit against anything, and his instinctive respect for love and for life that would have saved Charlotte is too weak to resist her will. He destroys her and in so doing destroys himself. Or rather, he completes the work of destruction which she has already made irreversible. Only in the end does he manage to salvage something from his own ruins by his refusal to escape or to commit suicide and by his determination to "grieve." Indeed, there finally emerges in him a kind of limited greatness, a tragic quietism, as if, sinking into his own nullity, he at last becomes united with the blind Tao of wind and finds in himself the acceptance of unbornness and unbeing which is for him his "salvation" and his entry into apophatic wisdom. Thus even Wilbourne is an "initiate" in a genuine traditional sense if we accept the idea that the devotee, as a Greek fragment says, is "not to learn but to suffer and to be made worthy by suffering."[9] The power of the last section of "The Wild Palms," the eerie sound of wind in hospital and jail, makes it one of the most impressive things Faulkner ever wrote.

The wisdom of *The Wild Palms* is barely what one would call "religious" wisdom. The "gods" dealt with, if one could call them that, are maiignant spirits, bent on destroying or at least frustrating man. The convict who wants nothing but to surrender to the police and get back to the prison farm which is "his place" is repeatedly thrust back, with all brutality and incomprehension, into the wild and hostile chaos of the flood. He feels himself to be up against "the old, primal, faithless manipulator of all the lust and folly and injustice," and his highest virtue consists in the cry of "final and irrevocable repudiation" of any such evil force. Here the "strange religion of Faulkner" becomes identical with the philosophy of Camus, his ethic of the absurd and of rebellion. But there is more to Faulkner's religion than this. It might be possible to interpret the voyage of the convict and the woman as a mythical "journey," like the medieval *Navigatio Brendani* with its visits to strange islands symbolizing spiritual states. The Indian mound where the baby is born is described as an "earthen Ark out of Genesis"; and its "cypress choked life-teeming constricted desolation," where the snakes respect the convict and the woman and where nothing harms anything else, is a kind of eschatological paradise in reverse. But one would still have to stretch Faulkner's symbols a long way to find in this "deluge" an unquestionably Christian meaning.

[9] Quoted in Hugo Rahner, *Greek Myths and Christian Mystery* (New York: 1963), p. 22.

However, the wisdom of *The Wild Palms* and of *Go Down, Moses* is not all of Faulkner, and it can be played in counterpoint to more explicitly Christian themes in his other works. That exercise does not concern us here. What matters is to show that a *sapiential* reading of Faulkner's works is both possible and rewarding. Such a reading protects the Christian against the temptation to claim Faulkner for the faith on the basis of a mythical development like that in "The Bear." At the same time it shows Faulkner's concern with the "old verities and truths of the heart" which flow from his classic view of the world as endowed with basic meaning and value. He embodies this view in symbols of a kind that man has always spontaneously recognized to be "religious" in a sense that is not confessional but sapiential.

What is the position of a believing Christian before the sick and bewildering gnosticism of modern literature? First of all, while respecting the truth and accuracy of his own religious belief, the Christian realizes that today he lives in a world where most people find Christian doctrine incomprehensible or irrelevant. Most modern literature speaks a language that is neither Christian nor unchristian. It seeks to explore reality in terms that are often symbolic, mythical, sapiential, vaguely religious. The modern reader is intolerant of dogmatism, whether it be Christian, Marxist, behaviorist or any other; and he demands of the novelist, the dramatist, and the poet that they seek their own kind of revelation. The present book is a sympathetic and reasonable survey in which scholars of varying beliefs and viewpoints have joined to explore this area in literature. Their studies show us that what we find in modern literature, when we find any religious wisdom at all, is not a coherent intellectual view of life but a creative effort to penetrate the meaning of man's suffering and aspirations in symbols that are imaginatively authentic. If God does appear in such symbols, we can expect to find Him expressed negatively and obscurely rather than with the positive and rewarding effulgence that we find in the poetry of other ages.

No sense can be made of modern literature if we are not willing to accept the fact that we live in an age of doubt. But even in the midst of this doubt we can find authentic assurances of hope and understanding, provided that we are willing to tolerate theological discomfort. Derek Stanford's quotation from Dylan Thomas sums up the casual but unimpeachable sincerity of modern sapiential literature:

> "These poems, with all their crudities, doubts, and confusions, are written for the love of Man and in praise of God, and I'd be a damn' fool if they weren't."

And many of our writers can be called, as Dylan Thomas is called in Stanford's essay, writers "of religious temperament nourished in a literary culture of doubt"; they make no commitments and they contrive to affirm and to deny the spirit at the same time.

FAULKNER AND HIS CRITICS

Thirty years ago, when Faulkner was at the height of his powers, the critics were doing their best to write him off as a failure. Even the few who, like Conrad Aiken, numbered themselves among his "passionate admirers" had serious reservations about Faulkner's style. In 1936, Clifton Fadiman reviewed *Absalom! Absalom!* in the *New Yorker* and decided that it represented "the final blowup of what was once a remarkable, if minor talent." However, Faulkner went on to publish *The Unvanquished* in 1938, *The Wild Palms* in 1939, *The Hamlet* in 1940, and *Go Down, Moses* in 1942. And at least two of these are admitted to be among his most important books. Nevertheless, by 1945 all seventeen of his early books were out of print. A period of silence, followed by *Intruder in the Dust* (1948) and the award of the 1950 Nobel Prize, reminded everyone that Faulkner was still around, but even then the critics tended to boycott him. He was dismissed as an irrelevant oddity, a pessimist, a sensationalist, a mere "Southern writer." Above all, he was out of touch with the times. He did not come up with the acceptable slogans. He wrote of the South, but what he wrote was trifling because it was myth rather than sociology. Those who grudgingly recognized that he had talent felt that this only made matters worse: his talent was being wasted in lamentable eccentricities. When he was awarded the Nobel Prize, *The New York Times* scolded him in terms which, though far milder, remind one a little of the Soviet objections to Pasternak receiving the award. It was felt that perhaps Faulkner was too well liked in Europe because he presented a disgusting image of the United States.

Of course this picture must not be oversimplified. Malcolm Cowley, who had at first treated him rather roughly, edited *The Portable Faulkner* in 1946 and to this Faulkner himself contributed some original material that was not without importance (the so-called "Compson Appendix"). This *Portable*, as Robert Penn Warren shows,[1] marked the "great watershed for Faulkner's reputation in the United States."

This review article was published in *The Critic*, April-May 1967. See Appendix III for two transcriptions of conferences of Thomas Merton given to the Community of Gethsemani about the same time as this essay and the preceding one were written.

[1] *Faulkner, a Collection of Critical Essays,* edited by Robert Penn Warren (Englewood Cliffs, N.J.: Prentice-Hall, Inc.).

Faulkner's "pessimism" and the dark mythology which depressed the social-minded critics in the days of the New Deal nevertheless seemed to have something to say to men returning from World War II. They found in it a validation of their own experience of a world that Camus and so many others were describing as absurd. Again, in Robert Penn Warren's terms, Faulkner was proving to be "one of the few contemporary fiction writers—perhaps the only American— . . . who really picks at the scabs of our time in the way that Dostoevsky, Kafka, Conrad, Proust and . . . Camus also do."

If Faulkner has been read with understanding and appreciation for this reason, it has been mostly in Europe. America still does not like scab-picking, especially when the scabs happen to be on our own hide. True, the Faulkner mythology has been much more widely accepted among us, and John L. Longley's study *The Tragic Mask* has taught us that we had a Sophocles in Mississippi and did not realize it. The mythical treatment of the wilderness-paradise theme in "The Bear" has also brought out the full positive scope of Faulkner's imaginative and quasi-religious vision of the South as a desecrated sanctuary. But myth itself is considered trivial in the minds of many American critics.

Faulkner was an outrageously and deliberately demanding writer. His tortuously involved time sequences, his interminable sentences, his multiplication of characters with the same name in the same book had one purpose above all: to ensure that the reader either became involved in the book or else dropped it altogether. Yet it is obvious, too, that Faulkner's style was often self-defeating. If it involved the reader enough to make him go back over a thirty-line sentence to puzzle out its meaning, and if after that the reader found the thirty-line sentence did not matter anyway, he would be likely to regret his involvement and throw the book aside. Faulkner's long sentences are perhaps meant more to obsess than to enlighten. But in any event involvement in Faulkner means something more than paying close attention to a story: it means entering into the power of his mythical obsessions. In the words of the French critic Claude Edmonde Magny, it means allowing Faulkner to cast his spells over you: for in her opinion Faulkner works like a prehistoric shaman who enmeshes the reader in numinous symbols and entrances him with sacred horror. To quote Conrad, the reader gets the feeling of "being captured by the incredible which is the very essence of dreams."

Unfortunately, there is a certain type of mind which fears and avoids this kind of witchery. The thing is dangerous. Too much is let loose. The spells are too awful. And there are various ways of defending oneself against them. The obvious refusal of assent is typified by the easy ridicule which Fadiman poured on Sutpen in *Absalom*. "He's the fellow you're supposed to shudder at, and if you understand Mr. Faulkner you'll shudder."

The only really serious Faulkner criticism is that which assents to the myth firmly enough to be captured by the incredible and then judges it from within: is it authentic, or phony? In between these two poles, of mere ridicule and serious involvement, is what one might call the standard American objection to Faulkner: the repudiation of an apocalyptic mystique of the absurd, which is Faulkner's way of celebrating the American destiny.

A typical example of this repudiation is found in Norman Podhoretz's criticism of *A Fable*—one of Faulkner's major failures. It would be well to detail the criticisms here.

To begin with, there is so much wrong with *A Fable* itself that it can easily be demolished. Writing not of the familiar South but of unfamiliar Europe and World War I, Faulkner tried to create a religious myth and succeeded only in concocting a pious allegory which has intentional Christian elements but which is without any of the usual tragic and metaphysical Faulknerian power. It does not really convince on any level. V. S. Pritchett called it a game of "rhetorical poker with the marked cards of myth and symbol." Of this equivocation Podhoretz says: it "is just another one of those proofs that an artist must either accept the religious view of the universe as literal truth or leave its myths alone." One might want to argue a little about the word "literal" here—because there is a definitely "religious view of the universe" behind a book like *Light in August*, though it is not something that is spelled out in penny catechisms. As Sartre said very rightly, writing on *The Sound and the Fury*, "a fictional technique always relates back to the novelist's metaphysics. The critic's task is to define the latter before evaluating the former." But critics like Podhoretz are not interested in metaphysics, whether Faulkner's or anybody else's. And the emptiness of *A Fable* gave Podhoretz an excuse for dismissing Faulkner's metaphysic instead of trying to define it. From the failure of *A Fable* Podhoretz goes on, as such critics often do, to generalize about Faulkner's work as a whole. The faults of this book are extended to all the others, and we learn that "Faulkner has *always* taken refuge from historical change in a vague sense of doom."

This is getting close to the heart of the matter, because in fact the great question in Faulkner—or one of the great questions—centers around his sense of time and of history. We cannot go into that here, but it is enough to say that Faulknerian time is a monstrous nonprogression dominated by the past event which casts a kind of implacable shadow over the present and paralyzes all action toward a definite future. "The unspeakable present, leaking at every seam" (says Sartre of Faulkner) lets in the monstrous obsessions of past evil. Man rides on the back of a train looking backward, and the swirl of objects going past him comes into focus, becomes "real," only as it falls behind. And even then the whole thing is "sound and fury, signifying nothing." The not-yet of the future is already overshadowed by the idiocies and brutalities of an implacable past.

The universe of Faulkner's early work thus becomes a closed universe of cyclic and tragic involvements in fate rather than a universe of hope in an eschatological redemption. Still less does he place any hope in historical development, evolutionary progress. Yet it is perhaps too easy to accuse Faulkner (as Sartre did, also on historical and political grounds) of being enmeshed in pure despair from which he attempts to escape "by mysticism." The great religious reality in Faulkner may not be the Incarnation or the Redemption, but it is certainly something close to the Fall: and where the Fall is fully realized the doors are silently open to eschatology if not to history.

The great question in Faulkner is this: does he even get beyond the sense of *doom* and arrive at the awareness of *judgment?* In my opinion he does. And furthermore *A Fable,* with all its faults, represents a position of conscious and positive affirmation instead of his early despair. Both "The Bear" and *Requiem for a Nun* are meditations on Judgment in history. But that is another very good reason for Faulkner to be unpopular with writers like Podhoretz, for whom eschatology has no meaning whatever. For Podhoretz, Faulkner is simply apocalyptic and this is bad manners. The middle class has brought into the world an "anti-apocalyptic style of life"—a style of life which, presumably, occupies itself with sociological changes which are all sweetness and light, guided by scientific ideas and led gently to a golden future by the peaceful hand of history.

The trouble with Faulkner, says Podhoretz, is that the Enlightenment has passed him by. "As far as Yoknapatawpha is concerned, the Enlightenment might just as well have never been." This is one of the most comical remarks in all Faulkner criticism. Not only is it a prize understatement, but it serenely ignores the fact that it is precisely in the midst of the "enlightened" middle class world that we have not only Yoknapatawpha but Auschwitz, Hiroshima, the Vietnam War, Watts, South

Africa, and a whole litany of some of the choicest atrocities in human history. On the basis of this diagnosis, Podhoretz goes on to deplore the fact that Faulkner is "out of touch with contemporary experience" and that though these are admittedly "difficult times" Faulkner's attempt at giving them a tragic and quasi-religious interpretation is "a typical literary symbol of a failure of nerve." Remember that at that time the *Partisan Review* was studying this "failure of nerve" in religiously inclined intellectuals. Finally, Podhoretz caps it all by saying that Faulkner shows "an unwillingness or an inability either to love or hate the world of the twentieth century enough to understand it." Proof? Well, for one thing, Faulkner did not appreciate "the moral sublimity (*sic*) of the Korean War."

This curious, artificially lucid, one-dimensional view of life, in which there is no place for madness or tragedy, will obviously fail to comprehend a Faulkner. It will accuse Faulkner of renouncing history and embracing tragedy instead. But there is also such a thing as the refusal to see any tragic possibilities in history, the exclusion of madness and cataclysm from life in favor of a pure rationale of historic development. Do not such suppressions make tragedy all the more terrible and unavoidable? Faulkner's point was that they do. The tiny ripples on the reasonable surface of history are perhaps indications of sea monsters below. As Michel Foucault has pointed out, the refusal of madness, the clear delimitation of reason and madness, creates a *demand* for madness. Far from getting on as if the Enlightenment had never been, Yoknapatawpha was made necessary by the Enlightenment—and was necessary to it. Faulkner saw that the reason, justice, and humanity of the Enlightenment and the lunacy, injustice, and inhumanity of the South were in reality two aspects of the same thing. How many rapes, murders, lynchings occur in the little city called, so ironically, "Jefferson"? When we look a little closer at the "demonic" Sutpen, we find that he evaluates his own motives in the language of the Enlightenment. He is convinced that "the ingredients of morality are like the ingredients of a pie or cake and once you measure them and balance them and mix them and put them into the oven it is all finished and nothing but pie or cake can come out." The tragic irony which Faulkner—like Freud—finds in this "enlightened" rationalistic view of life is that human reality is not quite so simple: you put in what seem to you to be reasonable and good ingredients and the result is far from what you expected. Translated into the context not of pies and ovens but of computers and nuclear weapons, the supposedly "rational" aims of contemporary Sutpens, of which there are always plenty, begin to seem a bit frightening. In other words, the Enlightenment has not passed these people by—they are fully aware of it and they appropriate its formulas to justify their own obsessions. Instead of imposing restraint on their unreason, the reasons of Enlightenment provide them with unique excuses for doing whatever they like, as long as it can be made to sound "scientific." Sutpen, says Hyatt Waggoner, is "the post-Machiavellian man consciously living by power knowledge alone, refusing to acknowledge the validity of principles he cannot or will not live by and granting reality to nothing that cannot be known by abstract rational clarity. He lives by calculated expediency." Sutpen is as much a creature of the Enlightenment as any other positivist, and his tragedy is not that he does not reason but that he does not *love*.

The points that Podhoretz makes are not unreasonable in their own limited context. The trouble is that Faulkner is not there, he is somewhere else. We find such arguments repeated over and over in literary criticism: the reasoning mind cannot understand the mad mythical shoutings of a William Blake. Socrates cannot abide to see tragedies and goes only when a play of Euripides is on, but only because Euripides is his friend. The Apollonian mind recoils from Dionysian dread and from the awful possibility of mantic seizure. But the Faulkners of this world are not to be judged in Apollonian terms, although, incidentally, Faulkner has a plainly classic side to him, and it comes out in his stoic ethic—the cult of the "old verities and truths of the heart" which he proclaimed on receiving the Nobel Prize. But Podhoretz will not accept this either. "It falls on the ears with a sound dangerously like irrelevant cant." But why? Because the metaphysical basis is ignored and dismissed as irrelevant. In point of fact, the verities of the heart which Faulkner praises turn out to be the same toilsome and inconclusive forms of patience which Podhoretz seems to laud in the soldiers of Korea. But in Faulkner these virtues are not alien to those of Camus's rebel who refuses to submit to the absurd. Podhoretz on the other hand seems more submissive.

In Horace Benbow, the well-intentioned, scholarly lawyer, Faulkner has shown that it is precisely the fully informed, cultured, and enlightened liberal who is often most helpless to cope with the tragic dilemmas of our time and who remains most completely "out of touch with contemporary experience" even when he pontifically defines for everyone else what that experience is.

The recent collection of Faulkner criticism edited with a long and important introductory essay by Robert Penn Warren contains most of the best positive and negative studies of his achievement. It is interesting to reread George M. O'Donnell's essay from one of the early numbers of *The Kenyon Review,* one of the first appreciations in depth of Faulkner's mythology and of the fact that Faulkner is "a traditional moralist in the best sense of the word." But the essay prematurely divides Faulkner's world into Sartorises and Snopeses, so that Faulkner becomes a Sartoris artist in a Snopes world. It would not be difficult to find Snopesism in some of Faulkner's less responsible critics, but Faulkner himself is not a Sartoris; he is more a McCaslin, and even his most positive hero, Ike McCaslin, is not idealized—in spite of a mystical baptism in the forest, he is a failed saint and a fallen monk in the end.

We have delayed too much with the adverse critics of Faulkner: his serious and friendly critics are here too. Conrad Aiken, Lawrence Thompson, Irving Howe, John L. Longley, Olga Vickery, Hyatt Waggoner, Cleanth Brooks, R. W. B. Lewis, and so on. An informative "Note on *Sanctuary*" by Carvell Collins is a valuable addition to the dossier. Some of the best French criticism is here, including Sartre's study of Time in Faulkner. The French, incidentally, take Faulkner seriously as a *religious* writer. The classic preface of Malraux to the French edition of *Sanctuary* is reprinted, along with three and a half lines of Camus quoted from the *Harvard Advocate.* But a much more relevant statement of Camus on Faulkner will soon be published in a new translation of Camus's essays— his preface to *Requiem for a Nun.* Unfortunately too there is nothing here by M. E. Coindreau, Faulkner's French translator and one of his best critics, whose preface to *The Wild Palms* brings out the true greatness of a neglected and misunderstood book.

What is one to conclude? This is a very important collection of reprinted essays, all of them in one way or another deeply interesting even when they are annoyingly prejudiced or unfair. Faulkner had his weaknesses, but now we can evaluate his strong points and find that he stands up very well against the strongest criticism. Time is giving us a better perspective, and we are beginning to see the relative importance of the American novelists who began publishing in the twenties. There was a day when Faulkner seemed dwarfed by people like Hemingway or even Steinbeck and Caldwell. Now we can understand that he was of far greater stature: a genius comparable to Melville, Hawthorne, Dickens, or Dostoevsky. A book like this is essential at a time when Faulkner is really coming into his own.

"TO EACH HIS DARKNESS":
NOTES ON A NOVEL OF JULIEN GREEN

Chaque homme dans sa nuit—

Julien Green creates a world of closely enmeshed contradictions: the young man who is regarded as devout, and is impure. The death of the impure old man "covered with Latin prayers." The horrid puritan who inflicts his determined will, his upright conscience on everyone, who is gifted with a frightful insight. He is hateful, yet can he after all be right?

> A constant uncertainty: that which is absolutely
>   worst must soon happen?
> That which is most dreadful must after all turn out
>   to be true?

The worst is never absolutely certain, and yet as we move along one evil possibility after another becomes certain and we are left with the final uncertainty—the one that cannot be resolved in a book or in this life—the last question: whether the final awful possibility, that of damnation, may turn out also to have been certain from the beginning, inflicted by an inexorable will.

The awful ease with which seduction takes place, not because it is desired but rather, perhaps, because it is part of an inexorable pattern from which there can be no escape.

The *inexorable consistency* of this world of fear!

A dream, a nightmare has that same consistency until we wake up. We can say: "But after all *he made this up!*" Yet we ask, in the end, if that explains anything. Maybe . . . ? His talent is to leave us with the tantalizing question which is his own torment.

What is the question? Salvation, damnation? or is it the question: *What is serious? What is really to be taken seriously?* What is the meaning of seriousness? What is to be doubted? What is to be dismissed as

---

This essay was written in 1964 and first appeared in the spring 1964 issue of *Charlatan*. It was later included in *Raids on the Unspeakable*, published by New Directions in 1966.

not serious? Is there *anything serious?* Is there *anything not serious?* It is perhaps the question of reality itself.

Hence he creates this awful consistent universe in which everything *may be* serious, very serious, vitally serious. Every little thing, every movement of a blade of grass in the wind may turn out to have been so serious that your whole destiny depended on it.

Is destiny serious? This he seems not to question.

Sometimes I ask myself whether Green's sense of guilt, his shame at his creative gift—a deeply religious shame in a way, as if God should be the only one with *any* kind of creativity—does not lead him to question the very structure of reality. Is "reality" itself only the false floor over an infinite void?

His gift enables him to conjure up people in a world of sin and drives him to damn them. Is creativity itself shot through with destruction, because it is from Eros, and Eros is also full of death? But if this is the question it implies a profound distrust of God himself. It suggests terrible analogies. It seems to imitate what He might do with His creative power. If He creates, is it only in order to destroy? Here we have the dilemma of the artist in Green: his fear of his own creative gift, his temptation to mistrust the danger of his art because he can never forget for one moment that it is rooted in Eros.

Is this the world of religion, or of magic?

There is, there should be, in religion, the power of magic, but transformed, transfigured, exorcised, clean, free.

We know we are never free from magic, never entirely free from obsession. To treat religion as if it could be entirely clear of obsession is, in one sweep, to rob it of all its seriousness (until the spirit of God delivers us Himself from our obsessions).

Yet when everything is serious, perhaps nothing is serious: since seriousness is relative, to destroy the relationship is to destroy seriousness.

Green makes relationship inexorable.

In this world it is terrible how things "hang together."

The enmeshing of passions, flame within flame, nets and ropes of fire that is pleasure, the world nested in a moving mesh of unending fire, passion, passion!

The consistency of the *massa damnata* in which all are dragged down into hell and *no one* is surely saved: neither the Calvinist with his grim determination that others should be damned, nor the priest with his impatient will that all should have been rescued by a sacrament, *ex opere operato*—since that is the business of a priest.

But where are they?

Is it enough that they have the will to be saved?

And to have the will to be saved, must one limit oneself very carefully *to a few select things that are taken seriously?* And must everything else be ignored? In other words, to be saved is to exclude from consideration the possibility that one might be damned?

To take that possibility of damnation seriously is, then, to be lost?

But how do anything else? How *not* take it seriously?

(Think of the unspeakable triviality of popular religion which consists in *not* taking the possibility of damnation seriously any more!

To be saved, is then, to be rescued from seriousness!

To fall into the ludicrous and satanic flippancy of false piety, *kitsch,* Saint Sulpice!—or the euphoria of busy and optimistic groups!)

So, unless you can falsify and dominate reality with will, you are lost—and if you can impose your own obsession on reality (instead of having reality impose itself as an obsession *on you*) then are you perhaps doubly lost?

The question of this book, the deeper question, is the very nature of reality itself.

Inexorable consistency. Is reality the same as consistency?

The "reality" of the world he creates is made of consistency, but the reality of the real world is not consistent.

The world of consistency is the world of justice, but justice is not the final word.

There is, above the consistent and the logical world of justice, an inconsistent illogical world where nothing "hangs together," where justice no longer damns each man to his own darkness. This inconsistent world is the realm of mercy.

The world can only be "consistent" *without God*.

His freedom will always threaten it with inconsistency—with unexpected gifts.

A god who is fitted into our world scheme in order to make it serious and consistent is *not God*.

Such a world is not to be taken seriously, such a god is not to be taken seriously. If such a god is "absent" then doubtless the absence is a blessing.

To take him seriously is to submit to obsession, to doubt, to magic, and then to escape these, or try to escape them, by willfulness, by the determination to stake all on an arbitrary selection of "things to be taken seriously" because they "save," because they are "his affairs."

(Note that even atheism takes seriously this god of consistency.)

But mercy breaks into the world of magic and justice and overturns its apparent consistency. Mercy is inconsistent. It is therefore comic. It liberates us from the tragic seriousness of the obsessive world which we have "made up" for ourselves by yielding to our obsessions. Only mercy can liberate us from the madness of our determination to be consistent—from the awful pattern of lusts, greeds, angers and hatreds which mix us up together like a mass of dough and thrust us all together into the oven.

Mercy cannot be contained in the web of obsessions.

Nor is it something one determines to think about—that one resolves to "take seriously," in the sense of becoming obsessed with it.

You cannot become obsessed with mercy!

This is the inner secret of mercy. It is totally incompatible with obsession, with compulsion. It liberates from all the rigid and deterministic structures which magic strives to impose on reality (or which science, the child of magic, tries to impose)!

Mercy is not to be purchased by a set way of acting, by a formal determination to be consistent.

Law is consistent. Grace is "inconsistent."

The Cross is the sign of contradiction—destroying the seriousness of the Law, of the Empire, of the armies, of blood sacrifice, and of obsession.

But the magicians keep turning the Cross to their own purposes. Yes, it is for them too a sign of contradiction: the awful blasphemy of the religious magician who *makes the Cross contradict mercy!* This of course is the ultimate temptation of Christianity! To say that Christ has locked all the doors, has given one answer, settled everything and departed, leaving all life enclosed in the frightful consistency of a system outside of which there is *seriousness and damnation,* inside of which there is the intolerable flippancy of the saved—while nowhere is there any place left for the mystery of the freedom of divine mercy which alone is truly serious, and worthy of being taken seriously.

LOUIS ZUKOFSKY—THE PARADISE EAR

All really valid poetry (poetry that is fully alive and asserts its reality by its power to generate imaginative life) is a kind of recovery of paradise. Not that the poet comes up with a report that he, an unusual man, has found his own way back into Eden: but the living line and the generative association, the new sound, the music, the structure, are somehow grounded in a renewal of vision and hearing so that he who reads and understands recognizes that here is a new start, a new creation. Here the world gets another chance. Here man, here the reader discovers himself getting another start in life, in hope, in imagination, and why? Hard to say, but probably because the language itself is getting another chance, through the innocence, the teaching, the good faith, the honest senses of the workman poet. Louis Zukofsky is such a poet, and I would say he is one of the best poets writing in America today—has perhaps been the best for many years. Certainly not the best known, for only now, after more than thirty-five years of poetic practice, is his work being published by one of the big commercial houses. Two volumes of short poems, of which this is the second,[1] bring together in collection all the short poems that have hitherto appeared in little magazines and out-of-the-way presses (Jargon Books, Trobar Books, the Wild Hawthorn Press at Edinburgh, etc.). The long poems will come later. They can now be read in magazines like Cid Corman's *Origin* (published in Japan) or, more accessibly, in *Poetry*.

At sixty-three, it is perhaps time for Louis Zukofsky to be recognized by more than a few poets: but poets have admired him since Ezra Pound wrote about him in the thirties.

Zukofsky has probably done more for the language of poetry than any other American writer. I say "probably" and cannot substantiate that claim in a brief review. Future studies will, I believe, show that this intuition was not wrong. The originality of his music is extraordinary. Not only does he have an inexhaustible, childlike curiosity about words,

---

This review article was written in November 1966, and was first published in *The Critic*, 25, February-March 1967, under the title "Paradise Bugged."

[1] Louis Zukofsky, *All: The Collected Short Poems, 1956–1964* (New York: W. W. Norton, 1966).

their resonances, their suggestions, their implications, the way they look, the way they behave: not only does he with marvelous tenderness place them in situations in which they quietly explode into new colors: he is also deeply attuned to the other music that is beyond the words, the music of the ideas, of the possibilities of new ideas, of the experience that has not yet been discovered behind the word, of the expectations that the word begins to open up for the first time. For this very reason his use of words is chaste and sparing: he does not waste any. He leaves a great deal for the reader's own ear and imagination to fill in. Those who cannot do this kind of work for themselves will not understand him. They will not contact him. The perfect music in themselves must be attuned to the gaps and silences in which his poetry really works. Because of all this exceptional sense of words, Zukofsky seems to be punning and playing, but if you pay attention you realize that the punning is not clever. It has classic resonances. Like new captious harmonies tried out quietly and casually by Mozart or by Thelonius Monk. He plays a couple of chords and walks away. He does not add what need not be added—only what can possibly excite attention to new possibilities—left unsaid. (Of course nothing *need* be added or even said in the first place. The poetry of Zukofsky has that nonnecessary necessity of classic art. Because it is, you can say it had to be, but there is never any sense of the poet being *driven* to it. He remains both modest and free in the classic liberality of the man who does not have to be a prophet. And who realizes that one life does not exhaust the possibilities of one man.)

Zukofsky, then, is modest enough to play with the language he loves, which is the language he uses in talking to *people* (rather than reviewers). His music is not different from talk: he explores all the musical possibilities of ordinary talk about ordinary things. "Talk," he says, "is a form of love/Let us talk." But because his music is well found (*ben trovato*), it is no longer ordinary (i.e., empty) talk, and the language of everyday becomes charged with expectations—the language of paradise. He often makes it be in fact the language of children. Many of his poems are the essence of conversation with a child. Therefore they are highly sophisticated and often difficult poetry, not baby talk, not cliché. To talk to a child is to participate in the discovery of language, to say words for the first time, thus recognizing their immensity. Baby talk is for adults only.

> Hello, little leaves
> Said not St. Francis
> But my son in the spring. . .

The speech of the child is paradise speech for it familiarly addresses all things, not yet knowing them as alien and anticipating nothing from them but joy: hence, it is Franciscan. And Zukofsky is my favorite Franciscan since he is one without any of the trappings, only the essentials (is in fact a Jew).

> "Because he was crying
> I like him most of all" says my son
> "Because he was crying"—the red fox
> With three porcupine quills in his paw
> Who brings tears to the eyes . . .

Or somewhere else:

> See:
> My nose feels better in the air

No man with children of his own needs to sentimentally idealize the child. He knows they can be a nuisance. But it doesn't matter. One of Zukofsky's best poems is "March First":

> Remarkably on this March first
> Would-be, small leaves are making a hell of a noise
> Littlest children fight with their fathers,
> The mothers are distracted or stark mad
> Rehearsing with them—
> Tiniest green and teemingest teen—
> Reciting
> "We are the generations of leaves."

There is so much compassion in Zukofsky that he can send repeated Valentines without irony, never the sadistic kind, Valentines to everybody, even though the world may be at war when he sends them:

> It never pours, it draws
> On St. Valentine's—
> An ocean
> Secret with mines.
> Magnetic hearts—
> Moving shoeshines—
> In the lines of force
> Of St. Valentine's.

The mined silences of water may have been partly suggested by the seas of World War II, but here, of course, they are the silences of life itself, and life's silences are mined with love, with unexpected encounters. In these, the heart must secretly blow up with the joy of being human and of being *for others* in all senses of the word: in favor of them, open to them, available to them, devoted to them. Yet there is no fussy activism about it. He loves his wife and children first, then his relatives and friends, then those he meets (like the sweet exile in the park with two two-headed kids). The true *ordo caritatis*.

This Valentine quotation gives us the key to Zukofsky's cosmology, which is a cosmology of love, and Valentines from the drugstore fit in naturally since he accepts it *all*. Franciscan, he knows that only when you accept the *whole thing* will evil be reduced to the last place in it, whereas those who start with the evil and never get beyond it, never find the whole, consequently never see that the whole can be paradise. Zukofsky's poems are about this wholeness, therefore they spring from a ground of immense silence and love which extends beyond them infinitely in all directions. This one must hear with a paradise ear. His poems in fact cannot be heard except against the vast background of silence and warmth that is the ground and the whole. His poems do not make sense except as part of the whole creation that exists precisely for love, for free, for nothing, unnecessary. In the whole that is unnecessary, every small thing becomes necessary, for when the All is gratuitous every small thing is seen to be wanted, to be important, to have its own unique part in the big gift of all things to each other.

> I'm a mosquito
> May I bite your big toe?
> Here's ten dollars
> Use it
> as you know.

Though everything is love I will not say that there is in Zukofsky no sign of any death wish. That would be absurd, for death too is part of it. But Zukofsky is one of those for whom death is only the weakest form of life (when life burns down so low that it appears to go out, only to flare up again later).

> My father praying at my mother's grave
> Heard his father's song.

So he is not divided. In a nation that is deeply troubled, torn with its own violence, fearing its own destructiveness and drawn to it at the same time, Zukofsky needs to bare nobody else's wound and does not fight the

other poets (for the poets are cutting each other up part of the time also).
Nor is he afraid to look at the psychopathology of everyday life. He does
not mind it because he sees more in it than the miserable frustrations and
the petty half-conscious smellings. He knows that these too have something to do with love in their way. So he loves life and loves it to live
itself in us, which it will if we let it. To all this, death is merely sub-
ordinate. Here is one short poem that comes up out of the silence and
the ground of love and stands for a moment like a world and returns
again to the silence. It says what I mean about Zukofsky being a "paradise hearer."

The poem begins so to speak in mid-air:

> And without
> Spring it is spring why
> Is it death here grass somewhere
> As dead as lonely walks
> As living has less thought that is
> The Spring.
> Spring it is spring why
> Is it death grass somewhere
> As dead walks
> As living has less thought that is
> A spring. And without.

This is typical of the mature and sometimes difficult verse of Zukofsky
but if we listen to it we see that it is really simple: it is not a question
of sacrificing meaning to music, but of structuring the ideas musically
instead of logically so that the music contains and communicates more
meaning than the mere words could—so much more that it cannot be
broken down easily into concepts and the poem has to be respected, left
alone, only to be read over and over. Then life and death and spring and
grass and walking and not-spring and not-thinking-about it, and not-
saying-it-is spring all become aspects of one unity. This gets very close to
the Zen-likenesses of ordinary life when it might be spring and one is in
the midst of a living-dying-life in all one's weakness and strength experienced together without contrast, and with no word at hand to signify it,
least of all "spring," yet it is spring. Or will be. The real subject of the
poem is then not just spring; a special season, a well-designated time, but
the unlimited curious sense of confused anticipation which is the very
stuff of ordinary life: an anticipation that is also aware of itself as a question. Zukofsky has understood as no one else has the reality of that ques-

tion and has been able to ask it in a way that preserves its purity: a way in which it cannot provoke any answer that would appear to dispose of it. So we never go on to the next question. Each poem is very much the same question, but brand new. Because here is a poet who has the patience and the good sense to listen. And look around at the Brooklyn he loves. And write a perfect poem about a dog looking out of a brownstone window.

THE ANSWER OF MINERVA:
PACIFISM AND RESISTANCE IN SIMONE WEIL

Like Bernanos and Camus, Simone Weil is one of those brilliant and independent French thinkers who were able to articulate the deepest concerns of Europe in the first half of this century. More controversial, perhaps more of a genius than the others, certainly harder to situate, she has been called all kinds of names, both good and bad and often contradictory: Gnostic and Catholic, Jew and Albigensian, medievalist and modernist, platonist and anarchist, rebel and saint, rationalist and mystic. De Gaulle said he thought she was out of her mind. The doctor in the sanatorium at Ashford, Kent, where she died on August 24, 1943, said, "she had a curious religious outlook and (probably) no religion at all."

Whatever is said about her, she will perhaps always be treated as "an enigma," which is simply to say that she is somewhat more difficult to categorize than most people, since in her passion for integrity she absolutely refused to take up any position she had not first thought out in the light of what she believed to be a personal vocation to "absolute intellectual honesty." When she began to examine any accepted position, she easily detected its weaknesses and inconsistencies.

None of the books of Simone Weil (seventeen in French, eight in English) were written as books. They are all collections of notes, essays, articles, journals, and letters. Though she has conquered a certain number of fans by the force of her personality, most readers remember her as the author of some fragment or other that they have found in some way both impressive and disconcerting. One cannot help admiring her lucid genius, and yet one can very easily disagree with her most fundamental and characteristic ideas. But this is usually because one does not see her thought as a whole.

The new biography by Jacques Cabaud[1] not only tells of her active and tormented life, but studies in detail a large number of writings (of

---

This essay, written in 1968, was first published in *Faith and Violence* (Notre Dame, Indiana: University of Notre Dame Press, 1968). Later it was included in *Thomas Merton on Peace* and in the revised edition brought out by Farrar Straus and Giroux under the title *The Nonviolent Alternative*.

[1] *Simone Weil, a Fellowship in Love* (New York: Channel Press, 1964).

which a complete bibliography is given), together with the testimony of those who knew her. Cabaud has fortunately avoided treating Simone Weil either as a problem or as a saint. He accepts her as she evidently was. Such a book is obviously indispensable, for without a comprehensive and detached study it would be impossible for us to see her in perspective. In fact, no one who reads this book carefully and dispassionately can treat Simone Weil merely as an enigma or a phenomenon, still less as deluded or irrelevant: few writers have more significant thought than she on the history of our time and a better understanding of our calamities.

On the other hand, probably not even Mr. Cabaud would claim that this book says the last word on Simone Weil or that it fully explains, for instance, the "Christian mysticism" that prompted her to remain deliberately outside the Church and refuse baptism even on the point of death because she felt that her natural element was with "the immense and unfortunate multitude of unbelievers." This "unbeliever," we note, was one who had been "seized" by Christ in a mystical experience the marks of which are to all appearances quite authentic, though the Catholic theologian has trouble keeping them clearly in a familiar and traditional focus. (Obviously, one of her charisms was that of living and dying as a sign of contradiction for Catholics, and one feels that the climate of Catholic thought in France at the time of Vatican II has been to some extent affected by at least a vague awareness of her experiences at Solesmes and Marseilles.)

Though her spirit was at times explicitly intended to be that of the medieval Cathars and though her description of her mystical life is strongly Gnostic and intellectual, she has had things to say of her experience of sufferings of Christ which are not only deeply Christian but also speak directly to the anguish and perplexity of modern man. This intuition of the nature and meaning of suffering provides, in Simone Weil, the core of a metaphysic, not to say a theology, of nonviolence. And a metaphysic of nonviolence is something that the peace movement needs.

Looking back at Simone Weil's participation in the peace movement of the thirties, Cabaud speaks rather sweepingly of a collapse of pacifism in her thought and political action. It is quite true that the pacifism of the thirties was as naïve as it was popular, and that for many people at that time pacifism amounted to nothing more than the disposition to ignore unpleasant realities and to compromise with the threat of force, as did Chamberlain at Munich. It is also true that Simone Weil herself underestimated the ruthlessness of Hitler at the time of the Munich crisis, though her principles did not allow her to agree with the Munich pact.

Cabaud quotes a statement of Simone Weil accusing herself of a "criminal error committed before 1939 with regard to pacifist groups and their actions." She had come to regard her earlier tolerance of a passive and inert pacifism as a kind of co-operation with "their disposition towards treason"—a treason she said she had not seen because she had been disabled by illness.

This reflects her disgust with Vichy and with former pacifists who now submitted to Hitler without protest. But we cannot interpret this statement to mean that after Munich and then after the fall of France, Simone Weil abandoned all her former principles in order to take up an essentially new position in regard to war and peace. This would mean equating her "pacifism" with the quietism of the uncomprehending and inactive. It would also mean failure to understand that she became deeply committed to nonviolent resistance. Before Munich her emphasis was, however, on nonviolence; after the fall of France it was on resistance, including resistance by force where nonviolence was ineffective.

It is unfortunate that Cabaud's book does not sufficiently avoid the clichéd identification of pacifism with quietist passivity and nonresistance. Simone Weil's love of peace was never sentimental and never quietistic; and though her judgment sometimes erred in assessing concrete situations, it was seldom unrealistic. An important article she wrote in 1937 remains one of the classic treatments of the problem of war and peace in our time. Its original title was "Let us not start the Trojan War all over again." It appears in her *Selected Essays* as "The Power of Words." Cabaud analyzes it in his book (pp. 155–60), concluding that it marks a dividing line in her life. It belongs in fact to the same crucial period as her first mystical experiences.

But there is nothing mystical about this essay. It develops a theme familiar to Montaigne and Charron: the most terrible thing about war is that, if it is examined closely, it is discovered to have no rationally definable objective. The supposed objectives of war are actually myths and fictions which are all the more capable of enlisting the full force of devotion to duty and hatred of the enemy when they are completely empty of content. Let us briefly resume this article, since it contains the substance of Simone Weil's ideas on peace and is (apart from some of her topical examples) just as relevant to our own time as it was to the late thirties.

The article begins with a statement which is passed over by Cabaud but which is important for us. Simone Weil remarks that while our technology has given us weapons of immense destructive power, the weapons do not go off by themselves (we hope). Hence, it is a primordial mistake to think and act as if the weapons were what constituted our danger, rather than the people who are disposed to fire them. But more precisely still: the danger lies not so much in this or that group or class, but in the climate of thought in which all participate (not excluding pacifists). This is what Simone Weil set herself to understand. The theme of the article is, then, that war must be regarded as a problem to be solved by rational analysis and action, not as a fatality to which we must submit with bravery or desperation. We see immediately that she is anything but passively resigned to the evil of war. She says clearly that the acceptance of war as an unavoidable fatality is the root of the power politician's ruthless and obsessive commitment to violence.

This, she believed, was the "key to our history."

If, in fact, conflicting statesmen face one another only with clearly defined objectives that were fully rational, there would be a certain measure and limit which would permit of discussion and negotiation. But where the objectives are actually nothing more than capital letter slogans without intelligible content, there is no common measure, therefore no possibility of communication, therefore, again, no possibility of avoiding war except by ambiguous compromises or by agreements that are not intended to be kept. Such agreements do not really avoid war. And of course they solve no problems.

The typology of the Trojan War, "known to every educated man," illustrates this. The only one, Greek or Trojan, who had any interest in Helen was Paris. No one, Greek or Trojan, was fighting for Helen, but for the "real issue" which Helen symbolized. Unfortunately, there was no real issue at all for her to symbolize. Both armies, in this war, which is the type of all wars, were fighting in a moral void, motivated by symbols without content, which in the case of the Homeric heroes took the form of gods and myths. Simone Weil considered that this was relatively fortunate for them, since their myths were thus kept within a well-defined area. For us, on the other hand (since we imagine that we have no myths at all), myth actually is without limitation and can easily penetrate the whole realm of political, social, and ethical thought.

Instead of going to war because the gods have been arguing among themselves, we go because of "secret plots" and sinister combinations, because of political slogans elevated to the dignity of metaphysical absolutes: "our political universe is peopled with myths and monsters—we know nothing there but absolutes." We shed blood for high-sounding words spelled out in capital letters. We seek to impart content to them by destroying other men who believe in enemy-words, also in capital letters.

But how can men really be brought to kill each other for what is objectively void? The nothingness of national, class, or racial myth must receive an apparent substance, not from intelligible content but from the will to destroy and be destroyed. (We may observe here that the substance of idolatry is the willingness to give reality to metaphysical nothingness by sacrificing to it. The more totally one destroys present realities and alienates oneself to an object which is really void, the more total is the idolatry, i.e., the commitment to the falsehood that the nonentity is an objective absolute. Note here that in this conext the God of the mystics is not "an object" and cannot be described properly as "an entity" among other entities. Hence, one of the marks of authentic mysticism is that God as experienced by the mystic can in no way be the object of an idolatrous cult.)

The will to kill and be killed grows out of sacrifices and acts of destruction already performed. As soon as the war has begun, the first dead are there to demand further sacrifice from their companions, since they have demonstrated by their example that the objective of the war is such that no price is too high to pay for its attainment. This is the "sledge hammer argument," the argument of Minerva in Homer: "You must fight on, for if you now make peace with the enemy, you will offend the dead."

These are cogent intuitions, but so far they do not add anything, beyond their own vivacity, to the ideas that prevailed in the thirties. In effect, everyone who remembered the First World War was capable of meditating on the futility of war in 1938. Everyone was still able to take sarcastic advantage of slogans about "making the world safe for democracy." But merely to say that war, in its very nature, was totally absurd and totally meaningless was to run the risk of missing the real point. Mere words without content do not suffice, of themselves, to start a war. Behind the empty symbols and the objectiveless motivation of force, there is a real force, the grimmest of all the social realities of our time: collective power, which Simone Weil, in her more Catharist mood, regarded as the "great beast." "How will the soul be saved," she asked her philosophy students in the Lycée, "after the great beast has acquired an opinion about everything?"

The void underlying the symbols and the myths of nationalism, of capitalism, communism, fascism, racism, totalism is in fact filled entirely by the presence of the beast—the urge to collective power. We might say, developing her image, that the void thus becomes an insatiable demand for power: it sucks all life and all being into itself. Power is then generated by the plunge of real and human values into nothingness, allowing themselves to be destroyed in order that the collectivity may attain to a theoretical and hopeless ideal of perfect and unassailable supremacy: "What is called national security is a chimerical state of things in which one would keep for oneself alone the power to make war while all other countries would be unable to do so. . . . War is therefore made in order to keep or to increase the means of making war. All international politics revolve in this vicious circle." But she adds, "why must one be able to make war? This no one knows any more than the Trojans knew why they had to keep Helen."

Nevertheless, when Germany overran France she herself found a reason for joining the resistance: the affirmation of human liberty against the abuse of power. "All over the world there are human beings serving as means to the power of others without having consented to it." This was a basic evil that had to be resisted. The revision of Simone Weil's opinion on pacifism and nonviolence after Munich does not therefore resolve itself, as Cabaud seems to indicate, with a practical repudiation of both. Munich led her to clarify the distinction between ineffective and effective nonviolence. The former is what Gandhi called the nonviolence of the weak, and it merely submits to evil without resistance. Effective nonviolence ("the nonviolence of the strong") is that which opposes evil with serious and positive resistance, in order to overcome it with good.

Simone Weil would apparently have added that if this nonviolence had no hope of success, then evil could be resisted by force. But she hoped for a state of affairs in which human conflict could be resolved nonviolently rather than by force. However, her notion of nonviolent resistance was never fully developed. If she had survived (she would be fifty-six now) she might possibly have written some exciting things on the subject.

Once this is understood, we can also understand Simone Weil's revulsion at the collapse of that superficial and popular pacifism of Munich, which, since it was passive and also without clear objective, was only another moment in the objectiveless dialectic of brute power. And we can also understand the passion with which she sought to join the French resistance. But she did not change her principles. She did not commit herself to violent action, but she did seek to expose herself to the greatest danger and sacrifice, nonviolently. Though her desire to form a "front line nursing corps" (regarded by de Gaulle as lunacy) was never fulfilled, she nevertheless worked—indeed overworked—until the time of her death, trying to clarify the principles on which a new France could be built. She never gave up the hope that one might "substitute more and more in the world effective nonviolence for violence."

ROLAND BARTHES—WRITING AS TEMPERATURE

In Camus' novel *The Plague,* there is a funny little character (called Grand) who is trying to write a novel. He never gets beyond the first sentence, which he tirelessly revises, always with the same words, in an infinite variety of combinations. He is obsessed by proper myths: literature, style, language, form, life, structure. He is, in fact, a fool. Yet he writes. And this puts him on the side of the angels, not because he writes well but simply because he writes as a matter of choice, indeed of fervent conviction. More than that (and this was something that neither he nor Camus could yet realize) like Moliere's M. Jourdain who was unaware that he spoke in prose, Grand was unaware that his labors could even qualify as "writing degree zero." He just thought he had style.

Roland Barthes does not refer to this character in his little book *Writing Degree Zero,*[1] although the "pale writing" (*écriture blanche*) of *The Stranger* is a standard example of writing that cools down close to zero. But the writer in *The Plague* will help us to understand what Barthes' book is about.

We also need to situate Barthes himself. To say he is one of the new French "structuralists" is no help: it is only misleading. What is "structuralism" anyway? We shall later see whether such a "school of philosophy" exists at all. Meanwhile, Barthes can be localized as a French critic and indeed as one of the most articulate and important literary critics writing today in any language, although *Writing Degree Zero* might not be enough, by itself, to convince anyone of the fact.

This is an extremely condensed little book, thick with esoteric language, highly charged with intuitions which may or may not be profound. You need some time to decide whether or not this is really a brilliant book or just another bag of critical tricks.

Barthes is at odds with Sartre on the question of *littérature engagée.* In other words he does not think the writer has a duty to arouse in the reader a revolutionary consciousness of some sort, though he does seem

---

The manuscript of this essay is dated September 1968. It was first published in *The Sewanee Review* in the summer issue of 1969.

[1] Roland Barthes, *Writing Degree Zero,* translated by Annette Lavers and Colin Smith, Preface by Susan Sontag (New York: Hill & Wang, 1968).

to think that "writing" is a subversive activity. On the other hand, he carries out an exemplary campaign of criticism against all forms of writing with a message, and particularly of writing with a political message. To be more precise, he separates the writing from the message and dissects the very mode of revolutionary writing (whether of the French or of the Marxist revolutions). He is, however, very much in favor of Brecht precisely as writer. And his model of "writing degree zero" is Robbe-Grillet. So that is where we begin.

Before we go any further, we must purify ourselves of the conventional anxieties which are likely to afflict us in the presence of someone who seems to be saying "literature is fradulent, only antiliterature is authentic." We are confronted with distinctions which, by knee-jerk reflex, we may assume to be distinctions between good and bad, right and wrong: as if *style,* for instance, had suddenly become sinful and *writing* virtuous (with "writing degree zero" at the summit of moral perfection). Barthes is the kind of writer who remains entirely closed to such a reading.

He is not saying that the "only good novelist" is Robbe-Grillet, or that the "only valid theater" is that of Brecht. He just wants to examine how writing works, whether in Robbe-Grillet (who refuses all complicity with the reader) or in Michel Butor (who takes the reader into his confidence). Barthes is not dealing with "good-bad" divisions at all. We must not confuse him with Sartre, a moralist who bristles with pastoral "shoulds" even while he prescribes to us the most austere and melancholy of freedoms, beyond all comfort of good-and-evil.

Barthes invents his new mystical category, "writing," and sets it up against all the "shoulds" of style. He confronts Sartre's distinction between language, which is "given," and style, which is "chosen" and "free" (therefore the region of commitment, lucidity, subversion, nobility, and revolution). He shows that this division will not work. Style (he thinks) is as much "given" as language. It springs "from the body and past of the writer." "Its frame of reference is biological, or biographical, not historical . . . it is the writer's solitude" (out of which he tends to fabricate communion with the solitude of the reader). "Under the name of style a self-sufficient language is involved which has its roots only in the author's personal and secret mythology." It therefore stands outside the "pact which binds the writer to society." In a certain way it places the author outside history—though this cannot be pushed too far, and it assumes too readily that style is merely personal, idiosyncratic: a description which might fit the romantics and is of course adequate for Rimbaud and René Char, who are "saturated with style." (Gide on the other hand has *art* rather than "style"—but let us not get carried away into still further distinctions!)

Style, in other words, is an expression of the writer's literary personality. If it be too consciously chosen, it becomes a fake, a mask, a persona, a fabricated self-image. And of course that is what often happens to "style." It becomes simply a bad habit by which an author reverts mechanically to the parody of his own *opus,* like the dog to his vomit.

To carry out his job, according to Barthes, the writer must accept his language and accept his style as given: what he has to choose is his *writing.* Not so much the *kind* of writing as the *act* of writing. If he is honest, he makes this choice in the full consciousness that what he is doing is merely *writing,* not something else ("expressing himself," "arousing a revolutionary consciousness," "exploring the metaphysical abyss of being," etc.). When the choice is completely lucid, when the writer chooses simply to *write* and renounces all the rest ("message," "expression," "soul," "revolution"), then the writing itself stands out clearly as writing. A distance is established which reminds the reader not to get lost in the writer or in the writing, not to immerse himself in false complicities with the message or the emotion, not to get swept away by illusions of an inner meaning, a slice of life, a cosmic celebration, an eschatological vision. When the writing is just writing, and when no mistake about this is possible because the very writing itself removes all possibility of error, then you have "writing degree zero."

How does writing cool down to this icy state?

Though in this early book Barthes cannot yet be accused of "structuralism," he does appeal to the linguistic theories of de Saussure (these have spilled over into other disciplines to create a big fashionable pond in which all the singing is said to be "structuralist"). The mania for arranging authors together in "schools" of thought or writing has become so obsessive that critics or novelists find themselves arbitrarily dumped together and, even worse, credited with all sorts of momentous effects in the world. So, for instance, though the men who have been summarily grouped as "structuralist" philosophers and critics are still protesting that no such school exists, the press continues to assure us not only that they are a school, that they are influential, but even that they exercised a decisive influence on the Paris student revolt in the spring of 1968. Barthes himself has shown in an essay (*"Il n'y a pas d'école Robbe-Grillet"*) how writers who are diametrically opposed have been solemnly welded together as members of one "school"—the school of the "new novel." The only thing they have in common is that they write novels that would tend to make one a conservative rather than a revolutionary. Or at least it would make one less likely to be sanguine about the inevitability of a glorious future, to be born of the right political formula.

De Saussure was concerned with the interrelationship of "semantic fields," and Barthes takes an analogous standpoint in his study of "writing." Semantic fields are constituted by the words which cover a given area in man's "representation of the world"—in the way man makes that world credible and livable for himself. One must not confuse historical (diachronic) development of understanding with a horizontal (synchronic) transfer of words from one field to another. Our assumption that ideas generate words and that words contribute to the evolution of ideas gives us a diachronic view which is perhaps less accurate than the synchronic. This latter shows us not so much a process of generation or of cause and effect as a haphazard migration of words into new fields, disappearing from one system and surfacing in another, in ways that affect *all the words in both systems,* and consequently alter man's view of his world. This may even create the illusion of a "new consciousness." The so-called structuralist approach is, however, austerely quantitative and does not concern itself directly with the changing quality of experience: only with different fields, areas (like style, writing, etc.).

The "writer" is conscious of words in synchronous interrelated systems (style, etc.) and if he knows what he is doing he can deliberately choose to subvert the systems by his use of words. It is here, and not in his doctrine, his "revolutionary message" or in a supposed "revolutionary style" that the writer really changes the world—(though he should be free of any obvious purpose to change anything).

A clear example of this is Joyce's *Ulysses,* which Barthes does not mention. The peculiar excellence of all of Joyce, but especially of *Ulysses,* is in the writing. Also in *Ulysses* we can easily see the distinction between writing and style: Joyce synchronizes "styles" in service of his writing, with a clear sense of personal distance from all of them. If Joyce comes at all close to having a "style" in his later work, it is in *Finnegans Wake,* where by dint of pure writing he ends with a highly personal idiom. Such a book can only be biography. And thus it is not "writing degree zero." It has style, however inscrutable. It is more like the "soul music," at once abstract and hermetically personal, of some of the new jazz saxophonists, whose playing is not as "cool" as it claims to be.

The point that Barthes wants to make about "writing" is that it is a genuine matter of choice. The writer's mere *decision to write* is what matters, not his decision to communicate a political message or share a human experience (say of passion, conviction, discovery, exaltation).

Here we come to the precise point where it is difficult to keep up with

Barthes. What precisely does the "writer" choose when he decides to write—and write cool? Where does he stand in relation to the rest of the world? His is not of course a childish and narcissistic choice: "I will be a writer—watch me write!" It has to imply a committed and responsible attitude toward the rest of the world. Where Sartre says that the writer becomes responsible to the world for a message or a style that awakens a new consciousness in man, Barthes sees it differently. For him the writer is more responsible to his writing than he is to his public. To be more exact: the "writer" (if he is cool) does not try to communicate something to the rest of the world, but only to define correctly the relation between writing and the world. This means that he knows his business is *to write* first of all, not to teach, to amuse, to inspire, to elevate, to shock, or to transform society. He does something to society not by pushing against its structures—which are none of his business—but by changing the tune of its language and shifting the perspectives which depend on the ways words are arranged. He systematically de-mythologizes literature. What the writer owes society is, then, *to refuse to communicate* with the reader if the urge to communicate interferes with his writing. And what the reader will look for is precisely this refusal. This, at least, is what he will look for in "writing degree zero."

The only thing that remains to be explained is: how does the reader keep awake when reading such writing? Barthes does not enlighten us. He assumes that one will follow Robbe-Grillet with alert attention, and without boredom. Maybe somewhere in "structuralism" there is magic or miracle about which we have not yet heard. Fortunately, Robbe-Grillet is not the *only* writer. Others are not quite so bleak.

Barthes' subtlety can easily reduce us to blind exasperation if we do not take into account his analysis of other kinds of "writing." When we read all he has to say about "political writing," "revolutionary writing," classicism, romanticism, the nineteenth century novel, and Mallarmé "the Hamlet of writing," we find that he is not just advocating solipsism for purity's sake and a Manichean rejection of art. He is really saying something both new and important about the nature of writing: that it is in fact *gestus*.

"*Gestus*" is more than "gesture," more than idiosyncrasy. It is the chosen, living, and responsible mode of presence of the writer in his world. But this *gestus* has been overlaid and corrupted with all sorts of elements which have turned it into posturing. Nowhere a more brilliant analysis of the rhetoric of the French Revolution—and its human or inhuman implications—than in this little book of Barthes. Nowhere a more devastating commentary on Racine and the whole culture of French classicism than in his essays on Racine. Nowhere a more ruthless unmasking of the phoniness of Marxist "literature" or of the "subwriting" of Zola, Maupassant, and Daudet. Naturalism and socialist realism are pure artifice and pure posture just because they claim to be entirely "real" and to induce, by "style," a new consciousness of reality. Their "realism" is an expression of the decay of a bourgeois consciousness which lost touch with reality a hundred years ago (with results we have had ample cause to regret since 1914). "No mode of writing was more artificial than that which set out to give the most accurate description of Nature." It was "loaded with the most spectacular signs of fabrication." It "flaunted the signs of literary convention with an ostentation hitherto unknown." Working zealously to supply that literature for which there was—and apparently still is—a voracious public demand, these "artists" have continued to turn out "good writing" and even to reap quite tangible rewards for so doing. But in claiming to write about life and to share with others a deeply meaningful experience of life, they have abandoned the living *gestus* by which alone the writer gives evidence that he is alive: they have adopted instead a mechanical kind of flag-waving, a conventional gymnastic, a signaling of assumptions which a torpid society wishes to see verified in "art." I can think of no better recent example of such "good writing" than Styron's book on Nat Turner. Barthes sums it all up: as "mechanizing without restraint the intentional signs of art." For what? To sell the stuff, of course. To make money by creating an illusion of significance.

The authentic *gestus* of writing begins only when all meaningful postures have been abandoned, when all the obvious "signs" of art have been set aside. At the present juncture, such writing can hardly be anything but antiwriting. The writer is driven back to the source of his writing, since he can no longer trust the honesty of his customary dialogue with the rest of society. But, Barthes argues, in doing so he recovers something of the numinous power of that *gestus* which is charismatic only because it is completely modest.

To do this, the "writer" must forget all charismatic exaltation, all aspiration to power, all *numen,* all that would seem to give him some ascendency over the reader. He must practice writing "without alibi, without thickness and without depth . . . the exact contrary of poetic writing." Here language no longer "violates the abyss" but slides away from us across an icy surface. "The silence of Robbe-Grillet about the romantic heart of things is not an allusive or sacral silence: it is a silence

which irremediably establishes the limits of the object, not its 'beyond.'"
(*Essais Critiques*).

What Barthes says about writing corresponds more or less exactly to what Ad Reinhardt said about painting—and said in painting. It is a kind of quietism, if you like; but a deadly, Zenlike stillness out of which —as you find out by reading Barthes himself—there does nevertheless spring a certain inscrutable excitement.

The ideas of *gestus* and of *distance* come of course from the theater of Brecht. Instead of creating an illusion, luring the audience into the experience and the passion of the players, Brecht insisted on reminding us at all times that we were merely *watching something that was being put on*. So, too, when we read writing we need to realize that what we are doing is not experiencing the deep things of life, penetrating the esoteric meaning of human existence, or being swept out of ourselves by rapture: we are just reading writing. Barthes says:

> The formalism of Brecht is a protest against poisoning by the fake nature of the bourgeois and petit bourgeois culture; in an alienated society art must be critical, it must cut off every illusion, even that of "Nature," the sign must be partly arbitrary. Failing this, you fall back into an art of "expression" and into essentialist illusions. (*Essais Critiques*)

Perhaps the best place to get acquainted with Barthes is in his fine essay on the staging and acting of Racine in the traditional French theater. Here we see clearly that he is not preaching art for art's sake but just the opposite. The theatrical conventions of the Comédie Française have come to demand that in acting Racine the actors cease to address one another and simply sing pure and perfect words which soar "vertically" to some imagined god of pure "meaning." If we are tempted to think "writing degree zero" means something of the sort, we must begin over again, we have not understood it.

Space does not permit an adequate treatment of Barthes' *Racine*.[2] It is a masterpiece of literary criticism, the power and impact of which may not be fully felt by one who has not had to study Racine in a French Lycée. The criticism goes far beyond Racine himself. It gets at the roots not only of French civilization but of the entire culture of the Western world. Let it suffice, in the present context, to say that one can hardly grasp the meaning of *Writing Degree Zero* if one does not also read Barthes' *On Racine*—or better still his *Essais Critiques*, which are not, unfortunately, translated into English.

[2] Roland Barthes, *On Racine,* translated by Richard Howard (New York: Hill & Wang, 1964).

J. F. POWERS—
MORTE D'URBAN: TWO CELEBRATIONS

Sooner or later someone will have to write a Ph.D. dissertation to examine the connection between *Morte d'Urban*[1] and *Morte d'Arthur*. A relationship is evident in the "Castle" scene, on Belleisle—a rather elaborately contrived incident which may disconcert Mr. Powers' clerical readers. (I presume he has some.) It is not easy, in terms of Thomas Malory, to account for the bishop who bounces the golfball off Fr. Urban's head, or for Msgr. Renton, a man of pungent verbal expressions, who hears the bounce but insists on interpreting it as the sound of a champagne cork popping out of a bottle. But ones does not need to account for characters who give such a very good account of themselves, with or without help from Arthurian legend.

The epic of Fr. Urban begins in the usual Powers style: sustained and withering irony. The first half of the book has an intensity about it that will perhaps discourage those who are disposed to mistrust and fear this seemingly cold, perhaps even clinical satire: it has never been so sharp and so incisive. But is it really cruel? Is it negative? Those who stay with the book will find a change of attitude in the last chapters, and they will discover that Fr. Urban has become a sympathetic, in some ways admirable person. The fact is that the "death" of Fr. Urban is the death of a superficial self leading to the resurrection of a deeper, more noble, and more spiritual personality. This novel is more than a ribald satire on the clergy. It is a valid and penetrating study of the psychology of a priest in what is essentially a spiritual conflict. The treatment is of course subtle, and the spiritual element in the story is deliberately understated: but we must clearly recognize not only that it is present but that it is essential to the book. Those who conclude that *Morte d'Urban* is purely negative and hostile to the clergy have not really read the story.

Perfectionists may worry that there are perhaps two Urbans rather than one. There is the more patently Arthurian Urban of the last third

---

This review article first appeared in *Worship,* November 1962, and was later published in a volume, *J. F. Powers,* compiled by Fallon Evans (St. Louis: Herder & Co., 1968).

[1] J. F. Powers: *Morte d'Urban* (New York: Doubleday, 1962).

of the book: and there is the unmitigated operator, the crass narcissist of the first two thirds. The more earthly Urban becomes suddenly volatile after "Twenty-Four Hours in a Strange Diocese," among a choice collection of lay freaks who make him seem very pleasant and human in contrast. He signs their visitors' book "Pope John XXIII" and takes off into legend in a borrowed sports car.

The presence, in our midst, of such a superb satirist as J. F. Powers is certainly a fact of major importance to American Catholicism. Much has been said, recently, about giving the laity a voice. Mr. Powers is there to prove that the American laity is not altogether passive and mute.

It is perfectly obvious that he speaks not as an embittered critic but as a very serious Catholic, profoundly concerned with the true mystery of the Church, of the priesthood, and of the Catholic faith. It is true that he will certainly appeal more to readers of the *New Yorker* than to those of *Our Sunday Visitor:* but it is a Catholic paradox that, since "Catholic" means universal, a writer who reaches only Catholics proves, by that very fact, that he is not yet Catholic enough. It is true that Mr. Powers may perhaps use his indisputable inside knowledge of the clergy ("How does he know so much about priests anyway?") to their apparent disadvantage. But let us reflect that the mere fact of portraying clerics as they are is not by itself an act of anticlericalism. To think otherwise would surely imply a pretty damaging admission!

Let us grant, then, that the simple frankness of Mr. Powers' satire is balanced by a certain modesty and charity which can make it, if we so desire, most salutary. One seldom finds him either really untrue or totally unkind.

Meanwhile a Council is in session, discussing ways of renewing Catholic life and the Catholic apostolate. It would seem that what Mr. Powers says in *Morte d'Urban* has a very distinct bearing on the need for renewal as it is now experienced in American Catholicism.

Every satirist is by implication a moralist, but as long as he keeps to his art, the morality is never more than an implication. Nor can it be otherwise.

If we are to learn from *Morte d'Urban,* we must take it in its own terms. How does Mr. Powers go to work?

A statement by V. S. Pritchett credits our author with a special "gift for recording natural speech." But there is more to it than that. Mr. Powers is remarkable for the sustained mastery with which he keeps up his sardonic parody of a glib, inexhaustible, semirational jargon. It is not natural speech that he records, but all the slogans, the fatuities, and the half-truths of which our minds are full. In such rhetoric, the right word is always, of course, the word that just happens to be wrong—the expression that glances off the truth, that just misses having real meaning.

To be more precise, the statements of a Powers character always mean at the same time less and more than they are intended to mean. The words are not quite accurate in saying what they want to say, and at the same time they speak infinitely damaging volumes by implication, thus confirming the words of Scripture: "A fool's mouth is his ruin, and his lips are a snare to himself" (Proverbs 18:7). The dialogue of Powers' characters then is always shot through with absurdity, and the cumulative effect of a few pages of it is to leave us convinced of the irrationality and fatuity of their attitudes and folkways.

J. F. Powers handles this instrument with incomparable dexterity, and he has never been so eloquent as in this new book. Evelyn Waugh praised the famous early story, "Prince of Darkness," as a masterly study of sloth. In some of the early chapters of *Morte d'Urban* the author communicates a sense of *acedia* which, if it were not so funny, would border on despair.

He portrays all the horror, all the tedium, all the frenzied inner protest of the extrovert who is reduced, in spite of himself, to living a plain religious life of poverty, monotony, and sacrifice.

The importance of *Morte d'Urban,* for a Catholic, is then not only that it is a work of literary genius, but that it makes a specifically religious statement: or at least a statement about religion. I say a statement, not a moral judgment. And this statement is contained principally in the character and the career of Fr. Urban. What kind of priest is he?

If we can extricate ourselves from the ironies of his creator and consider only the "hard facts" (as Fr. Urban himself would surely like us to) we will find him a very energetic and successful priest: one of the few members of the Order of St. Clement (founded by Mr. Powers) who actually amounts to anything.

When he preaches a mission, he has the people sitting on the edge of their pews. When he speaks to a mixed group of Catholics and separated brethren he leaves them all happy, with the feeling that the Church really fits right into our pluralistic society because *he* gets on so well with *them*. When he comes in to St. Monica's parish to help out Fr. Phil (another Powers priest who, like "Prince of Darkness," spends most of his time driving around in his car to get away from claustrophobia), he takes the parish census and gets everything set up for him to build a new church. Is it his fault if the bishop is not interested? And so on. Fr. Urban, in a word, is the kind people like to call a "good priest" without reservation and without resentment because his zeal is just the kind they have been taught to admire. He is not trying to be holy. He is not trying to encourage crackpot movements. He is not mixed up with radicals, pacifists, or integrationists. He is just a great guy with *people,* particularly if they happen to have money.

It is a familiar and not unacceptable picture.

But now if we tune out the other sounds and listen to his thoughts as they are relayed to us by Mr. Powers, we find in him empty gregariousness, not friendship. Verbalism, but not much to say. Cleverness, not talent or intelligence. His clerical zeal, though energetic, is based on an assumed equation between his own enlightened self-interest and the interests of the Church. He owes it to the Church to be a "winner," doesn't he? How else is the Church going to be respected in a competitive and affluent society? In a word, he is a public relations man, an operator, a ham.

It is not surprising, then, that he decides that the best way to put St. Clement's Hill Retreat House on the map is to add a golf course that will "draw the better kind of retreatant."

Fr. Urban is, then, a great priest, if by that you mean he is a clever salesman who can get everybody to buy his image of himself and of the Church as a good, wholesome, worthwhile American package.

Yet it would seem that Mr. Powers does not find this altogether satisfactory. As we watch Fr. Urban at work "with people" (he is not so good when he is not working with people) we become aware of profound religious ambiguities. Just as St. Clement's Hill consists of an old ramshackle retreat house and a fancy new golf course, so Fr. Urban's religion consists of a rather well-worn, though effective, road company act, to which he has added an up-to-date public relations routine. There are, with Fr. Urban, two celebrations always in progress: on one level his version of the ritual and the devotions of the Catholic Church, and on another, the profane ritual of marketing and advertisement.

Mr. Powers appears to think that Fr. Urban makes the sacred an occasion for the secular. The celebration of the more profane, monetary exchange seems to be the real basis for communion between Fr. Urban and his clients.

Happily, the story does not end there. And Fr. Urban certainly becomes heroic in the chivalric exploits by which he delivers himself from enslavement to his own commercially successful image. In the end, as a laconic provincial struggling with a brain tumor, he wins our sympathy and admiration.

This book is not a tract for or against anything: yet it can be taken perhaps as a witness and as a warning. The mission of the Church in America is not purely and simply to get itself accepted by wearing an affluent expression and adopting the idiosyncracies of American business. Preaching the word of God means something more than publicizing an acceptable and popular image of ourselves. We are here to celebrate the mystery of salvation and of our unity in Christ. But this celebration is meaningless unless it manifests itself in an uncompromising Christian concern for man and his society—the kind of concern expressed in *Mater et Magistra* and in the reiterated papal appeals for world peace.

It would appear that such concern is practically incompatible with the kind of superficiality in thought, in life, and in worship so trenchantly satirized in the works of J. F. Powers.

WILLIAM STYRON—
WHO IS NAT TURNER?

It is small wonder that in a year marked by the worst race riots in American history, William Styron's novel about the Negro prophet and revolutionary Nat Turner[1] should be a best seller. There is no doubt a real significance in the fact that Styron, a native of the Tidewater region of Virginia where Turner's slave broke out a hundred and forty odd years ago, should have been obsessed with the subject for years. The novel that has finally resulted is a tour de force. Its popular success is doubtless justified, and the book is a better piece of writing than most best sellers. Yet there are serious objections against it.

Is this book completely honest? Has a white author the right to identify himself, so confidently, with a black man of the last century, and propose this exercise of empathy as an answer to serious questions about contemporary crisis? Obviously, in so doing, Styron has taken liberties with historical fact. Few of his readers will have a chance to check his work carefully with the original document on which it is based—and that too was already the work of another white man with a characteristic bias of its own.

Styron has gone far beyond legitimate bounds in his artistic "transformation" of historic fact. Certainly the contemporary reader may wonder to what extent the character study of the prophet-revolutionary has been gratuitously overweighted with sex frustration and sadomasochism. Since in fact Styron engages in a full-scale character study of Nat Turner, and since he emphasizes the sexual aspects of that study, it comes as a shock to see that Nat, in historical reality a married man, is here portrayed as a celibate who never had any experience with women. Since Styron bases his whole resolution of the dramatic conflict upon Nat's frustrated feelings for a young white woman, and since the "religious" content of the book is also determined to a great extent by Nat's sexual inhibitions, we must admit from the start that we are not reading about the real Nat

---

This essay was written in January 1968 and published for the first time in *Katallagete*, Spring 1968.

[1] William Styron, *The Confessions of Nat Turner* (New York: Random House, 1967).

Turner. This character is purely and simply a creation of Styron's own imagination.

Is the creation then an improvement on the original? The historical Nat Turner was not only married, but married to a slave woman who was sold to another master and from whom he was therefore separated. The frustration and powerlessness of the real Nat Turner were something much deeper and more serious than the mere mental deprivation we read of in Styron's novel. The reader cannot help regretting that the novelist side-stepped the difficulties of this much more challenging situation. Or perhaps the facts were not known to him. What we have in this novel is not an authentic portrayal of a black rebel but simply a meditation of a sophisticated white Southerner, projecting upon a Negro character some of his own ambivalences about the culture based on slavery. This is all very well. But apparently people are reading the book with a misplaced conviction that they are learning some of the deep reasons behind Black Power and ghetto rebellion today. They are merely tuning in on another closed-circuit all-white program.

The book opens with Nat Turner in prison, ready for execution as leader of a slave rebellion in which numerous white planters and their wives and children have been brutally murdered. The revolt was the result of apocalyptic religious experiences, from which the prophet believed himself mandated by heaven to begin the extermination of a corrupt and unjust people. Praying and fasting in the woods, Nat had visions of a black angel overpowering a white angel in the storm clouds over the Tidewater pines. He methodically planned a massacre and carried it out, but the revolt failed, largely because the slaves were drunk and irresponsible and because other Negroes joined the whites and fought against them. Nat Turner stoically accepted the penalty visited upon him by a horrified white society. He faced death with indifference—since after all he still believed that he had only obeyed God. He refused to express any regret for his actions.

One very special question is raised during the course of his trial. Why did this Negro, who was in many ways privileged, take up arms in revolt against those who had gone out of their way to treat him with unusual fairness? Why did he direct his hatred against those who had been especially kind to him and with whom he had apparently lived on the best of terms? Why did it happen that the one person whom he killed with his own hands was a young white girl with whom, we learn from the novel, he lived on terms of intimate understanding very close to deep friendship? For this girl not only loves and understands him—and "the Negro"—with a deeply Christian compassion, but treats him with the openness and confidence one shows only to an equal. Why, finally, does the revolt occur just at a time when the Tidewater farmers are all getting rich on applejack and the slaves never had it so good?

The whole book is built around this question and the various answers (explicit and implicit) which the characters are prepared to give it. There is the crude racist answer: the Negro is essentially an animal, and all he understands is force. If you beat him down he will behave. If you treat him well he will get uppity and out of hand. Those who take this view, in the book, are the ones who really cause the revolt. But the more humane answer also proves ambiguous. Nat's first master, Turner, educates him for freedom, promises him freedom, then goes off and leaves him in the hands of the worst racists. Nat's own answer is quite plain: God told him to wipe out everybody that stood in his way. He had no special preference in the matter of victims. It just happened that some of his white friends were in the way along with the others. That was too bad. He could not change a divinely ordained plan on their account! For Styron, the main problem of the book is to "explain" how Nat might have arrived at such a curious position. He accepts Nat's prophetic urge only enough to explain it away. It is here the book fails.

Styron's question is first of all a reformulation, in simple terms, of what popularly appears to be the central paradox of the race conflict in the United States today. How is it that, though Negro and white are now officially equal, how is it that when the Negro seems to be getting ahead in American society, there should be so much violence and rebellion? Certainly one of the qualities of the book is in the fact that it grasps the real ambiguities of such a situation. It admits that Negroes are not really better off. It brings out all the brutal and suppressed tensions between a surface friendliness and a deep, pent-up, inarticulate hatred. These tensions provide all the necessary motive power for a violent, deeply disturbing narrative. The book plays hard on the reader's emotions: no question about that! All the more so since the tensions themselves are no mere fiction, but a present actuality felt by everyone in the country—indeed all over the world. Underlying the tensions themselves are the unresolved problems of guilt and retribution which, though they may be thrust out of consciousness or evaded by rationalization, remain objectively real. Styron recognizes all this and handles it with cool, objective power. His treatment is all the more effective because he "approves" the hatred and shows us some of the more unlovely white characters through the remorseless and bitter eyes of Negro contempt. Then, when he has aroused our instinctive hope for understanding and reconciliation—through those whites whom Nat himself admits as human and "good"—Styron dashes those hopes by the inexorable working out of a tragic nemesis against which ordinary sincerity and love remain completely powerless. So far, the book is an artistic success.

The ultimate failure of the book is due, I think, to too much "characterizing," too much psychology, too much analysis. Styron is still trying to do something with the novel that can no longer be done with full effect. Curious that on the very day this review is being written, an announcement comes in the mail that Styron will lecture, at Columbia University, on the subject: "Is the novel obsolete?" Doubtless he will say it isn't. In Nat Turner he is trying to say it isn't. He is trying to perpetuate the tradition of the psychological novel popular in the nineteenth and early twentieth centuries. But everywhere the strain for effect is evident. Fearing that his central character may become dull or unreal, the author has to inject a bit of sex once in a while (mostly masturbation fantasies and attempts at homosexual seduction). In so doing he defeats his supposed purpose: evading the more difficult task of creating the character of a prophet, he substitutes a frustrated masochist.

Now the formula: frustrated masochist equals prophet is not new. Flannery O'Connor used it very deftly. It is a good old Southern theme. But one suspects that the historic Nat Turner merits a different treatment. There are barely a dozen pages in the book where Styron's version of Nat Turner emerges as a credible religious figure of any kind, let alone a prophet. Those twelve pages are probably based more closely than the rest on the original source.

Styron's "character study" of Nat Turner is a project in alienation— and as such it is creditable enough. How is this arrived at? In order to make Nat stand out as "real," Styron begins by carefully and studiously isolating him from all the other Negroes. Because of his special talents— and privileges—he becomes aware of himself as *not* like the others. All right. He even feels secret contempt for the others. Whites and Negroes all. What then takes shape in young Nat is a kind of existentialist solipsism—a frigid, self-centered block of individuality struggling for a place in which to comprehend itself. That place is assigned to it entirely, and almost arbitrarily, by white society. But to have an identity and a role conferred upon one entirely by others is something else than choosing to make one's own identity in one's own world. Hence, in spite of all the best breaks, Nat experiences himself as a misplaced, cheated, alienated being. In order to choose himself he has to reject the identity proffered to him by whites—and in any event this identity itself breaks down as soon as his master's promise of freedom is seen to be a delusion. In order to choose himself authentically, he has to choose himself as black. But because he is alienated, his only way of doing so is to choose himself as a black rebel against the whites and finally to see himself as God's special instrument of judgment and vengeance, appointed to destroy white lives.

I have spelled this out in explicitly existentialist terms. I do not claim these terms were consciously in the mind of the author. I feel they were rather dictated by the cool, intense, and formal idiom in which his Nat Turner speaks and thinks. It is the same kind of icy, supercultivated, and ironic formality which we find in the writings of the more academic promoters of Black Power. It is the language of cold, implacable resentment, and it springs, precisely, from an acute sense of alienation—proper to the urban tensions of the nineteen-sixties. Pushed a little further, the treatment could have become an exercise in technical Marxism. But as it stands, it does nothing whatever to explain Nat Turner as a prophet. All we know is that suddenly he has a Bible and is quoting it more or less suitably. And then (in one of the few entirely credible "prophetic" passages) he is struck by a whip and soon after hears the heavenly voice saying "*I abide.*"

In the main, however, Nat's character is dictated by the choice of idiom in which he speaks interiorly. He creates himself in the language of his own inner and personal reflection. The idiom is cerebral, sardonic, aloof, proud, objective. But the tone of this interior monologue excludes the hearing of voices and the sense of religious terror in the presence of the "totally Other." Hence, to be consistent, Styron has to present Nat in jail as one who has all but lost his faith: as one for whom God "is dead." The solipsism of Nat Turner, in Styron's version of him, is that of a disillusioned and skeptical urban man, not the flaming and earth-shaking dread of a primitive Ezekiel who receives direct from God the identity and mission of which he has been cheated by society.

There is one great scene of Faulknerian gothic when Nat is entirely alone, in a thunderstorm, in the mansion abandoned by his first master. And another where he sees the angels fighting in the sky over the forest, during one of his fasts. But for the most part Nat is just not credible as a prophet—especially where, for some unknown reason, Styron tries to account for his religious impulses in terms of sexual frustration.

One thing that kept recurring to me while reading the book was the feeling that the obsessive shadow of Joe Christmas (in Faulkner's *Light in August*) has so come to dominate the typology of Negro revolt in white fiction that Styron just could not drag Nat Turner out from under it. Nat does not resemble a prophet, but he does in some ways resemble Joe Christmas. We find in him the same intense alienation, isolation, hatred, insensibility, and above all the same typological murder of the loved white woman who had been so kind. Yet Nat is not fundamentally cruel in the same way as Joe Christmas (in whom there is no such thing as compassion). Nor does he have the demonic unity and strength of Christmas. Nor is his alienation fraught with the deeper, more metaphysical ironies of Christmas' (the "blackness" of Christmas is purely a matter of imagination and arbitrary decree on the part of those whites who need him to be a Nigger).

What has happened to Nat Turner in these latest confessions? Due to the dominant influence of a Joe Christmas in art and of Black Power leaders in the news, he has lost his faith and abjured his prophecy. His religious drive is unreal, arbitrary, imposed from the outside, worn like a costume. This is a great shame. Because as a matter of fact, all over the world at the present time there are scores if not hundreds of Nat Turners—perhaps not all so murderous—but all discovering themselves to be messengers of the apocalypse, appointed to announce the doom of the white world and the beginning of a new creation. Though their message may at times be naïve and, in our sophisticated terms, quite absurd, they are to be taken seriously as manifestations of a "religious" drive that is not without deep significance. And some anthropologists are beginning to see the importance of understanding them in these terms. We need to understand these prophets of Doom, these preachers of apocalypse.

Nat Turner offers us no such understanding. On the last page of the book, Styron suddenly seems to realize that he has left some unfinished business: the whole crucial question of Nat's religion. What is he going to do about that? There will be a last glimmer of faith, or indeed a *first* glimmer. Nat will go to execution with an obscure awareness that he is really going to meet in heaven the lovely innocent white victim who forgave him as he bashed her head in—who indeed is waiting for him up above. *"Yet I would have spared one.* (he repents in italics) *I would have spared her who showed me Him whose presence I had not fathomed or maybe never even known."*

What's this? With amazement we look back at the pages of innocent and harmless piety in which this tender young lady whispered to Nat her loving concern for the dear Negro in general and for dear Nat in particular. During which time he had fantasies of raping her. All very fine! But now, on the last page, this mixture of milk and water is presented as the one real religious insight Nat Turner ever had! Here is more than Hollywood corn, more than a lapse into sheer humbug. It is a gratuitous betrayal of the Nat Turner whom the author has gone to such trouble to befriend. Styron has attempted to steal away the one reality Nat clung to: as final and absolute, his coal-black angel! He substitutes a message of reconciliation that is, in the artistic context, so completely undeveloped that it is merely a formal and perfunctory gesture. Such gestures, such theoretic afterthoughts only help to discredit Christianity.

FLANNERY O'CONNOR—A PROSE ELEGY

Now Flannery is dead and I will write her name with honor, with love for the great slashing innocence of that dry-eyed irony that could keep looking the South in the face without bleeding or even sobbing. Her South was deeper than mine, crazier than Kentucky, but wild with no other madness than the crafty paranoia that is all over the place, including the North! Only madder, craftier, hung up in wilder and more absurd legends, more inventive of more outrageous lies! And solemn! Taking seriously the need to be respectable when one is an obsolescent and very agile fury.

The key word to Flannery's stories probably is "respect." She never gave up examining its ambiguities and its decay. In this bitter dialectic of half-truths that have become endemic to our system, she probed our very life—its conflicts, its falsities, its obsessions, its vanities. Have we become an enormous complex organization of spurious reverences? Respect is continually advertised, and we are still convinced that we respect "everything good"—when we know too well that we have lost the most elementary respect even for ourselves. Flannery saw this and saw, better than others, what it implied.

She wrote in and out of the anatomy of a word that became genteel, then self-conscious, then obsessive, finally dying of contempt, but kept calling itself "respect." Contempt for the child, for the stranger, for the woman, for the Negro, for the animal, for the white man, for the farmer, for the country, for the preacher, for the city, for the world, for reality itself. Contempt, contempt, so that in the end the gestures of respect they kept making to themselves and to each other and to God became desperately obscene.

But respect had to be maintained. Flannery maintained it ironically and relentlessly with a kind of innocent passion long after it had died of contempt—as if she were the only one left who took this thing seriously. One would think (if one put a Catholic chip on his shoulder and decided to make a problem of her) that she could not look so steadily, so drily,

---

This prose elegy in memory of Flannery O'Connor was written in September 1964; it was first published in *Jubilee*, November 1964, and was included in *Raids on the Unspeakable* (New York: New Directions, 1966).

and so long at so much false respect without herself dying of despair. She never made any funny faces. She never said: "Here is a terrible thing!" She just looked and said what they said and how they said it. It was not she that invented their despair, and perhaps her only way out of despair herself was to respect the way they announced the gospel of contempt. She patiently recorded all they had got themselves into. Their world was a big, fantastic, crawling, exploding junk pile of despair. I will write her name with honor for seeing it so clearly and looking straight at it without remorse. Perhaps her way of irony was the only possible catharsis for a madness so cruel and so endemic. Perhaps a dry honesty like hers can save the South more simply than the North can ever be saved.

Flannery's people were two kinds of very advanced primitives: the city kind, exhausted, disillusioned, tired of imagining, perhaps still given to a grim willfulness in the service of doubt, still driving on in fury and ill will, or scientifically expert in nastiness; and the rural kind: furious, slow, cunning, inexhaustible, living sweetly on the verge of the unbelievable, more inclined to prefer the abyss to solid ground, but keeping contact with the world of contempt by raw insensate poetry and religious mirth: the mirth of a god who himself, they suspected, was the craftiest and most powerful deceiver of all. Flannery saw the contempt of primitives who admitted that they would hate to be saved, and the greater contempt of those other primitives whose salvation was an elaborately contrived possibility, always being brought back into question. Take the sweet idiot deceit of the fury grandmother in "A Good Man Is Hard to Find" whose respectable and catastrophic fantasy easily destroyed her urban son with all his plans, his last shred of trust in reason, and his insolent children.

The way Flannery O'Connor made a story: she would put together all these elements of unreason and let them fly slowly and inexorably at one another. Then sometimes the urban madness, less powerful, would fall weakly prey to the rural madness and be inexorably devoured by a superior and more primitive absurdity. Or the rural madness would fail and fall short of the required malice and urban deceit would compass its destruction, with all possible contempt, cursing, superior violence and fully implemented disbelief. For it would usually be wholesome faith that left the rural primitive unarmed. So you would watch, fascinated, almost in despair, knowing that in the end the very worst thing, the least reasonable, the least desirable, was what would have to happen. Not because Flannery wanted it so, but because it turned out to *be* so in a realm where the advertised satisfaction is compounded of so many lies and of so much contempt for the customer. She had seen too clearly all that is sinister in our commercial paradise, and in its rural roots.

Flannery's people were two kinds of trash, able to mix inanity with poetry, with exuberant nonsense, and with the most profound and systematic contempt for reality. Her people knew how to be trash to the limit, unabashed, on purpose, out of self-contempt that has finally won out over every other feeling and turned into a parody of freedom in the spirit. What spirit? A spirit of ungodly stateliness and parody—the pomp and glee of arbitrary sports, freaks not of nature but of blighted and social willfulness, rich in the creation of respectable and three-eyed monsters. Her beings are always raising the question of *worth*. Who is a good man? Where is he? He is "hard to find." Meanwhile you will have to make out with a bad one who is so respectable that he is horrible, so horrible that he is funny, so funny that he is pathetic, but so pathetic that it would be gruesome to pity him. So funny that you do not dare to laugh too loud for fear of demons.

And that is how Flannery finally solved the problem of respect: having peeled the whole onion of respect layer by layer, having taken it all apart with admirable patience, showing clearly that each layer was only another kind of contempt, she ended up by seeing clearly that it was funny, but not merely funny in a way that you could laugh at. Humorous, yes, but also uncanny, inexplicable, demonic, so you could never laugh at it as if you understood. Because if you pretended to understand, you, too, would find yourself among her demons practicing contempt. She respected all her people by searching for some sense in them, searching for truth, searching to the end and then suspending judgment. To have condemned them on moral grounds would have been to connive with their own crafty arts and their own demonic imagination. It would have meant getting tangled up with them in the same machinery of unreality and of contempt. The only way to be saved was to stay out of it, not to think, not to speak, just to record the slow, sweet, ridiculous verbalizing of Southern furies, working their way through their charming lazy hell.

That is why when I read Flannery I don't think of Hemingway, or Katherine Anne Porter, or Sartre, but rather of someone like Sophocles. What more can be said of a writer? I write her name with honor, for all the truth and all the craft with which she shows man's fall and his dishonor.

THE TRIAL OF POPE PIUS XII:
ROLF HOCHHUTH'S *THE DEPUTY*

Although *The Deputy*[1] is a bad play, it is a significant phenomenon, coinciding mysteriously with the great eruptions of race hatred in the United States, the Cuban crisis, the death of John XXIII, and the bitter struggle waged by the Curial forces in the Second Vatican Council to retain their unique position of power.

The play is an attack, a passionate aggression on the character and reputation of one who has been considered by many a great Pope. The playwright, Rolf Hochhuth, in his early thirties (he was fourteen when Hitler died), has earnestly dedicated himself to the mission of devil's advocate in the case (if not the "cause") of the Pope who allowed it to be said that he had visions of the Lord in his Vatican apartments and who defined the dogma of the Assumption in order, Hochhuth suggests, to assure himself an "important chapter in every history of the Popes."

The tone of the playwright throughout is one of moral outrage, not only at the infamy and inhumanity of genocide, or at Hitler and the SS, who were directly responsible, but above all at the white-clad universal Father in the Vatican, who was "ice-cold," who remained "indifferent," who "dared not protest." The Pope is accused of personally and deliberately choosing to sacrifice the entire Jewish people in order to carry on a policy of coexistence with Hitler—a policy which, it is alleged, would help to salvage the Church's power and "save Western Civilization" from the Communist hordes.

The unquestionable fact that the Holy See did, quietly and effectively, give unofficial aid and refuge to thousands of individual Jews is of course inescapable. But in admitting it, Hochhuth twists and distorts it into a pitiable evasion, a political comedy, without serious moral significance. Even before the curtain rises, the play is already white-hot with partisanship. Stage directions turn into three-page essays on political as well as religious morality, not excluding autobiographical confidences in which,

---

This critique of *The Deputy* was written in 1963 but has not been published previously.

[1] Merton translated *Der Stellvertreter* as "The Representative" instead of "The Deputy."

for example, Hochhuth explains what a tantalizing problem it was to recreate Auschwitz on the stage.

Pius XII is from the first on the same plane as Hitler (though in Act 3, scene 2, the parallel is ambiguously denied) and his fat Cardinal is explicitly compared with Goering.

The total effect of this is something more than a personal antipathy to Pius XII. It seems to be a systematic attack on the Papacy aimed at discrediting the Church herself for accepting and venerating such an institution. At least that is the impression I get from Hochhuth's free use of all the snide stereotypes that have been employed in this game for years. Nothing is lacking. The Cardinal is fat, sensual, cynical, opportunistic. We learn that "with advancing age he has become markedly more feminine." The Pope is portrayed as the most consummate hypocrite, avaricious, ambitious, a lover of flattery, obsessed with his "vast holdings" to the point of breaking off to inquire about his shares in the Hungarian railways in the middle of dictating an appeal for peace and clemency which is so general that it is meaningless. The Inquisition is alluded to: "Where would the Church be, gentlemen, if it had not lit up the stakes for the canaille in the Middle Ages?" Hochhuth's sociology of the Church is summed up in one sentence: "The number of whores increases in the provinces with the number of Churches."

I know others have argued that the play must not be regarded as conventional anti-Catholic propaganda. Well, I would say it should not be *dismissed* as that. It does have an importance that transcends the level of vulgar polemic against the Church. The issue which the play raises must by all means be taken seriously. But the play itself never rises to the level of that issue, and remains on the level of cheap verbal aggression and pseudo-tragedy. As drama it is every bit as absurd as the worst pomposities of Drury Lane in the eighteenth century.

This is not the first time that authority has been treated with savage satire in contemporary theater. It has been done, and done with terrible effect, by Sartre in *The Flies*. And of course the classic reproach against Catholic power is that of Dostoevsky in Ivan Karamazov's digression on the Grand Inquisitor. To mention Hochhuth in the same breath as these others is laughable. To compare him with Bert Brecht, as apparently some have done, is merely fantastic. The only thing Hochhuth would seem to have in common with Brecht is that his play would doubtless be just as acceable in East Berlin as it was where it was produced: in the western half of the city. Ponderousness, obviousness, crude caricature, heavy satire, labored melodrama, and stage directions that turn into interminable sermons on the author's *Weltanschauung:* these are the characteristics of Hochhuth, and they make him the exact contrary of Brecht in every way. Hochhuth cannot even make up his mind why his characters make this or that gesture. ("The Pope makes a couple of fidgety movements with his hands. He is silent either because he is so agitated that he is, as before, bereft of speech, or because he considers it beneath his dignity to answer." This at the high point of the play, Act 3, "Il Gran Rifiuto.")

Although the crudity of Hochhuth's attack (as virulent as it is naïve) on the Papacy does not allow us to take him too seriously, we must nevertheless admit that the issue he has raised is a momentous one. The play may not be important, but the issue it raises definitely is. The play asks a question that many honest, earnest, and unprejudiced people have asked themselves in the last fifty years, and not only in connection with the Jews. The same burning question arises in the American South, where some Bishops have been extraordinarily reticent about the struggle of the Negro for racial justice. Even though John XXIII was very explicit (as also was Pius XII) in declaring the Church's opposition to total war, whether nuclear or conventional, one still wonders how so many theologians and clergy can manage to take positions which distort the obvious sense of the encyclical.

Crudely stated (and Hochhuth states it crudely) the question is this: when the Church is faced with a critical choice between the most basic of all its moral laws, the law of love for God and for man, and the practical, immediate options of power politics, is she now so accustomed to choosing the latter that she is no longer able to see the former? In other words, has the Church finally come to the point where she is so concerned with preserving power and influence that she identifies her duty to God and man with the duty to preserve her power at any cost?

If this were true, then the chief responsibility of the Pope, the Bishops, and indeed all the faithful would be to help the Church keep going as a temporal institution, built into the pragmatic framework of all the other human institutions in the world. Obedience would then be seen *exclusively* in the context of the Church's interests in the struggle for power. The bishop, the priest, the layman who felt obliged in conscience to protest against injustice or inhumanity would be bound to keep silence if his statement were judged inexpedient by the "policy makers" in Rome. Policy would then usurp the place of conscience. This of course would tend to reduce the Church, in practice, to a human, sociological, and basically political entity on a level with any other such organization. The "spiritual" character of the Church would, in that case, be invoked, and frequently invoked, but only to justify and guarantee the supernatural rightness of blind obedience within a framework of political expediency.

I do not personally believe that Hochhuth is right in saying that this was the choice made by Pius XII. I do not believe his play explains the Pope's failure to make the clear, precise statement which all the world expected from the Holy See. There are a multitude of possible reasons why Pius XII did not make such a statement, the chief of which is, probably, that it would have been entirely useless and would have served only to make conditions much worse for thousands of Catholics.

Everyone knows, including Hochhuth, that when the Dutch Bishops protested against the arrest and deportation of Dutch Jews by the Nazis, raids were immediately made on all the convents and monasteries, and religious of Jewish origin were sent to the camps. (Edith Stein was one of these.) Hochhuth ignores this argument. He repeatedly insists that Hitler was so afraid of Pius XII that a mere word from the Pope would have blocked the "final solution." In order to convince us of this, Hochhuth has no less a historical figure than Eichmann himself appear in a beerhall scene, where, cursing and waving a stein, the chief engineer of the final solution declares that if the Church gets rough he will have to renounce the burning of Jews! Surely if Eichmann himself speaks, we must bow our heads in an act of devout faith. The only one who is not to be believed is the "Representative" ("Deputy") of Christ and the successor of St. Peter!

Hochhuth's Pope is not a person, he is an institution, and he is more than the institution of the Papacy. He is *all* Fatherhood. The "tragic" crisis into which the young Jesuit is plunged is a crisis of obedience to this paternal authority. It is curious that Riccardo first, quite seriously, thinks of murdering the Pope, blaming the murder on the SS and thus saving the honor and untarnished purity of Mother Church. But when he sees that this would not work, and when the Pope, icy and unbending, evading the issue with unctuous double talk, refuses to make an appeal for the Jews, then Riccardo pins the Star of David on his own soutane. This reduces the Pope to speechlessness and inarticulate horror. It is a kind of moral "death." Ricardo goes off to Auschwitz, finally completing the "father murder" in the most grandiose and acceptable fashion: it is pure heroism, an act of disobedience to corrupt, disloyal paternal authority. It is a martyrdom and at the same time a murder (in the person of the son) of the father's authority and prestige. Once Riccardo dons the yellow star, the Pope definitely ceases to exist as a being worthy of any kind of respect. He becomes a despicable ghost.

It would be temptingly easy to say that Hochhuth was a neurotic who had got away with what every neurotic secretly desires: he has acted out his conflict, and kept it, while at the same time cutting a figure as a heroic witness for justice and truth. He has killed the "father" who was indispensable for his neurosis, and yet he has kept his neurosis. But let us be both serious and fair. There is nothing uncommon or even especially reprehensible in having this kind of problem about authority in our day, and there is some reason to think that when the Church willingly and knowingly projects an image of grandiose, magical, and unearthly paternal authority, then some people are inevitably tempted and torn in the presence of such an image. Whatever may be the inner conflicts of this young playwright (and we must admit that they are none of our business), the fact remains that the official image of Pius XII, which was that of a super-Pope in every respect, did and still does constitute a psychological stumbling block for vast numbers of men and women in the world today. And this is true, to some extent, of the official image of the Papacy, and of the Episcopacy, and of the Clergy. Indeed, we must lament the fact that this has come to be, to some extent, the Church's image of herself, and it invites projections which even someone as obviously genuine as Pope John XXIII cannot entirely escape.

More than that: it would seem that this image quite naturally and spontaneously recommends itself to many who hold positions of authority in the Church. Who is not familiar with the type of Bishop or Pastor who is at once unctuous, evasive, and aloof with his subjects, and extremely shrewd and pragmatic in the business affairs? Who can put on a grandiose display in miter and crozier and can give authoritative and consoling messages on everything from space travel to midwifery, while refusing to commit himself on moral issues of crucial importance! Hochhuth is virulent, obsessive, and fanatical in attacking this authority image precisely because it constitutes such a huge, useless, and totally unwarranted provocation. Here is what he says in one of his stage directions about the Pope: "The Representative of Christ collects himself. The coldness and hardness of his face, lovingly described by the propagandists of the Church as 'unearthly spiritualization,' have reached freezing point simultaneously—he looks out, past all those around him, outward and upward as he liked to be photographed."

As regards the person of Pius XII, this is probably as unfair as it is cruel. But can we honestly say that this is a totally incomprehensible attack on the *image* that was created of this Pope, the image that he *allowed* to be created of himself? Is it a completely unwarranted reaction to the use of the "Papal image" to enlist blind obedience to all kinds of temporal and expedient causes that are by no means divine, but which are put forward as if they were God's will, without alternative, because they have been presented in close association with the magic image? Is it not the habit both of some who can speak officially in the name of the Church, and even of some who cannot, to evoke this image in support of interests and projects which are not, to put it mildly, those of God and of the Church?

Whatever may be the defects of Hochhuth's play, there may be comprehensible reasons why it was written. There is no question that he has appeared precisely as the devil's advocate, not in any official cause of canonization but in that rather regrettable "cause" which had already begun in Pius' own lifetime and which was promoted with such eagerness precisely by the type of Curial Churchman that so often, doubtless unconsciously, provides material for those who satirize the Church for "love of power."

WILLIAM MELVIN KELLEY—
THE LEGEND OF TUCKER CALIBAN

The deep elemental stirrings that lead to social change begin within the hearts of men whose thoughts have hitherto not been articulate or who have never gained a hearing, and whose needs are therefore ignored, suppressed, and treated as if they did not exist. There is no revolution without a voice. The passion of the oppressed must first of all make itself heard at least among themselves, in spite of the insistence of the privileged oppressor that such needs cannot be real, or just, or urgent. The more the cry of the oppressed is ignored, the more it strengthens itself with a mysterious power that is to be gained from myth, symbol, and prophecy. There is no revolution without poets who are also seers. There is no revolution without prophetic songs.

The voice of the American Negro began to be heard long ago, even in the days of his enslavement. He sang of the great mysteries of the Old Testament, the *magnalia Dei* which are at the heart of the Christian liturgy. In a perfect, unconscious, and spontaneous spirit of prayer and prophecy, the Negro spirituals of the last century remain as classic examples of what a living liturgical hymnody ought to be, and how it comes into being: not in the study of the research worker or in the monastery library, still less in the halls of Curial offices, but where men suffer oppression, where they are deprived of identity, where their lives are robbed of meaning, and where the desire of freedom and the imperative demand of truth forces them to give it meaning: a religious meaning. Such religion is not the "opium of the people," but a prophetic fire of love and courage, fanned by the breathing of the Spirit of God who speaks to the heart of His children in order to lead them out of bondage. Hence the numinous force of the great and primitive art of the American Negro, a force which makes itself felt precisely where men have lost the habit of looking for "art," for instance in that potent and mysterious jazz which has kept alive the inspiration of the traditional "blues," the con-

---

This review article on William Melvin Kelley's first novel, *A Different Drummer* (New York: Doubleday, 1962), first appeared in *Jubilee,* September 1963, and was later published in *Seeds of Destruction* (New York, Farrar Straus and Giroux, 1964).

temporary voice of the American Negro. And also in the "Freedom Songs" which he now sings, in the Baptist Churches of the South where he prepares to march out and face the police of states, already frankly Fascist and racist, which arm themselves against him with clubs, fire hoses, police dogs, and electric cattle prods, throwing their jails wide open to receive him. His song continues to resound in prison, like the songs of Paul and his companions in the Acts of the Apostles.

The Negro novelist and essayist has an important part in this creative expression of the present sense of *kairos* which is behind the great drive for "Freedom Now." We remember of course Richard Wright, whose warm voice is now silent, but who speaks still in his followers. We think especially of James Baldwin, who ranks with Martin Luther King as one of the most influential of Negro spokesmen today. *Go Tell it on the Mountain* is at once Baldwin's first novel and his best, as well as the one which has the most to say about the motives and the spirit of the Black Revolution in America. His hard-hitting tract, *The Fire Next Time,* which borrows its title from one of the Negro spirituals and which has an eschatological reference, is a manifesto of the Negro freedom movement which has done more than anything else to shock white readers into recognizing the seriousness and the unfamiliarity of the situation which they have been more or less taking for granted.

The title of the first novel of William Melvin Kelley, *A Different Drummer,* is taken, significantly, from Henry Thoreau. Thoreau, the hermit and a prophet of nonviolence, preached civil disobedience in protest against unjust laws a century ago, before the Civil War. He was an early champion of Negro freedom as well as a notorious nonconformist who seems to have believed that the American Revolution had either misfired or had never really taken place. Thoreau said: "If a man does not keep pace with his companions, perhaps it is because he hears a different drummer. Let him step to the music he hears, however measured or far away." It is an admirable title for the most mythical and in some sense the most prophetic of the Negro novels: one which makes quite clear the fact that the Negro hears a drummer with a totally different beat, and one which the white man is not yet capable of understanding. Yet it is imperative for him to pay attention. The trite and nasal hillbilly fiddling to which the white American mind continues its optimistic jig has long ago ceased to have a meaning, and the "most advanced country in the world" runs the risk of being, in certain crucial matters, precisely the most retarded. Certainly there is great risk for a nation which is still playing cowboys and Indians in its own imagination—but with H-bombs and Polaris submarines at its disposal!

A Different Drummer is more than a brilliant first novel by a young Negro writer. It is a parable which spells out some of the deep spiritual implications of the Negro battle for full civic rights in the United States and for a completely human status in the world today. This is more than a story of Negro protest; it is a myth endowed with extraordinary creative power bringing to light the providential significance of a tragedy in which, whether we know it or not, understand it or not, like it or not, we are all playing a part. Since we are all in the struggle, we might as well try to find out what it really means. The works of Negro writers are there to tell us. Such books cannot be ignored. They must be read with deep attention. They spell out a message of vital importance which is not to be found anywhere else at the present moment, and on the acceptance of which the survival of American freedom may depend.

The book opens as the loafers on the porch of a general store, in a small town of the deep South, watch a truckload of rock salt pass through on its way to the farm of a Negro called Tucker Caliban. It ends as the same loafers, after watching all the Negroes, mysteriously and without explanation, clear out of the state, lynch the last Negro available to them, a potentate from the North and founder of a black racist movement.

The heart of the story is the sense of *kairos,* the realization that the Negro's hour of destiny has struck. No one can deny that this is one of the most striking and mysterious characteristics of the Negro freedom movement. It is this sense which, awakening everywhere in the Negro masses of the South, especially in the youth, has brought them by the hundreds and thousands out of the ghettoes in which they have vegetated for a century of frustrated and despairing expectation. It is this that has moved them to action, not so much because a few inspired leaders like Martin Luther King have called them to action, but because the entire Negro race, and all the vast majority of "colored races" all over the world, have suddenly and spontaneously become conscious of their real power and, it seems, of a destiny that is all their own. Hence, inseparable from the sense of *kairos* is a conviction of *vocation,* of a providential role to play in the world of our time. With the awakening of independence in Africa the American Negro has become acutely conscious of his own underprivileged status and of his yearning not only to become a "part of White Society" (for this is now evidently a doubtful benefit in his eyes) but to play his own creative role in human history. One finds everywhere in American Negro society a more or less explicit anticipation of the end of the white domination of the world and the decline of European-American civilization. The Negro therefore cannot be content merely to be integrated into something he regards as already over and done with. And this is what the myth in Kelley's novel is all about.

Tucker Caliban is the central figure in the myth. He is the New Negro. The completely new Negro: not the Negro organizer from the North, not the Negro who has been to college, but a kind of preternatural figure, the lineal descendant of a giant African chief who came over with his tribe in a slave ship to be bought—and killed—by the first Governor of the mythical Southern state in which the story takes place. The giant "African" is the symbol of the Negro race and of its innate spirit, which the white man has tried first to tame for his own purposes, then to destroy. Tucker Caliban is not a giant. He is a small, intense, taciturn Negro, aligned with no group, no movement, and no cause. The implication is that he sees completely through even the best of movements and of causes. He also understands the problems of white people. He views them completely objectively and without bitterness. He harbors no delusions about them, and he places no hope whatever in the official benevolence of the white man. His is the spirit in which the Negro freedom movement must develop. In him the wisdom and strength of the African ancestor must one day awaken.

Meanwhile, the Calibans have served the family of the Governor for over a century, both as slaves and as freedmen. Tucker's father is typical of the venerable Negro servant, loyal and entirely devoted to his master; in other words, he is what the Negroes now regard with deepest scorn: he is an "Uncle Tom," or one who has fully accepted an inferior position in white society.

Tucker, without hatred and without rebellion, driven by an inner force which he does not quite understand himself and which baffles everybody who comes in contact with him, first buys a piece of land from the family his family has served so long. Then he leaves their service and farms his newly acquired land for about a year. Finally, following inscrutable interior messages, he sterilizes his field with rock salt, shoots his mule and his cow, sets fire to his house, and leaves in the night with his pregnant wife. He simply vanishes.

At this, all the Negroes in the state begin to leave. It is not necessary to know where they go. They just go. Out of the state, out of the South. In a few days they are all gone, leaving empty houses which they have not bothered to sell, with the doors wide open, furniture inside.

Their departure is a symbolic statement: it is the final refusal to accept paternalism, tutelage, and all different forms of moral, economic, psychological and social servitude wished on them by the whites. In the last analysis, it is the final rejection of the view of life implied by white culture. It is a definitive "NO" to White America.

The book is about the bewilderment with which this is observed and dimly understood by all the people who see them go: the poor whites, the child of a white sharecropper, the descendants of the first Governor, Southerners educated in the north, and finally the Reverend Bennett Bradshaw, founder of the Black Jesuits, a Northern Negro leader who is just as mystified as everyone else by the things that are happening. Though he, more than anyone, would have wanted to set all these things in motion, he has never been consulted or even dreamed of. He is not wanted any more than the benevolent white liberal is wanted, because he has no real power to do anything, to start anything, to move anyone. Yet for the Southern whites there has to be some explanation that fits their picture of life and reassures them that things are what the South has always believed them to be. In a final tragic irony, the loafers at the store follow the irresponsible inspiration of one of their number and blame the Black Jesuit for engineering the hegira. After beating him up they drive him in his own Cadillac to Tucker Caliban's gutted farm, and his screams in the Southern night ring down the curtain on this strange morality play about the evil of our time.

Evil is the word! Those who have seen, at first hand, the eerie glow in the eyes of the racist, those who have heard their peculiar silences as they stand together in the shadows waiting for the forces within them to reach some mysterious point where inner confusion and self-hate turn into violent fury—those who have seen this are aware of what it means to see apparently good and harmless men possessed with an evil so total and so complete that they prefer not to understand it, or refer to it, or treat it as if it existed.

Yet this evil is not something purely and simply confined to "white trash" in the South. What is open and expressed in the South may perhaps be hidden and implicit everywhere in the nation that is so fascinated with violence and with the myth of power that it seems to have lost interest in anything else—with the possible exception of sex.

There is no need to intone a litany of clichés in a useless attempt to convey some idea of the power with which this story is told. It is a power without the bitterness and frustration that give such bite to the works of James Baldwin. Kelley, a Northern Negro like Baldwin, is much more tranquil and reflective. The force of the myth itself seems to have absorbed and tamed the bitter rage that might have gone into such a story. There is no rage. Resentment is sublimated into irony. This accounts for the book's unforgettable impact. The myth of Tucker Caliban tells the same kind of truth as dreams tell us in our moments of personal crisis, spelling out to us in symbols, ranging from idyll to hallucination and to nightmare, the truths that are struggling for acceptance and for expression in our hearts.

That is the particular value of such a book. It gives us a message which, like all prophetic messages, is mostly in code, so that we can both hear and not hear, we can accept just as much of it as we are able. But if we really want to, we can understand completely. What, then, is the message?

The message of this book is very much the same as that which we read in James Baldwin's *The Fire Next Time* (written and published after *A Different Drummer*). It is the same message which the best American Negro writers are now, with a rather astonishing unanimity and confidence, announcing to the white world as their diagnosis of that world's sickness, with their suggestions for escaping the death which is otherwise inevitable.

First of all, we must seriously face the magnanimity of the statement. It would be all too easy for the Negroes simply to write the whites off as a total loss (as indeed the Black Muslims are doing) and be done with them forever. This solution is appealing not only in its simplicity, but also in its correspondence with the deepest psychological need of the Negro, the need to recover his belief in his own autonomous reality, the need to get the white man, spiritually and psychologically, off his back. But in point of fact, such a solution is not really possible, as the best Negro writers see quite clearly. They have certainly rejected, with all their force, the gross and subtle forms of alienation imposed on them by white society, even where it claims to do most to make them "free." But the thing that so many readers have failed to see in these books is the rather convincing assurance that there is one *kairos* for everybody. The time that has providentially come for the black man is also providential for the white man.

This implies a profoundly Christian understanding of man's freedom in history—a point that must be underscored.

The Negro revolution is a real revolution, and it is definitely not Marxian. It may have some very violent and destructive potentialities in it, but they have nothing to do with Soviet Communism. To identify the Negro freedom movement as a red-inspired revolt against Western democracy is a totally ludicrous evasion and one which involves complete and incurable ignorance of what is actually happening. This is of course precisely why it is accepted with total satisfaction by the entire South. In Alabama, Mississippi, Georgia, Louisiana, it is an article of faith that "all this trouble with the Nigras" has been fomented by Communist agents.

Though writers like Baldwin and doubtless Kelley lay no claim to be Christians, their view is still deeply Christian and implies a substantially Christian faith in the spiritual dynamism with which man freely creates his own history, not as an autonomous and titanic self-affirmation but in obedience to the mystery of love and freedom at work under the surface of human events.

In the light of this, then, the hour of freedom is seen also as an hour of salvation. But it is not an hour of salvation for the Negro only. The white man, if he can possibly open the ears of his heart and listen intently enough to hear what the Negro is now hearing, can recognize that he is himself called to freedom and to salvation in the same *kairos* of events which he is now, in so many different ways, opposing or resisting.

These books tell us that it is the Negro who hears, or believes he hears, the true voice of God in history and interprets it rightly. The white man has lost his power to hear any inner voice other than that of his own demon, who urges him to preserve the *status quo* at any price, however desperate, however iniquitous, and however cruel. The white man's readiness to destroy the world rather than change it is dictated by this inner demon, which he cannot recognize, but which the Negro clearly identifies.

The tragedy of the present crisis in race relations (say the Negro writers) is therefore essentially the white man's tragedy, and he will destroy himself unless he can understand and undergo the *metanoia* that will bring him into harmony with the awakened forces that are being revealed to him in the struggle of his black brother. The Negro may have much to suffer, and the times ahead may yet prove most terrible: but essentially, for him, the days of tragedy are over. He has awakened and taken his destiny into his own hands.

Tucker Caliban, when he burned his house down and took off into the night, was not a "tragic" hero. On the contrary, the implication of tragedy is all affixed to the comfortable and secure life which his father led as a loyal servant of the white Governor's family. Tragedy is not in freedom but in moral servitude. We are no longer in the world of Aeschylus and Sophocles, in which the aspiration to freedom is linked with unbearable guilt and punished by the gods. We are in a Christian world in which man is redeemed, liberated from guilt by the inner truth that makes him free to obey the Lord of History. It is the Lord of History who demands of the Negro a complete break with his past servitudes. And the break must be made by the Negro himself, without any need of the white man's paternalistic approval. It is absolutely necessary for the Negro to dissolve all bonds that hold him, like a navel cord, in passive dependence on the good pleasure of the white man's society.

The real tragedy is that of the white man, who does not realize that though he seems to himself to be free, he is actually the victim of the same servitudes which he has imposed on the Negro: passive subjection to the lotus-eating commercial society that he has tried to create for himself and which is shot through with falsity and unfreedom from top to bottom. He makes a great deal of fuss about "individual freedom," but one may ask if such freedom really exists. Is there really a genuine freedom for the person or only the irresponsibility of the atomized individual members of mass society?

The presence of the Negro in a state of humiliation and dependence may serve perhaps to perpetuate the illusion of power and autonomy which the white loafers on the porch of the village store imagine they enjoy. Actually, their own lives are empty, pointless, absurd, totally lacking in freedom. The departure of the Negroes suddenly makes that truth inescapable. Hence the frustrated whites confront the meaninglessness of their world. They know no other way of "facing" such facts than violence.

This, then, according to our Negro writers, is the plight of the white American and indeed of the whole Western world. Europe cannot save face by sitting back complacently and viewing with pity the conflicts and confusions of white America. When the house next door is on fire you too are in danger. America does not stand judgment alone. It is the whole white world, including Russia, that stands accused of centuries of injustice, prejudice, and racism. All white men together, in spite of their fantasies of innocence, are prisoners of the same illusion, seduced by their own slogans, obsessed by the voice of an inner demon. They have no better alternatives than the passivities and oral fantasies of the consumer's dream-world and the violent barbarities with which they react, when briefly awakened, to all that threatens to contradict their infantile dream.

In such a situation, it is absurd for the Negro to place any hope either in the white liberal or in the affluent Negro leader. Though there may be, in each of these cases, some awareness of the problem, the awareness is not deep enough to mean anything. On the contrary, it only makes matters worse by bringing a new element of delusion into the minds of those concerned. The liberal and the Negro leader are, each in his own way, completely committed to the comforts and securities and therefore to the falsities of the *status quo*. Each in his own way has sold out to the establishment. And his defection is all the more vicious because, with his seeming awareness of the problems and his demonstrations of great good will, he only encourages the Negro to continue in hapless submission, to "wait" and to hope for that same magic solution which continues, as always before, to recede further into the future.

To neither of these, says Kelley, can the Negro profitably or even safely listen. The most pitiful character in the book is perhaps the Southern white liberal who was once a promising young radical writer and crusader in the halcyon days of the thirties, but who allowed himself to be intimidated and silenced in order to protect his family. His life thereafter is doomed to sterility, impotence, uselessness. He may be prosperous and secure, but he is a total failure. He has betrayed his truth and his vocation, and is therefore miserable.

This comes close to being a standard formula in the new Negro literature. It calls white society before the bar of history and hands down the judgment that it has lamentably failed. Christianity itself is prominently associated in the failure. Without delaying here to make certain distinctions and to defend the basic truth of Christianity, we must admit that the judgment is not altogether without foundation. The practical conduct of many Christians, of whole groups and entire "Churches," lends it a great deal of support. Christians have perhaps too often been content to delude themselves with vague slogans and abstract formulas about brotherly love. They have too easily become addicted to token gestures of good will and "charity" which they have then taken as a total dispensation from all meaningful action and genuine concern in the crucial problems of our time. As a result they have become unable to listen to the voice of God in the events of the time, and have resisted that voice instead of obeying it.

What is the conclusion? The white man is so far gone that he cannot free the Negro because he cannot even free himself. Hence these books are not in any sense demanding that the whites now finally free the Negroes. On the contrary, the magnificent paradox they utter is that the Negro has a mission to free the white man: and he can begin to do this if he learns to free himself. His first step to freedom must be the clear realization that he cannot depend on the white man or trust him for anything, since the white man is hopelessly impotent, deluded and stupefied by his own alienation.

Such is the "message" of the Negro to white America, delivered by men who, to my mind, are the most impressive and inspired writers in our country today. Is the message "true"?

I must say that messages like this cannot be clearly declared to be either "true" or "false" until time itself lays out all the evidence before us. But that is precisely our difficulty. We cannot wait. We have to decide *now*, before the truth or falsity of the message becomes evident. We have to be willing to make it evident.

The question is, then, not whether the message is true, but whether it is *credible*. And to this I can only give the answer of one man's opinion. Comparing the spiritual earnestness of the message, the creative vitality of the messengers, the fruits of the message, with all the fumbling evasions and inanities of those who disbelieve the message, I can come up with no better choice than to listen very seriously to the Negro and what he has to say. I for one am absolutely ready to believe that *we need him to be free, for our sake even more than for his own.*

The school children of Birmingham would have convinced me, if I had not been already convinced. I find the message entirely credible. Doubtless, it may not be infallibly true, but I think there is no hope for us unless we are able to take seriously the obvious elements of truth which it contains.

II
SEVEN ESSAYS ON ALBERT CAMUS
(1966–68)

THE PLAGUE OF ALBERT CAMUS:
A COMMENTARY AND INTRODUCTION

Preface

The Plague is a modern myth about the destiny of man. Speaking as an artist rather than as a professional philosopher, Camus comes to grips with the problems of evil and unhappiness, not only on the level of the individual person and of society but also in their metaphysical dimension. He directly confronts the ancient problem which Christianity discusses in terms of original sin, actual sin, suffering and redemption. Like traditional Christianity, Camus solves the problem in terms of human freedom; but where Christianity introduces a higher dimension of liberty, the gift of divine freedom which is called grace, Camus finds the concept of grace impossible to accept. Is that perhaps because he has been deceived by the distorted notion of grace which some Christians find amply sufficient? The present commentary will pay particular attention to this problem. But meanwhile, the novel must be read not simply as a drama or as a psychological study, but as a myth of good and evil, of freedom and historical determinism, of love against what Hopkins called "the death dance in our blood."

For Camus, this "death dance," this hidden propensity to pestilence, is something more than mere mortality. It is the willful negation of life that is built into life itself: the human instinct to dominate and to destroy—to seek one's own happiness by destroying the happiness of others, to build one's security on power and, by extension, to justify evil use of that power in terms of "history," or of "the common good," or of "the revolution," or even of "the justice of God."

Man's drive to destroy, to kill, or simply to dominate and to oppress comes from the metaphysical void he experiences when he finds himself a stranger in his own universe. He seeks to make that universe familiar to himself by using it for his own ends, but his own ends are capricious and ambivalent. They may be life-affirming, they may be expressions of comprehension and of love, or they may be life-denying, armored in legalism

---

This study of *The Plague* was written in June 1967 and was first published as a pamphlet by The Seabury Press in 1968. Significantly, it was dedicated to Dan Berrigan.

and false theology, or perhaps even speaking the naked language of brute power. In any case, the message of Camus is that man cannot successfully seek the explanation of his existence in abstractions: instead of trying to justify his life in terms of abstract formulas, man must create meaning in his existence by living in a meaningful way. In the words of Maurice Cranston, for Camus "the world has no ultimate meaning . . . but something in it has meaning . . . man, the only creature to insist on having one."[1]

The Plague affirms this clearly. The frightful visitation of pestilence is met with men's insistence on retaining their meaning. The book is a protest against all forms of passive submission to unhappiness and un-meaning. It is a protest against the passive acceptance of alienation. This protest is explicitly nonreligious. Camus even called *The Plague* "the most anti-Christian" of his books. Yet Camus was at once too honest and too modest to be rigidly doctrinaire in his attitude toward religion. He was not an "atheist," still less a "militant atheist." He simply confessed that the Christian experience was something entirely foreign to his life and that he therefore could not really identify himself with Christians. His treatment of Christianity is ironic and severe, but not totally without sympathy. It is typical of the "post-Christian" mentality which bases its criticism of Christianity on the historic gap between a glorious Christian ideal and a somewhat less edifying reality. There are elements in Camus himself which suggest that Christian grace and liberty may perhaps have contributed unconsciously to the formation of his own austere and compassionate ethic.

Camus is sometimes represented as having preached "the absurd." Nothing could be more mistaken. He wants his reader to recognize "the absurd" in order to resist it. "The absurd" is simply one face of "the plague" which we must resist in all its aspects. The Plague is the tyranny of evil and of death, no matter what form it may take: the Nazi occupation of France, the death camps, the bourgeois hypocrisy of the French system (which Camus had observed in action in the colony of Algeria), Stalinism, or the unprincipled opportunism of certain French Marxists. All such types uneasily sensed that *The Plague* was talking about them— and we might add that the same Plague is not absent from the United States today.

One thing must be made quite clear. Camus is resolutely opposed to a facile historicism which, in the name of "progress" and of the "future," exploits and sacrifices living man here and now. In an interview in New

[1] Maurice Cranston, in *Encounter*, February 1967.

York in 1946, Camus said: "If the problem of mankind boils down to a historical task, whatever that task may be, man is no longer anything but the raw material of history, and one can do with him what one wishes." The presence in our world of a cynical, unprincipled appetite for power which seeks to "do with man what one wishes" is what Camus has symbolized, in this myth-novel, by the hideous figure of the Plague. If Camus is severe with Christians, it is because he thinks they have abdicated their mission of opposing the Plague and have instead devoted their talents to excusing and justifying it in terms of an ambiguous theology or (as in his story of "The Renegade") by compromise with political absolutism.

Life of Albert Camus

Though he fully identified himself with Algeria, where he was born in 1913 and grew up among working-class people of European extraction, Camus could not really be considered a voice of the "Third World." On the other hand, he could not be called a spokesman for France or for Europe, where he always felt himself to be to some extent a stranger and an exile. Actually, Camus is a cosmopolitan twentieth-century man born in Africa, familiar with Europe, South America, and the U.S.A. Citizen of a colony which, during his lifetime, took up arms to free itself from a European mother country, he lost his father in World War I (at the battle of the Marne). Rejected by the armed forces because he was tubercular, he nevertheless took an active part in the French resistance to Nazism in World War II. Though he was, like many others in the thirties, drawn to Communism, he later repudiated Stalinist power politics and remained aloof from Marxism, which he thought to be basically antihumanist. On the other hand, he did not, like so many other ex-Marxists, go over to the right wing, but maintained a precariously conscientious and personal attitude which was critical of all doctrinaire positions and earned him a great deal of obloquy from all sides.

Camus grew up in a poor working-class section of Algiers, in the care of his mother, a Spaniard who had given up all practice of her Catholic faith. He adopted her attitude of quiet contempt for the religiosity of old people in the neighborhood, especially his own devout grandmother, considering that their religion was simply an evasion from life and an attempt to find justification for an existence that drifted helplessly toward death. His first book of essays and sketches, *L'Envers et l'endroit* (1937), ironically observed the religion of the old and preferred the frank, skeptical, life-loving paganism of the Algerian youth on the sunny Mediterranean beaches. The sun, the sea, the shore, the Algerian countryside dotted with half-hidden Roman ruins—all spoke to Camus of what he most valued: the life-affirming heritage of Mediterranean culture, particularly Greek. But he was also alert to the ambiguities of the Greek tradition, sensitive to the tragic view of life that was born of the Athenian theater and to the dualistic spirituality of Neoplatonism.

At the University of Algiers Camus wrote a thesis (1936) on early Christianity, Neoplatonism, Gnosticism, and St. Augustine. He attempted to explain the Augustinian attitude toward evil, which he found deeply repugnant, by the influence of Manichaeism and Neoplatonism. This theme still concerned him in *The Plague,* where the Augustinian preoccupation with physical evil as the punishment of sin obsesses the Jesuit Père Paneloux.

During his university studies Camus contracted an unsuccessful civil marriage, which broke up in 1935. Meanwhile, he joined the Communist party and worked among the Moslems. His most productive work after leaving the University was in the theater, where he wrote and produced plays, with strong political implications, for a cast of working-class actors. After leaving the Communists in 1937, he joined the Algerian movement of National Liberation and, working for a left-wing paper, did a highly competent series of articles on the famine in Kabylia. When his paper was suppressed by the government in 1940, Camus went to France, which was by this time at war. Unable to enlist because of his health, Camus continued his newspaper work in Paris and finished his first novel, *The Stranger,* published two years later (1942). A second marriage, a series of breakdowns in health, trips back and forth from North Africa, periods of convalescence and rest in central France, publication of the philosophical essay *The Myth of Sisyphus,* work on his first plays, activism in the French resistance: all this occupied Camus during the war years, and out of this activity came *The Plague,* which certainly, on one level at least, reflects the tension, the fatigue, the struggle, the sense of frustration and dogged rebellion which dominated France under the Nazis.

Camus lived and taught school in Oran, the scene of the Plague, for a brief period in 1941. During that time there was an epidemic of typhoid in the city. The first notes for *The Plague* were written in April 1941.

> The liberating plague
> Happy town. People live according to different systems. The plague: abolishes all systems. But they are all the same.
> Doubly useless . . .[2]

[2] Albert Camus, *Notebooks 1935–1942* (New York: Alfred A. Knopf, 1963), p. 193.

Elsewhere he reflects that people are always ready to write books on Florence or Athens—but who would write of a place like Oran? "No one would have the idea of writing about a town where there is nothing to attract the mind, where ugliness has played an overwhelming role and where the past is reduced to nothing."[3]

He was already tempted to write about Oran, for if the town was ugly and boring, there was nevertheless something to write about. "My reply is: human beings."

When it appeared in 1947, *The Plague* was an instant success, and everyone recognized the experience of the war years as well as a deeper, more universal question about the meaning of life itself in the contemporary world. The war had shown Camus—and everyone else—that the placid surface of routine and prosperous middle-class existence opened out into a metaphysical and moral abyss that was both incomprehensible and frightening. Though Camus was no philosopher and no existentialist, his two first novels displayed all the irony, the austerity, the bizarre, laconic, and ruthlessly critical analysis of man and society which readers expected from Sartre.

Thus far, Sartre and Camus were friends, though there were always obvious and significant differences between them. In 1952, however, after Camus' essay on revolution, *L'Homme révolté,* the two authors broke with one another and became embroiled in one of those interminable, acid controversies which seem so necessary in the intellectual world, particularly in Paris.

In May 1956 Camus published his third and last novel, *The Fall.* Thereafter he devoted his time and energy to work in the theater, writing and producing plays based on Faulkner (*Requiem for a Nun,* 1956) and Dostoevsky (*The Possessed,* 1959). Meanwhile he was awarded the Nobel Prize for Literature in 1957, when he was still in his forties. Camus never reached the age of fifty. On January 4, 1960, when driving from southern France to Paris with his publisher, he was killed in an accident.

The work of a brilliant French writer—one of the best of his time— was thus cut off at the peak of his development. We know from his *Notebooks* (which have since been published) that he had other and perhaps more important work in progress. We know that having started with the problem of "the absurd" in his first novel and in *Sisyphus,* he had gone on to develop the ethic of revolt—above all in *The Plague. The Fall,* brilliant though it may be, represents a dead end, a *ne plus*

[3] *Ibid.,* p. 197.

ultra in futile self-examination. Clamence, the penitent-judge, is the re-
duction to the absurd of all that Camus has to say about the sterility of a
society that is built (as Tarrou in *The Plague* observes) on institutions
whose chief aim seems to be to justify evil and injustice and death.
Perhaps *The Fall* belonged to what the *Notebooks* call "the cycle of
Nemesis" which would also have included a book on the Nazi death
camps. Finally, however, Camus was planning to deal with what most
attracted him: a "certain kind of love"—a fuller development of those
life-affirming themes which we find in some of his early essays and also
in the conversations between Rieux and Tarrou in *The Plague*. Camus
never had a chance to develop further the austere, almost stoical idealism
of the "healer" who fights against disease and death because living man
remains for him an ultimate, inexplicable value. He never more fully
explored the mysterious and controversial heroism of "the saint without
God" that Tarrou wanted to be—and that Camus himself could never
quite accept. But Camus was always attracted to the cryptic idealism of
Tarrou, just as he had been to the quasi-mystical spirituality of Plotinus.

In the end, Camus' deepest affirmation is that of an almost traditional
and classic humanism with a few significant modern doubts, austerities,
and reservations. Camus is definitely not an existentialist. He rests his
work on basic assumptions about the nature of man, even though he
never spells out these assumptions in clearly essentialist terms. The work
of Camus is a humanism rooted in man as authentic value, in life which
is to be affirmed in defiance of suffering and death, in love, compassion,
and understanding, the solidarity of men in revolt against the absurd,
men whose comradeship has a certain purity because it is based on the
renunciation of all illusions, all misleading ideals, all deceptive and
hypocritical social forms.

What Camus really wanted to explore was the possibility of a new and
authentic humanism based not on religious or on political ideologies, to
which the individual may all too easily be sacrificed, but on a deeply
authentic relationship between living human persons. In the words of
his Nobel Prize acceptance speech: Camus wanted to show men how to
"fashion an art of living in times of catastrophe, to be reborn by fighting
openly against the death instinct at work in our society." Nowhere in all
his work did he achieve this aim more convincingly than in *The Plague*.

The Story of the Plague
A typical French colonial city, banal, placid, engrossed in its business and
in its routine pleasures, a little city without ideas, a community without

character, where nothing special is supposed to happen, is suddenly struck by a disease which has vanished from the civilized world: bubonic plague. Oran, Algeria (described elsewhere by Camus as a labyrinth where the wanderer is destroyed by the minotaur of boredom), is presented as typically "modern." Not of course that it is frantically progressive, or that it moves particularly fast or that it sees far ahead. Yet it is modern in the sense that it "has no past." Modern, too, in the sense that it is populated entirely by enlightened humanists who do not believe in bubonic plague.

The measure of Oran is the measure of modern man in his banality, his love of system, his routine practicality, his indifference to life in depth, whether in sorrow or in joy. The Oranais shares a universal modern conviction that the action is taking place somewhere else. Well, for once, the action takes place at Oran. In fact, the city, visited by pestilence, is entirely cut off from the outside world for ten months. Oran becomes a hectic and beleaguered little world in which the struggle for existence is a bizarre and incredibly difficult affair. A large proportion of the population is killed off. That their town should have "been chosen out for the scene of such grotesque happenings" is, for the Oranais, a rude and salutary shock. It inspires reflection, at least for a while. And then life itself becomes so exacting that one can hardly think: but all, in one way or other, come to realize that the fight against the Plague is everybody's concern. Some dedicate themselves completely to the work of keeping the Plague in check, saving lives, caring for the sick, burying the dead. Many lay down their own lives not as "heroes" but simply because it is what they have to do.

It was said above that Oran is "typical." The citizens are supposed to be the most ordinary kind of people: modern middle- and working-class Frenchmen living in Algeria. But Oran is not a typical *Algerian* city. Nowhere in the book does an Arab appear. The characters are all Europeans or of European descent. This is perhaps significant. The Plague described by Camus is a plague for *Europeans*—who happen also in this case to be "colonialists." That is why he chose Oran instead of Algiers or Constantine as the scene of his story. Oran is a new city, a completely French city with no Kasbah. The fact that the people in the book are for the most part French (there are one or two Spaniards) reminds us that the book, on one of its levels, is also a story of the Nazi occupation in France. The Plague is not only the physical epidemic but also the moral sickness of men under oppression by a hateful regime—a typological reign of evil.

We observe the plague-stricken city through the eyes of a detached, coolly objective witness who speaks in matter-of-fact tones, avoiding all drama and all overstatement, and yet with an authentic personal involvement in the struggle to save lives. Sometimes he draws on the notebook of another witness, Tarrou, a man of ironic and compassionate humor who turns out to be a kind of "saint without God"—or at least who aspires to that condition. Tarrou's notes, as quoted by the narrator, may also be found in the *Notebooks* of Camus himself, but we cannot say that Camus identifies himself with Tarrou. The central character of the book is Dr. Rieux, who is one of the first to identify the Plague and one of the few who, in spite of his constant daily contact with the victims, comes through unharmed.

The narrative begins when Dr. Rieux finds a dead rat on the landing outside his apartment. Within a few days, scores and then hundreds of dead rats show up everywhere. Soon humans begin to fall ill and die. Dr. Rieux diagnoses bubonic plague but has a difficult time getting the city officials to admit the facts and take the necessary measures. Finally the city is closed off, and since it is surrounded by fortifications, this is not difficult. All contact with the outside world except by telephone, telegraph, and radio comes to an end. There is no plague serum on hand. The supply ordered from Paris is a long time coming and proves ineffective. The sickness takes hold of the population. All available public buildings are turned into hospitals. Quarantine camps are set up in various places (for instance in the municipal stadium); food grows scarce; a black market flourishes. However, the cafés continue to be well frequented and so do the movie houses, in spite of the fact that the same pictures have to be shown over and over again.

Meanwhile, religion offers an answer to the tragic problem of pestilence. Père Paneloux, a prominent local Jesuit with a reputation for solid scholarship as well as for militant Christianity, preaches a sermon on the Plague. The sermon contains "vigorous home truths." Oran has the Plague because this is what the people deserve. God is disappointed with the modern world in general and with them in particular. But in his mercy God is giving the city another chance. The Plague is a summons to awaken from religious indifference. Perhaps this is a seedtime for a future harvest. Perhaps the Plague lights the path to future salvation. With St. Augustine (whom Paneloux acknowledges as his master) he believes the Plague "reveals the will of God in action unfailingly transforming evil into good." The theme of the Plague as punishment for sin here echoes the preaching of many French Catholic priests and bishops after the fall of France during "the great penitence of Vichy."

Meanwhile a journalist, Rambert, is working on an elaborate plan to escape from the city and rejoin his young wife in France. On the other hand, Tarrou organizes volunteer sanitation squads, whose members risk their lives in order to fight the Plague, under the immediate direction of Rieux. A great deal of suspense is created by the fact that when Rambert's plan for escape has, after repeated difficulties, finally reached the point of probable success, he renounces it and joins Tarrou.

The Plague drags on, the men who fight it are growing more and more exhausted. One of the doctors develops a serum taken from the victims themselves, and this is tested on a child, who dies in horrible suffering. But the unusual suffering of the child is due to the fact that the serum gave him power to fight the disease. Eventually the serum does prove effective. Meanwhile the suffering and death of the child, in the presence of priest and doctor, Paneloux and Rieux, once again bring up the problem of evil. Challenged by Rieux to justify the death of the innocent in religious terms, the Jesuit revises his previous declarations. He admits that his first sermon was "uncharitable," and instead of promulgating easy and definitive answers confesses that he does not claim to "understand" the mystery of evil but that he nevertheless continues to "love what he cannot understand." His conclusion is no longer expressed in terms of judgment and punishment but of self-abandonment and sacrifice. And, in fact, Paneloux also lays down his life in the struggle against the Plague, as a member of a sanitary squad. It is clear that the "sanitary squads" are meant to suggest the French resistance units, and the change of heart of Paneloux, who ends up fighting on the side of Rieux and Tarrou, represents the part played by some of the French Catholic clergy in the resistence against Nazism.

Finally the new serum begins to work. Patients who seem hopelessly condemned suddenly recover. The Plague is obviously beaten, but just as victory becomes certain Tarrou catches the plague and dies.

The last pages of the book describe the opening of the city gates, the coming of the first train, the reunion of Rambert with his wife, the death of a black marketeer, Cottard, who suggests the French collaborationists. Amid the general celebration, Rieux walks the streets alone, reflecting on the struggle and on its meaning, deciding "that there are more things to admire in man than to despise," but also thinking that the joy of the crowds is perhaps not as secure as they imagine: "the plague bacillus never dies or disappears for good . . . it can lie dormant . . . perhaps the day would come when, for the bane and the enlightening of men, it would rouse up its rats again and send them forth to die in a happy city."

In spite of these final words, *The Plague* remains the most positive and conclusive of all Camus' novels. The real drama of the book is found in the contrapuntal treatment of the theme of evil on two levels: the Plague as physical evil and the Plague as a deficiency in the human spirit, a challenge which summons up the deepest resources of the human conscience in its capacity for courage and love.

The Face of the Plague

"They fancied themselves free," said Rieux of the Oranais, "and no one will ever be free as long as there are pestilences." And "there have been as many plagues as wars in history; yet always plagues and wars take people equally by surprise."

In one of Camus' plays, *The State of Siege,* the Plague appears in person as a totalitarian dictator. In this novel, the Plague is in a way the "central character" though it remains faceless and impersonal. The Plague acts as though with an arbitrary mind and will of its own. Breaking through the placid surface of everyday routine existence, it rudely imposes upon the citizens the dreadful facts of suffering, isolation, and sudden death. The Oranais are not prepared to believe in the Plague because it is not made to their measure. The Plague teaches them that there are certain things which are not made to man's measure, and not exactly to his liking, which he must nevertheless confront as fundamental realities of human existence.

> A pestilence isn't a thing made to man's measure; therefore we tell ourselves that pestilence is a mere bogey of the mind, a bad dream that will pass away. But it doesn't always pass away, and, from one bad dream to another, it is men who pass away, and the humanists first of all, because they haven't taken their precautions. Our townsfolk were not more to blame than others; they forgot to be modest, that was all, and thought that everything still was possible for them, which presupposed that pestilences were impossible. They went on doing business, arranged for journeys, and formed views. How should they have given thought to anything like plague, which rules out any future, cancels journeys, silences the exchange of views?[4]

Plague here represents all the forms of evil which break in upon human existence and curtail the freedom of man by destroying the basic assumptions upon which he builds his plans for future action. Thinking which does not adequately account for evil cannot be called realistic. Freedom that presupposes such unreal thinking is not free. Camus summons the

[4] Albert Camus, *The Plague* (New York: Alfred A. Knopf, 1948), p. 35.

Plague to bear witness to the fact that no systematic thinking can be fully realistic if it excludes the radical *absurdity* of an existence into which evil or irrationality can always break without warning. Yet we seem to assume that human affairs can be laid out neatly in reasonable patterns, as if everything were always in order and as if this order were completely accessible to any mind that carefully studied causes and their effects. Dr. Rieux, by all odds the most objective and scientific mind in the book— the most authentic humanist—is also the one who comes closest to "knowing" the Plague. He is apparently the only one who is able to situate this epidemic in a historical context of bizarre and unpredictable disasters. He is aware that the clanging bells of the Oran trolley cars which proceed to the cemeteries loaded with bodies belong in long procession with the death carts of London and Marseilles, and draw our gaze back to the beaches of Attica where the Athenians kindled huge pyres and fought fiercely with torches in order to throw their dead into the flames rather than into the sea.

"They forgot to be modest, that was all." *Modesty* is a key word in this book. It is an understatement, chosen half in irony. What is it? The sanity of that realistic self-assessment which delivers men from fatal *hybris*. The citizens of Oran were unaware of the "miasma" of evil which a keener moral sense would have quickly detected. The self-assurance of those who know all the answers in advance and who are convinced of their own absolute and infallible correctness sets the stage for war, pestilence, famine, and other personages we prefer to leave unnoticed in the pages of an apocalypse. *Modesty,* in the vocabulary of Tarrou's notebook and of Camus himself, implies a capacity to doubt one's own wisdom, a hesitancy in the presence of doctrines and systems that explain everything too conveniently and justify evil as a kind of good. In Camus, this modesty is a lesson taught in the school of the absurd. It therefore has metaphysical—or antimetaphysical—resonances. The modesty of Tarrou and Rieux is antimetaphysical in the sense that it refuses to adorn with big words a mystery of being which it admits it cannot penetrate. But it is also metaphysical, at least in a sense acceptable to Gabriel Marcel, because it respects the more or less impenetrable truth, the baffling presence of the limitations imposed on man's existence as though by an arbitrary power. It is fully aware of the reality both of man's being and of his inexorable limits. It experiences at once the nobility and the poverty of man's freedom. It refuses to substitute grandiose and heroic ideals for the reality—the *modest* reality—of what man is actually capable of doing.

We find Rieux musing about the seriousness of the Plague which has just been discovered. Will the Plague die out just because it has been identified and resisted? Are lucidity and care and patience all that are needed? "He pulled himself together" (at the point where he was tempted to spell it out in a message of hope), he hears the sound of a man at work with a machine saw. "There lay certitude; there in the daily round. All the rest hung on mere threads and trivial contingencies; you couldn't waste your time on it. The thing was to do your job as it should be done."[5]

The Modest Certitudes

What is the difference between Rieux and the other people of Oran who also do their job each day more or less as it should be done? His lucidity. They imagine that their everyday existence *proves something*. Indeed, they are satisfied with the thought that they themselves prove something, if not everything. They are engrossed in lives which they imagine to be, if not actually significant (because, after all, they may be bored, frustrated, secretly confused or disillusioned), at least potentially so. They are convinced of the fact that there is a clear and simple meaning which is quite conclusive, which is the answer, the right answer, and that it is somehow embodied in an order to which they themselves bear witness insofar as they are happy, prosperous, comfortable, secure. They may not know that answer, or if they think they have dimly grasped it, they may not be able to formulate it. Never mind, they will delegate that responsibility to specialists. There are the officials of the city. They know the law. They represent the order which reflects a basic immutable truth. Or, if you happen to be a believer (a few of them have their moments of belief, which rarely last) there are theologians like Père Paneloux. And then there are doctors. And beyond all these there are still higher powers: higher governing officials, higher church dignitaries, and in Paris super-doctors, who will send a serum to save everyone from the Plague. Unfortunately the serum arrives late and proves ineffective.

The Plague breaks in upon all these people as a visitation of cosmic irony and tragedy. Suddenly their existence, their reasonable answers, their established order, their official clichés, are seen to be absurd. Dr. Rieux and his friend Tarrou are among the few who are able to defend themselves in such a position, precisely because they have no desire *to prove anything*. They are willing to do their job, do it well, and even

[5] *Ibid.*, p. 38.

lay down their lives, *without insisting that anything is proved by their action*. In other words without declaring that they were *justified* in doing what they did. The word "justified" is here used in a strong, quasi-theological sense. As if their action proved them to be in harmony with some Absolute Power.

Such is the modesty of Camus, refusing justification both by works and by faith. It is the modesty which simply elects to fight against death because life is a value beyond question. A modesty which also at the same time refuses to watch itself performing "praiseworthy acts" or "doing good" or even "being heroic." It refuses to preach about its acts, as if to imply "these are the acts everyone should perform." For example, Rieux refuses to argue that Rambert ought not to escape. He does not try to persuade Rambert to stay and fight the Plague with him. On the contrary, he admits that human love—for which Rambert wants to save his own life—is also something of an absolute or at any rate a primary value.

Rieux has standards which he has chosen for himself, but he hesitates to impose them on anyone else. When Tarrou offers to form "sanitary squads" and risk his life fighting the Plague, his motives are "modest" and he finds them almost laughable. They seem to imply that he has a code of morals. But he cannot quite define what that code is. Finally he tries to dismiss it in one admittedly inadequate word: "comprehension." This too, one can guess, is going to turn out to be another key word. Camus' key words are usually unexpected, chosen perhaps for a kind of obliquity which glances off the nail instead of pretending to hit it on the head. Another form of modesty! Only people like Judge Othon and Père Paneloux claim to hit nails squarely on the head. And they, too, must learn a more modest vocabulary from the Plague.

Perhaps one reason for this Camusian modesty and its distrust of formal virtuousness is that Camus is suspicious of success. Not that he entertains a superstitious fear of it, but he is repelled by an ethic of material success as the implicit reward for virtuousness—one of the more complacent myths of bourgeois society. It is ironic that *The Plague* itself was a great success and won the French Critics' Prize for 1947. Camus then reacted in his *Notebooks*:

Melancholy of success. Opposition is essential. If everything were harder for me, as it was before, I should have much more right to say what I am saying. The fact remains that I can help many people—in the meantime.[6]

[6] *Notebooks 1942–1951* (New York, Alfred A. Knopf, 1965), p. 158.

Camus was obviously aware of the fact that his critique of French society and of its criteria for success became ambiguous when that same society gave him the highest praise it could give a moralist precisely because he distrusted virtue.

In the same notes, and in a rather subtle analysis, Camus tries to come to grips with this ambiguity. "Distrust of formal virtue—there is the explanation of this world." The Marxists, he reasons, proceed from this to call everything impure except what contributes to the Marxist cause: and that becomes "virtue." But the conviction that "nothing is pure" has, Camus says, "poisoned our century." He admits that "everything I have ever thought or written is related to that distrust (it is the subject of *The Stranger*)." But even more than formal virtue, he distrusts the nihilism that negates all virtue in order to dedicate itself to revolutionary action in history, regardless of whether it be "moral" or not. "There are some who take up falsehood as one takes up a religious life." (Here he is alluding to the Marxists and to the Sartrian ethic.) Camus would try to solve this problem in *L'Homme révolté*: could one engage validly in historical action without on the one hand indulging in the narcissism of "the virtuous conscience" and without on the other being a nihilist and ignoring all good and evil? His solution is sketched out in *The Plague*, and in the end the followers of Sartre would condemn Camus as a "pure soul."

At any rate the modest narrator in *The Plague* refuses to praise the members of the sanitary squads as if they were heroes. He will not give them "more importance than is their due. . . ." The narrator is inclined to think that by attributing overimportance to praiseworthy actions one may by implication be paying indirect but potent homage to the worse side of human nature. "For this attitude implies that such actions shine out as rare exceptions . . ."

The modesty of Rieux and Tarrou is based therefore on a fundamentally *optimistic* view of human nature, while the idealism it rejects may perhaps often conceal an actual pessimism in regard to human reality. What is "good" about the activity of Tarrou is not precisely the courage, which many others share, but the *comprehension* which saw and loved the goodness of his fellow man and subordinated that value to everything else. Ignorance, the lack of comprehension, becomes an incorrigible vice and a great source of evil when it turns to dogmatism, "fancies it knows everything and therefore claims for itself the right to kill." The modesty and comprehension of Camus are then based not only on a realistic sense of the absurd, but also on a deeply compassionate respect for life and for the concrete human person. The ignorance which Camus rejects ignores the absurd, and fancying itself to be wisdom, prefers its own rightness to the values that are worth defending. Indeed it sacrifices those values by its willingness to kill men in honor of its dogmatic self-idolatry.

Camusian modesty and comprehension are therefore antiheroic. They speak in sober understatements, in quiet irony. They remain cool. Camus is not Promethean. His revolt is not that of the Titan who stormed heaven to steal fire from the gods, but of Sisyphus, the hero of the absurd (that is to say the nonhero) who simply pushes a rock again and again to the top of a hill, and starts all over again each time the rock rolls back to the bottom. The work of Rieux and Tarrou against the Plague is just as dogged, in many ways just as absurd, as that of Sisyphus. There are moments when their exhausting and dangerous struggle seems utterly hopeless: but they continue anyway, not in order to prove themselves better than the Plague, but simply because they are alive and they want to help others to stay alive also.

> Those who enrolled in the "sanitary squads" . . . had indeed no such great merit in doing as they did, since they knew it was the only thing to do, and the unthinkable thing would then have been not to have brought themselves to do it. These groups enabled our townsfolk to come to grips with the disease and convinced them that now that the plague was among us, it was up to them to do whatever could be done to fight it. Since plague became in this way some men's duty, it revealed itself as what it really was: that is the concern of all.[7]

The narrator goes on to say that one does not praise a schoolmaster for teaching children that two and two make four. However, he does admit that there are times in history "when the man who dares to say that two and two makes four is punished with death." Here we are once again reminded that the power and conviction of Camus' statements about the Plague derive from his own participation in the French resistance. His modesty is enhanced by the fact that he almost daily wrote editorials for which he could have been tortured and shot. He said that two and two made four, knowing that this was not acceptable to the enemy that occupied his country.

The true touchstone of merit in the kind of action described by Camus is not that it justifies the agent in comparison with other men who have acted less worthily, but that *it communicates the same lucid consciousness*

[7] *The Plague*, p. 121.

to other men and enables them to act in the same way. It awakens the
same "modesty and comprehension" and the same dogged courage—we
might say the same "Sisyphean spirit"—a spirit which is satisfied to act
on the grounds not of moral good or evil, still less of reward and punishment, but simply as a witness to human truth. "There was nothing admirable about this," says Camus, "it was merely logical." The irony of
that sentence is that its logic is rooted not in coherence but in absurdity,
and what gives it consistency is not reason but *love.*

Here Camus seems to contradict himself. After all, is not love itself the
highest good, the one virtue that gives all other virtues their reality and
meaning? He would not deny it. But we must place this thought in its
right context. By "virtue," Camus generally refers to what *society considers to be virtue,* that is to say, the normative system of conduct that
is preached with a certain amount of fallacious rhetoric. Such virtue is
admired by all and practiced by few. It merely sets the tone for forensic
condemnations, for moral and political witch hunts, for censorious self-
righteousness, and is easily evaded by everyone rich or powerful enough
to get away with it. In other words, virtue is for Camus a kind of social
disease, an endemic state of hypocrisy and doublethink which he called
la moraline ("moralitis"). It is a matter of talk, of conventional attitudes,
of cliché thinking and has nothing whatever to do with the classic idea
of *virtus.*

The whole satiric theme of *The Stranger,* where the hero is condemned
to death as a murderer chiefly on the grounds that he did not weep at
his mother's funeral (thereby proving himself a "criminal type") is that
the standards of right and wrong, law and order, virtue and vice upheld ,
by the court are in fact pure absurdities.

The same irony appears in *The Plague,* but in a much less evident way:
the "normal" life of the city retains a certain tranquility and order by
virtue of certain assumptions which break down under the stress of the
epidemic. But then they are replaced by other standards, less grandiose,
less easy to preach and to praise, but certainly more basic and more real:
the standards of men like Rieux, Tarrou, and all the others who sacrifice
themselves to save the city. What actually happens, of course, is that
instead of the convenient automatic functioning of a social system in
which at the same time everybody and nobody really participates (all
are implicated but few are actually *committed*), there arises a new order
of freedom and of love in which all who take an active part do so by
their own deliberate choice and out of the two motives Camus approves:
revolt against the absurdity and arbitrariness of an evil destiny, and de-

termination to give their lives in the affirmation of man, of life, and of love. Those who do not manage to arrive at this solution are either passive and helpless victims of the Plague or, worse still, its accomplices.

Absurdity—Revolt and Love
This whole attitude, which is of course a highly ethical attitude, is summed up in Camus' *Notebook* of 1946:

"THUS STARTING FROM THE ABSURD, IT IS NOT POSSIBLE TO LIVE REVOLT WITHOUT REACHING AT SOME POINT OR OTHER AN EXPERIENCE OF LOVE THAT IS STILL UNDE- FINED."[8]

This progression is basic in the whole work of Camus. In his early successes (*The Stranger* and *The Myth of Sisyphus*) Camus is exploring the world of the absurd. Those who have never read any other books of his often remain under the impression that Camus was *preaching* the absurd as a way of life. They have an entirely defective view of Camus' real philosophy, especially if they attach too much importance to the "ethic of quantity" which he propounded in some chapters of *Sisyphus* and which he later, quietly, retracted and altered.

The lucid realization of the absurd is, for Camus, only a first step. The function of this lucidity is not simply to negate and to deride the illusory standards of bourgeois society. Still less is it merely a groundwork for an ethic of austere and ironic despair. It is the first step toward a kind of modest hope. *The Myth of Sisyphus* is explicitly directed against sui- cide. Where one might be tempted to think "because life is absurd, let's get it over with," Camus replies, "because life is absurd that is all the more reason for living, and for refusing to surrender to its absurdity."

Life then becomes a revolt against negation, unhappiness, and inevi- table death. It is, under these conditions of lucidity and courage, a valid affirmation of freedom: the only freedom man has, the freedom to keep going even though a certain logic might seem to prove that resistance is useless. Camus detects this logic subtly at work in society itself and in the apparent "order" and "truth" by which society lives.

Indeed, what society preaches in *justification* of man's existence usually turns out upon examination to be a derisory, almost satanic repudiation of that existence. What society preaches as "the good life" is in fact a systematically organized way of death, not only because it is saturated

[8] *Notebooks 1942–1951,* p. 138.

with what psychologists call an unconscious death wish, but because it actually rests on death. It is built on the death of the nonconformist, the alien, the odd ball, the enemy, the criminal. It is based on war, on imprisonment, on punitive methods which include not only mental and physical torture but, above all, the death penalty.

The ambiguities of social thinking spring from the fact that while life, joy, love, and peace are theoretically extolled, what actually keeps the machine running is murder, greed, violence, hatred, war. This ambiguity is common both to affluent conservative establishments and to revolutionary dictatorships. In either case, the mode of conduct that is extolled as "right" is in fact a covert justification for cruelty, lying, killing—for all the evil and injustice upon which society itself actually rests. All this is discovered by Tarrou, when he realizes that his father, a prosecutor, sets his alarm clock and gets up very early on certain days: the days when he goes dutifully to watch his victims perish under the guillotine.

As long as one is content to justify one's existence by reference to these automatically accepted norms, one is in complicity with the absurd, with a murderous society, with death, with "the Plague."

When one comes face to face with absurdity itself, when one confronts the death wish in oneself, the question of suicide arises. He who gives in to the temptation consciously ratifies the absurdity which he has always unconsciously accepted. He dies as a passive victim of an absurd and alienated psychology. His first step toward freedom must be the acceptance of life on an entirely new basis: the affirmation that though the reasons which are supposed to justify existence do not, in fact, justify anything at all, he will go on living anyway as a matter of stubborn "Sisyphean" choice. This first step, this basic revolt against the absurd, this affirmation of freedom, sets man on the right path. After affirming his own life, his own existence, as a fundamental value in itself, he existentially realizes the value of life and existence for others as well. It is here that, in Christian terms, man begins to love others as himself. He is able to experience them as other selves insofar as he has actually *chosen his own life* in opposition to absurdity and death. Thus he also *chooses their lives* in defiance of an absurd philosophy or social system which, at any moment, may decree that they are to be killed in war, executed, exiled, or in some way ostracized, disgraced, and repudiated for defying the generally accepted myths. The steps follow one another with an inexorable "logic" which is, however, not the logic of syllogism but a logic based on *choice*. Once this "logic of preference" has experienced the free choice of life as the basic value and the starting point of all action, then it follows: 1) that one must live in constant revolt against an absurd social philosophy which, in one form or other, is nihilistic and based on murder. 2) One must live in solidarity and love with those whom one is ready to defend against the attacks of "the absurd"—against the death drive built into the structure of social existence. One must in other words make every effort to build a new order of love to supersede the false order which, for all its ideology of humanitarian love or of supernatural grace, is in fact a justification for murder and for hate. 3) But here the real difficulty begins: how is one to build this new order? Revolution, as Camus shows in *L'Homme révolté,* is also a facile justification of mass murder. *Can there be any historic action that does not eventually end in mass murder?*

This was a question which Camus had the honesty not to answer. He admitted that he did not know. But because he did not know, he remained to some extent uncommitted, undecided, and hence to some extent an accomplice of the established disorder. Therefore, what he said about love was ambiguous. Therefore, he had to be very "modest" about it indeed. Therefore, what he said about it was said almost in an undertone, almost as an aside, though it was in fact central to his thought.

Once again we turn to the *Notebooks:*

> The end of the absurd, rebellious etc. movement, the end of the contemporary world consequently, is compassion in the original sense; in other words ultimately love and poetry. But that calls for an innocence I no longer have. All I can do is recognize the way leading to it and to be receptive to the time of the innocents. To see it, at least, before dying.[9]

This is a significant passage, because it reflects something of the deep inner struggle with which Camus confronted the work he wanted to do after finishing *The Plague.* He said somewhere that he wanted to get *The Plague* out of his system, "after which I tell myself that I shall write about happiness." And he added, elsewhere, that this meant writing about "a certain kind of love."

The unusual hesitations, the profound moral scruples which kept Camus so often silent and which prevented him from ever fulfilling this intention, are rooted in his sense of lost innocence. The pages in which he best speaks of the love of life, and of an almost Franciscan happiness, are concentrated in his early essays. At the end of his life he was turning

[9] *Ibid.,* p. 157.

back toward these, to recapture the luminous and abandoned innocence of his Mediterranean existence, after the foggy hell of Amsterdam and *The Fall*. He never had time to go back. And one wonders if he ever really expected to. The sense of lost innocence, of complicity in a world of horror which exceeded the power of imagining, remained dominant in Camus up to the end. Yet he confidently looked for others who were innocent. Did he feel that he had lived to see "the time of the innocents"? Those of us who have learned to be deeply moved by the sincerity and the "innocence" of a new generation that remembers nothing of World War II and seeks only to prevent World War III may be inclined to think that Camus, in these words as in so many others, gave evidence of prophetic insight.

Why did Camus not turn to Christianity as to a source of hope, an affirmation of life? We shall discuss this in connection with the sermons of Père Paneloux. For the moment, we can content ourselves with saying that for Camus the Christian idea of grace had, like that of virtue, become distorted beyond recognition. "Grace" was, in the eyes of Camus, nothing more than the state of smug self-assurance by which the elect convinced themselves of their election. Grace was nothing but the secure self-satisfaction of respectable members of a society that "justified" its basically murderous and destructive activity by means of abstract ethical ideas. "Grace" for Camus was then the capacity to adjust without resistance to the demands of an establishment and to believe oneself thereby chosen by God and destined for eternal salvation. Obviously, this is a complete reversal of the Christian doctrine of justification. Yet who can deny that the caricature has, in fact, a basis which has been accurately described by writers like Mauriac, Julien Green, Graham Greene, Flannery O'Connor, J. F. Powers, and others? In any event, the *Notebooks* of Camus ironically observe:

"Happy Christians, they kept grace for themselves and left us charity." This was written shortly after the publication of *The Plague,* and it could well refer to the kind of charity practiced by Rieux and Tarrou as "saints without God"—therefore without grace. Once again, the distorted notion of grace must be noted. Like virtue, "grace" here supposes a kind of social justification, a logic of acceptability, an affirmation of *rightness*. What is done out of "grace" in such a case is justified by the fact that it *proves something beyond itself*. It is not only an act good in itself, but it proves that one is a Christian, or it proves that God exists, or it proves that the establishment is forever right, or it proves curial infallibility, the Immaculate Conception of St. Joseph, or a million other things.

Camus and Kafka

At this point it is essential to discuss, at least briefly, the obvious resemblances between Camus and Kafka. This is made easy for us by the fact that Camus himself devoted a chapter to "Hope and the Absurd in Kafka" in *The Myth of Sisyphus*. *The Plague* and Kafka's *The Castle* have something in common in that they deal symbolically with the relation between man and the inscrutable powers that influence his destiny without his being able to understand them. The mythical dimension of this relationship is much more elaborate in *The Castle* than in *The Plague*. We need only recall the fact that K. lives as a stranger in the village outside the Castle, insisting that he has been summoned there to work as a surveyor but never able to make any decisive contact with the elusive officials inside the Castle. He never enters the Castle and wastes his time in an exhausting, fantastic struggle with the Byzantine protocol that governs all communication between the Castle and the village. Obviously Kafka is speaking, in terms at once satirical and tragic, of religious alienation: man's struggle to bridge the gap between himself and a realm of utterly inaccessible transcendence.

It must be clear, of course, that what Kafka describes is man's attempt to imagine and to understand grace in terms of hierarchic organization, that is to say, in terms of "law." For anyone who understands the New Testament it is clear that this involves a contradiction that is beyond any solution. But for anyone who knows Church history it is also clear that for most people the contradiction is in fact inevitable. They cannot understand grace in any other terms.

One of the villagers is the girl Amalia, whose whole family is cursed and disgraced because she has refused a most insulting proposition from one of the Castle officials. She is in the right, but in the eyes of the village she has violated a basic moral axiom: the officials of the Castle are always to be obeyed. Faced with a decision between truth to her own integrity and loyalty to a corrupt but accepted "moral" standard, she prefers to do what is regarded as "wrong." She refuses unquestioning obedience to an arbitrary and revolting command. Her act is precisely the kind of choice which Camus describes as "revolt" against the arbitrary and the absurd, in affirmation of one's own personal life, one's own authenticity and existential truth.

Camus' commentary on this is very revealing. It expresses exactly his own critique on conventional notions about "grace," "virtue," and "religion." In his eyes, this is the kind of choice that is forced on one who seeks a transcendent solution to the mysteries of life: he is bidden to renounce his human dignity, his honor, his assertion of his personal truth and worth, and submit blindly to "answers" and "commands" which are an insult to his humanity. His act of submission makes him "worthy of grace." He who has thus surrendered his dignity in a blind act of self-prostration before the unknown has passed the test of faith, has made the "leap" into the dark, and is thereafter "justified." All further activity rooted in this submission is "right" and "good." It is "virtuous" and it "proves something." What? It proves that he is one of the elect, that his relations with the Castle are perfectly correct, and that he has a place in the village (that is to say, in human society).

On the other hand, he who refuses to surrender his human dignity in a blind act of obeisance to what is essentially inhuman becomes a pariah in the village. The morality of Camus demands precisely this refusal.

The ambiguity of Camus' answer is, however, evident to anyone who sees that it is based on a caricature of faith and grace. But let us be quite clear: the caricature cannot be blamed on Camus. Christians themselves are the ones responsible for it. He is simply expressing repugnance for a twisted and degraded form of "Christian morality" which has evolved historically in the framework of a civilization whose social institutions have tended to preserve "Christian values" by embalming them instead of allowing them to renew their own intrinsic life.

Without stopping to clarify this entirely wrong concept of grace, we need only admit once again that it is in fact all too common. But it is, of course, a contradiction of the theological concept of grace. An act which springs from grace is *purely gratuitous* and seeks no justification other than its own gratuitousness, that is to say, its freedom from any limitation, any need for an explanation other than itself. An act that has to be justified by an appeal to something other than its own intrinsic content of love becomes by that fact a legalistic action. It is justified by a norm outside itself.

Camus, without knowing it, was in the thick of the old argument of grace versus the law and, without being aware of the fact, was on the side of grace. He found himself disputing in grace's favor against those who had turned grace into a purely arbitrary law. This is not to say that Camus was a secret Christian, but only that a Christian is free, if he likes, to understand Camus in a Christian sense which Camus himself did not realize.

Rieux and Tarrou
The main characters in *The Plague* are all, in their various ways, solitary

people. But their lives are built into a dialectic of solitude and solidarity, of isolation and integrity on the one hand, commitment, compassion, and love on the other. This is fitting, because the mystery of death is after all a mystery of inexorable solitude, and yet it is something shared by everyone. The Plague intensifies this mystery and brings out, in sharp relief, the Camusian problems of the absurd, revolt, compassion, common action to affirm and protect life against death. Naturally, the two main characters of the book, the "heroes" of the Plague (in the qualified sense we have given to the word hero) are Dr. Rieux and the ironic, lonely Tarrou. The Plague brings them together in a common battle and both—though Rieux vigorously repudiates the allegation—are in a certain sense "saints without God." Who are they? Or perhaps it would be better to ask: what kind of people are they?

What Camus gives us is not so much detailed history or formal characterization. He portrays his characters two-dimensionally in their attitude toward life and toward the crisis in which they are involved. Yet they are men of flesh and blood, not mere abstractions. Of the two, Rieux is the more massive, more serious being: a man who has known work and suffering and who, as the book opens, has just had to send his wife away to a T.B. sanitarium, knowing he will probably never see her again. We are introduced to Rieux as a man who is somewhat weary and disillusioned but firmly committed to the service of other men and to an uncompromising refusal of what he considers dishonest. Serious, reflective, he is not an abstract thinker. In his conflict with the city officials, who are unwilling to accept the fact that the epidemic is really the Plague, he shows himself to be one who starts with facts rather than with definitions. Having determined the facts, he then finds a definition to fit them accurately. He has little patience with the official mind that goes at things the other way round, that starts with a definition of how things are supposed to be and then does all it can to make the facts keep fitting the definition, even when the two have long since parted company.

Ultimately, the difference between the two types of thinking boils down to this: Rieux is concerned with facts because he is interested above all in the needs of living persons. The others are concerned with definitions and legal principles because they are interested above all in the established institutions by which they themselves live.

Rieux is, however, so objective, so reticent, so little inclined to pass judgment, that he is thought by Rambert to be without feeling. Only later does Rambert discover the truth of Rieux's human suffering in his separation from his wife.

Above all, Rieux is the one who sees deepest into the real nature of the

Plague and who fully understands what it means for the whole life of the town to become "a dreary struggle between each man's happiness and the abstractions of the Plague." He cannot in any way agree with the theology of Paneloux, who *justifies* the Plague and tries to make people love their sufferings. His criticism of Paneloux has two aspects. First, he does not take him too seriously: *"Christians sometimes talk like that without really thinking it,"* he says. *"They're better than they seem."* A devastating compliment! Secondly, he reasons that Paneloux is a scholar and therefore judges evil and suffering in terms of what he has read in his theology books: "That's why he can talk with such assurance of the truth with a capital T. Every country priest . . . who has heard a man gasping for breath on his deathbed thinks as I do. He'd try to relieve human suffering before trying to point out its excellence."

Rieux has the same quarrel with Paneloux as he does with the city officials. Paneloux, he thinks, is more interested in justifying the ways of God to man than in the plight of man himself. In other words what Paneloux is really interested in—until he learns better from his own experience of the Plague—is to prove that his religious establishment is right rather than to help men struggle against the Plague. Rieux is not a believer. Not that he is a militant atheist; he is simply a modern man who does not quite know what so much talk about God can possibly mean. He admits it all leaves him fumbling in the dark, and arguments of men like Paneloux are no help whatever.

Rieux's chief problem with the idea of God is that of innocent suffering. If those who seek to justify God explain suffering by saying it is directly willed by God, then they make God a monster of injustice. Suffering is a punishment for sin? But why should God punish an innocent child who has never sinned? The forensic idea of an original guilt which makes evreyone *a priori* subject to punishment and damnation whether he himself does any wrong or not does not satisfy Rieux. He manages, with the help of the Plague, to make Paneloux himself see the difficulty all too clearly. But is this all? Actually, Rieux has a deeper intuition, shared with Tarrou—a sense that this pessimism about man, this degrading repudiation of man in order to justify the authoritarian image of God, is in reality bound up with a social structure that depends on force, cruelty, prison, death sentences, and war. What the doctrine seeks to justify with its inquisitional fires is not simply the Father Image of God, but the authoritarian social establishment and its cruel laws.

The Plague draws its real power from the death wish and the destructiveness that are built into man's own life. It is not merely a visitation from outer space, a punishing angel sent from heaven. It comes to full view on emerging from its hiding place, the city and its inhabitants. The people's *indifference to life and to authentic values*—an indifference which is justified and enhanced by their ideology and their social mores—allows the Plague to take undisputed possession of them. This indifference itself is already an indication of the Plague's dormant presence. Germaine Brée has summed up Camus' idea—which is expressed by Rieux and Tarrou—very succinctly.

> Unopposed, [the Plague] organizes all that is bad in human life into a coherent and independent system: pain, death, separation, fear and solitude. And it disorganizes and destroys all that is good: freedom, hope, and most particularly love . . . The Plague is not the symbol of an outer abstract evil; it merely applies and *carries to their logical limits the values implicit in the unconscious attitudes of the citizens of Oran.*[10]

This makes the Plague an excellent typological device for discussion of Nazism and other absolutisms, which operate in exactly the same way. The power of a dictator and of an authoritarian and violent party is made possible by the attitudes and dispositions already present in the people who submit to them, because in the depths of their hearts they want to submit. That is why, in Camus' eyes, the sermon of Paneloux urging people to submit to the Plague as a just punishment is—like the sermons of French clerics urging acceptance of Nazi rule—simply a form of collaboration with the evil in man, an act of obedience to the innate fury of pestilence and of death. But how can Rieux believe this if he does not also, in some form or other, believe in something remarkably like original sin? This Camus fails to explain.

Tarrou is somewhat less stolid than his friend Dr. Rieux. He is a poet of sorts, a more articulate thinker, more ironic, a "singular man" who is a bit of a poet and who frequents "Spanish dancers." He has a sharp eye for curious and human detail—it is he who observes the old man who likes to spit on cats (a real individual, enshrined in Camus' *Notebooks*). Tarrou is given to understatement. He looks at things through the wrong end of the telescope. He does not believe in heroism—certainly not the heroism of a Malraux, still less of a de Gaulle. Yet he aspires to a kind of sainthood. He wonders if it is possible for him to be a "saint without God." Can he be? He once thought of himself as "innocent." But was he ever in reality innocent? "I had the plague already before coming," he said. His whole history is, he recognizes, a history of Plague.

---

[10] Germaine Brée, *Camus,* rev. ed. (New Brunswick, N.J.: Rutgers University Press, 1961), p. 118.

His father was a prosecutor, and one day in court Tarrou, as a boy, suddenly realized what his father was doing: dressed in legal robes, haranguing the jury, demanding the death penalty for a criminal, he was permitting himself to become the incarnation of socially approved blood lust. He was acting as the willing and righteous instrument of a society that delighted in murder, provided the murder could be carried out in socially acceptable ways. Tarrou ran away from home and became a rebel against society. *"The social order around me was based on the death sentence and by fighting the established order I'd be fighting against murder."* But then, Tarrou asks, can one really wash his hands of society and its evil by a mere good intention? Can one become innocent by one's own declaration, backed up by some symbolic gesture (burning a draft card for example)? This is not a foregone conclusion. The great problem remains to be faced. "We can't stir a finger in the world without the risk of bringing death to somebody." But does that not make all life unlivable? Once again, if every act of man is involved in murder, one fails to see the difference between the doctrine of Camus and Augustine's pessimism on original sin. Innocence is equally impossible whichever way you look at it. But Tarrou reaches certain practical conclusions. First: it is possible to refuse all conscious and deliberate co-operation in any social action, any doctrine, any policy, whether revolutionary or conservative, which *justifies murder in order to exploit it freely.* In other words, though one cannot avoid all implication in some form of violence (Camus did not believe consistent nonviolent action was possible), one can at least refuse to co-operate with the social machinery of *systematic and self-justifying violence.* One can reject specious ideologies which permit massive killing in war, in pogroms, in nihilistic violence on the grounds of race, religion, class, nationalism, and so forth.

"On this earth," Tarrou declares in words which Camus explicitly made his own elsewhere, "there are pestilences (an early draft has "executioners") and victims, and it's up to us, so far as possible, not to join forces with the pestilences."

Starting from this, Tarrou builds his ethic of "comprehension." Indeed it is more than an ethic, it is almost a monastic ascesis: it demands constant *attention* (compare the old monastic idea of "vigilance" and "custody of the heart"). It is a monastic spirituality of *exile,* because he who refuses to co-operate with the "pestilence" which is part and parcel of every social establishment cannot really be accepted by that establishment. He remains a stranger in his own city. But in that city he nevertheless retains his sympathy for and concern with those whom he sees to be potential or actual victims of hidden plagues. Finally, one can perhaps be a "saint without God" insofar as one does all these without expecting a reward and without calling on God to justify and approve one's acts.

The expression "saint without God" sounds more anti-Christian than it really is. In fact, the Christian idea of disinterested sanctity is not too remote from this. St. John of the Cross somewhere remarked: "You should do your good actions in such a way that, if it were possible, God himself would not know you were doing them."

As for Rieux, he does not condemn Tarrou's idea but merely remarks that for his own part he does not want to be a saint or a hero: what interests him is simply "being a man." And to tell the truth that is already heroic enough.

Grand, Cottard and Rambert

Since Grand and Cottard are neighbors, we might as well consider them together. But one is on the side of the angels, the other is with the devils. In other words, Grand is on the side of life, with Rieux and Tarrou. Cottard is on the side of death and the Plague. Why? As the book opens, Cottard has just tried to hang himself. He is wanted by the police. When the Plague comes, all official attention is diverted to the crisis, and the police forget about him. The Plague for Cottard means freedom, respectability, and even a certain material well-being. He makes money on the black market and goes about in public, visits the cafés, enjoys life. The Plague is his element. He wants it to go on forever. When the statistics begin to promise an improvement, he refuses to believe them. When the Plague finally ends, he goes out of his head and starts shooting indiscriminately at everything that moves. He is captured by the police and brutally killed.

Cottard is the one character in the book who most obviously points to the Nazi occupation. He is a typical "collaborator."

Grand, on the other hand, appears at first sight to be nothing more than a dull, self-important civil servant, a failure in life who tries to console himself by his absurd obsession with writing a novel. But because he is a perfectionist—and not endowed with much creative imagination—he never gets beyond the first sentence, which he rewrites over and over, this way and that, on page after page.

He knows he is getting nowhere but he keeps working in his spare time, Plague and all, because he dreams of the day when his manuscript will be discovered by a great publishing house and the editor-in-chief will cry out to all the assembled staff "Gentlemen, hat's off!" This, in Grand's opinion, is what happens in publishing houses when a new masterpiece is discovered.

And yet, for all his failure, for all his devotion to a civic service job that undoubtedly should make him (if Tarrou is right) a collaborator with a murderous system, Grand is nevertheless something of a "hero." Why? Because he is, after all, like Sisyphus. His mild megalomania is no obstacle to this: it fits in. In can be approved. It helps him, in his own way, to revolt against the absurdity of his meaningless existence, because it keeps him valiantly pushing away at his own Sisyphean boulder—the first sentence of an impossible masterpiece.

We can better appreciate the sympathetic character of the journalist Rambert if we contrast him with another character which filled the same position in the first draft of the book and was later eliminated. This character, Stephan, is abandoned by his wife and then, though he survives the Plague, commits suicide. Rambert is totally different both in his story and in his attitude. He is a completely positive, life-loving character. He is a stranger in Oran and seeks to escape in order to rejoin his wife, whom he loves passionately. He makes repeated efforts to get out of the city. But finally, when he seems likely to succeed, he changes his mind and decides to remain and help Tarrou and the sanitary squads. In the end, however, he survives the Plague and is reunited with his wife in an almost ecstatic scene at the railway station. This serves as a striking contrast to the loneliness of Rieux, who has lost his own wife and also lost his friend Tarrou. But in reality the reunion scene is not altogether consistent with the story, since there is no reason why Rambert's wife should come to the Algerian town. Logic would seem to demand that Rambert go to meet her at their home in France, which is what he has been trying to do all along. Nevertheless, Rambert plays an important part in the artistic structure of the book. As a character he is aesthetically "right": he contrasts with the reflectiveness of Rieux and Tarrou. He is a straight type with healthy and deep impulses, grounded in the love of life and of his woman. He wastes no time in discussion, though he does at times become engaged in the issues raised by the two protagonists. But in the main he moves in a sober and simple world—that of the Spanish soccer player Gonzalez and of the sentries who are supposed to help engineer his escape.

One more minor character must be mentioned. In a book where there are few women—the solitude of men separated from their beloved is one of the emphatic themes of the novel—the whole weight of femininity is carried by Rieux's mother. She does little. She says practically nothing: but she is a "presence." She is there when Tarrou dies. She is a very considerable support for her son in his loneliness and his exhaustion. She remains shadowy, and is very real: a kind of silent incarnation of the "comprehension" about which Tarrou talks so much. This is the true role of woman in Camus' world: she is there to embody wisdom and love because she is capable of a dimension of understanding that too easily escapes the logic-machine which is the active mind of man.

The Bossuet of Oran: Père Paneloux

Finally we come to a character whom the Christian reader cannot help but find a little perplexing. Paneloux tends to polarize the thought of those who fight the Plague at Oran. But Paneloux himself remains quite ambiguous. What does he finally add up to? The answer is never quite certain, and Camus intended to leave it a mystery. This contributes to the unusual interest of a priest figure that was intended to bear the burden of traditional Christianity and of historical Christendom in a book which blames both for contributing to the modern pestilence. More than that: we shall see that in fact Paneloux bears other burdens as well. At times we hear him echo the justification of evil which Camus, in his university thesis, attributed to the Gnostic Basilides. He explicitly defends the doctrines of Augustine. But in later modifying these, Paneloux ends up with a curiously Nietzschean position. He takes refuge in a pure voluntarism which makes him a kind of Nietzschean *with* God, just as Tarrou's doctrine of charity without grace tends to make him a saint without God. Discussing Nietzsche's last period Camus in *L'Homme révolté* attributes to him the same "active fatalism" which he attributes to Paneloux. It would be interesting to examine the implications of all this, but space does not permit. At any rate, Paneloux is presented as a "compleat" Jesuit. His voluntarism masks a hidden will to power under a doctrine of total submission to seemingly arbitrary decrees of God.

We have already briefly outlined the two sermons of Paneloux. The first sermon is typical of French classic pulpit oratory. A vibrant, forceful, authoritarian delivery of all the right answers: just the kind of thing that Judge Othon must declare to be "absolutely irrefutable." Paneloux obviously models himself on the great Bossuet and echoes Bossuet's conservative idea of history. In the beginning God showed man the difference between right and wrong. Man consistently refused obedience, and history is simply the record of man's infidelities and of the repeated punishments he has to endure in consequence. The lessons of history are perfectly simple. But when will we ever learn? The Plague gives Paneloux an admirable opportunity to accuse, to judge, and to chastise in the name of God. He does not associate himself with his hearers: he calls them "you." He tells them that *they* have sinned, and that the Plague has been sent to *them* in order to bring them to their senses: the means by which they can effectively do this is to heed his message and fall on their knees.

A better understanding of the power complex behind the first sermon of Paneloux can be gained by a reading of Camus' story "The Renegade." Here the megalomanical missionary seeks nothing but a chance to affirm his own power by using the word of the Gospel to subdue the most wicked savages. Ironically, it turns out that the wicked savages are a lot more powerful and persuasive than he, even though they never say anything at all. They just *do:* and what they do is naked evil in its most brutal and uncompromising form. In either case, in "The Renegade" and *The Plague* we find the message of evangelical judgment pitted against straight evil, and evil goes its way in complete indifference. The announcement of judgment and punishment merely serves to reinforce the submission of weak humans to the evil that afflicts them, though that is obviously not the preacher's intention.

Though in the second sermon there is an even stronger emphasis on obedience to the will of God, Paneloux has obviously changed. He has learned a new attitude toward the Plague and toward life itself—indeed he has almost learned a new attitude toward God. Now he is much humbler—more "modest." Now he does not say "you" to his congregation. He says *we*. He includes himself among the sinners, the sufferers, and above all *among those who do not understand*.

The great difference between the vibrant and irrefutable Bossuet of Sermon 1 and the much more chastened preacher of Sermon 2 is that the second does not claim to have all the answers. He does not propound a simple view of life and of history that is merely a record of God commanding and man rebelling. He does not conclude that the only solution is "not to rebel." On the contrary, he almost, but not quite, admits that the suffering and death of the innocent boy, Othon's child, have made him hesitate. Not that he has doubted God's existence. He has faced the question of revolt. Is God to be loved or hated? Paneloux no longer dares to solve the problem with a sweeping apologetic argument. He is much more hesitant. Can the answer really be found without any resort to double talk and subterfuge? He no longer trusts formulas, but he has another answer: not of the mind but of the will. It is a question of choice. Either/or. Either one must deny God entirely and reject him entirely, or one must accept *everything*. Love him in everything, including the death of the innocent child. Including one's own death. Including (he hints at this) a sacrifice and death which are apparently without justification, without meaning.

At this point we realize that Paneloux anticipates his own demise and takes upon himself a course of action that is in fact not easy to understand or to justify—his ambiguous death is one that will never merit canonization. His loyalty to the Church is doubted by some of his fellow clerics. Some wonder if his faith has been shaken. But the death of Paneloux is definitely consecrated by an act of stubborn, personal choice.

One element in the choice is clearly bizarre. Paneloux decides that if his faith in God is to be perfectly "pure," he must refuse the aid of a doctor, for to have recourse to human science would be to resist the will of God.

Camus does not say so quite clearly, but we divine that Paneloux, in heroic Christian fashion, has doubtless asked God to lay upon him the punishment of all, all the unrelieved suffering of the worst kind of death by pestilence, and to do this in such a way that Paneloux will receive no praise or credit from men. So, in fact, he dies a mysterious, ambiguous, and stubborn kind of death: he gets precisely what he asks for, whatever it may have been. And, paradoxically, in blindly submitting to God he also manages at the same time to impose his own will on God.

In the tortuous scheme of his own secret spiritual will to power, Paneloux emerges an absolute winner, but in a victory no one else can possibly find either the time or the casuistic subtlety to comprehend. The implicit conclusion of Camus is that this is the limit of good will which can be expected from a present-day Catholic: an individual drama buried in the solemn and absurd secrecy of a Byzantine, casuistical theory of evil.

Conclusion

Camus, "the conscience of his generation" and indeed of a generation that has followed, is a stumbling block to Christians. He deliberately intended to be one. He is a typical "post-Christian" thinker in the sense that he combines an obscure sense of certain Christian values—the lucidity and solidarity of men in their struggle against evil—with an accusatory, satirical analysis of the Christian establishment and of the faithful.

His portrait of Paneloux is prehaps bizarre, but it is not pure and simple caricature. One might easily find Christian books—whether of theology or of "spirituality"—which treat the question of evil exactly as it is treated by Paneloux. Admittedly, Paneloux's idea that to consult a doctor would be to resist God is plainly eccentric and erroneous by Catholic standards. Even then, some of the saints have had bizarre ideas and gotten away with them.

But Paneloux is plainly no saint, and we must even admit that his Christianity is defective. Why? Because one looks in vain for any evidence of a really deep human and Christian compassion in this stern, logical mind. He seems to have no authentic Christian sense of mercy, no realization of the love of God for sinful and suffering man, no awareness of divine forgiveness overflowing in the love of man for his brother. Paneloux is learned, he is austere, self-sacrificing, disciplined, and indeed, in a certain sense, heroic. But his heart is sealed off from other men. He is isolated in himself.

Paneloux lives alone with an abstract God, whom he serves with exemplary fidelity, seeking in all things to justify him by logical argumentation and by the stern devotion of an implacable will. The solitude of Paneloux, immured in the stone cell of his own logic and his own will, makes the existential reality of human problems incomprehensible to him. Certainly, he knows that they are problems and he understands his duty to participate in solving them, but this duty itself is abstract. His *idea* of God, his *abstractions* about God come between him and other human beings. God is therefore not the infinite source of love and forgiveness in whom men are reconciled to one another in charity: he is for Paneloux a cause of opprobrium and of division.

The crisis of the Plague, in which Rieux and Tarrou become spontaneously *united* with others by their unobtrusive service, becomes for Paneloux an occasion for tortuous intellectual problems which, in spite of his good will, eventually cut him off from everyone else. He finally crowns his desperation (which he believes to be "hope") in a bizarre exploit of dying according to some casuistical pattern sanctioned by his own will and offered, for approval, to his inscrutable and abstract Judge.

One of the most shocking sentences uttered by Paneloux is his self-righteous exclamation, when Rieux protests against the "injustice" of the innocent child's death. "Ah," Paneloux sighs, *"now I understand what grace is."* In other words, "Now I know what it is that distinguishes me from this unbeliever here. He cannot see that God is to be loved even when he arbitrarily destroys the innocent. He does not have the grace to believe; consequently he sees only cruelty, and thinks God is wrong.

But I have the grace to see that even when he is arbitrary and cruel, God is always right." Grace, then, is that which gives one the ability to submit to a God who acts like an arbitrary tyrant. It gives us the power to submit to a will we do not understand and even to adore and love what appears horrible. This is an idea that Camus finds revolting. And he is right. It is also an idea which Camus believes to be essential to Christianity, and he is wrong: the idea that God is essentially unjust, and to be loved as such!

Christian faith is not simply the *credo quia absurdum* of Tertullian. Pascal could speak of faith as a wager, and this expression is quite valid in the context of his thought and work: but it is not the last word on all faith and on every problem of the believer. In other words, faith does not reduce itself always and everywhere into a demand that the believer lovingly and dutifully accept an image of God which is in fact a monstrous and arbitrary theological idol. This perversion of the idea of faith results from an overemphasis on the aspect of authority in faith and from the impasse reached by theological controversy on grace and free will, predestination, and evil since the Reformation. The God of Paneloux may be adorned by Christian terminology, but he is not the God of Christian revelation. He is the perverse abstraction distilled from centuries of futile argument. He is anything but the living God of the prophets, of the New Testament, and of the saints. Indeed, the most awful thing about Paneloux is that he is fanatically loyal to a God that is stone dead, and the stubborn intensity of his well-meant faith does nothing whatever to bring this idol back to life. People like Paneloux, with their combination of stern rationalism and a dogged will to believe, have brought about the death of God. Camus does not use this expression; he simply finds the God of Paneloux absurd, not because of the exactitude of the theological language about him, but precisely because it is only language *about* him. Paneloux has knowledge, discipline, will power, determination, sacrifice, and even a bizarre kind of grace. But he is without love. In portraying him as a Christian without love, Camus is portraying Paneloux as an unchristian Christian. In showing him as a Christian who knows *about* God but obviously did not *know God,* he displays him as a witness to the death of God. The only quarrel we can have with this is to differ with Camus on one point: that *a Christian must inevitably be someone like Paneloux.*

Here a Christian will be likely to suffer a salutary access of Camusian modesty. What one of us can be sure of demonstrating in his life that Camus is not right about Christians? It is a great deal easier, in many ways, to be a Paneloux than it is to be the kind of Christian that will measure up to Camus' exacting standard. But perhaps that is partly due to the fact that we are too self-conscious about ourselves and that, as Christians, we have become more and more habituated to a bad conscience in a world that is fed up with everything about us—not only with our double talk but also with our best efforts at sincerity, not only with our bad faith but also with our flashes of authenticity.

The current apologetic reply to Camus' dismissal of Catholicism goes something like this: Camus was exposed to Augustine when he was not ready for him. He paid too much attention to Pascal and to "sick" Christianity like that of Kierkegaard. And of course he was not favorably impressed by the French Catholic collaborationists and their jeremiads over sin and punishment at the time of the Nazi occupation. But it would have been a different story if Camus had been able to read Teilhard de Chardin.

Is it that easy? To begin with, let us state the question more exactly. It would be impossible to say whether or not Camus, under this or that set of "favorable circumstances," would ever have become "a believer." Such surmises are usually nonsense. The problem with Camus was that he simply could not find Christians with whom he was able completely to *identify himself on every level*. The closest he got was with some of the French priests in the resistance, and evidently that was not close enough.

What would Camus have liked about Teilhard?

Obviously, first of all, he would have been happy with Teilhard's complete acceptance of nature and of material creation. Teilhard came as close to developing a Christian mystique of matter as anyone has ever done; and Camus, in some of his essays, extols the material, the phenomenal, the sensible, the experience of the fleeting moment, in quasi-mystical language.

A study of Teilhard's writings and especially of his own spiritual development shows us to what extent he rebelled against the mentality we have seen in Paneloux: the self-righteous, censorious repudiation of a beautiful world created by God's love. Writing from the trenches in World War I, Teilhard confessed, in a letter to a friend, that even in the midst of war he was meditating and keeping notes on the "real problem of my interior life"—"the problem of reconciling a passionate and legitimate love of all that is greatest on earth, and the unique quest of the Kingdom of Heaven." He explicitly rejects any concept of the world as "only an opportunity to acquire merit." Rather he sees it as a good creation, coming from the hand of God and given us "to be built up and embellished."

It is of course typical of the spirituality of Paneloux to regard the created world merely as something to be manipulated in order to amass an abstract capital of merit. Paneloux is a spiritual profiteer, and his kind of Christianity is a reflection of the social establishment, with which it exists in a symbiotic unity. Of such Christianity, Teilhard says it makes one less than a man and a traitor to the human race. Those who observe it from the outside are repelled and "blame my religion for it." That is precisely what Camus does in his portrait of Paneloux. Teilhard's criticism of this false supernaturalism is that in trying to divert man's capacity to love and turn it aside from concrete human reality to the purely abstract and spiritual, it deadens and distorts man. "The capacity to love cannot with impunity be dissociated from its object: if you try, mistakenly, to cut off our affectivity from love of the universe, are you not in danger of destroying it?" This is what has happened to Paneloux: a good, sincere, strong-willed man, with a strong tendency to intellectualize, he has fallen a victim to an abstract and inhuman spirituality. His power of love has atrophied. His affectivity has been channeled into will-to-power and rigid authoritarianism. When he tries to recover the warmth of love, he ends in a self-immolation which is part heroism and part algebra, an irrefutable conclusion to an argument which no one is able to understand.

Teilhard, on the contrary, wants to transform and divinize the human passions themselves. "I shall put the intoxication of pagan pantheism to Christian use, by recognizing the creative and formative action of God in every caress and every blow . . . I would like to be able to love Christ passionately . . . *in the very act of* loving the universe." And he asks: "Is there communion with God through the Earth, the Earth becoming like a great Host in which God would be contained for us?"

Camus' basic sympathy for the element of Greek *theoria* in Mediterranean culture would incline him to accept this "Christian gnosis" up to a point. He could identify with the "passionate love," if not with the theological elaboration. Teilhard also completely and totally accepts *man;* and the God of Teilhard is not simply a remote judge and creator, but a God who seeks to complete his epiphany in the world of man by bringing all humanity to convergence and unity in himself, in the Incarnation. The Incarnation for Teilhard is, then, not just an expedient to take care of sin and bring the kind of "grace" that Paneloux was happy about. The Incarnation is ultimately the full revelation of God, not just in man but in the "hominization" of the entire material world.

Camus would have heartily agreed with Teilhard's love of man and with his aspiration toward human unity. But it is rather doubtful whether he would have been able to accept the evolutionary and historical scheme of Teilhardian soteriology. To be precise, it is likely that Camus would have had a certain amount of trouble with the systematic progress of the world toward "hominization" and "christification" by virtue of laws immanent in matter and in history.

The point cannot be adequately discussed here, but anyone who wants to investigate it further had better read Camus' book on *Revolt* (*L'Homme révolté*), which he wrote after *The Plague* and which he thought out at the same time as *The Plague*. This study of revolt, which precipitated the break between Camus and the Marxists (especially with Sartre), is a severe critique of Hegelian and post-Hegelian doctrines which seek the salvation and progress of man in the "laws of history."

Camus was suspicious of the way in which totalitarians of both the left and the right consistently appealed to evolution to justify their hope of inevitable progress toward a new era of the superman. In particular, he protested vigorously against their tendency to sacrifice man as he is now, in the present, for man as he is supposed to be, according to the doctrine of race or party, at some indefinite time in the future. In Camus' eyes, this too easily justified the sadism and opportunism of people who are always prepared to align themselves on the side of the executioners against the victims. In other words, a certain superficial type of eschatological hopefulness, based on evolution, made it easy to ignore the extermination camps, the pogroms, the genocide, the napalm, the H-bombs that so conveniently favored the survival of the fittest, got rid of those who no longer had a right to exist, and prepared the way for the epiphany of superman.

At this point, it must be admitted that one of the most serious criticisms of Teilhard bears precisely on this point: an optimism which tends to look at existential evil and suffering through the small end of the telescope. It is unfortunately true that Teilhard, like many other Christians, regarded the dead and wounded of Hiroshima with a certain equanimity as inevitable by-products of scientific and evolutionary progress. He was much more impressed with the magnificent scientific achievement of the atomic physicists than he was with the consequences of dropping the bomb. It must be added immediately that the physicists themselves did not all see things exactly as he did. The concern of a Niels Bohr and his dogged struggle to prevent the atomic arms race put Bohr with Rieux and Tarrou in the category of "Sisyphean" heroes that are entirely congenial to Camus. After the Bikini test, Teilhard exclaimed that the new bombs "show a humanity which is at peace both internally and externally." And he added beatifically, *"they announce the coming of the spirit on earth."* (*L'Avenir de l'homme*)

No matter how much we may respect the integrity and the nobility of this dedicated Jesuit, we have to admit here that at least in one respect he resembles his confrère Paneloux. True, they are at opposite extremes of optimism and pessimism; but they do concur in attaching more importance to an abstract *idea*, a *mystique*, a *system*, than to man in his existential and fallible reality here and now. This is precisely what Camus considers to be the great temptation. Lured by an ideology or a mystique, one goes over to the side of the executioners, while arguing that in so doing one is promoting the cause of life.

There is no question whatever that Teilhard believes in the "new man," the *homo progressivus*, the new evolutionary leap that is now being taken (he thinks) beyond *homo sapiens*. Science certainly gives us a basis for hope in this development, and perhaps Camus needed to have more hope in the future of man than he actually seems to have had. Perhaps Camus was too inclined to doubt and hesitate. Perhaps his "modesty" tended too much to desperation. Perhaps there was much he could have learned from Teilhard. But it is not likely that he would purely and simply have agreed with Teilhard's statement in Peking, in 1945, that the victorious armies of Mao Tse-tung represented "the humanity of tomorrow" and "the generating forces and the elements of planetization," while the bourgeois European world represented nothing but the garbage (*le déchet*) of history. No doubt there may be good reason to think that a "new humanity" will arise out of the emerging Third World. Let us hope that it will. But Camus would not be so naïve as to identify this "new humanity" with a particular brand of Marxism, or to pin his hopes on a party which announced its own glorious future as a dogma of faith.

Both Camus and Teilhard firmly took their stand on what they considered to be the side of *life*. Both saw humanity confronted with a final choice, a "grand option," between the "spirit of force" and the "spirit of love," between "division" and "convergence." Man's destiny is in his own hands, and everything depends on whether he chooses life and creativity or death and destruction. Teilhard's scientific mystique and long-range view, extending over millennia, naturally did not delay overlong to worry about the death of a few thousands here and there. Camus could still pause and have scruples over the murder of an innocent child. He refused to justify that death in the name of God. He also refused to justify it by an appeal to history, to evolution, to science, to politics, or to the glorious future of the new man.

CAMUS: JOURNALS OF THE PLAGUE YEARS

Camus said of himself that he was "not a novelist in the usual sense . . . but rather an artist who creates myths to fit his passion and his anguish." The statement has a Gallic vibrancy about it, and existentialist anguish has ceased to be as acceptable as it was immediately after World War II. Passion is not "cool." Myths are out of fashion; art tends to be anti-art. One would think that in this sentence Camus had said everything that our contemporaries would feel to be wrong. Yet he remains a writer by whom people are still able to be not only convinced but even vehemently inspired. A new generation, dubious of the safely liberal and pragmatic homilies of its elders, goes to Camus for an ethic it can believe in, which is an ethic of revolt. But strangely enough the revolt, though expressly post-Christian, is also a return to traditional and classic values, indeed in some sense to implicitly Christian values.

Camus is honest, and his style, his sense of myth, his authentic passion, his ability to become involved in an issue without being dominated by a program, have earned him a hearing: so much so that he has been called "the conscience of a generation." He is indeed a "moralist" in a great tradition, that of La Rochefoucauld, Montaigne, Pascal. What is more, when he was alive he managed to use this gift of insight and of style to very good effect not only in his novels but in the newspapers.

Faulkner (whom Camus greatly admired) could also be called an "artist who creates myths to fit his passion and his anguish," and he saw the world around him much as Camus saw occupied France. But the myths of Faulkner had a way of getting outside of and away from their creator so that they stood by themselves. Camus tends to remain present in his own myth, and we attend more directly to the maker than to the myth he has made. In *The Fall*, some people have been tempted (I think quite absurdly) to ask if Jean Baptiste Clamence is Camus himself. But Clamence is so genuine an emanation (in Blake's sense) of Camus that one keeps wondering what Camus thinks about him, or what he means by him. In *Light in August* one does not ask what Faulkner thinks of Joe Christmas until it is all over and one has to write an essay on it.

This review article on the Camus "Journals of the Plague Years" was completed in April 1967 and was first published in *The Sewanee Review*, autumn 1967.

Even then, what matters is that Christmas lives and dies, not what the author may have thought when he wrote about it (though that too may be helpful). Doubtless one could say that in Christmas and in Clamence the two authors came to grips with something in themselves, some aspect of man's native desperation and falsity that they feared. In Christmas this desperation becomes incarnate in terms that are at once tragic, ironic, and theological. Clamence is the product of an even more sustained, but less tragic, irony; and he never becomes incarnate. He remains the author's idea, his "emanation" or his obsession. The obsessive quality is heightened by the dry, exasperating monotone in which Clamence talks and talks (his hearer never being allowed to reply) until everything is analyzed out of existence.

So Camus, the moralist of the absurd, finally shows the absurdity of moralizing about the absurd, not because he is subtle and clever but precisely because he sees that we are the victims of our own cleverness. We are being slowly consumed by a plague of cerebration. This is the source of Camusian anguish: Cartesian man, the detached subject, who is because he thinks (and thinks because he is Cartesian man), having started out with the assumption that everything thinkable is comprehensible, suddenly finds out that everything thinkable is absurd. Why? Not because of a metaphysical flaw in objective existents but because there is something the matter with the relation of the thinking subject to the object of thought. And what is wrong seems to be the relationship itself, to which Cartesian man has condemned himself by making it the ground of all his certitudes, including the certitude of his own existence. From this illness, this absurdity, follow inexorable evils and injustices: the persecution and the murder of innocent people, the falsification of moral and historic truth, the poisoning of existence itself for millions of human beings. In the presence of these evils man remains helpless and passive, equipped with a few gimmicks and slogans which do little more than excuse his own helplessness or, worse still, rationalize his collaboration with the forces set on destroying him.

Camus was one of those who saw most clearly this "banality of evil" which some still consider to be rather characteristic of our time. The Nazi occupation of France was merely one virulent outbreak of the plague which is everywhere endemic and dormant. In his *Notebooks*[1] Camus wrote: "I want to express by means of the plague the stifling air

[1] *Notebooks 1935–1942* (New York, Alfred A. Knopf, 1963); *Notebooks 1942–1951* (Alfred A. Knopf, 1965).

from which we all suffered and the atmosphere of threat and exile in which we lived. I want at the same time to extend that interpretation to the notion of existence in general. The plague will give the image of those who in this war were limited to reflection, to silence—and to moral anguish."

The peculiar intensity and honesty of Camus comes precisely from this tension in himself: his sense that he must give his life meaning by striving to make sense out of an absurd situation.

At this point it must be made clear that Camus is not a "philosopher of the absurd" in the sense of an *advocate* of the absurd. The popular image of him shows Camus as one who somehow prefers the absurd, who finds it more interesting, more real, than rationality, and who takes it as the basis for complete freedom from all law: since everything is absurd, do what you like. In actual fact he is at once more exacting and more traditional. He first shows that what seems to be rational in accepted ethical and social systems is in fact irrational and largely meaningless. But the discovery of this meaninglessness calls for a revolt that will replace empty forms with authentically significant acts. (The ethic of quantity, proposed in *The Myth of Sisyphus,* approved Don Juanism. But this was later radically revised. Camus' thought is essentially qualitative. Mere quantitative repetition does not give meaning to anything, and the assumption that it does is basically nihilistic.) This quest for significance is by no means arbitrary. Camus opposes to nihilism a certain "human measure" of which the best examples are to be found, he thinks, in the Greek and Mediterranean tradition. Camus is, if anything, a classic moralist on the stoic pattern rather than an existentialist thinker.

The situation of twentieth-century man is absurd (Camus believes) because it consistently forces him into radical self-contradiction. The final idiocy to which complacent modern man is tempted consists in using all his resources of logic and of science to demonstrate that his self-contradictions make perfect sense. Camus refuses to consent to this gigantic hoax, and decides that if there is a meaning to be found in life it must be sought in revolt, in resistance against the plague, the kind of heroic and seemingly hopeless resistance which he and his fellow-countrymen put up against overwhelming odds during World War II.

It was in this resistance that Camus, as editor of a clandestine resistance newspaper, *Combat,* learned the seriousness of words. When you realize that you may be shot for your editorial, he said, you weigh what you say. You make sure you mean it.

Though one must avoid any temptation to call Camus a Christian, he himself saw that his revolt had much in common with the primitive and authentic type of Christian witness (which has nothing in common with the conformist parody of Christianity derided by Kierkegaard). Camus wrote in his *Notebooks:* "There is no objection to the totalitarian attitude other than the religious or moral objection. If this world has no meaning then they are right. I do not accept that they are right. Hence. . . ." This aphorism is eventually developed into the thesis of *L'Homme révolté,* the long and difficult book in which he analyzes the difference between "revolt" and "revolution." Revolt has to be perpetually renewed to prevent revolution from hardening into a tyranny which inexorably contradicts all of its own first principles.

Basically, Camus can be called a "religious" thinker insofar as he appeals to an obscure and ultimate faith. No doubt it is not a theological faith, but a faith in man, a faith in revolt itself, a faith in the value of an existential witness which says "No" to the absurd. In this assertion of man himself as a kind of ultimate value, Camus says: "We have but one way of creating God which is to become him."

This aphorism is not to be interpreted as a purely dynamic and existentialist statement. On the contrary, as we have seen above, Camus' ethic is based on classic assumptions about human nature. Man is not "pure becoming," and his freedom is not capable of arbitrary self-determination. To say that man's destiny is entirely in his own hands and entirely in the future, with no basic natural pattern to be realized, but only with a historic finality to be created out of nothing, is for Camus the basis of nihilism. It is another form of absurdity. In the name of creation it justifies destruction. A truly creative ethic must be authentically human, and this presupposes that man already *is* something definite. Unless we accept man as a *being* we will never respect him. If he "is not," then his destruction is a matter of small consequence. A philosophy of pure becoming justifies mass murder, torture, the police state, what you will. "Instead of killing and dying to produce the being that we are not," Camus says, "our job is to live and to make live in order to create what we are." If to "create what we are" is to "become God" then the Camusian position is not far removed from a traditional and even religious metaphysic, in which created being is a potential epiphany of the uncreated.

The ethic of Camus aimed, as he said in his Nobel Prize acceptance speech, "to fashion an art of living in times of catastrophe, to be reborn by fighting openly against the death instinct at work in our society." Born in poverty, brought up among people even poorer than himself—the

Algerian Moslems—early afflicted by the tuberculosis against which he struggled all his life, Camus was particularly sensitive to injustice and to evil. His very sensitivity gave him a quality of probity and detachment which was misunderstood and criticized by those who more easily identified themselves with mass movements and abstract ideologies. Precisely because he would not identify himself with the Marxists, Camus was attacked by and isolated from the postwar intellectuals in Paris. He would not admit that the "art of living in times of catastrophe" was to be found in political slogans and in the opportunism of parties. But precisely because he was a lonely figure, one who maintained his own principles against this kind of pressure, he earned a respect which will be denied to his adversaries. He was faithful to his own principle of refusal and of revolt, even though this earned him condemnation as a "pure soul."

Camus was killed in a tragic accident at the height of his career. He was working on a book about the war and the death camps. In fact his plans for his future work were already quite definite. Camus was one of the rare authors who saw his entire production as a consistent unity. Germaine Brée sums up this unity as a succession of four "cycles," two of which had been completed. First the cycle of "The Absurd," with *The Myth of Sisyphus* and *The Stranger*. Then the "Promethean cycle of Revolt" in *The Plague* and *L'Homme révolté*. This was to be followed by the work on which he was engaged, in the "cycle of Nemesis." Perhaps *The Fall,*[2] with its gloomy futility, belonged in this cycle, which would concern itself above all with the violence and nihilism of the Nazis. The *Notebooks* sketch out some incidents in the death camps.

The final cycle was to deal with "a certain kind of love." This was evidently what Camus really wanted to come to: he said that he wanted to get the plague out of his system first. "After which I tell myself that I shall write about happiness." But as a matter of fact we can already see something of what he meant in his two first books, the Mediterranean essays, in which he resembles D. H. Lawrence. This final work was to be called "The First Man" (*Le Premier homme*), and Camus evidently regarded all four cycles as "one vast novel" even though half the books were essays. In actual fact it is hard to make a clear distinction in Camus between the essay and the *roman mythe*. In all his work there is a moral unity, the unity of his main ideas: absurdity, revolt, nemesis, love. His expression of them varies in poetic essays, in plays, and in mythlike stories, as well as in his notebooks. The *Notebooks* themselves are of absorbing

[2] *The Fall* and *Exile and the Kingdom* (New York, Modern Library, 1966).

interest and importance precisely because his whole work is a unity and they provide the explicit key to it.

Of the relatively numerous studies of Camus, three may be mentioned here. Cruickshank's *Albert Camus and the Literature of Revolt*[3] was written while Camus was still alive, and as the title suggests it stresses the essays of the middle period, treating Camus above all as an ethical and political theorist and attempting to justify his ideas before an English audience which is presumed to be critical. Cruickshank assumes, in the opening pages, that the cool pragmatic Anglo-Saxon will not be sympathetic to a literature of anguished myth and of outspoken protest. He prepares his reader for Camus with lines like these: "Among the themes which occur most frequently in his writings are the isolation of man in an alien universe, the insufficiency of certain traditional moral values, the estrangement of the individual from himself, the humanist failure of Marxism, the problem of evil, atheism, the pressing finality of death and the advocacy of a form of neo-paganism. Such subjects, particularly when treated by a gifted writer, are usually regarded as unfortunate aberrations by the practical English mind. They become objects of suspicion and are thought to be the undesirable products of humorlessness, excessive abstraction, or mental and moral unhealth."

Throughout the book, Cruickshank keeps these possible objections in mind, and he analyzes the ideas of Camus with great care. Unfortunately he is so careful and so logical—and so British—that he tends at times to get away from Camus himself, whose logic is that of the imagination as well as of reason.

In his *Notebooks* Camus distinguishes between "a philosophy of evidence and a philosophy of preference." It is obvious that he himself is interested in preferences rather than in proofs. When he seeks a meaning in life he does not seek to prove life has a meaning on the basis of philosophical evidence, but to make certain choices and decisions which, because they are in accord with the hidden value of life, bring that value out into full view. The philosophy of preference is one which starts with an obscure moral intuition and ends by making man himself evident. Or in other words, the basic moral intuition from which the Camusian ethic begins is the assumption of human values. "Start by looking for what is valid in every man." But if man is essentially absurd, how can human experience be a basis for an intuition of any validity whatever? In the

[3] John Cruickshank, *Albert Camus and the Literature of Revolt* (New York, Oxford University Press, 1959).

presence of the absurd all our actions can be "equally instructive" on one condition: that they are lucid; or, "that faced with the humblest or the most heart-rending experience man should always be 'present' and that he should endure this experience without flinching with complete lucidity." The existential and poetic logic of Camus starts from an intuitive preference for lucidity as a fundamental human value, through which man discovers his own meaning and *chooses* to mean what he in fact is. The philosophy which starts out with abstract evidence may easily miss the whole point and never arrive at man at all, never have anything to say about his actual condition, never really help him to understand himself as he is.

Cruickshank, while sympathizing with Camus, tends to judge Camus' arguments in the light of a logic which Camus has already set aside. This approach forces Cruickshank into a point of view where he has to pinpoint logical inconsistencies in Camus and to account for them. Really, these inconsistencies do not matter. For instance, the theme of *The Myth of Sisyphus* seems to Cruickshank to be that suicide is illogical. And *L'Homme révolté* seems to proceed from there to declare that therefore murder is illogical. Cruickshank says this does not follow. Camus is "confusing moral choice with logical necessity." It is true that Camus is saying that we should refuse suicide and murder, but he is not saying that we must refuse murder because we must refuse suicide. He is proposing one basic "preference"—for life—and saying that to hold human life cheap is to connive with the absurd and yield to its malignancy. It is the sign of our surrender to the absurd. To prefer abstractions to life is to end in absurdity and despair. Suicide is the collapse of the individual in the presence of the absurd. Murder—mass murder, war, genocide, and even capital punishment—is a moral collapse of society under pressure of the absurd. We must refuse both if we are to find any possible meaning or honesty at all in human existence. To declare that a political ideology can give meaning to life when it manifestly results in the deaths of millions of innocent people is to become an agent of the evil and the absurd—the death instinct which actively and urgently threatens the very survival of man. The logic with which Camus urges his convictions is not that of the mathematical and Cartesian spirit but of the *esprit de finesse*. An abstract line of reasoning can "prove" that the extermination of millions of people is reasonable and necessary. But in the face of such "absurd" reasoning, one can only respond by a concrete preference for life and a refusal to kill.

What Camus proposes is not an explanation of life nor a logical solution of its central problems but an attitude toward life which does not rest on a mere logical hypothesis. He does not "use the absurd as a source of values" (as Cruickshank accuses him of doing), and he does not proceed by "a sudden twist in the argument [to change] the absurd into a solution, a rule of life, a kind of salvation." It may be true that in a certain sense "Camus takes as his key to existence the very fact of not having a key." But he does not take the absurd as the key to a philosophical system, or as the heart of a religious mystery, or as the springboard for a leap into faith. Camus is simply saying that if you start out in life with the presupposition that there is a definite and logically demonstrable answer hidden in it somewhere, and that this answer can be discovered by a patient application of reason, you will end up telling yourself a lie and immolating other people to prove that your answer is the right one. The authentic answer is not something that you teach others, but that you work out with them; not something that you look for, but something that you bring to light in your own life by the choices that you make. Cruickshank does not ignore this, and he says well: "Camus' observations on the absurd serve usefully to remind us, in common with all forms of existential thinking, that existence cannot be grasped conceptually and that abstractness of thought will always fail to pin down the particularity and concreteness of things."

He goes on: "The frustrated search for truth which made him conscious of the absurd is at least satisfied on one point in that it attains the truth of the absurd itself." That is neatly turned, but insufficient. The term "truth of the absurd" is after all ambiguous. Camus is not content to formulate analytical propositions about the absurd. Where his thought really begins is in the refusal to adorn the absurd with meaningless statements that pretend to be answers or "solutions." The whole point of his first novel, *The Stranger,* is that innocence begins with the refusal to say what one does not and cannot mean, but that society demands of us that we repeat a whole series of prescribed declarations which we could not possibly mean if we reflected on their full implications.

This is more than a judgment that society tends to be absurd: society will kill the man who refuses to be absurd along with it. Lucidity is punishable by death. One does not merely point to the absurd and snicker. One takes note of the absurd and looks around desperately for another who has seen it too, and one joins him in fighting for survival. For Camus, life does not begin to acquire value in a logical axiom: "I think, therefore I am"; but in a moral commitment: "We rebel against the absurd, therefore we are." The revolt is itself the beginning of authentic existence.

Though Cruickshank has given us a most valuable, richly documented, sympathetic, and careful study which cannot be neglected by any serious student of Camus, he tends to do what the hostile critics of Camus have done, and what Camus himself always protested against. Chiaromonte interviewed Camus in New York in 1948, after *The Plague,* when Camus was being accused of absolute pacifism and of Gandhian non-violence. Camus (said the interviewer) "dislikes very much having his words carried to some ultimate logical conclusion and thrown back at him in the form of a dilemma." Obviously, one might say that if Camus objected to this he ought to have taken more care to prevent its happening. But within the context of Camus' own thought we can see his protest has some justification, because what he objected to above all was the rationalist absolutism in philosophy or in politics which followed its own reasoning down endless corridors of abstraction, without taking the trouble to notice that it was being unfaithful to changing situations and to the truth of the momentary context.

To appreciate Camus one has to be willing to do as he does, to mortify one's appetite for system (if one has such a thing) and to follow him freely along as his mind imagines new symbolic complexes of moral truth to fit new situations. The peculiar quality of Germaine Brée's book about Camus is that she does this better than any other critic.[4]

Germaine Brée's *Camus* was also written during his lifetime but was completely revised after his death to make a comprehensive statement about his work as a whole. It is the best treatment of Camus as an artist, and its peculiarly empathetic quality makes it a Camusian appreciation of the art and thought of the Algerian writer. To begin with, Brée studies the way in which Camus' first overambitious and still unpublished novel, which he wanted to be a kind of *Summa* of all life, contained in its matrix his first three books and foreshadowed other works which Camus was planning at the time of his death.

She is perfectly attuned to Camus' style of poetic meditation. "So basic to Camus is the essay or personal meditation that even his short editorials tend toward it . . . one may distinguish two different uses of the form: those essays in which Camus elucidates certain intellectual attitudes, giving the basic orientation of his thought, and those in which he pursues the type of lyrical meditation so successfully initiated by *Noces*."[5]

[4] Germaine Brée, *Camus,* rev. ed. (New York: Harbinger Books, 1964).

[5] Only very few of these essays have hitherto appeared in English translation. A volume is being prepared for publication by Knopf and will contain some of Camus' best writing. [See *Lyrical and Critical Essays* (New York: Alfred A. Knopf, 1967)— Ed.]

Her appreciation of this meditative insight in Camus saves Germaine Brée from going through the trouble of working out his ideas in logical analyses and then wondering why they do not always make perfect sense. Her approach is that of Camus himself: "The unification of an experience through the conscious medium of style is an aesthetic solution, not a logical or especially systematic one. To misunderstand this in the case of Camus is to open the door to quite futile controversy. The fusion of image and thought . . . is successful but the image often seems to be stronger than the thought, for Camus was not impervious to the pleasures of a rhetoric whereby rhythm and image carried the meaning beyond the control of thought." Here the criticism of Camus' vagaries in philosophizing is rigorously exact: and one who keeps this in mind need never worry too much about his slight inconsistencies. "It is fallacious to seek a logical system of abstract reasoning in Camus' works. Camus himself speaks of certainties, convictions. All his meditations are lyrical and eloquent in nature, though some tend toward demonstration. If a passionate logic does err, it errs gravely, as Camus himself recognized."

Thus in the heat of political argument Camus was sometimes led to adopt an attitude which he himself later deplored. Momentarily, after World War II, he approved the savage reprisals taken against those who had collaborated with the Nazis. But he was able to catch himself in time and to change his attitude completely. Usually, instead of letting political passion run away with his reason, he let passion charge his images with their peculiarly convincing violence, "thus polarizing some of the major intellectual assumptions which feed the often nebulous thought of the average reader." Camus possessed this gift to a greater degree perhaps than anyone in our time: "Camus coins his personal idiom: simple, easily recognizable entities become charged with an intense suggestiveness . . . and play a fixed role in his inner universe. . . . How much more accessible is this idiom to the average reader than the abstract vocabulary thrown into circulation by the followers of Sartre!"

Germaine Brée to some extent shares this Camusian articulateness and lucidity, so that she sums up Camus' thought in aphorisms that have his own authentic ring. "Camus had an almost desperate sense of our immediate need to impose a tolerable pattern upon the violently haphazard development of our civilization. To him our greatest temptation, obsessed by the powerful mechanical forces which we manipulate and do not control, is to abandon our ethical human standards and needs, identifying ourselves thereby with a world which denies us our rightful place."

This is a perfect bull's-eye. Not only does it sum up Camus' approach, but it impressively conveys his lucid awareness of what we are doing.

Such an awareness is not content with words and images. It must put words to work in the political arena where, though man sometimes reaches his most absurd and repellent extreme of cruelty and dishonesty, his destiny has to be forged. Camus was an *artiste engagé* not in the sense that he put his art at the service of a definite party program (which he certainly never did) but in the sense that he realized that his art would never be worth much without deep roots in human responsibility. One cannot be an artist if one is not first of all human, and humanity is not authentic without human concern and real involvement in common and critical problems. The lucidity of the artist and the lucidity of the free man must be one and the same. It is a lucidity in the presence of the absurd, and it refuses to say what it does not mean. Hence the artist, Camus says, "walks a tightrope in an uneasy equilibrium between insignificance and silence." Insignificance, I take it, is here not only the evasion of responsibility but the routine social consciousness and the loquacity of the party hack.

In the fifties, during the Algerian war, Camus' scruples of conscience kept him on this peculiar tightrope, and his refusal to identify himself with either extreme caused him to be condemned as a "pure soul" withdrawn in an ivory tower. A recent book by Emmett Parker[6] studies the political impact of Camus' writing as an "Artist in the Arena." It is particularly interesting and important not only for the information it gives us on Camus' part in the resistance, and his editorship of *Combat* right after the liberation of Paris, but above all because of the unpublished material it brings to light about his political activity in Algiers before World War II. Before going to Paris in 1940 Camus had worked for the left-wing press in Algiers, had written a series of important articles on the famine in Kabylia, and had investigated the frame-up of a minor civil servant, Hodent, by which the rich *colons* were attempting to discredit the socialist relief program of help to the starving Moslems. This book shows us Camus as a man who not only wrote about a certain kind of political action but practiced what he preached.

On the other hand, Camus could never be a mere "activist" in politics or in anything else. He was a philosopher, not an agitator. His peculiar lucidity, his refusal to say or do anything that he did not really mean, often left him in an equivocal position where a definite political choice

[6] Emmett Parker, *Albert Camus: The Artist in the Arena* (Madison, University of Wisconsin Press, 1965).

was hardly possible. He was keenly aware of the impasse that had been reached by so many Western intellectuals. The helplessness and sterility of a certain kind of intellectualism are etched with acid in *The Fall*.

Nowhere has Camus more pitilessly exposed the helplessness of "demonstration." *The Fall* portrays the curious mixture of solipsism, self-hate, moral impotence, pseudolucidity, and despair which afflicts alienated and individualistic man in mass society. Clamence, the Judge and Penitent of *The Fall,* is rational Western bourgeois man whose conscience has died of self-analysis and whose frustrated reasoning has become a kind of moral eczema. This guilty guru has nothing left to communicate to his disciples except a scrupulously ironic self-awareness that can only prey upon itself. His confession cures nothing and finds relief only in passing on the contagion of analysis to another. The "Plague," which in the novel of that name was physical, is here revealed as a moral sickness unto death, an utter despair which can do anything but live with itself and accept life without analysis—a plague of self-examination which turns narcissism into self-hate. Clamence is a member of a civilization which "reads the newspapers and fornicates" and then classifies its meaningless and routine experiences in terms of good or bad news. He cannot help admiring the diligence and patience with which Hitler "cleaned up" Amsterdam, for "when one has no character one *has* to apply a method." He is a false John the Baptist, the voice of one crying (*clamantis* = Clamence) in the smog-dark desert of Europe, with nothing to announce except that futility is irremediable, and no light to offer, in the darkness, but the pale glow of gin. For him, doubt is woven into the very fabric of existence and "to cease to be an object of doubt would be to cease to exist at all." He is like someone who has accidentally fallen out of a space-capsule and cannot be recovered: he just has the good fortune to find someone else in the same predicament, someone he can talk to without ever permitting him to reply.

There is a curious post-Christian eschatology in *The Fall*. If God is dead, the Fall and the Last Judgment turn out to be one and the same thing: they are perfectly continuous. There is no longer a Redemption in between. Man is no longer judged in reference to any law or in consideration of some promised grace. Life is reduced to pure justice: it is itself judgment, and judges itself to extinction. Clamence is perhaps a kind of "saint without God." He is activated not by life-giving grace but by the self-scrutiny of an ironic and hatefully lucid mind that is incapable of love. To be so activated is to be purified and damned at the same time, a kind of extreme Augustinianism in which to be judged is not a final end but only an endless fall in the void, a fall for which there is no ultimate landing. The only possible relationship with another is the relationship of subject to object, of judge to penitent—proving to the other that all have sinned and all are in despair, that all must condemn each other; proving that we are all in the void, that if God is dead all is permitted and all is meaningless. "For judgment, today, we are always ready—as also for fornication." In such a universe, Love does not exist.

Whether Nemesis or Plague, *The Fall* represented a dead end beyond which there was no further progress possible in Camus' artistic development. He had to take another course. The *Notebooks* show that he was planning to go back to the earlier praise of life that filled his first two books: the celebration of the Mediterranean light, the Greek measure, the luminous joy of the Florentine primitives. Camus believed, with Lawrence, that the only vital answers were to be found not in systems but in life. His essays on the Roman ruins in Algeria, on the Balearic Islands, on Italy, remind us of Lawrence's response to Sicily, to the Etruscans, and to Mexican-Indian culture.

Though he remained determinedly non-Christian, Camus nevertheless responded, as all poets have responded, to the mysticism of the early Franciscans: in them too he found what he was looking for, because they were real. Somehow their faith was not an "explanation" or a "justification" but simply part of their response to the beautiful world in which they lived; hence it was something they could honestly mean. Camus had no trouble fitting both Franciscan poverty and Franciscan joy into the theme of the marriage (*Noces*) of man and nature in Mediterranean civilization. For Camus, the wedding was not purely and simply "pagan." It was existential and free from dogmatic preconceptions. It was open to affinities with anything that was alive (Franciscanism included), provided that doctrines and explanations did not get in the way. Hence there are pages, in the early essays, that border on mysticism.

"If I seek to understand myself [he wrote in *L'Eté*], and to taste that delicate savor which delivers up the secret of the world, it is I myself that I find in the depths of the universe. I myself: that is to say this extreme emotion that delivers me from the setting [*décor*]. . . . What counts is to be true. . . . And when am I more true than when I am the world? I am sated before I have even wanted anything. Eternity is there, and I was hoping. . . ."

The hell to which Clamence has condemned himself is the hell of separation from the world, from other people, and from himself, by the vicious habit of seeing everything (himself included) as though from the outside. It is this vice that makes everything absurd. "The Absurd" is not an object. It has no metaphysical existence of its own. It is not there until you put it there. You put it there by standing outside reality and looking in. You make life absurd by holding it at arm's length. Once you step over the boundary line between subject and object, void and the absurd are no more. There is only that fullness which we begin to experience when we realize that "lucidity" is the light itself—the light we look not *at* but *with;* the light that we not only *have* but in some way *are;* the "true light that enlightens every man that comes into the world." What Camus needed still to discover was that this light is pure mercy and pure gift and not the reward for a subtle, ironic, and self-conscious ethical concern.

TERROR AND THE ABSURD:
VIOLENCE AND NONVIOLENCE IN ALBERT CAMUS

Author's Note

The purpose of these notes is to examine sympathetically some features of an ethic which is basically atheistic and characteristically modern. The examination is not apologetic in intent and confines itself to being expository rather than critical. With this approach, it is hoped that we can more clearly see those elements in Camus' thought which, though radically in accord with the Gospel, suggest possibilities too often neglected or overlooked by Christians. The weakness of Camus is by no means in the integrity of his moral feeling but in the obstinate refusal to integrate that feeling into the solidity of a consistent rational structure. This is the price he pays in order to preserve the purity of his intuition of the absurd, the importance of which he doubtless overestimates. The absurd can hardly be a firm basis for logical argumentation. It is rather the occasion of an existential wager. If we can provisionally respect the gambler in Camus we can also profit by his practical conclusions.

Albert Camus, the French-Algerian novelist, playwright and essayist, was perhaps one of the most serious and articulate ethical thinkers of the mid-twentieth century. Active in the French resistance, associated with the existentialist movement in literature, though he repudiated the title of existentialist philosopher, Camus declared himself an atheist and yet spoke as the moral conscience of an embattled generation. In reality he is typical of that secular and nonreligious thought of the so-called "post-Christian era" which seeks to defend values that are essentially those of Western and Christian tradition against the nihilism and violence that have arisen out of the breakdown of Western civilization. Though considered a revolutionary, Camus turns out in the end to be conservative in the sense that he preaches the recovery of a basic and primordial humanism, the seeds of which are implanted in man's own nature and which was favored, he thought, by the ancient cultural climate of pre-Christian Mediterranean culture.

This essay on violence and nonviolence in Camus was written in August 1966 and first published in the February 1969 issue of *Motive* in a somewhat abbreviated form. This version is from the original manuscript.

One of the tragedies of Western civilization, for Camus, is its infidelity to the Greek sense of measure, beauty, harmony, and natural limits. Modern Europe, in totalist frenzy, is the child of unreason and of extremes. "We light up in a drunken sky any suns that we please." And yet the limits remain. Those who sin against reason and measure will be pursued and found out by Nemesis. What is our Nemesis? We are delivered over to the god of power that we adore—our punishment is to have what we want. "God being dead there remain only history and power." And power is incarnate in the secular city. Camus disagrees very strongly with Hegel's declaration: "Only the modern city offers to the spirit a ground in which it can achieve consciousness of itself." For Camus, the alienated life of the dark and northern city is a life in which consciousness gets lost (he has a different idea of the Mediterranean city, as evident in his luminous essay on Algiers in summer). When Camus rejects the modern idea that values are to be created by the dynamism of history and realized in the future and returns instead to the Greek idea of eternal and essential values which are ontological and natural and provide a norm for rational conduct, we see how like an existentialist he really is! Yet he will not turn away from our world—it is the only one we learn to live in! And we cannot live in it by hating one another. Friendship, loyalty to man, lucidity, courage in accepting the absurd but only as the starting point of a new creation—these are the elements with which the creative and "rebel" spirit can reaffirm the wisdom of Greece in the face of police states and the new Inquisition.[1]

We are not concerned here with Camus' so called "neo-paganism" except to say that it accounts for a certain life-affirming and optimistic outlook in all his writing. It is true that his first novel, The Stranger, may have seemed morbid and bizarre in its description of an "absurd" and alienated character—or rather an absurd and alienated culture: our own. Because of this book Camus was labeled a pessimist from the start. No one can question the sense of the tragic and his keen eye for all that tempts us to despair. Yet actually, though he was not patient with the illusory optimism of the naïve or of organization men, his was one of the more hopeful voices of his generation. It has been said of him, and quite rightly, that "his need to establish a passionately loved life on intellectual foundations that seemed valid to him [was] the strongest driving force behind his work and made a writer of him."[2]

[1] Quotations so far from the essay "L'Exil d'Helene" in L'Eté (Pléiade edition), vol. II, pp. 853–57.

[2] Germaine Brée, Camus rev. ed. (New York: Harbinger Books, 1964), p. 27.

As is well known, Camus was deeply concerned with politics but determined to remain a nonpartisan and in some sense to keep out of the more bitter and complex struggle of those who had completely committed themselves to this or that revolutionary cause. This led to his open break with Sartre, who committed himself to a broadly Marxist position and to collaboration with the Communists. Camus chose the more difficult and less consoling course: that of continuing to hope for a third position between the capitalist bourgeois establishment of the West and the rigid totalist establishment of the Communists. He saw that the world had reached a deadlock between these two forces and that there was nothing to be hoped for in merely supporting one of these against the other. No matter which side one chose, both were wrong, both were corrupt, both were sterile. In the end the struggle between them could only end in an intensification of nihilism and terror.

The "two imperialisms"—Eastern and Western—were for Camus a pair of twins "who grow up together and *cannot get along without each other.*"[3] When it was objected that this confrontation was a reality he replied that cancer is also a reality, but that is no reason for not trying to cure it. He rejected the two systems along with their rival ideologies, which "born with the steam engine and naïve scientific optimism a century ago, are today obsolete and incapable in their present form of solving the problems posed in the age of the atom and of relativity."[4]

The only hope he saw was in a difficult and genuinely dialectical struggle to pass beyond either of these positions, and in the last analysis the success of such a struggle depended on the lucidity and integrity of individuals, "Rebels" in the special sense in which, as we shall see, he uses the word. Rebels both against a stagnant and ineffectual bourgeois culture and against a fanatical and arbitrary totalism. In an interview in 1952, Camus said: "We can no longer live without positive values. Bourgeois morality repels us by its hypocrisies and its cruelties. We find equally repugnant the political cynicism that reigns in the revolutionary movement. As for the independent left (Sartre, etc.) it is in fact fascinated by Communist power and entangled in a Marxism of which it is ashamed."[5]

At this point we may remark that though Camus remained resolutely un-Christian and indeed never concealed his scorn for the religious façade

[3] An interview, December 1948, in Camus, *Essais* (Pléiade edition), vol. II, pp. 1587–88.

[4] Quoted in Brée, *op. cit.* p. 57.

[5] "Réponse à E. d'Astier," *Actuelles, I,* (Pléiade edition), vol. II, p. 358.

and sham of pseudo-Christianity, he retained a deep respect for authentic Catholicism. Though his own philosophy demanded of him a "passionate unbelief" he wrote in a letter of August 1943, "I have Catholic friends and for those among them who are truly Catholic I have more than sympathy: I have the feeling we are fighting for the same things. In fact, they are interested in the same things I am. In their eyes, the solution is evident, in mine it is not . . ."[6]

Elsewhere he spoke of having deep respect for the person of Christ and of not believing in the Resurrection—a standard "good pagan" posture. However, though he clung with total loyalty to the ideals and values of Greece, and though he tended to blame Christianity in part for the loss of those ideals, he still respected true Christian values. Were they the specifically *Hellenic* elements in Christianity? At any rate we remember he wrote a philosophical thesis at the University of Algiers on "Plotinus and St. Augustine."

In his most difficult book, *The Rebel* (*L'Homme révolté*), Camus examines the great problem and scandal of modern revolutions which, starting out with the affirmation of absolute liberty, have speedily consummated their efforts in absolute tyranny, and having pleaded for a more abundant life, have ended in hecatombs of political victims. Though himself an atheist (perhaps more accurately, an agnostic) Camus views with concern the fact that revolutions which began with the "death of God" and put man in the place of God were unable to work out a morality worthy of man. Having rejected the Kingdom of God and the realm of grace, having put the realm of justice in its place, the revolution proceeded from justice to the reign of terror, demanding the complete suspension of all liberty in view of a perfect consummation postponed to the future. Having rejected God it proceeded to reject man in the concrete, in favor of man in the abstract. In the name of this abstraction every violence, every cruelty, every inhumanity became permissible and even logically necessary. Though in this book Camus is speaking for the Rebel, he is speaking against "the revolution" in its historic forms. The Rebel is, in fact, in rebellion not only against a static and conservative establishment but also against a rigid and totalist revolution that has crystallized into a police state and maintains itself in existence by violence.

The key idea of *The Rebel* is that revolution nullifies itself when it resorts to massive killing. The need for the revolution to kill in

[6] *Essais*, p. 1596.

order to maintain itself in power means that it no longer has the right to be in power. When the love of life that is at the root of revolution turns into a need for the death of hundreds and thousands of other men, then the "love of life" becomes a contradiction and a denial of itself, and revolution turns into absurdity and nihilism. To reject the Kingdom of God and of grace is to build a society on the abstract concept of "justice," and this leads inexorably to the concentration camp. "Absolute liberty becomes a prison of absolute duties"—including the duty to exterminate thousands of one's fellow men in the name not of a happy and life-affirming present but of a hypothetical happiness in the future. The "death of God" means in the end an imperialism of the spirit that seeks world hegemony and total control at the price of unlimited murder and terror. Note that this same logic operates not only in the death camps of a Hitler, the labor camps of the Soviets or Red Chinese, but also where the power of unlimited destruction is concentrated in nuclear and other weapons. It is the same logic of power and terror that grows out of a radical godlessness which leaves man to build his world alone. This is what happens to man when "refusing God, he chooses history" and seeks (with Hegel, Nietzsche, and Marx) the eschatological unity of the human race "deified" by its own exercise of absolute political power. Once God is dead, the vacuum caused by His "death" sucks into itself this huge drive toward total human political power. To accept the death of God in some sense means to accept passively the awful force of this drag and suction into the emptiness created by His absence.

Camus grants all this without ceasing to hold his atheist position. Why? In common with those who more truly merit the name of existentialists, he considers that to accept the idea of God as the explanation and justification of an otherwise absurd life is a kind of "cheating."

The man who resorts to God to give sense to an otherwise senseless life is, according to Camus, evading the austere and stoical duty of facing up to "the absurd" and deciding to live with it. It has been said that Camus makes Pascal's wager—but in reverse. Instead of gambling on the possibility of God, he gambles on his impossibility and accepts the resulting absurdity of the universe with all its consequences—violence, ruthlessness, terror. For Camus as for Sartre, theological faith is a temptation. It is "bad faith" by definition. But what is faith anyway? Camus as a typical modern starts with the assumption that the world is absurd and that God then becomes necessary for some minds to explain the absurdity. God is regarded somehow as a *need* of man's mind and heart: and indeed a certain kind of apologetic in the past has been all too ready to advance this distorted and inadequate view of God. Here God is seen simply as the projection of man's need for clarity, for rationality. The act of faith then becomes a determination to convince oneself that no matter how absurd things may *look,* they are in fact quite reasonable because God must make them reasonable. One believes because one refuses to despair of an absolute and infallible reason.

But this assumes that God is merely called in to our lives as a kind of logical *Deus ex machina* and that he is little more than a convenient hypothesis. Is this what is really meant by God in Christianity?

Camus, with Ivan Karamazov, examines the classic problem of evil in the world and rejects a hypothesis of a God whose rule may have to be justified at the price of the suffering of one innocent child. Camus, like Ivan Karamazov, says that if this is the case he will turn in his ticket to heaven. But then, resolutely facing a world that has become frankly absurd, he has to watch dry-eyed the suffering not of one innocent child but of millions of innocents: a suffering that is demanded by the logic of a world without God. Camus may realize the contradiction implied in this position: he shrugs it off. He does not bother to argue. He merely assumes that one cannot save the millions by bringing God back to life.

In spite of all this, one of the root problems of *The Rebel* (hence one of the root problems of our world in revolutionary crisis) is the problem of God. This problem as stated by Camus remains insoluble, and Camus simply bypasses it, not on the basis of any reasoning in metaphysics or theodicy, but simply because the historical forms of Christianity—and other religions—seem to him to demand of man a futile and degrading resignation that solves nothing and merely leaves him at the mercy of blind social forces that push him this way and that.

Yet Camus recognizes that the problem of God arises in another inexorable form as the problem of murder. If the most critical problem of our time is the problem of (mass) murder and if human life has been reduced to an entity without value, this is because "God is dead." Camus admits it, without feeling any need for God to be other than dead—bringing him back to life may no longer mean a recovery of the sense of man as a value. Those who claim to represent God have often done much to cheapen man. If conventional and institutional religious establishments have taught man to hold human life cheap, if they have trivialized death, exalted nationalist or political abstractions, and given a blanket permission to kill without practical limit in the name of patriotism or of revolution, then they have contributed their share to the "death of God" in the experience of twentieth-century man. When the problem of God necessarily reappears as the problem of the sacredness of life and prohibition of limitless killing, then Camus must grapple with it. The most tragic thing, the root of crime, is the *silence* and complicity which accept the supposed rightness and necessity for man-killing, whether in war or in prison camps.

"We live in terror because persuasion is no longer possible; because man has been wholly submerged in history, because he can no longer tap that part of his nature, as real as the historical part, which he recaptures in contemplating the beauty of nature and of human faces; because we live in a world of abstractions, of bureaus and machines, of absolute ideas and crude messianism. We suffocate among people who think they are absolutely right, whether in their machines or in their ideas. And for all who can live only in an atmosphere of human dialogue and sociability, this silence is the end of the world."[7]

The face of Camus' "Rebel" now begins to appear in its true character. He is a man who protests, but protests not against abstract injustice, nor in the name of a theoretical program. He protests in the name of man, individual and concrete man of flesh and blood, against the war-making arrogance of total power, against the abstractions on which power bases its claim to an absolute right to kill. The Rebel moreover refuses to be silent and insists on an open dialogue which will help others like himself to arrive at a lucid and common decision to oppose absurdity and death and to affirm man against all abstractions.

In a certain sense, the starting point of Camus' ethic of revolt is a protest against passive resignation. In 1937, visiting the famous Campo Santo of Pisa, he was revolted by the pious and conventional sentiments of the epitaphs and mortuary art he saw all around him. For him they were in fact a mockery of the awful seriousness and mystery of man's contingency, an evasion of the inscrutable reality of death. So too, the "black" first chapter of *The Stranger* in all its apparent indifference and heartlessness is a protest against the utter inadequacy of formal social rituals surrounding death. All social forms tend, in Camus' eyes, to cheat and play obscene tricks with the mystery of death.

The Campo Santo of Pisa and the tombs in the cloister of the Annunziata were after all noble compared to those in the city cemetery of Algiers. Of this he wrote: "Everything that touches on death is here made ridiculous or hateful. This people living without religion and without idols dies alone after living in a mob. I know no more hideous place

[7] "Neither Victims nor Executioners," in *The Pacifist Conscience*, ed. Peter Mayer (New York: Holt, 1966), p. 424.

than the cemetery of Bru Boulevard, facing one of the finest landscapes in the world . . ." He goes on to speak of the revolting vulgarity of tombs on which angels fly in stucco airplanes, of hearts inscribed with words like "Our memory will never abandon you"—or clusters of stucco flowers accompanied by the declaration: "Your tomb will never be without flowers." Here it is not religion that he derides but the awful religionless and godless secularity that has crept in behind a collapsing religious façade. What is the façade? Resignation. And Camus, speaking now as a pure "Rebel," declines to be resigned. Even in Italy, where there was still some religious substance in the renaissance monuments to honor the dead, he said: "None of this convinces me. All of them . . . had become resigned, doubtless because they accepted their other duties. I shall not grow resigned. With all my silence I shall protest to the very end. There is no reason to say: 'It had to be.' It is my revolt which is right, and it must follow this joy which is like a pilgrim on earth, follow it step by step."[8]

The Rebel of Camus is therefore first of all the man who refuses to accept, with passive and unreasoning resignation, a diminution or falsification of authentic and living possibilities. The Rebel is one who is not resigned to letting his life be destroyed or mutilated in the name of something else, whether it be business, or politics, or money, or revolution—or religion. He is, in a word, the man who refuses alienation. It is interesting to notice that a few pages later in the same notebook Camus speaks with approval of the early Franciscans. He describes their religious poverty as a liberating force. It is clear that in Camus' eyes, Franciscan poverty was an enrichment of life and not a mutilation. Meditating in a cloister in Fiesole he recognizes in himself a deep affinity with the early Franciscans, for they too are Rebels in his sense of the word:

Sitting on the ground I think of the Franciscans whose cells I have just visited and whose sources of inspiration I can now see. I feel clearly that if they are right then it is in the same way that I am. This splendor of the world (he alludes to the view from the monastery) seems to justify these men. I put all my pride in a belief that it also justifies me and all the men of my race who know that there is an extreme point at which poverty always rejoins the luxury and richness of the world. . . . Being naked always has associations of physical liberty, of harmony between the hand and the flowers it touches, of loving understanding between the earth and men who have been freed from human things. Ah, I should become a convert to this if it were not already my religion.[9]

[8] Albert Camus, *Notebooks 1935–1942* (New York: Alfred A Knopf, 1963), p. 64.
[9] *Ibid.*, p. 57.

If we consider all the implications of this passage we will be tempted to think that Camus has ended by standing Franciscanism on its head. Camus' own neopagan and naïve atheism rests on a refusal to trust anything that is not directly accessible to the senses. He knows and loves the world as he sees it, directly in front of his nose: it is for him a unique and inexhaustible value, though it also confronts him with an absurd and enigmatic silence. For there remains death, and Camus will not play around with any "explanation" that evades or minimizes the seemingly utter finality of death. His refusal is not metaphysical or logical but aesthetic. Life and death are realities directly accessible to experience. The immediacy with which they sometimes confront us may be so stark as to be absurd. No matter. The absurd too is real. But for Camus the religious and metaphysical arguments for another life, for Providence, and so on are not accessible. They are not a matter of experience or of immediate grasp. They are therefore, he thinks, arbitrary fabrications.

On the other hand, his approval of the Franciscans in the passage quoted is based on the fact that he thinks they see things his way. They have gambled as he has: not on reasonings and ideas but on immediate facts: the burnt hills of Tuscany, the vineyards, the poverty of the people, the poverty of Franciscan life. All these are immediately experienced. They are directly present in the Franciscan consciousness, they are not mere objects of rationalization.

There is something to this intuition. The vision of a St. Francis is not the vision of an abstract and purely transcendent God dwelling in eternity, but the immediate, overwhelming, direct, tangible confrontation of "God who is" simply in the "is-ness" of every day reality. The belief of a Franciscan in eternal life does not determine how he lives—it flows from his life and is part and parcel of that life. If Camus had been able to follow this through he would have realized that the abstract God he could not believe in was not, and never had been, the living God of authentic Christianity.

Camus contrasts the peace and joy of life-affirming love with the frenzy born of abstractions which followed the French Revolution. Reason, disincarnated by godless revolution, "floated off like a balloon into the empty sky of the great principles," and therefore it needed the support of force: "To adore theorems for any length of time, faith is not enough: one also needs a police."[10]

The root of Camus' ethic is then not a fanatically reasoned nihilism but on the contrary an affirmation of life which, we have seen, he spon-

[10] Albert Camus, *L'Homme révolté* (Pléiade edition), pp. 154, 155.

taneously correlates with Franciscan poverty. In fact, the root of his ethic is love. In his notebooks we find this:

> If someone here told me to write a book on morality, it would have a hundred pages and ninety-nine would be blank. On the last page I should write "I recognize only one duty, and that is to love." And as far as everything else is concerned I say *no*.[11]

We have so far seen that Camus' Rebel refuses the resignation of a life submissive to cynical travesty in a decadent postreligious culture, or a life obedient to the dictates of totalist police in a godless revolutionary state, and that the paradigm of the Rebel is strangely enough the poverty-loving, therefore liberated, Franciscan. Will he pursue his idea further? If the godless revolution denies itself and cancels itself out in the blood of human victims, will Camus turn to a nonviolent revolution in the name of God and of love? No, for since to him God is only an inadmissible logical hypothesis, he has to engage in an intricate dialectic between godless violence and religious nonviolence in order to reach a different synthesis.

It is interesting to see how he arrives at this synthesis. His thought in this matter has certain positive implications even for the Christianity that he rejects. But while we admit that his conclusions are somewhat different from those of an ideally Christian nonviolence, they are at the same time a more strict and rigorous rejection of force than we find in the traditional Christian "just war" theory. In practice, we can say that Camus while admitting that violence may be necessary, speaks and writes as a pacifist not only in the face of global war but also in the face of world revolution. He contends that the power struggle of our time, whether on the side of capitalism or on that of communism, is essentially nihilistic and therefore starts from the implicit or explicit proposition that God is dead in order to justify in practice (if not in theory) torture, genocide, the police state, the death camps, and the obliteration of nations by nuclear war. All this in the name of a humanism postponed to an indefinite future when full justice will have been carried out on the adversary.

At this point, we can let Camus explain himself succinctly in statements or notes from the *Carnets* during the period after World War II when he finally broke with Sartre and Merleau Ponty on this issue of humanism and terror.

---

[11] *Notebooks 1935–1942*, p. 54.

In 1946 Camus said: *"There is only one problem today, which is that of murder. All our disputes are vain. One thing alone matters: peace."*[12]

This problem faces everybody, and not just politicians, business men, military strategists, manufacturers of armaments, or revolutionists. All men confront the problem of co-operation in murder, perhaps even in genocide. "We are in a world in which one must choose between being a victim or an executioner."[13]

To face such a world and such a choice means to confront the absurd. Either we know it or we do not. If we accept the absurd choice as perfectly reasonable or at least as an inevitable necessity, we resign our human dignity and freedom, we surrender to unreason and unfreedom in the name of abstractions which ignore our human measure and inexorably lead to our own destruction. There is only one answer: to become a Rebel—*un homme révolté.* The Rebel is distinguished on the one hand from the conformist who accepts a conservative establishment and its injustices and on the other from the revolutionary who in the name of an ideology and an abstract humanism consents to the alienation and destruction of his fellow man, and indeed of his own human honor and integrity, for the sake of a future utopia. This precise sense of the Rebel must be remembered. The Rebel is one who squarely faces the absurdity and risk of a choice that may in fact be meaningless and inefficacious because it is in fact nullified and set aside by the ruthless dynamism of the power struggle that grinds on inexorably toward global suicide or the establishment of a nihilist and totalist police state. The Rebel refuses to be an executioner, and if he has to be a victim he will at least know why. But as soon as he takes up this position of refusal, autonomy, and self-determination in the presence of the absurd, as soon as he resolves to confront the absurd and work within the limits that it necessarily imposes, he finds himself in solidarity with other Rebels who have made the same commitment. Camus says that revolt gives the Rebel an identity and a viewpoint analogous to the Cartesian self-awareness, "I think therefore I am," which is the starting point of modern epistemology. The Rebel finds his identity in the Revolt which places him side by side with other Rebels in their common lucidity: "I revolt, therefore *we are.*" The Rebel is then not simply the disgruntled individual—certainly not the alienated and seemingly apathetic individualist like Mersault, the hero of *The Stranger,* that classic of the absurd. The true Rebels portrayed by Camus are Rieux and Tarrou

[12] *Essais,* p. 1569.
[13] *Ibid.,* p. 1567.

in *The Plague,* men who decide in the face of the tragic absurdity of the plague to affirm life and human solidarity as best they can, for the best motives they can muster.

Solidarity in revolt is the only thing that balances and nullifies the absurd. From this solidarity and from the compassion it implies emerge the reasons by which one can decide for or against violence.

> The aim of revolt is the pacification of men. Any revolt reaches the ultimate and reverberates in the assertion of human limits—and of a community of all men, whoever they are, within those limits. Humility and genius.[14]

The nature of revolt, as opposed to the rigid authoritarianism of a totalist revolution directed from above by "the Party," is that it springs from the warmth and authenticity of human solidarity and compassion. Revolt is based on love, revolution on a political abstraction. Revolt is therefore real, and its reality is defined by risk, limitation, uncertainty, vulnerability. It has to be constantly created anew by a renewal of fervor, intelligence, and love. Revolution is abstract, and it seeks to guarantee itself indefinitely by the exercise of power, therefore by murder, and it is by this resort to force in the name of justice directed from above that it cancels itself out and makes renewal impossible. Revolt is the only thing that can give to revolution the renewal and lucidity it needs. Hence one can see that Camus was *persona non grata* with the Communists since he demanded revolt against Communism itself as well as against capitalism. Revolt strikes at every form of power that relies on blood.

> My effort: to show that the logic of revolt rejects blood and selfish motives. And that *a* dialogue carried to the absurd gives a chance of purity. Through compassion? (suffer together)[15]

The logic of revolt demands dialogue, openness, speech. Therefore revolt protests against the conspiracy of silence which, everywhere, both under totalism and under capitalism, seals men's lips so that they do not protest against organized murder but approve it.

> What balances the absurd is the community of men fighting against it. And if we choose to serve that community we choose to serve the dialogue carried to the absurd against any policy of falsehood or of silence. That's the way one is free with others. . . .[16]

[14] *Notebooks 1942–1951* (New York: Alfred A. Knopf, 1965), p. 144.
[15] *Ibid.,* p. 125.
[16] *Ibid.,* p. 126.

The universal order cannot be built from above, in other words through an idea; but rather from below, in other words through the common basis which. . . . .[17]

The phrase is unfinished, but we can easily reconstruct the rest of Camus' idea from other passages in the notebooks: when men resolve to speak out, they define for one another the absurd. When they find themselves in the presence of the absurd and recognize the need for revolt against it, in affirmation of life against death, they undertake a struggle against absurdity, in solidarity with one another. In this struggle their own lives acquire the meaning and the direction which alone overcome the absurd. This is Love.

Thus starting from the absurd it is not possible to live revolt without reaching at some point or other an experience of love that is still undefined.[18]

In *The Myth of Sisyphus,* man who has come to terms with the absurd does not yield to the temptation of suicide—a form of "resignation" or demission. On the contrary, man makes something out of the absurd by not agreeing to it. "The absurd has meaning only insofar as it is not agreed to."[19]

But this "not agreeing" is in fact a constant and very exacting discipline. Faith, for one thing, is rigorously excluded. One must not forget the absurd, or dismiss it, or explain it away, or give it a good reason. One must spend the rest of his life rubbing his nose in it.

Once he has reached the absurd and tries to live *accordingly,* a man always perceives that consciousness is the hardest thing in the world to maintain. Circumstances are almost always against it. He must live his lucidity in a world where dispersion is the rule.[20]

This would be an intolerable exercise of solipsism if Camus went no further. Fortunately he does. The confrontation with the absurd, and the ability to be undistractedly, unflinchingly aware of it, is not final. It is purely provisional, it is only a beginning. It must under no conditions become a dead end. The experience of the absurd is not suggested as an absolute value in itself (or if you prefer an absolute nonvalue). It is a clearing of the ground for something else. This something else is not

[17] *Ibid.,* p. 147.
[18] *Ibid.,* p. 138.
[19] *The Myth of Sisyphus* (New York: Vintage Books, 1959), p. 24.
[20] *Notebooks 1942–1951,* p. 10.

mere individual lucidity and purity of heart, but solidarity in creative revolt—ultimately it is solidarity in love.

The refusal to agree to the absurd and to accept "the unreasonable silence of the world" opens up a new possibility: the possibility of a difficult and dialectical choice between a passive and religious resignation (the yogi) and active revolutionary commitment (the commissar)—a choice which Camus also describes as being "between God and history." The Rebel chooses neither the absolute and transcendent God who "explains everything" and gets rid of the absurd, nor a historical dynamic which promises to wipe out all absurdity in the future, while in the present it wipes out the people who are responsible for all the absurdity. In his refusal of either of these consolations, the absurd man maintains the possibility of a vocation to revolt. On the basis of a lucid indifference which "lives without appeal" (to systematic explanations which justify one's experiences and give them an appearance of quality) revolt acts without concern for quality. This, as Camus puts it, sounds a bit hardboiled, but we can perhaps understand it by correlating it with the Oriental idea of concentrating on the act itself and not on its results or on the merit accruing from it.

More exactly, the moral value of an act, for Camus, depends not so much on the object and intuition, the will behind the act, as on the lucidity of the act. To appeal to some other standard which lucidity does not verify, to call upon a quality which lucidity cannot vouch for, is to abandon and muddle lucidity itself. The will to destroy one's enemies automatically involves sins against lucidity since it seeks abstract and impossible justifications for murder—reasons why, for the time being, death is more important than life. These illusory reasons can, it is thought, be maintained if one's acts are carried out with a certain quality of ruthlessness, or heroism, or patriotism, or self-sacrifice and so on. Camus has no patience with any of this language, though the facts of heroism and self-sacrifice are not absent from his ethic. They are simply not preached, because for him preaching is irrelevant. At the same time the purely "quantitative ethic" suggested as a consequence of the absurd in *The Myth of Sisyphus* must not be taken too seriously. It obviously was repudiated by Camus himself when he joined the French resistance, and is repudiated in his ideas on murder and in the stoic generosity of the heroes in *The Plague*.

Relation of the absurd to revolt. If the final decision is to reject suicide in order to maintain the confrontation, this amounts implicitly to admitting life as the only factual value, the one that allows the confrontation, "the value without which nothing." Whence it is clear that to obey that absolute value, whoever rejects suicide likewise rejects murder, or the justification of murder. Ours is the era which having carried nihilism to its extreme conclusions has accepted suicide. This can be verified in the ease with which we accept murder or the justification of murder. The man who kills himself alone still maintains one value, which is the life of others. . . . But the men of Terror have carried the values of suicide to their extreme consequence, which is legitimate murder, in other words collective suicide. Illustration: the Nazi apocalypse in 1945.[21]

In other words, it is the men of terror who have fully implemented a "quantitative ethic." In *The Myth of Sisyphus,* the hero of the absurd by not agreeing to the absurd, yet confronting it in lucidity and without any spurious hopes, gives it meaning and affirms the value which enables him to give it meaning. Revolt repeats the process collectively and in solidarity. Revolt is the refusal to agree with an absurd and self-destroying social system. Revolt affirms the life which that system negates and destroys in the name of an abstraction. Revolt is also, *a fortiori,* the negation of this idolized abstraction.

The great danger to lucidity and to revolt is the silent acquiescence in absurdity: the homage of unquestioning acceptance which the majority of men offer to the idol. Hence the obligation to speak.

Mankind's dialogue has just come to an end. And naturally a man with whom one cannot reason is a man to be feared. The result is that—besides those who have not spoken out because they thought it useless—a vast conspiracy of silence has spread all about us, a conspiracy accepted by those who are frightened and who rationalize their fears in order to hide them from themselves, a conspiracy fostered by those whose interest it is to do so . . .[22]

The obligation is not so much to formulate a direct accusation of injustice and level it against this or that economic system or power structure. The purpose of speech in the presence of the absurd political situation is to point to the fact that power is in fact a denial of life and an affirmation of death insofar as it depends on the killing of so many thousands or millions of human beings and implements policies which sooner or later will demand and exact these deaths. Note that there are innumerable ways of inflicting death on man. A rich nation can in effect "kill" thousands of people in a poorer nation without even firing a shot or dropping a bomb, simply by keeping the poorer nation in a state of dependence

[21] *Ibid.,* p. 149.
[22] "Neither Victims nor Executioners," in *The Pacifist Conscience,* p. 424.

in which the reasonable development of its resources is blocked (in favor of the exploitation which is profitable to the rich nation) and consequently people starve.

> [We confront a world] where murder is legitimate, and where human life is considered trifling. This is the great political question of our times, and before dealing with other issues one must take a position on it. Before anything can be done, two questions must be put: "Do you or do you not, directly or indirectly, want to be killed or assaulted? Do you or do you not, directly or indirectly, want to kill or assault?" All who say No to both these questions are automatically committed to a series of consequences which must modify their way of posing the problem.[23]

It is obvious that neither side in the power struggle really claims to want death or killing. But Camus believes that the power struggle is essentially a dilemma in which both sides must in the end, in spite of all their professed humanistic and peaceful aims, be committed to unlimited killing because of their implicit or explicit justification of mass murder, a justification which is of the very essence of their absurdity. Camus cites with approval Simone Weil's remark that official history is a matter of believing the self-justifications of murderers. Simone Weil was for him an example of "authentic Christianity" (she refused to join the Church) and, in fact, of a genuine Rebel in her integrity, her solitude, and her capacity for renunciation.

But can one escape implication in a murderous power struggle? Is there another choice? What about the choice of religious nonviolence?

Since in fact Camus did at times speak like a pacifist and came so close to the nonviolent position, his adversaries thought that to refute Camus it was enough to refute nonviolence. To one of these critics (a Marxist) Camus replied in 1948:

> I have never argued for non-violence . . . I do not believe that we ought to answer blows with blessings. I believe that violence is inevitable, and the years of the [Nazi] occupation have convinced me of it . . . I do not say that one must suppress all violence, which would be desirable but, in fact, utopian. I only say that we must refuse all legitimation of violence, whether this legitimation comes from an absolute *raison d'état* or from a totalitarian philosophy. *Violence is at the same time unavoidable and unjustifiable.*[24]

Hence violence must always be confined to the strictest possible limits.

---

[23] *Ibid.*, p. 425.
[24] "Réponse à E. d'Astier," p. 355.

In an age of nuclear war, to canonize violence and force is an intolerable and criminal absurdity, and hence Camus is, in practice, a "nuclear pacifist." In the face of the disastrous consequences of atomic war, he has no other choice but "the fight against war and the very long effort to establish a true international democracy."[25]

If a "scientific" historicism starts from the denial of God and proceeds to build a world unity without God, the consequence will be nihilism, totalism, the deification of force and the police state. It is the world of justice and history instead of the world of God and grace. In effect, Camus lumps capitalism and Communism together under this heading, since in fact the religious motives which are so conveniently advertised by the capitalist West do not convince him as being very serious. On the other hand, what of an authentic Christian nonviolence? Camus admits that such a philosophy is possible and reasonable. In fact: "In today's world a philosophy of eternity alone can justify nonviolence."[26] He agrees here with Gandhi, for whom *ahimsa* was not really possible without faith in God. Unfortunately, to solve the problem of killing by a resort to God is, for Camus, no solution. It merely raises once again the whole question of the metaphysic of evil, and Camus stands by the side of Ivan Karamazov. If the suffering of one child . . . For this reason the lucid Rebel cannot choose a nonviolence based on faith in God because he cannot choose God. To choose God is, for Camus, to choose an *explanation* and hence to evade the bitter honesty of a full confrontation with the absurd without hope and "without appeal" to any force other than that of human honesty and courage within the confines of human limitation.

Camus does not argue against God. The absurd is not a denial of God. Like the radical Protestant "death of God" theologians who often appeal to him, Camus simply discards the whole notion of God as irrelevant because it is *inaccessible* to the mind and experience of so many modern people. He does not go so far as to make a basic act of faith that God *cannot* be accessible to any modern believer as some of the radical theologians seem to. He simply says: "If today one could neither live nor act outside of God, a great number of Westerners would perhaps be condemned to sterility."[27]

In Camus' eyes religious nonviolence is doomed to failure because it

[25] *Ibid.*, p. 359.
[26] *L'Homme révolté*, p. 354
[27] *Essais*, p. 1426.

is in fact unfaithful to the actual condition of (unbelieving) man. It is based on presuppositions which most men simply no longer find acceptable or even conceivable. Thus in fact, in his eyes, the choice of religious nonviolence based on an appeal to God and to eternity would end only in political quietism, in silence, in resignation, in acceptance of injustice, in final submission to one or other side in the worldly power struggle.

At the same time, religious nonviolence is to him suspect because it savors of the futile desire of the bourgeois to convince himself of his perfect innocence. Christianity itself is suspect to Camus, as it is to many moderns since Marx, for this reason. A religious nonviolence produces in its devotee a pure and virtuous conscience and therefore a sense of subjective righteousness which may blind him to the fact that he is still deeply involved in collective guilt and violence. We must be very careful not to impute this desire of moral unassailability to Camus' Rebel. If the Rebel rejects a purely religious nonviolence it is because he insists on not regarding himself as any more innocent and "pure" than anyone else. True revolt is not clothed in virtuous justification: it has nothing to be proud of but its own naked lucidity and anguish in the presence of the absurd—and its love of man who is caught in absurdity. Revolt is not reducible to a mere cult of integrity and sincerity without efficacy. This is another complaint against religious nonviolence. It is, Camus suggests, inclined to accept defeat virtuously rather than to engage in efficacious combat. For him, nonviolence in the pure state is demission, resignation or simply illusion. The true Rebel, according to Camus, is allowed to choose neither terror and murder on one hand nor resignation, nonviolence and silence on the other. The question arises why Camus so easily identifies nonviolence with silence, submission, and passivity when authentic nonviolent resistance is *active* and should be highly articulate, since, if it is understood in the Gandhian sense, it demands much more lucidity and courage than the use of force does.

In any case, Camus refuses to accept absolute nonviolence. His Rebel may take up arms, and may indeed be compelled by duty to do so, but with one most important reservation:

> Authentic action in revolt will consent to arm itself only for institutions which limit violence, not for those that give it the force of law.[28]

This is all very fine—but what war-making institution does not in practice claim to be limiting violence and fighting for peace? The escalation

[28] *L'Homme révolté*, p. 360.

of the Vietnam war by the Pentagon is all, allegedly, in order to *limit* violence!

Camus does, however, come in practice very close to the nonviolent position. While admitting that violence and killing may in certain circumstances be necessary he lays down one ideal condition which is supposed to close the door to all unnecessary violence: he who kills must do so only on the understanding that he is willing to pay for the adversaries' life with his own. In this, Camus points with approval to the revolutionaries of the 1905 uprising in Russia.[29]

In this example Camus is suggesting a paradigm that is perhaps aesthetically satisfying but has no real application in politics. It may remain as a symbolic and edifying instance, and it may help us to take a more reserved view of the efficacy and legitimacy of force. The rebels of 1905 are there, he says, to restore an authentic perspective to the twentieth-century revolution.[30] The real meaning of Camus' position is to be sought elsewhere. He was not a man of precise and doctrinaire solutions. It was for this reason that he rejected a mystique of nonviolence although he was in practice aware of the possibly fatal consequences of escalating violence. He did not want to dictate absolute formulas in the realm of political and historical action, where situations and circumstances are always new. Therefore he left the way open for the use of force, in a situation where there might be no other way of liberating oneself from intolerable oppression. He did not declare *a priori* that nonviolence was necessarily more efficacious in the long run than force, when he doubted that most people would be capable of understanding and practicing nonviolence in its highest religious sense. To preach an abstract and ideal nonviolence and deliver this doctrine into the hands of people who do not understand it, leaving them to improvise and experiment with it, would simply play into the hands of the violent. Perhaps, too, he was thinking of the problem that arises when the illuminated moralist, speaking from the Olympian heights of privilege, presumes to make choices for others whose situation is far from privileged. Camus then, at the risk of seeming inconclusive, does not prescribe a *method* or a *tactic*. He is concerned only with one thing: the integrity and the lucidity of revolt, or in other words the moral climate of insight, loyalty, and courage without which no tactic can be humanly fruitful or creative.

In conclusion, then, the Camusian Rebel "is not only [in rebellion] as

[29] *L'Homme révolté*, p. 207ff.
[30] "Defense de l'homme révolté," *Essais*, p. 1707.

slave against master, but *he is man against the world of master and slave*."[31] The logic of Revolt is not that of destruction but of creation.[32] It is basically "a protest against death."[33] The Rebel cannot take refuge in self-righteousness: he recognizes in himself the same universal tendencies toward murder and despair. "The value that keeps him on his feet is never given him once for all, he must constantly maintain it in existence.[34] He cannot take refuge, either, in the self-assurance provided by a religious or political system that guarantees infallible knowledge. He must admit a "calculated ignorance" and never affirm more than he actually knows. He must be faithful to "human limits" and the "human measure," and he must be ready to risk even inevitable violence, because to pretend exemption from this would seem to be a denial of the human condition and an attempted evasion from practical reality.

Yet the basic choice remains this: *the refusal to be a murderer or the accomplice of murderers,* and this demands above all the resolute refusal to accept any system which rests directly and essentially on the justification of killing, especially mass killing, whether by war or by more subtle forms of destructive domination.

> Over the expanse of five continents throughout the coming years an endless struggle is going to be pursued between violence and friendly persuasion, a struggle in which, granted, the former has a thousand times the chances of success than that of the latter. But I have always held that, if he who bases his hopes on human nature is a fool, he who gives up in the face of circumstances is a coward. And henceforth the only honorable course will be to take everything on a formidable gamble: that words are more powerful than munitions.[35]

[31] *Ibid.,* p. 351.
[32] *Ibid.,* p. 352.
[33] *Ibid.,* p. 352.
[34] *Ibid.,* p. 353.
[35] "Neither Victims nor Executioners," p. 438.

PROPHETIC AMBIGUITIES: MILTON AND CAMUS

Poets and poetic thinkers—men who construct myths in which they embody their own struggle to cope with the fundamental questions of life—are generally "prophetic" in the sense that they anticipate in their solitude the struggles and the general consciousness of later generations. Rereading Milton in the 1960s one cannot help realizing at once how close he is to us and how remote from us. He is remote, if you like, in his classic stamina—his capacity to develop his ideas in the longest and most noble periods. He is remote from us in his moral assumptions and his world view. Yet the ideas and experiences he develops are often (not always) strikingly contemporary. For instance his passionate concern with free speech in *Areopagitica*—an anti-Catholic tract if ever there was one—has borne fruit, through the effort of American Catholic bishops and theologians, in the Second Vatican Council's declaration on religious liberty. His concern with the dignity and liberty of the human person has now become everybody's cliché (though not everybody's dignity or liberty). As for *Paradise Lost*, without slandering the nobility of this great poem, we have to admit that there are times when it is structured like a movie or even like a comic strip. Milton sometimes has a very modern imagination. There are scenes in which Satan is Batman. More seriously, there are unquestionable affinities between Milton's Satan and the Superman not of the comics but of Nietzsche.

Without falling into the romantic exaggerations of those "satanist" critics of Milton who see Satan as the true hero of *Paradise Lost*, we are forced to admit that Milton was, if not all, at least partly on Satan's side. The Satan of *Paradise Lost* is the embodiment of heroic energy, of obstinately futile resistance, a "freedom fighter," a loser who cannot be kept down by superior odds. To say this is not to say that Milton approves of Satan, still less consciously sympathizes with him. But the element in Milton which was "modern," that which brought him close to us, was at work in the creation of this dynamic rebel, while that in Milton which was more remote, the classicist, the Biblical thinker, disclaimed the Rebel

This essay, written in October 1966, first appeared heavily edited in the *Saturday Review*, April 15, 1967, under the title, "Can We Survive Nihilism?" We have retained the original version and the original title here.

he had created. We are less disposed to see this because we have become habitually inattentive to the kind of cosmology and theology that Milton took for granted. The Satan of *Paradise Lost* is not for us part of a cosmic whole. He stands out against a background that does not concern us so much—a modern hero against the scenery of a baroque opera.

Milton's Satan can easily be seen as modern man, the activist, the tireless mover and shaker who acts, moves, and shakes because these are his only resources: they make him seem able to tolerate Hell. They constitute for him a kind of freedom, a pretense of dignity. For this reason he is attached to them—in fact he makes idols of them. They are his substitute for religion.

Paradise Lost opens with the fallen angels lying stunned in Hell, where they have just made a crash landing. They do not stay that way for long. There is something curiously American about them. They get up and go. They go from a very hot part of Hell to one that is slightly cooler, and there, in order to make the best of things, build a devilish city and draw up a plan of action, a diabolical program, an energetically satanic way of life. This way of life is an organized and systematic resistance to divine authority. Whatever God has done that is good (and nothing that he has done is not good) is to be methodically fouled-up by cunning or by violence. The city is a secular city, and in many ways rather like New York: perhaps the New York of the twenties and the Roxy Theater rather than the New York of today:

> Anon out of the earth a febrick huge
> Rose like an exhalation, with the sound
> Of dulcet symphonies and voices sweet
> Built like a temple, where pilasters round
> Were set, and Doric pillars overlaid
> With golden architrave; nor did there want
> Cornice or frieze with bossy sculptures grav'n,
> The roof was fretted gold.

Whatever this metropolis may be, the point is that they built it, and built it fast, by a brand-new method. Their work was itself a rebellion against inertia and defeat. Hence it was a kind of victory. And a special kind of victory at that, because it was gained entirely by their own ingenuity and their own resources. The unequaled verve of the first books of *Paradise Lost* enables us to surmise that Milton wrote these pages with special satisfaction, even though he was both emotionally and intellectually "against" this fantastic rebellion. But, in spite of himself, his own character, indeed his own heroic struggle against the inertia imposed by blindness, disposed him to sympathize with this "sublimation" of beaten energies.

Yet at the same time these heroic energies are important. All the power, the splendor, and versatility of satanic technology remain illusory and pointless. One might almost say that, beneath his unconscious sympathy with the rebels, Milton realized even more deeply this finality of their despair. And this sense of futility is his final judgment on their rebellion—a fact which his superficial readers seem unable to realize. Dazzled by the poetic brilliance they do not see the real meaning of the poem and its ultimate disillusionment with power.

There is ambivalence in Milton's Satan and also in Milton's Paradise. We cannot question the importance of the archetypal Paradise myth in *Paradise Lost*. The title itself states the problem: man is created for peace, delight, and the highest spiritual happiness. In traditional language, he is created for contemplation. Not a loss of self in mystical absorption but self-transcendence in the dynamic stillness which, as the Zen Masters said, is found not in rest but in truly spontaneous movement. But man's weakness and superficiality, his inordinate love of a self metaphysically wounded with contingency, makes the Paradise life impossible. There is in Milton a tension between his desire of this ideal and his feeling that it is unattainable. He never resolved the apparent contradiction. He could not find the secret of contemplation in action and so saw, in practice, no solution but action without contemplation. And yet here too was no solution, only a kind of despair. What for Milton was a blind alley has become, in modern consciousness, an obsession with illusory vitalism.

When he comes to describe the ideal life of Adam and Eve in Paradise, Milton is weak and unconvincing: the life is too contemplative for him, there is too much leisure, there is apparently no room for initiative, there is just nothing to *do*. E. M. W. Tillyard once compared Adam and Eve in Milton to "Old age pensioners enjoying a perpetual youth" because they have to live and work in a garden which of its own accord produces more than they will ever need. Strangely enough, this is precisely the kind of society that seems to be resulting from the fantastically energetic and versatile progress of our technology. If inertia and lack of outlet for creative energy create Hell, then it appears that the greatest threat to man is not that he may succumb to hostile nature or to a stronger species, but to the explosive violence generated from the utter boredom of his own conquests. Milton was certainly not thinking of this, but the archetypal patterns of the Paradise story already spelled it out for him. The

Fathers of the Church had long since explored some of those implications in ways that might be highly suggestive to Jungian psychologists.

If Milton is an ambivalent activist, prone to sympathize with action and even rebellion for their own sakes, and unable to tolerate the contemplation which he still believed to be best, his theology tends to reflect these ambiguities, and here too he is modern. True, there can be no question of the reality of God for Milton. He is not a "God is dead" theologian before the time. Far from it. But his Pelagian taste for action and his instinctive disposition to seek in man himself the solution to all man's problems make his Christ a rather incredible and superfluous Savior. True, the Divine Word in *Paradise Lost* is intended to be even more heroically powerful than Satan in the poem—indeed he cannot be otherwise. But somehow, just because he *must* be more powerful, his power is poetically less convincing: it can never be seriously challenged or tested. Hence a theological ambivalence which has struck deep into the modern Christian consciousness and led eventually to the poetic protest of nineteenth-century minds like Baudelaire and Rimbaud, making explicit the contradictions which were as yet only implicit in Milton. Thus, though Milton himself was consciously and devoutly Christian, there was in him a basic ambiguity which made it possible, perhaps inevitable, for a certain type of modern reader to interpret him as anti-Christ—if he bothers to read and interpret him at all.

One trouble with a superficial and "satanist" reading of Milton—the kind of reading to which a modern reader would be instinctively disposed by his modernity——is that it ignores the fruitful ambiguities and tensions of Milton's mind. It concludes, against Milton, that present disorder is the only possible reality and that dynamic struggle is the only law of existence. But Milton's view of the struggling world is profoundly pessimistic: the world of conflict is one in which power enables a few to pervert truth and justice to their own ends and persecute the innocent. Milton does not glorify the will to power and the satanic superman; he deplores them, and he fears that precisely because of them mankind will throw away its ultimate chances of happiness and salvation.

There was in Milton a radical tension between his own psychology, his heart, his character as formed in his own revolutionary struggle for a republican England, and then his battle with blindness, and the traditional structure of beliefs to which he consciously held. The traditional structure was classic, static, and contemplative, while Milton was romantic, dynamic, and active. Milton was a romantic hero who wrote as a great classic poet. These tensions doubtless help to account for his greatness. But they have led astray all those who are able to see only one side of the picture, who insist on taking one horn of the dilemma as the answer to all the questions and dismissing the dilemma. Hence they hail as power and truth what Milton saw to be impotence and illusion.

One modern mythology—which doubtless no longer refers consciously to Milton but still deals with much the same archetypal patterns—is filled with Milton's themes of power, rebellion, will, and the drive to excel. But these themes have all undergone serious if not radical modification.

For one thing, the modern tendency is to interpret the dignity and freedom of the person not as Milton did but in a more frankly "satanic" way. The freedom and dignity of the person, for most people, mean in fact the ability of the individual to assert himself forcefully, to get up and overcome obstacles, if necessary to knock a few bystanders down and generally get everybody to recognize that he is around. One of the cardinal satanic virtues is the absolute refusal to let anyone else change your mind for you, by any means, reasonable or otherwise. This means that you can never be prevented from being the boss at least in your own small patch of hell. And this is freedom. "Better to reign in hell than serve in heaven."

To assume that Milton endorsed such doctrine would be the most monstrous misapprehension. He knew better than that what freedom was and how liberty implied intelligence and adaptation to the objective realities of life. He rejected as impudence the completely irrational misconception of freedom. This misconception is first of all purely subjective and secondly a blind exercise of will. But a blind exercise of will is doomed to frustration. When purely subjective whims encounter the opposition of objective reality, there is only one way to overcome them: since intelligence will not serve, violence alone remains. But violence is self-destroying and hence absurd. The concept of freedom which demands that one be one's own boss at all costs, that one should never change his mind for anyone, is a concept that leads nowhere but to blind addiction to violence and ultimately to willful self-destruction. Much of the current talk of "freedom" today has no more validity than this, and therefore it is a potential source of catastrophic madness. What forms will this madness take? Anything is possible, from street fighting to a nuclear *Götterdämmerung*.

In his *The Myth of Sisyphus* Albert Camus recreated something like Milton's Satan in the "hero of the absurd" who resorts to a purely "quantitative ethic." There are all kinds of affinities between Sisyphus (or the other heroes of the absurd, like Don Juan) and Milton's Demon Rebel.

Again, there is a basically hopeless situation of stupefied inertia to be redeemed by action. What is fundamentally absurd (and Hell is surely the realm of the absurd) cannot be made to make sense in itself. But one can seek to do *something* that makes sense. The will to make sense out of free action can counteract the absurd. Here many readers of Camus seem to have parted company with Camus and, as with Milton, have turned his own myth against him.

Though Camus more and more articulately disclaimed the title of "philosopher of the absurd" he is still stubbornly thought to have been preaching "the absurd" as a fundamental value—or as a heroically despairing antivalue. As a result of this, Camus' doctrine of revolt is sometimes turned upside down and stood on its head. In point of fact, Camus' study of the whole anatomy of revolution ends in a classic humanism, directly opposed to that nihilism which, he thinks, is the automatic result of all absolute use of power, whether in the spiritual or in the temporal orders. Thus, though a superficial reading of his early work seems to give some the impression that Camus advocated nihilism, he is on the contrary a humanist and a moderate, a liberal who is left in the very uncomfortable position of rejecting all the facile and doctrinaire generalizations of the mass movements and finding his own way in solitude. This, as Camus learned by experience, is a very fine way to become *persona non grata* with practically everybody, because sooner or later you have to say a polite "No" to each one's favorite cause. Since you have to keep deciding over again in changing circumstances, you forfeit the luxury of that unfailing rectitude which is conferred simply by following a large or small flock of sheep.

Yet Camus was no individualist. He knew the value of true solidarity and community, but he also knew the difficulty of finding them. Certainly the hopeful claims of movements and parties—and Churches—did not seem to him to be automatic guarantees of communion in fruitful effort. But he did find true solidarity in the clandestine journalism of the French resistance and later in the theater to which he devoted the best of his energies in the late fifties, before his death.

Though Camus may have started with Sisyphus, a figure somewhat similar to Milton's Satan, he soon distinguished between liberty and anarchy, authentic rebellion and totalist nihilism, and in the end rejoined the kind of classic view of liberty which was the one Milton himself really held.

Camus is wrongly called a neopagan. The term pagan is much too vague, and at best it accounts only for the vitalist strain in Camus' writings (in early essays like *Noces*). Actually the classic humanism of Camus—which is also an essentially post-Christian humanism adopting Christian values in a classic guise—is best expressed in a tragic concept of life. The word "tragic" here is used not in the sense of "sad" or "threatened with an unhappy ending," still less merely pessimistic.

There are certain basic notions underlying Greek tragedy—notions about the meaning and moral structure of life. The most basic of these concepts are *hybris* and *nemesis*. When man, either through his own fault or simply through some chain of fatal circumstances, begins to defy the gods and assert his own power against the claims of a higher power (we would say: of reality), he is permitted for a while to get away with it. Then in the end the momentum generated by his rash and illusory self-confidence brings with it his own destruction. But this does not mean that tragedy is always and simply a victory of the gods over men. On the contrary, the greatest tragedies are conflicts between the claims of various orders—various gods perhaps—having almost equal rights. In this conflict, a character of true nobility can in fact emerge victorious, as Oedipus for example does in the final play of the Sophoclean trilogy. Antigone is both ennobled and destroyed by a tragic dilemma: her love for her brother or her obedience to the power of the state. Prometheus is caught between his love for man, his devotion to the older order of telluric gods, and the power of the new Olympians. Neither Prometheus nor Antigone can be said to be afflicted with *hybris*. But if even the guiltless or unconsciously guilty hero incurs destruction by defying certain forces, how much more will the natural tendency of ordinary man to *hybris,* or what we have described as satanic self-assertion, inevitably bring *nemesis—a fatal retribution in which man's power becomes his own destruction.*

Strictly speaking, neither Christ nor Satan in Milton's poem can be called a perfectly tragic figure, because Satan's *hybris* has reached a kind of dynamic stasis in impotent and rebellious deadlock, while in Christ there is no defeat at all. Satan is always ruined yet always coming back for more. Hence he is a figure not of tragedy but of melodrama—and incidentally, since tragedy requires a single unified action, one can never have tragedy in a serial, however appalling it may be.

The Greek sense of measure, to which Camus ultimately appealed in his humanistic ethic, is built on the fatality and distinctiveness of *hybris*. A healthy fear of *hybris* is something which apparently is entirely lacking in the modern consciousness. We have swallowed without question the melodramatic values and dynamisms of a misunderstood Miltonic Satan, and we have no tragic dread of *nemesis*. The Greeks, who were probably far wiser than we realize, were well aware that he who has no sense of *nemesis* is in fact very close to it. Those whom the gods would destroy they first make mad—with self-righteous confidence and unquestioning self-esteem.

It might be interesting to refer in passing to Teilhard de Chardin, whose cosmic optimism restores all the dynamic energies and heroism of Milton's Satan to the Teilhardian Christ. Perhaps Teilhard was able to do this because his complete acceptance of evolutionism destroyed the tension and contradiction that were set up in Milton between his modern temper and his ancient world view. In Teilhard, the coincidence of the modern temper and a modern cosmology resulted in a convergence of energies that remained, for Milton, in unresolved conflict. Whether or not this convergence was too optimistic and too facile remains a point of controversy in regard to Teilhard, and it need not be discussed here. But one thing is obvious: Teilhard's splendid poetic vision of his "Mass on the World" (in his *Hymn of the Universe*) strikingly resembles the splendid hymn to light at the opening of the third book of *Paradise Lost*. Teilhard is in many ways a Miltonic epic "poet" whose power depends precisely on the fact that he has, at least in his own imaginative and creative experience, resolved the conflict which kept Milton's Christ such a dubious figure and which made it impossible for Camus to become a Christian.

It is one thing to admire the literary power and ambiguity of Milton's Satan, but another to seek, unconsciously or otherwise, to make a satanic and activist nihilism one's way of life. Camus has shown, in his study of revolt, *how this kind of nihilism has in fact entered into the very essence of all the modern power structures that are now in conflict.* This leads to some frightening and salutary conclusions. The first and most important of these is that the satanic nihilism of the great modern power structures represents a fatal infestation of *hybris*. This leads infallibly to *nemesis* and to destruction if we cannot learn to do something about it. No free man can allow himself passively to accept and identify with any one of these power structures in an unqualified way. To do so means associating himself in its *hybris,* abdicating his moral and personal dignity and participating in the cosmic witches' sabbath to which we are all now being invited.

Most of us seem to have accepted the invitation without stopping to reflect that there is a choice. Camus insisted that there was a choice: and the choice was man himself. Man's true dignity must lead him, Camus thought, to a free rejection of any system which makes the power of state, money, or weapons absolute values in themselves. While we seem to be asked to choose between this or that ideology, this party or that, this power bloc or that, in reality the choice is quite different. If we examine all their claims, says Camus, we find that they eventually concur in placing ideologies above man himself, politics above humanity, nation or party above truth, and power above everything.

Thus in every department of life the cart is before the horse, ends are sacrificed to means, man is alienated and destroyed in order to serve what is supposed to serve him. The state is theoretically for man, money is theoretically to help him live more easily, arms are supposed to protect him, and so on. But in fact man now lives and works in order to assemble and to stockpile the weapons that will destroy him, in an effort to serve a power structure which he worships as an end in itself and which makes his life more and more meaningless and absurd. Instead of using money to make life reasonable, man makes life unbearable by living for money. Everywhere we look we find the same contradictions and the same disorder. All these contradictions are symptomatic of one truth: our seemingly well-ordered and well-functioning society is a nihilist city of pandemonium, built on *hybris* and destined for cataclysm.

Is this inevitable? Nothing is absolutely inevitable. Man is still free to make choices, and he is even capable of making intelligent choices if he tries hard enough. But our future depends above all on this: the recognition that our present nihilistic consciousness is fatal and the development of a totally new state of mind, a whole new way of looking at ourselves, our world, and our problems. Not a new ideology, not a new formula of words, not a new mystique: but as Tillich said—*a new man*. With a little humility, patience, native luck, and the grace of God, the hard years we are going to live through may teach us to open our eyes. Meanwhile a more accurate understanding of Milton and Camus, perhaps a less naïve reading of Teilhard, may certainly help.

CAMUS AND THE CHURCH

> "Why do you call me 'Sir'?" said the prison chaplain, "why don't you call me Father?"
>
> "You are not my Father," said the condemned prisoner, "you are with the others."

1.

At the end of Albert Camus' novel *The Stranger,* there is a long dialogue between priest and condemned prisoner. The chaplain, an average, sincere, zealous, and not overbright priest is trying to grapple with the stolid unbelief of a man whom he considers the worst possible type of hardened criminal. He finally drives the man to complete desperation which explodes at last into a curious blend of Zen-Satori and existentialist revolt: the unexpected result of priestly zeal! The prisoner is a single-minded Algerian clerk, Meursault, who in a moment of thoughtlessness shot a man. He felt himself to have been partly irresponsible but failed to realize the importance of defending himself in terms that his society was willing to understand and accept. As a result he got the death penalty when, in fact, there were enough extenuating circumstances to warrant a much lighter sentence.

One of the themes of the novel is the ambiguity and "absurdity" of a justice which, though logical and right in its own terms, is seen to be an elaborate tissue of fictions—a complicated and dishonest social game in which there is no real concern for persons or values. Meursault is condemned, in fact, for not playing that game, as is made abundantly clear when the prosecution proves to the jury's outraged satisfaction that the accused did not weep at his mother's funeral. In the trial the sentimental exploitation of this fact curiously assumes a greater importance than the murder itself. The whole prosecution is sensational, pharisaical, and indeed irrelevant to the actual case. All through the trial the accused, though not particularly smart, gradually realizes that society is interested

This essay first appeared in *The Catholic Worker,* December 1966, and later was published in *A Penny a Copy,* ed. Thomas C. Cornell and James Forest (New York: Macmillan, 1968).

not in what he really did, but only in completely reconstructing his personality and his actions to make him fit its own capricious requirements—its need for the complete evildoer.

And now the prison chaplain, having taken for granted all that has been decided in the courtroom, proceeds to work the prisoner over in the interests of other requirements: the need for a complete penitent. Since to repent one must first believe, the chaplain simply tries to convince Meursault that in his heart of hearts he "really believes" but does not know that he believes. Meursault replies that though he cannot be quite sure what interests him, he is quite certain of what does not interest him; and this includes the whole question of religion. Meursault is right to feel offended by the priest's self-assurance, which simply adds to the affront that the court has visited upon his dignity as a person.

All through the imprisonment and the trial, the prisoner has in fact been treated as if he were not there, as if he were so complete a nonentity that he was not able to think or even experience anything validly for himself. "I am with you," says the chaplain with smug assurance based on perfect moral superiority, "but you cannot realize this since you have a blinded heart." In the end the prisoner reacts with violent indignation against this cumulative refusal of lawyers (his own included), judges, jury, the press, the Church, and society at large to accept him as a person. There is considerable bite in the sentence: "I answered that he was not my Father, he was with the others." After all what is a Father whose relation with his "son" is no more than his relation with a chair or a table—and a chair that is about to be thrown out with the rubbish?

Another ironic sentence shows up what Camus thought of the Church, as exemplified at least by this priest: "According to him the justice of men was nothing and the justice of God everything. I remarked that it was the former that had condemned me." The chaplain appears to make a distinction between the justice of man and the justice of God, but in actual fact he has assumed that the justice of man *is* the justice of God and that the truth of the verdict is the truth of God. When *bourgeois* society speaks, God speaks. This is taken so much for granted by him that he does not even think of questioning it.

Another priest, more subtly portrayed by Camus, is the Jesuit Paneloux in *The Plague*. In this novel Camus created a great modern myth in which he described man's condition in this life on earth. It refers more especially to French society. We know that *The Plague* is also about the German occupation of France, and Paneloux represents in some sense the French clergy under the Nazis. But he also represents the Church as she confronts man in his moral and metaphysical estrangement—his "lostness" in an absurd world. What will she offer him? Can she give him anything more than a predigested answer and a consoling rite? Does she ask of him anything more than conformity and resignation? At the outbreak of the plague Paneloux delivers a hell-fire sermon on the Justice of God and the punishment of iniquity, the need for penance and for a return to decent church-going lives. In other words the plague is a punishment. But for what, precisely? Sin! Later he learns, by working with the doctors in the "resistance," that things are not quite so simple as all that and that such a black-and-white interpretation of social or moral crises no longer convinces anyone. He proceeds to a new position which is, however, still unconvincing because no one can make out quite what it is. He now, in fact, demands a wager of blind faith that sounds like fatalism. In the end he lays down his life, but his sacrifice is ambiguous because, for obscure motives of his own, he has refused medical help.

There is in *The Plague* a decisive dialogue between Rieux the doctor and Paneloux the priest after they have witnessed the sufferings and death of a child. Paneloux no longer has any glib explanation, but only suggests that we must love what we cannot understand. Rieux replies, "I have a different conception of love. And I shall refuse to the bitter end to love this scheme of things in which children are tortured." This is a caricature of the theology of evil. Does Christianity demand that one "love a system, an explanation, a scheme of things" which for its coherence demands that people be tortured? Is that what the Gospel and the Cross mean? To some Christians, unfortunately, yes. And it is they who present Camus with an absurdity against which he must revolt. This is not a question of ill-will or culpable scandal—only a tragic misunderstanding. Camus' evaluation of the Church is not unusual and not totally unsympathetic, but it is especially worth attending to, since Camus has retained a kind of moral eminence (which he himself often repudiated) as the conscience of a new generation. By reason of his personal integrity, his genius, his eloquence, and his own record in protest and resistance, Camus still speaks to our world with resounding authority. His judgments carry much more conviction than those of Sartre, for example, who has thrown in his lot with Marxist power politics, or those of Marcel and Mounier, who, though respected outside the Church, have exercised their influence mostly inside it.

2.

If we as Catholics wish to get some idea of what the secular world thinks of us and expects of us, we can still with profit turn to Camus and question him on the subject. As a matter of fact, shortly after the end of the war the *avant-garde* Dominicans at the publishing house of Le Cerf invited Camus to come and answer this important question. Notes on the talk were preserved. They were very instructive and have lost none of their vitality today.

Camus opened his remarks to the Paris Dominicans with some interesting observations on dialogue. We are by now familiar enough with the fact that dialogue requires openness and honesty, and this supposes first of all that on both sides there is a complete willingness to accept the other as he is. This also presupposes a willingness to be oneself and not pretend to be someone else. On the part of the nonbeliever (Camus courteously begins with the nonbeliever), it is essential to avoid a kind of secular pharisaism (*pharisaisme laique*) which in the name of Christianity demands more of the Christian than the secularist demands of himself. "I certainly believe that the Christian has plenty of obligations," Camus admits, "but the man who himself rejects these obligations has no right to point them out to one who has recognized their existence." This is charitable of him, indeed. Pharisaism works two ways: on one hand the man who thinks that it is enough to *recognize* an obligation by a purely formal and punctilious fulfillment is a pharisee. On the other the man who detects the failure and points to it, without fulfilling an equivalent obligation himself, is also a pharisee. Camus had an exquisite eye for this kind of a thing, as his novels show. (See especially the perfect pharisaism of Clamence in *The Fall*.) According to him, pharisaism is one of the worst plagues of our time. In *The Stranger* the whole trial is an exhibition of the pure pharisaism of French *bourgeois* culture. Camus is no less aware of the pharisaism of Marxists, as we see in the long section devoted to them in *The Rebel*.

If it is not the business of the nonbeliever to judge the Christian's behavior, it is nevertheless essential that the Christian be a Christian if he is going to engage, as Christian, in dialogue with somebody else. Already in those days Camus had run into Catholics who, in their eagerness to be "open," were willing to throw their Catholicism out the window. True, the example he cites is not convincingly scandalous. In a discussion with Marxists at the Sorbonne, a Catholic priest had stood up and exclaimed, "I too am anticlerical." There are a lot of us who know exactly what he meant and would, by now, be willing to join him in his declaration, if by "anticlericalism" is meant weariness and exasperation with the seminary veneer of self-assurance, intolerance, expert knowledge of inscrutable sciences, and total moral superiority to the laity. Nevertheless, if one is a priest, one cannot allow oneself the rather indecent luxury of repudiating one's fellow priests *en bloc* in order to indulge one's own vanity or wounded feelings. It is quite true, and we must admit it, that life as a priest in these times of questioning and renewal is neither simple nor easy. One has to live with things that do not seem to be authentic or honest, let alone agreeable. One is likely to be impatient for reforms that are not only long in coming but may never come at all. And one may at the same time be the target of criticism which, though ambiguous, has enough ground in fact to be irritating. A cleric might well be tempted to free himself of these distressing conditions by joining some radical minority and taking up a position from which he can righteously attack his fellow clergy. If what he seeks by this is comfort for his own ego and recognition by an in-group of his own choice, Camus warns him that he is deluding himself.

Nevertheless, we must not take Camus' dislike of "anticlerical priests" too absolutely. He did not mean to silence all public opinion and self-questioning within the Church. On the contrary, he called for such self-criticism and self-examination and he approved of it when he met it, for example, in his friend the Dominican Père Bruckberger ("Bruck"). Camus' notebooks abound in spiritual nosegays like these, culled from the garden of Bruck's conversation:

"G. has the look of a priest, a sort of episcopal unction. And I can hardly bear it in Bishops."

"Those Christian Democrats give me a pain in the neck."

Camus naïvely said to Bruck: "As a young man I thought all priests were happy." Bruck replied: "Fear of losing their faith makes them limit their sensitivity. It becomes merely a negative vocation. They don't face up to life." And Camus added: "His dream, a great conquering clergy, but magnificent in its poverty and audacity." Poverty and audacity were two qualities that appealed more and more to Camus. He looked for them, as we shall see, in the Catholic Church but did not always find them.

3.

It would unduly complicate this article to go into Camus' difficulties with the Augustinian theology of sin and grace, and the reasons why he took scandal at a certain pessimistic religious approach to the problem of evil. But we recall that at the University of Algiers, Camus wrote the equivalent of an M.A. thesis on "Plotinus and St. Augustine." It is not enough to say, as one recent writer has said, that if Camus had read Teilhard de

Chardin instead of Augustine he would have been more likely to become a Christian. Maybe so, maybe not. But he remained more or less impaled on the same dilemma as Ivan Karamazov: if there are evil and suffering in the world, and if God is omnipotent, then the fact that He permits the evil must mean that He is responsible for it. And if the evil has to exist in order somehow to justify the divine omnipotence, then Camus will return his ticket to paradise, he doesn't want to go there if it means admitting that this is "right."

Stated in the terms in which he states it, the problem becomes an aesthetic one which cannot really be solved by logic or metaphysics, a question of structure that is unsatisfactory because it lacks harmony and unity—it is in fact to him aesthetically and morally absurd. He cannot accept it because it repels his imagination. It is like a play that falls apart in the third act. To demand that one simply accept this with resignation and to say it is "right" (in the sense of satisfactory to man's deepest sense of fittingness and order) is simply an affront to man, thinks Camus. And a lot of other people go along with him. We need not argue the theoretical point here.

What is crucially important in our world is not evil as an abstract scenario but evil as an existential fact. It is here that Camus speaks most clearly to the Church. The unbeliever and the Christian both live in a world in which they confront evil and the absurd. They have different ways of understanding these facts, but this does not make too much difference provided they offer authentic protest and resistance. Camus then raises the question that recently has been hotly debated as a result of Hochhuth's *The Deputy*. Why did not Rome speak out more clearly and forcefully against the crimes and barbarities of Nazism?

Why shall I not say this here? For a long time I waited during those terrible years, for a strong voice to be lifted up in Rome. I an unbeliever? Exactly. For I knew that spirit would be lost if it did not raise the cry of condemnation in the presence of force. It appears that this voice was raised. But I swear to you that millions of men, myself included, never heard it; and that there was in the hearts of believers and unbelievers a solitude which did not cease to grow as the days went by and the executioners multiplied. It was later explained to me that the condemnation had indeed been uttered, but in the language of encyclicals, which is not clear. The condemnation had been pronounced but it had not been understood. Who cannot see in this where the real condemnation lies? Who does not see that this example contains within it one of the elements of the answer, perhaps the whole answer to the question you have asked me? What the world expects of Christians is that

Christians speak out and utter their condemnation in such a way that never a doubt, never a single doubt can arise in the heart of even the simplest man. *That Christians get out of their abstractions and stand face to face with the bloody mess that is our history today. The gathering we need today is the gathering together of men who are resolved to speak out clearly and pay with their own person. When a Spanish bishop blesses political executions he is no longer a bishop or a Christian or even a man. . . . We expect and I expect that all those will gather together who do not want to be dogs and who are determined to pay the price that has to be paid if man is to be something more than a dog.*

This is strong meat, and it has lost nothing of its strength since 1948. It can be repeated today and perhaps with greater effect than before, since the Vatican Council has so obviously and explicitly told all Catholics to listen to what the world has to say to them. This is it!

Camus' challenge is nothing new. We can say the same thing to ourselves, and we do when we are in the mood. And yet there remains always that fatal ambiguity, that confusion, the muddle, the fuss, the hesitation, the withdrawal into obscurity, and finally the negation of what we just said. We give it out with one hand and take it all back with the other. We promise everything and then cancel it all out by promising the opposite to someone else. In a word we have to please everybody. So we are uncertain, dubious, obscure. And finally we just give up and keep our mouths shut.

Fully to understand the implications of Camus' stark demand we have to see it against the background of his thought and not against the background of what has been standard practice in Christian society for centuries. We can accept with great good will Camus' declaration of the necessity to protest against injustice and evil. But when we look a little closer at society the picture is not so simple. It is on the contrary very intricate, and threads work within threads in a complex social tapestry in which, everywhere, are the faces of bishops, of priests, and of our fellow Catholics. We are involved everywhere in everything, and we have to go easy. . . . Perhaps that is why it is so simple to blast off against Communism. There are no bishops of ours in Russia, and we have nothing invested there except hopes. Communism has made it easy for us; by its single-minded hostility to the Church it has become the one force we can always condemn without compromise at any moment—until perhaps we start making deals with Communism too. Then there will be nobody left!

Where we see unavoidable, distressing, and yet "normal" complications,

Camus sees the "absurd." What we accept and come to terms with, he denounces and resists. The "absurd" of Camus is not the metaphysical absurd and *néant* of Sartre, and his "revolt" is not the Sartrian nausea. The absurd of Camus is the gap between the actual shape of life and intelligent truth. Absurdity is compounded by the ambiguous and false explanations, interpretations, conventions, justifications, legalizations, evasions which infect our struggling civilization with the "plague" and which often bring us most dangerously close to perfect nihilism when they offer a security based on a seemingly rational use of absolute power.

It is here we are forced to confront the presence of "the absurd" in the painful, humiliating contradictions and ambiguities which are constantly and everywhere evident in our behavior as Christians in the world. To mention only one: the scandal of men who claim to believe in a religion of love, mercy, forgiveness and peace, dedicating themselves wholeheartedly and single-mindedly to secular ideologies of hate, cruelty, revenge, and war and lending to those ideologies the support of a Christian moral casuistry. And when the Church officially examines her conscience before the world and repudiates this contradiction, many Catholics still find ways of ignoring and evading the consequences of what the Church has said. "The arms race is an utterly treacherous trap for humanity and one which injures the poor to an intolerable degree. . . . Divine Providence urgently demands of us that we free ourselves from the age-old slavery of war. But if we refuse to make this effort. . . ." Vatican Council II, *Gaudium et Spes*, 81.) Who is making a really serious effort? A few of us are perhaps thinking it over! Certainly the Church has spoken without ambiguity though still in official language: but if Christians themselves do not pay attention, or simply shrug the whole thing off, the ambiguity persists, and it is perhaps more disconcerting than it was before. The prisoner in *The Stranger* did not even hope that the chaplain would be any less absurd than the lawyers and the judges. He knew in advance he was "with all the others"!

To really understand what Camus asked of Christians that evening at the Dominican house of Latour-Maubourg, we would have to understand his difficult analysis of two centuries of cultural and political history in *The Rebel*. This book is, admittedly, a failure. But its insights remain nevertheless extremely precious, and they enable us still to see through the specious claims of the power politician (so often accepted without question by Christians both of the right and of the left) and to detect beneath the superficial arguments the absurd void of nihilism and mass murder. At this point we might quote a Catholic thinker, Claude

Tresmontant, who restates in purely Catholic terms exactly what Camus means by being a "Rebel" against the "absurd."

> But the child is going to inherit also, and especially by the education he is going to receive from his environment, a set of ready-made ideas, a system of judgments, a scale of values which, as often as not, he will not be able to question or criticize. This system of values, in the aggregate of nations, in large part is criminal. It is the reflection of a criminal world in which man oppresses, massacres, tortures, humiliates and exploits his brother. The child enters into an organized world, on the political, economic, mental, mythological, psychological and other planes. And the structure of this world is penetrated and informed by sin. The child is not born in Paradise. It is born in a criminal humanity. In order to have access to justice, to sanctity, the child, as it grows up, will have to make a personal act of judgment, of refusal, of choice. It will have to make a personal act of opposition to the values of its tribe, of its caste, of its nation or of its race, and of its social class, in order to attain justice. To a certain extent it will have to leave its tribe, its nation, its caste, its class, its race, as Abraham, the father of the faithful did, who left Ur of the Chaldees to go into a country that he did not know. Holiness begins with a breach. Nothing can dispense this child from breaking with "the world." In order to enter into Christianity, the child will have to choose between the values of the world, the values of the tribe, its nation or its social class, and the values of the Gospel. It must renew its scale of values. It must, as it were, be born anew from the spiritual point of view: it must become a new creature. Tertullian said one is not born a Christian. One becomes a Christian. The access to Christianity represents a new birth. One can then legitimately distinguish between the state which precedes this new birth and the state which follows it. The state which precedes this new birth is the state which the Church calls "original sin."[1]

But does the Catholic Church clearly and always define the relation of the Christian to secular society in these terms? Does it not, in fact, like the chaplain in *The Stranger,* identify itself at times with this society?

For Camus it is clear that a certain type of thinking and talking, a certain type of mental attitude, even though it may be vested in the most edifying clichés, betrays a firm commitment to economic and political interests which are incompatible in the long run with the message of the Gospel, the true teaching of the Church, and the Christian mission in the world. It is the commitment that speaks louder than any words. It manifests itself in the peculiar absurdity of official doubletalk, the

---

[1] Claude Tresmontant, *Christian Metaphysics* (Westminister, Md.: Christian Classics, 1965), p. 99.

language of bureaucratic evasion, which, while nodding politely to Christian principles, effectively comes out in full support of wealth, injustice, and brute power. For Camus it is axiomatic that any ideology, any program, whether of the right or the left, which leads to mass murder and concentration camps as a direct consequence is to be revolted against, no matter how "reasonable" and "right" it is made to appear.

Speaking in an interview in São Paulo, Brazil, in 1949, Camus said: "Only the friends of dictatorships, the people who set up concentration camps, can be in favor of war. It is the duty of writers to sound the alarm and to fight against every form of slavery. That is our job."

The Camusian "Rebel" fulfills the role of the prophet in modern society, and it is to the writer and the artists that Camus looks above all to carry out this essential task. Nowhere in his work do we find him expressing any real hope of this prophetic voice being in the pulpit or in the documents of the Church, though as we have seen, he still says it is the Church's job to speak out also. He no longer looks to her for guidance—but he does at least hope for a little support. If she cannot lead, she can at least follow!

In the same interview, speaking of the poet René Char, "the biggest event in French poetry since Rimbaud," he says he expects far more from poets than from moralists: "When you say 'poetry' you are close to love, that great force which one cannot replace with money, which is vile, nor with that pitiable thing they call 'La Morale.'" (Note that in French primary schools there is—or was—a weekly class in "La Morale" in which the children memorize the most appalling platitudes. One wonders if our catechism is much better.)

It was said above that *The Rebel* is not a fully successful thesis on revolt. In spite of some acute and detailed analysis and diagnosis nothing is very positively prescribed. But there remains a basic ambiguity in the book. In his study of modern revolutionary violence and his analysis of its inevitable trend toward tyranny and mass murder, Camus attributes this to the godlessness of modern revolutionaries. At the same time he admits that without God there can be no rational philosophy and practice of nonviolence. Yet he still cannot make the Pascalian wager of faith (by which he seems at times to be tempted). If there is to be a choice between faith and the absurd, his stoic conscience will, in the end, dictate the choice of the absurd. And the "absurd man" of Camus remains strangely isolated, even though, if he is consistently faithful to his steady view of the absurd, he should proceed to a revolt that joins him in solidarity with other men of his own kind. But this solidarity lacks human validity unless it is in the service of life and humanity. In other words, revolt is legitimate only if it refuses all complicity with mass murder and totalitarianism of whatever kind, whether of the right or of the left.

"There is one problem only today," said Camus in a statement of 1946, "and that is the problem of murder. All our disputes are vain. One thing alone matters, and that is peace."

However, Camus was never an out-and-out pacifist. He always admitted the possibility of a strictly limited use of force. He had various reasons for this, besides the rather complex one of his rejection of faith in God, which at the same time implied the impossibility, for him, of consistent nonviolence and pacifism. Since many can attain only an "approximation of justice" then it is futile for him to hope to avoid all use of force, but he must restrain himself and exercise full, indeed heroic responsibility in keeping the use of force down to the minimum, where it is always provisional and limited and never in favor of a cause that consecrates and codifies violence as a permanent factor in its policies.

The peculiar isolation of Camus' position comes from his inability to cope with the idea of God and of faith to which his sense of justice and his instinctive nonviolence nevertheless enticed him. In the same way, he was led up to the "silence of God" by his interest in the studies on phenomenology of language written by his friend Brice Parain, an existentialist who became a Catholic in the late forties, when he was closely associated with Camus. In fact we cannot do full justice to Camus' relations with the Church without taking into consideration his interest in the ideas of Parain. It is here that Camus' dialogue with Catholicism developed on the most intimate and profound level.

In an age of highly academic linguistic analysis, Camus appreciated the courage of Parain, who sees the problem of language as ultimately a *metaphysical* problem. The questioning of meaning raises the whole question of reality itself and in the end Parain is asking one thing above all: can language make sense if there is no God? In other words, what is the point of talking about truth and falsity if there is no God? Is not man, in that case, reduced to putting together a series of more or less arbitrary noises in the solitude of a mute world? Are these noises anything more than the signals of animals and birds? True, our noises exist in a very complex on-going context of development and are richly associated with one another and with other cultural phenomena: but can they be true? And does this matter? Or are they merely incidents in a developing adventure that will one day end in some kind of meaning but which, for the time being, has none?

Parain rejects this post-Hegelian position and returns to the classical ideas of language as able to provide grounds for at least elementary certitude. If language has no meaning then nothing has any meaning. Language has enough meaning, at least, to reassure us that we are not floating in a pure void. In other words, communication becomes possible, and with it community, once it is admitted that our words are capable of being true or false and that the decision is largely up to us. "To name a thing wrong is to add to the miseries of the world." We are thus called to take care of our language, and use it clearly. "The great task of man is not to serve the lie." These words of Parain might have been uttered—and have been uttered equivalently, many times—by Camus. And so Camus says in a review-article of Parain's books: "It is not altogether certain that our epoch has lacked gods: it seems on the contrary that what we need is a dictionary."

It is certainly true that the twentieth century has been distinguished for its single-minded adoration of political and cultural idols rather than for the clarity and honesty of its official speech. The sheer quantity of printed and broadcasted doubletalk overwhelms the lucid utterances of a few men like Camus.

But once again, Camus remains sober and unidealistic. Our task is not suddenly to burst out into the dazzle of utter unadulterated truth but laboriously to reshape an accurate and honest language that will permit communication between men on all social and intellectual levels, instead of multiplying a Babel of esoteric and technical tongues which isolate men in their specialities.

What characterizes our century is not so much that we have to rebuild our world as that we have to rethink it. This amounts to saying that we have to give it back its language. . . . The vocabularies that are proposed to us are of no use to us . . . and there is no point in a Byzantine exercise upon themes of grammar. We need a profound questioning which will not separate us from the sufferings of men. . . .

It is unfortunately true that the "Byzantine exercises" not only of logical positivism (which nevertheless has a certain limited value) but of all kinds of technical and specialized thinking tend to remove us from the world in which others, and we ourselves, are plunged in the dangers and the sufferings of an increasingly absurd and unmanageable social situation. As Camus and Parain have seen, we have to *rethink* that whole situation, and we no longer possess the language with which to do it.

Such a language will necessarily confine itself at first to formulating what is accessible to all men. But it will not talk down to them or cajole them. It will enable them to lift themselves up. Yet if the artist, the peasant, the scientist, and the workman are all going to communicate together, their language will have to have a certain simplicity and austerity in order to be clear to them all without degrading thought. This means not the attainment of a pure classic prose (though Camus admits he thinks of a "new Classicism") but rather of a kind of "superior banality" which will consist in "returning to the words of everybody, but bringing to them the honesty that *is required for them to be purified of lies and hatred.*"

It is at this point that we can see what Camus is asking not only of intellectuals but also of the Church: this *purification and restitution of language so that the truth may become once again unambiguous and fully accessible to all men, especially when they need to know what to do.*

I think that everybody will readily admit that the language of the Church is distinguished by a "superior banality," but this is not the kind that Camus was talking about. We can certainly say that the Church speaks without hatred and that she does not lie. On the other hand, as we saw, it is quite possible for her to speak in such complex, unclear, evasive, and bureaucratic language that her message is simply inaccessible even to a reader of some education and average patience. With a few outstanding exceptions, the clergy, Catholic thinkers, teachers, writers, too often speak so confusedly, so timidly, so obscurely, that even when they are telling the truth they manage to keep it out of circulation. In fact one sometimes wonders if some of the writers of official documents have not trained themselves to tell the truth in such a way that it will have no visible effect. Then one can say indeed that one has "told the truth" but nobody will have gotten excited or done anything about it!

After all, it was not Camus who said to the Church: "Go, teach all nations." And the teaching of the nations is not to be accomplished by the triumphant utterance of totally obscure generalities. It is not enough for us to be at once meticulously correct and absolutely uninteresting and unclear. Nor, when we have clarified our speech and livened it up a bit, can we be content that we have merely *declared* the truth, made it public, announced it to the world. Are we concerned merely to get others to *hear* us? We have a hearing. But how many of those that hear us, and understand what we are saying, are convinced? Perhaps we are satisfied with proving to them (and thereby to ourselves) that we are convinced. But the kind of rethinking that Camus—and the world—calls for demands not only the publication of official statements but the *common effort to arrive at new aspects of the truth,* in other words dialogue, community, not only among believers but between believers and unbelievers as well.

The whole truth of Albert Camus is centered upon the idea of *telling the truth*. The relation of words to the inscrutable presence of what he called the power of words to identify the absurd as such. The function of words in establishing community among men engaged in resisting and overcoming the absurd. The power of words to lead revolt in a creative and life-affirming direction. The power of words against murder, violence, tyranny, injustice, death. The novels, stories, and essays of Camus explore this question from many angles, and everywhere they reach the conclusion: we live in a world of lies, which is therefore a world of violence and murder. We need to rebuild a world of peace. We cannot do this unless we can recover the language and think of peace.

The tragedy that is latent behind the fair and true declarations of the Church on peace, justice, renewal, and all the rest is that these words of truth and hope are being devoured and swallowed up in the massive confusion and indifference of a *world that does not know how to think in terms of peace and justice because in practice the word peace means nothing but war and the word justice means nothing but trickery, bribery, and oppression.*

Anything the Church may say to such a world is immediately translated into its opposite—if indeed the Churchmen themselves are not already beguiled by the same doubletalk as the world in which they live. To all of us, Camus is saying: "Not lying is more than just not dissimulating one's acts and intentions. *It is carrying them out and speaking them out in truth.*"

THREE SAVIORS IN CAMUS:
LUCIDITY AND THE ABSURD

"Lucidity" in the presence of the "denseness and strangeness" of the world, solidarity in revolt against the absurd: these terms roughly define the familiar themes of Camus' published work, though they do not exhaust the full scope of his humanistic vision. The work he was planning when he was overtaken by an untimely death opened further horizons of love and compassion. But in any case, the central idea of Camusian humanism is the clarification of man's consciousness of his lot in the world.

In proportion as he becomes authentically aware of his own plight, man confronts the absurd—and finds it not in himself or in the objective world, but "in their presence together." Whereas he seeks to understand himself and his world by reason, he finds that the "only bond" between himself and the world is the absurd. He is caught by a desire for clarity that is frustrated by the irrational abuse of reason itself. If he consents to his situation, resigns himself to it, and convinces himself by his reasoning that things are just as they should be, he abdicates his dignity as a human person in order to enjoy the tranquillity of a delusive "order." This delusion must be refused. The absurd must be faced. Anguish must not be evaded, for it is "the perpetual climate of the lucid man." Language must then be used not merely to rationalize and justify what is basically absurd, but to awaken in man the lucid anguish in which alone he is truly conscious of his condition and therefore able to revolt against the absurd. Then he will affirm, over against its "unreasonable silence," the human love and solidarity and devotion to life which give meaning to his own existence. "The doctrines that explain everything to me also debilitate me at the same time. They relieve me of the weight of my own life and yet I must carry it alone." (*The Myth of Sisyphus*)

The work of Camus is essentially meditative, imaginative, and symbolic. He constructs myths and images in which he elaborates his main themes. The awakening and clarification of the "lucid consciousness" is of course

---

Written in September 1966, this essay was first published in *Thought,* spring 1968.

a matter of personal meditation: but it is much more than that. It depends most of all on the encounter and communion of persons. Camus frequently admits an attraction to solitude and silence—he had even read with approval Chateaubriand's life of Rancé, the seventeenth-century monastic reformer of La Trappe—but he always felt that this attraction was a mere temptation to be firmly resisted. He needed to be present among men, for his own sake as well as for theirs. He needed, with them, to develop a new and more human style of life in the absurdity of a world torn by a power struggle of immense magnitude. In the midst of this struggle it was the mission of a few men to preserve the purity of communication within a human measure and safeguard the clarity and sincerity of language in order that men might love. The "human task," he said, was "a humble and limited one: to find those few words by which to appease the infinite anguish of free souls." Of course he meant more than the phrase says by itself. He was concerned with the power of language—of truth then—to protect man against ferocity, murder, nihilism, chaos. Language used clearly and honestly in the service of a lucid consciousness would protect man against his tendencies to nihilism and self-destruction.

So Camus, deeply concerned as he is with the loneliness and estrangement of man, is also preoccupied even more deeply still with the problem of communication.

In his notebooks he writes, "Peace would be loving in silence. But there is conscience and the person; you have to speak. To love becomes hell." He has no naïve illusion that communication has become an easy matter in the age of TV. He is fully aware of its extreme difficulty, precisely because of the prevalence of sham communication and sham community. Curiously, in the next notebook entry he remarks on an actor who is a believer and who lies in bed listening to Mass on the radio. "No need to get up. He has salved his conscience." The great difficulty facing the man who really wants to communicate with his brother is not the lack of words or of media, but the fact that words and media are now so commonly and so systematically used in order to cheat and to lie.

The very first essay or, rather, triptych of character sketches in his youthful book, *L'Envers et l'endroit,* deals with two old women and an old man, each one struggling with the terror of isolation and death, each one coping with it in one way or another, not without defeat and desperation in spite of pitiful and futile efforts to cheat and to cajole the indifferent into giving them attention. This was Camus' first clear treatment of the question of estrangement and communication. The theme reappears everywhere in his work. The long, obsessed, and ironic monologue, the confession of his "penitent-judge" Clamence in *The Fall,* is an ancient-mariner-like effort to break down the wall which guilt has erected between the speaker and the rest of men. The theme of the book could be summed up as the total failure of garrulous analytical reasoning as a means of authentic communication. It describes this breakdown of the futile and individualistic self-awareness of the bourgeois ethos.

In treating this theme of human communication, Camus naturally made use of mythical false-prophet figures (Clamence is a sort of feeble twentieth-century John the Baptist preparing the way for nobody, bringing no news except the analysis of his own sins and those of his world, and announcing, with finality, nothing but general and irreversible guilt). In particular Camus creates symbolic personages who are "sent," who have an explicit or implicit mission to bring a message from a distant country, a message which is ultimately one of salvation. The purpose of the present essay is to briefly consider three of these. They are the "Renegade" Catholic missionary whose mission has collapsed and who is held captive by fierce idolaters in a desert city carved entirely out of salt. Then Jan, the son of the innkeeper in *Le Malentendu* who, returning home from a distant country with his fortune, hides his identity in order to surprise his mother and sister and is murdered by them for his money. Finally there is the French engineer, D'Arrast, in "The Growing Stone," who goes to build a dam near a small Brazilian town and becomes involved in a strange religious adventure which binds him to a half-caste ship's cook in the fulfillment of an "absurd" and difficult vow.

In all these three stories we confront the problem of communication between men of different countries, races, or religions—what has become one of the best-publicized questions of our day: we have learned to call it "dialogue." In the case of the Renegade we have a traditional situation: the missionary who comes to announce the word of God to pagan idolaters. Jan in *Le Malentendu* comes to bring his mother the liberation she has so long hoped for: to take her away from the dank and misty country where she lives and bring her to a land of happiness in the south. In the "Growing Stone" we might say that D'Arrast comes in the name of science and modern European civilization. He is a humanist. The dam he builds will protect the *favelas* of the poor against floods. Yet it is really he who hears a message of "salvation" in the primitive faith of the Brazilian natives. The "Renegade" with his message from Christian Europe is unfortunately preaching himself more than Christ, and the reward of his *hybris* is conversion to the atrocious cult of the idol he came to overturn. Jan comes with a message of life and hope, but because he is too complex and too mysterious in his communication of it, he pays for his fantasies with his life. In both the "Renegade" and *Le Malentendu* the messenger runs into a wall of hostility, opposition, refusal and, in the case of the "Renegade," total silence. Violence, torture and murder are the reply to inadequate language, and they effectually defeat it.

The Renegade

The Renegade missionary has no name. Indeed, he has no longer a mission. He has no more message. His tongue has been cut out, yet his story is a monologue. The gargled interior monologue of a perverted apostle whose tongue has been removed in the most savage and revolting fashion! The very style of the story has implications! This monologue is one of hate and resentment, and it obviously gives Camus an opportunity to express himself, ironically, about the Catholic Church. But the story is not merely a satire on the Church. It goes deeper and is more complex than that. It deals with the confrontation between Christianity and Communism. In a sense it displays the ironies and absurdities of a dilemma with which Camus felt that he, in common with so many others, was faced: the question of grace versus justice, revelation versus history, the Church versus Communism: should one be a yogi or a commissar? Should one resign oneself to be a victim or should one join with the executioners—as Sartre for instance was not unwilling to do? Should one, in other words, choose not so much between virtue and unscrupulous politics as between two kinds of power, two cults of the absolute: that of the Catholic Church with the subtle methods of Dostoevsky's "Grand Inquisitor," or that of the Communists and of the Stalinist secret police? Camus once remarked jokingly that his "Renegade" was really the picture of a "Progressive Christian," in other words, of a Christian who has been won over to Marxism in the course of an attempted "dialogue" with the Communists.

It would not be fair to say that "The Renegade" was intended to represent Christianity, even in caricature. Yet it is, nevertheless, a satire on a certain kind of Catholic triumphalism. In particular, it contains an ironic estimate of the distortions and perversions of the Christian message due to a secret resentment and love of power on the part of the messenger. The Renegade is shown to be a highly questionable Christian. And yet, together with an intense and obstinate zeal, he combines a spirit of opportunism and superstition which makes it easy and obvious for him to be perverted in a most shameful fashion. This shows, if you like, that his Christianity itself is false and perverse. In its fanatical theism it ends up by being a practical atheism: what it adores under the guise of God is simply brute power. Camus evidently intends to show that the very existence of such Christians prepares the way for totalist atheism and explains the existence of mass-man. Unfortunately the Renegade is in his rudimentary "character" closer to a right-wing integralist than to a *progressiste*. However the story is grimly entertaining for anyone who enjoys a little horror.

In reality the Renegade is more Manichaean than Christian. From the very start he is afflicted with the pride of those who resent their own inferiority. He does not know love, only hate—but his hate is masked in the language of the Gospel. Because he has been subject all his life to the indifference and contempt of others, he wants to assert himself by the exercise of power. He wants to be a misionary in order to "conquer" people who are inferior even to himself: primitives. But he wants them also to be morally inferior: they must be not only idolaters but the most wicked and perverse of idolaters. And he, the missionary, the pure one, the man of holy faith, will confront their wickedness, their inhumanity with the power of his word and of his virtue. He will have the delightful satisfaction of "reigning at last by the power of the word only over an army of the wicked." But he discovers that the power of their silent ruthless violence is greater than that of his virtuous speech. He is overcome. Far from being a Christian martyr, he becomes the dumb sacristan of the idol, and as we meet him he is planning to shoot another Christian missionary who is on his way, this time backed by the French military, to bring the message of mercy to the Salt city. "But I know," says the Renegade, "I know now what to respond to the message, my new masters have taught me the lesson, and I know that they have reason on their side, one must square accounts with love. . . ." "The day they cut out my tongue I learned to adore the immortal soul of hate . . . I abandoned myself (to the idol) and approved his order of evildoing, I adored in him the evil principle of the world."

In his notebooks for 1947, when planning his play on the Russian revolutionaries of 1905 (*Les Justes*), Camus mentions a Russian ascetic who was "mystical and scrupulous" and who, like the gnostic Marcion, lost his faith when confronted with evil. A few pages later he refers to Berdyaev's remark that a certain Procurator of the Russian Holy Synod (a religious autocrat and ideologue) was, like Lenin, a nihilist. Incidentally, Charles de Foucauld is mentioned about this time in the notebooks, but there is no sign of any connection between him and the Renegade in the mind of Camus. He notes ironically that Père de Foucauld thought it normal to furnish the French military occasional information on "the state of mind" of the Tuaregs. But we also note that at the end of "The Renegade" the only people for whom one can feel any sympathy are the French colonists and the missionary whose coming brings some semblance of human hope to the city of despair. So Camus also, to some extent, was able and willing to identify himself with the culture to which he belonged!

In "The Renegade," Camus is satirizing Russian Marxism even more than Christianity, and yet the language is that of his ordinary complaints against what he believed to be a Christian theology of evil. For Camus, Christianity was a servile submission to an unjust order which "had to be accepted" in blind faith in order to give "glory" to an inscrutable authoritarian God. For Camus, Christian faith in God necessarily implied the declaration that evil and suffering were "right" because they gave glory to God and were in some sense necessary to establish and confirm His power over the earth.

This, certainly, is caricature, and we need not pause to discuss it here. What is important, however, is that for Camus the affirmation of the absolute power and justice of God, even when completed by a reverent bow to His mercy, amounted to a denial and rejection of man. To affirm God was to justify the suffering of the innocent, to set up abstract values against the flesh and blood of living man, and to prefer ideas to persons.

This is a well-known stereotype—Christianity is said to involve a radical calumny, a devaluation and rejection of man. Ultimately this is Marx's idea, derived from Feuerbach, that man religiously alienates himself by making over all his own powers and capacities to an imaginary God and living as if he were deprived of what is essentially his own. But Camus turns this concept of alienation against Marxism itself (as he did in his treatise on revolution, L'Homme révolté), for Marxism has put history in the place of God and has projected all man's human value and reality into a future that he must achieve by revolution. For Camus, then, the choice between Christianity and Marxism is only a choice between two sides of the same coin, two kinds of absolutism and alienation in which abstract religious and political systems are preferred to existential human values—to man, his personal dignity and his human freedom.

The point Camus is making in "The Renegade" is, then, that there is nothing surprising about the conversion of a *progressiste chrétien* to Marxism. Christianity has in fact prepared the way for the Marxist cult of history and of absolute justice. The Renegade was a fanatic who from the beginning adored power, and his adoration was only thinly disguised under a Christian exterior of meekness and mercy: when he came face to face with brute violence he had to prostrate himself before what he really adored. Here at last he had found what he had always really sought: "implacable truth." The Renegade alleged that the dogmatic and authoritarian formation of his seminary days had deceived him: "They had fooled me: only the reign of wickedness had no fissures in it!" He who seeks an absolute perfection "with no fissures in it" will, according to Camus, eventually yield to the attractions of a totalitarian system built on murder. He who loves man will respect man in his weakness, fallibility, and contingency.

We can see by this that though Camus was ostensibly anti-Christian, he was instinctively groping toward an authentically Christian interpretation of man's condition—an interpretation which he thought he would no longer find in institutional Christianity and in its official pronouncements. He laid the blame not only on the Church as institution but on what he thought was the Christian concept of God as an absolute authority and implacable judge, demanding impossible perfection and creating evil in order to punish it.

Jan

The title of the play *Le Malentendu* ("The Misunderstanding") tells us what the problem will be. But it does not warn us that the question of communication will be openly discussed, ironically or symbolically, for entire scenes. Jan, a citizen of a Central European country, returns to his home village with a loving young wife he has recently married in North Africa. They are intensely happy in their love, and they are both, by the way, believing Christians. Jan has come to announce to his mother and sister that he has made his fortune and wants to take them away to a land where they can be happy. But he also wants the pleasure of surprising them, and in order to play a rather elaborate practical joke on them, he separates from his wife and presents himself at the inn as a solitary stranger. The mother and sister are closed, hostile, lugubrious beings—a pair of Charles Addams cartoon characters. Martha, the sister, is almost a parody of existentialist gloom, hatred, and despair. These two have been murdering their rare guests in order to save up money and go to a far country "where the sun shines" and where they can at last smile. The "misunderstanding" becomes very complex and begins to operate on several different levels: the root misunderstanding being in fact that of Jan himself. Maria, the only really lucid person in the whole play, senses the danger he faces and warns him to speak simply and directly, but he is incapable of doing this. And because he cannot speak out simply and say who he is, he becomes involved in one tragic complication after another and finally pays with his life for his inability to deliver the simplest of all human messages—the revelation of his own identity.

The play is definitely symbolic. In his notebooks, jotting down ideas before he actually wrote *Le Malentendu,* Camus suggested that the inn might symbolize the world. And the world, as Martha suggests, is only "a place to die in." Martha's philosophy is pure despair. Its bitterness gives it a certain clarity but she does not really see things as they are: hers is the pseudo-lucidity of willful distortion. The world is nobody's home. It is a place of absurdity and estrangement. Jan could have saved himself the trouble of coming into it, when his only reward would be death. Yet he must come into the world and receive death at the hands of its absurd inhabitants. Martha even speaks of Jan in a phrase which has overtones of Biblical messianism: "He who is to come!" But we cannot simply say that Jan represents Christ.

Martha's entirely closed and loveless view of the world and of life is certainly not that of Camus. She proposes a thesis which he himself questions: her arguments and actions are all based on the postulate that true communication is not possible. The real order of the world is one in which "no one is ever recognized." Absurdity, estrangement, loneliness, misunderstanding are basic facts, indeed a sort of metaphysical ground for a baseless and futile existence. Love is vain and pointless. Man has no home and no hope of peace. He can never find rest and reassurance in solidarity and mutual trust based on genuine understanding.

Maria does not share this view. She believes that if Jan would only speak out clearly, declare himself, show his love in plain and obvious terms, this nihilistic philosophy of Martha would be refuted. Maria comes closest to representing Camus' own ideas on love and communication, even though he does not share her Christian faith. For him, too, the great problem is that Jan refuses to speak out in all simplicity.

We know that Camus, in a talk to the Paris Dominicans after World War II, reproached the Church for not announcing a clear, unambiguous message to the troubled world. It is quite possible that the Christian Jan is meant to represent, among other things, the Church. However, he certainly does not carry this symbolic burden alone. Maria is more Christian than he is, and she has none of his ambiguity. The famous last scene of the play, in which—after the murder of Jan and the suicide of the mother and sister—Maria's faith is brutally rebuffed, certainly indicates that *Le Malentendu* is at least partly concerned with the Christian message in the world. But it is not to be taken merely as an attack on Christianity. Jan speaks with his curious and complicated ambiguities not because he is a Christian only but because he is a twentieth-century European. His absurdly contrived surprise is rationalized in familiar modern terms: it will enable him to "study his family objectively." He will thus be "better able to make them happy." And he will "invent ways of being recognized." This is supposedly the voice of "reason." It is the confidence of a scientific mind that speaks. Maria, one of Camus' own favorite characters, speaks rather with the wisdom of love. Why make difficulties where none exist? She urges Jan to walk in and tell them exactly who he is. "There are cases where one simply has to act like everybody else. When one wants to be recognized, one tells his name. . . . If you insist on appearing to be what you are not, you will get everything mixed up. . . . It's not healthy. . . . There is only one way: to say 'Here I am' and let your heart talk."

Maria goes on to spell out this simple theory of communication. She tells Jan exactly what he should say: "I am your son. This is my wife. I have lived with her by the sea, under the sun . . . but I was not yet happy enough and I have need of you. . . ." Jan objects to this presentation of things as inaccurate and "unjust." He wants to defend an image of himself as Savior, as one who is needed by his mother and sister but does not need them. This may perhaps, on examination, seem a bit arbitrary: but it is important for Camus' line of thought. He insists on it. Jan fails in communication because of his one-sided idea that he is bringing happiness to those whom he himself does not need. He is a generous Savior who has looked into their need, studied the problem, understood it, and responded to it. "J'ai *compris* qu'elles avaient besoin de moi. . . ." Everything is logical. And even the apparently playful business of hiding his identity is part of a logical—and complicated—plan. It will all help to make Mother and Martha a little more happy!

Jan is a Savior who observes those he wishes to save, analyzes them, understands them, studies them as their superior, and without consulting them arranges everything to suit his abstract plan for their salvation. He decides he will manipulate their lives (whether they like it or not) and surprise them with the gift of happiness. But his plan is not completely perfect. It is something of an improvisation. He does not quite know the "right words." And "while he was looking for his words they killed him!"

Maria told him from the first that he did not need to look for his words: he already had them. But he had to recognize the words that were his and distinguish them from the words that were not his. He had in fact too many words, some of them his own, many belonging to others: words of theories and worldviews, words of projects and politics, words to explain why things are what they are, words of justice and duty, words to excuse and rationalize his mistakes when it is too late to rectify them. Maria sees that the real source of all this confusion is not lack of intelligence but lack of love. If Jan really loved, he would be able to say what he meant because his love would by itself make that clear to him.

> Men never know how one ought to love. They are never content with anything. All they know how to do is dream, imagine new duties, seek new lands and new homes. But as for us we know that we have to make haste and love share our bed, give our hand, fear absence. When you love you don't dream of anything. . . . But the love of men in a tearing apart. They cannot prevent themselves from abandoning what they prefer.

The root of this error is Jan's distrust of love and his veneration for abstract reason. In order to "see clear" he wants to get away from Maria and from her love, which "confuses" him. But when he is away from her he dies. There is deep unconscious irony in Jan's last words to Maria: "I am doing what I have made up my mind to do and my heart is at peace. You are turning me over for one night to my mother and my sister. What is so terrible about that?" The irony consists in two things: first in the self-righteousness of the "man who has made up his mind," who is doing what he himself wills, and whose "heart is at peace" with itself. But the cost of that peace is the rejection of love. And then the ethical cliché with its implicit syllogism: "All mothers and sisters are loving and life-affirming beings. You turn me over to my mother and sister. Therefore you turn me over to loving and life-affirming beings"—who drug him and dump him in the river. The real "misunderstanding" is to "understand" according to this kind of naïve and unrealistic reasoning.

D'Arrast

So Jan too fails to deliver his message of salvation. What about D'Arrast? "The Growing Stone" is a myth of solidarity and communication, and the story has what the author obviously intended as a positive and "happy" ending. Is it convincing?

In 1949 Camus visited Brazil, and the tale of "The Growing Stone" incorporates some of his own experiences there. He attended a *Macumba* rite and used this material to create the *Macumba* described in the story. He visited Iguape, and many of the characters are based on those he met there. The driver who, in the story, is called Socrates is based on the chauffeur who brought Camus to Iguape and whom Camus in his notebooks nicknamed "Auguste Comte." Most significant of all, the strange vow of the ship's cook—to carry a huge stone on his head to the Church in a penitential procession—was actually witnessed by Camus at Iguape. There a "black-bearded man" carried on his head a rock ten kilograms heavier than the one in the story and, in spite of some difficulty, managed to get it all the way to the Church. In the story, the ship's cook collapses under the stone, and the foreigner, the French engineer D'Arrast, feels himself obligated to take up the stone and fulfill the vow for him.

The story is a *récit-mythe* which reflects the profound impressions of Camus himself in his most intimate contact with South America. It tells us of Camus' own inner feelings about his relationship, as a European, with the primitive and abandoned people of this remote continent: his responsibility toward them and his need for solidarity with them. "The Growing Stone" is in fact a meditation, in the form of a parable or myth, on the relationship between the old established European-American civilization and the colored and mulatto cultures of the emerging "Third World."

Whereas in both "The Renegade" and *Le Malentendu* the problem of communication is difficult and indeed impossible because of the closed and hostile attitude of the ones to whom the "messenger" comes with his message, here the situation is quite different. The people are simple, warm, and open. When they speak, they speak with an almost comical friendliness. Even their silence is expectant. The story reaches its climax in the long silence of the Negroes in the *favela* and ends when one of these breaks the silence, asking D'Arrast: "to sit here with us." But on the whole everyone is friendly, and there is a typical conversation in which Socrates pities the European for his "impoverished" civilized life. "In your country," says Socrates, "you have Mass but no dancing." D'Arrast confesses that he does not go to Mass. "What do you do then?" Socrates cannot conceive of a life with neither Mass nor dancing. Bad enough to be without dancing: but not even Mass? "You are a Lord without a Church, without anything! Stay with us! I love you!" D'Arrast's answer is that he does not know how to dance.

Here Camus is obviously confessing his own characteristic attraction to the pre-Christian primitive world, the world of dancing and nature rites, the world which he idealized in the Greek-Mediterranean culture which had been his dream from the time of his earliest work. Now he gets a glimpse of it still alive and actual in another form, in South America. It fascinates him as primitive art and culture have fascinated so many of us in the Western world since the Romantic revival. This implies a definite and expressed preference for the primitive over our own culture. The ship's cook, conversing with D'Arrast about Europe, sums up what he regards as an impossible situation: "You buy and sell! What filth! And where the police run things, dogs are in command!" It is a judgment of Europe with which D'Arrast expresses no disagreement. But this only accentuates his sense of homelessness and estrangement. "In Europe it was shame and anger. Here exile and solitude in the midst of these sick and agitated madmen dancing themselves to death. . . ."

The vow of the ship's cook (and of the black-bearded man in the real Iguape) obviously suggests Camus' favorite mythical figure, Sisyphus. For Camus, Sisyphus, the "hero of the absurd," is not beaten or frustrated by his impossible task. Having finally elected to give it meaning by freely embracing its absurdity, he has overcome absurdity, and we must "imagine that Sisyphus is happy." But in the curious religious procession of "The Growing Stone," so like the way of the Cross, the mythical figure of Sisyphus merges strangely with the historic and religious figure of Christ on his *via dolorosa* (a figure so alive in Brazilian folk art in any case!). D'Arrast has been compared to Simon of Cyrene. There is a definite resonance here which echoes the Gospel account of the Passion.

Impulsively and for no apparent reason, the ship's cook has roped D'Arrast into his vow: "You will help me keep my promise. . . . Did you ever make any promises yourself?" (D'Arrast lamely admits that he once "nearly" did.) "You are going to help me keep my promise and it will be as though you had made the promise yourself!"

The description of the procession, with the ship's cook struggling far behind it surrounded by a few penitents, is an exciting one. We foresee that when the cook finally collapses and is unable to rise again, D'Arrast will hastily leave his place of honor on the balcony among the "notables," will go down into the street, take the stone on his own head, and carry it to the end. But what end?

Instead of carrying the heavy stone into the Church (and this after all was a substantial element in the cook's vow) D'Arrast carries it down into the *favela* and sets it on the floor in the middle of the cook's poor cabin. There the Negroes slowly and silently gather around him, saying nothing at all, and evidently not fully able to understand how things came out this way. Finally one of them says, "Sit with us. . . ."

It is a curious ending, and it raises certain questions which we shall consider before ending this essay.

First of all, the intention of Camus is obvious enough. He cannot accept the Church as institution. In his eyes, the gesture of taking the heavy stone, at so much cost, and laying it down before the altar is meaningless. The alternative—laying it down in the cabin—is evidently meaningful in his eyes: but it remains quite ambiguous. What is he saying? It is a repetition of his thesis that acknowledgment of God means a depreciation and rejection of man. And that to set things right it is necessary to reject God and by that very fact to acknowledge man.

The Augustinian concept that the love of God was the ground of true communion among men because the *caritas* for God and man was one love, not two, apparently never struck Camus, though he knew his Augustine up to a point. One of Augustine's most characteristic doctrines is that the love of God is worthless if it does not imply communion with our brother: and the living unity of those united in charity forms one body, the Mystical Christ, "the City of God." Here, one would imagine, was a basis for the kind of communication and solidarity Camus was really looking for. But we cannot question the sincerity or the reality of his repugnance for the pseudo-Christianity that has so deformed the *veritas caritatis* and the *caritas veritatis* of Augustine!

Instead, Camus comes out with a rather feeble maxim of liberal and humanist morality. One respects his intention. Yet in reading the story one feels that the ending is inconsistent with what the story itself has told us about the people he claims to love. Whatever Camus himself may have thought about the Church, the ship's cook evidently believed that the meaning of his difficult and sacrificial gesture was precisely that it was a promise to God. And this could not be made clear except by the obvious means of taking the stone to the Church. Absurd, perhaps, but it fits in with a certain primitive logic which is that of the people by whose primitivism Camus feels himself attracted. If then he loves the cook, why does D'Arrast not respect this deep and sincere intention? The reader does not feel that the gesture of laying down the stone in the cabin means anything whatever to the poor Negroes. Camus tries to insinuate that it somehow does, but we are left with the uneasy feeling that he himself is not perfectly convinced. He ends his story on a note of victory: there has been communication. There is solidarity. Oh yes, there really *is*! All we can say is that we hear the author's shrill declaration, nothing more. The ending is dubious and a bit sentimental. The story turns out to be an edifying liberal daydream rather than an effective and poetically convincing myth.

At this point it is interesting to notice that Camus first considered another ending (in his notebooks). Curiously enough, in this alternative, D'Arrast takes the rock and disappears with it into the virgin forest! A return to the primitive origins! This was perhaps a bit too arbitrary and too stark: but it is significant to note that Camus' first impulse was itself an implicit denial of man, not in the name of God but in the name of a quasi-religious feeling of awe and attraction to primitive unspoiled nature or what Mircea Eliade calls "the myth of the eternal return." Then Camus had a second thought (perhaps accompanied by a twinge of conscience). The stone is laid in the hut, but "the most miserable of the huts. . . . Here we are the last, we take the last place among the last." Camus was always attracted by the Franciscan interpretation of Gospel poverty and humility, and this was perhaps what had come to his mind here: but he must have reflected that Communist critics would hoot at it, so he gave this up too.

Germaine Brée, who has written what is perhaps the best book on Camus to date, says in connection with "The Growing Stone" that Camus remained "fundamentally hostile to that humiliating image of man which Christianity presents. . . ." Here we find him turn to it rather spontaneously: and then, of course, regretting the fact. But it is hardly a "fundamental hostility."

His third attempt was, he thought, the lucky one. But when we discover his hesitations we are given grounds for doubt. Do they perhaps reveal to us a deep uncertainty in Camus himself? He cannot dance and he cannot go to Mass either. But he will settle if the poor Negroes in the *favela* say "sit with us." That is all very nice! But the main trouble with this ending is revealed when we ask the kind of question a child might ask at this point: "And what did they do then?"

They did not dance, they did not go to Mass, and the best the reader can do is to surmise that D'Arrast built the dam and went home to Europe, to the buying and selling, to "all that filth," and to a society run by the police, that is to say, "by dogs."

It is just not conceivable that he remained "sitting" with the silent Negroes in the *favela*. The symbolic gesture of D'Arrast is, then, a poignant and perhaps futile confession of nostalgia, the desire to return not to the virgin forest but to the primitive hearth, the sacred center of the neolithic hut, the silent family, the home ruled by the Great Mother, the place of dances. Mingled with this is the Judeo-Christian concept of the "poor" as the "sacred remnant," the true Israel, the *Anawim,* the eschatological people of the future. This concept of the poor in the "Third World"—the poor among whom Camus himself grew up in Algiers—is very important in his early essays, and in his later notebooks he thought of returning to this concept and developing it. But in "The Growing Stone" the idea is as yet only obscurely grasped. Hence we have an attempt at "communion" with primitives, but a communion without transcendence and without real immanence—a communion on the level of edifying fraternal sentiments, a love without metaphysical roots.

"The Growing Stone" is, of the three works we have considered, the one which gives the supposedly positive answer to the problem of communication. Where there is openness, humility, love, and the willingness to accept the obvious limitations of a certain human measure, communication, though never absolutely perfect, may become possible and may lead to solidarity. D'Arrast is open to the kindness and simplicity of the Brazilian people. He has enough sense to see that he needs them even more than they need him. This is certainly one point in his favor. He does not repeat this particular mistake of Jan. Yet at the same time, at the end of the story, one cannot help thinking that D'Arrast has imposed his own one-sided European solution on everyone else after all. He has worked out a message that is, like Jan's, rather contrived and arbitrary. Fortunately the people are all friendly to him. But one can easily imagine that this sudden reversal of meanings, this unexpected ritual ambiguity could mean instant death among real primitives, more open to transcendence and more truly concerned with the validity of their relations with superhuman powers. As it is, we reflect that at the *Macumba* (both the real one attended by Camus and the one in the story) the visitor (Camus-D'Arrast) is asked not to stand with his arms crossed as this will prevent "the descent of the Holy Spirit." Camus very promptly uncrossed his arms as did D'Arrast, and of course they were both right! One doubts if, the next day, Camus would have been able to carry the vowed stone of Sisyphus into "the most humble of the huts." He would have felt very strongly that this involved a radical and dangerous confusion, a failure of communication.

A joke is told about two men who lived in the same apartment to which there was only one key. One evening they were out together, and the one who returned first agreed to leave the key under the doormat. When the other returned he could find the key nowhere. He rang the bell, and the first one appeared at the door. "I thought you were going to hide the key under the doormat," said the other. "Oh yes," replied the first, "but on the way home I thought of a better hiding place. . . ." This is the tragedy of Jan. He wanted to invent better ways of being recognized. And it seems to some extent to be the failure of D'Arrast. Instead of accepting the terms in which his gesture could be understood without explanation, he sought to "invent a better way" of being recognized as a brother.

In the end, then, we must admit that the "successful" communication of D'Arrast is in reality much the same as the arbitrary and contrived game played by Jan: and there is no artistic reason why D'Arrast too should not have lost his life "while he was still looking for his words"— except of course that everyone was very friendly.

To solve the problem merely by making everyone friendly in advance is no solution. It just does away with the problem.

However, if the symbolism of "The Growing Stone" is not in every way artistically successful, the idea Camus is trying to express remains worthy of respect and sympathetic attention on its own level and in the context of his thought. Man on earth (says Camus) is faced with the absurd task of Sisyphus. The struggle to achieve human solidarity in a world of confusion and conflict may at times appear hopeless. Man is fatally attracted to nihilism and violence. His peace is constantly threatened by his incapacity to "recognize" his fellow man as his other self and to enter into frank, simple communication with him. In the past, Camus reflects, man hoped that a message would come from heaven, a Savior would enter the world to be received and understood by men: they would accept his Gospel of peace and would understand and love one another. Instead, thinks Camus, the message was perverted into an ideology of power and authority seeking to control the course of history for the advantage of the powerful, at the expense of the weak. To be a "believer" meant, in effect, to seek reassurance for oneself in persecuting "unbelievers." In other words, one must be willing to prove his fidelity to God by preferring God to man, by sacrificing man to God, not by loving one's neighbor but by burning him at the stake. And this led inevitably to secular mystiques of history and power like Marxism and Fascism. For Camus, then, Saviors and Messiahs are all discredited. Man himself, like Sisyphus, must take up his absurd task—his stone, or, if you prefer, his Cross. In the context of contemporary life, the white European, the South American mulatto, and the black African must roll the stone of Sisyphus together even though their labor seems futile. It is in their common effort that they will arrive at some sort of simple, rudimentary, but valid understanding. But in order to achieve this the European or American must learn to abandon his position of imagined superiority, come down from his eminence, and admit his own need of his underprivileged brother.

Here, although Camus is expressly non-Christian, we must admit that in practice his ethic seems to tend in the direction pointed out by authentic Christian charity. Though Camus failed to understand the full import of the Christian message, the failure is for many reasons understandable, and once again it suggests that even for the Christian the moral aspirations of a Camus retain a definite importance. They bear witness to the plight of man in that world with which the Christian still seeks to communicate, and they suggest conditions under which the communication may conceivably be more valid.

THE STRANGER:
POVERTY OF AN ANTIHERO

"And it was enquir'd Why, in a Great Solemn Assembly
The Innocent should be condemn'd for the Guilty."

Blake, Milton

"Récit: L'homme qui ne veut pas se justifier. L'idée qu'on
se fait de lui est préférée. Il meurt, seul à garder conscience de
sa vérité. Vanité de cette consolation."

Camus, Carnets, Avril 1937

This entry in Camus' *Notebooks* sums up the whole idea of *The Stranger*
—the alienated man who, discovering his alienation, prefers not to justify
it and is condemned by society for this refusal. A few pages later in the
same notes, Camus sketches out the final scene with the priest in the
condemned cell and the resistance of the prisoner who wants to "chew
all his fear" and not evade it.

In between there is a curious entry, a quotation from Luther on justification by faith: "It is a thousand times more important to believe firmly
in absolution than to be worthy of it. This faith makes you worthy and
constitutes true satisfaction." Camus does not tell us what he thinks of
this. Does he accept it or reject it? Usually, when Camus quotes a
Christian writer, it is because he disagrees. Certainly the notion of absolution, in the Christian sense, was foreign to his thought. Yet perhaps
he did incline a little toward Luther's idea of the utterly unworthy
sinner, in his total poverty, being justified in spite of his unworthiness.
Clearly Camus and Luther remain poles apart. But Camus had, after
all, written his dissertation on Augustine at the University of Algiers.
In any event, *The Stranger* is an ironic study in extreme poverty, the
man who has no interiority, who does nothing, makes no choice, has
no real purpose, cannot be justified, has no God; even his crime is not
really "his"—it is so automatic, so mechanical. Because he cannot choose

---

The manuscript of this essay is dated March 1968, but it was not published until the
fall 1968 issue of *Unicorn*.

a role in society, the Stranger is saddled with one by society, so that he has no identity except one which society has arbitrarily contrived for him and which does not fit him at all. An abstraction, a construction, is preferred to him. "The idea that they make of him for themselves is preferred to him." (Incidentally Philip Thody's translation of this in the English version of the *Notebooks* is inadequate: "Other people prefer their idea of him." It is not just that the court and the public are more pleased with their notion of the Stranger as a "born criminal" but that this notion is given official *preference,* so that it displaces his identity, substitutes for his own reality.)

Thus Meursault is finally isolated in his own consciousness of his identity, his truth, which no one else accepts. This sense of identity is something he has to arrive at with considerable labor throughout the trial. It is the fruit of the crime and the trial: the final conscious *acceptance* of his absolute poverty because it is *his* poverty: the act of choice by which he freely elects to *affirm his own absurdity* rather than submit to a convenient but false definition which claims to explain him in the eyes of society. Meursault's refusal to agree that he is what they say he is turns out to be the first real choice he has ever made, and it is his last. But it is a "vain consolation."

The question is: *does this choice justify him?* Is his free acceptance of poverty a spiritual enrichment? Is his admission of absurdity a final somersault into sense?

The Stranger in its tantalizing and condensed simplicity remains a complex, ambiguous book. But it is also famous, a "classic of the absurd." It is regarded, like Sartre's *Nausea,* as a typical "existentialist novel" (in spite of all Camus' protests that he was neither an existentialist nor a "philosopher of the absurd").

In this context it has become usual to interpret Meursault as a "hero of the absurd," as one who is in some sense *justified* by his refusal to justify himself. And of course this is to some extent true if by "justification" is meant the attainment of a final personal integrity of some sort.

The division of *The Stranger* into two parts, breaking at the precise point of the murder, is highly significant. Up until the murder, Meursault is a passive, mechanical sort of being with a fairly rich vegetative, sensuous life, existing in total indifference to abstract or formal questions of any kind. He is without ambition, without any drive whatever, integrated only in a kind of symbiotic existence with the rest of the world. If he is alienated, he doesn't know it, it does not hurt him, he couldn't care less. He is in many ways quite happy. He "loves life," but in a plainly superficial kind of way. He accepts his life in the North African city, his acquaintances, his girl friend, his job, without involvement and without comment. He responds when pushed, or when solicited: but without enthusiasm or even interest. Offered a good job in Paris, he declines it, saying he is all right where he is. When Marie proposes marriage, he says, "O.K., if you like." She asks, "Do you love me?" He says, "No." "Would you marry any other woman in the same circumstances?" "Yes." And so on.

The murder is the fruit of this passive, automatic existence—and an awakening from it. The shooting is almost entirely an accident. Completely unmotivated, it occurs under the blazing noonday sun of North Africa in a trance of *acedia* worthy of a Desert Father. It is a pure climax of that inner sloth which is at the heart of Meursault's "character." A study of *The Stranger* as a paradigm of *acedia,* of surrender to the "noonday demon" of Evagrius and Cassian, might prove revealing. *Acedia* is the demon of psychic exhaustion, listlessness, void, thirst, and the moral impotence which attacks the ascetic when he has been entirely burned out by the desert sun and seeks at all costs to find a little shade and clear water. *Acedia* is the desperation which drives the frustrated monk to escape his imprisonment in his own destroyed and meaningless being (his desert cell which has become a hell and a Babylonian furnace) and return to simple contact with the refreshment and interest of worldly life. Meursault kills the Arab as a result of an involuntary, reflex impulsion to take one more step in the direction of the cool water of the spring near which the Arab is resting. There is a profound significance in this whole chapter on the murder, a chapter which is not only consummate myth but rises to the level of prophecy.

The Arab is not seen as a person. Meursault does not kill out of personal hate. Nor is it a question of racist animosity. The violence which drives the Arab and Meursault together is the same symbiotic violence which accounted for all the hundreds of crimes in Algeria at that time— the murder of Arabs not by the French but by one another. It is not the hatred of the *colon* for the Arab or vice versa, but the more elemental collision of lower-class atoms in the symbiosis of alienation. The mindlessness of Meursault, a poor French Algerian, is radically the same as that of the poor Arab. Meursault's indifference, his "fatalism," have something of the same quality which colonial cliché assumed was purely Islamic or African.

If Meursault does not treat the Arab as a person, there is no discrimination involved: he does not regard himself as a person either. Two nonpersons meet in the blinding sun of an African beach. One is lying by the limpid spring in the shade. The other is drawn mindlessly to the coolness. It happens that fate has decreed, through a strange and arbitrary involvement, that they must be hostile to each other. One pulls a knife. The other happens by chance to have a revolver . . . But the impulsion that draws Meursault to the spring is not essentially violent at all. It could just as well have been a drift toward reconciliation and acceptance. In its deepest ground, it was simply a blind, instinctive urge to be by the same spring where the Arab happened to be: an inarticulate, and never to be articulated, gravitation toward unity in nature.

But this blind groping for a purely *natural* unity between the races, a return to some supposed primitive Eden of sinless and unselfish communion in nature, is doomed by history to frustration. Whether it may or may not ever have been theoretically possible, history has placed insuperable obstacles in the way of this reunion. There is a *karma,* a historic and pathological residue of crime, exploitation, hatred, and incomprehension which can only be sweated out in pain, turmoil, conflict.

After the murder, Meursault awakens to the *inevitability* of conscious suffering and conflict that comes from being, whether you like it or not, in history. He is brought up face to face with a society which has been determined by certain fatal historical choices: his passivity has not absolved him from the endemic and historical ills of the Algerian colony. He painfully awakens not to a full social awareness, but at least to "his own truth." His fidelity to that truth, as far as it goes, is heroic. I say *as far as it goes.* It does not go all the way.

Let us return to the main question: does Meursault's outburst of frustrated anger against the importunate priest in the death cell constitute a *justification?* The cliché interpretation of *The Stranger* assumes that it does. Meursault is presented as the lone individual in his absurdity and authenticity, who justifies his existence by exposing the lies and the massive organized hypocrisy of the social establishment and resisting them unto death.

According to Camus' original idea, quoted at the beginning of the article, Meursault does not wish to be justified, does not even attempt to justify himself. He permits the idea that people have of him to be preferred to him. *But he does not allow them to impose that idea upon himself.* That is to say, he neither considers himself justified nor does he accept as a substitute the proffered absolution by which the lack of justification is rectified. He knows he is not right, but he also knows that he is not really wrong. He knows that consent to the fictitious and absurd scenario of his wrong, concocted by a troubled society in order to allay its own anxieties, would be a greater wrong.

It turns out that there is enough sullenness, enough revolt, underlying his *acedia* to underwrite this refusal with some energy. Pushed to the wall, he no longer submits blindly to the force that pushes him. He turns violently against it. He rebels against everyone and everything, and in so doing shatters the grip that *acedia* has upon him. In the final breakthrough, he makes what is fundamentally a personal commitment of his entire life and his entire being: if he is to die, he will accept death in terms which are *his,* in terms which correspond to his own genuine experience of himself and not in a formula dictated to him by somebody else in terms of a fictitious identity which has been devised for him, in bad faith, by a misguided court of law. Ultimately this implies a recognition on his part that the guilt rests as much on the corrupt social organization as it does upon his own self, and that a legality which neatly separates out right and wrong in favor of an "order" which masks avarice, self-interest, and spite should not have the final say in determining the meaning and value of one's own personal existence. So he will allow the vindictive law to destroy him but not to meddle with his own self-definition.

This is "heroism" certainly. But Camus also intended it as a "vain consolation" rather than as a "justification," because this too was only another aspect of absurdity, and absurdity *does not justify.*

To make too much out of Meursault, to justify him as a splendid rebel who stands alone against the inhuman social monolith and defies it to his last breath, is to introduce stereotypes which falsify Camus' own ideas.

It is quite true that Camus belongs in a tradition of protest and resistance which, through Romanticism, goes back to the archetype of Romantic Rebellion, Milton's Satan. But it is equally true that Camus was, like Milton, a classicist. Neither for Milton nor for Camus is the mere fact of rebellion sufficient to justify either Satan or Meursault. (Of course it is clear that the utter poverty and in some ways the helplessness of Meursault, and above all his total refusal of rhetoric and declamatory self-justification, set him apart from the Satan of *Paradise Lost.*) But student and critics have habitually fallen into the temptation of thinking that the Satan figure is justified by his own rhetoric and by his own revolt.

Those who have made too much of a hero out of Meursault have forgotten not only his poverty and his somewhat provisional place in the scheme of Camus' work, but they have also misread the meaning of the

Camusian absurd. Meursault's revolt against society's interpretation of him and his crime is a revolt against *a total systematic explanation* of existence which falls down not because it happens to be an inadequate explanation but because it is total. *All total explanations* are inadequate and deceptive. For Camus, that included all philosophical systems (including existentialism insofar as it claimed to be "total") and all religious doctrines (note that he was better able to accept unformulated religious experience in primitive Franciscanism). Now insofar as justification implies integration into a system or a total explanation, to be justified means to enter into the general and specious deceptiveness of the system itself. Even to want to justify oneself is to yield to the temptation of thinking that there is, or can be, a "total explanation" whose claims can be verified and which can really solve all the basic questions.

The real import of the "absurd" in Camus is its direct confrontation with the gap between thought and actuality—a gap which is created and made absolute by attempts to "explain" it. Rational demonstration— or the Hegelian *Verstand*—claims to exorcize the absurd but only makes it inexorable. It divides consciousness from reality, thought from actuality, subject from object, in a canonization of estrangement, a systematic schizophrenia blessed by a purely abstract Reason. In other words, Camus is in revolt against French Cartesian rationalism, which pretends to have answers for everything. The absurd in Camus is his reply to the Cartesian *cogito*—a systematic doubt that goes deeper than "cogitation" and doubts the power of reason itself. Later, Camus was to replace Descartes' formula with another totally different one based on solidarity in love and action: "we revolt, therefore we are."

Now when a "philosophy of the absurd" takes on the appearance of a rational explanation, and when, in terms of that explanation or "system," one can be justified or make sense out of life by becoming a "hero of the absurd," then this too collapses into falsity and bad faith. Acceptance of the absurd, in Camus' terms, does not justify life, does not give it meaning; it is the lucid acceptance of unmeaning. Furthermore, this is not the end, only the beginning: for to live in meaninglessness and absurdity is not an end. That would be simple nihilism, and Camus was completely opposed to nihilism. But when one can face a life that is "without justification," one is, according to Camus, prepared to go beyond to that solidarity in revolt and ultimately to that unity in love which he intended to explore in his later works. One starts, in other words, by renouncing the desire to be justified—one renounces hope of a consoling sense of one's own clarity and rightness—in order to go on to that lucid solidarity in action and resistance that are conscious of their own limitations and respectful above all of life.

This is what, in Camus, is "beyond justification." It does not need to be justified. And in any case, it cannot be justified by being fitted into the context of something else that is less basic, less authentic, less real, but more easily reduced to rational formulas. The authenticity and love toward which Camus tended were, then, beyond formulas of justification and explanation. They were also in some sense beyond the apprehension of an interior spiritual insight, beyond any *trémoussement prophétique*.

Camus always strove for a lucid interior austerity in this regard. He recognized the temptation to substitute inner exaltation and spurious luminosity—emotional affectation and mystique—for genuine solidarity, lucidity, action, found only in the ordinary stuff of everyday life. "This battle by means of poetry and its obscurities, this apparent revolt of the spirit, is *what costs the least*. It is ineffective and tyrants know that well." (*Carnets*, 1942)

On the other hand, those who make too much of a hero out of Meursault tend to read his outburst at the end as if it were a final flash of mystic exaltation, a luminous deliverance from the tyranny of an alienating world, a breakthrough into transcendence, a kind of existentialist *satori,* an *ecstasy of the absurd.* Unfortunately the very ground of the Camusian absurdity is that it negates ecstasy. (This does not alter the fact that for Camus a certain neo-Platonic ecstasy in the immediate grasp of natural beauty was possible and was finely expressed in some of his early essays—*cf.,* "Le Désert.")

It must be admitted that Camus himself, in the preface of the American student edition of *The Stranger* (written in 1955), spoke in less moderate language of his Meursault. The Stranger "is a man poor and naked" who "refuses every mask" who "refuses to lie . . . by saying more than he feels" but who is "in love with the sun that casts no shadows" and is animated "by a profound passion . . . for the absolute and for truth." Camus goes on to give encouragement to those immoderate spirits who make Meursault a Christ-figure, by admitting that, well, he is "the only kind of christ we deserve." It must be remarked that this language is much more vibrant than that which Camus himself was using twenty years before. And its vibrancy does strike a definite note of "justification" and of "interiority" which are alien to the earlier work. But we must see them in the context of Camus' own development. *The Plague* and *The Rebel* have taken Camus far beyond the limitations of the "absurd" and committed him fully to an ethical vitalism in which he recognizes the shortcomings of nihilism. The "ethic of quantity" which he had approved in *The Myth of Sisyphus* seemed innocent enough at the time: but experience of Nazism had shown how easily it could become the ethic of Auschwitz. Nevertheless, Meursault's "love of life" had not progressed that far. It was not yet the profound human compassion of Rieux and Tarrou.

To have only the lucidity of Meursault is by no means enough. To recognize that life is absurd is certainly not to answer the question of its meaning: that answer, according to Camus, is not found by speculation but by making. One *gives* life a meaning by living it in openness and solidarity with others. But Meursault is utterly impoverished because he is utterly alone. He is caught in his own absurdity because, having rightly rejected the hypocrisy of systematic answers and explanations proposed by others, he has not entered into solidarity with anyone else. He does not love anyone else. He does not love Marie, or his mother, or his neighbors, or his friends. The fact that he frankly admits his lovelessness does not make him a hero.

This might seem to be painfully obvious, yet it is important to spell it out in a time when a lot of people, misled perhaps by a distorted appreciation of writers like Camus, think that it is enough to proclaim life absurd and confess that one's own existence is meaningless—as if this were a guarantee of instant lucidity and even of moral superiority over everyone else. But this only leads to the kind of sterility and defeat that Camus himself refused to tolerate. A disillusioned nihilism, dressed in the right kind of cool clichés, can be made to seem heroic: but it is only another feeble and ineffective attempt to justify one's own defeat.

There is a chapter in Fanon's *The Wretched of the Earth* which throws a decisive new light on the mentality of Meursault and on his *acedia*. This extremely important essay on "Colonial War and Mental Disorders" studies case histories of Algerians who were brainwashed and tortured by the French in the Algerian war, and does so against the background of an official racist psychosociology which was being officially taught at the University of Algiers when Camus studied there and when he planned his novel. Fanon's essay integrates all these elements in one consistent picture of the colonial structure of Algeria in which Camus grew up and in which the story of *The Stranger* takes place. What is remarkable above all is that the case histories of the victims of the colonialist repression in war show so many of the features we find in Meursault. Moreover, Meursault's character and his crime correspond in almost every detail with the kind of formula worked out by the official colonialist psychiatry of the thirties in Algiers. It is important to note that what applies to Algerian Arabs applies also to many French *colons* who were, in any case, formed by the same system. Thus Meursault is an *Algerian* before all else, rather than a white as distinct from an Arab Algerian.

Here is a passage from Fanon about a French girl whose father was killed after he had tortured many Arabs. The crisis and conflict produced in her by her revolt against the colonialism incarnated in him produced something of Meursault's apparent lassitude, disgust, and *acedia*.

> The death of her father . . . was mentioned by the patient with such light-heartedness that we quickly directed our investigations towards her relations with her father. The account which she gave us was clear, completely lucid, with a lucidity which touched on insensibility . . .
>
> "The funeral sickened me," she said, "all those officials who came to weep over the death of my father whose 'high moral qualities conquered the native population' disgusted me. Everyone knew that it was false. . . . They all came there to tell their lies about my father's devotion, his self-sacrifice, his love for his country and so on. I ought to say that now such words have no meaning for me. . . . I avoided all the authorities. They offered me an allowance but I refused it. . . ."

This of course reminds us of the funeral in *The Stranger*. Obviously, there are important differences, but the alienation is the same and it has the same roots. So too is the refusal of a proferred social role—this time as patriot and victim. The story of *The Stranger* is the story of a man who has been living in apparent happiness in spite of unconscious alienation, becomes conscious of his actual condition, and becomes able to articulate his protest and resistance against what has caused it.

Now in summing up the official psychiatric doctrine of French colonialism, Fanon lists characteristics which were accepted without question as being those of the Algerians: they are born lazy, they are slackers, cretins, liars, robbers, and murderers. This, incidentally, was thought to be "proved scientifically" by physiological study. The Algerian—and the African in general—"lacked a cortex" and was dominated like an animal "by his diencephalon." His life was therefore purely vegetative and instinctive. He had no interiority, no morality, no spirituality (unlike the superior European!). He was therefore impulsive, he murdered without motive, he was in fact driven to homicide by a kind of melancholia—in other words, we have a perfect description of Meursault and his *acedia*, as interpreted by the court which condemned him. Though not using the jargon of this psychiatric literature, the court started from the same assumptions and ended, naturally, with the same results. And it agreed perfectly with the official conclusion that there was only one way to control such people: force. Guns, or the guillotine. Camus' Stranger as defined by the court is identical with the "North African" as analyzed and dismissed by a colonialist pseudo-science based on the kind of shallow rationalism which inevitably condemned human beings to an alienated and absurd existence.

The official teaching of colonialist psychiatry was, in two words, that the African was a *lobotomized European.* Meursault is precisely that: a lobotomized European. But Camus, like Fanon, saw that the explanation was not physiological, it lay in history: "the history of men damned by other men."

The poverty of Meursault is the product of a social system which needs people to be as he is and therefore manufactures them in quantity—and condemns them for being what they are. Camus portrayed in Meursault not the physical misery of starvation, deprivation, and disease, but the psychic misery of alienation. He also portrayed the awakening of Meursault to identity through a quasi-accidental crime. But Meursault remained in his poverty, his absurd, solipsistic loneliness. He was not able to find and integrate himself completely by compassion and solidarity with others who, like himself, were poor.

III
INTRODUCING POETS IN TRANSLATION
(1963–66)

RUBÉN DARÍO

Nineteen sixty-six marks the hundredth anniversary of the birth of one of the greatest Latin American poets, Rubén Darío, in an obscure town of Nicaragua. The event is of course being celebrated in Spanish-speaking countries and will be dutifully noted, no doubt, where Spanish is taught on North American campuses. The poetry of Darío is not likely to be widely read in the United States today. Even more modern Spanish-American poets like César Vallejo and Pablo Neruda remain largely unknown. Yet Darío has something to say to us. The following lines, written for a volume of official tribute to be published in Nicaragua, may be of interest to North American readers.

All true poetic genius tends to generate prophetic insight. The poet cannot help but listen to awakening voices that are not yet audible to the rest of men. The greatness of Rubén Darío lay not only in the orphic power of the song by which he transformed the Spanish poetry of his own time but also in the prophetic apprehension in which he foresaw something of our own age. While we salute the eloquence, the creative freedom, the luminosity, the passionate fervor of this great spirit, we must also pay attention to what he tells us about ourselves: and this we are less likely to expect of him, since *modernismo* is no longer modern but dated, like the *art nouveau* which was its contemporary. Yet even in his poetic style Rubén Darío had at his command a rich diversity of tone and harmony, and (if one may express a personal preference) his admirable "Sonnet to Cervantes," at once limpid, casual, and profound, anticipates the less rhetorical poetic tastes of a later generation.

Darío was concerned not only with poetic renewal but with man himself, and especially with the future of the two Americas. In the universality of his genius and in the strength of his poetic aspiration to unity, Rubén Darío longed for a world that would be culturally and spiritually one in civilized harmony and fraternal co-operation. But he foresaw the danger to this dream of unity—the danger of power used blindly by men of personal sincerity and limited understanding (not to mention the abuse of power by others less sincere and perhaps more intelligent). He foresaw the perils of an age that would set too great a price upon ma-

---

Written in 1966, this essay was published in *Continuum*, autumn 1966.

chines and muscles and too little upon authentic civilized and ethical values. He foresaw above all the terrible difficulties that would beset the vitally necessary dialogue between the two Americas: the Anglo-Saxon north and the Ibero-Indian south. Rubén Darío was fully aware of the importance of mutual understanding between these great racial and national complexes. He foresaw, too, that the dialogue between them could all too possibly remain superficial and might perhaps one day be silenced in a violent, inarticulate frenzy. One has only to recall his devastating poem to (Theodore) Roosevelt, the bronco buster, tiger killer, and "professor of energy." In the "language of the Bible and Whitman" Rubén Darío appealed not only to the president but to the whole North American people for a better understanding of the complexities and needs of their brothers in the South. In spite of many earnest gestures of good will and sincere efforts at understanding, we are permitted to wonder if the desired results have ever been attained, except in the case of a few exceptional men. It is to be regretted that North America never appreciated Rubén Darío as did Europe, and his voice has been only imperfectly heard here.

Yet Rubén Darío, being magnanimous, remained an optimist. His admiration for Walt Whitman taught him to see the vast resources of human honesty and fraternal love in the people of North America. In his own blood and in his own spirit he experienced the riches of the South American civilization, which gave him even greater and more inexhaustible hopes for the future. It is highly significant that Rubén Darió blended in his veins the blood of the Spaniard, of the Indian, and the Negro. He experienced in himself both the anguish and the creative power of the fusion which is now closer to fulfilling its providential destiny in the world of man.

Not only in his writing but in his person Rubén Darío portrays for us the chances and challenges facing the Ibero-Indian America as it enters upon the period of its significant action in world history. What events will usher in the new era? We can hardly guess at present—and guesses may not always comfort us with easy answers to almost impossible questions.

Yet, facing the imminence of even greater and more critical changes than Rubén Darío was able to imagine, we can learn from him to advance into the future with trust not only in the goodness of man but in the infinite goodness of the Creator and Redeemer of man. And we can repeat after Darío these great words which were so often echoed, in substance, by Pope John XXIII: "Abominad los ojos que ven solo zodiaces funestos!" ("Abhor the eyes that see only fatal zodiacs!").

RAISSA MARITAIN

Jacques and Raissa Maritain were married in 1904 when they were both students at the Sorbonne, seeking not degrees but truth, in the midst of nihilism and despair. Their story is well enough known: how first they came upon Bergson and then discovered metaphysics. How they then met Léon Bloy living like a desolate and compassionate tiger in Montmartre, in utter destitution and prophetic holiness, cursed by respectable bigots as a follower of Satan. It was Bloy who in bringing them to the font of baptism (where he was their godfather) helped kindle the purest light in the Catholic intellectual renewal of the twentieth century.

Will we ever know how much of the best of Jacques' writing owed its realization to Raissa? One is aware of her influence in the last chapters of his *Degrees of Knowledge* on contemplative wisdom. Raissa left her imprint on the remarkable *Art and Scholasticism* and collaborated with Jacques in works on poetry and prayer which remain as classics.

Raissa Maritain was perhaps one of the great contemplatives of our time, great in her humility, her simplicity, her angelic purity of heart, her utter devotion to truth. Her whole life, all her thought and love were centered in the supernatural, that is to say in the Three Divine Persons considered as a source and finality more intimate and more ultimate to her than her own natural and contingent individuality. Their transcendent and immanent presence in turn gave everything around her a religious and spiritual transparency which sometimes shone with an indescribably pure and transfiguring light, the "Light of Thabor" of the Russian mystics, and yet a light which appeared only in pure and apophatic darkness. This is the real root of her poetic experience, even when her poetry seems to say nothing explicit about God. Her verse is so devoid of artifice, so pure of ornament and mannerism, that it has the immediacy of a Japanese drawing. One thinks instinctively of visual analogies for her poetic experience precisely because it is so immediate and so pure. It has the direct impact of painting, and in many of the poems one

This essay introducing Merton's translations of Raissa Maritain's poetry from the French first appeared in *Jubilee*, April 1963, and was subsequently published in *Emblems of a Season of Fury* (New York: New Directions, 1963). The translations were later included in *The Collected Poems of Thomas Merton* (New Directions, 1977).

irresistibly sees the subject through the eyes of the painters who were the Maritains' friends. "The Prisoner" for instance: even though she refers by name to Quentin Matsys, this is a rugged painting with all the dark labored and muted compassion of Rouault. "The Lake" is like a picture by Dufy or Matisse. And then, of course, there is their friend Chagall. Raissa not only herself sees things as does her compatriot, but writes with childlike wonder of what he beholds. Beyond "The Prisoner," however, and beyond the profoundly moving poem on the Mosaic of the Blessed Virgin in the Church of St Praxed, there is the prodigious and simple "dream" of angels ("The Restoration of the Pictures") recorded when Jacques was ambassador of France to the Vatican and when Raissa was with him in Rome. One feels that such a poem was more than a mere dream. In any case it is a comfort to know that even in a world of atomic bombs and extermination camps such "dreams" are possible. This alone would be sufficient reason for the publication of a few characteristic poems by a saintly Christian who, in her simplicity, was one of the glories of our kind in a century of torment, duplicity, and confusion.

FERNANDO PESSOA

Fernando Pessoa is a curious and original figure of the early twentieth century, in some sense an antipoet, who wrote under several pseudonyms in Portuguese besides publishing poems in English and Portuguese over his own name. *The Keeper of the Flocks* is a collection attributed by Pessoa to a fictitious personage called Alberto Caeiro—and the first line of the book is "I am not a keeper of the flocks." The interest of the poetic (or antipoetic) experience of Alberto Caeiro lies in its Zen-like immediacy, though this is sometimes complicated by a certain note of self-conscious and programmatic insistence. However, Pessoa-Caeiro may be numbered among those Western writers who have expressed something akin to the Zen way of seeing—the "knack of full awareness."

This short introduction to Merton's translations from the Portuguese of poems by Fernando Pessoa, from *The Keeper of the Flocks,* was written in 1965 and was found among Merton's unpublished manuscripts following his death. The translations are included in *The Collected Poems of Thomas Merton* (New York: New Directions, 1977).

CÉSAR VALLEJO

Certainly one of the greatest Latin American poets of the present century, César Vallejo hardly needs a long introduction. Born in a small town in the High Andes of Peru, in 1893, Vallejo was half Indian, and all his life he wrote verse full of colloquialisms and turns of phrase peculiar to Peru: in addition to which he invented words whenever he felt like doing so. He fled from the mountains to Lima, then to Paris. All his life he thought and spoke as a Peruvian of the Andes, and yet he became a "cosmopolitan" poet among so many others living in poverty on the Left Bank, in the twenties and early thirties. Picasso's drawing of Vallejo shows a rugged, sad, and serious man, sardonic and compassionate, not given to empty political rhetoric or to the trifling of literary fashion. He was too conscious of the suffering and the tragedy of twentieth-century man and of his own insoluble ambiguities. There are moments when he reminds one of Rimbaud and Baudelaire, but he is always more reserved and more austere, at once more virile and more humble, always jealous of his independence and of his originality, which were great. He is a poet of much more consistent excellence than his friend Pablo Neruda. Vallejo went to Madrid during the Spanish Civil War and then returned, broken and almost without hope, to die in 1938, torn apart by the inexorable forces that were plunging the world into disaster. Yet no one with such deep compassion and such inextinguishable humanity could ever be completely negative. The work of César Vallejo can be classed with the most authentic and creative achievements of our time.

Written about 1963, this introductory essay to Merton's translations from the Spanish of César Vallejo's poetry was first published in *Emblems of a Season of Fury* (New York: New Directions, 1963). The translations were subsequently included in *The Collected Poems of Thomas Merton* (New Directions, 1977).

ALFONSO CORTES

The story and figure of this unknown Nicaraguan poet are fantastic. He has never before been published in any language but Spanish, and he has barely been published in that language, even in his native country. Yet there he is a kind of symbol and portent, discovered years ago by Coronel Urtecho, and looked upon with awe by the young poets of the Nicaraguan avant-grade today; for Cortes went mad one February night, more than thirty-five years ago, in the house of the one Nicaraguan poet who has enjoyed a world-wide reputation: Rubén Darío. Ernesto Cardenal, as a child, going to the school of the Christian Brothers in León, used to look in the door of Darío's house and see Cortes inside, chained to a beam. Since that time Cortes has been transferred to a hospital, and there, visited by the young poets, he declaims about the defects of his "rival" Darío (who died in 1916).

Yet Cortes has written some of the most profound "metaphysical" poetry that exists. He is obsessed with the nature of reality, flashing with obscure intuitions of the inexpressible. His poetic experience is quite unique. There is no explanation for its sudden appearance in an obscure Central American township, at such a time, under such circumstances.

It cannot be said without qualification that Cortes' verse is that of a madman. His best poetry, which is completely individual, has been written now in "lucid" moments and now in moments which would be considered "insane." But then, too, he has written some very bad verse, both when "sane" and when not so sane. The good verse is at once metaphysical and surrealistic, with a deep, oneiric, and existentialist character of its own. The bad verse is simply conventional. There has been *no evolution* in his poetry, but he sometimes rewrites poems that he had written forty or fifty years ago. "Truth" is one such poem, a recent version (considerably improved) of an earlier piece. It can be said that Cortes is a man of a few basic poetic experiences which have continued to stay explosively alive in his subconscious and which enable him completely to

This essay introducing Merton's translations from the Spanish of poems by Alfonso Cortes was written in the early sixties and was first published in *Emblems of a Season of Fury* (New York: New Directions, 1963). The translations appear in *The Collected Poems of Thomas Merton* (New Directions: 1977).

transcend his condition by breaking through to the world which he calls "theological."

His idea of "man" (that is, of himself) is that of a "mystical tree" on which space and time are fruits produced by the life that is within him: but man's business is not so much to "comprehend" these fruits of space and time (or, as we might say, to have a history) but rather to live in the full, bewildering, and timeless dimension of a life so shattering in its reality that it seems to be madness. Hence Alfonso Cortes has no history, for he lives in "the origin of things which is not anterior to them, but permanent." This gives his poetry (and it is perhaps only in his poetry that he is fully present as himself) the strange, unerring certitude of Zen.

RAFAEL ALBERTI

It is almost forty years since Rafael Alberti's series of poems *Concerning the Angels*[1] first appeared in Spain. The publication of an English version of the complete series will probably not be regarded as an important event. Yet it is. And perhaps it is also timely. More somber, more austere and arresting than Lorca's *The Poet in New York*. The intensity and concentration of this series makes it capable of a valid and generative effect which our poetry could use at the present time.

The Spanish poets of the "Generation of 1927" are, with one exception, not well known outside Spanish-speaking countries. The one exception is García Lorca, who died a dramatic and violent death in the first days of the Spanish Civil War. Rafael Alberti, an Andalusian like Lorca, survived the war and has since lived in exile in various places—now in Rome. He is sixty-four years old and continues to write. His latest is a privately printed book of poems presented in homage to his friend Picasso in the latter's eighty-fifth year. The poems for Picasso are illustrated by Alberti himself, who began as a painter and turned to poetry in the early twenties, winning the Spanish National Prize for Literature with his first book of verse, *Marinero en Tierra,* in 1924.

The tag "Generation of 1927" refers to the fact that in that year a group of young Spanish poets, among them García Lorca, Alberti, Aleixandre, Guillén, Salinas, and Gerardo Diego, decided to celebrate the tercentenary of the baroque poet Góngora. Since Góngora was considered an impossible and unreadable poet by the literary establishment at the time, this celebration constituted an act of defiance and a new beginning in Spanish verse. Critics are divided on the point whether the result can be called "surrealism." The point is academic. In any case one can say that the peculiar chaotic intensity of this verse results from a rich profusion of unconscious images jarring against one another in creative dissonances and dreamlike shock effects with a result quite different from the dry, dead-pan parade of objects (and "objective correlatives") with which we

---

This essay, written in 1966, first appeared in *Continuum,* spring 1967, under the title "Rafael Alberti and His Angels."

[1] Rafael Alberti, *Concerning the Angels* in *New Directions in Prose and Poetry 19* (New York: New Directions, 1966).

have become familiar (and perhaps so exhausted) in English and American verse since the First World War.

Alberti experienced in Spain the same Wasteland that Eliot had confronted in England and America, but Alberti's response to it was different. It would be wrong to accuse Eliot of having no "spirit" and no "interiority," but the mysticism of *Four Quartets* remains distinctly sober, objective, barely hinted at in spare and traditional austerities of roses and flame, ashes and dark explosions and silences, frost and stone, a bell in the sea. Alberti (struggling as did Gerontion with what has since become fashionable as the "death of God") created or rather discovered the depths of his subjective struggle and came to spiritual terms with himself in a world of disconcerting forces which he called angels. His poems *Concerning the Angels* are most powerful in their controlled anarchy and their sustained ironies which plunge much further than Eliot into the hidden dynamism of our extraordinary world and of our own predicament in it.

We may remark here that in the world where God is claimed to be dead and where religion, in despair, seeks to content itself with the synthetic foods of sociology, pseudo-politics, and liturgical cliché, artists have been unexpectedly concerned with angels. True, there is no agreement on that subject, and angels do not get very far these days in pale English. But remember Rilke and the *Duino Elegies* above all. Be reminded of the revival of interest in Blake. The restoration of Milton in honor after Eliot seemed to have demolished him for good. Think, too, of Chagall in painting. Alberti's angels tend to be monochrome, and he has nothing of Chagall's colors. Visually, the angel world of Alberti is more like Picasso's *Guernica* than like Chagall. And yet in one of his early books (a year or two before the *Angels*) his poems remind us at once of Chagall and of the early silent movies for, as he said, he owed to the films a kaleidoscopic development of sensibility:

> I was born with the movies, heaven help me!
> Under a net of planes and cables,
> When the stately coaches of kings were done
> And the Pope climbed into an auto.

In the same poem he watches an outdoor movie in a Spanish village, where Anne Boleyn is all mixed up with the nearby sea and a policeman "dissolves her with the flower of his flashlight." Another poem of this series is a charming celebration of Buster Keaton's search through the forest "for his sweetheart a full-blooded cow." The picture is pure Chagall.

So the poetry of Alberti begins not with a refusal of the world of those

new media which, both "hot" and "cool," have lately come to be celebrated by Marshall McLuhan, but with an acceptance of their devastating
effect on the old patterns of imagination, the old way of seeing and singing. Some of Alberti's early poems remind me of the songs of Bob Dylan,
who bravely jumbles together all the mad collection of cultural ikons
that have been stuffed into the heads of our kids in high school ("Shakespeare, *he's* in the alley / with his pointed shoes and his bells / He's talking with a French girl / who says she knows him *well. . . .*" Obviously
Shakespeare is in the alley because everybody else who was ever heard of
is there too).

The *Angels* of Alberti belong to a period of personal crisis in the late
twenties, followed by a time of objectivity, recovery, and political consciousness during the Spanish Civil War. The latter poems are by far less
interesting: Alberti having become a success on the Left and having enjoyed the usual free trips to Russia was now well-to-do—a member, in
fact, of a particular poetic establishment in which there was no more
place or need for angels.

Quotations from Alberti's autobiographical notes, *La Arboleda Perdido,*
are given in the introduction to the Englished *Angels* and provide an
essential basis for an understanding of them. The angels are in part forces
of life struggling for freedom against a capricious and arbitrary sense of
quiet and in part forces of alienation and death reinforcing that guilt.
They create a kind of spiritual snake pit, a "pit of disasters" in which the
poet is trying to recover some sort of elementary strength to liberate himself. Sometimes the angels are helpful, sometimes they bring only new and
more inscrutable accusations. Alberti's solution is not to escape the
struggle and the ruins—for escape is impossible, but:

> Submerging myself, burying myself deeper and deeper in my own ruins,
> pulling the rubble over my head, with my entrails torn and my bones splin-
> tered. And then were revealed to me the angels. . . .

This is no doubt Spanish violence, incompatible with our nice optimism.
And yet observe that when the "ruins" are frankly seen and accepted the
angels are revealed. It is not good news that tells us that the ruins are
not there. And in the ruins too is met Christ, but a strange Christ who
destroys by his presence all holy-card images of himself—a burning presence, a "hound of heaven":

> Endless, intense, white hot glow
> The steady shade of the hound.
> His still shadow.

The extraordinary baroque effect of Alberti's *Angel* poems is due in part to the way in which matter dissolves into spirit and spirit congeals into marble or plaster, with the human element left out—without even a spectator. Such is the "uninhabited" condition of alien man in whom angels (the good hard to tell from the bad) fight with objects, walls, glass, membranes, garments, fabrics, or simply draughts of air. Yet the human is not always completely negated. Sometimes the zombie rouses himself and drives the angel out. (Or is it a zombie angel driving out the real one?) In any case, to be without the angel is not the ultimate in good fortune:

> My body's empty black sack
> Stood by the window alone.
> It went.

> Down streets, round corners it started.
> My body walked off deserted.

So the angel is desperately needed.

> Dead angel, awaken
> Where are you? Send your lightning
> to light my homeward road.

But nothing is definitive. There are alarms, battles, reconciliations. The uninhabited suit which is man is sometimes peopled with revived expectations, anonymous hopes, too pale to step forward by themselves, too used to deception, but still capable of being pushed by some exasperated spirit. Yet the spirit himself hesitates, and does not reveal his own intentions—or let us know if he *has* intentions.

All this is given not in analysis, not in argument, but in hard and resistant imagery.

> There once was a light that had
> for its bone a bitter almond.

> . . . only two unwavering matches from an electric nightmare
> fixed on his dusty earth and judging it.

> . . . A King is a hedgehog of eyelashes.

The angels are sometimes furies, sometimes driving and teaching storms of fire, sometimes ice and snow, sometimes empty frames. Always they invade our empty homes and ask why there is no inhabitant. Why? Perhaps because there are too many bodies and there is no room to breathe. We can no longer leave each other enough room to be lucky.

And so Alberti laments the man who had a city inside him, and then lost it. After which he became a tunnel. You shout into the tunnel, and there is no echo. Then the angels reduce him to ashes. They char all his dreams to rubble. Methodically, furiously. And suddenly we hear echoes of the Bible:

> —You, in downfall
> you, overthrown,
> the finest city of all.

The angelic poems of Alberti are prophetic "burdens" like the burdens of Isaiah and the laments of Ezekiel over Babylon and Tyre, and as such they can be attended to with a certain pity and fear appropriate to the awareness of tragedy and of accursedness—an awareness to which our own poets have seldom been attuned though a few of our prose writers—Faulkner above all—certainly have. One can agree with the translator of these poems that this book can be considered one of the greatest poetic works of the twentieth century. It has been published entire, in an excellent translation, in the latest New Directions annual (*New Directions in Prose and Poetry 19,* 1966).

JORGE CARRERA ANDRADE

Humanity, tenderness, and wit in the sense of *esprit* characterize the innocence and seriousness of Jorge Carrera Andrade. He is one of the most appealing of the fine Latin American poets of our century. One is tempted to call him an incarnation of the genius of his humble and delightful country, Ecuador: a land of green volcanoes, of hot jungles and cold sierras, of colonial cities set like jewels in lost valleys; a land of Indians and poverty. The voice of Ecuador (which sings in his verse) is a soft, humble voice: a voice, oppressed but without rancor, without unhappiness, like the voice of a child who does not get much to eat but lives in the sun. Ecuador is a hungry wise child, an ancient child, like the child in the Biblical proverbs who was always playing in the world before the face of the Creator. An eternal child, a secret Christ, who knows how to smile at the folly of the great and to have no hope in any of the strong countries of the world. Ecuador has always been, and will always be, betrayed by the strong. It can despair of them without sorrow, because to despair of shadows is no despair at all. It is, in fact, a pure and sacred hope. This kind of truth, this kind of confidence, strong nations, preparing ruin, cannot understand. . . .

Some sixty years ago Carrera Andrade was born in Quito, and in the dawn of his life the cobbled streets of the sleepy capital echoed for him with the rhythms of Verlaine and Góngora. He read the Symbolists under the eucalyptus trees and meditated baroque conceits in the green-and-white presence of the volcano Pichincha. Yet his poetic sensitivity remained simple and happy, for he walked among the cornfields and Indians of the country, sharing their blood and their silence, thinking and making their poems in his heart. He has remained pre-eminently a South American poet.

He had taken an active part in the politics and journalism of his

---

This essay, which served as an introduction to Merton's translations from the Spanish of Jorge Carrera Andrade, first appeared in *New Directions in Prose and Poetry 17* (New York: New Directions, 1961), and was also included in *Emblems of a Season of Fury* (New Directions, 1963). It was later published in *A Thomas Merton Reader,* ed. Thomas P. McDonnell (New York: Harcourt Brace & World, 1962). Merton's translations of Jorge Carrera Andrade's poetry are included in *The Collected Poems of Thomas Merton* (New Directions, 1977).

country. He had already published more than one book of poems when, in 1928, he boarded a Dutch steamer in Guyaquil and headed for Europe.

> In a ship of twenty bugles
> I took my trunk of parrots
> To the other end of the world.

His bags and his money were stolen in Panama. He wandered through Holland, Germany, France, Spain. He lived as poor people live, traveling third class, carrying everywhere his light burden of poetry and of Indian blood. More and more alone in the ancient cities, he wrote poems, first one book then another. In the strikes, the riots, the movements of the day, he stood with the poor. He sided with the Left, hoping for a better world. But the ambiguities of power politics making use of the humble and defenseless to increase its own power did not satisfy him. He broke away from Communism. He found himself more alone.

He set up a small publishing house in Paris. He married. He came home to South America. Later he went to Japan, China, and England, in the consular service of his country. In 1941 he came to the United States as Ecuadorian Consul in San Francisco. He found the city exciting, and he responded gladly to the friendship and to the hard-boiled mystery of North America. He wrote a "Song to the Oakland Bridge" which was to him a symbol of strength and peace:

> Thy spans are of peace,
> Thy sea-chains set men free.
> From thy unceasing journey thou returnest,
> Dragging a city and a handful of orchards.

Yet I do not think Carrera Andrade has built his hopes definitely on any earthly or political power. He has learned a new geography, the world which has to be discovered sooner or later by those who do not believe in power, violence, coercion, tyranny, war. "I embarked for the secret country, the country that is everywhere, the country that has no map because it is within ourselves."

It is in this secret country that I have met Carrera Andrade, and here we have become good friends. Here without noise of words we talk together of the mountains of Ecuador, and of the silent people there who do not always eat every day. The secret country is a country of loneliness and of a kind of hunger, of silence, of perplexity, of waiting, of strange hopes: where men expect the impossible to be born but do not always dare to speak of their hopes. For all hopes that can be put into words are now used by men of war in favor of death: even the most sacred and living words are sometimes used in favor of death.

During the last war the poet was silent, except for the quiet irony of his parachute jumper. He looked about him at the desolation of man, at the prison without a key in which man had enclosed himself, or so it seemed, forever. Carrera Andrade has not reproached anyone, has not joined the harsh chorus of the prisoners in despair. He has listened, silently, to other voices and other harmonies. Can prophecy be so humble, so unassuming? Can the voice of a new world be so quiet? Is this the voice of the gray-green Andes, of the long-hidden America, of the dim and cool twilight of the Sierra dawn out of which peace, perhaps, will one day be born?

Who can answer such absurd questions? It is foolish perhaps to ask them outside of the secret country in which, unasked, they retain their meaning and prepare the hearer, quietly, for the answer they already contain.

PABLO ANTONIO CUADRA

Unquestionably one of the leading intellectual figures of Nicaragua, Pablo Antonio Cuadra has earned, by his sincerity and maturity, a central position in the tormented political life of Central America, in which dictators and left-wing revolutionists alike turn to him as arbiter in their disputes. Editor of one of the most outspoken newspapers in Central America, *La Prensa* of Managua, he is also a fine poet, not in the "modernist" tradition of Rubén Darío but in that powerful "indigenist" movement which has tapped the deepest and most authentic sources of Latin American poetic inspiration, in Mexico, Peru, Ecuador, and other predominantly Indian countries.

Like César Vallejo, Pablo Antonio Cuadra has dedicated himself with passion to the frank expression, in Spanish, of the Indian within him. He has therefore joined the ranks of those who have created what is undoubtedly the finest and most authentically "American" poetry of Latin America. We have long been familiar with the corresponding tradition in the plastic arts, and it is years since Orozco, Diego Rivera, and later Rufino Tamayo became famous in North America. The poets have not enjoyed a similar good fortune.

Cuadra's verse owes its vitality not to a sentimental and romantic meditation on the "Indian past" of Central America, but to its roots in a grim and vital Indian present, in which the past still lives with an unconquerable and flourishing energy through the unmatched prestige of the ancient plastic arts, architecture, folklore, and music, as well as in the texts of ancient Indian poems and dramas. Cuadra himself is so directly inspired by the pre-Colombian Chorotega pottery of his own native country that these poems were written, so to speak, to be "inscribed on ceramics."[1]

This introductory essay to Merton's translations from the Spanish of Pablo Antonio Cuadra's poetry was written about 1963 and first appeard in *Emblems of a Season of Fury* (New York: New Directions, 1963). It was later brought out in a handsome edition by Unicorn Press. The translations were subsequently included in *The Collected Poems of Thomas Merton* (New Directions, 1977).

[1] See Samuel K. Lothrop, *The Pottery of Costa Rica and Nicaragua* (New York: Museum of the American Indian, 1926). Cuadra tells us that the Chorotega culture was probably pre-Mayan, later being mingled with that of the Nahoas, or Nicaraos, in Nicaragua. In addition to their polychrome ceramics, the Chorotegas left stone sculpture which often expressed the mythic conception of the *alter ego*—an animal covering a human figure as a guardian angel—a theme which has inspired some of Cuadra's poetry.

Actually, the original Spanish versions were accompanied by drawings by the author, taken from stylized Nahoa ceramic themes. The combination of poem and picture was singularly effective, and the book, *El Jaguar y la luna,* received the Rubén Darío prize for Central American verse in 1959.

Cuadra, then, absolutely refuses to regard the Indian heritage of Central America as a matter of archaeology or of lavish color pictures in *Life* magazine. It is to him something living, something that boils and fights for expression in his own soul, and in the soul of his people. Certain aspects of his verse are social and political. He cannot do otherwise than attempt, as so many others have attempted, to clarify contemporary aspirations in the language of ancient myth. It is a singularly fruitful and necessary combination, and there is no longer any question of its validity. Cuadra himself has spoken of his attitude in the following words:[2]

On this road, we refuse to treat the Indian legacy as archaeology and we believe that this legacy contains a life that we can continue to exploit in order to express ourselves as Americans. This is the last step, and a difficult one, because the Indian legacy is shrouded in mystery. . . . My first task therefore was to reduce the great inheritance of the Toltecs, Olmecs, Mayas, Aztecs, and Incas to that which was most directly my own. I made the acquaintance of the arts of the ancient peoples of Nicaragua. I saturated myself in the culture of the Nahoas, or Nahuas, and Chorotegas. I studied their pictorial expressions (in ceramics) and their sculpture (in stone) in order to gain possession of their spirit and of the artistic outlook with which they saw the world and their lives, in order to express them. I called upon the ancient texts of Indian poems to help me in the verbal forms of expression they employed. Folklore also helped me in this matter of expression, above all the popular street theater. For the rest, I waited in study and in love for the answer. . . .

The answer came in these poems, *The Jaguar and The Moon,* in which the social, cultural, and political struggles of Central America are invested with the passion and eloquence of a primitive tradition.

[2] From an unpublished letter to the translator of these poems [T. Merton].

ERNESTO CARDENAL

Born in 1925 in Granada, Nicaragua, Ernesto Cardenal is one of a number of significant young poets who have reached maturity in the poetic movement begun, in that country, by José Coronel Urtecho and Pablo Antonio Cuadra. Educated at the University of Mexico and Columbia University, Cardenal was involved in a political resistance movement under the dictatorship of the elder Somoza, and this experience is reflected in a volume of *Epigrams* written before he entered Gethsemani, and published in Mexico, as well as in a long political poem, *La Hora O.*

Cardenal applied for admission to Gethsemani, and we received him into the novitiate in 1957. He had just exhibited some very interesting ceramics at the Pan American Union in Washington, and during his novitiate he continued modeling in clay. He was one of the rare vocations we have had here who certainly and manifestly combined the gifts of a contemplative with those of an artist. However, his poetic work was, by deliberate design, somewhat restricted in the novitiate. He set down the simplest and most prosaic notes of his experiences, and did not develop them into conscious "poems." The result was a series of utterly simple poetic sketches with all the purity and sophistication that we find in the Chinese masters of the T'ang Dynasty. Never has the experience of novitiate life in a Cistercian monastery been rendered with such fidelity, and yet with such reserve. He is silent, as is right, about the inner and most personal aspects of his contemplative experience, and yet it shows itself more clearly in the complete simplicity and objectivity with which he notes down the exterior and ordinary features of this life. No amount of mystical rhetoric could ever achieve so just an appreciation of the unpretentious spirituality of this very plain monastic existence. Yet the poet remains conscious of his relation to the world he has left and thinks a great deal about it, with the result that one recognizes how the purifying isolation of the monastery encourages a profound renewal and change

This introduction to Merton's translations from the Spanish of Ernesto Cardenal's poetry was written in the early sixties and was first published in *Emblems of a Season of Fury* (New York: New Directions, 1963). The translations appear in *The Collected Poems of Thomas Merton* (New Directions, 1977).

of perspective in which "the world" is not forgotten but seen in a clearer and less delusive light.

I do not know how much the selections from "Gethsemani, Ky." (Mexico City, 1960) will mean to someone who has never listened to the silence of the Kentucky night around the walls of this monastery. But Cardenal has, with perfect truthfulness, evoked the sounds of rare cars and trains that accentuate the silence and loneliness by their passage through it.

He was not destined to remain for life in this particular solitude. His health was not sufficiently strong, and indications were that he should go elsewhere. He is still pursuing in Central America his vocation as priest, contemplative, and poet. He is much published in Mexico and Colombia, where he is rightly recognized as one of the most significant of the newly mature generation of Latin American poets.

IV
RELATED LITERARY QUESTIONS
(1953–68)

POETRY, SYMBOLISM AND TYPOLOGY

The Psalms are poems, and poems have a meaning—although the poet has no obligation to make his meaning immediately clear to anyone who does not want to make an effort to discover it. But to say that poems have meaning is not to say that they must necessarily convey practical information or an explicit message. In poetry, words are charged with meaning in a far different way than are the words in a piece of scientific prose. The words of a poem are not merely the signs of concepts: they are also rich in affective and spiritual associations. The poet uses words not merely to make declarations, statements of fact. That is usually the last thing that concerns him. He seeks above all to put words together in such a way that they exercise a mysterious and vital reactivity among themselves, and so release their secret content of associations to produce in the reader an experience that enriches the depths of his spirit in a manner quite unique. A good poem induces an experience that could not be produced by any other combination of words. It is therefore an entity that stands by itself, graced with an individuality that marks it off from every other work of art. Like all great works of art, true poems seem to live by a life entirely their own. What we must seek in a poem is therefore not an accidental reference to something outside itself: we must seek this inner principle of individuality and of life which is its soul, or "form." What the poem actually "means" can only be summed up in the whole content of poetic experience which it is capable of producing in the reader. This total poetic experience is what the poet is trying to communicate to the rest of the world.

It is supremely important for those who read the Psalms and chant them in the public prayer of the Church to grasp, if they can, the poetic content of these great songs. The poetic gift is not one that has been bestowed on all men with equal lavishness, and that gift is unfortunately necessary not only for the writers of poems but also, to some extent, for those who read them. This does not mean that the recitation of the Divine

---

This essay formed a chapter in Merton's *Bread in the Wilderness,* a study of the Psalms of the Old Testament as poetry (New York: New Directions, 1953). It was later included in *A Thomas Merton Reader,* ed. Thomas P. McDonnell (New York: Harcourt, Brace & World, 1962).

Office is an aesthetic recreation whose full possibilities can only be realized by initiates endowed with refined taste and embellished by a certain artistic cultivation. But it does mean that the type of reader whose poetic appetites are fully satisfied by the Burma Shave rhymes along American highways may find it rather hard to get anything out of the Psalms. I believe, however, that the reason why so many fail to understand the Psalms—beyond the fact that they are never quite at home even with Church Latin—is that latent poetic faculties have never been awakened in their spirits by someone capable of pointing out to them that the Psalms really are poems.

Since, then, they are poems, the function of the Psalms is to make us share in the poetic experience of the men who wrote them. No matter how carefully and how scientifically we may interpret the words of the Psalms, and study their historical background, if these investigations do not help us to enter into the poetic experience which the Pslams convey, they are of limited value in showing us what God has revealed in the Psalms, for the revealed content of the Psalter is *poetic*. Let it therefore be clear, that since the inspired writer is an instrument of the Holy Spirit, who, according to the Catholic Faith, is the true Author of the Psalms, what is revealed in the Psalter is revealed in the *poetry* of the Psalter and is only fully apprehended in a poetic experience that is analogous to the experience of the inspired writer. However, when I speak of the poetry of the Psalter and the content conveyed by its poetic form, I do not mean to imply that it is necessary for everyone to read or recite the Psalms in their original Hebrew, in which alone they possess their authentic and integral artistic form. I imagine that every contemplative would, at some time or other, wish that he could chant the Psalms in the same language in which they were chanted by Jesus on this earth, and in which He quoted them when He was dying on the Cross! This is a longing that very few of us will ever be able to satisfy. But it is accidental.

Actually, the simplicity and universality of the Psalms as poetry makes them accessible to every mind, in every age and in any tongue, and I believe that one's poetic sense must be unusually deadened if one has never at any time understood the Psalms without being in some way moved by their deep and universal religious quality.

The Psalms are more than poems: they are *religious* poems. This means that the experience which they convey, and which the reader must try to share, is not only a poetic but a religious experience. Religious poetry—as distinct from merely devotional verse—is poetry that springs from a true religious experience. I do not necessarily mean a mystical experience. Devotional poetry is verse which manipulates religious themes and which does so, perhaps, even on a truly poetic level. But the experiential content of the poem is at best poetic only. Sometimes it is not even that. Much of what passes for "religious" verse is simply the rearrangement of well-known devotional formulas, without any personal poetic assimilation at all. It is a game, in which souls, no doubt sincere in their piety, play poetic draughts with a certain number of familiar devotional clichés. This activity is prompted by a fundamentally religious intention, if the poem be written for the glory of God or for the salvation of souls. But such poems rarely "save" any souls. They flatter those who are comfortably "saved" but irritate the ones who really need salvation. A truly religious poem is not born merely of a religious purpose. Neither poetry nor contemplation is built out of good intentions. Indeed, a poem that springs from no deeper spiritual need than a devout intention will necessarily appear to be at the same time forced and tame. Art that is simply "willed" is not art, and it tends to have the same disquieting effect upon the reader as forced piety and religious strain in those who are trying hard to be contemplatives, as if infused contemplation were the result of human effort rather than a gift of God. It seems to me that such poetry were better not written. It tends to confirm unbelievers in their suspicion that religion deadens instead of nurtures all that is vital in the spirit of man. The Psalms, on the other hand, are at the same time the simplest and the greatest of all religious poems.

No one will question the truly religious content of the Psalms. They are the songs of man—and David was the greatest of them—for whom God was more than an abstract idea, more than a frozen watchmaker sitting in his tower while his universe goes ticking away into space without him. Nor is the God of the Psalms simply an absolute, immanent Being spinning forth from some deep metaphysical womb an endless pageantry of phenomena. The Psalms are not incantations to lull us to sleep in such a one.

The human symbolism of the Psalter, primitive and simple as it is, should not deceive us into thinking that David had an "anthropomorphic" God. Such a mistake could only be made by materialists who had lost all sense of poetic form and who, moreover, had forgotten the violent insistence of the great Jewish prophets on the transcendence, the infinite spirituality of Jaweh, who was so far above all things imaginable that He did not even have an utterable name. The God of the Psalter is "above all gods," that is to say, above anything that could possibly be represented and adored in an image. To one who can penetrate the poetic content of the Psalter, it is clear that David's concept of God was utterly pure. And yet this God, who is "above all the heavens," is "near to those who call upon Him." He who is above all things is also in all things, He is capable of manifesting Himself through them all.[1]

The men who wrote the Psalms were carried away in an ecstasy of joy when they saw God in the cosmic symbolism of His created universe.

The heavens declare the glory of God, and the firmament proclaims the work of his hands.

Day unto day heralds the message, and night unto night makes it known.

There is no speech nor words, whose voice is not heard:

Their sound goes forth unto all the earth, and their strains unto the farthest bounds of the world.

There he has set his tabernacle for the sun, which like to the bridegroom coming out from the bridal chamber, he exults like a giant to run his course.

His going forth is from one end of the heavens, and his circuit ends at the other . . .[2]

Praise ye the Lord from the heavens, praise ye him in the high places.

Praise ye him, all his angels, praise ye him, all his hosts.

Praise ye him, O sun and moon, praise him, all ye shining stars.

Praise him, ye heavens of heavens, and ye waters that are above the heavens:

Let them praise the name of the Lord, for he commanded and they were created,

And he established them for ever and ever: he gave a decree, which shall not pass away.

Praise the Lord from the earth, ye sea-monsters and all ye depths of the sea.

Fire and hail, snow and mist, stormy wind, that fulfill his word,

Mountains and all hills, fruitful trees and all cedars,

Beasts and all cattle, serpents and feathered fowls,

Kings of the earth and all people, princes and all judges of the earth,

Young men and even maidens, old men together with children:

Let them praise the name of the Lord, for his name alone is exalted.[3]

---

[1] Cf., *The Roman Missal: Collect for the Mass of the Dedication of a Church.*
[2] Psalm 18: 2–7.
[3] Psalm 148: 1–13.

Although we tend to look upon the Old Testament as a chronicle of fear in which men were far from their God, we forget how many of the patriarchs and prophets seem to have walked with God with some of the intimate simplicity of Adam in Eden. This is especially evident in the first days of the Patriarchs, of which the Welsh metaphysical poet Henry Vaughan speaks when he says:

> My God, when I walke in those groves,
> And leaves thy spirit doth still fan,
> I see in each shade that there growes
> An Angell talking with a man
> Under a *juniper* some house,
> Or the coole *mirtles* canopie,
> Others beneath an *oakes* greene boughs,
> Or at some *fountaines* bubling Eye:
> Here *Jacob* dreames, and wrestles: there
> *Elias* by a Raven is fed,
> Another time by th' Angell, where
> He brings him water with his bread;
> In *Abr'hams* Tent the winged guests
> (O how familiar then was heaven!)
> Eate, drinke, discourse, sit downe, and rest
> Untill the Coole, and shady *even*.

As age succeeded age the memory of this primitive revelation of God seems to have withered away, but its leaf is still green in the Psalter. David is drunk with the love of God and filled with the primitive sense that man is the *Leitourgos* or the high priest of all creation, born with the function of uttering in "Liturgy" the whole testimony of praise which mute creation cannot of itself offer to its God.

The function of cosmic symbols in the Psalter is an important one. The revelation of God to man through nature is not the exclusive property of any one religion. It is shared by the whole human race and forms the foundation for all natural religions.[4] At the same time the vision of God in nature is a natural preamble to supernatural faith, which depends upon distinct and supernatural revelation. Hence even those modern readers who may be repelled by the "historical" Psalms will nevertheless be attracted by those in which the keynote is struck by cosmic symbolism and by the vision of God in nature.

[4] Cf., Romans I: 18 and Acts 14:15.

However, the cosmic symbolism in the Old Testament is something much more than an element which Judaeo-Christian revelation shares with the cults of the Gentiles. The Old Testament writers, and particularly the author of the creation narrative that opens the Book of Genesis, were not only dealing with symbolic themes which had made their appearance in other religions of the Near East: they were consciously attempting to purify and elevate the cosmic symbols which were the common heritage of all mankind and restore to them a dignity of which they had been robbed by being degraded from the level of theistic symbols to that of polytheistic myths.

This question is so important that I hope I may be permitted a brief digression in order to touch upon it.[5]

Everyone knows with what enthusiasm the rationalists of the late nineteenth century berated the Judaeo-Christian revelation for being fabricated out of borrowed materials, because the religious themes and symbols of the Old Testament were similar to those of many other Eastern religions, and because the New Testament made use of language and concepts which bore a great resemblance to the formulas of Platonic philosophy, the ritual language of the mystery cults, and the mythological structure of other Oriental beliefs. Even today the world is full of honest persons who suppose that this parallelism somehow weakens the Christian claim to an exclusive divine revelation. The writers of the Old and New Testaments were simple men, but St. John the Evangelist was certainly not so simple as to imagine that the Greek word *logos,* which he may well have borrowed from the Platonists, was a personal discovery of his own. The fact that the Biblical writers were inspired did not deliver them from the common necessity which compels writers to clothe their ideas in words taken from the current vocabulary of their culture and of their time. When God inspired the author of Genesis with the true account of the creation of the world, the writer might, by some miracle, have set the whole thing down in the vocabulary of a twentieth-century textbook of palaeontology. But that would have made Genesis quite inaccessible to anyone except a twentieth-century student of palaeontology. So instead, the creation narrative was set down in the form of a poem which made free use of the cosmic symbolism which was common to all primitive mankind.

[5] I am especially indebted to the article by Père Jean Danielou, S.J., "The Problem of Symbolism," in *Thought,* September 1950. See also his book *Sacramentum Futuri* (Paris: 1950).

Light and darkness, sun and moon, stars and planets, trees, beasts, whales, fishes, and birds of the air, all these things in the world around us and the whole natural economy in which they have their place have impressed themselves upon the spirit of man in such a way that they naturally tend to mean to him much more than they mean in themselves. That is why, for example, they enter so mysteriously into the substance of our poetry, of our visions, and of our dreams. That too is why an age, like the one we live in, in which cosmic symbolism has been almost forgotten and submerged under a tidal wave of trademarks, political party buttons, advertising and propaganda slogans, and all the rest—is necessarily an age of mass psychosis. A world in which the poet can find practically no material in the common substance of everyday life, and in which he is driven crazy in his search for the vital symbols that have been buried alive under a mountain of cultural garbage, can only end up, like ours, in self-destruction. And that is why some of the best poets of our time are running wild among the tombs in the moonlit cemeteries of surrealism. Faithful to the instincts of the true poet, they are unable to seek their symbols anywhere save in the depths of the spirit where these symbols are found. These depths have become a ruin and a slum. But poetry must, and does, make good use of whatever it finds there: starvation, madness, frustration, and death.

Now the writers of the Bible were aware that they shared with other religions the cosmic symbols in which God has revealed Himself to all men. But they were also aware that pagan and idolatrous religions had corrupted this symbolism and perverted its original purity.[6] The Gentiles had "detained the truth of God in injustice"[7] and "changed the truth of God into a lie."[8]

Creation had been given to man as a clean window through which the light of God could shine into men's souls. Sun and moon, night and day, rain, the sea, the crops, the flowering tree, all these things were transparent. They spoke to man not of themselves only but of Him who made them. Nature was symbolic. But the progressive degradation of man after the fall led the Gentiles further and further from this truth. Nature became opaque. The nations were no longer able to penetrate the meaning of the world they lived in. Instead of seeing the sun a witness to the power

[6] The classical passage in this connection is the first chapter of St. Paul's Epistle to the Romans.

[7] Romans I: 18.

[8] Romans I: 25.

of God, they thought the sun was god. The whole universe became an enclosed system of myths. The meaning and the worth of creatures invested them with an illusory divinity.

Men still sensed that there was something to be venerated in the reality, in the peculiarity of living and growing things, but they no longer knew what that reality was. They became incapable of seeing that the goodness of the creature is only a vestige of God. Darkness settled upon the translucent universe. Men became afraid. Beings had a meaning which men could no longer understand. They became afraid of trees, of the sun, of the sea. These things had to be approached with superstitious rites. It began to seem that the mystery of their meaning, which had become hidden, was now a power that had to be placated and, if possible, controlled by magic incantations.

Thus the beautiful living things which were all about us on this earth and which were the windows of heaven to every man, became infected with original sin. The world fell with man, and longs, with man, for regeneration. The symbolic universe, which had now become a labyrinth of myths and magic rites, the dwelling place of a million hostile spirits, ceased altogether to speak to most men of God and told them only of themselves. The *symbols* which would have raised man above himself to God now became *myths,* and as such they were simply projections of man's own biological drives. His deepest appetites, now full of shame, became his darkest fears.

The corruption of cosmic symbolism can be understood by a simple comparison. It was like what happens to a window when a room ceases to receive light from the outside. As long as it is daylight, we see through our windowpane. When night comes, we can still see through it, if there is no light inside our room. When our lights go on, then we see only ourselves and our own room reflected in the pane. Adam in Eden could see through creation as through a window. God shone through the windowpane as bright as the light of the sun. Abraham and the patriarchs and David and the holy men of Israel—the chosen race that preserved intact the testimony of God—could still see through the window as one looks out by night from a darkened room and sees the moon and stars. But the Gentiles had begun to forget the sky, and to light lamps of their own, and presently it seemed to them that the reflection of their own room in the window was the "world beyond." They began to worship what they themselves were doing. And what they were doing was too often an abomination. Nevertheless, something of the original purity of natural revelation remained in the great religions of the East. It is found in the *Upanishads* in the *Baghavad Gita*. But the pessimism of Buddha was a reaction against the degeneration of nature by polytheism. Henceforth for the mysticisms of the East, nature would no longer be symbol but illusion. Buddha knew too well that the reflections in the window were only projections of our own existence and our own desires, but did not know that this was a window and that there could be sunlight outside the glass.

So much, then, for cosmic symbols. In the Psalms we find them clean and bright again, where David sings:

O Lord, our Lord, how glorious is thy name in all the earth, thou who
    hast exalted thy majesty above the heavens . . .
When I gaze at the heavens, the work of thy fingers, the moon and stars,
    which thou hast made:
What is man, that thou art mindful of him? or the son of man, that thou
    hast care of him?
And thou hast made him a little lower than the angels,
    thou hast crowned him with glory and honour;
Thou hast given him dominion over the works of thy hands;
    thou hast put all things under his feet:
Sheep and oxen, all of them, and the beasts of the field, too,
The birds of the heaven and the fishes of the sea:
    and whatever traverses the paths of the seas.
O Lord, our Lord, how wonderful is thy name in all the earth![9]

But it is not the cosmic symbolism that is the most important symbolism in the Bible. There is another. This is the symbolism we have already referred to as *typology*. The typological symbolism of the Bible is not common to other religions: its content is peculiar to the Judaeo-Christian revelation. It is the vehicle of the special message, the "Gospel" which is the very essence of Christian revelation. And it is typology above all that makes the Psalms a body of religious poems which are, by their own right altogether unique.

[9] Psalm 8: 2, 4–10. Every line of this Psalm has antipolytheistic repercussions. Man, who can see God *through* His creation, is in possession of the truth which makes him free. (John 8: 32) Thus he leads a spiritualized existence "a little less than the angels" and stands in his rightful place in the order of creation, above the irrational animals. The Gentiles, on the other hand, have descended lower than the animals, since they have lost the knowledge of God though God remains evident in His creation. For by their ignorance of God, they have doomed themselves in the worship of beasts. (Romans I: 23) Compare also: St. Bernard, *De Diligendo Deo*, Chapter II, n. 4; *Patrologia Latina*, Volume 182, column 970.

I have already brought up the subject of the typical sense of the Psalter. I have discussed the significance of type and antitype, and suggested briefly that the important antitypes in Scripture all have something to do with the Incarnation of the Word of God, and with man's Redemption by the Sacrifice of Christ on Calvary, for this is the central Mystery of the Christian faith. It is now time to add a few remarks on the importance of typology in the Psalms.

Pope Pius XII said, we remember, that "By assuming human nature, the Divine Word introduced into this exile a hymn which is sung in heaven for all eternity." The context of this important declaration suggested to us that if the Psalter and the Liturgy can become for us means to contemplation, it is simply because they are capable of uniting us with Christ in this "hymn which is sung in heaven." That is as much as to say that if the Psalter is to lead us to contemplation we must know how to find Christ in the Psalms. Apart from a few clear messianic prophecies it is typology that reveals Christ to us, even in some of the most unexpected lines of the Psalms.

Scriptural typology is a special kind of symbolism. It is something far purer and more efficacious than allegory. I would even add that in the Psalms allegory is altogether negligible. There is almost nothing in the Psalter that reminds us of the tissue of allegorical complexities which goes to make up a poem like Spenser's *Faerie Queene*. It seems to me that the personification of moral abstractions is foreign to the spirit of true contemplation.

The relation of types and antitypes in Scripture is a special manifestation of God: it is the testimony of His continuous providential intervention in human history. Unlike the universal cosmic symbols, which repeat themselves over and over with the seasons, historical and typical symbols are altogether singular. Cosmic symbols reflect the action of God like the light of the sun on the vast sea of creation. Typological symbols are meteors which divide the dark sky of history with a sudden, searing light, appearing and vanishing with a liberty that knows no law of man. Cosmic symbolism is like clouds and rain: but typology is like a storm of lightning wounding the earth unpredictably with fire from heaven.

Consider for a moment the typology of the Deluge. In the Deluge, God purifies the world, destroying sin. The Deluge is simply a type of the one great redemptive act in which God destroyed sin: Christ's Passion and death. But the symbolism of the Deluge goes further: it also manifests to us the activity of God destroying sin in the souls of individuals by the

336

sacraments, for instance Baptism and Penance, in which the merits of Christ's Passion are applied to our souls. This also corresponds to another Old Testament type: the crossing of the Red Sea by the people of Israel. Finally, all these symbols are tied together in one, final, climax of significance. All Scriptural types point to the last end, the crowning of Christ's work, the establishment of His Kingdom, His final and manifest triumph in His Mystical Body: the Last Judgment. There again the same creative action by which God manifested Himself in the Deluge will once more strike the world of sin. But this time it will have the nature of a final "accounting" in the sense that then all men will come forth to give testimony to their personal response to God's action in the world. Those who have believed, and who have freely accepted the light and the salvation offered to them from heaven, will pass, like the Israelites, through the Red Sea; they will be rescued in Christ as Noah's sons were saved in the Ark; they will have lived out the meaning of their Baptism because they will have died and risen with Christ. Those who were not with Christ—and all who are not with Him are against Him—will manifest what they too have chosen. It will be their own choice that they will drown in the Deluge and perish with the chariots of Egypt in the closing waters of that last sea.

Not only do many of the Psalms literally foretell the suffering and glory of Christ, but David is a "type" of Christ. The Psalter as a whole is "typical" of the New Testament as a whole, and often the particular sentiments of the Psalmist are, at least in a broad sense, "typical" of the sentiments in the Heart of the Divine Redeemer. Even the sins of David belong to Christ, in the sense that "God hath laid upon Him the iniquity of us all."[10]

[10] Isaias 53: 6.

POETRY AND CONTEMPLATION: A REAPPRAISAL

Author's Note
Ten years ago I wrote an article called "Poetry and the Contemplative Life"
which was published first in Commonweal *and then appeared in a volume*
of verse, Figures for an Apocalypse.

In its original form, this article stated a "problem" and tried to apply a
rather crude "solution" which, at the time, was rather widely discussed
by people interested in religious verse and, at least by implication, in
religious experience. Many of them were inclined to accept the "solution"
that was proposed. Others wisely rejected it because of its somewhat puri-
tanical implications.

As time passed I have found that the confident pronouncements made
in my early writing lay more and more heavily on my conscience as a
writer and as a priest, and while it is evidently impossible to correct and
amend all my wrong-headed propositions, at least I would like to revise the
essay of 1948. The revision is unfortunately not fully satisfactory precisely
because it is no more than a revision. But I do not want to write a whole
new article, approaching the subject from an entirely different angle. I
believe it is necessary to revise the earlier article and to restate the case in
the same context, arriving at a different conclusion.

One of the unavoidable defects of this kind of revision is that it retains
an altogether misleading insistence on the terms "contemplation" and
"contemplative life" as something apart from the rest of man's existence.
This involves a rather naïve presupposition that "contemplation" is a
kind of objectivized entity which gets "interfered with" by such things as
aesthetic reflection. There is a certain amount of truth behind this supposed
conflict, but to state it thus crudely is to invite all sorts of misunderstand-
ing. In actual fact, neither religious nor artistic contemplation should be
regarded as "things" which happen or "objects" which one can "have."
They belong to the much more mysterious realm of what one "is"—or

---

This reappraisal of "Poetry and Contemplation" first appeared in *Commonweal,*
October 24, 1958, and was included in the first edition of *Selected Poems of Thomas
Merton* (it does not appear in subsequent editions). It was also published in *A
Thomas Merton Reader,* ed. Thomas P. McDonnell, (New York: Harcourt, Brace &
World, 1962).

rather "who" one is. Aesthetic intuition is not merely the act of a faculty, it is also a heightening and intensification of our personal identity and being by the perception of our connatural affinity with "Being" in the beauty contemplated.

But also, and at the same time, the implied conflict between "contemplation" as rest and poetic creation as activity is even more misleading. It is all wrong to imagine that in order to "contemplate" divine things, or what you will, it is necessary to abstain from every kind of action and enter into a kind of spiritual stillness where one waits for "something to happen." In actual fact, true contemplation is inseparable from life and from the dynamism of life—which includes work, creation, production, fruitfulness, and above all love. Contemplation is not to be thought of as a separate department of life, cut off from all man's other interests and superseding them. It is the very fullness of a fully integrated life. It is the crown of life and of all life's activities.

Therefore the earlier problem was, largely, an illusion, created by this division of life into formally separate compartments of "action" and "contemplation." But because this crude division was stated so forcefully and so frequently in my earlier writings, I feel that it is most necessary now to try to do something to heal this wound and draw together the two sides of this unfortunate fissure.

In this present article, the wound is still evident, and it is meant to be so. I am attempting to patch it up, and probably do not fully succeed. If this is true, I do not care so much, as long as it is clear that I am stitching and drawing the wound together, pouring in the disinfectant, and putting on a bandage.

1

In an age of science and technology, in which man finds himself bewildered and disoriented by the fabulous versatility of the machines he has created, we live precipitated outside ourselves at every moment, interiorly empty, spiritually lost, seeking at all costs to forget our own emptiness and ready to alienate ourselves completely in the name of any "cause" that comes along. At such a time as this, it seems absurd to talk of contemplation: and indeed a great deal of the talk that has been bandied about timidly enough on this subject is ludicrous and inadequate. Contemplation itself takes on the appearance of a safe and rather bourgeois "cause"—the refuge of a few well-meaning Christians who are willing to acquaint themselves with St. Thomas and St. John of the Cross, and to disport themselves thereafter in such Edens of passivity and fervor as cannot be disapproved by the so-called "Masters of the Spiritual Life." For others, safer still, contemplation means nothing more than a life of leisure and of study: in many cases more a fond hope than an accomplished fact.

The relative timidity of these adventures, and the hare-brained chase after more exotic forms of spirituality, should not make us too prone to laugh at every symptom of man's acute need for an interior life. For one of the most important and most hopeful signs of the times is in the turbulent, anarchic, but fully determined efforts of a small minority of men to recover some kind of contact with their own inner depths, to recapture the freshness and truth of their own subjectivity, and to go on from there not only to God but to the spirit of other men. In the face of our own almost hopeless alienation, we are trying to get back to ourselves before it is too late. One of the most outstanding examples of this struggle is seen in the almost symbolic career of Boris Pasternak, whose more recent poetry and prose can most certainly qualify in a broad and basic sense as *contemplative.*

The contemplative is not just a man who sits under a tree with his legs crossed, or one who edifies himself with the answer to ultimate and spiritual problems. He is one who seeks to know the meaning of life not only with his head but with his whole being, by living it in depth and in purity, and thus uniting himself to the very Source of Life—a Source which is infinitely actual and therefore too real to be contained satisfactorily inside any word or concept or name assigned by man: for the words of man tend to limit the realities which they express, in order to express them. And anything that can be limited cannot be the infinite actuality known to the contemplative without words and without the mediation of precise analytical thought. We can say, then, that contemplation is the intuitive perception of life in its Source: that Source Who revealed Himself as the unnameable "I Am" and then again made Himself known to us as Man in Christ. Contemplation is experience of God in Man, God in the world, God in Christ: it is an obscure intuition of God Himself, and this intuition is a gift of God Who reveals Himself in His very hiddenness as One unknown.

Contemplation is related to art, to worship, to charity: all these reach out by intuition and self-dedication into the realms that transcend the material conduct of everyday life. Or rather, in the midst of ordinary life itself they seek and find a new and transcendent meaning. And by this meaning they transfigure the whole of life. Art, worship, and love penetrate into the spring of living waters that flows from the depths where man's spirit is united to God, and draw from those depths power to create a new world and a new life. Contemplation goes deeper than all three, and unites them, and plunges man's whole soul into the supernal waters, in the baptism of wordless understanding and ecstatic prayer.

There can be various levels of contemplation. There is contemplation in a broad and improper sense—the religious intuition of the artist, the lover, or the worshiper. In these intuitions, art, love, or worship remain in the foreground: they modify the experience of ultimate reality, and present that reality to us as the "object" of aesthetic vision, or adoration, or love. In an even less proper sense, "contemplation" loses sight of ultimates and becomes preoccupied with a beautiful thing, or a meaningful liturgy, or a loved person.

But in its proper meaning, contemplation transcends all "objects," all "things," and goes beyond all "ideas" of beauty or goodness or truth, passes beyond all speculation, all creative fervor, all charitable action, and "rests" in the inexpressible. It lets go of everything and finds All in Nothing—the *todo y nada* of St. John of the Cross.

On a dark night, kindled in love with yearnings—oh happy chance—
I went forth without being observed, my house being now at rest.

In darkness and secure, by the secret ladder, disguised,—O happy
    chance—
In darkness and concealment, my house being now at rest.

In the happy night, in secret when none saw me
Nor I beheld aught, without light or guide save that which burned in
    my heart

This light guided me more surely than the light of noonday
To the place where He (well I knew who!) was awaiting me
A place where none appeared.

Now when we speak of a possible conflict between poetry and contemplation, it is clearly only contemplation in the last, most perfect sense that is intended. For when we speak of contemplation in the more broad and improper sense, we find it uniting itself with art, with worship, and with love. It is not only compatible with poetic creation, but is stimulated by it, and in its turn inspires poetry. And in the realm of worship, contemplation in this broad sense is stimulated by meditation, by prayer, by liturgy, and arises out of these religious activities. Above all, in the sacramental life of the Church, we find contemplation in this broad sense should normally be the fruit of fervent reception of the sacraments, at least sometimes. That is to say that the reception of the sacraments should produce, once in a while, not only interior and unfelt grace but also a certain dim awareness of the presence and the action of God in the soul, though this awareness may be very fleeting, tenuous, and almost impossible to assess. Nor should people trouble their heads about whether or not they feel it, because some are not supposed to feel it: feelings are not important, and what they will experience without realizing it too clearly is the fervor of love and the desire to dedicate themselves more perfectly to God. Such things we can call in a broad and improper sense "contemplative" experiences.

This is *active* contemplation, in which grace indeed is the principle of all the supernatural value and ordination of our acts, but in which much of the initiative belongs to our own powers, prompted and sustained by grace. This form of the contemplative life prepares us for contemplation properly so called: the life of *infused* or *passive* or *mystical* contemplation.

Contemplation is the fullness of the Christian vocation—the full flowering of baptismal grace and of the Christ-life in our souls.

Christian contemplation is not something esoteric and dangerous. It is simply the experience of God that is given to a soul purified by humility and faith. It is the "knowledge" of God in the darkness of infused love. "This is eternal life, that they should know Thee, the One True God, and Jesus Christ Whom Thou hast sent" (John 17:3) or "But we all, beholding the glory of the Lord with open face, are transformed into the same image from glory to glory, as by the Spirit of the Lord." (2 Corinthians 3:18). St. Paul, in his Epistle to the Hebrews, rebuked those who clung to the "first elements of the words of God" when they should have been "Masters," and he urged them to relinquish the "milk" of beginners and to desire the "strong meat" of the perfect, which is the contemplation of Christ in the great Mystery in which He renews on earth the redemptive sacrifice of the Cross. "For every one that is a partaker of milk is unskillful in the word of justice: for he is a little child. But strong meat is for the perfect: for them who by custom have their senses exercised to the discerning of good and evil" (Hebrews 5:13-14). *Omnis qui ad Dominum convertitur contemplativam vitam desiderat,* said St. Gregory the Great, and he was using contemplation in our sense: to live on the desire of God alone; to have one's mind divested of all earthly things and united, insofar as human weakness permits, with Christ. And he adds that the contemplative life begins on earth in order to continue, more perfectly, in heaven. St. Thomas echoed him with his famous phrase: *quaedam inchoatio beatitudinis* (contemplation is a beginning of eternal blessedness). St. Bonaventure goes further than any of the other Doctors of the Church in his insistence that all Christians should desire union with God in loving contemplation. And in his second conference on the Hexaemeron, applying Christ's words in Matthew 12:42, he says that the Queen of the South who left her own land and traveled far to hear the wisdom of Solomon will rise up in judgment against our generation, which refuses the treasure of divine wisdom, preferring the far lesser riches of worldly wisdom and philosophy.

Infused contemplation is a quasi-experimental knowledge of God's goodness "tasted" and "possessed" by a vital contact in the depths of the soul. By infused love, we are given an immediate grasp of God's own substance, and rest in the obscure and profound sense of His presence and transcendent actions within our inmost selves, yielding ourselves altogether to the work of His transforming Spirit.

By the light of infused wisdom we enter deeply into the Mystery of Christ Who is Himself the light of men. We participate, as it were, in the glory that is radiated mystically by His risen and transfigured Humanity. Our eyes are opened to understand the Scriptures and the mystery of God's intervention in man's history. We become aware of the way in which the infinite mercy and wisdom of God are revealed to men and angels in the Mystery of the Church, which is the Body of Christ. The contemplative life is the lot of those who have entered most fully into the life and spirit of the Church, so that the contemplatives are at the very heart of the Mystery which they have begun really to understand and to "see" with the eyes of their soul. To desire the contemplative life and its gifts is therefore to desire to become in the highest sense a fruitful and strong member of Christ. But it means also, by that very fact, to desire and accept a share in His sufferings and death, that we may rise with Him in the participation of His glory.

Now whether we speak of contemplation as active or passive, one thing is evident: it brings us into the closest contact with the one subject that is truly worthy of a Christian poet: the great Mystery of God, revealing His mercy to us in Christ. The Christian poet should be one who has been granted a deep understanding of the ways of God and of the Mystery of Christ. Deeply rooted in the spiritual consciousness of the whole Church, steeped in the Liturgy and the Scriptures, fully possessed by the "mind of the Church," he becomes as it were a voice of the Church and of the Holy Spirit, and sings again the *magnalia Dei,* praising God and pointing out the wonder of His ways. The Christian poet is therefore the successor to David and the Prophets, he contemplates what was announced by the poets of the Old Testament: he should be, as they were, a mystic, full of divine fire. He should be one who, like the prophet Isaias, has seen the living God and has lamented the fact that he was a man of impure lips, until God Himself sent Seraph, with a live coal from the altar of the heavenly temple, to burn his lips with prophetic inspiration.

In the true Christian poet—in Dante, St. John of the Cross, St. Francis, Jacopone da Todi, Hopkins, Paul Claudel—we find it hard to distinguish between the inspiration of the prophet and mystic and the purely poetic enthusiasm of great artistic genius.

Consider also what a tremendous mine of literary inspiration is in the Liturgical life. The Liturgy itself contains the greatest literature, not only from Scripture but from the genius of the Patristic and Middle Ages. The Liturgy stands at the crossroads of the natural and supernatural lives, and exploits all the possibilities of both in order to bring out every possible meaning and implication that is in them with respect to our salvation and the praise of God. It surrounds those founts of all supernatural vitality, the Sacraments, with a music that is perfect in its integrity and dignity, and with ceremonies that are most meaningful by reason of their tremendous, dramatic simplicity, not to mention all the resources of pictorial and plastic art still unknown in this land which has never yet possessed a Chartres or an Assisi.

The Liturgy is, then, not only a school of literary taste and a mine of marvelous subjects, but it is infinitely more: it is a sacramental system built around the greatest Sacrament, the Blessed Eucharist, in which Christ Himself is enthroned, in mystery, in the very heart of His wonderful creation.

Christ on the Cross is the fount of all art because He is the Word, the fount of all grace and wisdom. He is the center of everything, of the whole economy of the natural and the supernatural orders. Everything that is made subsists in Him and reflects His beauty. Everything points to this anointed King of Creation Who is the splendor of the eternal light and the mirror of the Godhead without stain. He is the "image of the invisible God, the firstborn of every creature . . . in Him were all things created, by Him and in Him . . . He is before all and by Him all things consist . . . in Whom it hath pleased the Father that all things should dwell . . . for in Him dwelleth all the fullness of the Godhead corporeally," that in all things He may hold the primacy. (Colossians, 1 and 2)

The Christian's vision of the world ought, by its very nature, to have in it something of poetic inspiration. Our faith ought to be capable of filling our hearts with a wonder and a wisdom which see beyond the surface of things and events, and grasp something of the inner and "sacred" meaning of the cosmos which, in all its movements and all its aspects, sings the praises of its Creator and Redeemer.

No Christian poetry worthy of the name has been written by anyone who was not in some degree a contemplative. I say "in some degree" because obviously not all Christian poets are mystics. But the true poet is always akin to the mystic because of the "prophetic" intuition by which he sees the spiritual reality, the inner meaning of the object he contemplates, which makes that concrete reality not only a thing worthy of admiration in itself, but also and above all makes it a *sign of God*. All good Christian poets are then contemplatives in the sense that they see God everywhere in His creation and in His mysteries, and behold the created world as filled with signs and symbols of God. To the true Christian poet, the whole world and all the incidents of life tend to be sacraments—signs of God, signs of His love working in the world.

However, the mere fact of having this contemplative vision of God in the world around us does not necessarily make a man a great poet. One must be not a "seer" but also and especially a "creator"—a "maker." Poetry is an art, a natural skill, a virtue of the practical intellect, and no matter how great a subject we may have in the experience of contemplation, we will not be able to put it into words if we do not have the proper command of our medium. This is true. But let us assume that a man already has this natural gift. If the inspiration is helpless without a correspondingly effective technique, technique is barren without inspiration.

2

Christ is the inspiration of Christian poetry, and Christ is at the center of the contemplative life. Therefore, it would seem fairly evident that the one thing that will most contribute to the perfection of Catholic literature in general and poetry in particular will be for our writers and poets to live more as "contemplatives" than as citizens of a materialistic world. This means first of all leading the full Christian sacramental and liturgical life insofar as they can in their state. Obviously, the poet does not have to enter a monastery to be a better poet. On the contrary, what we need are "contemplatives" outside the cloister and outside the rigidly fixed patterns of religious life—contemplatives in the world of art, letters, education, and even politics. This means a solid integration of one's work, thought, religion, and family life and recreations in one vital harmonious unity with Christ at its center. The liturgical life is the most obvious example of "active contemplation," but it is hard enough to find a parish where the liturgical life is anything more than a bare skeleton. The eccentricities and obsessions of occasional faddists should not prejudice us against the immense vitality and permanent value of the true liturgical revival. It is quite certain that one of the most valid achievements in the realm of Christian art in our time is to the credit of the monks of Solesmes, with their revival of Gregorian chant.

A sincere and efficacious desire to enter more deeply into the beauty of the Christian mystery implies a willingness to sacrifice the things which are called "beautiful" by the decadent standards of a materialistic world. Yet the Christian contemplative need not confine himself to religious, still less to professionally "pious" models. He will, of course, read Scripture and above all the contemplative saints: John of the Cross, Theresa of Avila, John Ruysbroek, Bonaventure, Bernard. But no one can be a poet without reading the good poets of his own time—T. S. Eliot, Auden, Spender, Rilke, Pasternak, Dylan Thomas, García Lorca. One might add that a fully integrated vision of our time and of its spirit presupposes some contact with the genius of Baudelaire and Rimbaud, who are Christians turned inside out.

Contemplation has much to offer poetry. And poetry, in its turn, has something to offer contemplation. How is this so? In understanding the relation of poetry to contemplation the first thing that needs to be stressed is the essential dignity of aesthetic experience. It is, in itself, a very high gift, though only in the natural order. It is a gift which very many people have never received, and which others, having received, have allowed to spoil or become atrophied within them through neglect and misuse.

To many people, the enjoyment of art is nothing more than a sensible and emotional thrill. They look at a picture, and if it stimulates one or another of their sense-appetites they are pleased. On a hot day they like to look at a picture of mountains or the sea because it makes them feel cool. They like paintings of dogs that you could almost pat. But naturally they soon tire of art, under those circumstances. They turn aside to pat a real dog, or they go down the street to an air-conditioned movie, to give their senses another series of jolts. This is not what one can legitimately call the "enjoyment of Art."

A genuine aesthetic experience is something which transcends not only the sensible order (in which, however, it has its beginning) but also that of reason itself. It is a suprarational intuition of the latent perfection of things. Its immediacy outruns the speed of reasoning and leaves all analysis far behind. In the natural order, as Jacques Maritain has often insisted, it is an analogue of the mystical experience which it resembles and imitates from afar. Its mode of apprehension is that of "connaturality"—it reaches out to grasp the inner reality, the vital substance of its object, by a kind of affective identification of itself with it. It rests in the perfection of things by a kind of union which sometimes resembles the quiescence of the soul in its immediate affective contact with God in the obscurity of mystical prayer. A true artist can contemplate a picture for hours, and it is a real contemplation, too. So close is the resemblance between these two experiences that a poet like Blake could almost confuse the two and make them merge into one another as if they belonged to the same order of things.

This resemblance between the experiences of the artist and of the mystic has been extensively discussed in the long and important article on "Art and Spirituality," by Fr. M. Leonard, S.J., in the *Dictionnaire de Spiritualité*.

This theologian pushes the dignity of the aesthetic intuition practically to its limit. He gives it everything that it is ontologically able to stand. He insists that the highest experience of the artist penetrates not only beyond the sensible surface of things into their inmost reality, but even beyond that to God Himself. More than that, the analogy with mystical experience is deeper and closer still because, he says, the intuition of the artist sets in motion the very same psychological processes which accompany infused contemplation. This would seem to be too much: but no, it is not. It fits in with the psychology of St. Augustine and St. Bonaventure and the latter's notion of contemplation *per speculum,* passing through the mirror of created things to God, even if that mirror may happen to be our own soul. It also fits in with the ideas of the Greek Fathers about *theoria physica,* or "natural contemplation" which arrives at God through the inner spiritual reality (the *logos*) of the created thing.

The Augustinian psychology, which forms the traditional substratum of Christian mystical theology in the Western Church, distinguishes between an *inferior* and *superior* soul. Of course, this is only a manner of speaking. There is only one soul, a simple spiritual substance, undivided and indivisible. And yet the soul insofar as it acts through its faculties, making decisions and practical judgments concerning temporal external things, is called "inferior." The "superior" soul is the same soul, but now considered as the principle or *actus primus* of these other diverse and multiple acts of the faculties which, as it were, flow from this inner principle. Only the superior soul is strictly the image of God within us. And if we are to contemplate God at all, this internal image must be re-formed by grace, and then we must enter into this inner sanctuary which is the substance of the soul itself. This passage from the exterior to the interior has nothing to do with concentration or introspection. It is a transit from objectivization to knowledge by intuition and connaturality. The majority of people never enter into this inward self, which is an abode of silence and peace and where the diversified activities of the intellect and will are collected, so to speak, into one intense and smooth and spiritualized activity which far exceeds in its fruitfulness the plodding efforts of reason working on external reality with its analyses and syllogisms.

It is here that mystical contemplation begins. It is into this substance or "center" of the soul, when it has transcended its dependence on sensations and images and concepts, that the obscure light of infused contemplation will be poured by God, giving us experimental contact with Himself without the medium of sense species. And in this contact, we are no longer facing God as an "object" of experience or as a concept which we apprehend. We are united to Him in the mystery of love and its transcendent subjectivity, and see Him in ourselves by losing ourselves in Him.

Yet even in the natural order, without attaining to God in us, and without perceiving this "inner spiritual light," the aesthetic experience introduces us into the interior sanctuary of the soul and to its inexpressible simplicity. For the aesthetic intuition is also beyond objectivity—it "sees" by identifying itself spiritually with what it contemplates.

Obviously, then, when the natural contemplation of the artist or the metaphysician has already given a man a taste of the peaceful intoxication which is experienced in the suprarational intuitions of this interior self, the way is already well prepared for infused contemplation. If God should grant that grace, the person so favored will be much better prepared to recognize it, and to co-operate with God's action within him. This, as a matter of fact, is a tremendous advantage. The artist, the poet, the metaphysician is, then, in some sense already naturally prepared and disposed to remove some of the principal obstacles to the light of infused contemplation. He will be less tempted than the ordinary man to reach out for vulgar satisfactions and imaginable thrills. He will be more "spiritual," if not more "religious." He will be more ready to keep himself detached from the level of crude feeling and emotionalism which so easily corrupt the integrity both of the artist and of the man of prayer. The mere fact of the artist's or poet's good taste, which should belong to him by virtue of his art, will help him to avoid some of the evils that tend to corrupt religious experience before it has a chance to take root and grow in the soul.

3

Mystical contemplation is absolutely beyond the reach of man's natural activity. There is nothing he can do to obtain it by himself. It is a pure gift of God. God gives it to whom He wills, and in the way and degree in which He wills. By co-operating with the work of ordinary grace we can—and, if we really mean to love God, we must—seek Him and even find Him obscurely by a love that gropes humbly for truth in the darkness of this life. But no amount of generosity on our part, no amount of effort, no amount of sacrifice will make us into mystics. That is a work that must be done by God acting as the "principal agent" (the term is that of St. John of the Cross). If He is the principal agent, there is another agent: ourselves. But our part is simply to consent, to listen, and to follow without knowing where we are going. All the rest that we can do amounts to the more or less negative task of avoiding obstacles and keeping our own prejudiced judgments and self-will out of His way. St. Bonaventure tells us in many places that prayer and ardent desire can persuade God to give us this gift, and that *industria* on our part can open the way for His action. The term *industria* stands for active purification, and St. Bonaventure means, by that, precisely the same thing that St. John of the Cross talks about all through the "Ascent of Mount Carmel," namely the active emptying of the soul, clearing it of all images, all likenesses of and attachments to created things, so that it may be clean and pure to receive the obscure light of God's own presence. The soul must be stripped of all its selfish desires for natural satisfactions, no matter how high, how noble, or how excellent in themselves. As long as it rests in things for their own sake, seen and possessed as "objects" to gratify our own self-love, it cannot possess God and be possessed by Him, for the love of the soul for objectivized beings is darkness in the sight of God.

It is the common doctrine of Christian mystical theologians that a great obstacle to "unitive" or "connatural" or "affective" knowledge of God by infused contemplation (the terms are those of St. Thomas and his followers) is attachment to objectivized human reasoning and analysis and discourse that proceeds by abstraction from sense images, and by syllogizing, to conclusions. In other words, a man cannot at the same time fly in an airplane and walk along the ground. He must do one or the other. And if he insists on walking along the ground—all right, it is no sin. But it will take him much longer and cost him much more effort to get to his destination, and he will have a much more limited view of things along his way. What the Holy Spirit demands of the mystic is peaceful consent and a blind trust in Him: for all this time, since the soul does not act of itself, it remains blind and in darkness, having no idea where it is going or what is being done, and tasting satisfaction that is, at first, extremely tenuous and ineffable and obscure. The reason is, of course, that the soul is not yet sufficiently spiritualized to be able to grasp and appreciate what is going on within it. It remains with nothing but the vaguest and most general sense that God is really and truly present and working there—a sense which is fraught with a greater certitude than anything it has ever experienced before. And yet if one stops to analyze the experience, or if one makes a move to increase its intensity by a natural act, the whole thing will evade his grasp and he will lose it altogether.

Now it is precisely here that the aesthetic instinct changes its colors and, from being a precious gift, becomes a real danger. If the intuition of the poet naturally leads him into the inner sanctuary of his soul, it is for a special purpose in the natural order: when the poet enters into himself, it is in order to reflect upon his inspiration and to clothe it with a special and splendid form and then return to *display it to those outside.* And here the radical difference between the artist and the mystic begins to be seen. The artist enters into himself in order to *work.* For him, the "superior" soul is a forge where inspiration kindles a fire of white heat, a crucible for the transformation of natural images into new, created forms. But the mystic enters into himself, not in order to work but to pass through the center of his own soul and lose himself in the mystery and secrecy and infinite, transcendent reality of God living and working within him.

Consequently, if the mystic happens to be, at the same time, an artist, when prayer calls him within himself to the secrecy of God's presence, his art will be tempted to start working and producing and studying the "creative" possibilities of this experience. And therefore immediately the whole thing runs the risk of being frustrated and destroyed. The artist will run the risk of losing a gift of tremendous supernatural worth, in order to perform a work of far less value. He will let go of the deep, spiritual grace which has been granted him, in order to return to the reflection of that grace within his own soul. He will withdraw from the mystery of identification with Reality beyond forms and objectivized concepts, and will return to the realm of subject and object. He will objectivize his own experience and seek to exploit and employ it for its own sake. He will leave God and return to himself, and in so doing, though he follows his natural instinct to "create," he will, in fact, be less creative. For the creative work done directly in the soul and on the soul by God Himself, the infinite *Creator Spiritus,* is beyond all comparison with the work which the soul of man itself accomplishes in imitation of the divine Creator.

Unable fully to lose himself in God, doomed by the restlessness of talent to seek himself in the highest natural gift that God has given him, the artist falls from contemplation and returns to himself as artist. Instead of passing through his own soul into the abyss of the infinite actuality of God Himself, he will remain there a moment, only to emerge again into the exterior world of multiple created things whose variety once more dissipates his energies until they are lost in perplexity and dissatisfaction.

There is, therefore, a likelihood that one who has the natural gift of artistic intuition and creation may be unable to pass on to the superior and most spiritual kind of contemplation, in which the soul rests in God without images, without concepts, without any intermediary. The artist may be like the hare in the fable, who far outstrips the tortoise without talent in the beginnings of the contemplative life, but who, in the end, is left behind. In a word, natural gifts and talents may be of great value in the beginning, but contemplation can never depend on them. They may, indeed, prove to be obstacles, unless by some special grace we are completely detached from them. And so the artist may well receive the first taste of infused prayer, for, as St. John of the Cross says, that is granted to relatively many souls, and often quite soon in their spiritual life, especially where conditions are favorable: but, because of this tragic promethean tendency to exploit every experience as material for "creation," the artist may remain there all his life on the threshold, never entering into the banquet, but always running back into the street to tell the passers-by of the wonderful music he has heard coming from inside the palace of the King!

4

What, then, is the conclusion? That poetry can, indeed, help to bring us rapidly through that early part of the journey to contemplation that is called active: but when we are entering the realm of true contemplation, where eternal happiness is tasted in anticipation, poetic intuition may ruin our rest in God "beyond all images."

In such an event, one might at first be tempted to say that there is only one course for the poet to take, if he wants to be a mystic or a saint: he must consent to the *ruthless and complete sacrifice of his art*. Such a conclusion would seem to be dictated by logic. If there is an infinite distance between the gifts of nature and those of grace, between the natural and the supernatural order, man and God, then should not one always reject the natural for the supernatural, the temporal for the eternal, the human for the divine? It seems to be so simple as to defy contradiction. And yet, when one has experience in the strange vicissitudes of the inner life, and when one has seen something of the ways of God, one remembers that there is a vast difference between the logic of men and the logic of God. There is indeed no human logic in the ways of interior prayer, only Divine paradox. Our God is not a Platonist. Our Christian spirituality is not the intellectualism of Plotinus or the asceticism of the Stoics. We must therefore be very careful of oversimplifications. The Christian is sanctified not merely by always making the choice of "the most perfect thing." Indeed, experience teaches us that the most perfect choice is not always that which is most perfect in itself. The most perfect choice is *the choice of what God has willed for us,* even though it may be, in itself, less perfect, and indeed less "spiritual."

It is quite true that aesthetic experience is only a temporal thing, and like all other temporal things it passes away. It is true that mystical prayer enriches man a hundredfold in time and in eternity. It purifies the soul and loads it with supernatural merits, enlarging man's powers and capacities to absorb the infinite rivers of divine light which will one day be his beatitude. The sacrifice of art would seem to be a small enough price to lay down for this "pearl of great price."

But let us consider for a moment whether the Christian contemplative poet is necessarily confronted with an absolute clean-cut "either/or" choice between "art" and "mystical prayer."

It can of course happen that a contemplative and artist finds himself in a situation in which he is morally certain that God demands of him the sacrifice of his art, in order that he may enter more deeply into the contemplative life. In such a case, the sacrifice must be made, not because this is a general law binding all artist-contemplatives, but because it is the will of God in this particular, concrete case.

But it may equally well happen that an artist who imagines himself to be called to the higher reaches of mystical prayer is not called to them at all. It becomes evident, to him, that the simplest and most obvious thing for him is to be an artist, and that he should sacrifice his aspirations for a deep mystical life and be content with the lesser gifts with which he has been endowed by God. For such a one, to insist on spending long hours in prayer frustrating his creative instinct would, in fact, lead to illusion. His efforts to be a contemplative would be fruitless. Indeed, he would find that by being an artist—and at the same time living fully all the implications of art for a Christian and for a contemplative in the broad sense of the word—he would enjoy a far deeper and more vital interior life, with a much richer appreciation of the mysteries of God, than if he just tried to bury his artistic talent and be a professional "saint." If he is called to be an artist, then his art will lead him to sanctity, if he uses it as a Christian should.

To take yet another case: it might conceivably be the will of God—as it certainly was in the case of the Old Testament Prophets and in that of St. John of the Cross—that a man should remain *at the same time a mystic and a poet* and ascend to the greatest heights of poetic creation and of mystical prayer without any evident contradiction between them. Here again, the problem is solved not by the application of some abstract, *a priori* principle, but purely by a practically practical appeal to the will of God in this particular case. We are dealing with gifts of God, which God can give as He pleases, when He pleases, to whom He pleases. It is futile for us to lay down laws which say when or how God's gifts must be given, to whom they can be given, to whom they must be refused. It remains true that at a certain point in the interior life, the instinct to create and communicate enters into conflict with the call to mystical union with God. But God Himself can resolve the conflict. And He does. Nor does He need any advice from us in order to do so.

The Christian life is the life of Christ in the soul. Christian wisdom is the wisdom of God's only-begotten Son, Who is begotten Wisdom—*sapientia genita*. To be wise with the wisdom of Christ, we must let Christ be born and live within us in His own way. He does not come to all in the same way, because we all have different functions in His Mystical Body. "There are diversities of graces, but the same Spirit, and there are diversities of ministries but the same Lord: and there are diversities of operations, but the same God Who worketh all in all. And the manifestation of the Spirit is given to every man unto profit." (I Corinthians 12:4–7)

We may apply the last words of this text to our present case. If the Christian poet is truly a Christian poet, if he has a vocation to make known to other men the unsearchable mystery of the love of Christ, then he must do so in the Spirit of Christ. And his "manifestation of the Spirit" not only springs from a kind of contemplative intuition of the mystery of Christ, but is "given to him for his profit" and will therefore deepen and perfect his union with Christ. The Christian poet and artist is one who grows not only by his contemplation but also by his open declaration of the mercy of God. If it is clear that he is called to give this witness to God, then he can say with St. Paul: "Woe to me if I preach not the Gospel." At the same time, he should always remember that the hidden and more spiritual gifts are infinitely greater than his art, and if he is called upon to make an exclusive choice of one or the other, he must know how to sacrifice his art.

THEOLOGY OF CREATIVITY

The most obvious characteristic of our age is its destructiveness. This can hardly be doubted. We have developed an enormous capacity to build and to change our world, but far more enormous are our capacities for destruction. It is significant that the age of atomic war is the one in which man has become preoccupied with what he calls "creativity," and preoccupied with it almost to the point of obsession. The problem of creativity, when approached from the semantic viewpoint, reveals itself almost as a problem of guilt. The function of this paper is by no means the investigation of this admittedly fascinating and timely question. But the possibility has to be taken into account, otherwise a discussion of creativity, which is supposed, in the end, to be theological, will not make sense at all.

We must begin by facing the ambivalence which makes so much of our talk about creativity absurd because it is fundamentally insincere. Why insincere? Because it is so glib, so all-embracing. The popular use of the word creativity is so facile that one feels immediately that it is a pure evasion. It is a trick to avoid thought, and to avoid real communication. When everything is "creative," nothing is creative. But nowadays everything is called creative: we have creative salesmanship, meaning probably obnoxiously aggressive and vulgar salesmanship. We have creative advertising, which is merely outrageously whimsical or arbitrary. We have creative ways of doing everything under the sun, and in every case what is called "creative" is not even more original than what it is supposed to supersede: it implies nothing but a more ponderously stupid emphasis on what is already too familiar. In a word, being "creative" seems to mean little more than rushing forward with breakneck impetuosity into the conventional, the vulgar, or the absurd.

But there is a more serious complaint against our obsession with creativity. The inanity of the popular, commercialized degradation of this concept is merely an innocent "cover" for its self-contradictions when it is

---

This essay first appeared in the September–December 1960 number of *The American Benedictine Review* as the first section of a three-part article, along with William Davidson, M.D., and Brother Antoninus, O.P. (William Everson). An excerpt was published in *A Thomas Merton Reader,* ed. by Thomas P. McDonnell (New York: Harcourt, Brace & World, 1962).

used on a deeper level. And here we come face to face with the implication of guilt.

The term "creativity" may be seen, if we observe carefully how it is used, to be in some cases nothing less than a justification of destructiveness. It is a negation, an un-making, justified by a positive-sounding name: "creation." There are, admittedly, almost infinitely interesting possibilities in broken pieces of machinery, ruined houses, even the smashed bodies of human beings. The revelation of these grim but arresting qualities in horrifying objects, contemplated from a certain detached viewpoint, is in fact a positive aesthetic value, and all the more positive by its implied contrast with empty and formalistic attempts at conventional "beauty." Nevertheless, it should be clear that to take delight in a symbolic, or represented, destruction is not far removed from taking delight in actual destruction. The artist may have a perfect right, perhaps even a duty, to protest as effectively and as vocally as he can against man's present state of alienation in a world that seems to be without meaning because of the moral, cultural, and economic crises of society. This protest certainly can be creative, and there is no doubt that it can bring forth great and living art. But when the protest has so taken possession of the artist that he is no longer articulate, and can only express it by gestures equivalent to dashing his brains out against the wall, then there is no longer question of creativity. What we have is destruction. It may be terribly pitiable, it may be a matter of urgent importance, but creativity is just not the honest word for tongue-tied frustration, helplessness, and self-hate. This means that not every expression of frustration and despair is creative, only such as are really articulate.

Our misuse of the word and concept of creativity has robbed us of a standard of judgment. We can no longer tell when an artist is expressing something human or merely screaming: we do not even try to interpret the noise, we just react to it one way or another, believing that the mere fact of having a reaction is somehow "creative." One reason for this seems to be that we have begun, out of resentment, to dissociate the creative from the human. We now tend to assume that a humanistic outlook frustrates the real creative urge, which is in some way subhuman, or even antihuman. But this makes our "creativity" nothing more than a destructive and negative reaction against that very element of life and spirit upon which true creativity depends.

At this point, though a partisan declaration is really not called for, it is necessary to make a personal statement in regard to modern art movements, including those that are most experimental and extreme. I want to say quite clearly and emphatically that I am for the people who experiment in modern art. I have in other places and contexts made known my admiration for Picasso, Matisse, Rouault, etc. In this I share the taste of my time and society. I do not intend to call into question the "creativity" of such great artists, though I must admit that the traditional, classic art of the past, especially primitive Italian, Byzantine, and Oriental sacred art, seem to me to be vastly more important and significant. I am interested in abstract art, surrealism, fauvism, action painting, and all the rest. It seems to me that the men who experiment in action painting have every right to do what they are doing, and that they have a claim upon our respectful attention, though I do not believe the publicity and money they receive are in proportion to their so far slight achievements. And though I am persuaded that they have every right to do what they are doing, I find it hard to get very excited about the results. Most action painting is to me little more than a pleasantly intriguing accident, no more worthy of insult than of praise. It is what it is. Comment on it would be absurd, and I suppose that is why the enormous amount of favorable comment that is actually made is couched in peculiarly earnest doubletalk which, if it were worth interpreting, would probably turn out to mean nothing whatever. Or perhaps it is simply a justification of its own meaninglessness.

When I reflect that the artistic history of the past decade recorded, among other things, the "first one-ape show" held in London, it becomes clear to me that the term "creativity" is all too likely to be used today as a pure cliché. There may well be a fortuitous design in the ape's "paintings," and one could probably find in them as many forms as in a Rorschach inkblot. But this applies to everything else under the sun: the grain in wood, stains on a damp wall, the fence of a vacant lot covered with tattered posters and, for that matter, even the paintings of the most absurd and conventional academicians. If we include the ape, there is no reason for excluding the professional bootlickers who painted portraits of Hitler and Stalin, though doubtless in their case it is not the "art" that is creative but the "action painting" of the tongue on the leader's boot.

We find ourselves confronted with a situation where everything is creative. The sweaty palms of the frustrated business man are "creating" for him a symbol of his frustration. But what does this mean? Frustration is due precisely to the incapacity for positive, constructive, creative activity. Creation in this sense is then nothing else but frustration failing to express itself freely and normally, calling desperately for help in a way that fails to be heard or understood. It is quite true that a neurotic symptom is a positive sign, but it is a sign of a negation, of a lack of creativity, or of a frustrated creativity. When everything is creative, nothing is creative. When nothing is creative, everything tends to be destructive, or at least to invite destruction. Our creativity is in great measure simply the expression of our destructiveness, the guarded, despairing admission of destructiveness that cries for help without admitting it. The only positive thing left in our destructiveness is its bitter anguish. This, at least, can claim to be. This has creative possibilities.

These initial reflections may seem to be unnecessarily pessimistic. They are not proposed as anything more than suggestions, or questions. I do not know how true they may be, but it seems to me they offer material for serious thought. I will not insist on the paradoxes I have proposed. Putting them aside, it can be said quite fairly and objectively that there are four misleading senses of creativity in current use. No doubt there are more than four, but these seem to be characteristic of our confusions on the subject.

In order to understand what is wrong with these conceptions we must first begin with what is right in them. They all seem to be a more or less vital reaction against lifeless formality and aesthetic cliché. Three of them are explicitly concerned with the sincerity and spontaneity of the artist and with the reality of his art. They encourage him to fight for the spiritual freedom he needs if he is to be a genuine artist who makes something new, something that lives with a life of its own, a new "creation." Creativity in this sense is a healthy reaction against conventionalism and academic inertia.

I. We find the word "creativity" quite often used to signify original and spontaneous self-expression, particularly in art. This meaning of the term is popular wherever men are concerned with the self-realization of the individual, with personalist values. Creativity is a fruit of personalism. The free and spontaneous person has something original to say, and he is able to say it in paint, in poetry, in music, in his house, in his work, or simply in his way of confronting life. Conversely, if his "creativity" can be allowed to develop without restraint when he is young, he will stand a better chance of growing into a well-rounded person.

I have used these clichés seriously and with respect. The need for spontaneity, for spiritual freedom, for personal growth, is certainly urgent: nothing more so. But when "creativity" and "personalism" slide into the context of popular mythology, they are not going to help us achieve this end. On the contrary, they may all too easily frustrate it. It should not be hard to see that this thoroughly understandable and commendable idea of personalist creativity has been corrupted by the mass media. Once corrupted, it is no longer creativity but mere wishful thinking. It is part of an optimistic myth, the myth that we can somehow escape the responsibilities of laboring, suffering, disciplining ourselves, sacrificing ourselves in order to carry out a difficult vocation. In the name of "life," creativity substitutes itself for responsibility and becomes an evasion of responsibility. But life is superficial and invalid as long as it is a mere evasion. The use of fine long words is no help. If "creativity" is mere laziness, narcissism, and self-display, then no amount of spontaneity can justify it, enliven it, or make it "original."

Hence the danger is apparent of a "creativity" that is merely a matter of relaxing and "doing what you want." This illusion is supported by the false idea that it is easy for us to know what we really want, and that as soon as we stop doing what someone else, what society demands of us, we can become "creative." One is tempted to say that this concept of creativity, when applied to primary education, has been notable above all for its effectiveness in producing juvenile delinquents. That might be unfair. But at any rate this concept is too tolerant, too vague, too dim, and by its light the artist cannot see his way to anything except doodling.

II. If the characteristic error of the capitalist world, in this matter, is to equate creativity with individualistic self-expression, Communists go to the other extreme. Creativity is not in the individual but in the party, or rather in history: but the party is the only infallible interpreter of the enigma of history. The party is creative because it is the midwife of history. Creative work is done only when the artist expresses the hidden dynamism of historical events and situations, and this means nothing more nor less than acting as the servant of a political program which is conceived to be based on a correct understanding of this hidden dynamism. The artist does not contemplate the inner creative spirit at work in history—this would be a noble and indeed a Christian conception. He merely paints pictures that make the worker happy about "creating" the new world which will be the inevitable result of overfulfilled production quotas. This concept of creativity really does not take art seriously. Art is only a superstructure whose creativity, if any, depends on the economic base upon which it stands. The worst art can be creative if its politics are correct, for then it is presumably built on a creative foundation.

There is no need to deplore what this sophistry has produced in art: everybody knows the story. However, it would be a mistake to suppose that this delusion is confined to Russia. Besides the personalist approach which is the more popular one here, there is a very widespread belief in

American business and scientific circles that creativity is a matter of team-work. It is not the individual who is creative but the team, and the more the individual submerges his originality and personal differences in the collective project, the more creative that project will turn out to be. This has been fully discussed in books like *Organization Man*.

III. A third delusion would be to equate creativity with productiveness: a quantitative view which tempts everyone in a consumer society. An obsession with fecundity might well frustrate genuine creative potentialities in the artist. Once you get started, it is always easy to do too much, to keep on reproducing over and over again the one or two works the public has come to expect from you. Of course this makes money. It means popularity, a vulgar error. But the mass media give it such encouragement that it ruins very many. We ought to remember that an artist who paints only one or two pictures in his lifetime may well be more creative than one who paints one or two a week.

IV. The fourth delusion brings us back, in some respects, to the first. We return to the idea of original self-expression, but this time we consider it on a deeper level. We find ourselves face to face with another myth, the myth of the genius as hero and as high priest in a cult of art that tends to substitute itself for religion. This delusion is serious, and it is here that "creativity" sometimes takes on a demonic quality which makes it one of the tragic temptations of our era. One of the most tragic of its aspects is the fact that the weaknesses of conventional religiosity are in some sense to blame for this apostasy of the artist. It is the inarticulateness of the preacher that moves the artist to assume a prophetic irresponsibility intended to justify not so much his art as his cult of himself. For here what matters is no longer art or the work of art as such. Here art stands out as the monument of genius, not as the symbol of a transcendent spiritual reality but as the ikon of the artist himself. The artist becomes fascinated by his own gifts and by their superhuman quality. He renounces everything else, including morality and sanity, in order to devote himself exclusively to their magic. His life becomes a deliberate cultivation of experience intended to open up new depths in his genius. Indeed it sometimes seems to him that a full, connatural acquaintance with evil and with despair has become a sacred obligation for him because only in this way can he fully assert his protest against the conventions and hypocrisies of a society he despises. His vocation is to devote his magic gifts as fully as possible to negation and to defiance, and if in saying "no" he can also explode with self-satisfaction, then all the better for him and for his art. He is a professional mystic-in-reverse.

It does not matter how sombre or perverse his experiences may be: what matters is not their beauty, their significance, or even their reality, but the fact that they are his experiences. If they are sinful, degraded, subhuman, this makes no difference. Indeed it makes his experiences even more significant. The genius with his magic soul has descended into hell for a season of satanically detached lucidity which frightens ordinary men. This assures him of his own superiority and confirms him in "prophetic" vocation.

Unfortunately this is a complacency that is no less complacent for being impure. It offers no escape from bourgeois smugness, for it is the same smugness turned inside out. This accounts for the dullness, the sameness, the conventionality, and the absurdity of all the second-rate followers of the few rare ones whose voices, speaking out of the shadows with Baudelaire and Rimbaud, impose upon the hearer the silence and the awe that are fitting in the presence of tragedy.

Here again, we cannot help being impressed by the inherent destructiveness of this kind of creativity, even when it is also genuinely creative.

As Jacques Maritain has pointed out, the artist who assumes this tragic role also takes upon himself the burden of forming the consciences of the lost, and guiding those who have not been able to find meaning or orientation in traditional philosophies.

In this cult of art, in which the artist is hero and high priest, and the work of art is an ikon or a fetish of the creative genius which produced it, we find a pitifully deluded hope of immortality. Though all must die and be forgotten, all must vanish into the void, the work of art remains as a monument to the options made by the unusually gifted one, the supersoul, the magic genius who dared to experience everything and who, in doing so, transcended everything—life, society, ethics, even his own art.

This is the religion of some modern intellectuals who are incapable of committing themselves to a religious, philosophical, or political ideal. They devote themselves to a cult of experience, a cult of "creativity" for its own sake. And creativity here becomes synonymous with despair. Hence it is not hard to see why a careful investigation of the word has been necessary.

In caricaturing the postures of those I believe to be deluded I have not intended in any way to minimize the residue of truth in their delusions. Of the various philosophical approaches to the problem four are chosen which have very much in common. They are all religious, and three of them are also existentialist. These existentialist and religious views all express a sympathy and respect for the real responsibility of the artist to his gifts. They take into account the importance of the aesthetic experience, its need for sincerity and depth. They well know art's exigencies for honesty at any price, even at the price of clarity, beauty, and so-called perfection of form. They pay full respect to the subjectivism which seems to be the only guarantee of honesty at the present moment. In a word they take into account the originality and genius of the artist, and they recognize his broadly "prophetic" role. But at the same time, in one way or another, they remind him of his responsibility toward the work done, and they introduce an element of salutary objectivity into the discussion. They strike a note which distracts the artist from complete obsession with himself and with his experience. They bring him back from the world of devils into the world of men and perhaps even of angels. Such things are still possible.

I. Paul Tillich has clearly seen the dialectic of creativity and destructivity which underlies the art of our time, a dialectic which expresses man's alienation from reality. Man is no longer able to preserve any depth in his encounter with reality, which has "lost its inner transcendence, . . . its transparency for the eternal."[1] Struggling to adjust himself in a world which becomes opaque and replaces God, man tries to endow himself with God's own creative powers. But in order to do so he has to forget his own limitations, his own essential reality. He lives in contradiction with himself. The reaction of religious thought and art against this demonic trend has been abortive: a feeble insistence on conventional symbols, expressed in a new style.

For Tillich, the only valid way out for the artist is to face squarely the very anxiety and meaninglessness inherent in contemporary technological culture and "live creatively, expressing the predicament of the most sensitive people of our time in cultural production."[2] A valid religious art in our time will then be a "creative expression of destructive trends." This is a sound justification of modern art when it is the expression of humility and anguish, not of pride and revolt. It is precisely pride that prevents modern man from achieving depth, even when he most seeks it.

II. The Buddhist existentialist thinker Daisetz Suzuki, well known

[1] Paul Tillich, *Theology of Culture* (New York: Oxford University Press, 1959), p. 43.
[2] *Ibid.,* p. 46.

362

as the major modern spokesman of Zen, has profoundly significant pages on Japanese art, and these have the advantage of being lavishly illustrated.³ Writing only of Japanese and Chinese art, Suzuki is interested in the work of art as an expression of Zen experience. The experience and its expression must not be separated, for, as he says, "In Zen, experience and expression are one."⁴ What is this Zen experience? It is often explained by the term "self-realization," but this can easily be interpreted in a sense exactly contrary to its intended meaning. The "self" that is "realized" in Zen is by no means the "personality of the genius" discussed above. On the contrary, whereas the demonic experience of pseudo-creativity involves the affirmation of man's false, exterior self, the Zen experience is a deliverance from this false self. Rather it is an emptiness, an "original suchness" in which no such false and illusory self can be present at all. Zen tolerates no phenomenal ego that can be affirmed and placed over against other selves, other objects. Suzuki claims that the Zen experience is a leap out of relative, subject-object confrontations into pure "isness," in which there is no reflection upon self, no awareness of oneself as knower, or of one's own knowledge. There is simply "what is," an immediate grasp of existential fact, undimmed and undisturbed by mediate reflection or conceptual analysis. Is the "suchness" discovered by Zen a higher and more spiritual self? At times this is explicitly stated. Suzuki, at certain moments, talks like a Western personalist. But always behind his personalism we face the protean metaphysic of Buddhism. It is my own opinion that Buddhism is not as negative in its attitude to man's personality as is generally thought. The "ego" is not the "person" in the highest and most spiritual sense of the word. In abolishing the ego to discover the higher self Zen, which Suzuki explicitly claims is "not pantheistic," asserts a peculiar, indefinable personalism of its own.

The Zen artist does not "study Zen in order to paint." He does not, as is sometimes thought, practice meditation as a means to artistic experience and expression. Zen meditation is not a preliminary step to artistic creation. Indeed the Zen man does not strictly speaking practice meditation at all, in any sense familiar to us in the West. Rather he enters into a purifying struggle against conceptual knowledge, in which he "sweats out" his attachment to images, ideas, symbols, metaphors, analytic judg-

³ Cf., *Zen and Japanese Culture* (Princeton, N.J.: Princeton University Press, 1959).

⁴ *Ibid.*, p. 6.

ments, etc., as means for grasping, appreciating, and understanding reality. Instead of this, he seeks to recover an immediate, direct intuition: not so much an intuition "of" being as an intuition which is rooted in and identified with his very existence: an intuition in which the existent knows existence, or "isness," while completely losing sight of itself as a "knowing subject."

In the case of a Zen artist, there is then no artistic reflection. The work of art springs "out of emptiness" and is transferred in a flash, by a few brush strokes, to paper. It is not a "representation of" anything, but rather it is the subject itself, existing as light, as art, in a drawing which has, so to speak, "drawn itself." The work then is a concretized intuition: not however presented as a unique experience of a specially endowed soul, who can then claim it as his own. On the contrary, to make any such claim would instantly destroy the character of "emptiness" and suchness which the work might be imagined to have. For the Zen man to pretend to share with another "his" experience would be the height of absurdity. Whose experience? Shared with whom? The artist might well be brusquely invited to go home and consider the question: "Who do you think you are, anyway?" I do not know if this question is recorded among the traditional *koans,* but it deserves to be.

The chief thing about Zen in its relation to art is precisely that the "artist," the "genius as hero," completely vanishes from the scene. There is no self-display, because the "true self," which functions in Zen experience, is empty, invisible, and incapable of being displayed. A disciple once complained to a Zen master that he was unsettled in his mind. The master said: "All right, give me your mind and I will settle it for you." The disciple's helplessness to pick up his mind and hand it over to somebody else gave him some idea of the nature of his "problems." One cannot begin to be an artist, in Suzuki's sense, until he has become "empty," until he has disappeared.

These might seem like gratuitously confusing paradoxes. But fortunately Suzuki's numerous contacts with the West have given him the ability to explain himself in Christian terms. He translates his basic Zen idea of art into terms familiar to us:

When an art presents [the intuitively grasped mysteries of life] in a most profound and creative manner, it moves us to the depths of our being; art then becomes a divine work. The greatest productions of art, whether painting, music, sculpture or poetry, have invariably this quality—something approaching the work of God. The artist, at the moment when his creativeness is at its height, is transformed into an agent of the creator. This supreme moment in the life of an artist, when expressed in Zen terms, is the experience of *satori*. To experience *satori* is to become conscious of the Unconscious [*mushin,* no-mind] psychologically speaking. Art has always something of the Unconscious about it. The *satori* experience cannot be attained by the ordinary means of teaching and learning. It has its own technique in pointing to the presence in us of a mystery that is beyond intellectual analysis. . . . Where *satori* flashes, there is the tapping of creative energy.[5]

This same Oriental concept of the artist was developed in a masterly way by the late Ananda Coomaraswamy, in various articles now buried in the files of art magazines. These articles ought to be gathered together and published. Speaking of Balinese dancers, Coomaraswamy alludes to their essentially passive and "limp" attitude, which enables them to respond to the will of an invisible master who, so to speak, moves them in the sacred dance.[6] Coomaraswamy quotes the Gospel, in which Christ says, "I do nothing of myself," and adds a beautifully significant line of Boehme: "Thou shalt do nothing but forsake thy own will, that which thou callest 'I' or 'thyself.' By which means all thy evil properties will grow weak, faint and ready to die; and then thou wilt sink down again into that from which thou art originally sprung."

Coomaraswamy comments:

The dancer is in fact not expressing "herself" but altogether an artist, inspired: her condition is quite properly described as one of trance or ecstasy. The whole procedure is a carrying over into art of the vital principle of resignation. Religion, and culture, sacred and profane, are [here] undivided.[7]

III. Coomaraswamy joined with his friend Eric Gill in a vehement protest against the modern heresy of a pseudo-personalist art cult in which the genius is hero and high priest. Both Gill and Coomaraswamy derided this myth of our marketing society in which the artist, the practitioner of the "fine arts," is a very "special kind of man" whose "highly developed sensibility" is put on display. They protested against the dishonest use of the "fine arts" to justify the alienation of man in modern industrial society by providing him with a second-hand spirituality in art for art's sake. According to this view, we might describe the artist as the Orpheus in a kind of modern mystery cult. He immolates himself on the altar

[5] *Ibid.,* pp. 219–20.
[6] Cf., Ananda Coomaraswamy, "Spiritual Paternity," *Psychiatry, Journal of the Biology and Pathology of Interpersonal Relations,* III, August 1945, pp. 17–36.
[7] *Ibid.,* p. 28.

of art, and the devout public is saved from the Hades of industrialism in a vicariously salvific bath of "culture." Coomaraswamy and Gill declared that the artist is not a special kind of man, but every man is a special kind of artist. Both Coomaraswamy and Gill insisted with the greatest emphasis on the artist's responsibility to his work. He had to "make things right" irrespective of the quality of his artistic experience. In no circumstances was his experience to be exploited or displayed for its own sake. This strong and salutary reaction against the narcissistic cult of genius, with its false "creativity," can only be commended.

IV. Jacques Maritain, while clinging to St. Thomas as fervently as Eric Gill, has insisted more on the creative intuition of the artist and poet.[8] He proposes a reconciliation between Eastern and Western views. Whereas the Orient is utterly unconcerned with the artist's conscious "self," it nevertheless reveals his creative subjectivity. While Western art has in the last few centuries concentrated on the artist's subjectivity, it also tends to grasp and disclose the hidden mystery of things. However, Maritain takes account of the modern artist's tragic "craving for magical knowledge and his dismissal of beauty." He points out that certain modern art movements have consciously taken upon themselves a prophetic function precisely in the denial and rejection of beauty for the sake of the artist's own self-assertion or for the manifestation of his magic and prophetic gifts. In a more recent book,[9] Maritain stresses the artist's responsibility to his own gifts, to his subjectivity, to his creativity, which demands his complete, dedicated loyalty as artist. But he also shows that as a member of society the artist has other loyalties and obligations which cannot be "sacrificed" on the altar of his art.

Of the four views discussed, those of Maritain and Tillich are most sympathetic to the modern artist and the most ready to accept him on his own terms. True to the Western and personalist climate in which they write, these distinguished Christian thinkers are willing to excuse and accept very much that is negative, even much that is sick and decadent, in the name of the inherent dialectic between creativity and destruction in the modern world. Chiefly concerned with modern and Western art, Maritain and Tillich obviously have much to say about, and in favor of, the hidden spiritual possibilities in overtly secular creativities. More intent on modern nonreligious art, their viewpoint is generally less explicitly spiritual than that of the Orientals quoted. Our own

[8] Cf., Jacques Maritain, *Creative Intuition in Art and Poetry* (New York: Pantheon, 1953).

[9] *The Responsibility of the Artist* (New York: Scribner's, 1960).

Christian tradition is just as rich as the Oriental in examples of the higher "selflessness" of the truly creative art. Maritain says of Dante:

> The ego of the man has disappeared in the creative Self of the poet. Theological faith itself, the most sacred belief, has entered the work through the instrumentality of creative emotion and poetic knowledge and passed through the lake of disinterestedness and of creative innocence.[10]

Having taken account of four religious philosophies of creativity and having carefully dismissed the main secular delusions on the subject, our conclusion can now be drawn. This conclusion will not be a fully developed theological statement, only a few hints and suggestions as to how some such statement might eventually be formulated. How shall we prepare ourselves to consider the theology of creativity?

The secular caricature is a futile and demonic attempt to squeeze divine powers out of man. Since there is no genuine creativity apart from God, the man who attempts to be a "creator" outside of God and independent of him is forced to fall back on magic. The sin of the wizard is not so much that he usurps and exercises a real preternatural power, but that his postures travesty the divine by degrading man's freedom in absurd and servile manipulations of reality. The dignity of man is to stand before God on his own feet, alive, conscious, alert to the light that has been placed in him, and perfectly obedient to that light. Wizardry and idolatry obscure the light, dim man's vision, and reduce him to a state of infatuated self-absorption in which he plays at unveiling and displaying powers that were meant to remain secret, not in the sense that they must be concealed from others, but in the sense that the artist ought not to be wasting his own attention upon them or calling the attention of others to them. He should be using them in an "empty" and disinterested manner for the good of others and for the glory of God instead of exploiting them to draw attention to himself. The commandment "to make no graven image" is designed first of all to protect man against his inveterate temptation to make gods in his own image, gods in which he can objectify and venerate the divinely given powers he finds in himself. By this magic man seeks to enjoy in himself those powers that were given him as means to find fulfillment beyond and above himself. This bending back upon self, this fixation upon the exterior self was, for St. Augustine, one of the principle elements in the fall of Adam.[11]

Man's true creativity is lost, then, with his loss of innocence, selfless-

[10] *Creative Intuition*, p. 379.
[11] *De Trinitate*, xii, ii (*PL*, XLII, 1007).

ness, and simplicity. Oblivious of his external self and empty of self, man was originally one with God his creator. So intimate was their union that the creator could live and act with perfect freedom in his created instrument. Having fallen, and been redeemed in Christ, man is once again able to recover this state of innocence and union, in and through Christ. The Spirit of God, the *Creator Spiritus* who brooded over the waters before the world came into being, dwells in man and broods over the abyss of his human spirit, seeking to call forth from it a new world, a new spiritual creation, in union with the liberty of man redeemed in Christ. The theology of creativity will necessarily be the theology of the Holy Spirit re-forming us in the likeness of Christ, raising us from death to life with the very same power which raised Christ from the dead.[12] The theology of creativity will also be a theology of the image and likeness of God in man. The restoration of our creativity is simply one aspect of our recovery of our likeness to God in Christ. The image of God in man is his freedom, say St. Bernard and St. Gregory of Nyssa. The likeness of God in man is fully restored when man's freedom is perfectly united with the divine freedom, and when, consequently, man acts in all things as God acts. Or rather when God and man act purely and simply as one. Since "God is love" then for man to be restored to the likeness of God, all his acts must be pure and disinterested love, lacking all taint of that *proprium* which makes him aware of himself as a separate, insecure subject of inordinate needs which he seeks to satisfy at somebody else's expense. Creativity becomes possible insofar as man can forget his limitations and his selfhood and lose himself in abandonment to the immense creative power of a love too great to be seen or comprehended.

A theology of creativity might, then, meditate at some length on the first few chapters of Genesis, the narrative of the creation and the fall. Especially important is Genesis 2: 15-24, in which Adam appears as God's collaborator in governing paradise and in which he is given the power to name the animals as he sees fit: "for whatsoever Adam called any living creature, the same is its name." The most significant part of this passage would be sought in the typical sense of verses 21-24, on the creation of Eve. The mystery of Christ and his Church would be the very heart of any fully developed theology of creativity. Patristic works like St. Gregory of Nyssa's *De Hominis Opificio* might furnish a rich variety of intuitions from which to start building a synthesis. We would,

[12] Ephesians, 1: 17–21.

of course, have to ransack the works of Origen and St. Augustine. Among the scholastic sources, we ought not to neglect the magnificent *Collationes in Hexaemeron* of St. Bonaventure. Valuable materials for study can only be briefly indicated here.

It would above all be necessary to disentangle the various threads of thought about man's creativity as individual person and man's creativity in society. There can be no doubt that a theology of creativity would give an entirely new perspective to the distorted view produced by undue emphasis on the exceptional personality of the "genius" and his complete independence from all ethical and aesthetic norms by virtue of his talented personality. But the theological view would do nothing to diminish the value of the person: on the contrary, situating the person in his right place in relation to other men and to God, our theology would liberate in him the deepest potentialities of his nature and the highest, most secret endowments of divine grace.

The creativity of the Christian person must be seen in relation to the creative vocation of the new Adam, mystical person of the "whole Christ." The creative will of God has been at work in the cosmos since he said: "Let there be light." This creative *fiat* was not uttered merely at the dawn of time. All time and all history are a continued, uninterrupted creative act, a stupendous, ineffable mystery in which God has signified his will to associate man with himself in his work of creation. The will and power of the Almighty Father were not satisfied simply to make the world and turn it over to man to run it as best he could. The creative love of God was met, at first, by the destructive and self-centered refusal of man: an act of such incalculable consequences that it would have amounted to a destruction of God's plan, if that were possible. But the creative work of God could not be frustrated by man's sin. On the contrary, sin itself entered into that plan. If man was first called to share in the creative work of his heavenly Father, he now became involved in the "new creation," the redemption of his own kind and the restoration of the cosmos, purified and transfigured, into the hands of the Father. God himself became man in order that in this way man could be most perfectly associated with him in this great work, the fullest manifestation of his eternal wisdom and mercy.

The Christian dimensions of creativity are then to be meditated in the light of such texts as Ephesians 1: 8–10 (the re-establishment of all things in Christ); Colossians 1: 9–29 (the work of God building the Church of saints united in Christ, the "firstborn of every creature," and through him reconciling all things to himself). In this text, particularly, we see the creative role of suffering. This is very important. It is the reply to the secular and demonic overemphasis on the individual, his self-fulfillment in art for its own sake. Here, on the contrary, we see that the cross is the center of the new creation: the tree of life, instead of the tree of the knowledge of good and evil. He who has approached the tree of the knowledge of good and evil has tasted the intoxicating fruit of his own special excellence but he dies the death of frustration. He becomes the prisoner of his own gifts and he sticks to his own excellence as if it were flypaper. There is no joy for him because he is alienated from life, love, and communion in creativity by his own demonic self-assertion, which automatically involves a rejection of suffering, of dependence, of charity, and of obedience.

On the contrary, it is the renunciation of our false self, the emptying of self in the likeness of Christ, that brings us to the threshold of that true creativity in which God himself, the creator, works in and through us. The fact that the Christian renounces his own limited ends and satis-factions in order to achieve something greater than he can see or under-stand means the sacrifice of immediate visible results. But it also means that the efficacy of his action becomes lasting as well as universal. Such creativity does not stop with a little ephemeral success here and there: it reaches out to the ends of time and to the limits of the universe.

This may sound like hyperbole: but this is creativity in a new and spiritual dimension, which is its full Christian dimension. And this ap-plies not only to the artist, but to every Christian. To adapt Coomara-swamy's phrase, one might say "the creative Christian is not a special kind of Christian, but every Christian has his own creative work to do, his own part in the mystery of the 'new creation.' " Would that we were all more aware of this. Our awareness would produce a climate that would have a special meaning for the artist. The way for sacred art to become more "creative" is not just for the artist to study new and fashion-able trends and try to apply them to sacred or symbolic themes. It is for the artist to enter deeply into his Christian vocation, his part in the work of restoring all things in Christ. But this is not his responsibility alone. This is the responsibility of the whole Church and everybody in it. We all have an obligation to open our eyes to the eschatalogical dimensions of Christian creativity, for, as St. Paul says, "all creation is groaning" for the final manifestation of this finished work, the only work that has an eternal importance: the full revelation of God by the restoration of all things in Christ.

MESSAGE TO POETS

Author's Note
This message was read at a meeting of the "new" Latin-American poets—
and a few young North Americans—Mexico City, February 1964. This
was not a highly organized and well-financed international congress,
but a spontaneous and inspired meeting of young poets from all over the
hemisphere, most of whom could barely afford to be there. One, for in-
stance, sold her piano to make the trip from Peru.

We who are poets know that the reason for a poem is not discovered until the poem itself exists. The reason for a living act is realized only in the act itself. This meeting is a spontaneous explosion of hopes. That is why it is a venture in prophetic poverty, supported and financed by no foundation, organized and publicized by no official group, but a living expression of the belief that there are now in our world new people, new poets who are not in tutelage to established political systems or cultural structures—whether communist or capitalist—but who dare to hope in their own vision of reality and of the future. This meeting is united in a flame of hope whose temperature has not yet been taken and whose effects have not yet been estimated, because it is a new fire. The reason for the fire cannot be apparent to one who is not warmed by it. The reason for being here will not be found until all have walked together, without after-thought, into contradictions and possibilities.

We believe that our future will be made by love and hope, not by violence or calculation. The Spirit of Life that has brought us together, whether in space or only in agreement, will make our encounter an epiphany of certainties we could not know in isolation.

The solidarity of poets is not planned and welded together with tactical convictions or matters of policy, since these are affairs of prejudice, cunning, and design. Whatever his failures, the poet is not a cunning man. His art depends on an ingrained innocence which he would lose in

Written in 1964, excerpts of this essay first appeared in *Americas*, 16, April 1964, and was subsequently published *in toto* in *Raids on the Unspeakable* (New York: New Directions, 1966).

business, in politics, or in too organized a form of academic life. The hope that rests on calculation has lost its innocence. We are banding together to defend our innocence.

All innocence is a matter of belief. I do not speak now of organized agreement, but of interior personal convictions "in the spirit." These convictions are as strong and undeniable as life itself. They are rooted in fidelity to *life* rather than to artificial systems. The solidarity of poets is an elemental fact like sunlight, like the seasons, like the rain. It is something that cannot be organized, it can only happen. It can only be "received." It is a gift to which we must remain open. No man can plan to make the sun rise or the rain fall. The sea is still wet in spite of all formal and abstract programs. Solidarity is not collectivity. The organizers of collective life will deride the seriousness or the reality of our hope. If they infect us with their doubt we shall lose our innocence and our solidarity along with it.

Collective life is often organized on the basis of cunning, doubt, and guilt. True solidarity is destroyed by the political art of pitting one man against another and the commercial art of estimating all men at a price. On these illusory measurements men build a world of arbitrary values without life and meaning, full of sterile agitation. To set one man against another, one life against another, one work against another, and to express the measurement in terms of cost or of economic privilege and moral honor is to infect everybody with the deepest metaphysical doubt. Divided and set up against one another for the purpose of evaluation, men immediately acquire the mentality of objects for sale in a slave market. They despair of themselves because they know they have been unfaithful to life and to being, and they no longer find anyone to forgive the infidelity.

Yet their despair condemns them to further infidelity: alienated from their own spiritual roots, they contrive to break, to humiliate, and to destroy the spirit of others. In such a situation there is no joy, only rage. Each man feels the deepest root of his being poisoned by suspicion, unbelief, and hate. Each man experiences his very existence as guilt and betrayal, and as a possibility of death: nothing more.

We stand together to denounce the shame and the imposture of all such calculations.

If we are to remain united against these falsehoods, against all power that poisons man and subjects him to the mystifications of bureaucracy, commerce, and the police state, we must refuse the price tag. We must refuse academic classification. We must reject the seductions of publicity.

We must not allow ourselves to be pitted one against another in mystical comparisons—political, literary, or cultural orthodoxies. We must not be made to devour and dismember one another for the amusement of their press. We must not let ourselves be eaten by them to assuage their own insatiable doubt. We must not merely be *for* something and *against* something else, even if we are for "ourselves" and against "them." Who are "they"? Let us not give them support by becoming an "opposition," which assumes they are definitively real.

Let us remain outside "their" categories. It is in this sense that we are all monks: for we remain innocent and invisible to publicists and bureaucrats. They cannot imagine what we are doing unless we betray ourselves to them, and even then they will never be able.

They understand nothing except what they themselves have decreed. They are crafty ones who weave words about life and then make life conform to what they themselves have declared. How can they trust anyone when they make life itself tell lies? It is the businessman, the propagandist, the politician, not the poet, who devoutly believes in "the magic of words."

For the poet there is precisely no magic. There is only life in all its unpredictability and all its freedom. All magic is a ruthless venture in manipulation, a vicious circle, a self-fulfilling prophecy.

Word-magic is an impurity of language and of spirit in which words, deliberately reduced to unintelligibility, appeal mindlessly to the vulnerable will. Let us deride and parody this magic with other variants of the unintelligible, if we want to. But it is better to prophesy than to deride. To prophesy is not to predict, but to seize upon reality in its moment of highest expectation and tension toward the new. This tension is discovered not in hypnotic elation but in the light of everyday existence. Poetry is innocent of prediction because it is itself the fulfillment of all the momentous predictions hidden in everyday life.

Poetry is the flowering of ordinary possibilities. It is the fruit of ordinary and natural choice. This is its innocence and dignity.

Let us not be like those who wish to make the tree bear its fruit first and the flower afterward—a conjuring trick and an advertisement. We are content if the flower comes first and the fruit afterward, in due time. Such in the poetic spirit.

Let us obey life, and the Spirit of Life that calls us to be poets, and we shall harvest many new fruits for which the world hungers—fruits of hope that have never been seen before. With these fruits we shall calm the resentments and the rage of man.

Let us be proud that we are not witch doctors, only ordinary men.

Let us be proud that we are not experts in anything.

Let us be proud of the words that are given to us for nothing, not to teach anyone, not to confute anyone, not to prove anyone absurd, but to point beyond all objects into the silence where nothing can be said.

We are not persuaders. We are the children of the Unknown. We are the ministers of silence that is needed to cure all victims of absurdity who lie dying of a contrived joy. Let us then recognize ourselves for who we are: dervishes mad with secret therapeutic love which cannot be bought or sold, and which the politician fears more than violent revolution, for violence changes nothing. But love changes everything.

We are stronger than the bomb.

Let us then say "yes" to our own nobility by embracing the insecurity and abjection that a dervish existence entails.

In the *Republic* of Plato there was already no place for poets and musicians, still less for dervishes and monks. As for the technological Platos who think they now run the world we live in, they imagine they can tempt us with banalities and abstractions. But we can elude them merely by stepping into the Heraklitean river which is never crossed twice.

When the poet puts his foot in that ever-moving river, poetry itself is born out of the flashing water. In that unique instant, the truth is manifest to all who are able to receive it.

No one can come near the river unless he walks on his own feet. He cannot come there carried in a vehicle.

No one can enter the river wearing the garments of public and collective ideas. He must feel the water on his skin. He must know that immediacy is for naked minds only, and for the innocent.

Come, dervishes: here is the water of life. Dance in it.

ANSWERS ON ART AND FREEDOM

Author's Note

These lines were written in reply to nine questions asked by readers of the magazine Eco Contemporaneo, *Buenos Aires, and were reprinted in the* Lugano Review. *I no longer have the questions, but they may be guessed. They were simple enough, and were all concerned with the familiar topic of the artist's autonomy in his own sphere. The artist is responsible first of all for the excellence of his work and his art should not be used for an ulterior purpose that conflicts with this primary aim. All this is obvious enough in theory. Not being perfectly informed, I do not know how far, in practice, the artist is perversely "used" or controlled by society. I assume that the questions were formulated chiefly with a mind to protest against all forms of official—especially political—censorship. Taking for granted that political oppression is obnoxious, these answers seek deeper motives and principles of freedom within the artist himself, and they concern themselves chiefly with the artist in Western society.*

I am asked whether or not the artist, writer, poet, is a docile servant of institutions, or whether he can and should work in complete freedom. Stated in these terms the proposition would seem to be deceptively simple. One would mechanically answer that the artist is by his very nature free and autonomous. He can be nobody's slave. There is no problem. Everyone sees the answer. It is even *to the interest of those who control him* to allow the artist his autonomy. The relative freedom that is suddenly granted to a Soviet poet becomes a matter of great importance to the whole world. It tends to make people think more kindly and more hopefully of Soviet Russia. Whereas the poet who rebels completely against conventional Western society (Rimbaud, Baudelaire, the Beats) establishes that society more firmly in its complacent philistinism, he also

This article on art and freedom was originally written for Miguel Grinberg and was published in Spanish translation in *Eco Contemporaneo* and then appeared in English in the first issue of *Lugano Review* in 1965. It was subsequently included in *Raids on the Unspeakable* (New York: New Directions, 1966).

strengthens its conviction that all artists are by necessity opium fiends and feeds its sense of magnanimity in tolerating such people.

What I mean to say by this is that the enemies of the artist's freedom are those who must profit by his *seeming* to be free, whether or not he is so.

And the artist himself, to the extent that he is dominated by introjected philistine condemnations of his art, pours out his energy and integrity in resisting these tyrannical pressures which come to him from within himself. His art then wastes itself in reaction against the antiart of the society in which he lives (or he cultivates antiart as a protest against the art cult of the society in which he lives).

The artist who expends all his efforts in convincing himself that he is not a nonartist or the antiartist who struggles not to become "an artist" cannot justify his vexations by appealing to an ideal of freedom. What he needs is not an ideal of freedom, but at least a minimum of practical and subjective autonomy—freedom from the internalized emotional pressures by which society holds him down. I mean freedom of conscience. This is a spiritual value and its roots are ultimately religious. Hence my first principle is that since in our society everybody is already more or less concerned with a theoretical and doctrinaire approach to the question of art and freedom, maybe the artist himself has something better to do—namely his own job. There have grown up so many myths about the business of "being an artist" and living the special kind of life that artists are reputed to live, that if the artist is too concerned with "being an artist" he will never get around to doing any work. Hence it is to his advantage, first of all, to be free from myths about "Art" and even from myths about the threat which society offers to his "freedom." This applies, at least, to artists living in "the West," where in fact nobody is seriously interfering with his freedom. On the other hand, under Communism the poets and painters seem to be the most serious prophets of a genuine liberation for thought, life, and experience. They protest more articulately than anyone against the general servility to boredom and official stupidity.

Yet the artist who is held by dope or drink is just as much a prisoner of a corrupt commercial or political power structure as the artist who is held by the coercion of the Writer's Union. Each in his own way is turning out propaganda by producing something according to the dictates of the society in which he lives. The artist who is really free and chooses this particular servitude is perhaps less worthy of admiration than one who, being subject to all kinds of harassment, still makes the choice for which Sartre praised the men of the French resistance under Nazism.

1. What is the *use* of art? The artist must serenely defend his right to be completely useless. It is better to produce absolutely no work of art at all than to do what can be cynically "used." Yet anything can be used—even the most truculently abstract paintings. They decorate the offices of corporation presidents who have quickly caught on to the fact that to pay ten thousand dollars for something explicitly "useless" is a demonstration of one's wealth and power—as well as of sophistication.

And tomorrow the abstract paintings will be on the walls of the Commissars.

Works of art can be and are used in many ways, but such uses are beyond the range of this question. "Art" considered as an immanent perfection of the artist's own intelligence is not improved by nonartistic use. Let us set aside the question of a supposed cult of pure art, art for art's sake, etc. Is this an actual problem? I doubt it. Who is to say what poets and artists as a species are thinking and doing? The world is full of poets, novelists, painters, sculptors: they blossom on all the bushes. Who can generalize about them, except perhaps to say that they all tend to start out looking for something that can't be found merely by selling insurance or automobiles.

The problem arises when art ceases to be honest work and becomes instead a way to self-advertisement and success—when the writer or painter uses his art merely to sell himself. (It is an article of faith, in Western society at least, that a poet or painter is by nature "more interesting" than other people and, God knows, everybody wants in the worst way to be interesting!)

2. The artist cannot afford passively to accept, to "reflect," or to celebrate what everybody likes. The artist who subscribes to the commercial slogan that the customer is always right will soon be deserted by everybody. The customer has now been trained to think that the *artist* is always right. Thus we have a new situation in which the artist feels himself obligated to function as a prophet or a magician. He sees that he has to be disconcerting, even offensive. Who will ever read him or buy him unless he occasionally insults the customer and all he believes in? That is precisely what the customer wants. He has delegated to the artist the task of nonconforming on his behalf—the task of not conforming with "ordinary decent people." Where does the artist go from there? In desperation he paints a meticulously accurate portrait of a beer can.

3. The writer who submits to becoming "an engineer of the soul" is in complicity with the secret police—or with the advertising business. He is worse than the policeman, who does an honest job of work beating up his prisoner and extracting a confession. The "engineer of the soul"

simply dictates routine and trivial testimonials to the rightness of an absurd society without any cost to himself and without need to make use of art in any form whatever. For this he receives certain rewards with which he is content.

4. *The artist in uniform.* Precisely when does it cease to be respectable to be seen marching with the political police? It is a nice question in countries where, rightly or wrongly, one is considered to be alive only if he is agitating for revolution. Putting the question in another form: how do you know when *your* revolution has developed sclerosis?

5. *Art and ethics.* Certainly the artist has no obligation to promulgate ethical lessons any more than political or economic ones. The artist is not a catechist. Usually moral directives are lost when one attempts to convey them in a medium that is not intended to communicate conceptual formulas. But the artist has a moral obligation to maintain his own freedom and his own truth. His art and his life are separable only in theory. The artist cannot be free in his art if he does not have a conscience that warns him when he is acting like a slave in his everyday life.

The artist should preach nothing—not even his own autonomy. His art should speak its own truth, and in so doing it will be in harmony with every other kind of truth—moral, metaphysical, and mystical.

The artist has no moral obligation to prove himself one of the elect by systematically standing a traditional moral code on its head.

6. Is the artist necessarily committed to this or that political ideology? No. But he does live in a world where politics are decisive and where political power can destroy his art as well as his life. Hence he is indirectly committed to seek some political solution to problems that endanger the freedom of man. This is the great temptation: there is not a single form of government or social system today that does not in the end seek to manipulate or to coerce the artist in one way or another. In every case the artist should be in complete solidarity with those who are fighting for rights and freedom against inertia, hypocrisy and coercion: e.g., the Negroes in the United States.

The American Negroes are at once the ones who fight for their freedom and who exemplify a genuine and living creativity, for example in jazz.

7. "Formalism"—a meaningless cliché devised by literary and artistic gendarmes. It is a term totally devoid of value or significance, as are all the other cultural slogans invented in the police station.

8. I do not consider myself integrated in the war-making society in which I live, but the problem is that this society *does* consider *me* in-

tegrated in it. I notice that for nearly twenty years my society—or those in it who read my books—have decided upon an identity for me and insist that I continue to correspond perfectly to the idea of me which they found upon reading my first successful book. Yet the same people simultaneously prescribe for me a contrary identity. They demand that I remain forever the superficially pious, rather rigid, and somewhat narrow-minded young monk I was twenty years ago, and at the same time they continually circulate the rumor that I have left my monastery. What has actually happened is that I have been simply living where I am and developing in my own way without consulting the public about it, since it is none of the public's business.

9. Society benefits when the artist liberates himself from its coercive or seductive pressures. Only when he is obligated to his fellow man in the concrete, rather than to society in the abstract, can the artist have anything to say that will be of value to others. His art then becomes accidentally a work of love and justice. The artist would do well, however, not to concern himself too much with "society" in the abstract or with ideal "commitments." This has not always been true. It applies more to our time when "society" is in some confusion. It is conceivable that the artist might once again be completely integrated in society as he was in the Middle Ages. Today he is hardly likely to find himself unless he is a nonconformist and a rebel. To say this is neither dangerous nor new. It is what society really expects of its artists. For today the artist has, whether he likes it or not, inherited the combined functions of hermit, pilgrim, prophet, priest, shaman, sorcerer, soothsayer, alchemist, and bonze. How could such a man be free? How can he really "find himself" if he plays a role that society has predetermined for him? The freedom of the artist is to be sought precisely in the choice of his *work* and not in the choice of the role as "artist" which society asks him to play, for reasons that will always remain very mysterious.

To conclude: the artist must not delude himself that he has an infinite capacity to choose for himself and a moral responsibility to exercise this unlimited choice, especially when it becomes absurd.

If he does this, then let him take my word for it, he will find himself with the same problem and in the same quandary as those monks who have vegetated for three centuries in a moral morass of abstract voluntarism. There is a great deal of ambiguity in the facile rationalization which says that even in the worst and most confined of situations you can become perfectly free simply by *choosing* the situation you are in. Freedom consists in something more than merely choosing what is forced upon you—and doing so with a certain exultation at the absurdity and the humiliation that are involved. It takes more than this kind of choice to make one "the incontestable author of an event or of an object"(Sartre). At the same time, I wonder if this *need to be an incontestable author* points to freedom at all. On the contrary, maybe it is one of the roots of unfreedom in the psychology of the modern artist. As long as I am obsessed with the need to get myself or my work recognized as "incontestable" and "authentic," I am still under servitude to the myths and anxieties of my society and unable to attain the complete freedom of the artist who chooses his work of art in its own terms and in his, not in those of the market, or of politics, or of philosophy, or of the myth of pure experience, absolute spontaneity, and all the rest.

The impiety of the Sartrian who chooses the ugly, the absurd, and the obscene as an act of which he is the "incontestable author" rejoins the piety of the monastic novice who chooses the most arbitrary and most pointless acts of self-mortification in order to see himself as pleasing to God. In either case there is a naïve and narcissistic emphasis on the pure voluntaristic choice for its own sake. The supposed purity of this voluntarism is not purity at all: it is merely abstract willfulness.

True artistic freedom can never be a matter of sheer willfulness or arbitrary posturing. It is the outcome of authentic possibilities, understood and accepted in their own terms, not the refusal of the concrete in favor of the purely "interior." In the last analysis, the only valid witness to the artist's creative freedom is his work itself. The artist builds his own freedom and forms his own artistic conscience by the work of his hands. Only when the work is finished can he tell whether or not it was done "freely."

WHY ALIENATION IS FOR EVERYBODY

If we want to understand alienation we have to find where its deepest taproot goes—and we have to realize that this root will always be there. Alienation is inseparable from culture, from civilization, and from life in society. It is not just a feature of "bad" cultures, "corrupt" civilizations, or urban society. It is not just a dubious privilege reserved for some people in society. In Louisville, it is not just for the West End. In my opinion the East End may be even more alienated than the West because it is not aware of the fact.[1]

Alienation begins when culture divides me against myself, puts a mask on me, gives me a role I may or may not want to play. Alienation is complete when I become completely identified with my mask, totally satisfied with my role, and convince myself that any other identity or role is inconceivable. The man who sweats under his mask, whose role makes him itch with discomfort, who hates the division in himself, is already beginning to be free. But God help him if all he wants is the mask the other man is wearing, just because the other one does not seem to be sweating or itching. Maybe he is no longer human enough to itch. (Or else he pays a psychiatrist to scratch him.)

Modern literature is by and large a literature of alienation, not only because we are painfully living through the collapse of a culture but because today we have more culture and more civilization than we know what to do with. There are not only the simple, beautiful, wild, honest ceremonial masks once affected by the Kwakiutl Indians (and which were well understood because they had their "right" place in life and went with some pretty good dancing): but today we smother under an overproduction of masks and myths and personae. We all have to try to be fifty different people. We all can refuse some of the more absurd and unacceptable roles, but not many can refuse as much as they would like to, and no one can refuse them all.

This essay was written in early 1968 for a "Prospectus of Writings" in Louisville's West End, but for some unknown reason has remained unpublished. It was discovered among the Merton manuscripts following his death.

[1] Louisville's West End is poor and mostly black, while the East End is made up of the more affluent.

The result is the painful, sometimes paranoid sense of being always under observation, under judgment, for not fulfilling some role or other we have forgotten we were supposed to fulfill.

The peculiar pain of "alienation" in its ordinary sense—alienation as a kind of perpetual mental Charley horse of self-conscious frustration—is that nobody really has to look at us or judge us or despise us or hate us. Whether or not they do us this service, we are already there ahead of them. We are doing it for them. WE TRAIN OURSELVES OBEDI-ENTLY TO HATE OURSELVES SO MUCH THAT OUR ENE-MIES NO LONGER HAVE TO. To live in constant awareness of this bind is a kind of living death. But to live without any awareness of it at all is death pure and simple—even though one may still be walking around and smelling perfect.

There has to be a culture, obviously. The best cultures have always been those which achieved the most workable balance between custom and nature, discipline and impulse, conscious and unconscious. Primitive cultures on the whole did this well. The great traditional religious cultures managed it well (Mayan, Zapotecan, the Buddhist-inspired King-dom of Asoka, some medieval Christian cultures). Our culture is doing a disastrously bad job of it.

What can the artist do about it?

It is not enough to complain about alienation, one must exorcise it. One must refuse the most useless and harmful role it imposes on us: that of causing and judging our own pain and condemning ourselves to nonentity on account of it. The constant, repeated, compulsive self-annihilation is due to the short circuit which puts a conventional judg-ment, dictated by culture, fashion, literature, style, art, religion, science, sociology, politics, what have you, IN THE PLACE OF OUR OWN IMMEDIATE RESPONSE however unconscious, irrational, foolish, un-acceptable, it may at first appear to be. (Immediate response is not "knee-jerk" response, and it does imply some cultural formation and expe-rience.)

Yes, we have to learn to write disciplined prose. We have to write poems that are "Poems." But that is a relatively unprofitable and secon-dary concern compared with the duty of first writing nonsense. We have to learn the knack of free association, to let loose what is hidden in our depths, to expand rather than to condense prematurely. Rather than making an intellectual point and then devising a form to express it, we need rather to release the face that is sweating under the mask and let it sweat out in the open for a change, even though nobody else gives it a prize for special beauty or significance.

What follows may be mystifying.[2] Partly because it comes from a different city, and a completely faceless part of that city (freightyards in Long Island City, a stadium, an Italian ghetto, etc.—all this back in the thirties). It consists mostly of free-flowing unconscious images mixed in with the "real" places and events (left very nebulous). The language is deliberately compressed, nothing is spelled out. It is meant to be only half penetrable (important for the alienation-pro.) One clue: the "funnel house" which smokes and has eyes is in fact the presence of death, in terms of the crematory that reduced most of my family to ashes. No, not Auschwitz, just an ordinary American burning ghat for the respectable.

In that way we accumulate a lot of material which may be fresh and new and which may, by itself, suggest new forms. We may have to do a lot of rewriting and discard most of what was first put down. But gradually, out of this, comes work that is free from the obsessions and pre-digested formulas of everybody else's "art."

This present "Prospectus of Writings" by Louisville writers reflects something of the struggle I have been talking about. There are some fine pieces in it, and the best are precisely ones in which experience has got loose from obsessions about form and imposed something of its own form. One feels though that many of the writers were overawed by the topic and could not quite get out from under it—hence a tendency to write editorials and sermonettes. On the other hand, when I meet the poem "Christianity" and find:

"God unknown, wrapped in a cellophane bag, oversees all," I am immediately impressed. This poet dares to express the reality of religious alienation—an alienation which I myself know.

"The bull nuzzles the lamb while an un-eyed Moslem sees many things." That is a fine line of real poetry that needs no label.

In "18 yr olds die young" there is another kind of freedom, verging on concrete poetry, but also promising in the future something of the same thing. Coltrane and Pharaoh Sanders did and are doing with their instruments the visual gesture of squawk that builds ironic and suffering personages out of sound, spirit figures posturing, hurting, living, dying, enigmatic.

From the title on, "To Die Is Human, to Rot Something Else" the piece on the funeral is a powerful insight into the heart of alienation.

[2] A section of Merton's long booklength prose poem, *The Geography of Lograire,* published posthumously (New York: New Directions, 1969).

The culture built on death: the convergence of affluence and death wish, the root of our tragedy.

I have been invited to contribute something myself, and I am more than happy to do so, and to confess my own alienation in good company. The piece is part of a long section of a booklength poem. It is about my own youth in New York, alienation in the thirties. A peculiarly drab section of Queens between the Long Island Railway tunnel and the place where I used to live. It is largely dream writing so do not expect to be swept off your feet by a message. And thanks for the hospitality of these pages.

APPENDIX I
NATURE AND ART IN WILLIAM BLAKE:
AN ESSAY IN INTERPRETATION
(1939)

Submitted in partial fulfillment of the requirements for the degree of Master of Arts in the Department of English and Comparative Literature, Faculty of Philosophy, Columbia University. February, 1939. (Thomas Merton)

2 December 1953
Constance M. Winchell
(Reference Librarian)
Columbia University Library
New York, New York

Dear Constance Winchell:

If you wish to reproduce my Master's Essay, *Nature and Art in William Blake*, it is perfectly all right for you to do so. You may have my permission to reproduce it in any way convenient to you, in order to meet the requests of other libraries. It is therefore perfectly agreeable to me if you have the essay microfilmed.

However, I would like to ask you the favor of including this present letter in the microfilming of the essay. My reason for this will be understandable, when I say that it is fifteen years since I have looked at the essay, or had a copy of it in my hands. As far as I can remember, the thesis contains quite a few statements which I would like to have changed. I have no chance to go over the essay now, and the changes I would like to make would probably involve the re-working of several important passages in it. Anyone who reads the essay should therefore take into account its many mistakes, especially in the field of of scholastic philosophy and theology, and not hold me too strictly responsible for them at the present time.

If this essay can in any way be useful to students, I will feel myself more than amply rewarded for having written it. I hope the religious minded among them will pray for its author.

With best wishes,

Sincerely yours in Christ,

Fr. M. Louis Merton, O.C.S.O.
    (Thomas Merton)

Table of Contents

PREFACE

It is a pity that Blake, a good artist and, though scarcely orthodox, a good Christian, should be so often treated as some strange pagan freak, whom we draw upon for stray remarks to support whatever prejudices of the moment we happen to want to defend. Such criticism will be discussed later in connection with Mr. Middleton Murry.

But it is a greater pity still to try and take Blake apart piece by piece and spread him in the sun to dry out while we examine the shreds of his poetry for traces of this Gnostic or that Manichaean, finally getting so lost that we talk entirely about his knowledge of the occult, and never about his greatness as a poet.

This essay will not, therefore, attempt to examine any precise historical influences upon Blake. And the discussion in detail of Blake's relationship to India is no indication that I am yielding to the temptation to juggle with influences. I think that the affinities between Christian thinkers and Oriental mystics are interesting in themselves. To break them up into influences in one direction or another always encourages arbitrary, false, and pigheaded statements, without adding anything at all to our understanding of the way these thinkers and mystics looked at life.

This essay aims toward a clearer understanding of Blake's ideas about art; no more. To this end, I have compared him with the aestheticians I think he most resembles. More than that, I have used the aesthetic ideas of St. Thomas Aquinas (as presented by one of the greatest of living philosophers, Jacques Maritain) as a touchstone by which to test Blake's thought, without meaning to insinuate that Blake and St. Thomas are exactly like each other, or, worse still, that Blake ever read a line of St. Thomas. As mystic, Blake belongs to the Christian tradition of the Augustinians and the Franciscans; in this tradition the influence of the Neo-Platonists is strong. Thomism, especially in its views about the nature of matter, and the created world, differs widely from the more mystical tradition, as is well known. But I have chosen to study Blake in comparison to the Thomists, because the latter are so clear, so acute, so well balanced, that they fill the whole subject with a light by which we may more clearly see into the depths of Blake's own more recondite thought. In any case, the similarities between Blake and St. Thomas on the subject of art are more numerous than their differences, as will be shown.

The function of the first part of this essay is, I think, self-evident. I have attempted to sketch in lightly Blake's intellectual background, to give some idea what he was struggling for, and to dispel the illusion that he lived exclusively in the tabernacles of ecstatic puritan cranks.

Finally, a word about the confusion Blake often throws one into because of his lack of a set of comfortable second-class philosophical abstractions. As Henry Adams says (in *Mont St. Michel and Chartres*): "Children and Saints can believe two contrary things at the same time."

CHAPTER I
BACKGROUND AND DEVELOPMENT

Blake was the son of a Swedenborgian hosier and was born in London in 1757. He was a boy of "a strangely romantic habit of mind,"[1] and he would wander through the fields and woods outside of London, across the Thames. Returning from Peckham Rye near Dulwich Hill one day he told how he had seen a tree full of angels: "bright angelic wings bespangling every bough like stars,"[2] and his father, in spite of Swedenborg, decided to beat such nonsense out of him right away. His mother seems to have interceded for him; at any rate, his father changed his mind in time and let the boy go wandering where he pleased, not only in the country, but in the art galleries and print shops around London. He even began to encourage the boy's taste for art and bought him plaster casts of "The gladiator, the Hercules, Venus Medicis, and various heads, hands and feet"[3] to draw from. When Blake was ten, he was sent to Pars' Drawing School in the Strand.

At the print shops, Blake spent his pocket money on engravings of Raphael, Hemskeerk, and Dürer, and he was well known in the Auction Rooms, especially at Langford's where "Langford called him his little connoisseur and often knocked down to him a cheap lot with friendly precipitation."[4] Of course, Blake did not have much pocket money; but according to Gilchrist[5] bidding in those days began at threepence. And then, it was easy enough to pick up a Marc Antonio at a time when stipple was at the height of fashion and the old style of clear and vigorous engraving was neglected:

> I am happy I cannot say Raffaele ever was from my earliest childhood hidden from me. I saw and I knew immediately the difference between Raffaele and Rubens.[6]

[1] Alexander Gilchrist, *Life of William Blake*, London, John Lane Ltd., 1907, page 6.

[2] *Ibid.*, page 7.

[3] Benjamin Heath Malkin, *apud* Arthur Symons, *William Blake*, New York, Dutton & Co., 1907, page 312.

[4] Malkin, *op. cit.*, page 313.

[5] Gilchrist, *op. cit.*, page 10.

[6] "Annotations to Reynolds," *The Writings of William Blake*, edited by Geoffrey Keynes, London, Nonesuch Press, 1925, Vol. III, page 8.

By the time Blake was ten his father was apparently willing to do anything to help him become an artist, buying him the casts Malkin spoke of and sending him to Pars' School. This school was one of the most fashionable of its kind, and was run by the "Incorporated Society of Artists" which Hogarth had helped to found. Pars himself had studied in Greece and brought back with him a portfolio of sketches which were probably familiar to his students. In this school there was no life class; the boys learned to draw from casts.

While he was copying Michelangelo, Raphael, and Greek sculpture, and undergoing the discipline of art school, Blake had become an eager but perhaps haphazard reader and was even writing poetry. The song "How Sweet I Roamed" antedates his fourteenth year.[7] The first contemporary criticism of Blake, Benjamin Malkin's remarks in his preface to *A Father's Memoirs of His Child,* tells us something of this early reading. The information probably came from Blake himself. There were, of course, Milton and the Bible. Then:

> Shakespeare's Venus and Adonis, Tarquin and Lucrece and his Sonnets. . . . These poems, now little read, were the favorite studies of Mr. Blake's early days. So were Jonson's Underwoods, his Miscellanies, and he seems to me to have caught his manner rather than that of Shakespeare in his trifles.[8]

Blake himself adds:

> Milton lov'd me in childhood and showed me his face
> Ezra came with Isaiah the prophet, but Shakespeare
>   in riper years gave me his hand,
> Paracelsus and Boehme appeared to me . . . .[9]

It is apparent enough that this reading was altogether free and casual. The Bible and Milton were probably on his father's shelves, and he would have been led to Paracelsus and Boehme by his father's Swedenborgian friends. The influence of "Ossian" and the Graveyard school is fairly evident in the *Poetical Sketches;* for instance, in the ballad "Fair Eleanor" and in the prose pieces. Blake probably knew Isaac Watts' "Horae Lyricae," and the first review of his poems compared him unfavorably with Watts.[10]

[7] Malkin, *loc. cit.*

[8] Malkin, *op. cit.,* page 323.

[9] "Letter X, To John Flaxman," *The Writings of William Blake,* Vol. II, page 150.

[10] Mona Wilson, *The Life of William Blake,* London, Nonesuch Press, 1927, page 183.

But still the strongest influence on the *Poetical Sketches,* which include "Lines in Imitation of Spenser," is that of the Elizabethans. Of course, the attempt at a tragedy, *King Edward III,* is the result of his reading Shakespeare. Osbert Burdett, in his *Life of William Blake* says:[11]

The *Poetical Sketches* show Blake at the only period of his life when he read books as works of art simply. Already his first artistic zeal was being definitely transferred to drawing, and, left entirely to his own devices in his intellectual studies, for which the atmosphere of his home set the seal on peculiarity of opinion, he soon came to read only to confirm, and never to correct his peculiar and dogmatic preferences. . . . After his boyhood was over he read to justify visionary intuition, never to learn how best to reach his readers by communicating his ideas in an apprehensible form.

This is a seemingly reasonable but really misleading remark. It is based on too simple an idea of Blake's character and development. Twenty years after he had ceased, according to Burdett, to read except for the support of his mysticism, he began to learn Greek. He had read Winckelmann and praised Cowper's *Letters.* Then he read Chaucer with great admiration and wrote some critical notes on him[12] that Charles Lamb praised as "most spirited."[13] A precis in a Sale Catalogue of a lost letter to Hayley[14] quotes Blake as saying Richardson has "won his heart." Tatham tells us he enjoyed Ovid's *Fasti,*[15] and Crabb Robinson that he liked Wordsworth, although he called Wordsworth's love of nature "atheism."[16]

Indeed, it is absurd to say Blake read to "justify" his visions. To his mind there was probably no book but the Bible that could justify them. Milton and Dante, his two favorite poets, were both defective. Dante, for his political interests, was too much in the "world," and as for Milton, Blake had to write a whole poem to correct his errors.[17]

---

[11] Osbert Burdett, *William Blake,* London, Macmillan and Co., 1926, page 10.

[12] "Descriptive Catalogue," *The Writings of William Blake,* Vol. II, p. 95 ff.

[13] *The Works of Charles and Mary Lamb,* Editor, E. V. Lucas, New Haven, Yale University Press, 1935.

[14] *The Writings of William Blake,* Vol. II, page 379.

[15] Frederick Tatham, *Letters of William Blake together with a Life by Frederick Tatham,* edited by Archibald Russell, London, Methuen and Co., Ltd., 1906, page 32.

[16] *Ibid.,* page 15.

[17] Milton's Emenation, Ololon, is the one who creates the detested Natural Religion. The accusation this implies against puritanism is only just beginning to be realized. ("Milton", *The Writings of William Blake,* Volume III)

True, he drew on occultists and mystics of all kinds for ideas, symbolism, and cosmography. But to say he read only mystics is false, and even to suggest he used them to justify himself is misleading.

Meanwhile he left Pars' in 1771 and entered upon his apprenticeship under James Basire, engraver to the Society of Antiquaries. Basire had studied in Rome and had done some engravings after Hogarth which the master had highly praised.[18] Basire himself was to have a great influence over Blake's technique as an engraver. This influence added nothing to Blake's popularity, because Basire was of the old school, and Hogarth's style was giving way in popular favor to the softer, trickier technique of Bartholozzi and Strange, while Basire confirmed the young Blake in his love of vigorous and clean outlines.

He sent Blake out to make drawings from churches and old buildings for an antiquary named Gough.[19] This was very important to Blake's development. For several years he was busy sketching Gothic architecture and sculpture in Westminster Abbey and other churches. "There," says Malkin,[20] "he found a treasure which he knew how to value. He saw the simple and plain road to the style which he aimed." He was above all impressed by the Gothic sculpture on the tombs and monuments of the kings and queens around about the Chapel of Edward the Confessor. These studies occupied him entirely between the ages of fourteen and twenty-one, and the influence on his own work is obvious; for example, in his treatment of drapery. But the influence of this Gothic atmosphere upon his aesthetic thought was even more important. In fact, Blake understood and loved the Gothic so well that he came to understand the Christian ideals underlying Gothic art far better than the amateurs and virtuosi of his century could ever hope to.

When he was twenty-one he ended his apprenticeship with Basire and went to study at the Royal Academy under Moser, a Swiss, and a favorite with Reynolds and with royalty. Moser admired the fashions of his day, and Blake argued with him fiercely over the relative merits of Raphael and Rubens.[21] It was here that Blake had his first chance to draw from life. His reaction was one of violent disgust; he could hardly draw at all, he had no inspiration. This seems to us strange only because we know little more than the Renaissance and Romantic traditions, which

---

[18] Gilchrist, *op. cit.*, page 14.
[19] Gilchrist, *op. cit.*, page 17.
[20] Malkin, *op. cit.*, page 314.
[21] *The Writings of William Blake*, Vol. III, page 11.

are highly naturalistic; in these traditions the artist's model is as necessary to him as his palette. We forget that this was not the case with a Fra Angelico; nor was it so with Blake. He not only preferred to draw without a model—he could not draw with one. "Natural objects," he said, "always did, and do weaken deaden and obliterate imagination in me." (Notes on Wordsworth)[22] He was willing to copy tirelessly from traditional forms, but copying nature seemed to him futile. Art was to him a purely intellectual thing, and the love of sensuous beauty for its own sake was unthinkable. In other words, that was idolatry, as the Christian thinkers of the Middle Ages put it. This is why Blake calls Wordsworth an atheist.

But at the same time, Blake does not ignore natural beauty. We shall see exactly what its place is in art for him. Meanwhile, this antinaturalism in him had developed in his earliest years and went hand in hand with his belief that art appealed first of all to the "imagination." We shall see he uses "imagination" to include all that we understand by "spirit" and "intellect" at the same time.

Meanwhile he was working for such booksellers as Harrison and Johnson, and in the course of his work engraving and illustrating, he met a young artist, Stodhard, who introduced him to John Flaxman.

Flaxman had already exhibited and won several prizes at the Free Society of Artists and, later, at the Royal Academy. He was at this time doing classical designs for the Wedgwood pottery, and at the same time he worked on the plans for a monument to Chatterton to be erected in Bristol. Works of this kind eventually made him very famous. He was already well known. Romney was his good friend, and so was William Hayley, who was later to be a patron of Blake's. But the man who really discovered Flaxman was the Reverend Henry Mathew, whose bluestocking wife invited Blake to her salon. It was Mathew who had the *Poetical Sketches* printed for Blake in 1783.

Flaxman was the Mathews' first and most important "find," and out of gratitude for their kindnesses to him he had redecorated their house in the "Gothic style." That is, he placed little models of clay and putty in niches "in the Gothic manner,"[23] and the bookcases were also Gothic. Another protégé, Oram, painted the windowpanes in imitation of stained glass. This all contributed to the success of the salon, which was frequented by such important "Blues" as Mrs. Montague, Mrs. Vessey, Mrs. Chapone, and Mrs. Barbauld.

[22] *Ibid.*, page 377.
[23] Gilchrist, *op. cit.*, page 46.

Here Blake was, for a time, a success. But the atmosphere of polite society, as we see from *Island in the Moon,* soon got on his nerves. He had just married Catherine Boucher, and although she has become almost legendary as the perfect wife (in spite of Saurat's entirely unfounded comparison of Blake's married life with Milton's)[24] she could neither read nor write at that time, and certainly could not have fitted into the conversations with Mrs. Montague or Mrs. Vessey. Their attitude toward his wife probably helped Blake to become estranged from the Mathews. It is not clear what the real reason for that estrangement was. But at any rate it came about. J. T. (Nollekens) Smith says, in his highly imperfect style:

> In consequence of his unbending department, or what his adherents were pleased to call a manly firmness of opinion, which certainly was not at all times considered pleasing by everyone, his visits were not so frequent.[25]

Although the *Island in the Moon* was written sometime after the break with the Mathews (Keynes gives the date as circa 1787), yet much of the satire seems to be directed at the frequenters of the salon. Blake must have thought the conversation about literature and ideas there was trivial; and although these people were not necessarily ignorant of art, they were incapable of really appreciating it.

The *Island in the Moon* is not directed entirely at the friends of the Mathews. S. Foster Damon,[26] logically enough, takes "Inflammable Gass, the wind-finder" to be a caricature of Priestley, the radical chemist, in whom Blake mocks both science and Deism. Blake probably met Priestley through the bookseller Johnson. Then there are a lawyer, the "Dean of Morocco," "Etruscan Column the Antiquarian" (he knew his antiquarians through Basire), and so on.

There is always a tendency on the part of those who have studied Blake's occult sources to leave their readers with the impression that he lived either out of the world altogether, or else only in the company of quacks, astrologers, and religious maniacs. As a matter of fact, he lived in a circle of fairly well-known and successful artists and engravers. He also knew publishers, booksellers, antiquarians, and for a while, radicals; Paine, Godwin, Priestley, Horne Tooke, Holcroft. He was one of the

---

[24] Denis Saurat, *Blake and Milton,* London, Stanley, Nott and Company, Ltd., 1935.

[25] J. T. Smith, *Book for a Rainy Day,* quoted in Gilchrist, *op. cit.,* page 51.

[26] S. Foster Damon, *William Blake, His Philosophy and Symbols,* London, Constable and Co. Ltd., 1924, page 32.

intellectuals who formed the nucleus around which the London Corresponding Society was later formed, in 1792.[27]

However, Blake probably did know the eccentric Thomas Taylor, the Platonist, who revived polytheism and is supposed to have sacrificed to the gods in his lodgings. Damon assumes that Taylor figures in *Island in the Moon* as "Sipsop the Pythagorean."[28] One might add that the experiments carried out by "Inflammable Gass" and the explosion that follows might have some remote connection with Taylor's invention of a "perpetual lamp" which blew up while he was demonstrating it at the Freemason's Tavern.

Following that explosion, George Cumberland, an artist and Blake's friend, helped Taylor to get work, which soon led to his giving a series of six lectures on Plato in Flaxman's house, in the early '80s.[29] Besides this, Taylor already knew Flaxman's friend Romney. This, by the way, was long before he was supposed to have sacrificed goats to Zeus. He was originally a mathematician and was led toward Plato and Plotinus in searching for a metaphysics of mathematics.

It is practically certain that Blake's ideas on Plato and the Neo-Platonists grew directly out of a personal acquaintanceship with this Thomas Taylor. This is especially plausible since he stresses the fact that Plato's idealism is "mathematical" and, by implication, lifeless. This also is why Plato, whether justly or not I may not decide here, is continually attacked by Blake for abstraction and mathematical idealism.

Another of Thomas Taylor's interests was in the Greek mystery religions. In 1787 he published a translation of the Orphic Hymns and in 1790 a work on *Bacchic and Eleusinian Mysteries*.

Blake seems also to have been influenced by this side of Taylor's studies, for Damon has carefully pointed out the affinities between *The Book of Thel* and the Persephone legend, with all its surrounding ritual.[30]

Meanwhile, Taylor was translating Plotinus. In 1787 he published his translation of *Enneads* I, vi, "Concerning the Beautiful," followed by translations of Proclus, Plato, Aristotle, Sallust, Apuleius, Iamblichus, Porphyry, and Maximus Tyrius. We shall later examine the affinities between Blake and Plotinus in reference to the place of Nature in Art.

[27] H. N. Brailsford, *Shelley, Godwin and their Circle,* New York, Henry Holt and Co., 1913.

[28] Damon, *op. cit.,* page 33.

[29] Wilson, *op. cit.,* page 23.

[30] Damon, *op. cit.,* page 74.

Although Blake, then, was certainly influenced by Taylor's studies of Greek philosophy, there is no reason to suppose that he was very friendly toward the "Platonist." He never mentions him, and there is no indication anywhere that he had any feelings of respect or admiration for him. In fact, there is no absolute proof that he ever knew Taylor. We can only infer that he must have met him through Flaxman or Cumberland since so much in his work implies familiarity with Taylor and what he was doing.

The tradition of Blake's connection with the radicals of his time is better known and better established. Their influence on his work has very little importance in this discussion of aesthetic ideas, but it is just as well to remark upon it in passing. He came in contact with this group through Johnson, the bookseller who published Wordsworth's *Descriptive Sketches* and Mary Wollstonecraft's *Vindication of the Rights of Women* (which her friend Thomas Taylor satirized). In 1791 he published Blake's *French Revolution*. He was well known in literary circles for his dinners, which were the meeting place of radical intellectuals. Mary Wollstonecraft and Godwin were frequently there; Mary even tried to start a love affair with Blake's friend Fuseli, who was also a frequent guest. Blake cannot have had much patience with Godwin's ideas of perfectibility and the Calvinism behind them. At any rate, Mona Wilson records that Godwin "is said to have been antipathetic to Blake."[31]

The story that Blake saved Thomas Paine's life is well known. Although he hated Deism, he seems to have been a good friend of Paine's, and he sided with him against the Anglican Bishop, Watson, who wrote *An Apology for the Bible in a series of letters addressed to Thomas Paine.* Blake calls Paine "a better Christian than the bishop" and ends his annotations to Watson's *Apology* with this:

> I have read this book with attention and find that the bishop has only hurt Paine's heel, while Paine has broken his head. The Bishop has not answered one of Paine's grand objections.[32]

The influence of these eighteenth-century radicals upon Blake is clear and important. But it has no effect on his ideas of art. He does, indeed, have a tendency to talk about "society" in terms that remind us of Rousseau (as, for instance, where he talks of the growth of religious institutions in *The Marriage of Heaven and Hell*). Here, too, he seeks a way to formulate his hatred of commercial imperialism[33] and his interna-

[31] Wilson, *op. cit.,* page 40.
[32] *The Writings of William Blake,* Vol. II, page 170.
[33] "Four Zoas VII" from *The Writings of William Blake,* Vol. II, page 90 ff.

tionalism. Blake is, of course, not the nationalist Saurat would have us believe he is,[34] an idea which is entirely misleading, because it does not go deeply enough into his symbolism. Saurat's argument is based on shallow interpretation of such symbols as "The Giant Albion" and "Druids."

The only connection this early radicalism has with Blake's ideas on art is in his ideas about the place of the artist in a commercial society. And this is only secondary; it is a sociological, not an aesthetic problem.

Henry Fuseli, the artist, who also frequented Johnson's dinners, was probably Blake's warmest and best friend. He certainly appears to have been more congenial to him than the cold and precise Flaxman. Fuseli had a sense of humor and a racy tongue, was almost as full of enthusiasm as Blake himself, and was just as impatient of stupidity and sham as the poet. When one of his duller students at the Royal Academy kept pestering him for praise of a drawing he answered: "It's bad. Take it into the fields and shoot at it, there's a good boy."[35] And like Blake, he was enough of an idealist to feel that pictures were not just "copies of nature." When a critic of the other school protested that the boat in his painting of the miracle of the loaves and fishes was too small, he merely answered that was "part of the miracle."[36]

Once he turned on his students with: "God, you are a pack of damned wild beasts and I am your keeper."[37]

In every line that we read about Blake's friendship with Fuseli we find that this was the friend who most nearly shared Blake's point of view. Fuseli is characterized by the same passionate indignation against pettiness and fakes that we find in Blake. And also, the two seemed to meet on a common ground of thoroughly humorous frankness. And Fuseli's admiration for his friend is transparent behind the jokes he kept making, that Blake was "damned good to steal from."[38]

Fuseli expressed this admiration without reserve in his introduction to the edition of Blair's *Grave* which Blake illustrated.

---

[34] Denis Saurat, *Blake and Modern Thought,* New York, Lincoln MacVeagh, The Dial Press, 1929.

[35] Harold Bruce, *William Blake in This World,* London, Jonathan Cape, Ltd., 1925, page 63.

[36] *Ibid.,* page 64.

[37] *Ibid.,* page 64.

[38] *Ibid.*

Every class of artists in every stage of their progress or attainments, from the student to the finished master . . . will find here materials of art and hints of improvement.

Now Blake was almost unknown to the public in his own time, and these illustrations to Blair, which had a wider circulation than any of his other work, were violently criticized in the press. Robert Hunt in the *Examiner* considered that "all the allegory is not only far-fetched but absurd, inasmuch as a human body can never be mistaken, in a picture, for its soul," and that "an appearance of libidinousness intrudes itself upon the holiness of our thoughts and counteracts their impression."[39]

This pruriency about the "naked form" led another subscriber to the edition to get rid of his copy as "unfit to lie on the parlor table," but he "regretted his haste when the work became rare and more valuable."[40]

In that time only a few, like Flaxman, had a genuine appreciation of Blake's genius. But Fuseli went further than them all. He was the only one who believed the age had anything to learn from Blake.

Fuseli, a Swiss and a friend of Lavater's, had come to London and attracted the attention of Sir Joshua Reynolds, who helped send him to Italy, where he studied art for nine years. He met Blake sometime after his return in 1779. They knew each other at least before 1788, when Blake engraved a portrait of Lavater after a design by Fuseli, as frontispiece to the *Aphorisms* of Lavater which Johnson published in that year.

Now, although Fuseli had been brought up on the early Romanticism of Bodmer and Breitinger at Zurich and loved Shakespeare, Richardson, Milton, Dante, and Rousseau, yet in his painting he was entirely Neoclassical and in 1758 he translated Winckelmann's *Reflections on the Painting of the Greeks*. After that he held a professorship at the Royal Academy from 1799 to his death in 1825. He was also deeply interested in Greek literature. He was a good linguist, and Greek was one of the languages he knew well. He even helped Cowper with his translation of the *Iliad*.[41]

James Barry, R.A., another Neoclassical painter, of greater importance than either Fuseli or Flaxman because he was very popular with his contemporaries, was also a friend of Blake. He had been discovered in Ireland by Burke, found favor with Reynolds, and went, like Fuseli, to study in Italy. There his taste in art became exclusively classical; he admired only

[39] Wilson, *op. cit.,* page 193.

[40] *Ibid.,* page 193.

[41] Lionel Cust, "Henry Fuseli," *Dictionary of National Biography,* edited by Sir Sidney Lee, London, Smith Elder and Co., 1889, Vol. XX, page 334 ff.

the antique and, among the Italians, the Florentines, especially Raphael.

> Rubens, Rembrandt and Van Dyke . . . are beyond the pale of my church; and although I will not condemn them, yet I must hold no intercourse with them.[42]

During the 1770s he ceased to exhibit at the Academy, disgusted with the reception of his *Death of General Wolfe,* in which the figures were nude, while West's painting of the same subject with the figures dressed up, even to the latest wigs in the current fashion, was very popular. In spite of quarrels with the Academy as a whole and with Reynolds in particular, Barry later obtained a professorship there.

Like Blake, he was always poor, but he shared Blake's belief in the duty of the artist to devote himself entirely to his art; painting could exact from him the greatest personal sacrifices.[43] Art was his whole life. In 1777 he offered to decorate the rooms of the Society of Arts for nothing although he only had sixteen shillings in his pocket, and he proceeded to cover four walls with murals. During this time, Blake tells us,[44] he lived on "bread and apples." In the evenings he sketched for printsellers to keep alive.

> I have taken great pains, he says, to form myself for this kind of quixotism. To this end I have contracted and simplified all my wants and brought them into a very narrow compass.[45]

He issued an account of these paintings in a pamphlet which coincided with the public exhibition of these murals, *An Account of a Series of Pictures in the Great Room of the Society of Artists.* This exhibition took place in 1777, and Blake owned a copy of this *Account,* in which he sketched a portrait of Barry.[46]

We must therefore add Barry to the number of friends who consciously or otherwise were drawing Blake toward Neoclassicism. In Barry, as well as Fuseli, Blake found much that appealed to him. Not only was Barry passionately devoted to art as we have seen, but like Blake, remember,

[42] W. Cosmo Monkhouse, "James Barry," *Dictionary of National Biography,* Vol. III, pages 321–24.

[43] Consider the contrast between him and Reynolds, of whom Tatham says, in his *Life of William Blake,* page 13, "Sir Joshua Reynolds was indeed a clever painter, but he was too fond of the comforts of life to give even an hour a day for any other experiments but those which would enable him to paint with greater celerity.

[44] "Descriptive Catalogue," *The Writings of William Blake,* Vol. III, page 86.

[45] W. Cosmo Monkhouse, "James Barry," *loc. cit.*

[46] G. L. Keynes, *A Bibliography of William Blake,* New York, The Grolier Club of New York, 1921.

he had quarreled with Reynolds and the "stuffed shirt" element of the Royal Academy. Also, like Blake, he was in frequent conflict with cheating printsellers. Barry was a religious man, a devout Catholic, and we recall that Blake was later to say that only the Catholic church, of all churches, taught the forgiveness of sins.[47]

Although he detested Reynold's criticism and Burke's *On the Sublime,* yet Blake praises Barry's paintings in the grand style, and for once puts himself in the same camp with Dr. Johnson. Was this entirely out of loyalty to Barry? Rather it means that for some time Blake was not entirely opposed to Neoclassicism, to which he allowed the virtues of clarity, precision, and definiteness of outline. Indeed, he may never have accepted the metaphysics of the Sublime in art, but now because of his friends and possibly his readings in Greek philosophy, he was under a Neoclassical influence that exerted pressure on him up until his return from Felpham, when he made a clean break with it in 1803.

A letter of 1799 shows a curious compromise in Blake between "Inspiration" and "Greek" as the symbol of Classicism:[48]

> I find more and more that my style of Designing is a Species by itself, and in this which I send you have been compelled by my Genius or Angel to follow where it led; if I were to act otherwise it would not fulfil *the purpose for which alone I live, which is in conjunction with my friend Cumberland, to renew the lost art of the Greeks.*

The Cumberland to whom he refers is, of course, George Cumberland, Thomas Taylor's friend, whom we mentioned above as having arranged for Taylor to lecture on Plato at Flaxman's house. Blake met Cumberland some time before 1795;[49] he was the cousin of Richard Cumberland, the dramatist. He was one of Blake's lifelong friends, and the last work of any kind Blake did was to engrave a visiting card for Cumberland in 1827, shortly before his death.

In 1796 Cumberland published his *Thoughts on Outline,* a copy of which Blake acknowledges receiving from him in a letter of December 23, 1796.[50] About the same time Cumberland was busy with a scheme for

[47] Blake's friend, Samuel Palmer, wrote in a letter to Anne Gilchrist (quoted in Mona Wilson's *Life of William Blake,* p. 287): "He quite held forth one day to me on the Roman Catholic Church being the only one which taught the forgiveness of sins; and he repeatedly expressed the belief that there was more civil liberty under the Papal government than any other sovereignty."

[48] "Letter IV, To Dr. John Trusler," *Writings of William Blake,* Vol. II, page 173.

[49] Wilson, *op. cit.,* page 23.

[50] *The Writings of William Blake,* Vol. I, page 345.

founding a National Gallery; Blake was enthusiastic about it, and the way he speaks of the project shows him accepting "Greece" more completely than at any other time in his life.

> I have to congratulate you on your plan for a National Gallery being put into execution. All your wishes shall in due time be fulfilled; the immense flood of *Grecian light and glory* which is coming on Europe, will more than realize our warmest wishes.[51]

It is obvious from this last quotation that Blake had two entirely different ways of looking at Greece, for the "Grecian light and glory" he anticipates here is scarcely "mathematical form." He must have thought for some years that his search for clarity and intelligibility in all things might be satisfied by the study of Greece. Classicism was not entirely alien to him, because of its simplicity and vigor and cleanliness of line: a quality Blake demanded in all art. Yet he was never able fully to accept the Classicism either of Greece or of his contemporaries. On the contrary, one aspect of his life at this time is that it became a struggle between Classicism and something else; call it, if you will, Romanticism, although there is in Blake a quickness of imagination and intellectual acuteness and a mysticism that no other Romantic possesses.

So this period in Blake's life has something of a dramatic quality about it. This drama is one of the things he has written in the Prophetic Books.

Urizen, in the Prophetic Books, represents empiricism, rationalism, "the philosophy of the Five Senses": that is, Urizen in the world at large. But in Blake's own private drama Urizen is the Classical spirit which tried to capture him and against which he continually had to struggle. When Urizen dethrones Urthona, in *The Four Zoas,* wisdom is replaced by rationalism, imagination by blindness, knowledge by doubt. The result is that the other Zoas, Luvah (passion, emotion) and Tharmas (the vegetative body) are also thrown into turmoil. A struggle of this type is common to the systems of all mystics, and it represents in the same terms the Creation, the Fall, and the Birth of Christ. All these tell us the same kind of thing, for they imply the descent of Intellect from the peace and harmony of pure being into the turmoil and blindness of a changing, contingent world. The punishment for eating the fruit of the forbidden tree was the knowledge of good and evil and fall from paradise, where evil is unknown, into generation, flesh, which is half blind to good and condemned to die.

Now as far as this study is concerned, what interests us in *The Four*

[51] *The Writings of William Blake,* Vol. II, page 180.

Zoas is that Urthona, dethroned, is no longer pure wisdom, but becomes Los, art. Los is the only one who works (at his anvils) to preserve some kind of harmony and order and intelligibility in the created world.

The Lambeth Books were all written during the period of this struggle with Greek influences and they are concerned entirely with the struggles of Los and Urizen. Urizen is the lawgiver, the maker of rules, who not only binds man with moral codes, but tyrannizes over art with artificial rules. These shorter books represent Blake's intellectual struggles at the time. It was important that he find the proper place for Classicism without letting it usurp anything that was not its own. To his poetry "Greece" did not matter; he was ready to ignore all rules of prosody, and he had never really accepted the Classical spirit in poetry beyond a few short lyrics in the *Poetical Sketches*. In his poetry he is completely free; one might say in his longer works, too free. But insofar as he is concerned with Classicism in the Prophetic Books they are a commentary on his development as a graphic artist.

This is quite natural, in any case, since in literature he was subject to no strong private influences and had never had any literary discipline of any kind imposed upon him. He read and wrote as he chose and never consulted any criterion on this earth. But in his art he had had a strict training in schools and as an apprentice, and most of his friends were Neoclassical artists. Add to this, of course, that he depended on art for his living and, consequently, had to try to compromise with the popular tastes of his time as they were exemplified; for instance, in Dr. John Trusler, the author of *Hogarth Moralized*.

The struggle reached its height when Flaxman introduced Blake to William Hayley, "Hermit of Eartham," author of *Triumphs of Temper,* "forever feeble and forever tame."[52] Hayley gave Blake some engraving to do on illustrations for his *Essay on Sculpture* and his *Life of Cowper*. In order to do this Blake moved down to a cottage at Felpham in Sussex. At first he was happy and really grateful to Flaxman for what he believed was a chance to do the creative work he wanted to do in peace. But actually Flaxman and Hayley were busying themselves deciding what kind of work Blake ought to be doing for his own good as an artist. Mona Wilson quotes a letter of Flaxman to Hayley:[53]

[52] Byron, "English Bards and Scotch Reviewers," in *Don Juan and Other Satirical Poems,* edited by Louis I. Bredvold, Garden City, New York, Doubleday Doran and Co. Inc., 1935, page 15.
[53] Wilson, *op. cit.,* page 126.

I see no reason why he [Blake] should not make as good a livelihood there as at London if he engraves and teaches drawing, by which he may gain considerably, also by making neat drawings of various kinds; but if he places any dependance on painting large pictures for which he is not qualified either by habit or study, he will be miserably deceived.

Hayley, as a matter of fact, soon put Blake to work doing miniatures. Their whole purpose was to keep him so busy at steady money-making work that he should have no chance to write his unprofitable poems or do his incomprehensible mystical drawings. Of course, it was all meant in perfect kindness. Hayley also put him to work in tempera doing busts of poets on the walls of his library; then there were the engravings for the life of Cowper and the designs for *Comus*. Besides all this, in his spare time Blake acted as Hayley's amanuensis. It was with Hayley also that Blake began to learn Greek.

In the first months at Felpham Blake, because the change made him happy, gladly accepted anything Hayley said as wise and good. Consequently, he even began to submit his own wildly independent genius to Hayley's milder ideas and opinions. In Blake this is unbelievable: yet here is what he says in a letter to Thomas Butts:[54]

> I labor incessantly and accomplish not one half of what I intend because my *abstract folly* hurries me often away while I am at work, carrying me over mountains and valleys which are *not real*, in a Land of Abstraction where spectres of the dead wander. This *I endeavour to prevent and with my whole might chain my feet to the world of duty and reality*.

These are certainly among the strangest words Blake ever wrote. Hayley's influence must have been very subtle and very strong to make him mistrust imagination even for a minute. This was the nearest Blake ever came to a compromise with Neoclassicism. A compromise that had in view his own material gain. But at the same time he made another compromise for that same reason, hoping to fall in with the taste of his time, and this also brought him unhappiness. What Flaxman may have meant by the "large pictures" Blake was not fitted to do were probably paintings in oil and tempera. As early as his twenty-first year Blake had begun studying the Flemish and Venetian painters who were so much in vogue, and he began experimenting in studies of these great colorists and their handling of light and chiaroscuro, in spite of the fact that he believed it was all more or less trickery. In 1799 he writes to Trusler:

[54] *The Writings of William Blake*, Vol. II, page 196.

If you approve of my manner and it is agreeable to you, I would rather Paint Pictures in oil of the same dimensions than make drawings, and on the same terms; by this means you will have a number of cabinet pictures which, I flatter myself, will not be unworthy of a scholar of Rembrandt and Teniers, whom I have studied no less than Michelangelo.[55]

It is not surprising to read that Blake had studied Rembrandt and Teniers; but it is amazing, in the light of the *Annotations to Reynolds,* that he should want to be thought their imitator.

The *Descriptive Catalogue* (1809) lists several "experimental" pictures done over a ten-year period when Blake was interested in oils. He worked over them time and again, trying out different effects, as he explains[56] in his notes.

Now no matter what he may have said to Dr. Trusler, Blake's tempera paintings have nothing in common with Rembrandt or Teniers. Blake is much closer to Giotto and the Byzantines before him, as Roger Fry has pointed out,[57] than to any Renaissance influence. But although these paintings are fine, he was not at home with this medium, and painting in it was a struggle to him. The *Descriptive Catalogue* is concerned not only with the difficulties he found in oils, but, even more important, with the havoc Titian and the Venetians threw him into when he tried to imitate their effects.

They cause that every thing in art shall become a machine. They cause that execution shall be all blocked up with brown shadows. They put the original artist in fear and doubt of his own original conceptions. The spirit of Titian was particularly active in raising doubts concerning the possibility of executing without a model, and when once he had raised the doubt it became easy for him to snatch away the vision time after time for, when the artist took his pencil to execute his ideas his power of imagination weakened so much and darkened that memory of nature and of Pictures of the various schools possessed his mind.[58]

This is the explanation of his much misunderstood condemnation of Rembrandt and Titian. Emotional art critics who are as much partisans as they are averse to serious study regard Blake's ideas on Rembrandt as bigoted and incomprehensible. It is not necessary to agree with Blake's

[55] *The Writings of William Blake,* Vol. II, page 174.
[56] *Ibid.,* Vol. III, page 117.
[57] Roger Fry, *Vision and Design,* London, Chatto & Windus, Ltd., 1920, page 140.
[58] *The Writings of William Blake,* Vol. III, page 118.

judgment, here, but it is certainly very clear what he means by it; it is not incomprehensible at all.

In the first place, it is false to say he was never able to see anything at all in Rembrandt or the Venetians, because, after all, he tried to imitate them. What is essential is that Blake's art has no place in it for naturalism, nor was Blake capable of approaching art through an enjoyment of physical beauty in itself. Color, line, light, beautiful bodies, in themselves meant nothing to him, and he was incapable of drawing directly from a living model. Of course it is hard for us to understand this since, after all, these other masters are still the popular artists and their tradition dictates what we believe art should be. But Blake belongs to another tradition, and is related to the artist of the European Middle Ages and of the Orient. Blake is a religious artist, and as such he wants the world to be not beautiful and appealing to him, but intelligible. In other words, he does not love nature for and in herself, but looks at natural objects *sub speci aeternitatis,* as they are in God. It is God he loves and not nature (and to think you can love God through nature is still to love only nature and be an atheist, Blake would say).

His technique, then, is to "copy" a "vision"; not natural objects but "mental images," a practice which does not at all isolate him, for it is one of the fundamentals of Hindu art,[59] besides being implicit in all Medieval art. Blake hated naturalism, and this precipitated his struggle to understand the rich, broad effects of light and color of the Venetians, their tendencies toward pure sensuousness, and their tricks of light to heighten this sensuous appeal. All this was not what he meant by art, for to a religious artist, art is part of the worship of God. And he was all the more convinced of this when the imitation of the Venetians muddled up his own clear ideas about art and imagination. So he naturally swung to the other extreme and condemned them bitterly: he had the right to, for they had given him much misery in making him lose the direction he had first chosen.

This, then, is one aspect of the drama of the Prophetic Books—a very minor aspect, as all the autobiography in the Books is, for the most part, irrelevant. But here, in the struggles of Los and Urizen, we do see reflected Blake's doubts, self-examinations, experiments, and failures to compromise with the taste everyone else shared for the Neoclassicists, the Flemish painters, and the Venetians.

[59] A. K. Coomaraswamy, *Transformation of Nature in Art,* Harvard University Press, Cambridge, Massachusetts, 1934.

None can know the spiritual acts of my three years of slumber on the bank of the Ocean [Felpham was near the coast] unless he has seen them in the spirit, or unless he should read my long poem descriptive of those acts.[60]

The dramatic content of the Prophetic Books, once again, is expressed in Blake's mystical symbols, as this quotation shows. He always deals with the fall into a violent, tragic conflict of ideas, and the subsequent regeneration into spiritual and intellectual harmony. This is the drama which mystics understand to underly the whole of human life. It is the pattern of the contingent universe.

In Jerusalem, for the last time Blake gave this fall, struggle, and regeneration its complete exposition. From then until his death, twenty years later, he hardly wrote anything more except notes and pamphlets defending his ideas on art and some shorter poems. Surely when he left Felpham, the struggle ended. By finally making a clean break with Hayley (and, incidentally, he was estranged with Flaxman after this) he seemed to throw off all ideas of following the influences that were pernicious to him. Once the struggle was over, long poems growing out of it were unnecessary, and he deliberately gave up writing them.[61] Now, too, he realized that it was useless to try and become a popular or successful artist: not that it was impossible for him, but because it involved too great a sacrifice and too much suffering.

Whatever natural glory a man has is so much taken from his spiritual glory. I wish to do nothing for profit, I wish to live for art. I want nothing whatever, I am quite happy.[62]

This is no bohemian pose of some fin-de-siècle banker's son seeking some excuse to live in Paris on a comfortable allowance: these are the words of a man who refused the position of art teacher to the royal family.

Giving up all attempt at compromise with the taste of his contemporaries, he returned to London in 1803 and threw himself wholeheartedly back into the tradition he loved and understood: the great tradition of Christian art, the Middle Ages, and the Florentine painters.

He found new inspiration in a collection of pictures that went on exhibition in that year, the "Truchsessian Gallery." This collection, belonging to a Polish nobleman, Count Truchsess, included over a thousand paintings.[63] Truchsess had been ruined by the French Revolution and was try-

[60] *The Writings of William Blake,* Vol. II, page 243.

[61] H. Crabb Robinson, *Diary,* edited by T. Sadler, Boston, Fields Osgood Co., 1869, Vol. I, page 303.

[62] *Ibid.,* Vol. II, page 26.

[63] Wilson, *op. cit.,* page 174.

ing to start a company for the purchase of his pictures and the foundation of a permanent art gallery.

Mona Wilson quotes Sir Thomas Lawrence's opinion of this show as it is recorded in Farington's diary.[64] He, as a matter of fact, thought the whole collection was worthless. This opinion, of course, referred to the money value of the collection, the price Truchsess was asking for his paintings. Lawrence was an admirable judge of what his contemporaries would like and represented eighteenth-century taste at its best.

> It was a varied collection . . . by German, Dutch, Italian, Flemish, Spanish and French masters. The masters included Albrecht Dürer, Hans Holbein senior, Brueghel, Vandyke, Michelangelo, Leonardo da Vinci, Bourdon, Watteau.[65]

Of these Blake would have been most interested in his favorites, Dürer and Michelangelo. But there are other good reasons why the show might have filled him with such enthusiasm as it did. Blake, unlike most of the artists of the time, had never been abroad and so had hardly ever had a chance to see original canvases of the great masters: as a matter of fact, he knew Raphael mostly from the engravings of Marc Antonio. But it is also possible that among a thousand pictures, a number were the work of Italian primitives, Duccios, or Fra Angelicos, which would help to explain not only Blake's enthusiasm but Lawrence's disgust. In any case, it would be safe enough to say that a collection of that size contained a great number of pictures in the tradition of Christian Medieval art. At any rate, Blake writes to Hayley:

> Suddenly, on the day after visiting the Truchsessian Gallery of pictures, I was again enlightened with the light I enjoyed in my youth, and which for twenty years has been closed from me as by a door and window shutters.[66]

Twenty years, that is, since the days when he had been studying Gothic art. In 1783, exactly twenty years before, was the date of the publication of the *Poetical Sketches* and was the time of his contact with the Mathews' circle. Twenty years before he had ended his apprenticeship with Basire, and the long hours of delightful study in the Gothic churches of the city came to an end. From then on he had been, as we have seen, in closer and closer contact with Neoclassicism and all the fashionable tastes in art,

---

[64] *Ibid.*

[65] Charles Gardner, *William Blake the Man*, London, J. M. Dent and Sons, Ltd., 1919, page 42.

[66] *The Writings of William Blake*, Vol. II, page 282.

literature, and ideas involved in a society of which Reynolds was the artistic leader. A society which was largely skeptical or Deistic. A society which believed in "nature" with a vague, a good humored, and entirely ill-founded optimism. And, of course, Nature was a goddess more akin to Common Sense than to Wordsworth's Goddess: the landscape through which shines a "visionary gleam." One of the eighteenth-century ways of looking at nature is well reflected by the term they gave Deism, that is, "natural religion." This does not mean that Deism is the worship of nature in a vague anthropomorphic sort of way, as one might suppose, but it is, above all, "natural" religion as opposed to "supernatural." It is a religion, in other words, that comes as close as it can to doing without any God at all. It is a religion which makes God as vague as he can possibly be; as distant and as unthinking as possible. To the Deists, God was little more than a good feeling pervading the universe. God is thus relieved of all his supernatural attributes, and religion is whittled down to walking out on the terrace of a Sunday morning, taking a few deep breaths, and slapping your chest contentedly as you wait for your breakfast.

Blake was perfectly right when he pointed out there was no natural religion. It is an impossibility and a contradiction in terms. Incidentally, how can Mr. Middleton Murry so glibly say Blake did not believe in the supernatural in the face of this?

Blake got no closer to the Deists than his brief acquaintance with Paine allowed him. But this vagueness, this misty confusion in considering the relation of the Creator and the Created, or the natural and the supernatural, pervaded the whole of fashionable thought. That is, I am not necessarily accusing Hume or Berkeley of vagueness: I am not talking of philosophers, but saying that this vagueness was fashionable and prevailed in literature and polite conversation. It was nowhere better represented than in William Hayley. Blake had been in conflict with this all along, with his insistence on "distinctness" and "single and particular detail." When he was finally thrown in with Hayley and steeped in this awful saccharine tameness all day long, every day, it is no wonder he finally revolted altogether.

Incidentally, Blake's best friends were mostly religious men with very clear and definite ideas as to what they believed in, and no hesitation in expressing their beliefs forcibly: we have seen this in Fuseli, generally speaking. Flaxman was a Swedenborgian, a pious and, above all, a strict man. As for Barry, whom Blake so admired, he was a devout Catholic.

Then there was the rather silly artificiality of the Mathews' salon, with its pretenses at culture, its superficiality which Blake satirized in *Island in the Moon;* yet at the same time, in contrast to this gentility on the surface, there was still a rich substratum of filth, violence, and vulgarity, a contradiction characteristic of the whole century. Blake sometimes remarked on this contradiction. As an artist, he was not interested in going for material to either one side or the other. He was not interested in painting portraits or conversation pieces of the genteel, but even less was he going to follow Rowlandson in his robust satire which exploited the eighteenth-century substratum of filth. Blake, as a matter of fact, complains against the popularity of caricature in one of his letters to Trusler.[67]

It was the return to the tradition of Christian art that had inspired his early days, then, that brought Blake out of the "dark night," the despair into which he had been plunged by his misgivings about his own art, after his experiments at compromise had failed.

But now:

> I am really drunk with intellectual vision whenever I take a pencil or graver in my hand, even as I used to be in my youth, and as I have not been for twenty dark, but very profitable years.[68]

The only poem of importance written between 1808 and his death is *The Everlasting Gospel* (*circa* 1818). Almost all of his writing at this time has to do with his art. It includes critical notes, catalogues, prospectuses, the *Lacoon Plate* (1820), the *Annotations to Reynolds,* and such things as the *Descriptive Catalogue* and the *Public Address.*

The Prophetic Books had dealt with the period of his struggle. But now, to judge by his remarks to Crabb Robinson, he deliberately gave up all ambitious projects in poetry. Or, as he put it, "angels had commanded him to write, but he refused."[69] Perhaps he felt Jerusalem had finally said all that he wanted to say, for we have remarked that all the Prophetic Books use the same material and the same story over and over again, sometimes with greater complexity, sometimes from the point of view of another "state." Perhaps, also, he felt that since no one was reading his poetry, while his pictures were better understood and appreciated, that he should concentrate entirely on painting and engraving. It is, at any rate, certain that at this time Blake began to achieve greater and fuller power as graphic artist than ever before.

What was this early tradition to which he now returned with such fortunate results? Saurat says:

[67] *The Writings of William Blake,* Vol. II, page 174.
[68] *Ibid.,* Vol. II, page 283.
[69] Robinson, *Diary,* Vol. II, page 33.

Mingling therefore, with the great modern movements of liberalism, nationalism, idealism, we shall at every turn find in Blake a reversion to the old lore, cabalistic, Gnostic or occultist of every kind, also a rummaging among pseudo-scientific theories of the origin of races and crude knowledge of Indian religion.[70]

This broad and sketchy statement does not quite cover the whole ground it so agilely seems to traverse. Whether Blake is a liberal, a nationalist, or an idealist has still not been proved by M. Saurat's gymnastics with ill-interpreted symbols. It is, however, true that he was "rummaging among pseudo-scientific theories of the origin of races." The most important of these were the theories proposed[71] by Jacob Bryant and based on the highly imaginative etymological technique of a man who knew no Oriental languages. We know that Blake knew Bryant from a reference to him in the *Descriptive Catalogue*[72] and can trace Bryant's influence through his work, principally in his ideas on the Greeks *not* being the fountainhead of Western civilization. Bryant, starting with the proposition that "There was once but one language among the sons of men"[73] works his way backward, beyond the Greeks, tracing his way by etymology through ancient religions, which he finds have everything in common. His method is pleasantly slipshod and lacks only a dash of psychoanalysis to make it completely modern.

Bryant insisted that Greece was not the fountainhead of all our culture. Rather than owing her our civilization we are, he thinks, lucky to have had any civilization at all after the original heritage had passed through their hands:

> We must be cautious in forming ideas of the ancient theology of nations from the current notions of the Greeks and Romans, and more especially from the descriptions of their poets. Polytheism originally vile was rendered ten times more base by coming through their hands.[74]

Bryant's etymologies, as we have said, failed because he knew no Oriental languages, and the great Sanskritists, Richardson and Sir William Jones, effectively demolished him in his own time. But it is interesting to know that Blake, because of Bryant's influence, looks beyond Greece toward the

[70] Saurat, *Blake and Modern Thought,* Introduction, page xiv.

[71] Jacob Bryant, *A New System, or an analysis of ancient mythology,* London, T. Payne, 1774.

[72] *Writings of William Blake,* Vol. II, page 3.

[73] Bryant, *op. cit.,* Vol. I, page 54.

[74] *Ibid.,* Vol. I, page 141.

Orient for the origins of our heritage, especially as there is so much that is Oriental in Blake's mysticism. Besides, such an idea was not cherished by Bryant alone. The beginnings of Sanskrit studies had led scholars like Sir William Jones to muse upon the similarity between the religious and poetic traditions of Greece and India.

Blake seems to have welcomed this idea, partly because it fit in with his anti-Hellenic reaction, of course, but partly, also, because he must have known enough about India to feel drawn toward her culture.

Saurat has shown that Blake did know some elementary facts about Indian religion, mythology, and iconography. We know that Blake knew the *Bhagavad-Gita,* because he did a picture of Sir Charles Wilkins translating it,[75] and Wilkins' translation appeared in 1785, with a prefatory note by Warren Hastings. Saurat assumes that Blake knew various travel books about India, and this is a safe assumption. There were many travel books being published at this time,[76] and that Blake read this kind of literature and had drawn on it for symbols and ideas is also known. He mentions a subject in the *Descriptive Catalogue* taken from one of these books called *The Missionary Voyage.*[77] Another book he might have known was the famous collection of pictures of Indian art, architecture, and landscape, *Daniell's Oriental Scenery,* published in 1808. Blake does speak of

> those apotheoses of Persian, Hindoo and Egyptian antiquity preserved on rude monuments, being copies from some stupendous originals now lost or perhaps buried until some happier age.[78]

Blake was a voracious reader, we know, but it is not so easy to find out just what he read. In general, however, we can say that no matter what he did read, the books on the Orient in that day merely scratched the surface. Little more than outward descriptions of religious rites and repetitions of tales and legends were given, without any true understanding of the philosophy behind them. The great scholars, Jones, Wilkins, Halhed, were interested only in the language and the laws, as befitted members of the East India Company. Sir William Jones does speak frequently of Oriental literature in terms of art, but when he does so, he stands and

[75] "Descriptive Catalogue," *The Writings of William Blake,* Vol. III, page 117.

[76] G. Boucher de la Richardière, *Bibliographie Universelle des Voyages,* Paris, Treutel et Wurtz, 1808.

[77] *The Writings of William Blake,* Vol. III, page 115.

[78] *Ibid.,* Vol. III, page 94.

views it from a distance, a bit suspiciously, as a good Neoclassicist should. He goes to great lengths to explain away Oriental excesses of imagination and symbolism[79] and makes every effort to palliate the "enthusiasm" in these works. Finally, he explains their mystical content in terms as close to Plato as he can get: "Sweet musick, gentle breezes, fragrant flowers perpetually renew the primary idea, refresh our fading memory and melt us with tender affections."[80] (In this case he is talking about the poetry of the Sufis.) Whether or not this is a distortion of the Oriental viewpoint, Jones is certainly far from seeing the same things in it that Blake would have seen. Whether Blake read Jones' works we cannot tell; yet there is a faint possibility that Blake might have known Jones himself. He certainly knew of him, for Jones had been a famous radical and a member of the Price, Godwin, Holcroft circle which later became the London Corresponding Society. Jones had even given up the idea of running for Parliament because of his radicalism; not, of course, that a radical had scruples about sitting in the Commons, but because he had no possible chance of being elected to that House. It is just barely possible that Blake did meet Jones. It depends on how early he knew Johnson, the bookseller, for Jones sailed for India in 1783 and lived there until his death in 1794. In any case, Jones could not have told Blake much, since all his studies in Sanskrit had been made in England. However, Jones was admired and respected in the radical group. A poem of his was read aloud at the meeting of the Corresponding Society that celebrated the Terror in 1794. Whether Blake was still there to hear it or had thrown away his liberty cap in disgust is irrelevant: in any case, it is interesting to speculate whether he heard anything interesting about India, Indian art, Indian religion through radical friends who were in touch with Sir William Jones in India.

There is another important early Sanskritist whom Blake is much more likely to have known, and that is Nathaniel Brassey Halhed.[81] Halhed was a school friend of Sheridan and had been at Oxford with William Jones. He had gone to India with the East India Company and, as one of the pioneers of the philological movement, began the translation of the Gentoo Code. He returned to England and ran for Parliament, being elected to the seat for Lymington, Hampshire. He held his seat until 1794.

[79] Sir William Jones, Works, London, John Stockdale, 1807, Vol. IV, page 212.
[80] Ibid., Vol. IV, page 220.
[81] Alexander Gordon, "N. B. Halhed," Dictionary of National Biography, Vol. XXIV, pages 41–42.

His study of Sanskrit must have prepossessed him in favor of mysticism without teaching him to understand it, for his Parliamentary career is distinguished for the way he became converted to the ideas of one maniac, Richard Brothers, and championed his claims to the throne of England (as being the "nephew of the Almighty") single-handed against the whole House.

In 1794, Brothers had revealed himself to be a direct descendant of King David and published his claims to the English throne. He proposed to do several things once he became King, one of which was to "rebuild Jerusalem." There is no need to assume that Blake got any ideas from this man Brothers, but the familiarity of "rebuilding Jerusalem" to the Blake student makes this a thing of at least passing interest. Now, although Blake did not live entirely among fortunetellers as has been pointed out, yet both he and Flaxman knew a great many people belonging to out-of-way sects and cults. We remember that Thomas Taylor was a friend of Flaxman. Flaxman also knew an engraver called William Sharp, who was apparently quite a gullible fellow and took after more than one prophet in his time. At the moment, he was a loyal follower of Richard Brothers. He had done two portraits of him, made plates of them,[82] and was as enthusiastic a supporter of his claims to the throne as Halhed himself.

Blake had probably met Sharp through Flaxman some time before this, but in any case he knew Sharp before 1815, for in that year Crabb Robinson tells us of Sharp ("the dupe of any fanatic") trying to convert Blake to the ideas of Joanna Southcote and not being at all successful at it. Blake must surely have known Sharp as far back as 1794. First, because he was then very intimate with Flaxman, with whom he later became estranged, so then he would have known most of Flaxman's friends. Then Sharp was an engraver, which makes the meeting all the more likely. If he knew Sharp it is highly probable that he met Brothers, and if he met Brothers, he may just as well have also met Halhed, the Sanskritist. Besides, it is interesting to wonder whether Brothers' idea of "rebuilding Jerusalem" was not something he picked up from a conversation with Blake and turned to his own uses.

It is possible then that Blake knew Nathanial Halhed, and he may have heard directly from him ideas on Indian philosophy and Indian art, although the latter is not too likely. He could have got something from him

[82] Alexander Gordon, "Richard Brothers," *Dictionary of National Biography,* Vol. VI, pages 442–45.

to serve as basis for the general insight into Indian art we discover in some of his chance remarks in the *Descriptive Catalogue.*

But it is only for the sake of exploring every possible contact of Blake with India that we have investigated his possible meeting with Halhed. It is not necessary for him to have known Halhed to have known about Indian thought and art. We have seen he read the *Bhagavad-Gita.* We have surmised he knew some travel books about India, although we can only guess which ones. Not only this, we definitely do know he had one close friend who had been in India, and that was Ozias Humphrey.

Ozias Humphrey was a miniaturist who apparently enjoyed some success. He was, at any rate, successful enough to know the Countess of Egremont, and it was through his intercession that this lady ordered from Blake a drawing of *The Last Judgment.* Now Humphrey had been in India, not only as a visitor, not as a business man, not as an imperialist interested in law codes as Jones and Halhed had been, but as an artist. He had carried on with his painting in Indian courts and had been successful with it there. This is what Gilchrist says of him:

Ozias Humphrey, a miniature painter of rare excellence, whose works have a peculiar sweetness of painting and a refined simplicity in a now old-fashioned style, was himself a patron as well as a friend, for whom Blake had expressly colored many of his illustrated books. Humphrey had passed three years of his life, 1785–88, in India and had reaped a golden harvest in Oude by painting miniatures of the native princes. What has become of these I wonder . . . His sketches and notebooks during the period are in the British Museum . . . His eyes failed him altogether in 1799 after which he lived at Knightsbridge.[83]

What is in his notebooks? Unfortunately, I do not know. But it is certain that Humphrey could tell Blake much about Indian art, at least superficially. He may not have fully understood it, just as Sir William Jones surely never fully understood all the deeper implications of Indian or Persian poetry, but it would be unwise to say he did not appreciate it at all.

It is especially interesting to notice that Blake's *Last Judgment* is not without its resemblances to Hindu art. Of course, the resemblance is remote, yet the way the picture is crowded with clear, well-rounded figures, flying up and down, all in a quite formal pattern, reminds us of a Hindu bas-relief, equally crowded and equally formalized, in a way which Michelangelo's *Last Judgment* in the Sistine Chapel could not possibly do. In his correspondence with Humphrey concerning this *Last Judgment* Blake says, after describing this picture:

[83] Gilchrist, *op. cit.,* page 236.

Such is the design which you, my dear sir, have been the cause of my producing, and which, but for you, might have slept till the Last Judgment.[84]

It is just possible that he means Humphrey has not simply procured him the order for this design, but also inspired in him, this particular treatment of it, by descriptions of Indian art? That is perhaps suggested by the last half of the sentence (and, incidentally, the idea of art lying dormant in the artist is one we shall come upon later). But there is absolutely no proof to support this guess any further.

On the other hand, Blake did not always agree with Humphrey's ideas on art. Humphrey, who like most eighteenth-century artists had been to Italy, attacked Blake's ideas on the Florentines and Venetians. Blake, in sending him a copy of the *Descriptive Catalogue,* writes:

You will see in this little work the difference between you and me. You demand of me to mix two things that Reynolds has confessed cannot be mixed . . . Florentine and Venetian art cannot exist together.[85]

So Blake disagreed with Humphrey, as he did with practically everyone else on this question. But, as he himself says, it is in this that the difference between them lies. There is no reason to doubt that they shared a common enthusiasm for Indian art.

So, Blake had more points of direct contact with India than Saurat or anyone else has pointed out. But in addition to this, we must take into account all the vaguely Oriental elements which he got from the Neo-Platonists he read in Thomas Taylor's translations.

It is not generally realized that the great intellectual ferment in Egypt, Greece, and Asia Minor in the earlier centuries of the Christian era owed no little of its character to influences from the East. And, long before this, it is possible to trace Oriental influences in Pythagoras; his ideas on transmigration and vegetarianism are followed by Herodotus as far as Egypt. But this is because Egypt is the most ancient authority the historian could think of, and it is doubtful whether such beliefs were held in early Egypt.[86] The ideas of metempsychosis and *karma* reappear in Plato. The Hindu idea of the world egg (Blake's "Mundane Shell") appears in Orphism. Eusebius even records that Indian sages visited Socrates at Athens.[87]

[84] *The Writings of William Blake,* Vol. II, page 4.
[85] *Ibid.,* Vol. II, page 123.
[86] G. T. Garratt, editor, *Legacy of India,* Oxford, Oxford University Press, 1937, page 5.
[87] *Ibid.,* page 8.

Since the Persian Empire extended from the Aegean to the Indus, and the Persian army contained both Greek and Indian mercenaries, Persia was the intermediary through which these influences passed. In 327 B.C. Alexander took with him to India at least nineteen learned men who filled their notebooks and diaries with material on India that later historians used. After Alexander, diplomatic relations between Indian kings and princes of the Near East and Egypt were still kept up.

Buddhist missionaries were sent to the courts of Antiochus of Syria, Ptolemy, Antigonus Gonatas, Magas of Cyrene, and Alexander of Epirus. That trade between the Mediterranean and India was active then is proved by the number of Greek coins of the period found in India.[88]

In fact, when Alexandrian merchants discovered the regularity of the monsoons, the trip to India was cut down to sixteen weeks and India was brought into closer contact with the Occident than it was ever to be again until the eighteenth century. But the intellectual contact was closer even than it is today. In spite of Rudyard Kipling, East and West did once meet. Then Palmyra, Antioch, and Alexandria were thronged with Indian merchants and men of letters. Dio Chrysostom mentions the great numbers of Indian students there were in Alexandria.[89]

Meanwhile, as early as 50 A.D. Apollonius of Tyana went off to India and studied under the Hindu monks at Taxila.[90] He returned to the Roman world, convinced that the Hindus were the only wise men, and went about preaching Hinduism from Ephesus to Spain. He continued to practice the "Indian discipline" he had learned, even cutting short a talk with the Emperor Vespasian when the hour came for his meditations.[91]

From our point of view, Apollonius is most interesting, once again, because he too observed and studied Indian art. He had traveled all over the known world, but Philostratus devotes more space to Apollonius' remarks on Indian art than to those he made on the art of any other country. Apollonius not only stands quite opposed to the Platonic idea that art copies the illusions of nature, but rejects naturalism altogether and talks about art in more or less Indian terms.

He opposes imagination to "mimicry" in a way that reminds us immediately of Blake,[92] and he even identifies the whole Hindu way of life

[88] *Ibid.,* page 12.

[89] *Ibid.,* page 17.

[90] Philostratus, *Life of Apollonius of Tyana,* translated by J. S. Phillimore, Oxford, Clarendon Press, 1912.

[91] *Ibid.,* Vol. II, page 75.

[92] *Ibid.,* Vol. I, pages 75–77.

with art. S. Foster Damon,[93] commenting on Blake's remark that he was walking down a lane one day and, coming to the end of it, touched the sky with his stick, points to a similar sentence in Philostratus and suggests on these grounds that Blake read the *Life of Apollonius*. It is quite possible that he did.

There is an element of anti-Hellenism in Apollonius that sounds curiously like that of Blake and Jacob Bryant. Iarchas, the Brahmin, says to Apollonius:

> Troy was ruined by the Achaean armada, but the legends about it have been your ruin. You have no ideas beyond the heroes who went against Troy and no regard for all the rest, the many more and diviner men whom your country and Egypt and India has produced.[94]

This is surely echoed by Blake when he says:

> Sacred truth has pronounced that Greece and Rome, as Babylon and Egypt, so far from being parents of Arts and Sciences as they pretend, were destroyers of all Art. Homer and Virgil and Ovid confirm this opinion and make us reverence the Word of God, the only light of antiquity that remains unperverted by War. . . Rome and Greece swept Art into their maw and destroyed it; a warlike state can never produce Art. It will rob and plunder and accumulate into one place and translate and copy and buy and sell and criticize, but not Make.[95]

Blake, like Iarchas, the Brahmin, disliked Greece for its warlike mythology and ideals: this is one of the main reasons for his pronounced anti-Hellenism. This hatred of Greece and Rome as "conquerors," strengthened by Bryant's theories, prompted Blake to say Greece stole her art from "ancient Hindu monuments."

Here are two other remarks Philostratus attributes to his traveler; their similarity to Blake is too obvious to require comment: "Imagination is more cunning craftsman than mimicry." And "Imitation can portray in art what it has seen, Imagination even what it has not seen."[96] Owing to the influence of Apollonius and the numerous travelers from India to the Mediterranean, the attraction of India had become so great by the time of Plotinus that this philosopher in 242 A.D. joined the army of the Emperor Gordian in the hope of reaching India. The expedition came to grief in

[93] Damon, *op. cit.*, page 422.

[94] Philostratus, *op. cit.*, Vol. II, page 112.

[95] "On Homer's Poetry and on Virgil," *The Writings of William Blake,* Vol. III, page 362.

[96] Philostratus, *Ibid.*, Vol. II, page 123.

Mesopotamia, and Plotinus was disappointed. It has been pointed out, however, that he probably knew enough about Indian philosophy to work out most of its deeper implications for himself. Emile Brehier says:[97]

Il n'est donc pas necessaire de faire de Plotin un Indianiste; it suffit qu'il ait eu connaissance des quelques breves formules ou aimait à se consenser la philosophie indienne pour avoir matière a un travail de pensée qui en penetrat le sens profond.

As for the Gnostics, Bardesanes the Babylonian knew the Indian diplomats who were sent to Elagabalus from 218 to 222 B.C., and Basilides[98] drew many of his ideas from India, especially from the Buddhists. Finally, all the Neo-Platonists are continually referring to Hindu, Buddhist, and Jain ideas and ascetic practices.

Now we have seen that the philosophers who most influenced Blake were the Neo-Platonists. It is also from this period that spring the occult influences that operated upon him. Consequently, much that was Oriental originally came to Blake in this way: came to him, that is, if we are content to look at it in a very crude light. To say that Blake would have had none of these ideas if he had never read any books would be absurd. Nor is it fair to assume that all these Oriental elements, that is, elements which are in Blake and have their counterparts in Indian artists and philosophers, came to him through Gnostics or other heretic sects or pagan philosophers. Much of Alexandrian philosophy passed on into Christianity, especially Augustinianism, and Blake's Christianity is predominantly Augustinian. Incidentally, the Neo-Platonists, through Augustine, strongly influenced Blake's beloved Dante.

Our task is not, however, to explain Blake's ideas on Nature in art in terms of Oriental or Gnostic or Neo-Platonic or any other "influences." Blake's point of view is entirely that of a religious and, specifically, a Christian thinker. But it happens that in these other essentially religious approaches to art the same hatred of naturalism and the identifying of it with idolatry is everywhere apparent. The attitude of Christian schoolmen and of Hindu thinkers toward this problem is the same, as Dr. Coomaraswamy has pointed out.[99] Blake's ideas about art are similar to Medieval Christian ideas of art, as we shall see, for we shall use the ideas of the schoolmen to elucidate Blake's. And because Blake is closer to

[97] Emile Brehier, "La Philosophie de Plotin," *Revue des Cours et Conferences,* Paris, 1922, 2e serie, page 275.

[98] Another Gnostic.

[99] A. K. Coomaraswamy, *op. cit.,* page 3.

422

Medieval Christians than to his own contemporaries, he is also closer to the religious thinkers of the East. Coomaraswamy says:

> There was a time when Europe and Asia could and did actually understand each other very well. Asia has remained herself, but subsequent to the extroversion of the European consciousness and its preoccupation with surfaces it has become more and more difficult for European minds to think in terms of unity.[100]

This, then, is the background for Blake's ideas on naturalism. It is from this starting point that we can investigate these ideas and better set out to understand his quarrel with Sir Joshua Reynolds.

[100] *Ibid.*

CHAPTER II
BLAKE'S IDEAS ON THE PLACE OF NATURE IN ART

We know that Blake was in reaction against the eighteenth century because he was a mystic. We know how the eighteenth century used the
words "nature" and "natural religion." We know that mysticism despises
the world and believes that man by God's good grace, and Free Will, can
transcend the material world, with its confusions and deceits, and rise into
a visionary supernatural world of True Being and unity. Nature itself is
not intelligible, and intelligibility only exists on this transcendental plane.

Blake used the word nature in two ways: first, in the current vague
way of his contemporaries when he was actually attacking them; that is,
as it is used in "natural religion." We have already seen that he could not
abide this nebulous idealization of scenery, plus the infusion of some
unidentified benevolent spirit that this conception implies. That is, nature
is the created world of matter as opposed to the supernatural world of
Intellect, Love, and Pure Being. Tharmas, in the Prophetic Books, represents "Nature," that is, the "vegetable universe" or the world of perishing,
blind, created things.

J. Middleton Murry[101] points out the way he uses the word in yet another sense—where he speaks of "true nature" in one of his *Annotations
to Swedenborg*. Nature as seen by the five senses and nature transfigured
by the imagination are two entirely different things to Blake. We recall
these familiar lines:

> Now I a fourfold vision see
> And a fourfold vision is given to me
> 'Tis fourfold in my supreme delight
> And threefold in Soft Beulah's night
> And Twofold always: May God us keep
> From single vision and Newton's sleep.[102]

But from this Mr. Murry goes on to the startling conclusion that Blake
believed nature was everything. There would be opposition between na-

---

[101] John Middleton Murry, *William Blake*, London, Jonathan Cape and Co., Ltd.,
1935, page 327.
[102] *The Writings of William Blake*, Vol. II, page 207.

ture with a small "n" and Nature capitalized. The latter, nature transfigured by Christ, the former whatever it is the scientists look at. But, says Mr. Murry, since for Blake Nature was everything,[103] therefore, there was no supernatural.[104] Consequently Blake must have been an atheist. By this token, when Blake called Wordsworth an atheist, he was presumably condemning him for being such a fool as to believe in God. Mr. Murry has performed the amazing feat of trying to oversimplify one sentence in Blake and thereby making everything else he ever wrote twice as complicated as it already is.

To begin with, we have to suppose that the Christ who transfigures Nature so conveniently for Mr. Murry is not himself supernatural. Such an idea is full of insoluble mysteries which we can hardly attempt to elucidate here.

Mr. Murry supports his theory with Blake's statement that "God only acts or is in existing beings, or men." But he forgets that for a mystic, "action" belongs to the contingent world, to time and not eternity. Actions begin at a given point in time, and they are ordered to the fulfillment of a desire. But desire itself belongs to a created and material world. We all know that the Hindu mystic seeks his way into eternity because there all desire is annihilated. For the mystic, even the creation of the world is not an "action" of God. It did not take place in time, according to Blake, or the Neo-Platonists or the Hindus (but, of course, the Catholic mystics would not necessarily hold to this). Blake shows Los forging the chains of Time and Space around Urizen after the eternals have fallen into the Wheel of Existence.[105] And Plotinus believed that "The world in space was necessarily produced because its production was possible."[106] And this production did not become possible at a given minute of a given day.

It seems much more likely that Blake meant that God fills all eternity with His love and beauty, but that in eternity they are static; activity implies corruption, and imperfect love and imperfect beauty "act" in the contingent world. But they only act there for men, for in men only, in all God's material creation, is there imagination and intellect.

Finally, if Blake's visions were not visions of a supernatural world, why did he pray for them to be restored when they would not come to him?

[103] Murry, *op. cit.,* page 327.

[104] *Ibid.,* page 322.

[105] William Blake, *The Book of Urizen.*

[106] Thomas Whitaker, *The Neo-Platonists,* 2nd edition, Cambridge, University Press, 1918, page 60.

Or how could he say such a thing as "The Lord our Father will do for us, and with us according to His divine will, and for our good"?[107]

By far the silliest conclusion Mr. Murry's theory leads him into is that when Blake attacked naturalism in art he was confused and did not quite know what he was about. Mr. Murry explains this as follows:

> Because the symbolical and mystical character of his art demanded that he should sacrifice natural appearances for symbolic significance, he began to insist that naturalistic art was false art, a "pretense of art to destroy art." *This was quite definitely a delusion on Blake's part.*[108]

Mr. Murry is driven to this extremity because he has made Blake believe in nothing but "Nature." But since Blake's ideas are the ideas of religious art, as we shall later see without any shadow of doubt, he not only believes that literal truth is to be sacrificed to symbolism or iconography, but that the reproduction of natural beauty for its own sake is idolatrous and misleading. To understand just what all the implications of "Nature" were for Blake, it is necessary to examine, briefly, his ideas on matter.

For Blake, as well as for the Gnostics and the Cabalists, matter is inextricably tied up with the idea of the fall, the expulsion from Eden. It is common among mystics to identify the creation of man with the fall; that is, the creation of man in time and space. In Eden, man was eternal. But he fell from eternity into time, into matter, illusion, chaos, and death. The creation of the universe as we know it resulted from the fall of one of the "eternals," Urizen, from eternity into matter, and he dragged all the others with him.[109]

Blake's cosmography has no Purgatory and no Hell: but as far as he is concerned, Ulro, the state of almost complete materialism, is equivalent to Hell. It is almost, but not quite, complete nonexistence or death. So also believed the Neo-Platonists. For them, "The death of the soul would be to be wholly plunged in matter."[110] Matter and evil, roughly speaking, are bound up together and are opposed to spirit and the good. By way of clarification, we might compare this with the somewhat similar idea in St. Thomas Aquinas, that matter is the limit of form, that form only is intelligible; that matter is the principle of change, and change denies intelligibility; and that, therefore, things are intelligible insofar as they are immaterial.

[107] *The Writings of William Blake,* Vol. II, page 187.
[108] Murry, *op. cit.,* page 339.
[109] William Blake, *The Book of Urizen* and *The Four Zoas.*
[110] Whitaker, *op. cit.,* page 67.

It is self-will that causes the fall from intelligibility into the blindness of matter: then the spirit is locked up in the flesh. The five senses are thus only "chinks in a cavern," and whereas before the intellect contemplated Truth face to face, now "Five windows light the cavern'd man . . ."[111] and "if the doors of perception were cleared away, everything would appear to man as it is: infinite."[112] Now, when the spirit falls from eternity, it nevertheless brings with it form from the ideal world and imposes it upon matter. This form is not, however, the reflection of some vague general pattern. Plotinus believes there are as many formal differences as there are individual men and things, and all pre-exist in the ideal world. These forms are imposed on matter and so exclude one another: hence arise all temporal and spatial differences in the material world. Plotinus' theory of matter is essentially Aristotelian,[113] and Blake's ideas follow the same line of argument.

When he says, "Man has no body distinct from his soul," he is saying what St. Thomas said, that all Catholics say after him: that the soul is the "form" of the body.

But as to the reason for there being matter:

> Matter is necessary because the principle of all things having infinite productive power, that power must manifest itself in every possible degree; *there must therefore be a last term which can produce nothing beyond itself,* and this is matter, having nothing of its own. This is the necessity of evil.[114]

This is analogous to what Blake means when he says that "Reason is the outward bound and circumference of energy."[115] Reason is "the last term, which can produce nothing beyond itself." "Energy (imagination) is eternal delight." Of course, Blake's "reason" and matter go together. Skepticism, empirical reasoning are the kind of mental activity that seeks nothing beyond matter. It is Urizen who represents empiricism and doubt, and also dogmatism, because he is blind to imagination, passion, spirit. Consequently, he cannot really understand life or experience at all.

---

[111] "Europe," *The Writings of William Blake,* Vol. I, page 294.

[112] "The Marriage of Heaven and Hell," *The Writings of William Blake,* Vol. II, page 189.

[113] Whitaker, *op. cit.,* page 68.

[114] *Ibid.*

[115] "The Marriage of Heaven and Hell," *The Writings of William Blake,* Vol. I, page 182.

He in darkness clos'd viewed all his race
And his soul sicken'd and he curs'd
Both sons and daughters, for he saw
That no flesh nor spirit could keep
His iron law one moment.[116]

And Urizen himself says:

Read my books, explore my constellations,
Enquire of my sons and they shall teach thee how to war.[117]

The tyranny of Urizen consists in trying to govern by abstract codes based on mathematical reasoning and materialism, and it brings about a vicious circle of oppressions and wars. This tyranny of abstraction, for example, leads to "one law for the lion and the ox" and, consequently, oppression for either lion or ox.

The Prophetic Books, it has been pointed out, all dramatize the same great myth.[118] The same things continually recur with only a slight shift of emphasis or viewpoint: *The Book of Urizen, The Song of Los,* and "Night IV" of *The Four Zoas* all repeat the same incident in the same story.

This story is that of *The Four Zoas* and, complex as it is, it is the drama of the whole world, and at the same time the drama of any individual in it. The fall of the spirit from eternity corresponds to the inevitable fall of the individual from innocence into experience.

A unique and central part is played in the struggle of the Zoas by Los, who is the temporal form of the Zoa Urthona, (spirit, intellect). Los, in fact, is art, imagination. And while the others, Urizen, Tharmas, and Luvah, fall into the revolving "circle of destiny" (a typical mystical wheel of life), Los stands somehow apart with his anvils eternally giving forms to the others and re-creating them to keep them from sinking into undivided and undistinguishable matter, or nonexistence.

Beating still on his rivets of iron
Pouring Sodor of iron: dividing
The horrible night into watches.[119]

---

[116] "The Book of Urizen," *The Writings of William Blake,* Vol. I, page 319.
[117] "The Four Zoas," *The Writings of William Blake,* Vol. II, page. 77.
[118] W. B. Yeats and E. J. Ellis, *Works of William Blake with a Memoir and Interpretation,* London, Bernard Quaritch, Ltd., 1893, Vol. II, page 370.
[119] "Urizen," *The Writings of William Blake,* Vol. I, page 310.

>   . . . the Thund'ring
> Hammer of Urthona forming under his heavy hand the hours
> The days the years in chains of iron around the limbs of Urizen
> Link'd hour to hour and day to day and year to year.[120]

Los is art, imagination as a whole, but here he is specifically poetry, and hence the divisions he creates are appropriately those of time. But it is implied, of course, that it is the forms poetry imposes upon matter that help to give it significance and keep us from falling into despair, because we would otherwise see nothing but chaos around us.

Art, too, participates in the fall. The fall from eternity into matter is a "fall from unity into division." Los, who was himself only a part of Urthona (Urthona is divided into Los, art, and his own specter, metaphysics) now loses part of himself, and his emanation Enitharmon is created from him. She is inspiration: so Art is fallen, too, into division once more. Whereas Art and inspiration used to be one, Los now has to court Enitharmon and pursue her: "I am dead till thou revivest me with thy sweet song."[121] But although she waits until he is nearly exhausted, she brings him back to life with her song, telling him that all matter is still transfigured by form and the radiance of spiritual beauty and that even God himself will descend into the flesh as Christ.

> Arise you little glancing wings and sing your infant joy!
> Arise and drink your bliss!
> For everything that lives is holy, for the source of life
> Descends to be a weeping babe.[122]

Later the specter of Urthona, that is metaphysics, tells Los, "Without a created body the spectre is eternal death."[123] Los, the specter, and Enitharmon together build the City of Art,[124] creating forms which the specters behold: and they become the things they behold and love,[125] so they are redeemed from the Hell of utter materialism. This is also called "giving error a form that it may be cast out," and is not unrelated to the idea, from medieval psychology, that the beauty or ugliness inside a man determine his outward form.

[120] "The Four Zoas," *The Writings of William Blake*, Vol. II, page 50.
[121] *Ibid.*, page 32.
[122] *Ibid.*, page 34.
[123] *Ibid.*, page 86.
[124] *Ibid.*, page 86.
[125] *Ibid.*, page 89.

So also Enitharmon weaves "bodies" on the looms of Catherdron and sings to them to keep them from despair.[126]

Finally, however, it is when the example of Christ's sacrifice shows the Zoas how they may be reconciled that Urizen gives up his idea of dominating all the others and retires to his proper place, on an equal footing with them. Then Los and Enitharmon and the specter are reconstituted as one, the perfect intellect, the "Last Judgment" has taken place, and the world is accepted back into eternity, or Heaven if you will.

This is a brief summary of the drama: and it shows not only the importance of art and its religious function, but shows Blake to be no pagan, no naturalist, and above all, essentially Christian.

One of the things that we gather from the story of Los is that art appeals purely to the intellect. So it does not serve any social end. It has no exclusive concern with moral values. Los remembers eternity where good and evil do not exist, while his enemy Urizen is the one who sets up codes and laws: codes which are tyrannical insofar as they are abstract and do not consult real individual needs. Nor is art concerned with the delight of the senses and nothing else: we have seen that Blake believed living according to the evidence of the senses alone was living in darkness and illusion, cut off from God and "reality." As an artist, Blake found in art a way of knowing and loving the principle of all Being. But truth, as St. Thomas points out, is what the intellect seeks. In art, truth is brilliant form imposed upon matter. Art, for Blake, appeals entirely to the intellect. "What kind of intellects must he have who sees only the colours of things and not the forms of things,"[127] he says, and:

Allegory addressed to the intellectual powers while it is altogether hid from the corporeal understanding is my definition of the most sublime poetry.[128]

Of course, we must not confuse Blake's use of the word "intellect" with the eighteenth-century conception of reason. This should be sufficiently clear from the foregoing remarks on Urizen, in the previous section. Once again, Blake is closer to medieval Christian thought, for intellect to him is a divine gift; intellect is one of the attributes of God; intellect, in an imperfect state, still remains to man as part of his supernatural inheritance; by it he seeks the truth he no longer sees face to face.

But since we are considering Blake not only as aesthetician but as Chris-

126 *Ibid.*, page 101.
127 *The Writings of William Blake*, Vol. III, page 123.
128 *The Writings of William Blake*, Vol. II, page 246.

tian, it is useful to approach him from the point of view of a Christian aesthetics; that is to say, Thomist ideas about art.[129] By this we are not trying to prove that Blake was influenced by the thought of St. Thomas directly or otherwise. He may well have been, but with this we are no longer concerned. Blake's Christianity is far more Augustinian than Thomist, and we are only using the ideas of St. Thomas as a key to help us unlock some of the more difficult problems in Blake's thought about art: and, we may say, these problems are likely to remain unsolved as long as people refuse to interpret Blake as a Christian and continue to seek explanations for everything he said among Gnostics, astrologers, and alchemists.

At the same time, Indian ideas also can help us in this task, because they are essentially similar to Christian ideas about art, as has been pointed out.[130]

That art appeals first of all to the intellect is the starting point of Thomist thought on the subject. It is not simply intellectual in a vague way, but in the technical language of the schools, it is a "virtue of the practical intellect." As distinguished from intellectual activity of the speculative order, the practical intellect operates in two spheres: first, in that of action, where human ends are concerned, and where the means to these ends are selected on a moral basis. Secondly, in the sphere of "making." This is the sphere of productive action, considered not in relation to the *use to which we put our freedom* but in relation to the *thing produced*. The ends are here extrahuman. The artist does not have to consider our needs or desires but only the perfection of the work of art itself.

Art is a "virtue" of the practical intellect. Perhaps it would be well to explain the word "virtue" not only to divest it of its modern colloquial connotations, for in the language of movies and editorials virtue has become synonymous with chastity, but also in order to understand its precise technical meaning. The idea of a virtue is the ancient's idea of *habitus*. *Habitus* is a "permanent condition perfecting in the line of its own nature the subect which it informs."[131] There are "entitative habits" like Grace, which tend to perfect being in its very nature, and "operative habits," which have for subject the faculties of the Soul, and these habits are acquired by exercise and customary use.

[129] Jacques Maritain, *Art and Scholasticism,* translated by J. F. Scanlan, New York, Scribners, 1930.
[130] Coomaraswamy, *op. cit.*
[131] Maritain, *op. cit.*, page 9.

Such a habit is a virtue, that is to say a quality, which, triumphing over the original indetermination of the intellective faculty, at once sharpening and hardening the point of its activity, raises it in respect of a definite object to a maximum of perfection and so, of operative efficiency.[132]

The presence of virtue in the workman is necessary to the goodness of the work. As a man is, so are his works. The tree is known by its fruits.

Then as we examine this virtue of the practical intellect a little further, and consider its relation to the things it knows, we find the Schoolmen consider that the conception of knowledge and being as independent has only a logical but not an immediate validity. The knower and the thing known actually become identified. This identification of being and intelligence is also made by the Hindu,[133] and it is implicit in Blake's remark, "Every eye sees differently. As the eye, such the object."[134] St. Thomas says, "The thing known is in the knower according to the mode of the knower."[135] This concept of the "connaturality" of the artist and his object is Aristotelian and is also found in Plotinus. "Mind knows its objects not, like perception, as external to itself but as one with itself."[136] But even if Blake in his aphorisms shows that he understands this concept of the *adaequatio rei et intellectus* which is bound up with the idea of art as a virtue of the practical intellect, does he have any idea of art which would correspond to that of virtue or *habitus*?

We return to the basis of the Prophetic Books. What is real, true, beautiful, good, is transcendental. This is real existence. Complete nonexistence, on the other hand, if it were possible, would be an utter chaos of matter without the least trace of form or intellect. According to the Neo-Platonists, "We may even say that Beauty is the authentic existence and ugliness is the principle contrary to existence."[137]

As the Thomist idea of virtue is a quality which *perfects* the soul, and enables it to strive toward its ends with a stronger and purer life, so evil is deficiency, lack of strength and purpose, lack of intellect and the im-

---

[132] *Ibid.*, page 11.

[133] Coomaraswamy, *op. cit.*, page 11.

[134] William Blake, *Annotations to Reynolds,* 34. (References to the *Annotations* will be given as above. The numbers refer to the pages of the original edition of Reynolds in which Blake wrote his marginalia. The remarks are so numbered in all editions of Blake. The *Annotations* will be found in *The Writings of William Blake*, Vol. III.)

[135] St. Thomas Aquinas, *Summa Theologica*, I, q. 59, a. 2.

[136] Whitaker, *op. cit.*, page 60.

[137] Plotinus, *Enneads VI.*, translated by S. McKenna, Library of Philosophical Transactions, London, Medici Society, 1916, page 85.

possibility of participating in God's Grace and, in the last analysis, hatred of God, or according to mystics, nonexistence. Remember that Dante's Hell is Blake's Ulro. Blake shows us Urizen, after the fall from eternity into sin (to use the Christian term) an old man, blind, sometimes chained, sometimes imprisoned in rock, or frozen up on ice. But Los, imagination, we remember, created forms, builds the City of Art to keep eternals from falling into his nonentity (or sin). In the end he leads them back to eternity, truth, real existence (heaven). This parallel is apparent enough, although Blake does not, of course, speak of virtue or *habitus* at all, and does not even see it in the precise clear sense in which St. Thomas uses it.

Of course, when Blake speaks of belief in good and evil he is not necessarily in conflict with St. Thomas, nor does that have anything to do with this Thomist idea of virtue. On the contrary, Blake in attacking good and evil as misleading ideas is attacking shortsighted and fanatical moralists of the Puritan variety. Rigid and sweeping distinctions between right and wrong infuriated him. But the Thomist believes that in ethics every case is to be judged strictly on its own merits, and no two moral cases are ever identical.[138] Besides, we repeat, our investigation here is not at all concerned with morals, for in neither Blake nor in St. Thomas does ethics enter into the discussion of art.

Since art is a virtue of the practical intellect, and virtue tends only to good, art tends always to the good of the intellect which is truth. That is to say, it involves infallible correctness. So, when in the preface to *Reynolds' Discourses* Blake read that we should excuse the "errors of genius" he replied, "Genius has no errors. It is ignorance that is error."[139] Genius, in other words, implies a highly developed *habitus* of art. The virtue of genius is infallible. But, of course, the infallibility of art only concerns the regulation of the work itself. Infallible knowledge of the kind of truth the speculative intellect seeks is not involved here. The speculative intellect knows in conformity with what *is*. The infallibility of art concerns only *direction,* toward the perfection of art in itself.

Consequently, defects in the actual work of art, proceeding from faulty tools, lack of materials, a trembling hand, do not affect the *virtue* of the artist. The work may be imperfect, but the art in the artist is unimpaired. Therefore manual dexterity is necessary to produce works of art but is extrinsic to art itself. That is to say, that virtuosity[140] and facility alone never constitute art.

138 Maritain, *op. cit.,* page 17.
139 Blake, *Annotations to Reynolds,* introduction, page iii.
140 Virtuosity has nothing to do with virtue in the Thomist, or any other sense.

The labour by which the virtuoso who "plays the harp" acquires agile fingers does not increase his art itself or produce any special form; it merely removes a physical impediment to the practise of the art.[141]

And so Blake could say also:

In my brain are studies and chambers filled with the books and pictures of old which I wrote and painted in eternity before my mortal life; and those works are the delight and study of archangels. Why then should I be anxious about the riches and fame of mortality?[142]

The quotation from Blake, while it has nothing directly to say about virtuosity, at least shows clearly that what is important is the virtue of the artist. Execution comes afterward and, important as it is, this importance is secondary. If you have virtue of art, you may never paint a picture and still retain that virtue. But if you only possess facility, no matter how many pictures you paint you are not a good artist. The created work is not art, it is the result of art.

I write [he said to Crabb Robinson], I write when commanded by the spirits and the moment I have written I see the words fly about the room in all directions. It is then published and the spirits can read. My Manuscript is of no further use.[143]

A line from *Milton* tells us the same thing in another way: "Whatever can be created can be annihilated: forms cannot."[144] So, too, St. Thomas, toward the end of his life, looked at the immense and unfinished work of his life, the *Summa Theologica,* and turned away with, "Omne istud videtur ut palea"—"all straw!"

But if manual dexterity is no intrinsic part of art, the same holds good for the exact copying of natural objects. Naturalism is no more important to art than virtuosity, and for the same reason.

From the Scholastic point of view, "Imitation . . . materially considered is merely a means, not an end. It no more constitutes art than manual dexterity."[145] The artistic process demands that the work should be already half done in the artist's mind before he begins to study any natural model. And even then he does not copy it slavishly but imposes upon it the form which his mind, his intellect, is prepared to see in it. This in-

---

141 Maritain, *op. cit.,* page 58.
142 *The Writings of William Blake,* Vol. II, page 137.
143 Robinson, *op. cit.,* Vol. II, page 36.
144 "Milton," *The Writings of William Blake,* Vol. II, page 356.
145 Maritain, *op. cit.,* page 58.

tellectual approach goes quite naturally with the Aristotelian theory of matter which the Schools adopted for their own. Just as the soul is the form of the body, so the art in the artist is the form of the work of art.

According to the rules of art in the Orient as they are summarized by Dr. Coomaraswamy,[146] the aesthetic process is understood to be threefold. First, the arising of the image in the mind; second, study of the image by the intellect; and last, and least of all, giving it outward expression.[147]

So a special kind of artistic vision is necessary: vision to which the eye itself, by itself, is unimportant. For the eye, by itself, sees things by virtue of a substantial kinship to them (as like to like) and is merely a mirror: the formal relations of objects to one another are perceived not by the eye but by the intellect through the eye. "My eye sees flat, but I see in relief; this relief is not necessarily a fact, but an idea of relation which would have validity for me even supposing the total unreality of the external world."[148] At the same time it is never possible to see things purely as the eye alone would see them. We always know things rationally; we pick out what is significant for us; we perceive the relationships that interest us; as we look at nature, we interpret it.

The only perfect likeness to a natural object would be a pure reflection, a sensation not interpreted or understood, and it would remain incomprehensible. Yet even then, the material image would be only commensurable with a natural species in substance and fundamentally irreconcilable in terms of material or life. In fact, a perfect reproduction of a creature would have to be self-moving. Art would have ceased, and we would be involved in necromancy.

The logic of the pure naturalist in art finally breaks down when we observe that making a recognizable image of your subject, say painting a portrait of a man, does not mean making an image that one would mistake for the person himself. The perfect portrait is not one that people will go up and say "good morning" to in all good faith and try to shake hands with it. Otherwise, to judge by the familiar jokes about Madame Tussaud's Wax Works, there is more good art there than there is in the National Gallery. A man's portrait is his "essential image," his image as he "is in God"; that is, it expresses his own character, whatever it is that makes him who and what he is.

Dr. Coomaraswamy points out the similarity between Blake and the

---

[146] Maritain, *op. cit.,* page 76.
[147] *Ibid.,* page 77.
[148] *Ibid.,* page 79.

great Christian mystic Meister Eckhart.[149] He finds ideas common to Blake and Eckhart upon naturalism, in Hindu philosophy also.

We now have only to add to these remarks Blake's own familiar ideas about the artist's vision:

> For a double vision my eyes do see
> And a double vision is always with me
> With my inward eye 'tis an old man gray
> With my outward a thistle across my way.[150]

And, "All forms are perfect in the poet's mind, but they are not abstracted or compounded from nature, they are imagination itself."[151] In a letter to Dr. Trusler, Blake explained:[152]

Some see nature all ridicule and deformity and by these I shall not regulate my proportions: and some scarce see nature at all. But to the eye of the man of Imagination, Nature is Imagination itself.

The man of imagination, the artist, because of the "virtue" of his art, sees more than his eyes present to him. He does not rely like Urizen entirely on the evidence of his senses, accepting nothing else at all. Urizen is always blind and in chains, and is trying continually to impose that blindness on the whole world. Los and Enitharmon on the other hand:

> . . . walk'd forth on the dewy earth
> Contracting and expanding their all flexible senses
> At will to murmur in the flowers small as the honey bee
> At will to stretch across the heavens and step from star to star.[153]

By virtue of artistic vision, they enjoy nature *sub specie aeternitatis* and not merely as it is in itself.

> To see the world in a grain of sand
> And a heaven in a wild flower
> Hold infinity in the palm of your hand
> And eternity in an hour . . .[154]

The artist, then, does not attempt imitation of natural objects, nor does he love nature for its own sake. Yet from the above quotation, Blake cer-

---

[149] Coomaraswamy, *op. cit.,* page 57, note.
[150] *The Writings of William Blake,* Vol. II, page 207.
[151] Blake, *Annotations to Reynolds,* page 158.
[152] *The Writings of William Blake,* Vol. II, page 175.
[153] "The Four Zoas," *The Writings of William Blake,* Vol. II.
[154] *The Writings of William Blake,* Vol. II, page 207.

tainly loves nature in the sense in which we say any poet loves nature who even talks about its beauties, no matter what the beauties are he sees in it. But when nature has become "imagination itself," he who sees her so is no naturalist. The Thomist point of view is, "Nature concerns the artist essentially simply because it is a derivation from the divine art in things, *ratio artis divinae indita rebus*."[155] Pure naturalism, on the other hand, aims to yield "sensations as nearly as possible identical with those aroused by the model itself."[156] This, however, is idolatrous, for idolatry is the love of creatures as they are in themselves and not as they are in God.

"Everything," Blake says, "is Atheism which assumes the reality of the natural and Unspiritual world."[157] According to Quintillian, "Docti rationem artis intellegunt, indocti voluptatem," and Blake adds:

> Some look to see the sweet outlines
> And beauteous forms that love does wear:
> Some look to find out patches, paint,
> Bracelets and stays and powdered hair.[158]

Blake's ideas on art display this severity toward all adventitious aspects of art and stress the essential, intellectual character of art, because Blake feels that the artist who forgets these essentials becomes meretricious, or a trickster, or a clown. This condemnation of idolatry in art is once again not a moral judgment. Nor does it amount to a categorical statement that sensuousness has no place in art: on the contrary, Hindu iconography, which follows strict rules built up out of this theory of the aesthetic process, is richly sensuous. Good art delights the senses as well as the intellect, but the delight of the senses must never become the artist's only end. "If art seeks to please it commits a betrayal and tells a lie."[159] This is why Blake made such frequent attacks on the Venetian and Flemish painters:

Salvator Rosa was precisely what he pretended not to be. His pictures are high laboured pretensions to Expeditious workmanship. He was the quack doctor of painting. His roughness and smoothness are the production of Labour and trick. As to Imagination he was totally without any.[160]

---

[155] Maritain, *op. cit.,* page 64.
[156] Coomaraswamy, *op. cit.,* page 80.
[157] Robinson, *op. cit.,* Vol. II, page 27.
[158] Blake, *Annotations to Reynolds,* introduction, page xiv.
[159] Maritain, *op. cit.,* page 65.
[160] Blake, *Annotations to Reynolds,* page 132.

His condemnation of Rembrandt, which is generally taken to be the result of eccentricity and bad temper combined, is based on his belief that chiaroscuro is a melodramatic trick; and, incidentally, such a belief does not necessarily prove insanity in a critic.

"Any fool," he says, "can concentrate a light on the middle."[161] The reason why he said the Flemish and Venetian painters "could not draw" was because in his eyes they seemed to achieve their effects by trickery, by technical dodges, and not by the infinite patient and loving humility of the artist who lives only for the perfection of his work. "The difference between a bad artist and a good one is this: the bad artist seems to copy a good deal, the good one really does copy a good deal."[162] So, if it is not sufficient to catch the play of color and light, or the beauty of a landscape to make a work of art: if art must appeal not to the senses and emotions alone but first of all to the intellect, what does the good artist see to paint in the world? When Blake says "Nature is Imagination itself," what does he mean? How does he "see" imagination in created things?

Crabb Robinson puzzled his head over Blake's conversation, full of deliberately provoking exaggerations and teasing references to angels, planned especially to shock an unimaginative and literal-minded man. He wondered confusedly at Blake's mysticism and fumbled about for some catalogue number or index card that would fit Blake's philosophy. So, in his *Diary:*

> It would be hard to fix Blake's station between Christianity, Platonism and Spinozism. Yet he professes to be very hostile to Plato, and reproaches Wordsworth with being not a Christian but a Platonist.[163]

This confusion, it seems, is one which is bound to beset any lover of card indexes that begins to read Blake. There are two reasons why card indexers get into a muddle by trying to file all mysticism on their card marked "Plato." To begin with, they probably cherish natural sympathy with Plato himself, who filled heaven with a lot of ideal card indexes of his own; and then, in the second place, the advanced scholarship of our day, which prefers to disbelieve in real mysticism, such as that of a St. Theresa, or a St. John of the Cross, finds the idealism of Plato a comfortable rule by which to judge all mysticism. Seriously, however, Crabb Robinson's confusion was natural, for Blake had willy-nilly accepted much from Neo-

---

161 *Ibid.,* page 251.
162 *Ibid.,* page 32.
163 Robinson, *op. cit.,* Vol. II, page 25.

Platonism, where Plato is modified by Aristotle, and India, and Persia, and Christianity, and Hebraism. But Plato himself Blake could never stand.

From what we know of his hatred of naturalism, and his insistence that imitation, naturalism, have no place in art, we can soon see where Blake would take issue with the ideas on art in the tenth book of the *Republic*. It is not that he would have disagreed that slavish copying had nothing to do with truth and beauty, for Plato believed that, too: but Blake detested Plato for thinking that imitation of natural objects was the end of the artist, in fact, his only end, all that he was capable of attempting. Now, Plato, no less than Blake, believed that nature was illusory: and so, if the artist copies nature, we get a double illusion, a copy of a copy. From this, Plato runs on to make the most extravagant conclusions about art:

> For example, the painter will paint us a carpenter . . . *without knowing anything about his (the carpenter's) trade.* And notwithstanding this ignorance on his part let him be but a good painter and if he paints a carpenter and displays his picture at a distance *he will deceive children and silly people by making them think he is really a carpenter.*[164]

Or, speaking of Homer, a poet he himself loved, we find Plato falling into this, which could not have helped striking Blake as complete absurdity. Plato argues that since, in the *Iliad,* Homer speaks of the government of a city and the conduct of a war, this presupposes *knowledge* of these subjects on his part, but, "If he knows these things so well, what wars has he won, what cities has he governed?" So, he goes on to his moral condemnation of poetry. First, "That part which relies on measurement and calculation must be the best part of the soul . . ."[165] Now, poetry does not appeal to this part of the soul: "Poetry, portraying emotions, excites the meaner instead of the better part of the soul and is therefore bad."[166] We are frequently told how Blake's Urizen represents Plato's Demiurge, but no one has troubled to find out if Urizen does not represent Plato himself, along with so many other things. At any rate, Plato is playing Urizen's game here of setting up clear-cut, arbitrary distinctions between the good and bad parts of the soul, and piling this on top of a complete misunderstanding of the nature of the artistic process, he condemns art

---

[164] Plato, *Republic X,* translated by J. Llewellyn Davies and D. J. Vaughan, London, Macmillan, 1923, page 340.

[165] *Ibid.,* page 346.

[166] *Ibid.*

on moral grounds. And this was what Blake hated in Plato most of all: This is what he called

> eating of the tree of the knowledge of good and evil. This was the fault of Plato. He knew nothing but the virtues and vices, good and evil. There is nothing in all that, everything is good in God's eyes.[167]

Obsessed as he was with his search for ultimate truth, Plato made the mistake of looking at art entirely as a means of cognition. It pretended to know beauty, and beauty was truth. Why could philosophers not go to art for their information? Because art copied the world's deceptive beauty and existed in order to give information about that. This second error throws him completely off on the wrong path. Maritain says:

> Plato, with his theory of various degrees of imitation and poetry as an illusion, misconceives like all extravagant intellectualists, the peculiar nature of art . . . it is clear that if art were a means of knowledge it would be wildly inferior to geometry.[168]

However, even if we agree that Plato, as far as Blake was concerned, misconceived the nature and function of art, we are still faced with Blake's transcendentalism and tempted to associate it somehow with Plato. Even though Plato hardly had a word to say about art that Blake could have agreed with—even though he grudgingly admits the possibility of inspiration in the Ion—it may still be thought that Blake's ideas about the "Imagination" may have something to do with Platonic archetypes.

We have heard Blake speak of "seeing a world in a grain of sand," and we are familiar with the Platonic idea of ideal beauty and ideal types which are somewhat poorly reflected in this world. Do not Blake and Plato meet here?

When he attacked Reynolds, Blake was attacking an admittedly distorted and misunderstood and diluted Platonic idealism which came down through the Renaissance together with Aristotle (mangled beyond all recognition) to help make up what we call Neo-Classicism. Where, in a footnote, in the introduction to *Reynolds' Discourses,* we read, "This disposition to abstractions, to generalizing, and classification is the great glory of the human mind." Blake replies, "To generalize is to be an idiot, to particularize is the alone distinction of merit."[169] Later, he adds, "Dis-

---

[167] Robinson, *op. cit.,* Vol. II, page 26.
[168] Maritain, *op. cit.,* page 56.
[169] Blake, *Annotations to Reynolds,* introduction, page xcviii.

440

tinct general forms cannot exist: distinctness is particular, not general."[170] Indeed, it is no exaggeration to say that every time he attacked the Classicists as generalizers he was attacking Plato, at any rate as he was understood in the eighteenth century. If we are puzzled by Blake's concept of "particular beauty," it will be clarified, perhaps, if we look at the term in contrast with Plato's ideal forms.

Plato's archetypes are types of being external to the world, entirely separate from it, and above it, they are faintly reflected in the things of this contingent world. Blake found these archetypes so vague that they were nothing more to him than "mathematical diagrams" (Greek form is mathematical form);[171] broad, general types, abstract classifications, into which living individual created things had to be fitted somehow, even if it took a little mutilation. One of the things cut off and thrown away was art, because it did not happen to be something it was never intended to be. This is what Plato meant to Blake.

Now, we have seen that there is some difference between Plato and Plotinus precisely on this problem. Plotinus' Aristotelian theory of matter is the same as that of the Schoolmen; he believes that there are as many formal differences as there are individuals and all pre-exist in the intelligible world.[172] As to Oriental types (like Yang and Yin), they are still more remote from Plato. They

> are not thought of as mechanically reflected in phenomena but as representing to our mentality the operative principles by which we explain phenomena . . . Thus Indian types representing sentences or powers are analogous to those of Scholastic theology and the energies of science but not comparable with Plato's types.[173]

What Blake called generalizing, for one thing, was giving to a particular subject a kind of ideal or typical beauty, a standard beauty by which we might presumably judge all men. To Blake it was unthinkable to consider beauty in terms of standards—to draw an individual figure so as to make it resemble a broad, ideal model.

This is one of the familiar distinctions made between Classic and Romantic artists. The latter are assumed to have sought out subjects with an individual, or weirdly strange, or even exotic character. This brings

---

[170] *Ibid.,* 74.
[171] *The Writings of William Blake,* Vol. III, page 362.
[172] Whitaker, *op. cit.,* page 61.
[173] Coomaraswamy, *op. cit.,* page 17.

us to Romantic naturalism as well as to Romantic assertions of the validity of an artist's individual tastes and viewpoints. But, of course, Blake's reaction was not at all in the direction of naturalism. His mysticism is stronger and purer than that of any other Romantic poet, and his reaction against Classical generalizing is not that of the other Romantics. Hardly any of the others were in reaction against Platonism. On the contrary, some of them steeped themselves in a deeper, purer Platonism than the Classicists had ever known. How can we further distinguish his mysticism from Plato's idealism?

In this case we may once more approach the subject through Scholastic and Hindu thought.

Meister Eckhart, a great medieval Christian thinker, believes that there are as many ideas (forms) in the Divine Intellect as there ever can be things in the created world. "There are as many types as there are grades of nature to be typified."[174] "To call a tree a tree is not to name it, for all the species is confused,"[175] and (reflecting once again Aristotle's theory of matter) "every creature makes innate denial; the one denies it is the other."[176]

So, since no two creatures are ever the same, we get into confusion as soon as we try to reduce them to general types in order to identify them properly and not vaguely; in order to recognize their *quidditas,* their own individual character, that makes them what they are and not something else. Reducing things to general and unchanging rigid types is misleading because in essence there can be no such thing as likeness or image; there can be only sameness. "Every nature emanates from its appropriate form,"[177] and "Ideas are living, not merely existing like standards fixed and deposited for safe keeping—Ideas not merely of static shapes but ideas of acts."[178] This lies behind Blake's attacks on Plato, on Greece, of Classicism as a whole. This is exactly what he means by saying, "The Gods of Greece and Egypt were mathematical diagrams—see the Works of Plato."[179] How does this apply to beauty? Beauty, in Thomist words, is "a certain excellence or perfection in the proportion of things to the mind," and this excellence depends upon three conditions: integrity, proportion, and clarity.

[174] Coomaraswamy, *op. cit.,* page 70.
[175] *Ibid.*
[176] *Ibid.*
[177] *Ibid.*
[178] *Ibid.,* page 71.
[179] "Lacoön Plate," *The Writings of William Blake,* Vol. III, page 77.

Now this beauty is not perceived by the intellect alone; only the angels perceive beauty by a direct intuition without the intermediary of the senses, and for us beauty is *id quod visum placet.*[180] Plotinus begins his discussion of beauty by saying it "addresses itself chiefly to sight."[181] Although a metaphysician can enjoy purely intelligible beauty, yet the beauty that is "connatural" to him becomes intelligible after reaching the mind through the senses. It is integrity, clarity, and proportion in a beautiful object that delight the mind.

> Integrity because the mind likes being; proportion because the mind likes order and likes unity, lastly and above all brightness or clarity because the mind likes light and intelligibility.[182]

The most important idea is that of *claritas:* and the brightness of *claritas* is the *splendor formae;* the glory of form shining through matter.

> Form, that is to say the principle determining the peculiar perfection of everything which is, and completing things in their essence and their qualities, the ontological secret, so to speak, of their innermost being . . . is above all the peculiar principle of intelligibility, the peculiar clarity of everything.[183]

Now we see how much closer we are to Blake than to Plato. Form is a revelation of essence; to see a thing as it is essentially, and how it is filled with God's glory with which all things alike are charged, this is what Blake means by "particularizing." "Distinctness is Particular, not general,"[184] and so beauty does not conform with certain ideal and unchanging types. Seeing the world in a grain of sand is the perception of *claritas.*

To see the splendor of form in matter is to look through matter into eternity, it is to abandon "single vision and Newton's sleep" and to realize that:

> Every generated body in its inward form
> Is a garden of delight and a building of magnificence.[185]

Here then, from the poem *Milton,* we take a good example of the way Blake looks at nature, or rather through nature.

[180] St. Thomas Aquinas, *Summa Theologica,* I Q39, A8.
[181] Plotinus, *Enneads VI,* page 77.
[182] Maritain, *op. cit.,* page 24.
[183] *Ibid.*
[184] Blake, *Annotations to Reynolds,* page 74.
[185] "Milton," *The Writings of William Blake,* Vol. II, page 345.

These are the Sons of Los, and these the laborers in the vintage.
Thou sees't the gorgeous clothed flies that dance and sport in summer
Upon the sunny brooks and meadows, each one the dance
Knows in its intricate mazes of delight artful to weave:
Each one to sound his instruments of music in the dance
To touch each other and recede, to cross and change and return
These are the children of Los. Thou sees't the trees on mountains
The wind blows heavy, loud they thunder through the darksom sky
Uttering prophecies and speaking instructive words to the sons
Of men: these are the sons of Los: these the visions of eternity
But we see only as it were the hem of their garments
When with vegetable eyes we view these wondrous visions.[186]

In Wordsworth and the other Romantics, it is always the nature that
presents itself to the senses of the poet that comes first: after that we find
the "something far more deeply interfused" that makes nature, so to
speak, God's mouthpiece. Consequently, Wordsworth is often closer to
the Deists and to Thomson than he is to Blake. And for Blake the nature
that we see merely with our eyes is nothing, it is dross, nothing but the
"hem of the garment" of the sons of imagination. "The material thing,"
says Plotinus, "becomes beautiful by communicating in the thought that
flows from the Divine . . . ,"[187] and this emphasis is entirely different
from Wordsworth's. Wordsworth finds nature beautiful *per se*.

Since *claritas* implies essential beauty it implies also intelligibility, and
this is what Blake always insists on when he defends imagination against
scientific reason, "the philosophy of the five senses." Empirical skepticism
only explores phenomena, the created world. Mathematics strips things
down to quantitative abstractions, symbols of physical properties in time
and space. But poetry and metaphysics (remember, the specter of Urthona
helps Los build the city of Art) seek a still higher kind of truth and intelligibility. However, Blake is not concerned with metaphysics. The work
of reason and logic which gives us in the end only an approximate understanding of first causes does not interest Blake: he, rather, inextricably
linking up the poetic instinct with his own mysticism and all his religious
feeling, finds, through poetry, the possibility of direct intuitive contacts
with pure intelligibility. Blake believes the poet may see God face to face,
but it is not the poet as poet that does so, of course. This seizure of intelligible realities without using concepts as a formal means is something

[186] *Ibid.,* page 344.
[187] Plotinus, *Enneads VI,* page 80.

444

analogous in both the poet and the mystic, but they both operate differently and on different planes. Blake saw that the artist and the mystic seemed to have the same kind of intuitions, for he himself, as mystic and artist, certainly did: therefore he never troubled to distinguish between aesthetic emotion and the mystic graces. And, although the Thomists make the distinction quite clear, the Hindu thinkers come closer to identifying art and mysticism just as Blake does:

> Pure aesthetic experience is theirs in whom knowledge
> of ideal beauty is innate, and is known intuitively,
> in intellectual ecstasy, without the accompaniment
> of ideation, at the highest level of conscious being.[188]

To return from this brief digression, then, the brilliance of form the artist sees is intelligible, but does not possess the kind of intelligibility the scientist seeks. It is ontological splendor that is revealed to us here, but certainly not conceptual clarity. It is the perfection of an antelope or a flower, not the perfection of a theorem or of a syllogism. The artist sees into the very essence of things, but that essence is not necessarily immediately clear to us, nor can it be communicated to us in logical concepts without losing the purity in which the artist first perceived it. But the Thomists, as well as Blake, think that in the presence of *claritas* the intellect is spared any effort of abstraction and analysis and can enjoy beauty, directly and intuitively. The beauty it thus enjoys is that which is connatural to man.

Blake has an exceptionally keen feeling for this idea of connaturality, witness the following lines:

> Each grain of sand
> Each rock and each hill
> Each fountain and rill
> Each herb and each tree
> Mountain, hill earth and star
> Cloud meteor and star
> Are men seen afar.[189]

Blake, of course, also firmly believed that God created man in his own image and speaks continually of "the human form divine." These lines are typical of Blake, and they show us how filled he was with two im-

---

[188] Coomaraswamy, *op. cit.,* page 49.
[189] *The Writings of William Blake,* Vol. II, page 190.

portant Scholastic concepts, the concept of *claritas* and that of connaturality: the two are completely worked together here.

However, the Thomists make yet another distinction that Blake and the Hindus do not trouble to make. Beauty is distinguished from truth: that is, beauty is related to truth but is not itself a kind of truth. To see a beautiful object is, in a sense, to know truth, and added to this knowledge, there is delight. But if in beauty there is delight, that is why it appeals to our desires, causes love, and becomes an object of the appetite. Beauty is thus a "good," and the apprehension of beauty implies at once knowledge and ecstasy. But truth alone can illuminate.

Blake is simply not interested in truth as a matter of analysis and concept. Metaphysics can only show us God as an object of thought, vaguely foreshadowed in analogies: can create in us the desire to love God but cannot satisfy that love. Blake, on the other hand, has forgotten all intellectual distinctions, all labels and categories, in the ecstasy of the mystic who surely knows God, and is dazzled by the glory of all His attributes at once. So Blake makes no distinctions between truth and beauty, knowing and loving, but puts them all together in "Imagination," a word that also covers the experience of "fourfold vision," the mystic ecstasy. But it is here that Blake becomes an extremist. St. Thomas was a mystic, too, but on the other hand, his mysticism seems to have given him an even more keen and clear sense of balance in his metaphysics and logical reasoning, so that more than any other philosopher he comes to conclusions which astonish us with their brilliance and yet delight us with their perfect soundness and consonance with our experience and our intellectual needs. So St. Thomas balances the love of beauty with judgment in the artist: *perfectio artis consistit in judicando,* while Blake rushed fearlessly ahead, forgetting about judgment and putting complete trust in the critical discretion of the angels who guided him.

It would be an unrewarding task to seek a direct literary cause for Blake's enthusiasm outside Blake himself; mystics are born, and so are poets and artists. Blake himself says, "Man is born like a garden ready planted and sown. This world is too poor to produce a single seed."[190] However, Blake was thoroughly familiar with the eighteenth-century pre-Romantic writers, and from them, as well as from Swedenborg and Boehme, and the Catholic mystics, and the Methodists, he could draw literary warrant for enthusiasm and inspiration. The subject of my essay is not Blake's ideas on genius and enthusiasm, so it is not for me to ex-

[190] Blake, *Annotations to Reynolds,* page 157.

446

amine in detail the relation of Blake to a Byron, a Parnell, or an Isaac Watts. But still there are interesting similarities between Blake and Edward Young's *Conjectures on Original Composition* (1759). Blake was, of course, a great reader of Young, as were all the English middle class at that time, and besides that, he illustrated the *Night Thoughts*. Young's conjectures did not have to "cause" Blake's claims of inspiration and feelings of enthusiasm. Literary criticism which makes such categorical claims is always absurd. But the conjectures probably gave him much encouragement to never be critical of the least thing that his own genius told him. "Genius," says Young, "can set us right in composition without the works of the learned as conscience sets us right in life without the laws of the land."[191] Again, "All eminence and distinction lie out of the beaten road, excursion and deviation are necessary to find it; and the more remote your path from the highway, the more reputable."[192] And here is a passage which may be compared with Blake's "Proverb of Hell": "Bring out number, weight and measure in a year of dearth."[193] "Rules, like crutches, are a needful aid to the lame though an impediment to the strong."[194] Then:

> Genius often, then, deserves most to be praised when it is most sure to be condemned; that is when its excellence is mounting high to weak eyes is quite out of sight.[195]

This could have been taken from any one of Blake's letters from Felpham, and so could this: "Thyself so reverence as to prefer the native growth of thine own mind to the richest import from abroad."[196] All this may never have influenced Blake beyond encouraging him to go on in the direction he had already chosen: yet that encouragement may have been important. Blake must have returned to this kind of thing again and again, until he became so uncritical of everything that flowed from his pen that *The Four Zoas* and *Milton* were written almost automatically, as he tells Butts in one of his letters.[197]

[191] Edward Young, "Conjectures on Original Composition," in *Works of Edward Young*, London, Tegg, 1854, Vol. II, page 558.

[192] *Ibid.*, page 555.

[193] "The Marriage of Heaven and Hell," *The Writings of William Blake*, Vol. I, page 184.

[194] Young, *Works*, Vol. II, page 557.

[195] *Ibid.*

[196] *Ibid.*, page 564.

[197] *The Writings of William Blake*, Vol. II, page 244.

This was certainly not the case with the *Poetical Sketches,* or *Innocence and Experience,* or the lovely *Book of Thel.* There indeed he shows more refinement of artistic judgment, more critical poise than any other Romantic except Coleridge.

Now, art is impossible without inspiration. More than that, inspiration is not something that has to be halfheartedly admitted into the discussion of art in the grudging way Plato assented to it in the Ion. It is not a matter of learning: genius was not taught in schools, as Reynolds seemed to have believed: "Reynolds' opinion was that Genius could be taught and that all pretence to inspiration was a lie and a deceit."[198] But, on the other hand, it is not necessary to go as far as Blake did in contradicting Reynolds' "mere enthusiasm will not carry you very far" with "mere enthusiasm is the all in all."[199] *Perfectio artis consistit in judicando.* The virtue or *habitus* of art does not spring full grown in the artist's mind, it has to be cultivated by definite means. Education alone cannot make an artist; sometimes it kills art in the bud, especially if it teaches nothing but technical tricks to catch a buyer's eye. But strict training is important. The interior light given the artist by God must be cherished, that it may strengthen and come to burn brilliantly in the end. The most important thing of all, in training, is to come to possess an infallible critical judgment. "A good disposition of the appetite is necessary, for everyone judges his particular ends by what he himself actually is."[200] And one of the most important disciplines is that of contemplation. This implies a kind of asceticism, that is self-sacrifice, sacrifice of immediate physical goods for the good of the spirit, for the success of the work of art. The Hindu artist accompanies the artistic process with a strict routine of asceticism and contemplation. First of all, he must purge himself of all personal desires, all distracting influences. Then he visualizes his subject as it is described in a given canonical prescription (mantram); he contemplates this ideal model until he comes to "reflect" it, becomes identified with it, holds it in view in an act of nondifferentiation, then draws it.[201] Blake spoke of "copying a vision"; if anyone would like to see a systematic exposition of all this meant, here it is. It might seem the ultimate limit of folly to associate Blake, who is popularly regarded as anti-intellectual and anti-ascetic, with such rigid discipine, both moral and intellectual, in the artistic process, especially when he made such a remark as:

---

[198] Blake, *Annotations to Reynolds,* page 2.
[199] *Ibid.,* page 35.
[200] Maritain, *op. cit.,* page 148.
[201] Coomaraswamy, *op. cit.,* page 145.

He who has nothing to dissipate cannot dissipate; the weak man may be virtuous enough but will never be an artist. Painters are noted for being dissipated and wild.[202]

Readers who must draw general rules from every little sentence will make a generalization out of this and get lost. They will take it to mean, perhaps, some recommendation of drunkenness as an aid to art. Such people are the same who are confused by a simple Catholic idea that the capacity for great sin can also be the capacity for great saintliness. Those who are absorbed in Calvinist ideas about predestination will doubtless puzzle at this, thinking it to mean that we should all go out and be great sinners.

Blake is talking about the "energy" of imagination and not at all about ethics, even though the words "weak" and "virtuous" might imply it. He is saying that artists have been drunkards without necessarily being bad artists. But since Blake loved Fra Angelico,[203] we may be sure he would have agreed with the only recorded words of the Dominican painter, a remark reflecting a faith that shines in all his work. "Art," said the Blessed Angelico, "demands great tranquillity, and to paint the things of Christ the artist must live with Christ."[204] Blake was too great a man not to recognize instinctively the necessary balance between the uncontrolled energy of genius and the devotion of the artist to his work, which must involve a willing sacrifice of everything in the world.

We are all too ready in this day to talk about the antiasceticism of some of Blake's remarks and forget that he willingly bore the asceticism imposed on him by poverty—chose it in preference to sacrificing his art to a more comfortable living. Blake chose poverty as deliberately as any Franciscan brother. We must remember that, after all, Blake said:

> Prayer is the study of Art
> Praise is the practice of Art
> Fasting etc all relate to Art
> The outward ceremony is antichrist.[205]

And we find this "anti-intellectual" Blake coming to preach a thoroughly rigid discipline in art. What he condemns as "outward" ceremony" is of course not technical ability but technical *tricks*. He always stands for perfection of technique, and we have seen that he believed the technique of the Venetians and so on was imperfect and shoddy. So he says,

---

[202] Blake, *Annotations to Reynolds,* page 14.
[203] Gilchrist, *op. cit.,* page 230.
[204] Quoted in Maritain, *op. cit.,* page 71.
[205] "Lacoön Plate," *The Writings of William Blake,* Vol. III, page 357.

Mechanical excellence is the only vehicle of genius. Execution is the chariot of genius.[206]

A facility of composing is the greatest power of art.[207]

Without minute neatness of execution the sublime cannot exist. Grandeur of ideas is founded on precision of ideas.[208]

All these statements were directed against Reynolds' ideas of technique, and they are apt to be surprising in view of the popular belief that Blake stood for a typical Romantic reaction, an attempt at liberation from Classical emphasis on form and strict technical perfection. For Blake, Reynolds' technique was not perfect enough, but the liberation he did strive for was liberation from arbitrary rules for their own sake. He was fighting against Aristotle as he had been corrupted and misinterpreted by the Renaissance, and, did he but know it, he was on the side of Aristotle as the Christian medieval thinkers understood him. To mangle art to fit a Procrustes' bed of rules was not, in Blake's eyes, a way to achieve technical perfection. (However, these remarks apply mostly to his ideas on drawing and painting and have little to do with the verse of the Prophetic Books.)

It may possibly be objected that Blake said, "What has reasoning to do with the art of painting?"[209] and say the Schoolmen insist that the first principle of all human work should be reason, while logic takes first place among the liberal arts. But it only has to be pointed out:

that a work of art should be logical means that its truth is taken to be *per ordinem et conformitatem ad regulas artis* . . . not in the pseudologic of clear ideas, not in the logic of knowledge and demonstration (i.e. reasoning) but in the working logic of every day . . . the logic of the structure of the living thing—the innate geometry of nature.[210]

And compare this with the following words of Blake, "Ideas cannot be given but in their minutely appropriate words nor a design be made without its minutely appropriate execution."[211] This is where Blake stood in relation to the eighteenth century. His reaction was entirely individual, perhaps because he was the most deeply religious artist of his time in

[206] Blake, *Annotations to Reynolds*, page 14.

[207] *Ibid.*, page 3.

[208] *Ibid.*, page 56.

[209] Blake, *Annotations to Reynolds*, page 56.

[210] Maritain, *op. cit.*, page 52.

[211] *The Writings of William Blake*, Vol. III, page 129.

England. Because of this, his reaction was not medievalistic as Coleridge's was, yet more than any other poet of his time Blake seems to build on the groundwork of a philosophy that is essentially Christian and medieval. There is none of the medieval surface in Blake: but, on the other hand, perhaps all that other English nineteenth-century poets ever recaptured from the Middle Ages was their own vague idea of what it looked like on the surface.

One of the most important ideas in Blake is that nature, simply as the eye sees it, is utterly unimportant to art. In this he is diametrically opposed to Wordsworth and Coleridge and Shelley and Keats. He found it literally impossible to draw directly from nature. We have seen what confusion and despair he fell into when he tried to do so. Yet once nature had been assimilated and transformed by his imagination, it blazed before him in a vision fired with the glory of God. Nature, for Wordsworth, was God's greatest and most important creation, and so he, too, saw God in nature. But for Blake, nature is only the hem of God's garment.

It is impossible to understand Blake with the analytical tools his own century used—by judging him by preconceived and arbitrary standards, and, worst of all, by seeking out his moral ideas and attempting to judge his art by them. He must be approached with a broader, deeper, more flexible understanding. Hold Blake up beside the Scholastic philosophers, and many of his apparent contradictions resolve themselves out, many dark places become light. And this is true simply because Blake as a devout Christian, as a mystic, as an artist, living a semiretired and almost saintly life, brought up on the beauties of Gothic art, perhaps not unfamiliar with the traditions of religious art in the Orient, which is closer to medieval art than the late Renaissance ever was, could not help but live in the same kind of intellectual climate as a Saint Thomas, or a Saint Augustine, or a Saint Francis. His thought cannot but become clearer by comparison with theirs.

But if we approach him as materialists and skeptics—as his enemies, Blake will mock us as he mocked many of his unenlightened friends, teasing us with more and more extravagant visions until we are forced to walk away shaking our heads and murmuring like Dr. Trusler:

"Blake, dim'd with superstition."

BIBLIOGRAPHY

Berger, Pierre, *William Blake, Mysticisme et Poésie*, Paris, Société Française d'Imprimerie et de Librairie, 1907.

Bhagavadgita, The, translated with notes by John Davis, London, Trubner, 1882.

Blake, William, *The Writings of William Blake*, 3 volumes, Edward Geoffrey Keynes, London, Nonesuch Press, 1925.

Boucher, de la Richardière, G., *Bibliothèque Universelle des Voyages*, 4 volumes, Paris, Treutel et Wurtz, 1808.

Brailsford, H. N., *Shelley, Godwin and their Circle*, New York, Henry Holt, 1925.

Bruce, Harold, *William Blake in This World*, London, Jonathan Cape, 1925.

Bryant, Jacob, *A new System, or an Analysis of Ancient Mythology*, 2 volumes, London, T. Payne, 1774.

Burdett, Osbert, *William Blake*, London, Macmillan, 1926.

Coleridge, Samuel T., *Letters*, edited by E. H. Coleridge, Boston, Houghton Mifflin, 1895.

Coomaraswamy, Ananda K., *The Transformation of Nature in Art*, Cambridge, Massachusetts, The Harvard University Press, 1934.

Damon, S. Foster, *William Blake, His Philosophy and Symbols*, London, Constable, 1924.

de Selincourt, Basil, *William Blake*, London, Duckworth, 1909.

Eliot, T. S., *The Sacred Wood*, London, Methuen, 1920.

Ellis, E. J., *The Real Blake*, London, Chatto and Windus, 1907.

Fry, Roger, *Vision and Design*, London, Chatto and Windus, 1920.

Gardner, Charles, *William Blake the Man*, London, J. M. Dent, 1919.

Garratt, G. T., editor, *The Legacy of India*, Oxford, Clarendon Press, 1937.

Gilchrist, Alexander, *The Life of William Blake*, edited by W. Graham Robertson, London, New York, John Lane, 1907.

Jones, Sir Wiliam, *Works*, 13 volumes, London, John Stockdale, 1807.

Keynes, Geoffrey, editor, *A Bibliography of William Blake*, New York, Grolier Club of New York, 1921.

Maritain, Jacques, *Art and Scholasticism*, translated by J. F. Scanlan, New York, Scribners, 1930.

M'Crindle, J. W., *The Invasion of India by Alexander the Great*, Westminster, Archibald Constable, 1896.

Middleton Murry, J., *William Blake*, London, Jonathan Cape, 1933.

More, Paul Elmer, *Shelburne Essays*, 4th series, New York, Putnam's, 1907.

Ogden, C. K., Richards, I. A., Wood, James, *The Foundations of Aesthetics*, London, Allen and Unwin, 1922.

Percival, Milton O., *William Blake's Circle of Destiny*, New York, Columbia University Press, 1938.

Philostratus, *In Honor of Apollonius of Tyana*, translated by J. S. Phillimore, 2 volumes, Oxford, Clarendon Press, 1912.

Plato, *Republic*, translated by John Llewellyn Davies and David James Vaughan, London, Macmillan, 1923.

Plotinus, *On Beauty, Enneads I-VI*, translated by Stephen McKenna, Library of Philosophical Transactions, London, Medici Society, 1916.

Porphyry, *Select Works*, translated by Thomas Taylor, London, Thomas Rodd, 1823.

Robinson, Henry Crabb, *Diary*, edited by T. Sadler, 2 volumes, Boston, Fields Osgood, 1869.

Saurat, Denis, *Blake and Milton*, London, Stanley Nott, 1935.

　　　　　Blake and Modern Thought, New York, Lincoln MacVeagh, The Dial Press, 1929.

Spurgeon, Caroline, *Mysticism in English Poetry*, Cambridge, University Press, 1913.

St. Thomas Aquinas, *Summa Theologica*, translated by the Fathers of the English Dominican Province, London, Burns Oates and Washbourne, 1922.

Symons, Arthur, *William Blake*, New York, Dutton, 1907.

Tatham, Frederick, *Letters of William Blake together with a Life by F. Tatham*, edited by Archibald Russell, London, Methuen, 1906.

Taylor, Thomas, *Selected Works of Plotinus and Extracts from a Treatise of Synesius on Providence*, London, Black, 1817.

Whitaker, Thomas, *The Neo-Platonists*, 2nd edition, Cambridge, University Press, 1918.

Wilson, Mona, *The Life of William Blake*, London, Nonesuch Press, 1927.

Winckelmann, J. J., *Reflections on the Painting and Sculpture of the Greeks*, translated by Henry Fuseli, London, J. Millar, 1765.

Yeats, W. B., and Ellis, E. J., *Works of William Blake with a Memoir and Interpretation*, 3 volumes, London, Bernard Quaritch, 1893.

Young, Edward, *Conjectures on Original Composition*, in *Works*, 2 volumes, London, Tegg, 1854, Volume 2, page 547 ff.

APPENDIX II
EARLY BOOK REVIEWS
(1938–40)

HUXLEY AND THE ETHICS OF PEACE

> "Before I go off into my trance I concentrate on the subject I wish to be inspired about. Let us say I am writing about the humble heroisms; for ten minutes before I go into the trance, I think of nothing but orphans supporting their little brothers and sisters, of dull work patiently done, and I focus my mind on such great philosophical truths as the purification and uplifting of the soul through suffering, and the alchemical transformation of leaden evil into golden good. Then I pop off. Two or three hours later I wake up again and find that inspiration has done its work. Thousands of words, comforting and uplifting words, lie before me. I type them out neatly on my machine and they are ready for the printer."
>
> Aldous Huxley, *Crome Yellow,* 1922

The publication of *Eyeless in Gaza* filled American and English readers with perplexity over what they chose to call the "New Huxley"; and they gave that adjective, "new," all the quaint, sinister implications it possesses in "new thought" and "new Jerusalem." This is more than ever true since the publication of his latest book, *Ends and Means,* in which he makes a statement that is heresy in our day: that it is impossible to live without a metaphysics.

Since this is an article about Huxley, not about philosophy, it is expedient to take this statement for granted. What it is more relevant to show here is that it is not a new statement on Huxley's lips, and consequently offers no good reason for so many dropped jaws and such patronizing astonishment.

It is important to show that the Huxley in *Ends and Means* is not so new, after all, because the accusation implies no small inconsistency on his part. He is supposed to have abandoned safe, scientific ground and retreated towards magic. He is supposed to be at one, now, with the Barbecue Smith he satirized in the quoted passage from *Crome Yellow.*

A review of *Ends and Means,* by Aldous Huxley (New York: Harper, 1937).
This article appeared in the March 1938 issue of *The Columbia Review.*

Why must it be imagined that, in sketching this charlatan, he was flaying a mystic? On the contrary, it is evident that he was, as usual, satirizing vulgarity, stupidity, sham. And to suppose that Huxley would not be prepared to laugh at the sticky, Oxford-groupish falseness of Barbecue Smith today would be as absurd as saying that when he laughed at the biologist sweating away on his stationary bicycle at the end of *Antic Hay,* it meant that he didn't "believe in biology." Besides, it is apparent that the critics who were so astounded by the demise of a materialist in *Ends and Means* had either never read, or else forgotten, *Those Barren Leaves,* published only a few years after *Crome Yellow,* in which Huxley leaves an interesting, not unsympathetic character, Calamy, meditating quite mystically in his own Thebaid. Indeed, we have every reason to believe that Huxley was as interested in mysticism, particularly Buddhist mysticism, then as he is now.

Whatever change there has been can only be expressed in terms of development, of expansion. To talk of it as if it were the minor, personal revolution of a lecher suddenly running to the cloister (which is what the critics have done) is to confess unfamiliarity with most of Huxley's books.

It is true enough that the Huxley of *Point Counter Point* had nothing to preach, but preferred to remain satisfied, as a whole, with what has been called "mechanomorphism." This philosophy is content with a pointless universe, accepts things as they are, finds enough satisfaction in work and diversions to fill up life. It is a good enough philosophy, but one that tends to break down under strain and uncertainty. It is a philosophy that goes better with prosperity than depressions, and Huxley himself has probably always realized that it was a rationalization especially appropriate to the twenties, and to the reaction against Victorian customs, in particular those surrounding sexual intercourse.

Since 1929, there are many who have abandoned this pleasant and after all sensible kind of skepticism and run to the cover of various religious or nationalistic dogmas that have far less philosophic or scientific soundness. Biology and economics in their most elementary forms have been hashed up into various theories of the sovereign state to fill our uncritical need for some kind of philosophy. And Huxley is one of the few who has avoided the inconsistency of transferring his belief to one of the popular fetishes. Ortega y Gasset remarked:

"If a man believes in rationalism in the way people believe in the holy Virgin of the Pilar, it means that he has fundamentally ceased to believe in rationalism."

Society has changed remarkably in the last ten years. Millions have regressed, in their beliefs, from monotheism to the worship of local fetishes, national symbols. And the unintelligent, flooded with the propaganda of hate, are taught that certain superstitions about race or class are "scientific." It is logical and consistent that the mind which, in *Point Counter Point,* was able, principally by taste, intuition, and good sense, to detect sham and pastiche, should have continued to develop along those lines toward *Ends and Means.*

The most shocking newness about *Ends and Means* may, perhaps, be run to earth between the two virtues that Huxley places above all others: they are Intelligence and Love.

There can be no possible doubt that Intelligence was always the highest of virtues in Huxley's eyes. And his treatment of Intelligence as a virtue, in *Ends and Means,* follows the same pattern as his treatment of it in other books. His ideas about propaganda, for instance, were quite fully expressed in the *Olive Tree* and *Beyond the Mexique Bay,* but were foreshadowed in practically every book he ever wrote. *Beyond the Mexique Bay* develops practically the same ideas on peace and nationalism as *Ends and Means,* but this is one topic, perhaps, on which Huxley was not quite so clear in his earliest work.

After all, what shocks us more perhaps than anything is the fact that Huxley puts Love by the side of Intelligence at the head of all the virtues. And the fact that we are shocked is as much a question of language as anything else.

In any context of social control, the word Love has so often been used by charlatans, evangelists, and movie producers that it is less convincing than the better advertised patent medicines. But, besides this, the impression has always prevailed that Love, in a book by Huxley, stood for a mixture of Darwin, Metchnikov, and Crébillon fils. It was all glands, but it also manifested itself, socially, as seduction, a game rather like chess.

In *Ends and Means,* Love is a shorthand term for a number of things that are hard to understand because they rest on assumptions utterly alien to the philosophy of rugged individualism. Love, in Huxley, stands for something that is just about diametrically opposed to fascism. Understanding this symbol implies familiarity with lines of reasoning and sets of values that are mostly Oriental. It implies a discipline, both physical and intellectual, which seems impossible in a society that bases its conduct on movies, novels, radios, editorials, and magazines: in other words, savage incantation that merely lacks the aesthetic qualities inherent in some kinds of voodoo.

The word implies negation of all those values which go to make up a military hero, a successful advertising man, a movie star. It means denial of ambition, self-assertion, or even that seemingly harmless exhibitionism inseparable from a society where men are judged by their material possessions.

It is related to the Buddhist doctrine that separateness is synonymous with pain, and that such manifestations of "separateness" as anger, greed, self assertion, or even boasting are the lowest degradation.

But over against the values emphasized by Gautama, Confucius, Tsze-Sze, and Lao-Tsu, which combined to shelter most of China from disastrous wars for centuries at a time, we have all the varied Western systems of organized paranoia, where Napoleons and Caesars are gods, Hitlers, and Caligulas, Mussolinis and Tiberii get themselves worshiped in their own lifetime. Here all political philosophies are based on gangsterdom or tyranny, and consequently, there seem to be no methods of achieving social change that do not rely on violence.

Thus we are still in the position where "just one more war" will save everything, either from communism or from fascism: we are told that we have to resort to violence in order to choose between two kinds of violent dictatorship.

So long as men continue to worship Caesars and Napoleons, Caesars and Napoleons will duly rise and make them miserable. The proper attitude toward the hero is not Carlyle's but Bacon's. "He doth like the ape," wrote Bacon of the ambitious tyrant, "He doth like the ape, that, the higher he climbes the more he shows his ars. The heroe's qualities are brilliant, but so is the mandril's rump."

There are many critics who have chosen to quarrel with the above and its corollary, that you cannot abolish violence with violence. Huxley's plausible reason is that to practice violence is to train for more violence. An unscathed war veteran is the best material, if he is still young enough, for war. And however much he may be disposed toward peace, he will still retain much that is warlike in his ways of doing things, in his habits and his beliefs, the rationalizations he will pass on to his children.

The only two virtues that can never have anything to do with war are these two, Love and Intelligence. This is axiomatic. These virtues must therefore dominate any system of ethics framed to exclude war.

Huxley's plan of action is clear and uncompromising. But it depends on cultivation of a discipline and training that seem difficult to the point of asceticism in this overstimulated age. He postulates the necessity of education in this discipline before anything effective can be done to build a stable, civilized society once again. The purpose of this training would be to promote intelligence and "awareness," the latter being possibly best described as a combination of complete self-possession along with complete lack of self-consciousness, a superior variety of conscious self-control. He is very much indebted, in this, to the work of F. Matthias Alexander, which is not as well known as it deserves to be, although it has had considerable influence on the thought of John Dewey among others.

This awareness constitutes a sound weapon against propaganda because it depends on freedom from addiction to all the current mental narcotics, from the funny sheet to speeches about the constitution.

It also depends on a certain detachment, the love of intellectual curiosity for its own sake. All that Huxley postulates is that we should love wisdom enough to behave like wise men, a point that Henry Hazlitt saw fit to obscure completely in the Sunday *New York Times* review of *Ends and Means.*

Under these conditions, non-violence and non-cooperation, including boycott and folded arms strike, would even gain in effectiveness.

Ends and Means is, in fact, much more than the book that was being prepared by Anthony Beavis, the hero of *Eyeless in Gaza*. In a sense, it is a clear, persuasive summary of the main ideas and much of the learning that has delighted Huxley's readers since the publication of his first book. As long as these ideas were mere casual fragments, in essays, or the conversations of his characters, no one thought that they had to be justified or defended. It is strange that they should now require explanation or defense. More than strange, it is a little frightening; for if such simple truths have to be justified, it means that readers are so accustomed to the raving of fanatics that the voice of a civilized man has come to sound unconvincing and thin.

JOHN CROWE RANSOM—
STANDARDS FOR CRITICS

Mr. Ransom has written a distinguished book about poetry—a volume of essays that consider the subject from various standpoints, dealing now with the aesthetics of poetry, now the theory of criticism as well as with poetry itself. He has chosen examples for discussion from Milton, Shakespeare, and Donne, as well as from different levels of contemporary poetry represented by T. S. Eliot and Edna St. Vincent Millay.

Turning to aesthetic theory, he examines Plato and Aristotle and finds occasion to disagree with two significant moderns, I. A. Richards and George Santayana. But he has not attempted to give us any systematic theory of literary criticism. The book is simply intended as a collection of ideas that may serve as a basis for some such system.

His ideas are characterized by the word "reactionary," in a technical not political sense. Where poetry is concerned—and that is all that concerns us here—the word implies stress on form and technique and a distaste for homiletics in poetry. Mr. Ransom dislikes, for instance, the poetry of vague moods that associates romantic landscapes with man's fate and ends on a moral text.

One of his best arguments against the romantics develops out of his examination of Milton's "Lycidas," which is, of course, a pastoral poem. The pastoral type, with its rigid conventions, forced the poet to step out of his own personality and to put on a mask for poetic purposes. Mr. Ransom points out what a valuable technical resource this "anonymity" was: and this was one of the first things the romantics threw away. Expanding this idea into that of "aesthetic distance," the author describes it as a process in which the poet inhibits direct response to the object in order to approach it in a roundabout way through convention and form. The advantages of this "technique of restraint" must be obvious detachment, objectivity, control of the material, and so on.

Going deeper into the subject, he attempts a definition of poetry in

---

A review of *The World's Body,* by John Crowe Ransom (Scribners), first published in *The New York Herald Tribune,* May 8, 1938. It was later included in *A Thomas Merton Reader,* ed. Thomas P. McDonnell (New York: Harcourt, Brace & World, 1962).

terms of cognition. It is a kind of knowledge, and a knowledge that cannot be gained by any other means, for the poet is concerned with the aspects of experience that can never be well described but only reproduced or imitated.

However, for long periods at a time men have attempted to repeat, in poetry, the conclusions of science or philosophy, with the result that a great number of poems are badly disguised sermons and not much more. This Mr. Ransom calls the "poetry of ideas" or "Platonic poetry," and it forms a category large enough to hold the traditional enemies, Pope and Wordsworth, at the same time.

Besides this, there is pure, or "physical," poetry, of which Imagism is one type, but the works he finds most significant are those he classifies as metaphysical. He has stretched this term considerably in order to include Milton and some of Shakespeare. This is architecturally the finest and soundest poetry.

This brings the reviewer to the essay "Shakespeare at Sonnets," which will certainly make many of Mr. Ransom's readers angry. It is one of the most stimulating essays in the book, not only because it is a bit startling, but because it is one in which Mr. Ransom examines specific poems instead of poetry in the abstract. Recognizing that Shakespeare's greatness can withstand any attack, he sets upon the sonnets with all his force. He begins bluntly by showing that they are badly constructed, which may be true enough. And then, they are diffuse, self-indulgent pieces of emotionalism: not only that, but he blames Shakespeare for most of the bad romantic poetry that has been written since his time. Naturally Shakespeare cannot too seriously be held responsible for his bad imitators. But there is more: as soon as he has finished Shakespeare off as a romantic, he sets him up as a metaphysical in order to demolish him all over again for not being as good as Donne. This attack is unfortunate in its unnecessary and disproportionate violence, but that does not mean that it is uninteresting or, especially, false. It is simply unnecessary; Mr. Ransom is only saying, after all, that Donne is a better lyric poet than Shakespeare, and he will easily find many who will agree with him on that. It is not necessary to try to demolish the sonnets in order to prove it: and besides, he has pitted Shakespeare against Donne in the latter's own well-fortified territory.

It is clear that the further Mr. Ransom gets from poetry, the less sure he is of himself. The closer he is to actual works of art the more are his statements clear, succinct, and provocative.

VLADIMIR NABOKOV—
REALISM AND ADVENTURE

Laughter in the Dark, written by a Russian emigré living in Paris, has already enjoyed some acclaim in Europe under the title of *Camera Obscura,* and, indeed, it is a strange, exciting, and unusual book. It does not lack vitality, but, as the story closes, its vitality simply resolves itself into a kind of crazy hectic movement across a plane surface—like oil burning on the face of a pond.

Stated baldly, the plot is both tragic and familiar. It is the story of a man, Albinus is his name, who was "rich, respectable, happy: one day he abandoned his wife for the sake of a youthful mistress: he loved, was not loved, and his life ended in disaster." The author, however, treats this theme more and more in the comic manner as his story goes on. This is, of course, a harder task, and one which he does not finish with complete success.

The book begins well and holds us as long as the author does not commit himself to either a tragic or a comic tone of voice. Here we watch the pathetic, rich little puritan Albinus being drawn out of his respectable orbit by the girl, Margot. We can understand how it happens. We are aware of her fascination and are not unable to appreciate Albinus' discontent with his comfortable life when this is pointed out to us. And as we follow the rapid movements of these two about the windy, rainy Berlin streets, we are never sure if we love or hate the lovers, or admire or despise them. Far from being a fault, it is this ambiguity which keeps the book alive, and once the author resolves it, he robs his book of most of its reality. At the climax of the story the least convincing of the major characters is introduced: one wordly cynical fellow by the name of Rex. Here the author comes out openly for comedy. Albinus goes into a decline and takes the whole book with him. From now on we are sure he is too much of a fool to be pitied and that Margot is far too sluttish to remain even a

---

A review of *Laughter in the Dark,* by Vladimir Nabokov (Bobbs-Merrill), published in *The New York Herald Tribune,* May 15, 1938. It was subsequently included in *A Thomas Merton Reader,* ed. Thomas P. McDonnell (New York: Harcourt, Brace & World, 1962).

little bit fascinating. Uncompromising comedy has thrown too strong a light on them, and their transparencies become too obvious.

However, it is amusing enough to watch Rex, who is a very unpleasant character, use Horner's trick from Wycherley's comedy *The Country Wife* to replace Albinus in Margot's affections while Albinus continues to support him. But Albinus finds out: Margot talks him out of shooting her, for the moment. Before much else can happen he gets a broken head in an automobile accident and goes blind.

So she bundles him off to the Swiss Alps. Rex, who has announced he is going to America, follows them to Switzerland, where he contrives to live with Margot in the same chalet with Albinus, without the blind man finding out. And, as if the dexterity required for this were not enough to keep Rex amused, he has to invent a lot of practical jokes to play on the poor fellow.

It is here that the author has outdone himself, for Rex's jokes are at the same time stupid and frightful. But we are neither amused nor horrified, because they carry little conviction. Rex is too artificial a character for his actions and ideas to have much force: they are uninteresting, and so is he. Mr. Nabokov lacks the finesse of a Gide or a Huxley in describing an intellectual cad. Rex is little more than a story-book cynic.

However, a word about the style. This is a rapid, colorful, lively, and frequently witty book. The author has a keen eye for movement and outline. In two words he can create the image of a girl getting out of a wet coat or a goalkeeper in a hockey game. The economy and justness of his observation of externals are as striking as the speed and facility with which he tells his story.

JOHN COWPER POWYS—
IN PRAISE OF BOOKS

When Mr. Powys calls his book *The Enjoyment of Literature* he really means what he says. Not only does he take us through all the rich fields of poetry, drama, and fiction from Aeschylus to Hardy and from Job to Proust, but his introduction is, itself, one of the most delightful and enthusiastic essays in praise of books that it is possible to find anywhere.

Yet he has set himself not only the task of celebrating the wonders of great literature but also that of finding out the philosophies of the great writers he praises. These two threads of investigation and appreciation run through the whole book. He ties them together in the conclusion, where he speaks briefly of literature and life. So, rather than a collection of random essays, the work is a well-knit unity.

This, of course, gives him another opportunity to enlarge upon the philosophy, or rather religion, for which he is well known: that is, a vague paganism that detests all doctrine, all metaphysics, all scientific rationalism, and only seeks to enjoy sensuous and emotional richness wherever it can be found. Now Mr. Powys is entitled to talk about his beliefs if he wants to, but we must remember that the judgments he makes, in its light, are not strictly speaking literary criticism.

So, when he tempers his praise of the *Divine Comedy* by calling it "wicked" and "diabolical" he means that the undefeatable logic which dooms pagans to Hell is distasteful to him because, as a pagan, he would rather see the pagans in Paradise. At the same time he does not speak of Goethe's *Faust* as diabolical, but on the contrary, he looks to it for "assistance in our mental and emotional quandaries." He prefers the way Goethe's vague pantheism understands the world to the kind of understanding offered, for example, by Dante's Catholicism or, on the other hand, by any positivistic or rationalistic system you would care to mention. Then the orgies of *Walpurgisnacht* and the whole dark mystical universe peopled with demons and satyrs are more congenial to his own unsystematized mythology than Christian orthodoxy or cold, scientific

A review of *The Enjoyment of Literature,* by John Cowper Powys (Simon and Schuster), published in *The New York Herald Tribune,* November 20, 1938.

skepticism. But, of course, he does not decide the greatness of a work of art by the beliefs it expresses. In fact, for him, the three greatest of all writers are Homer, Shakespeare, and Rabelais. In Rabelais it is not only the man's boundless appetite for life that appeals to him, but also his bookishness, the delight in learning for its own sake that makes him truly what he is.

The task of discovering Shakespeare's message is, at best, an unrewarding one, but Mr. Powys embarks on it with the excuse that if we can determine what Shakespeare believed, we may, possibly, find out why his personality is completely submerged in his plays.

And the reason is, he says, that Shakespeare's philosophy was a mixture of agnosticism and superstition and was therefore so completely the philosophy of the common man that he not only easily projected himself into his characters but became entirely lost in them. By this token Shakespeare uttered his philosophy through Hamlet and through Polonius, too, and contradicted himself so often that we may wonder if he believed everything or nothing at all. And this is not very helpful.

From the first pages of the introduction the reader notices the similarity of Mr. Powys' style to Herman Melville's, and, indeed, in his essay on Melville the author claims to be a "congenital disciple of the particular kind of imagination, both mystic and realistic, both monstrous and grotesque, that was so natural to Melville." So his analysis of Melville is very interesting indeed. He dwells particularly on Meville's "humor," a humor that never aims at being funny but is rather a great naïve buffoonery, expressed in rich, fantastic language, with undertones of inarticulate pessimism. He mentions the obvious comparison between Melville and Sir Thomas Browne: it is a pity he did not contrast him with Rabelais.

This is by no means a book that pretends to teach us how to read. It is addressed to those who already love books, and they will certainly enjoy it. It is not necessary to agree with everything he says: Mr. Powys has chosen a subject in which an author may say what he pleases, provided only he loves his subject and talks about it well.

CHRISTINE HERTER—
IN DEFENSE OF ART

Miss Herter calls her book a "defense" of art, but she emphatically believes the best kind of defense is an attack. So she condemns not only contemporary critics, like Roger Fry, John Dewey, Thomas Craven, Herbert Read, and Sheldon Cheyney, but also all the modern "abstract" and "expressionist" painters.

Modern critics, she says, have done altogether too much theorizing about art without really understanding it: they use too many long, vague words; they appear to be full of deep wisdom, but they are really only obscure. They exaggerate half-truths about art, they misunderstand the function of art, and they attribute to dead artists aims and ideas they can never possibly have had.

Now the artist is not primarily a theorist, as Miss Herter points out. As often as not he is entirely unconcerned with abstract principles. When he paints a picture his task is not to develop some new theory of color or form but to paint a good picture, that is, one in which the relation of parts to the whole, of the subject to its treatment, is harmonious, significant, and delightful. But the fact remains that he treats his material according to his own lights and his own abilities. Forms and ideas in the artist's mind predetermine the final form his work will take on.

Now Miss Herter contends that Cézanne was a good artist solely because of the intensity of his absorption in his subjects, but that his distinctive treatment of nature was not deliberate or studied; rather, it was an inveterate clumsiness in him. This stupid ineptness of his hampered his attempts to represent natural forms, and his paintings were only "broken fragments of what he hoped to achieve." In the same way El Greco's characteristic distortion was a weakness he could not conquer. Miss Herter attributes it to defective eyesight.

If the artists themselves were, or should have been, ashamed of these failings, the critics have gone to extremes in elaborating on them and so

---

A review of *Defense of Art,* by Christine Herter (W. W. Norton), published in the December 25, 1938, issue of *The New York Herald Tribune.*

creating theories which allow a Picasso or a Matisse to commit any outrage he pleases. Miss Herter hates these two and all their disciples; she plainly thinks they are fakes.

We are very clear, then, what *Defense of Art* attacks, but it is much harder to find out what it defends. Random references to "Tradition" are only vague and unsatisfactory clues. We gather that Tradition embraces Paolo Uccello, Leonardo da Vinci, and Manet. But these painters are not defended, except we know that for Miss Herter "traditional" implies praise rather than abuse. While she has uncovered many of the weaknesses of contemporary criticism and scolds the critics with great fervor and sincerity, yet she remains no less confusing than she accuses them of being.

AGNES ADDISON—
LOVE OF CHANGE FOR ITS OWN SAKE

Miss Addison has written an interesting study of the connection between Post-Reformation Gothic architecture and the growth of Romanticism in literature. She begins by discussing some of the 11,396 different definitions of Romanticism, selects half a dozen of them for very summary consideration, and finally decides upon one which fits her topic. As far as she is concerned, Romanticism is the "love of change for its own sake."

Then she briefly describes the development of various Romantic (or pre-Romantic) tendencies in eighteenth-century England, paying particular attention to the growing interest in the Gothic and the medieval. "Gothic," she reminds us, was first used as a term of abuse synonymous with "barbaric"; but soon Young's *Night Thoughts* or Gray's "Elegy" were to express a change in the taste of the age and a new delight in the eerie and mysterious effect produced by Gothic buildings or old ruins in an appropriate natural setting. Then the poet Shenstone embellished his gardens in Warwickshire with a "ruined Priory" and the aristocrat Horace Walpole made the Middle Ages acceptable in polite society by remodeling Strawberry Hill in what he conceived to be the Gothic manner. Finally the Romantic poets and the Anglicans of the Oxford Movement helped to produce the great Gothic revival with which we are familiar.

Now this ground has already been well covered by scholars and critics of English literature, so Miss Addison's eighteenth-century material, while interesting, is nothing new. It simply serves as a valuable introduction to the main part of her book, where she contemplates the dubious, graceless glory of Victorian Gothic at its zenith.

Miss Addison has done the student of nineteenth-century art and ideas no mean service in emphasizing the importance of the younger Pugin to the architecture of his time. His emphasis on sound construction and organic ornament anticipates the work of Viollet-le-Duc and, like Henry Adams, he was one of the rare souls who understood Gothic art from its

A review of *Romanticism and the Gothic Revival*, by Agnes Addison (Richard B. Smith), published in *The New York Times*, January 29, 1939.

very roots. If we have forgotten him, it is because Ruskin, who was no architect and was responsible for the plague of "streaky bacon" Gothic in England, sneered him almost out of existence. Miss Addison points out how much Ruskin really owed to Pugin and does much to correct the popular error that Ruskin engineered the whole Gothic revival by himself.

If the chapters on the Gothic in France, Germany, and America are sketchy, nevertheless her treatment of this one issue, the relative importance of Pugin and Ruskin, makes Miss Addison's book valuable to specialists as well as interesting to the general reader. Occasionally she makes flat, dogmatic statements of cause and effect where only the vaguest of influences can be discerned. There does not by any means exist so plain a cause and effect relationship between Romantic nationalism and Gothic architecture as Miss Addison speaks of in her concluding chapter. Naturally the two tendencies are often related, but to state, categorically, that the Gothic revival is *the expression* of nationalistic sentiments can only lead to confusion and error.

R. H. S. CROSSMAN—
RESTAGING THE *REPUBLIC*

The title of this book might lead us to suspect it contained a discussion of Plato's followers in philosophy today or, perhaps, of the part played by Plato in our own intellectual and political chaos. But it is nothing so technical: Mr. Crossman has chosen a rather more fanciful task, calling up the historical Plato out of Hades and confronting him with various figures of our own day in an attempt to "restage the *Republic* in modern dress." It would take a man with much more active imagination than Mr. Crossman's and a more brilliant wit, and much more assurance and expertness in the handling of dialogue, to do this job well. But unfortunately, this is not all he attempts to do.

He had the wisdom to confine himself for more than half the book to the history of philosophy, in which he himself has received the training of an expert. He devotes his earlier chapters to a keen and succinct study of Plato and Socrates against the background of decadent Greek civilization, showing that the decadence of Athens was in many ways analogous to our own. A quotation from Thucydides on the use of power politics against Melos reveals a situation very similar to that in which Czechoslovakia perished last autumn. Now Plato devoted his life to an unsparing critique of his dying civilization, when Athens was struggling to preserve freedom without anarchy; trying to stifle class war, fighting against atheism, greed, and political corruption. Excellent as his diagnosis may, at times, have been, yet when he had a chance to administer his cures in the city-state of Syracuse, they all failed.

The *Republic* offers too simple a solution to the problem of class war, suggesting it can be forestalled by two things: taking away all political freedom from the "civilians" and taking away all property from the rulers. Now, since the rulers are "philosopher-kings," they will naturally want no reward anyway. And, although the ignorant will be kept so by force and noble lies, yet we know they will always be treated justly, since the philosopher-king is assumed to be as impartial as an adding machine. In one

A review of *Plato Today*, by R. H. S. Crossman (Oxford University Press), published in *The New York Herald Tribune*, March 19, 1939.

respect the *Republic* should be anathema to liberals; but Mr. Crossman does not point out that Plato and the liberals agree on at least one thing, that human reason is capable of being infallibly correct and impartially just.

As soon as the author finishes this preliminary analysis of the *Republic* he embarks upon the second part of the book, and the whole thing changes completely. Plato himself appears and strikes up a conversation with a member of Parliament. His Majesty's Government comes in for little more than mild irony, and finally Plato, with the gestures of a bad amateur magician whisks the "democratic" mask off Britain and reveals— the scarcely less kindly face of "Benevolent Oligarchy." America is treated rather more harshly in a dialogue on education and a letter on the New Deal. But we are left with a feeling that the notorious lightheadedness of our nation could have been better satirized than it is in this same old string of stale and obvious jokes.

This second part, however, is not uniformly bad. There are great fluctuations from the poorest attempts at Socratic irony to some of the most excellent critical analysis. There is a splendid digression on slavery in Athens, and the discussion of the relations between Plato's *Republic* and the dictatorship of the proletatiat is both dispassionate and illuminating. The irony is perhaps least bad in the chapter on Nazism.

Mr. Crossman has many ideas which would have gained from a strictly prosaic and critical presentation, such as a chapter on "Why Plato Failed."

Plato, says our author, too glibly supposed that the common man was unreasonable and incapable of self-government. And he took it for granted too readily that there existed a constant supply of supremely wise potential rulers in the landed gentry. Finally he believed human reason was so godike as to be capable of infallibility. Because of these and other flaws in Plato, less sincere, less scrupulous, and less philosophical persons can take up the *Republic* and turn it into a complete apologia for power politics, although Plato himself hated military dictatorship and continually denounced it.

Mr. Crossman has to admit in his epilogue that he was forced into the position of devil's advocate in order to show that, in spite of Plato's greatness as a metaphysician, and in spite of the fact (he believes) that the *Republic* is one of the greatest books on political science, yet we must not let ourselves be duped by the mistakes Plato's exaggerated idealism led him to commit.

WILLIAM NELSON—
JOHN SKELTON, SCHOLAR, POET AND SATIRIST

John Skelton is one of the great English satirists; but in his own time he was a famous scholar, almost as renowned as Erasmus and Sir Thomas More. Besides that, he was a man of almost legendary wit. So great was his reputation as a humorist that his biographer has to deal with a mass of apocryphal stories, probably the product of that familiar trick of tagging jokes with the names of famous wits. We have not abandoned the practice, for how many of our modern stories begin with the words: "Dorothy Parker said—"?

However, Skelton's great reputation for wit, for poetry, and for scholarship perished within a century. In his language, in his Catholicism and in his hatred for the "new men," the parvenus, he belonged more to the Middle Ages than to the Renaissance. Yet the poets of our own time have rediscovered him: Robert Graves and Richard Hughes have imitated his verse. W. H. Auden has written about him and shows his influence. Skelton has been enjoying a kind of vogue. This vogue has been accompanied by good criticism, but only a very slight amount of it. J. M. Berdan discusses Skelton in *Early Tudor Poetry*, Hughes and Auden have essays on him, and that has been all there was to read, of any value, about Skelton up until now. Mr. Nelson, only indirectly influenced by the fact that Skelton happens to be in fashion, has written the first full-length biographical study of the poet against his background. His book is the fruit of painstaking research and frequently brilliant scholarship and makes a valuable contribution to the study of Tudor literary history.

Skelton's reputation for scholarship won him the position of Royal Tutor in the court of Henry VII, where he taught the arts of grammar, rhetoric, and government to the Duke of York. But the pupil grew up and was crowned Henry VIII, forgot his lessons, and turned his ear to wicked counsel. Skelton's bitter satires are all aimed at the *Realpolitik* of Cardinal Wolsey. Mr. Nelson's first chapter, then, is a study of humanism at the court of Henry VII, for it is not generally known that humanistic

---

A review of *John Skelton, Laureate*, by William Nelson (Columbia University Press), published in *The New York Times*, May 28, 1939.

studies flourished under this king a generation before Erasmus and More. Ciceronian Latin had become a diplomatic necessity, and it was cultivated in England by a rather tedious group of continental grammarians. There is, indeed, no injustice in rating that age a literary backwater; and, although Skelton was among these Ciceronians, and was a better grammarian than many who came after him, what is really important is that he developed into the best poet England had seen since Chaucer. It seems, however, that the sixteenth century scarcely distinguished between accomplishment in rhetoric and in poetry.

Skelton's real greatness is in the clangor of the rough, rocking verse style he invented. The drone and beat of a prolonged sequence of short lines rhyming five and six together produces effects that are to be found in medieval Latin poetry; in fact, J. M. Berdan has an attractive theory linking Skelton to accentual Latin verse. Mr. Nelson rejects this theory only to better it by tracing "Skeltonics" not to any verse (for this would mean ignoring many prosodic irregularities) but to rhymed Latin prose. This is a brilliant and original theory, and, thanks to the recent discovery of a short treatise by Skelton in Latin prose, Mr. Nelson succeeds in proving his point conclusively.

The book attacks and solves many other problems having a much more limited scope. The date of the poet's birth, and dates of his poems, his life as a parish priest, his life as Henry VIII's court poet, and his conflict with Wolsey are studied in detail. Careful and laborious research takes our author through everything from account books and parish registers to minor problems in astronomy; to say that the problems solved concern not the critic but the historian of literature, not poets but bibliographers, is not to disparage the work but merely to indicate its nature. Yet the book does suffer from the faults of the type to which it belongs, for it is not the biography of a man but the biography of some documents. The materials of the book are given to us raw. The style is completely colorless. Skelton's passionate, humorous, indignant, and tender personality only gets into the background of the book by force, and in spite of all the facts, dates, and figures appropriate to the arguments of scholars, Mr. Nelson, although he admires Skelton's poetry, refrains from talking about it, only discussing its history. But after all, the author himself explains he is aware of the limitations of such a study, and he is offering it not as a definitive biography but as the material for one. His research has been exhaustive, his analyses illuminating, and his conclusions eminently sound, so perhaps after all we are not entitled to ask more of him.

E. M. W. TILLYARD AND C. S. LEWIS—
A SPIRITED DEBATE ON POETRY

E. M. W. Tillyard has gained a considerable reputation for critical acumen in recent years by the publication of two studies of Milton and a more general work called *Poetry, Direct and Oblique;* while C. S. Lewis' *Allegory of Love* puts him in the front rank of scholars of English literature. It is therefore a not unimportant event to all readers, but especially to critics, when two such men hold a debate about the fundamentals of poetic theory. Such a controversy recently occupied space in several issues of an English scholarly journal and is now made accessible in an interesting little volume.

The discussion began with an article by Mr. Lewis, and from that article is taken the title of the book; and throughout the debate it is Mr. Lewis who dominates the whole subject, maintaining an intensity of conviction and a forcefulness of dialectic that his opponent cannot overcome. This is frequently so obvious, indeed, that Mr. Tillyard seems only to be presenting a mere foil for Mr. Lewis' ideas, which serves to clarify and strengthen them as the debate proceeds.

What is the question they are attempting to decide? Generally speaking, it is the relation of the poet to his work. It would be misleading to say they are trying to decide just what poetry is about, since most of the argument centers on one thing that Mr. Lewis maintains poetry is *not* about: and it is in this connection that he finds a use for his term *The Personal Heresy.*

What does this mean? It means the illusion we would be under if we read poetry mainly in order to find out what kind of man the poet was who wrote it. Reconstructing verses into personalities and using the images of poetry for the experiments of psychoanalysis constitute heresy. Of course, it is quite legitimate to psychoanalyze anybody you please, provided you are aware that this is not the same thing as "reading poetry." A poem may be read as a poem, as a philological document, and as a case history all at one time; yet its value as poetry cannot be judged in terms

---

A review of *The Personal Heresy*, by E. M. W. Tillyard and C. S. Lewis (Oxford University Press), was published in *The New York Times*, July 9, 1939.

of Freud or the history of the language. In the same way, grammarians and psychologists are not really concerned whether a poem is good or bad when they are using it to prove one of their theses. Now what Mr. Lewis condemns is the notion that poets are so concerned with their own state of mind as they write that it is really this their poems describe and not the things that are apparently being talked about. So, in the first pages of the book, he rates Mr. Tillyard a heretic for attaching too much importance to the theory that Milton, in describing Satan, was really describing himself. This theory may have some truth in it, but any disproportionate emphasis will falsify that truth and turn it into a source of stupid errors. So we see that Mr. Lewis is using the term "heresy" not ironically but in its technical and Catholic sense.

Some poems, however, cannot fail to communicate a vague idea of their author's personality. The verse of Donne proves him to be a different kind of a man from Milton. The imagery, the grammar, and the rhythms Blake loved proclaim him another kind of person than, say, Swinburne, who nevertheless admired him passionately. A poet like Marvell, even, has a very individual and personal kind of charm. It is hard not to imagine the man who wrote "A Portrait of Little T. C. in a Prospect of Flowers" as having a character made up of a singularly happy combination of attractive qualities. But such fancies must keep within a certain just proportion, for they are not part of the direct apprehension of poetry. That apprehension is the recapture of what the poet once apprehended, but not the reconstruction of his state of mind or of his character.

Besides, the poet in love and the lover he puts in his sonnet are never quite the same person, just as writing a poem to a beautiful woman is not the same kind of experience as making love to her. And then, both these experiences demand a heightening of intensity above the normal tenor of a poet's everyday life, in which he may be anything from a duke to an inspector of schools. Beyond these arguments, Mr. Lewis insists that a poet's personality is merely a starting point for his poetry and to study that personality is really only to study the limitations within which his poetry was written, not the poetry itself. The critics have fallen back on the catchwords of psychology in an unhappy compromise between complete materialism and the views of any religious person. Both these philosophies tend to discard the importance of the poet's personality, the one in favor of uncompromising determinism, the other by considering the human intellect open to divine illumination.

Mr. Tillyard's argument in favor of "personality" changes considerably under pressure of Mr. Lewis' arguments, but he does arrive at an interesting definition of his position. For him, contact with the poet's normal, everyday personality is an important part of any poem. This is not as simple as it sounds, for he is driven to exclude from this all items of literary gossip and details about the kind of shoes the poets wore and the kind of rooms they lived in. What he is talking about is described as a "mental pattern" which we can recognize in the poet's style, his imagery, his rhythm: Marvell is one of his examples. And when Keats compares oaks to senators in "Hyperion," it is the fact that he was prepared to do so that constitutes, for Mr. Tillyard, his personality. What is important, then, is to pay attention to "all the accumulated predispositions" that led up to just such a metaphor. These are, briefly, the two ways presented of looking at the main question, but in the later articles this yields its importance to another topic, one that is inseparable from the *Personal Heresy*.

One of the unfortunate results of that heresy is poet-worship. There are biographies of Keats and D. H. Lawrence that are simply exercises in hagiography. The tendency to make saints out of poets has been strong since the Romantic revival, and the debunking biographies that have grown up in the last century are merely the reverse of the medal. Mr. Lewis points out the confusion between the response of love or hatred, which is appropriate to personality, and that of imaginative enjoyment more proper to poetry itself. Mr. Tillyard's reply is the unconvincing one that although poetolatry is admittedly foolish, yet it may have the good result of inspiring its victim by the example of his poet surmounting the difficulties of this life. That may be all very well if the poet's name happens to be St. Francis of Assisi, but there we are out of the range of poet-worship.

In the last pages of the book each of the debaters finds something to say about the nature of poetry itself, and while the remarks are interesting and valuable on both sides, yet the main interest of the whole book lies in the discussion of this less usual topic of "personality." The urgency of such a discussion may be greater than Mr. Tillyard at first believed and, at any rate, this is a book which all critics of poetry should find time to consult.

HOXIE NEAL FAIRCHILD—
BACKGROUND OF ROMANTICISM

The title of this book may prove misleading to readers who are not aware that its author is a noted authority on the Romantic revival in literature. Professor Fairchild has written several volumes on the so-called "pre-Romantics"—the writers who laid the foundations for Romanticism even in the Classical golden age of the eighteenth century. This is another book of the same kind, and it is a detailed inductive study of every line of early eighteenth-century poetry that has the remotest claim to the name of "religious." The author's purpose is to find out whether an immense quantity of semireligious verse bore any relationship to the Romanticism of Coleridge and his contemporaries.

Professor Fairchild does not confine himself to "divine" poets. Indeed, his first chapter is devoted to atheists and libertines—men on the extreme periphery of his subject. The "divine" poets themselves he treats only in passing, as he does political pamphleteers. His true quarry is not such a man as the Calvinist hymnologist Isaac Watts but a more vaguely religious writer like Thomas Parnell, in whom sentimentality, love of nature, and the praise of genius combine with a vaguely religious mysticism to give us an admirable type of the pre-Romantic poet.

Where, we ask, did such poets find their origin?

After the Low Church won her final and most complete victory in 1688, the zeal of dissent was allowed to abate while Puritans and dissenters turned their hand to making money in the new and favorable situation they had created. Presently Low Church ardor became confused with political zeal; the Puritans, as quickly as they filled their pockets, turned into Whigs. The grim tenets of Calvinism yielded before a milder faith in materialism, commerce, and Isaac Newton.

This was an age in which religion reached a very low ebb in both the High Church and the Low; the bibulous parson is a familiar eighteenth-century figure. At this time, sentimentality, the cult of "feeling," and the love of nature began to assume an important place in poetry, because these

---

A review of *Religious Trends in English Poetry*, by Hoxie Neale Fairchild (Columbia University Press), published in *The New York Herald Tribune*, July 23, 1939.

little emotional luxuries provided your solid Whig with a necessary supplement to his lukewarm Deism, or to the kind of Christianity that was anemic enough for his "reason" to accept. At the same time, the Puritan concept of original sin was undergoing a subtle metamorphosis into the Romantic notion of original genius; and Newtonian physics, formulated in defense of Christianity, was now turned against it by the Deists.

Professor Fairchild's careful investigations show that the typical pre-Romantic sentimentalist is a Whig, a Deist, perhaps a vague pantheist. He admires Newton and, most important of all, he has a kind of pseudo-religious attitude which the author attributes to the degeneration of Protestantism into Whigery. In proportion as the dissenter lost faith in dogma, he allowed himself the luxuries of sentimental optimism or literary melancholy.

The conclusions reached in this, the first volume of a lengthier study, suggest, among other things, that the Communists today are the heirs of this Whig and Calvinist tradition.

Whether Professor Fairchild's investigations will take this course no one can predict; nor is it important to do so. But here is a book rich in valuable material for the historian of ideas to draw upon. It is the most detailed and voluminous work the author has attempted so far, and the most courageous, for he has had to wade through many volumes of the world's very worst poetry; but that is a historian's misfortune. Out of it all he has made a great contribution, perhaps his greatest contribution so far, to the history of the background of Romanticism.

G. WILSON KNIGHT—
THAT OLD DILEMMA OF GOOD AND EVIL

The poet William Blake despised Plato for seeing nothing in the world but "good and evil." Whether that aphorism expresses a true criticism of Plato does not matter: Blake's meaning is the important thing, and here the sentence implies that philosophy is imperfect without charity, and that the charitable man cannot see a clear division between good and evil because, for him, evil is not a positive thing. In much the same way G. Wilson Knight seems to imply in his judgment of Spenser and Milton as men who saw too much of "good and evil" that poets as well as philosophers need to be crowned with charity. This does not mean that Professor Knight, in his scholastic reasoning, in any way resembles Blake. Nor does it mean that he judges the *Faerie Queene* and *Paradise Lost* as "Magnificent Failures" on ethical grounds: he is too good a critic for that.

The principal contribution of Dr. Knight to modern literary criticism has been his studies of what he calls "impressionism" in Shakespeare. Impressionism, by means of symbolism, imagery, mood, tone, and so on, awakens automatic recognition, in the hearer, of the truth the author wants to tell him: and so that truth does not have to be told directly. What Professor Knight calls "impressionism" is really the *raison d'etre* of all poetry, and the most familiar examples of it are the parables of Christ. The term, however, means more than words like allegory, symbolism, metaphor, imagery, and so on: and it includes them all. The organic compactness of *Hamlet* results from the perfect appropriateness of the imagery, the sound of the verse, the ideas and emotions developed to one another and to the theme; everything here is perfectly integrated. The result is we only feel the effect of the play, and it takes a lot of study to find out how that effect was achieved. In Spenser, on the other hand, the machinery of the symbolism is always before our eyes. Not only that, but his symbols all too frequently lack imaginative common sense. The result is that the whole poem is diffuse, seems to stand on a weak foundation, is

---

A review of *The Burning Oracle*, by G. Wilson Knight (Oxford University Press), published in *The New York Times*, September 24, 1939.

often fluid to a fault. This is the fault of the poet, not of his medium, for Dante used allegory not only without sacrificing any organic integration, but even making the *Divine Comedy* the most perfectly constructed epic we know.

One of the reasons that Spenser's imagination is often peculiarly dull is that he is a little too concerned (still using the words of Blake) with the rigid separation of "good and evil." Every man and every poet is at one time or another forced to face dilemmas arising out of such dichotomies as that of flesh and spirit, and Shakespeare is just as much concerned with those problems in *Hamlet* as Milton is in *Paradise Lost;* but what Milton lacks is Shakespeare's ability to become identified, inwardly, with whatever he is writing about (example: the hare in *Venus and Adonis*) and to be in complete imaginative sympathy with all kinds of things without having to find out first if they are good or bad. St. Augustine and Shakespeare are two who know that nothing is, or can be, completely evil: Milton does not know that. *Paradise Lost* mechanically contrasts two positive forces of evil and of good and leaves us with the strange confusion that the one real character in the great struggle is Satan, the personification of evil. The "good and evil" dilemma concerns Spenser too, especially in terms of sacred and profane love.

Space does not permit more than the briefest indication of what the book is about. The "good and evil" dilemma is only one of the problems it faces, but it is the most important of the problems because it is the one that serves to tie seven otherwise disparate essays together. Besides the authors mentioned, Pope and Swift and Byron are also treated, and the essay on Byron is one of the most interesting of them all. Many topics are discussed in these pages packed with brilliant analysis: for instance, the nature of irony and of symbolism, Milton's theology, and Shakespeare's ideas of kingship. But everything is subordinated to problems of literary technique and of aesthetics, for Dr. Knight, unlike many literary critics in this day, sets himself up only as a critic and not as a moralist or a theologian.

THE ART OF RICHARD HUGHES

Richard Hughes is fascinated by a story for its own sake, the proof of this is not hard to find. Ten or a dozen times, if not more, in each of his novels, characters surprise each other with strange and brilliant tales, striking sometimes for their humor, sometimes for their strangeness, and often for their barefaced overstatement. These are never digressions; they never take more than a few sentences; they never hold up the action, but on the contrary, the swift stimulus they give us in passing adds greatly to the speed of the whole enterprise. But it is important to notice that Hughes tends to create characters which reflect his own passion for stories.

For example, the Bas-Thornton children in *High Wind* overcame the first embarrassment upon meeting some other children from a different part of Jamaica by telling them "disproportionate" stories about their own home. Not the least impressive part about *In Hazard* is when, in the story of the sinking *Archimedes,* we find the Chinese seamen huddled together telling weird and humorous ghost stories out of China. The children in *High Wind* have a *sense* for the kind of story they want to tell themselves. Other characters in Hughes' novels display some genius in the telling of tall and "disproportionate" stories to others.

The most attractive among these appears in *In Hazard*: I mean the sixteen-year-old daughter of an old Virginia family, a girl called Sukie. Her character is of the kind that combines innocence with complete desperateness, and she drinks, on one occasion, enough corn whiskey to paralyze several grown men. The result is that she starts solemnly telling of a series of five or six of the most inspired tall stories you may ever hope to hear. Sukie is a kind of an artist. Under the stress of furious illumination vouchsafed her by corn liquor she rises above herself and becomes a minor genius. The character Lochinvarovic, hero of the short story which bears his name, achieves a genius for banditry in the same way: in a bout of drunkenness. But Hughes is careful to explain that he is not talking about the effects of a casual glass, or even about the effect of a great many upon a commonplace drinker. As he sees it, there are certain

This essay on Richard Hughes was published in the November 1939 issue of *The Columbia Review*.

men who get drunk and reach, through a stage of furious concentration, to a kind of inspired clarity which is probably the closest a nonascetic may get to imagining what the mystic graces may be like. The other characters in Hughes who reach this height of illumination do not necessarily get there through drink: but it comes out under any other kind of stress and strain. And the greatest artists in Hughes are brought out by the presence of death. Perhaps in the captain of the *Archimedes* it is much more than death: it is a complex situation in which he is completely surrounded by alternative disasters, of which death is merely the greatest and most immediate at the time. But at any rate, in the height of the storm, he is suddenly carried out of himself and achieves a perfect genius for seamanship.

> Yes, he had been worried, but that was only at first. For soon the storm reached such a height that plainly this was no longer an issue between himself and his owners but between himself and his Maker. That altered things. That suited him better. From then on he was like an artist in a bout of inspiration.
>
> . . . as the storm increased to its immense height so the flame brightened: his whole mind and body were possessed by an intense excitement. No room for thought of his owners. No room in him for anything but a gigantic exhilaration, and a consciousness that, for the time being, all his abilities were heightened.

But Hughes is not only interested in the artist who is an inspired genius. This is too rare a creature in the first place: and even when we find him, we find him half the time uninspired anyway. Hughes is interested just as much in men who possess skills and use them well. Too many inspired geniuses on board a sinking ship might become unwieldy. In fact, everybody on board besides the captain has become an automaton: yet they go on automatically doing jobs they know how to do, or even learning new and rough techniques, makeshifts appropriate to a helpless ship in a great gale. Now one of these makeshift skills that has to be learned is the completely humble and dirty one of pouring oil on the water to keep the ship from being swamped. And since it would waste oil to pour it over the heavily listing lee side, it has to go out, bit by bit, through the latrines, which are themselves admitting sea water from time to time. One of the young officers learns this technique briefly and sets about practicing it until he is in a delirium and is conscious of nothing else but his job: indeed he is only half conscious of that.

> The boy stuck to his post pouring oil without food or rest for twenty hours on end, till midnight Saturday: and though at the end of that time he was dog-tired and dreaming on his feet, he never felt bored.

Nor was it long before dreams and technique had woven themselves together.

Most frequently he imagined himself in a lecture room where a dreary lecturer droned out a discourse on pouring oil. Sometimes he was himself the lecturer, explaining in balanced periods the Whole Art of Oil Pouring, its every thrust and parry, and riposte: while an entranced audience of students scribbled down his sections and subsections *a* and *b* in their notebooks.

This is not by any means a poor example to take. It is not a piece of morbid psychology; and even if it is slightly humorous, (very slightly, though) it reflects Hughes' own quite serious and passionate interest in skills and techniques for their own sake. The slightest and most varied skills do not escape his appreciative eye. He even devotes a few sentences in *High Wind* to describing how a Negro taught John Bas-Thornton to make tree-springes for catching birds.

He is interested in people who know a good story when they see it, in men who, in occasional bouts of inspiration, really transcend their powers, and in men who possess a skill and use it well and sternly. He is interested in artists.

Now he himself knows quite a little, at least about the surface of various techniques: such as that of navigation. But the one technique he does possess in perfection is that of his own craft. In a word, Hughes is a very skillful storyteller, perhaps the most skillful we have. In fact, when in the first part of *In Hazard* he appears to be solely interested in navigation, he is really all the time using his own technique to build up a terrific suspense.

High Wind is also very exciting, but the excitement is different in kind and in degree. Its material is as tragic as that of the later novel, but the story has less stark tragedy in the telling.

The interest in mechanical skills is pretty much the same kind of thing for Richard Hughes as the interest in manners and conventions, for conventions are to behavior what tools are to a craft, and also require no little skill. *A High Wind in Jamaica* happens to be a study of manners.

Three kinds of social groups (if a slight but illuminating distortion will be permitted here) are brought into play against one another in this book. That of the average middle-class grownup (whose conventions are kept well in the background of this story, and only serve as a standard of comparison), a far from average group of children, and a shipload of nondescript malefactors labeled as pirates.

These pirates are not kidnappers. They are only after money and odds and ends of cargo. It is only by an unlucky accident that they become saddled with these children. The fact is the children did not realize exactly what had happened until weeks later. Indeed, at the time of the raid, Emily had misinterpreted the whole thing, for although she had heard the actual word "pirates" she only understood it as "pilots"; and since it is of the nature of pilots to "come aboard" (witness a famous chromo: "The Pilot Comes Aboard") the matter was at once accepted as the most proper and logical thing in the world.

What problems will arise out of this situation? Problems of manners. This is immediately clear, since the author first of all shows the pirates and the children eating dinner together, finding it hard to keep a polite conversation going, and finally falling back into silence and mutual embarrassment. From then on we follow the interactions of two mutually exclusive sets of social conventions.

Now pirates may be expected to have a certain way of life in which no provision is made for taking care of young children, at any rate on expeditions. This is complicated by the fact that these pirates are no longer in a pure state: a convention that had once been essential to piracy (the liberal practice of murder) has become for these men too dangerous a weapon to use. For this reason, the purity of their piratical state is completely interfered with by the presence of these children, who must at all costs be returned safe to civilization. And this will take a long time. Time for this more vital little society to completely put to rout the weakened conventions of piracy. But the children have no immediate difficulties. They flourish as vigorously on this boat as anywhere else. Only one of them, Margaret, finds the situation at all confusing; she cannot in all animal innocence run with the rest of her pack, and the result is physical and social disaster. In attempting to compromise with the standards of the other side, she is destroyed, and therefore suffers contempt from both sides that is directly proportionate to the childhood she has belied.

Otherwise the children have admirable poise and impeccable decorum. When they finally find out that these are pirates, they wisely pretend to know nothing about it: but they immediately incorporate into their games of make-believe a fiercer and truer kind of piracy than these men ever knew.

And so the story climbs from one surprise to another until it finally leads us up to the final surprise of all: then we realize that not only are the pirates harmless, but that the children are actively and unconsciously dangerous: and that the pirates as a group, with their group customs and manners and skills, are being swallowed up and destroyed by a rival set of conventions, a set of dreadful, fierce, innocent conventions of make-believe.

What has been said about Hughes' interest in mechanical techniques on one hand and social conventions on the other does not, of course, mean that his book offers any message to politicians or sociologists, and it is a pity it should be so necessary to sound this warning in our days. All this is mere raw material that has become firmly embodied in the form of the novels themselves. Certainly, whatever Hughes thinks about our social and economic conditions must lie somewhere at the back of all this, but the man who goes digging them out will completely miss and destroy for himself what is really important about Hughes: his art. We might, for example, hazard a guess that Hughes is probably philosophically close to Lawrence of Arabia, in a kind of stoicism that respects nothing so much as a devotion to duties and conventions and techniques, that withstands the impact of any misfortune or dishonor. But what possible good will it do a man to ferret out all this and then determine either to believe in it or hate the belief, and above all to judge Hughes by it, rather than by his book? I strongly suspect that even radicals who have discovered that Hughes believes a sailor's allegiance to be to his ship and not to the Second International are simply keeping quiet about it and enjoying the books without crying "fascist!"

This is perhaps a secondary question, but after all it seems necessary to say this sort of thing over and over again. Hughes is *not* some D. H. Lawrence, in whom you have to take what is artistically good with a whole lot that is philosophically foul. Hughes scrupulously avoids moral observations that attract our eye beyond the framework of the work of art itself. Morals are only involved, in these books, in the relations of motives to moral patterns the personages themselves possess. The only preferences Hughes shows are for motives and situations that lend themselves to a good story, and it is because of this formal strictness and integrity that we must confine ourselves to the essentials of art in talking about him. It is impossible to admire him for the wrong reasons.

WILLIAM YORK TINDALL—
D. H. LAWRENCE: WHO SAW HIMSELF AS A MESSIAH

D. H. Lawrence sincerely condemned James Joyce's *Ulysses* as "obscene," and yet he himself wrote *Lady Chatterley's Lover*, which achieved a certain notoriety of its own. Whether either of these books is obscene is relatively unimportant here: but we must assent to the paradox that Lawrence's judgment of Joyce was the judgment of a moralizing man whose religious aspirations were as intense as they were misdirected. A comparison between the two authors is something that Dr. Tindall's book only suggests; it would be an illuminating one, for they both remained intellectually true to the religions which they abandoned. Joyce's work is built squarely and firmly upon St. Thomas Aquinas, and although his use of Christian literary and liturgical symbol is free and even facetious, yet he never denies the truths which those symbols have always striven to express. That he lost sight of those truths is a thing which *Ulysses* and *Finnegans Wake* do not boast of, but rather lament.

Lawrence's background is Protestantism, which allows a relative freedom in making religion just what you want it to be, and Lawrence's private religion demonstrates the abuse of this privilege; but, while Joyce remains a kind of Christian, Lawrence becomes a complete pagan and preaches a return to gods that were forgotten even before Jupiter and Venus and Dionysius. Yet all the while it is the Protestant in Lawrence that condemns the Catholic in Joyce: condemning the intellectual subtlety and the perfection of formal, imaginative unity in *Ulysses*, which strives after artistic, and not moral, success. Joyce and St. Thomas believe the aims of a work of art and those of a moral act to be, in a certain sense, distinct. Lawrence conceives the function of the writer to be to write sermons about dark and primitive love, about the moral relationship of man to the earth, to the sun, and to cows like "Susan."

At the same time Lawrence is continually using his own very acute intellect to attack intellectuals and to defend the process he calls "thinking with the blood." He bitterly detested all Catholics, all scientists, all Communists and, finally, all "international bankers." He went off on a disappointed hunt for the "noble savage": the closest he got was the New

---

A review of *D. H. Lawrence and Susan His Cow*, by William York Tindall (Columbia University Press), published in *The New York Times*, January 14, 1940.

Mexican Indian, and that was not close enough, by any means, to nobility. He found his ideal, finally, only in the pages of Frobenius, of Jung, and of Sir James Frazer. Lawrence's gospel culminated in the proclamation of himself as a messiah, as one who had come to save the world from intellectualism and give back to men the joyful "mindlessness" of the Hopi snake dance.

Now the fact of Lawrence's restlessness and dissatisfaction in the presence of the sterile materialism of our age and of its deadly, barbarous wars is a very easy thing to understand and sympathize with. But unfortunately the conclusions he reached are too often laughable. Lawrence was a man who never resisted the temptation to write nonsense, and so he was not afraid to state, for example, that the best cure for labor unrest was to teach the workers the Hopi snake dance, or perhaps, to English workers, it would be better to teach the more appropriate nine-men's morris.

Extreme nonsense of this type could not fail to attract the interest of the Nazis, who long ago claimed Lawrence as their very own. In spite of that, nonsense of another sort makes some Communists still reluctant to let go of him altogether, and thus, although the extreme right seems to have captured him completely, he is still secretly adored in certain cenacles of the left.

Dr. Tindall's interesting and important volume treats of all these matters and does so with the thoroughness of impeccable scholarship. At the same time the author turns upon his subject more than the keen eye of the historian; he flays Lawrence with the bitter mockery of an accomplished ironist. His irony is as undoubtedly unfair to Lawrence as it is diverting to the reader, yet if it appears extreme its violence may be mitigated by the fact that it is directed less at Lawrence the man than at certain ideas which are brought to a focus *through* him. Lawrence the man is as unimportant as Lawrence the writer in the study of Lawrence the philosopher.

Now this poor philosopher is almost too easy to put in the pillory, but Dr. Tindall seems to think that is necessary because there does exist a very flourishing cult of Lawrence the Messiah. This new piece of research shows that no scorn for this false Christ or for his Apostles could be excessive, but it is unfortunate that Dr. Tindall cannot see more in Lawrence than this. Lawrence was undoubtedly a writer of exceptional power and brilliance, yet Dr. Tindall, except perhaps in *The Plumed Serpent,* seems to find him all but unreadable, and he refuses to discuss his poetry. His contention that Lawrence's work suffers tremendously from the burden of his private religion is, of course, true. But it is only true that Lawrence's books bow down under that burden; they do not fall to earth.

HUXLEY'S PANTHEON

A few years ago Aldous Huxley wrote *Eyeless in Gaza,* a novel which disappointed his followers for two reasons. First it was not a very good novel, and second it indicated his disillusionment in the comfortable and materialistic skepticism with which he had been, until then, apparently satisfied. His new opinions, instead, appeared to be those of a theosophic crank, but it was not altogether true that these opinions were as new or as startling in Huxley as they seemed. They had their roots in earlier work, like *Those Barren Leaves,* in which Huxley exhibits the sneaking curiosity which intellectuals often feel toward mystics, who say they contemplate the truth face to face.

In all justice to Huxley he was always more than a mere intellectual. He is also an intelligent man. He even now sees more clearly than most of his contemporaries the end for which man was created, but he shows himself both perplexed and confused in his discussion of the means of attaining that end. He is still a capable writer. He still makes criticisms of literature that are as full of erudition as they are of perspicacity. His personal charm is equal to his wit and his good intentions; but unfortunately as a philosopher he is not distinguished.[1]

His *Ends and Means* seemed a little better than *Eyeless in Gaza* because he avoided, in it, some of the limitations that are imposed upon metaphysical concepts by the language of imagination and the accents of cultured dialogue. But the contradictions which were so perplexing in *Ends and Means* have become even more obvious in *After Many a Summer Dies the Swan,* his latest novel.

There is a good enough reason why his opinions frequently sound theosophic: it is that they often really are so. He has gone from one mystic to another, Christian and Oriental, and he has reached his own kind of pantheistic idealism, at last, not without having stopped by at the doors of Spinoza, Kant, and Bergson. He now believes that the world is completely illusory. Matter does not exist, and it is evil. Of course it is evil by

---

This review article was first published in *The Catholic World,* November 1940.

[1] Merton later repudiated this critique of Huxley "as a philosopher" in *The Secular Journal of Thomas Merton* (New York: Farrar Straus & Giroux, 1959), p. 266.

privation of reality, truth, and goodness, which are only to be found in the single substance that exists, God. This substance is also life itself; but although all living things participate in it, they are separated from it by matter, and imprisoned in the realm of death or *karma*. Existence on earth, then, is not good, and we are meant to escape from it by purification, detachment from matter, and union with the selfless One. Material attachments only bind us down to evil: they cannot help us to reach God in any manner. Huxley follows Buddhism this far, but abandons it on the question of metempsychosis, adding a further complicated twist of his own that makes it impossible in his system. He says that good is only impossible on the "human level," and exists not only above it, in eternity, but also below it on the level of animals!

The reason for this is probably a reminiscence of the old *Point Counter Point* days, in which animal instincts were good for their own sake: he thinks they still are, but they must be evil in men because they are self-conscious.

Matter, in any case, can be symbolized as death. That is a familiar enough convention in mystical literature, and that explains all the death symbols upon which Huxley's latest novel is built.

In the very first pages of the book we come upon a rather oppressive description of a cemetery called, not without reason, a pantheon, on the outskirts of Los Angeles. It is one of the great commercial enterprises of one of the characters, Stoyte, and it is a flamboyant place adorned with every possible kind of vulgarity and pagan display. Its more ambitious features include a Fountain of Rainbow Music, a Vestibule of Ashes, a tiny Taj Mahal, an Old World Mortuary, some catacombs, and a perpetual Wurlitzer. But the most offensive thing about the place is that some of the graves are decorated with erotic statuary: for it is Stoyte's pride that he has "put sex appeal into death."

This heavy-handed joke would appear to be too extreme, if only it were not all too possibly, if not actually, true. But the importance of it is that it is a device Huxley uses to satirize materialism. For the materialist has to look for all goodness, all beauty and truth (if any) in materially desirable things. But since beauty, goodness, and so on are not in material things alone, this is as absurd and as bad as trying to "put sex appeal into death." Nevertheless, the pagan hopes to get for himself as many material things and pleasures as possible before he dies: and if it ceases to be a case of every man for himself, at least one has a chance of getting his fair share if he unites to fight for it with other members of his "oppressed class." An extremely happy consummation, for him, would be to live on earth forever, enjoying everlasting youth and health: that is a character-istically pagan paradise. Therefore, the central theme of *After Many a Summer* is not death in general, but physical immortality.

The title of the book is taken from Tennyson's poem about a man to whom the gods gave everlasting life in return for some favor. But un-fortunately they did not give Tithonus everlasting youth, and he just got older and older and older, until he finally begged to be allowed to die like all other creatures.

Huxley has created a Tithonus of his own; one who did the gods no favor but whom at least the reader should thank for being the material cause of the only readable parts of the novel, the "Hauberk Papers." He is an English nobleman who found that he could be immortal on a diet of fishes' intestines and lived for two hundred years in a hidden cave in Surrey. Unlike Tennyson's Tithonus, Huxley's does not lose his youthful vigor. Instead he suffers a different degradation. That degradation is only revealed in the surprise ending of the book, so perhaps it would not be just to reveal it. But in any case, it is very effective and constitutes the most forceful indictment of materialism that ever came from Huxley's pen, even though somewhat the same idea was used, more crudely, in a Laurel and Hardy comedy in 1933.

The central theme is not at all a bad one, but it should have been treated in all its simplicity. Instead of that, it is buried in a lot of extra-neous material. The interminable philosophizings of one Mr. Propter, the dullest character in the whole history of the English novel, are allowed to impede the movement of the story and to spoil the effect of the whole plan.

In the course of these soliloquies Huxley at the same time condemns most of the religious systems in the world and struggles with the contra-dictions of his own. His principal contention, in this, is a perfectly good one: it is that too many men have created God in their own image, and after they have done so, have called upon the God they have created to justify their own violent depredations upon their neighbors. The lowest form of anthropomorphic god is the dictator, who is not only a god in the form of a man but is a man and who sets himself up as the embodi-ment of all the desires and strivings of his followers. Above this come polytheism and primitive monotheism, and so on up the scale: and all the way up, even where God is the purest spirit, He does not cease to retain, in Huxley's eyes, some taint of anthropomorphism.

So he goes as far as he can and reaches the same extreme as the Bud-dhists, to whom God is pure nothingness. But He is not nothingness in the metaphorical sense that no concept of ours can represent Him (which is the Christian view), He is really absolute nothingness. But at this point Huxley seems to realize that to say that God is nothingness is simply atheism, and so he falls back hurriedly upon the Christian notion of God as pure actuality, or "pure working" as he says in the words of the German mystic John Tauler.

Nevertheless Huxley cannot assent to the Divinity of Christ (although he doesn't say how he feels toward the many incarnations of God worshiped in the East), and he thinks that Christianity, although it has "the merit of being simple and dramatic," is categorically "wrong."

He thinks that men like St. John of the Cross, by a lucky accident, transcended these "errors" and managed to get a glimpse of pure and actual truth, but he condemns in the Spanish mystics a "strain of negative sensuality" which only reaffirmed their self-will more strongly when they believed they were annihilating it.

But for Huxley any expression of will at all is "self-will." He believes all our acts are evil, and thus it would be absurd to designate special acts as sources of sin. He is convinced that "the level of man is the level of evil," and he wants to lift the mind by main force out of that level, so that it may attain union with God through not love, but knowledge.

In *Ends and Means,* love was an important virtue, but now Huxley only mentions the word to say how much it embarrasses him. His mysticism operates exclusively in the order of speculation. Love, by which the will is directed to its proper end, the good, has no place in that order. So naturally, since that is the only order Huxley accepts, love must go.

Even the best-intentioned activity only leads to evil consequences, and there is no longer any reason for Huxley to want to do anything for others. Gone, therefore, are the little groups of eight or ten proselytizers, familiar to readers of *Eyeless in Gaza,* schooled in self-control by the methods of F. M. Alexander, traveling about making speeches and opposing violence with nonresistance. In his new book, Huxley admits he does not want to save anyone, except perhaps three or four well-disposed individuals.

Yet in spite of all these opinions which are put into his mouth Mr. Propter is a very active person. He is as busy as he is talkative. He spends much time in a workshop, and he cares not only for his orange trees but for the bodies and souls of itinerant fruit-pickers. He dreams of a small agrarian community in some fertile valley, a sort of beaverboard Shangri-la in which a few chatty contemplatives might wait out the war in seclusion and safety.

All Mr. Propter's attempts to help others seem false because of their inconsistency. Neither Propter nor Huxley really believes he can do anything for anybody else, and if they have any vocation at all, it is to the hermitage. There they will have no more worries about self-contradiction because they will no longer have to argue. There Huxley would be able to sit and think in peace, in between visits from cultured and amusing friends, and it would be very good for him. He should do that. He should stop writing about Mr. Propter and, retiring to a suitable retreat, work in the medium in which he is really good: the essay.

APPENDIX III
TWO TRANSCRIPTIONS OF MERTON'S TALKS
ON WILLIAM FAULKNER
(1967)

TIME AND UNBURDENING
AND THE RECOLLECTION OF THE LAMB:
THE EASTER SERVICE IN
FAULKNER'S *THE SOUND AND THE FURY*

Editor's Note

Thomas Merton resigned his post as Master of Novices at the monastery of Gethsemani in mid-August of 1965 and entered upon a more solitary life, living in a small, cinderblock hermitage in a wooded area overlooking the old abbey in Nelson County, Kentucky. Each Sunday afternoon, however, he could be seen hiking down through the woods and jumping over the creek in blue jeans with an empty water jug hung from his shoulder. He was returning to continue his conferences, or informal talks, to the novices and young monks. Later he opened them up to the entire community, where the attendance grew as he began to explore more literary themes, such as the poetry of Rilke and the German poets after World War II in the winter of 1965 and on into the spring of 1966. Later that year he spoke on the poetry of Edmund Muir, Thich Nhat Hanh (who visited Gethsemani), and the antipoets.

In January of 1967, Father Merton commenced his lectures on "The Classical Values in William Faulkner," which continued for several months. These included an excellent commentary on "The Bear"—a pattern of development in hunting and in the spiritual life. An article entitled, "Baptism in the Forest: Wisdom and Initiation in William Faulkner," which grew out of these studies, was written by Merton as an introductory essay to George Panichas' Mansions of the Spirit *(New York: Hawthorne, 1967). Then came readings from* The Wild Palms, *with its buried baptismal imagery—the theme of the Deluge. And finally in March of 1967, he concluded this series of talks with* The Sound and the Fury. *To each, Merton brought a wealth of wisdom and insight, often punctuated with a dash of humor. As in any subject treated in these Sunday afternoon talks, the fire of Merton's enthusiasm made Faulkner come alive to his audience.*

Merton wrote a long review article for the April-May 1967 issue of The

---

This transcription of Merton's conferences on Faulkner's *The Sound and the Fury* was edited by James Y. Holloway for the Summer 1973 issue of *Katallagete*.

Critic *on* Faulkner: A Collection of Critical Essays, *edited by Robert Penn Warren. He concluded his essay with these eulogistic lines which bear quoting: "There was a day when Faulkner seemed dwarfed by people like Hemingway or even Steinbeck and Caldwell. Now we can understand that he was of far greater stature: a genius comparable to Melville, Hawthorne, Dickens or Dostoevsky . . ."*

Father Merton had been in close contact with the editor at Katallagete *during this time, and had agreed to contribute an article on Faulkner for a project he and they had been working on for some time. Unfortunately, his plan never materialized. What we have here, with a minimum of editing, is a transcription of a tape-recording made by the Trappist monks of Merton's commentary on the deeply moving Easter service in* The Sound and the Fury. *The message for us today is so obvious that it requires no further comment. The words of Thomas Merton (and William Faulkner) speak eloquently for themselves in "the unburdening and the recollection of the Lamb."—Brother Patrick Hart*

1

The Sound and the Fury is one of William Faulkner's greatest stories.

It has one of his greatest saints. Faulkner had many saints. And it is absolutely wrong to say that he had a "negative view of women." Faulkner had a very positive view of women: two of his most "saintly" saints are women. The Christian saint in *The Sound and the Fury,* a mystic, you might say, is, of course, Dilsey. She's a fantastic, wonderful person, and what I want to lead up to in these talks is the climax of *The Sound and the Fury:* the Easter service at the black church, which Dilsey attended that particular Sunday morning. This service is one of the most beautiful things Faulkner ever wrote. The Easter experience of Dilsey occurs in the midst of all "the sound and the fury" of the story. The event is much more impressive when you see it in the middle of all that "sound and fury" which takes place in the household where Dilsey works—and that is just how Faulkner develops the theme in this story.[1]

Now to get all this clearly in focus, let me fill you in on some of the background. We will want to look especially at some of the great ways

---

[1] There is a passing reference to the Easter service in Merton's *Opening the Bible,* written about the same time as these talks were given (Collegeville, Minnesota: The Liturgical Press, 1970, pp. 42–49). Merton saw in this episode a contemporary example of Biblical time and a powerful community experience of "hearing the Word."

Faulkner handles his theme. (By the way: this is an extremely difficult book to read; so it is a book that could easily be read around monasteries. Any segment of it could utterly "disedify," but it is so obscure you probably won't be aware that you're being "disedified!") In any case: one of the things Faulkner does in all of his books—and does so very effectively, indeed—is to deal with the question of *time*. He has a really amazing way of handling *time*. By that I mean not just the way he might begin at the end of a story and work backward, or with the tricks he plays with the sequence of events in a story. Rather: in *The Sound and the Fury,* he divides the book into five parts, and each part represents the experience of time by a particular person in the household of the family Compson.

One of the things that marks the differences between and establishes the character and identity of each person in the Compson household is their totally different experience of *time*. The great thing about Dilsey is her completely Christian experience of time. Basically, it seems to me that Faulkner's own treatment of time is itself Biblical. Of course, in his stories, there are many experiences of modern, abstract time—the time of the villains, the bad ones, who follow linear, clocked, calendar time. But that and other kinds of time are seen and understood against the Biblical view of time, and the more sympathetic, deeper characters have just this understanding of time.

Now we know that the Biblical sense of time is not linear. For us, today, this is hard to comprehend, since we live on a time-line. Our experience of time is wholly linear, and therefore wholly artificial. In fact, we, today, have no *real* experience of time, for our experience of it is wholly abstract. For example: I don't even have to look at the clock to tell you that, right now, it is 4:12 (well, 4:15, I'm three minutes off!). In fifteen minutes, our gathering here must stop; Vespers will be exactly at 4:34 (or whenever it is!). Then, we know that supper will be exactly at 5:15. And we know this is 1967. Our time is like the railway line, and we know that there are stations we are going to pass, eventually, and that we will, sure enough pass them along this linear time-line. But the Biblical conception of time is not this way at all. The Bible measures time not by a line into which things fit, a line into which to put in slots of 1965, 1966, 4:30 P.M., 5:15 P.M., etc. Rather, the Biblical conception of time is a matter of ripening, fullness. It is more like that little dog of our recent experience: she knew what was going on inside her belly, and it was quite different from the time that was going on inside the head of Brother, who had consulted his time-line calendar and thought he knew when, on that line, the puppies were due to come. She had her puppies when she had her puppies. When the time came for her to have her puppies, she *had* her puppies. But her time had to do with fullness, ripening, not time-lines. And so the Bible is not concerned with what's going on in anybody's head about time on a line, any more than the little dog gave a hoot about what was going on in Brother's head. The Bible is concerned with time's *fullness,* the time for an event to happen, the time for an emotion *to be felt,* the time for a harvest or for the celebration of a harvest.

In Faulkner one finds a type of people who have just this Biblical sense of time, time which goes with the fullness of things. Dilsey is one of these people, and Faulkner sees these characters as having a special capacity for pity which those with other conceptions of time simply don't have. These folks are more compassionate, more loving, more understanding of others because they are more in touch with the natural rhythm, the movement and growth of life. So, the more these characters in *The Sound and the Fury* get away from this Biblical notion of time, the more their evil becomes apparent. The villain in the story is Jason Compson, a miser, who lives entirely by clock time, by telegrams, telephones, timetables—things like that. He is a sly, crafty man who has no sympathy for anyone, hates everyone, makes life miserable for everyone. I am not saying (and certainly Faulkner is not saying, either) that if you look at your watch you are an evil person (You! fellow! right there! Looking at your watch! You'll just have to wait for that drink of water or Coke!) But it *is* to say that one can live by clock time and become a slave to it and so not care for people. It *is* to say that clock time cannot measure what is real, significant, full of meaning: clock time cannot permit us to live in expectation, anticipation, fullness.

Time, and each of the characters' sense of time, is a key factor in *The Sound and the Fury.*

So, let's identify the characters in the story by the *time* which dominates them. First, there is Benjy Compson, a thirty-three-year-old idiot. The story begins, in fact, on his thirty-third birthday. Benjy's sense of time is completely whacky. He has no sense of *any* kind of time: everything is present to him at once. Even his wailing Faulkner describes as seeming "to begin before the sound itself had started, seemed to cease before the sound itself had stopped." Even his vocal sounds—not words, though full of meaning for Dilsey—were timeless. The past is present, always immediate to him. That is why Benjy's section is so difficult to read. Everything in time is coming and going, and only after you get through, say, a hundred pages or so, do you realize that all of the events which Benjy is experiencing are not happening on the same day! On the contrary, some of them happened thirty years ago!

There is this beautiful girl, Caddy Compson (possibly she is Faulkner's favorite girl character). She is always in the background of the book, but never quite gets in, and you see her only through the eyes of the others—and of the time they live by, and on, and in. But she's there, throughout the Benjy section, from when she's five years old to when she's fourteen, maybe older. Then, later on, she's married and out of the picture, and when we get Benjy in focus, she's gone.

Another thing about Benjy is that he cannot talk. He has no way of communicating anything, with anyone, directly. He just sounds off, like a factory siren or something like that. What bothers Benjy the most is that Caddy's gone away. There are a few things Benjy likes: Flowers. Firelight. Caddy (but she's gone). The pasture next to the house: It *used* to be a pasture, but they sold it and made a golf course out of it so Benjy's brother, Quentin, could go to Harvard. Benjy likes to watch the fellows play golf, but he disturbs the players by bellowing at them as they play on his pasture.

Now, for me, this Benjy section is a beautiful part of Faulkner's story. It is a wonderful vision of life through the eyes of Benjy, the idiot. In fact, the thing that is most beautiful is Benjy's immediate reaction to everything. He doesn't think about anything or anybody, he just reacts to simple things, like color and people and golf players, as a child might react. But, he's not a child. Benjy has no personal identity. He's just a sort of nature. Some ridiculous critics have said, as you might well guess, that "it is not possible to 'identify' with Benjy." But the fact is, he is *just* the sort of person you *do* identify with—or, at least, I do! Because, all Benjy's got is a nature, so, you simply absorb his reactions as if they were your own. There is no "personality" in the way. It is just this natural mechanism of Benjy's which reacts to simple things, to warmth, color, light, love, etc., etc. And when something beautiful is taken from him—for example, when he's looking at the fire in the stove, as if in a trance, they shut the door of the stove, and he starts bellowing because the fire went away . . .

In sum, Benjy has no sense of time, whatsoever.

Then there is Quentin, who goes to Harvard. Quentin is all fouled up about time. It's a very difficult section to discuss, but we can't go into it now, for it's a very tricky, modern section. Sartre, for example, read the book and picked up Quentin's section and said, "A-hah! Look at all this about *time!*" Quentin breaks his watch—this is the first thing he does, in his section of the story: it's time to get up, out of bed and go to class. But instead of that, he gets out of bed, breaks his watch, puts it in the drawer, shuts the drawer, and goes back to bed. Of course, that sort of thing could happen at any college—you don't have to go to Harvard for that! But the point of Quentin's section is that he has no capacity to get away *from time*. He's haunted by it, even though that day, in his section, is his birthday (a different day than Benjy's, of course). Quentin cuts all his classes and rumbles around Cambridge, Massachusetts. He hears each striking of the clock, so he's constantly aware of time. In fact, he's *hyper-aware* of time, in a way that is very, very bad. He's doomed because of it, because he's so dominated by it.

And there is the mother of the Compson family. She's always upstairs, a hypochondriac. She has a notion of time, measured by her headaches, her need for her hotwater bottle, all the things she's always asking for and worrying about. Faulkner's portrayal of her is an admirable one—with her funny, yet depressing, pathetic personality. She, too, has a destructive idea of time, turned forever in on herself.

It is Jason Compson who's on *business* time, a miser. Actually, his idea of time seems the most normal, the most real to us, and yet it's the most destructive time of all. It's Jason, actually, who seems to set the action for *The Sound and the Fury*. Caddy Compson, his sister, after a wild, teenage life, gives birth to a child, a girl, and Caddy—somehow or other, Faulkner never makes it quite clear—goes away, ending up in Europe. But Caddy leaves her daughter (named *Quentin!*) in the care of Jason. But Jason takes the money that Caddy sends for the support of her daughter, and, of course, in the process treats the daughter very badly, tormenting her, abusing her. The girl is aware what is going on. Finally, on Holy Saturday night (before the climactic Easter service), Caddy's daughter steals the money which Jason had kept hidden in a box on the floor of a closet in his room, slips down a rain pipe (or pear tree), and gets away. So on Easter Sunday morning, there is a great explosion of wrath by Jason when he discovers that the girl has made off with the money he had been stealing from her. And this, of course, upsets the whole household: the mother frets; Jason thinks he knows where to find the girl, but he never does. He rushes madly over the countryside in his car, trying to get the sheriff, to get a telegram off, to use the telephone—all sorts of things—but he never catches up with her. And the Compson household is in an uproar on that Easter morning.

In the middle of all this Dilsey (along with Benjy) and the other blacks make their way to their church for this beautiful Easter service. Here, Dilsey has a great illumination about Christian truth; the beginning, the end, and everything. It's a wonderful thing. Really beautiful.

Now, we're ready, I think, to look at a few passages in *The Sound and the Fury* more closely. First, let's get introduced to an obvious passage about *time*. There has been a lot of byplay between Dilsey and Luster (her son, who takes care of Benjy). And, of course, there is all that commotion going on, everywhere, in the household, as each of the Compsons wake up: the hypochrondriac mother is yelling for her hotwater bottle; Jason knows that Caddy's daughter has escaped with the money, etc., etc., and Dilsey is trying to make bread by getting the stove ready . . .

> Dilsey put some more wood in the stove and returned to the bread board. Presently she began to sing again.
>
> The room grew warmer. Soon Dilsey's skin had taken on a rich, lustrous quality as compared with that as of a faint dusting of wood ashes which both it and Luster's had worn, as she moved about the kitchen, gathering about her the raw materials of food, coordinating the meal. On the wall above a cupboard, invisible save at night, by lamp light and even then evincing an enigmatic profundity because it had but one hand, a cabinet clock ticked, then with a preliminary sound as if it had cleared its throat, struck five times.
>
> "Eight oclock," Dilsey said. She ceased and tilted her head upward, listening: But there was no sound save the clock and the fire.

This is a typical example of Faulkner's direction. Here is this household beset by *time:* the clock strikes five, and Dilsey says, "eight o'clock! . . ." She knows it's three hours slow. The thing about Dilsey is that, as Faulkner sets this question about time in the story, she is on Benjy's time, and Quentin's time, and Jason's time—completely on everyone else's time. She is able to understand all these different times, in each of these different characters, and she correlates them into one, natural, and Christian experience of time, time which transcends them all. That is one of the keys— maybe the most important key—of Faulkner's story.

Another key is that an estimate can be made of the characters by how they treat Benjy. Each one treats him consistent with the *time* they are on: the great characters understand and love Benjy; the others don't. Dilsey loves Benjy; Caddy loves Benjy; some love him more, some less; some don't love him at all; some think he's an idiot and try to get him away from the house, for good, because he's always bellowing. But Dilsey understands. She understands why he starts bellowing, and she knows what to do to calm him down.

It seems to me that when a story is built on leads and thrusts such as these, it becomes a totally different experience when you read it—different, that is, from reading what we might call a "straight" story. You can see what Faulkner is doing with us: the story releases in us—it's really like a *meditation!*—it releases in us a certain capacity for deep feeling and emotion. Emotions and feelings we do not get from reading a straight, surface story—stories which are just any novel, among many. But when stories do what Faulkner is doing here, they are deep *meditations* on life. What one invariably receives in reading Faulkner is something qualitative. There is a deep quality to be found in just one, tiny, beautiful passage.

Just to read one gives you some indication of who Dilsey is: Here, of course, the theme is *identity:* For the Compsons (or, the mother) it becomes necessary to give Benjy a new name, because it becomes obvious he is an idiot. So he's named "Benjy," changed from Maury (from his mother's family) early in his childhood, when he was three or four years old. "Benjy" is a "Biblical" name:

> *His name's Benjy now, Caddy said.*
>
> *How come it is, Dilsey said. He aint wore out the name he was born with yet, is he.*
>
> *Benjamin came out of the Bible, Caddy said. It's a better name for him than Maury was.*
>
> *How come it is, Dilsey said.*
>
> *Mother says it is, Caddy said.*
>
> *Huh, Dilsey said. Name aint going to help him. Hurt him, neither. Folks dont have no luck, changing names. My name been Dilsey since fore I could remember and it be Dilsey when they's long forgot me.*
>
> *How will they know it's Dilsey, when it's long forgot, Dilsey, Caddy said.*
>
> *It'll be in the Book, honey, Dilsey said. Writ out.*
>
> *Can you read it, Caddy said.*
>
> *Wont have to, Dilsey said. They'll read it for me. All I got to do is say Ise here.*

I believe that this is one of the best statements about what identity means for a Christian: it is a perfect statement of what identity is *in* Christ: identity *as response*. But a response *to a name you already have!* You are given a name: *the name to which you will respond, when it is called out!* In this passage, there is *identity*. And *vocation!* (So, we *all* ought to be careful about changing our names: when we get *up there*, they may read it to us out of a book!)

2

Now, I believe we are ready for the move to the church, for the Easter service, for this preaching of the Word about Easter. Here we have this holy Faulkner character, Dilsey, going to the church. The theme is resurrection.

Resurrection is also one of the themes in Faulkner's early stories. In some of them, he treats the resurrection theme as a member of his own generation, the World War I generation. It is about men coming back from that war, men whose lives have been completely dislocated by the war and are unable to readjust to normal life. In his novel, *Sartoris,* he really moves with this theme: in this story, Faulkner depicts the various attempts and various means of that generation trying to get back into normal life. But nothing works. The character gets a fast car, and speeds all over the country, but cannot settle down. Then, he falls in love, and this holds him a while, but not completely. Then something happens: his father is killed in the automobile accident, and the character is completely dislocated by it and takes off into the hills with some countryfolk and lives there, in a sort of daze, but this doesn't settle him, either. Then follows a sort of Christmas scene, where he is in a cabin with some Negroes, finding himself caught up on Christmas day, experiencing Christmas with them. But, he himself has no place to go. *But he has to go somewhere!* These moves are treated as ritual situations, situations which *could* have brought about his resurrection from the state of collapse the war had left him in. But they all fail. Again, the question of time in this *Sartoris* story is critical: there are moments (which Faulkner handles beautifully) in which the man lives a natural, ordinary life, where all the beauty and sense of time move in a slow, organic quality of life. But then the character is off again, dashing about, madly. *Sartoris* is a beautiful book. "Does he *ever* get settled?" No. He commits suicide. But, in fact, he doesn't commit suicide. He disappears from home and ends up in Chicago. Some crook there has a new kind of airplane and needs a test pilot for it! The character is drunk, and says, "Sure, I'll test it for you!" As soon as he gets the plane off the ground, the wings fall off! And he cracks up. That is *Sartoris.*

But, this Easter service, with Dilsey: that is an absolutely beautiful thing. Really beautiful! It is the resurrection theme. Let's remember now the different tempo, the different levels of the time and action of the people in *The Sound and the Fury.* Jason Compson, the godless, avaricious man, the liar, the cheat, who cons everybody, who's interested only in himself—Jason is rushing down the road in his car after his niece, seeking to get the money she had taken from his room, but which he conned her out of, but he never finds her.

Faulkner's thrust here in the Easter scene is beautiful: this small, beat-up Negro church, with all these black people together. A beautiful picture of them being *called* from their poor, beat-up cabins—the *ecclesia:* called together, to this church, their church, for Easter service. All of them are black, except Benjy, the idiot: he must go to their black church. Understand what Faulkner is saying: these are *the elect,* these are the ones who are *chosen* in this mad, crazy world of nutty people. These are *God's* own: Benjy; and Dilsey, who loves him and calms him and takes care of him; and all the other black people, going to that Easter service.

Let's start out where Benjy is wailing over something. What he's wailing over now is that his niece (Caddy's daughter) is gone. When something like that happens, he just moans, and wails . . . Here's a bit of that moaning and wailing:

> Then Ben wailed again, hopeless and prolonged. It was nothing. Just sound. It might have been all time and injustice and sorrow become vocal for an instant by a conjunction of planets.
>
> "Listen at him," Luster said, "He been gwine on dat way ev'y since you sont us outen de house. I don't know whut got in to him dis mawnin."
>
> "Bring him here," Dilsey said.
>
> "Come on, Benjy," Luster said. He went back down the steps and took Ben's arm. He came obediently, wailing, that slow hoarse sound that ships make, that seems to begin before the sound itself has started, seems to cease before the sound itself has stopped.
>
> "Run and git his cap," Dilsey said. "Dont make no noise Miss Cahline kin hear. Hurry, now. We already late."
>
> "She gwine hear him anyhow, ef you dont stop him." Luster said.
>
> "He stop when we get off de place," Dilsey said. "He smellin hit. Dat's whut hit is."
>
> "Smell whut, mammy?" Luster said.

This is a kind of cosmic woe, coming out in Benjy. This is what the Fathers of the Church call the *planctus creaturatum,* the moaning of the creatures, the lamentation of the fallen world. But Benjy is not fallen: you see, this is the lamentation of innocent creation, innocent dislocation— creation just wailing its *un*-understood sadness:

> "You go git dat cap," Dilsey said. Luster went on. They stood in the cellar door, Ben one step below her. The sky was broken now into scudding patches that dragged their swift shadows up out of the shabby garden, over the broken fence, and across the yard. Dilsey stroked Ben's head, slowly and steadily, smoothing the bang upon his brow. He wailed quietly, unhurriedly. "Hush," Dilsey said, "Hush, now. We be gone in a minute. Hush, now." He wailed quietly and steadily.

Dilsey knows that just as soon as they get Benjy away from that Compson household, Benjy will stop his howling: it is the doom over the house that makes him wail the way he does.

So now they start off, down to the church. And there is this lovely procession, and as they go down, the other black families, one by one, join them. This is a real *procession* to Church: a ceremonial procession:

> They reached the gate. Dilsey opened it. Luster was coming down the drive behind them, carrying the umbrella. A woman was with him. "Here dey come," Dilsey said. They passed out the gate. "Now, den," she said. Ben ceased. Luster and his mother overtook them. Frony wore a dress of bright blue silk and a flowered hat. She was a thin woman, with a flat, pleasant face.
>
> "You got six weeks' work right dar on yo back," Dilsey said. "Whut you gwine do ef hit rain?"
>
> "Git wet, I reckon," Frony said. "I aint never stopped no rain yit."
>
> "Mammy always talkin bout hit gwine rain," Luster said.
>
> "Ef I dont worry bout y'all, I don't know who is," Dilsey said. "Come on, we already late."
>
> "Rev'un Shegog gwine preach today," Frony said.
>
> "Is?" Dilsey said. "Who him?"
>
> "He fum Saint Looey," Frony said. "Dat big preacher."
>
> "Huh," Dilsey said, "What dey needs is a man kin put de fear of God into dese here triflin young niggers."
>
> "Rev'un Shegog gwine preach today," Frony said. "So dey tells."

See! this is a kind of incantation. We are being led into a different world! These people who are *getting themselves ready,* getting themselves into a certain mood, to hear the Word of God. There is a kind of incantation about the visiting preacher, Reverend Shegog.

> They went on along the street. Along its quiet length white people in bright clumps moved churchward, under the windy bells, walking now and then in the random and tentative sun. The wind was gusty, out of the southeast, chill and raw after the warm days.
>
> "I wish you wouldn't keep on bringin him to church, mammy," Frony said. "Folks talkin."
>
> "Whut folks?" Dilsey said.
>
> "I hears em," Frony said.
>
> "And I knows whut kind of folks," Dilsey said, "Trash white folks. Dat's who it is. Thinks he aint good enough fer white church, but nigger church aint good enough fer him."
>
> "Dey talks, jes de same," Frony said.
>
> "Den you send um to me," Dilsey said. "Tell um de good Lawd dont keer whether he smart er not. Dont nobody but white trash keer dat."

A street turned off at right angles, descending, and became a dirt road. On either hand the land dropped more sharply; a broad flat dotted with small cabins whose weathered roofs were on a level with the crown of the road. They were set in small grassless plots littered with broken things, bricks, planks, crockery, things of a once utilitarian value. What growth there was consisted of rank weeds and the trees were mulberries and locusts and sycamores—trees that partook also of the foul desiccation which surrounded the houses; trees whose very burgeoning seemed to be the sad and stubborn remnant of September, as if even spring had passed them by, leaving them to feed upon the rich and unmistakable smell of negroes in which they grew.

From the doors negroes spoke to them as they passed, to Dilsey usually:

"Sis' Gibson! How you dis mawnin?"

"I'm well. Is you well?"

"I'm right well, I thank you."

They emerged from the cabins and struggled up the shading levee to the road—men in staid, hard brown or black, with gold watch chains and now and then a stick; young men in cheap violent blues or stripes and swaggering hats; women a little stiffly sibilant, and children in garments bought second hand of white people, who looked at Ben with the covertness of nocturnal animals:

"I bet you wont go up en tech him."

"How come I wont?"

"I bet you wont. I bet you skeered to."

"He wont hurt folks. He des a loony."

"How come a loony wont hurt folks?"

"Dat un wont. I teched him."

"I bet you wont now."

"Case Miss Dilsey lookin."

"You wont no ways."

"He dont hurt folks. He des a loony."

And steadily the older people speaking to Dilsey, though, unless they were quite old, Dilsey permitted Frony to respond.

See! This is again a ceremonial. Wherever Dilsey is, she's the queen of it, all dressed up! And Frony (her daughter) goes along, answering questions about her, addressed to her, or speaking for her: "How are you?" Or whatever:

"Mammy aint feelin well dis mawnin."

"Dat's too bad. But Rev'un Shegog'll cure dat. He'll give her de comfort en de unburdenin."

Now, all this may sound very quaint to us, but it is part of the story Faulkner is telling here, part of what *The Sound and the Fury* is all about.

508

Here are these black people, who *are burdened, really* burdened. And they are going to church with their sadness and burden and grief. The Lord is going to *unburden* them: they are going to the church to be *unburdened* of a *real* burden, not an imaginary one:

The road rose again, to a scene like a painted back drop. Notched into a cut of red clay crowned with oaks the road appeared to stop short off, like a cut ribbon. Beside it a weathered church lifted its crazy steeple like a painted church, and the whole scene was as flat and without perspective as a painted cardboard set upon the ultimate edge of the flat earth, against the windy sunlight of space and April and a midmorning filled with bells. Toward the church they thronged with slow sabbath deliberation. The women and children went on in, the men stopped outside and talked in quiet groups until the bell ceased ringing. Then they too entered.

See! They are inside: *gathered* there. The people come in. The preachers come in:

The second man was huge, of a light coffee colour, imposing in a frock coat and white tie. His head was magisterial and profound, his neck rolled above his collar in rich folds. But he was unfamiliar to them, and so the heads were still reverted when he had passed, and it was not until the choir ceased singing that they realised that the visiting clergyman had already entered, and when they saw the man who had preceded their minister enter the pulpit still ahead of him an indescribable sound went up, a sigh, a sound of astonishment and disappointment.

The visitor was undersized, in a shabby alpaca coat. He had a wizened black face like a small, aged monkey. And all the while that the choir sang again and while the six children rose and sang in thin, frightened, tuneless whispers, they watched the insignificant looking man sitting dwarfed and countrified by the minister's imposing bulk, with something like consternation. They were still looking at him with consternation and unbelief when the minister rose and introduced him in rich, rolling tones whose very unction served to increase the visitor's insignificance.

"En dey brung dat all de way fum Saint Looey," Frony whispered.

"I've knowed de Lawd to use cuiser tools dan dat," Dilsey said. "Hush, now," she said to Ben, "Dey fixin to sing again in a minute."

When the visitor rose to speak he sounded like a white man. His voice was level and cold. It sounded too big to have come from him and they listened at first through curiosity, as they would have to a monkey talking. They began to watch him as they would a man on a tight rope. They even forgot his insignificant appearance in the virtuosity with which he ran and poised and swooped upon the cold inflectionless wire of his voice, so that at last, when with a sort of swooping glide he came to rest again beside the reading desk with one arm resting upon it at shoulder height and his monkey body as reft of all motion as a mummy or an emptied vessel, the congregation sighed as it waked from a collective dream and moved a little in its seats. Behind the pulpit the choir fanned steadily. Dilsey whispered, "Hush, now. Dey fixin to sing in a minute."

They get this *thunderclap!* Who can ever forget it when he reads it? All of a sudden, this preacher changes. Completely:

Then a voice said, "Brethren."

The preacher had not moved. His arm lay yet across the desk, and he still held that pose while the voice died in sonorous echoes between the walls. It was as different as day and dark from his former tone, with a sad, timbrous quality like an alto horn, sinking into their hearts and speaking there again when it had ceased in fading and cumulate echoes.

"Brethren and sisteren," it said again. The preacher removed his arm and he began to walk back and forth before the desk, his hands clasped behind him, a meagre figure, hunched over upon itself like that of one long immured in striving with the implacable earth, "I got the recollection and the blood of the Lamb!" He tramped steadily back and forth beneath the twisted paper and the Christmas bell, hunched, his hands clasped behind him. He was like a worn small rock whelmed by the successive waves of his voice. With his body he seemed to feed the voice that, succubus like, had fleshed its teeth in him. And the congregation seemed to watch with its own eyes while the voice consumed him, until he was nothing and they were nothing and there was not even a voice but instead their hearts were speaking to one another in chanting measures beyond the need for words, so that when he came to rest against the reading desk, his monkey face lifted and his whole attitude that of a serene, tortured crucifix that transcended its shabbiness and insignificance and made it of no moment, a long moaning expulsion of breath rose from them, and a woman's single soprano: "Yes, Jesus!"

As the scudding day passed overhead the dingy windows glowed and faded in ghostly retrograde. A car passed along the road outside, labouring in the sand, died away. Dilsey sat bolt upright, her hand on Ben's knee. Two tears slid down her fallen cheeks, in and out of the myriad coruscations of immolation and abnegation and time.

"Brethren," the minister said in a harsh whisper, without moving.

"Yes, Jesus!" The woman's voice said, hushed yet.

"Breddren en sistuhn!" His voice rang again, with the horns. He removed his arm and stood erect and raised his hands. "I got de ricklickshun en de blood of de Lamb!" They did not mark just when his intonation, his pronunciation, became negroid, they just sat swaying a little in their seats as the voice took them into itself.

Now what follows is a sacred poem. I can't read it right, but I'll do the best I can. A fantastic, sacred poem!

"When de long, cold—Oh, I tells you, breddren, when de long, cold— I sees de light en I sees de word, po sinner! Dey passed away in Egypt, de swingin chariots; de generations passed away. Wus a rich man: whar he now, O breddren? Was a po man: whar he now, O sistuhn? Oh I tells you, ef you aint got de milk en de dew of de old salvation when de long, cold years rolls away!"

"Yes, Jesus!"

"I tells you, breddren, en I tells you, sistuhn, dey'll come a time. Po sinner saying Let me lay down wid de Lawd, lemme lay down my load. Den whut Jesus gwine say, O breddren? O sistuhn? Is you got de ricklickshun en de Blood of de Lamb? Case I aint gwine load down heaven!"

He fumbled in his coat and took out a handkerchief and mopped his face. A low concerted sound rose from the congregation: "Mmmmmmmmmmm!" The woman's voice said, "Yes, Jesus! Jesus!"

"Breddren! Look at dem little chillen settin dar. Jesus wus like dat once. He mammy suffered de glory en de pangs. Sometime maybe she helt him at de nightfall, whilst de angels singin him to sleep; maybe she look out de do' en see de Roman po-lice passin." He tramped back and forth, mopping his face. "Listen, breddren! I sees de day. Ma'y settin in de do' wid Jesus on her lap, de little Jesus. Like dem chillen dar, de little Jesus. I hears de angels singin de peaceful songs en de glory; I sees de closin eyes; sees Mary jump up, sees de sojer face: We gwine to kill! We gwine to kill! We gwine to kill yo little Jesus! I hears de weepin en de lamentation of de po mammy widout de salvation en de word of God!"

"Mmmmmmmmmmmmmm! Jesus! Little Jesus!" and another voice, rising:

"I sees, O Jesus! Oh I sees!" and still another, without words, like bubbles rising in water.

"I sees hit, breddren! I sees hit! Sees de blastin, blindin sight! I sees Calvary, wid de sacred trees, sees de thief en de murderer en de least of dese; I hears de boasting en de braggin: Ef you be Jesus, lif up yo tree en walk! I hears de wailin of women en de evenin lamentations; I hears de weepin en de cryin en de turnt-away face of God: dey done kilt Jesus; dey done kilt my Son!"

"Mmmmmmmmmmmmmmm. Jesus! I sees, O Jesus!"

"O blind sinner! Breddren, I tells you; sistuhn, I says to you, when de Lawd did turn His mighty face, say, Aint gwine overload heaven! I can see de widowed God shet His do'; I sees de whelmin flood roll between; I sees de darkness en de death everlastin upon de generations. Den, lo! Breddren! Yes, breddren! Whut I see? Whut I see, O sinner? I sees de resurrection en de light; sees de meek Jesus sayin Dey kilt Me dat ye shall live again; I died dat dem whut sees en believes shall never die. Breddren, O breddren! I sees de doom crack en hears de golden horns shoutin down de glory, en de arisen dead whut got de blood en de ricklickshun of de Lamb!"

Now, what is this? This is a man announcing the Story. The sacred history of salvation in the most simple possible, straight terms. They are not just the terms of the preacher, but they are the terms of the people in his hearing. *They are ready for it!* The way he presented it at the beginning of his sermon, he was *not* telling them *anything:* he was preaching to them as a white man. But *now* he is simply saying not only what they know, *but what is present among them!* Now: he is *re-creating* in them their realization of the great truth: *Jesus lives!* And these people realize this. They *know* that they know *this.*

So what happens?

In the midst of the voices and the hands Ben sat, rapt in his sweet blue gaze. Dilsey sat bolt upright beside, crying rigidly and quietly in the anneal-ment and the blood of the remembered Lamb.

As they walked through the bright noon, up the sandy road with the dis-persing congregation talking easily again group to group, she continued to weep, unmindful of the talk.

"He sho a preacher, mon! He didn't look like much at first, but hush!"

"He seed de power en de glory."

"Yes, suh. He seed hit. Face to face he seed hit."

Dilsey made no sound, her face did not quiver as the tears took their sunken and devious courses, walking with her head up, making no effort to dry them away even.

"Whyn't you quit dat, mammy?" Frony said. "Wid all dese people lookin. We be passin white folks soon."

"I've seed de first en de last," Dilsey said. "Never you mind me."

"First en last whut?" Frony said.

"Never you mind," Dilsey said. "I seed de beginnin, en now I sees de endin."

This is an impressive statement because this is what the story builds up to. It is really the climax of the whole book. This Christian statement . . . about *time!* The Word of God breaks into time, into the community of *the chosen,* into those who belong to God. It reveals the beginning and the end-ing: *at once!* It reveals the *meaninglessness* of time and the *full meaning* of time. Dilsey sees all this because she is a person filled with love. All her functions in the Compson family, their household, is to hold together those who are separated by conflict, *by time.* Dilsey has a love that reaches out and embraces all of them. So, *she's* the one who is burdened. And *she* sees at this Easter service the beginning and the ending. And this is just what worship is. This is what contemplation is.

Let's put it this way: worship and contemplation is to hear the Word of God and to see it *all,* in *one* thing.

Now, just what is the beginning and the ending? As Frony says, "the beginning and the ending of *what?" That is* an order! I think this scene is a prelude to the terrible theology of another Faulkner story, one that follows this one, *Light in August:* a terrifying book, but also a great book about the crucifixion. It is a very strange story (and I know we don't have the chance to go into it here). But the center of it is Joe Christmas, a bootlegger and murderer who is . . . lynched, I guess . . . but he is, nevertheless, a sort of Christ-figure, and how he gets that way is a very strange tale.

But in this picture we have of Dilsey, the answer is very simple. There are no complications, no funny theology. There is simply the *Word of God.* Remember that what goes through all this preaching, this sermon, is the refrain coming up from the chorus: "Yes, Jesus! *Yes, Jesus!"* That is what is important. That is the secret of the whole thing. Hearing the Word of God, opening one's self to it with a complete: *"Yes, Jesus!"* Not a "Yes!" off the top of the head. Not a "Yes!" as individuals. But a kind of a—well, try to think to yourself what it means: This kind of *"Yes, Jesus!"*

What is this response, this *"Yes, Jesus?"* Of course, Faulkner doesn't tell us. He leaves us in the dark about Reverend Shegog. That is, it is not altogether clear whether Reverend Shegog did what he did on purpose— whether he had some trick up his sleeve. Why did he start out preaching as a white man and then all of a sudden shift to preaching as a black? I don't know. *But it doesn't matter.* That is not the point.

The point is what Dilsey said, from the start that Easter morning: she is going to church for the unburdening, and while Reverend Shegog is a funny little man, the Lord has used "cuiser" things than that! The Lord is going to speak to her! *This* is the whole story. It isn't what kind of person you are, or what you do. But it is a matter of your *expectation.* What you expect is what you get is pretty much what the answer is in *The Sound and the Fury.* Each of the characters gets what they're looking for: Benjy isn't looking for anything, so he doesn't get anything; Jason expects trouble, and gets trouble; Quentin is all tied up in his trouble with time, and that is what happens to him; Dilsey is looking for the recollection and the blood of the Lamb and the unburdening, and that is what she gets.

3

And that is why this seems to me to be a very great book. One of the things that is so marvelous about it is that the Easter service is a statement of the Gospel in a wholly American idiom: Dilsey's expectation, Reverend Shegog's sermon, Dilsey's unburdening. It is a fine example of an authentic way to preach the Word of God, here.

There is, after all, something very fundamental about the Word of God in America. There is something very fundamental about the "theology" in the sermon of Reverend Shegog. There are some very special slants that are not at all our "conventional" Christian theology of expiation and redemption. Rather, there are some different twists in what the Reverend Shegog says: for example, what happens when Christ *dies,* in the Reverend Shegog's sermon? God the Father is spoken of as "de widowed God," who "shet His do'": the One most disconsolate and sad at the crucifixion is God in Heaven. *He's* all broken up about it: *"Look at what they did!"*

But that's not the way the Gospels are usually presented: conventional theology has God in Heaven, waiting for Christ to die! "You've got to pay the price," God is represented as saying: "I'm waiting to get this bill paid off!"

But that's not what Reverend Shegog says. He says something else: something familiar, of course, to mystics and to others who have a deep sense of other aspects of the redemption given by Christ. It is what you find in the Gospel and the parables. Nowhere in the four Gospels do you find anything about God sitting up in heaven and waiting for this blood debt to be paid off. This idea of God waiting to get "paid off" is later theology—a lot of it is German, bringing in their tribal, feudal idea of responsibility incurred that must be "paid off."

What is critical, after all, is the theology of this church service on Easter, where Dilsey is unburdened by the message of Reverend Shegog and its contrast with the gathering at the white, Presbyterian church in *Light in August,* where a truly gruesome Sunday service takes place, attended by those who the very next day are determined "to get" Joe Christmas.

So all in all, the Easter service in *The Sound and the Fury* seems to me to be an authentic example of the way in which the Word of God is preached: the point is the fulfillment of one's life and the fulfillment of one's identity *in response to the Word of God preached in a community.*

That is the unburdening and the recollection of the Lamb.

FAULKNER MEDITATIONS: *THE WILD PALMS*

Editor's Note

These "meditations" belong to the conferences between Thomas Merton and the community of the Abbey of Gethsemani, in Kentucky, recorded on tape by the brothers, as was their custom. The informal quality of the conferences on Faulkner needs emphasis: Merton used few notes and moved his own concerns by directing questions to and eliciting comments from those participating in the conferences. For publication, he might well have rearranged the order and gone into more detail and depth on matters touched here only in passing. For a number of years, Merton had been studying Faulkner and spoke of bringing the work together in a book. Had he lived to do so, he would probably have related other Faulkner novels and themes to his consideration of The Wild Palms. *The opening section hints of this in the reference to "The Bear" and other stories in* Go Down, Moses.*

This printed version of the informal talks is a studied effort to maintain the continuity of Merton's informal presentations and preserve his own phrasings. One or two awkward sentences may slip in, but not many. Merton's speaking about Faulkner was as clear as his thinking about him. To retain the direction and language of these talks and avoid an overlay of editorial judgments was an obvious decision. That is why these "meditations" hold the power of Merton's insights despite the minimum of editing necessary to prepare it for print. The chief regret editorially is the failure to be able to include all of Merton's "asides"—those splendid examples of his robust humor and humanity.—James Y. Holloway

1

The Wild Palms! A rough but an excellent book. Actually, as we shall see, it's best to read it as a meditation. Yes: *a meditation!* For *The Wild Palms* is another of Faulkner's symbolic presentations of deep, classic truths about man and human values. Strangely enough, the novel has never been widely appreciated. Many critics have failed to realize just how marvelous

---

This second transcription of Merton's conferences on Faulkner's *The Wild Palms* appeared in the Summer 1975, issue of *Katallagete*, edited by James Y. Holloway.

it is. O.K. So it's a rough book—and not refectory reading for a monastery! But it is nevertheless a profoundly moving work.

Faulkner's "The Bear," you'll remember, was concerned with the archaic world of nature, a world no longer with us—the world of man the hunter, man in direct contact with the wilderness, man brought up to understand nature, to live in direct contact with it and so be deeply united with God's plan for the world. The boy, Ike McCaslin, was initiated into this real, natural wisdom of the values of creation by the episodes Faulkner relates in "The Bear." And what was the result? What effect did this have? What was the value of this in his life? Well, Ike made a kind of *monastic* renunciation when he gave up his property. That renunciation was his response to the conviction that the South was under a curse, that to own land in the South was to be part and parcel of a system built on slavery, making money and destroying nature. Ike wanted no part of this. The fourth part of *Go Down, Moses* (where "The Bear" appears) contains a long discussion between Ike and a cousin which one critic says is the traditional argument between the contemplative and the active life. The cousin argues against Ike's decision to give up his property, insisting that it's a useless gesture; no matter what he does he is still part of the South and should work his land like everybody else. So a big question of "The Bear" cycle of stories is where Ike finally comes out. Is his renunciation "successful"? Does he become, as it were, a kind of saint? Or is he a kind of failure?

Keeping this in mind we want to pass to another kind of world—the world of *The Wild Palms*. Actually, this book is a "double-novel," two novels-in-one, two *apparently* unrelated stories which open up some new themes for Faulkner while continuing others we have already considered: monastic vocations (at least, in Faulkner's "world"), time, nature, man, honor, duty, and love. First of all, we need to underscore "*apparently* unrelated stories," for good critics have argued that these two stories ("The Wild Palms" and "Old Man" are the titles given to the two stories published as one novel, *The Wild Palms*) are in fact unrelated and each novel must be dealt with as a unit. (Malcolm Cowley's famous *The Portable Faulkner,* for example, carries only "Old Man," and it comes off pretty good, but in the final analysis "Old Man" is insufficient if it stands alone.) When the *connection* between the two stories that Faulkner was trying to bring about is grasped, the double-novel takes us to a much deeper level of meaning than if we tried to deal with each one by itself.

Now what are these two stories? They are pitched on entirely different levels. Faulkner gives us a little of one story, then a little of the other, piece by piece, one on top of the other, and I'll try to do something like this for our considerations. Suddenly, you realize that there's a real "counterpoint" at work (and "counterpoint" is the word Faulkner used to describe what he was trying to do in *The Wild Palms*). While they are pitched on two different levels, they have one fundamental thing in common: each is the story of a man and a woman thrown into situations where they are completely alone and isolated from the rest of the world, engulfed in a flood, a "tidal wave" that threatens to destroy them.

With a theme like *that,* we can be sure Faulkner is going to do something very basic! It's man's solitude, the story of the cosmic, existential solitude of man. Not just man-as-an-individual, but man in the *complete* sense; that is, man-and-woman, the complete human being. For "man" is never alone. The complete human being is man-and-woman: the message of Genesis. God made man in his own image, man-and-woman-he-created-them. What we have in this double-novel is a meditation on the first chapter of Genesis: the mystery of evil, sin, even a Genesis-type paradise theme, but Faulkner paints it with deeply ironic hues, a paradise-in-disaster from two levels of disaster. One goes deeper and deeper into despair; the other becomes more and more a story of hope. On the one hand are two modern, extremely vulnerable, and ultimately wrecked people; on the other, two totally indestructible people, the "tall convict" and the woman from Mississippi. In one sense, it is the old Faulkner contrast between city people and those less touched by modern civilization, but it is not simply that. The two utterly wrecked are modern bourgeois people, the other two are Mississippi woods people. One level is the modern, psychological, social novel; the other is on an almost preternatural level, becoming more and more myth. The thing that begins to emerge as Faulkner moves the two stories is that these mythologically cast woods people are even more real and human than the modern ones. *They're* the ones who are totally human! In them Faulkner seems to be presenting a sort of quintessential humanity: *they* are man-and-woman and the other two, the moderns, are simply a couple of poor, beat-up, ruined people.

So what Faulkner has going here is a very interesting story. But beyond that is the solitude of *man-and-woman*—man completely human—against destiny; and beyond that the many contrasts between two stories of two people facing destiny. Let's get into this fantastic Faulkner meditation by treating the two levels as he does, in a sort of counterpoint.

Behind the story in "Old Man" is a monastery, namely a penitentiary. The "tall convict" is out of his monastery because of the great 1927 Mississippi river flood. The convicts in the monastery-penitentiary are turned out to help in the disaster of the flood. The one idea, the one passion of the "tall convict" is to get back into that penitentiary and away from the woman who had been cast into his life by the flood. In the penitentiary everything was quiet, peaceful, and well ordered, no surprises, no great events. The tall convict and another one ("short, plump, hairless, quite white") are ordered out in a row boat to rescue a woman stranded in a tree and a man stranded on the roof of a cottonhouse. But one of them, the "tall convict," gets caught up alone in the rowboat and carried off in the currents of the flood, around in circles, getting bashed up at every turn. He rescues the woman by accident, coming up under the tree where she is perched, and she says simply, "You took a long time getting here"! Then they are swept off together in the rowboat, down one river, up another, since the rivers are running backward in the flood, and several times they are almost killed. On top of all this, the woman is pregnant and has her baby with the help of the "tall convict" on the top of an Indian mound covered with cottonmouth moccasins. They bathe the newborn with flood water from an old tin can and tie the umbilical cord with one of his shoestrings. They are then washed up and down the Mississippi, end up in Louisiana where they live for a time with some Cajun alligator hunters. By this time, the tall convict had been officially registered as dead, and so "free." But his one determination has always been to get back to the penitentiary. So after many months, with all these fantastic adventures up and down the floodwaters, he returns with the boat and woman and child and gives himself up to a sheriff, saying, "Yonder's your boat, and here's the woman. But I never did find that bastard on the cottonhouse"! A strange, fantastic story that Faulkner builds up with his tremendous description of the river and the two indestructable people in the boat. That is the level of "Old Man."

"The Wild Palms" story is quite different. It is not as the other a Mark Twain tall story, or a heroic story, rather just a sordid tale of modern, urban people. Faulkner pitches this one on the psychological level. An intern in New Orleans meets a married woman; they fall in love and decide that they are going to have the perfect life of love. It's going to be *love,* not marriage. Just *love.* The well-known modern pitch: "We are going to live in 'sin' for it does not matter what anybody says, we have one life to live come what may," etc., etc., etc. That is what they do, and you see as Faulkner builds the story up that they are wrecking themselves. This story begins with a charactertistic Faulkner twist of time sequences: the beginning of the story of "The Wild Palms" (in fact, the first scene in the book) is actually the *end* of the story of these two wrecked people.

It begins on a beach on the Gulf Coast. Two people (Harry and Charlotte) are in a run-down beach cabin. Faulkner lets us see them as driftwood washed up on the beach, through the eyes of their neighbor, a doctor who by his agent rented them the cabin. The doctor wonders who these people are, for they obviously have little money, appear to be trash, obviously not married, the woman "in them pants that was just exactly too little for her in just exactly the right places." At the end of this first section of "The Wild Palms" the man Harry comes to the neighbor, without knowing he's a doctor, seeking help, because the woman Charlotte is bleeding. The doctor goes to see about her and discovers that she is bleeding because of a failed abortion. And that is where Faulkner cuts off this story and begins the story in "Old Man" about the tall convict and the woman in the flood. But the beginning is that Charlotte is bleeding to death because she insisted that the intern she had been living with during the months recorded in other sections of "The Wild Palms" perform an abortion on her. He is reluctant but finally attempts it, makes a complete mess of it, and they rent a shanty on the Gulf Coast to wait out the consequences. In the last section of "The Wild Palms" Harry is sent to the same prison the "tall convict" finally gets back to after his adventures with the woman in the Mississippi flood. Faulkner moves the two stories in counterpoint, ending, so to speak, at the same station.

Now: the important thing about the way Faulkner moves these two stories together in a counterpoint is that the convict story is the account of the tremendous power of the river ("Old Man"), which becomes a kind of mythical, symbolic expression of the tragedy of life itself. It is Faulkner's expression in *symbolic terms* of the forces that have been let loose in the lives of these other, modern, bourgeois people in "The Wild Palms." Where the novel gets interesting is in the correspondence between the material on a cosmic scale in "Old Man" and the modern man and woman in "The Wild Palms" who are also engulfed in a flood, a deluge, a tragedy of their own making, but they don't realize it. They are typical, modern people who don't believe in anything, are convinced that death is the end of it, we live our lives since that's all there is. This is the basic faith of modern man! This is what people today think! I want to get something out of life before it's too late! This faith is what Faulkner's two-level novel finally torpedoes as he describes its shallowness and stupidity: *That's not the way to live!* People who try it let loose in their lives a titanic flood, a tremendous force, without even knowing what they are doing, without even knowing they are also in a "flood."

Reading these two stories together, you get from Faulkner a far more effective description of how these two modern people, with their modern faith, without realizing it are gradually destroying their lives by their own willfulness. On this level of the psychological, modern story, there are no "cosmic" events, yet we witness the meaning of the willfulness of this man and woman as we see it in counterpoint to Faulkner's cosmic descriptions of the tall convict and the woman in "Old Man." There are many, many correspondences. One example, the themes of life and death. On the one hand the fantastic birth story of the child in the flood on top of an old Indian mound and the baby living and thriving amidst all the events of the flood sweeping them from Vicksburg, Mississippi, to Louisiana and back again. And on the other level, the denial of life in the abortion of "The Wild Palms" which takes the woman's life (and the child's) and brings the man to the penitentiary. The novel as a unity is loaded with correspondences of this sort. That is why the two stories must be read together.

To read a book like this, to see how Faulkner refers things back and forth in counterpoint is a fantastic way of understanding life. In a certain sense, it's like a *meditation* on the Bible, or parts of the Bible. We know Faulkner was full of the Old Testament. Flood is an eschatological symbol, and Faulkner is saying that *our life* is like being in the flood. *We are in the deluge*. The novel is dominated by this eschatological deluge theme. Once you see it in the tall convict and the woman from Mississippi, the deluge which overwhelms Charlotte and Harry is seen more deeply, with more significance. On the near-mythological, Faulkner presents one level of dealing with the deluge in the episodes faced by the tall convict and the woman; on the other level, in the behavior of the two modern people who try to defy everything to live together for life and love alone. Faulkner is saying that *this too is the deluge!* Charlotte and Harry are living in it and don't know it—the counterpoint to the tall convict and woman in the flood of "Old Man." Charlotte and Harry have been judged by God; they are, so to speak, living under divine judgment and in disaster.

This is a great, as well as unique, statement for a modern writer to make. In fact Faulkner continually excels in saying things just like this. His novels and stories are far more prophetic in the Biblical sense than the writings of any theologian writing today (at least, any that I know!). Faulkner doesn't express himself in terms that can be easily used in the pulpit. O.K. But in *The Wild Palms,* as in other Faulkner meditations on life and nature (as in "The Bear"), I am convinced that we have before us a better idea about man and nature and values and God than can be found in the whole Spiritual Directory, and everything else on the Mystical Theology Shelf as well. That is why it seems to me so important to read *The Wild Palms* as a meditation.

Let's begin with the archetypical deluge in "Old Man" and read Faulkner's wonderful description of the convicts being removed from the penitentiary—which is actually more like a prison farm, no walls or fences, only guards with shotguns—and into the deluge of the 1927 Mississippi River flood. He describes how they get further and further into this void of the flooding river. They go by truck and by train to find themselves on a levee. Here they see water for miles in all directions, houses and buildings floating by, some convicts jump into the water and tear a barn apart until it disappears. Much of this section reminds you of a picture by Hieronymus Bosch: strange things happening—a plantation unaccountably burning in the middle of the flooding water, this flame going up and no human being there; just the flame in the middle of the water.

Faulkner creates an atmosphere with these apocalyptic signs. The convicts get deeper into the situation created by the flood and finally arrive on a levee for rescue work. Here, the tall convict becomes aware of the tremendous force of the *flow* of the water. Before that time, it had simply been a lot of water. Now, all of a sudden, in a manner typical of Faulkner, the tall convict realizes something more than just a lot of water. An immense *power* is at work!

The convicts arrive by train:

> Sometime after dark the train stopped. The convicts did not know where they were. They did not ask. They would no more have thought of asking where they were than they would have asked why and what for. They couldn't even see, since the car was unlighted and the windows fogged on the outside by rain and on the inside by the engendered heat of the packed bodies. All they could see was a milky and sourceless flick and glare of flashlights. They could hear shouts and commands, then the guards inside the car began to shout; they were herded to their feet and toward the exit, the ankle chains clashing and clanking.

> When they reached the top of the levee they could see the long line of khaki tents, interspersed with fires about which people—men, women and children, negro and white—crouched or stood among shapeless bales of clothing, their heads turning, their eyeballs glinting in the firelight as they looked quietly at the striped garments and the chains; further down the levee, huddled together too though untethered, was a drove of mules and two or three cows. Then the taller convict became conscious of another

sound. He did not begin to hear it all at once, he suddenly became aware that he had been hearing it all the time, a sound so much beyond all his experience and his powers of assimilation that up to this point he had been as oblivious of it as an ant or a flea might be of the sound of the avalanche on which it rides; he had been travelling upon water since early afternoon and for seven years now he had run his plow and harrow and planter within the very shadow of the levee on which he now stood, but this profound deep whisper which came from the further side of it he did not at once recognise. He stopped. The line of convicts behind jolted into him like a line of freight cars stopping, with an iron clashing like cars. "Get on!" a guard shouted.

"What's that?" the convict said. A negro man squatting before the nearest fire answered him:

"Dat's him. Dat's de Ole Man."

"The old man?" the convict said.

"Get on! Get on up there!" the guard shouted. They went on; they passed another huddle of mules, the eyeballs rolling too; the long morose faces turning into and out of the firelight; they passed them and reached a section of empty tents, the light pup tents of a military campaign, made to hold two men. The guards herded the convicts into them, three brace of shackled men to each tent.

They crawled in on all fours, like dogs into cramped kennels, and settled down. Presently the tent became warm from their bodies. Then they became quiet and then all of them could hear it, they lay listening to the bass whisper deep, strong and powerful. "The old man?" the train-robber convict said.

"Yah," another said. "He don't have to brag."

Then the tall convict sees the river by daylight:

At dawn the guards waked them by kicking the soles of the projecting feet. Opposite the muddy landing and the huddle of skiffs an army field kitchen was set up, already they could smell the coffee. But the taller convict at least, even though he had had but one meal yesterday and that at noon in the rain, did not move at once toward the food. Instead and for the first time he looked at the River within whose shadow he had spent the last seven years of his life but had never seen before; he stood in quiet and amazed surmise and looked at the rigid steel-colored surface not broken into waves but merely slightly undulant. It stretched from the levee on which he stood, further than he could see—a slowly and heavily roiling chocolate-frothy expanse broken only by a thin line a mile away as fragile in appearance as a single hair, which after a moment he recognised. *It's another levee*, he thought quietly. *That's what we look like from there. That's what I am standing on looks like from there.* He was prodded from the rear; a guard's voice carried forward: "Go on! Go on! You'll have plenty of time to look at that!"

This last is a very ironic sentence, because the tall convict is going to have plenty of experience with that river and what it's about before the story ends!

Now let's look back into these passages and consider the contrasts of the different kinds of tonality Faulkner employs. All these people are moving around almost mechanically, people turned out of their homes by the flood, hovering around fires, watching the convicts come in from the penitentiary. The convicts are also moving mechanically, like animals, into the tents. And in the midst of this picture of mechanical movement Faulkner paints for us, the tall convict suddenly becomes aware that there is *another level* of being. The river here is *being-itself*—and "being and becoming"—and all the jazz you can think of as "the metaphysical ground of life"! The tall convict "did not begin to hear it all at once, he suddenly became aware that he had been hearing it all the time, a sound so much beyond all his experience and his powers of assimilation that up to this point he had been as oblivious of it as an ant or a flea might be of the sound of the avalanche on which it rides . . ."! This is an awakening, a realization, and enlightenment!—which Faulkner excels in recording! It is a kind of existential description of what happens to people in real life: all of a sudden you are fifty-two (or however many) years old, you wake up to find this immense roar that has been going on under your feet *all the time! Now,* everything is moving! And way over *there* is a little thin line; and where *you're standing* . . . well! that's what it looks like from there! "a slowly and heavily roiling chocolate-frothy expanse broken only by a thin line a mile away as fragile in appearance as a single hair, which after a moment he recognised. *It's another levee,* he thought quietly. *That's what we look like from there. That's what I am standing on looks like from there.*" Everything seemed so solid and real and dependable and suddenly . . . swoosh! . . . you find yourself suspended . . . "as fragile in appearance as a single hair . . ."

And remember also: this is a tremendous statement of something that happens not just to individuals but to the human race. When? Well, toward the end of the Middle Ages, for example. As if all of a sudden, the whole picture changed and Western man found that things weren't nearly as solid and definite as they had been before. The earth was not the center of the cosmos, with all those concentric circles around it and God exactly seven miles up. Moreover, what Faulkner is talking about in these passages is not the archaic world of "The Bear." It is the world of Pascal, the world of infinite spaces, of a void, and neither you nor anyone else knows where it's going.

Then there is the account of the convicts moving along in their clanking chains, when suddenly the tall one stops and they all have to stop like cars in a freight train but nobody knows why they stop. But the Negro knows why and answers his question immediately: The tall convict asks, "What's that?" and the Negro says, "Dat's him. Dat's de Ole Man." Again, different levels of *being*. The primitives are the ones who are aware of the nature of things, while the more civilized people, the guards and white convicts move along mechanically on their line, not aware of it. But later on, settled down in their tents, they all become aware of it. One of them resents the river's bragging: "Then they became quiet and then all of them could hear it, they lay listening to the bass whisper deep, strong and powerful. 'The old man?' the train-robber convict said. 'Yah,' the other said. 'He dont have to brag.'"

The "tall convict" and another ("short, plump, hairless, quite white") are ordered into a rowboat to pick up two people stranded in the flood—a man on a cottonhouse and a woman in a cypress snag. Almost immediately, they are separated, the tall convict swept along in the rushing floodwaters but hidden in the rowboat from the other, who reports him drowned to the warden of the penitentiary. Let's pick up the story where the tall convict is clinging to the rowboat and oar as they are tossed around in the current:

> Things had moved too fast for him. He had not been warned, he had felt the first snatching tug of the current, he had seen the skiff begin to spin and his companion vanish violently upward like in a translation out of Isaiah, then he himself was in the water, struggling against the drag of the paddle which he did not know still held each time he fought back to the surface and grasped at the spinning skiff which at one instant was ten feet away and the next poised above his head as though about to brain him, until at last he grasped the stern, the drag of his body becoming a rudder to the skiff, the two of them, man and boat and with the paddle perpendicular above them like a jackstaff, vanishing from the view of the short convict (who had vanished from that of the tall one with the same celerity in a vertical direction) like a tableau snatched offstage intact with violent and incredible speed.
>
> He was now in the channel of a slough, a bayou, in which until today no current had run probably since the old subterranean outrage which had created the country.

Typical! But bad geology. Faulkner geology has nothing to do with the geology of Mississippi, which is not the result of igneous rock being pushed up and down but of a flat sea bottom being eroded. Geologically, there was no "subterranean outrage"! But you can see how it fits into the picture Faulkner is painting for us. Just try to grasp the implications he would have us consider when he regards the origin of all this as a "subterranean outrage"!

> There was plenty of current in it now though; from his trough behind the stern he seemed to see the trees and sky rushing past with vertiginous speed, looking down at him between the gouts of cold yellow in lugubrious and mournful amazement. But they were fixed and secure in something; he thought of that, he remembered in an instant of despairing rage the firm earth fixed and founded strong and cemented fast and stable forever by the generations of laborious sweat, somewhere beneath him, beyond the reach of his feet, when, and again without warning, the stern of the skiff struck him a stunning blow across the bridge of his nose. The instinct which had caused him to cling to it now caused him to fling the paddle into the boat in order to grasp the gunwale with both hands just as the skiff pivoted and spun away again. With both hands free he now dragged himself over the stern and lay prone on his face, streaming with blood and water and panting, not with exhaustion but with that furious rage which is terror's aftermath.

I dare say that this is an admirable description of a man being beaten up by his own boat in a flood! But more than that, we must consider the implications Faulkner is trying to get before us! The picture is not one simply of a man getting beat up and tossed around in a flood. Rather, *this is life!* This is the way life goes! And there are times (including the monastic life!) when we know life gets to be exactly like the deluge Faulkner gives us here.

My notion is that this particular deluge journey is close to what is called a mystical *navigatio*. It's like the *Navigatio Sancti Brendani*—the navigation of St. Brendan—during which he goes to those fabulous mythical islands.

2

Now that we're into *The Wild Palms,* let's try to get some impression of the *two layers of being* Faulkner superimposes one on top of the other, by the way he moves these two stories. One thing that comes through in each of the stories is his use of an element of nature to create a special kind of atmosphere. Maybe we should call it a "double element." In "The Wild Palms," air; in "Old Man," water. Water, we all know, is a very ambiguous element: life and death, as the liturgy has it. Baptism is both death and life. And while Faulkner was not being explicitly Christian here, it is clear that the deluge in "Old Man" is symbolic of life and death. For in the midst of this deluge by water, the tall convict meets the woman perched in a tree trying to escape the flood. She is pregnant, the two are swept madly back and forth, wholly unable to help themselves. Just as she is about to have the baby—and he's ready to "ditch" her, but he knows he can't—the flood dumps them on an Indian mound sticking up above the water, which Faulkner pictures as one of superabundant life: everything that can swim is on it, deer, water moccasins, rabbits, chipmunks, living together in the deluge. It is Isaiah's description of the eschatological kingdom, the "end of the world," dangerous and menacing animals living together in peace, not in a man-made zoo but on an old Indian mound and, in the midst of this deluge comes new life, a human being. It is almost a kind of virgin birth, for no one knows about the father, he's totally irrelevant to the point that the woman gives birth to the child, miraculously, in a flood on a strange, eschatological mound. A shattering thing! Without giving this any explicit Christian message, Faulkner does present us with an eschatological event, *a renewal of life in the midst of the deluge*. And the convict realizes that he is involved in this great renewal.

This must be put in counterpoint, as Faulkner does, to the totally sterile, windy hospital where everything is spic and span—the symbol of death with the element of wind and air and their sounds in "The Wild Palms." The title itself suggests the palm tree outside Harry's jail cell where he is imprisoned following the death of Charlotte. The rattling of the dry palm in the wind creates—with the use of the sounds in the hospital where Charlotte is dying because of the abortion aimed at life—a fantastic *atmosphere of guilt!* By merely suggesting the sounds in the hospital, Faulkner is able to convey the picture of Harry, who exhibits no expression of sadness, dejection, or despair. Faulkner gives us merely the *sounds* which are going on around Harry—sounds of wind, of air in movement— and somehow or other the sounds are so real that *we* are put in the other's place, in Harry's place. Now, it's *our* guilt because we have identified so completely with the sound enveloping Harry in the hospital. We have in ourselves this awful feeling of desolation created by Faulkner's description of the wind blowing up the seashore and into the hospital, and later into the jail. This is one of the best things ever written by Faulkner!

There are many other counterpoints in *The Wild Palms* which symbolize life and death. On one level, the birth of the child in the utterly impossible environment of the flood on the Indian mound, surrounded by all kinds of animals and reptiles, with nothing of use to aid in the birth but a tin can and the fire and hot water and the convict's shoestring: here, the symbol of life. On the other level, the absence of life in the totally sterile, windy hospital, the woman dying because she insisted willfully on an operation which strikes directly at life: here, the symbol of death. You can work out here other fantastic correspondences between two levels of life and death.

And from another angle, *The Wild Palms* presents contrasting notions, or two levels, of man-and-woman destined to be part of each other as "one body." For Harry and Charlotte, sexual fulfillment was obviously not enough to make them "one body" that is, fully human. It gets them nowhere, and in the end Charlotte continues only as a "neutral reality" or memory. There is no renewal for Harry, just a prolonged "enduring (*"between grief and nothing I will take grief"*). On the other level, there is no sexual relationship between the tall convict and the woman, yet between them is the birth of the child presented as a renewal amidst all the scenes of destruction caused by the deluge. Perhaps because of his own acceptance of responsibility for the woman and the child, the tall convict is renewed also.

Now let's look a bit closer at a few more of the texts to bring out these contrasts. The tall convict is again beaten flat on his face in the rowboat by the floodwaters:

> This time he did not get up at once. He lay flat on his face, slightly spread-eagled and in an attitude almost peaceful, a kind of abject meditation. He would have to get up sometime, he knew that, just as all life consists of having to get up sooner or later and then having to lie down again sooner or later after a while. And he was not exactly exhausted and he was not particularly without hope and he did not especially dread getting up. It merely seemed to him that he had accidentally been caught in a situation in which time and environment, not himself, was mesmerised; he was being toyed with by a current of water going nowhere, beneath a day which would wane toward no evening; when it was done with him it would spew him back into the comparatively safe world he had been snatched violently out of and in the meantime it did not much matter just what he did or did not do. So he lay on his face, now not only feeling but hearing the strong quiet rustling of the current on the underside of the planks, for a while longer. Then he raised his head and this time touched his palm gingerly to

his face and looked at the blood again, then he sat up onto his heels and leaning over the gunwale he pinched his nostrils between thumb and finger and expelled a gout of blood and was in the act of wiping his fingers on his thigh when a voice slightly above his line of sight said quietly, "It's taken you a while," and he who up to this moment had had neither reason nor time to raise his eyes higher than the bows looked up and saw, sitting in a tree and looking at him, a woman.

A beautiful section! No one wrote like this before the movies! You can see this thing being filmed, with orders from the director about camera angles, zooming in on the man spitting blood, the woman in the tree . . . (As a matter of fact, "Old Man" was on TV not long ago. I didn't see it, of course! But I've heard it was pretty good. But the book is better!) The convict gets the woman into the boat, still determined to pick up his partner, get the woman and boat back to the authorities so he can return to the penitentiary. But immediately they are swept madly away into the Yazoo River, which in the flood is running backward, not, as he thinks, toward, but away from Vicksburg. Then, the tidal wave:

> And he was not alarmed now either because there was not time, for although the visibility ahead, for all its clarity, did not extend very far, yet in the next instant to the hearing he was also seeing something such as he had never seen before. This was that the sharp line where the phosphorescent water met the darkness was now about ten feet higher than it had been an instant before and that it was curled forward upon itself like a sheet of dough being rolled out for a pudding. It reared, stooping; the crest of it swirled like the mane of a galloping horse and, phosphorescent too, fretted and flickered like fire. And while the woman huddled in the bows, aware or not aware the convict did not know which, he (the convict), his swollen and bloodstreaked face gaped in an expression of aghast and incredulous amazement, continued to paddle directly into it. Again he simply had not had time to order his rhythm-hypnotised muscles to cease. He continued to paddle though the skiff had ceased to move forward at all but seemed to be hanging in space while the paddle still reached thrust recovered and reached again; now instead of space the skiff became abruptly surrounded by a welter of fleeing debris—planks, small buildings, the bodies of drowned yet antic animals, entire trees leaping and diving like porpoises above which the skiff seemed to hover in weightless and airly indecision like a bird above a fleeing countryside, undecided where to light or whether to light at all, while the convict squatted in it still going through the motions of paddling, waiting for an opportunity to scream. He never found it. For an instant the skiff seemed to stand erect on its stern and then shoot scrabbling and scrambling up the curling wall of water like a cat, and soared on above the licking

crest itself and hung cradled into the high actual air in the limbs of a tree, from which bower of new-leafed boughs and branches the convict, like a bird in its nest and still waiting his chance to scream and still going through the motions of paddling though he no longer even had the paddle now, looked down upon a world turned to furious motion and in incredible retrograde.

From this point on, he hasn't even a paddle. On the Indian mound, he picks up a board, which he loses, and then tries to burn a tree limb into the shape of an oar. But this gives you some idea of what it's like to be on a Mississippi River flood.

Then they reach the mound; he's carrying the woman up, and she's ready to have the baby:

"Let me down!" she cried. "Let me down!" But he held her, panting, sobbing, and rushed again at the muddy slope; he had almost reached the flat crest with his now violently unmanageable burden when a stick under his foot gathered itself with thick convulsive speed. *It was a snake,* he thought as his feet fled beneath him and with the indubitable last of his strength he half pushed and half flung the woman up the bank as he shot feet first and face down back into that medium upon which he had lived for more days and nights than he could remember and from which he himself had never completely emerged, as if his own failed and spent flesh were attempting to carry out his furious unflagging will for severance at any price, even that of drowning, from the burden with which, unwitting and without choice, he had been doomed. Later it seemed to him that he had carried back beneath the surface with him the sound of the infant's first mewling cry.

Now there's a child born into the world. The tall convict still wants to leave the woman and return to the penitentiary, but he doesn't. He knows he cannot, regardless of how badly he wants to. (This is the end of a section of "Old Man," which is followed by a terrible section of "The Wild Palms"—a mine in Utah, scenes in San Antonio and New Orleans. It becomes clear that Harry has bungled the abortion demanded by Charlotte, so "I will be all right and it will be us again forever and ever.")

Then, back to the tall convict, the woman and the child. He's trying to light a fire:

When he returned with the wood and the dead rabbit, the baby, wrapped in the tunic, lay wedged between two cypress-knees and the woman was not in sight, though while the convict knelt in the mud, blowing and nursing his meagre flame, she came slowly and weakly from the direction of the water. Then, the water heated at last and there produced from some where he was never to know, she herself perhaps never to know until the need comes, no woman perhaps ever to know, only no woman will even wonder, that square of something somewhere between sackcloth and silk—squatting, his own wet garments steaming in the fire's heat, he watched her bathe the child with a savage curiosity and interest that became amazed unbelief, so that at last he stood above them both, looking down at the tiny terra-cotta colored creature resembling nothing, and thought, *And this is all. This is what severed me violently from all I ever knew and did not wish to leave and cast me upon a medium I was born to fear, to fetch up at last in a place I never saw before and where I do not even know where I am.*

What is the tall convict saying? With Faulkner, you know, half of it is music. But the convict suddenly realizes, "I've gone through all this, I've been brought here because of this little thing that looks like a piece of clay!" A tremendous religious message, a fantastic statement about providence. Faulkner has brought us, with the convict and the woman, through all these wild experiences in floods and tidal waves, beaten continually by the rowboat, to the Indian mound and the cottonmouth mocassins, a baby born with only a tin can and shoestrings . . . *for what?* That somehow God—or providence—wanted this child to be born and safe! God will go to all this trouble for one little bit of human flesh, one bit of life! The convict sees this when, so to speak, an enlightenment comes to him about the whole experience, the meaning of reality, what *life* is in God's sight: it is worth all this trouble that a child might be born and be safe: "looking down at the tiny terra-cotta colored creature resembling nothing, and thought, *And this is all. This is what severed me violently from all I ever knew and did not wish to leave and cast me upon a medium I was born to fear, to fetch up at last in a place I never saw before and where I do not even know where I am.*

This level of Faulkner's meditation on life we must hold in counterpoint to death in "The Wild Palms." Here, the young, modern, urbanized, sophisticated, educated, and talented woman wants neither the trouble of childbirth nor, more importantly, the implications of children in her relationship with her lover. To perform an abortion is easy—Harry had been an intern, he had successfully performed the operation on another woman during their stay at the mining camp in Utah. Here with Charlotte and Harry the resistance to life is seen in counterpoint to the affirmation of life in the birth scene in "Old Man." Faulkner makes here (and in 1938, remember!) a precise statement about the world we live in. It is a judgment on modern society and modern man. Say only, the birth control issue—and we may as well face up to it, there is going to be a lot of fuss in the next few years about the issue of birth control. At the moment, let's not pass judgment, but simply record the tremendous swing in progress toward a wholly different point of view about life than the one Faulkner is making in *The Wild Palms*. What is being argued is the difference between the "person" and "nature," and the judgment is going down more and more on the side of "person" against "nature." There is certainly an element of this in Charlotte's argument. Moreover, I know Catholic women who argue solemnly about a time when the differences between the sexes may be eliminated by some kind of biological stroke. In other words, it's not simply that women become "equal" to men, it's that women refuse to be held down by what they call a "binary life-style." Faulkner takes the other view: here is life, given by God. Here is death. Man doesn't inflict death: *Thou shalt not kill!*

O.K. Let's get further into these contrasts seen in "The Wild Palms," the hospital where Charlotte is dying, for here we have those elements (and sounds) of air and wind in counterpoint to the water of "Old Man." Harry is waiting in one of the corridors of the hospital; in the operating room the doctors are trying to save Charlotte's life. Harry is with an officer, who talks to him, goes in and out for a smoke . . . that sort of thing. They wait and wait, nothing much really "happens," except that they keep on waiting. And listening. And we listen to Faulkner's description of the noises, the sounds. This first section is a description of what it is like to be in a hospital:

> "Yes," Wilbourne said. There was no wind in here, no sound of it, though it seemed to him that he could smell, if not the sea, at least the dry and stubborn lingering of it in the oyster shells in the drive:

Now this idea of the smell of low tide is very important here: the tragic miasma, the smell of evil, which is the source of the tragic disaster and the punishment of the gods, symbolized by the low-tide smell, this awful sense of a completely rotten existence that comes when the wind blows ashore. The passage continues:

> and then suddenly the corridor became full of sound, the myriad minor voices of human fear and travail which he knew, remembered—the carbolised vacuums of linoleum and rubber soles like wombs into which human beings fled before something of suffering but mostly of terror, to surrender in little monastic cells all the burden of lust and desire and pride, even that of functional independence, to become as embryos for a time yet retaining

still a little of the old incorrigible earthy corruption—the light sleeping at all hours, the boredom, the wakeful and fretful ringing of little bells between the hours of midnight and the dead slowing of dawn (finding perhaps at least this good use for the cheap money with which the world was now glutted and cluttered); this for a while, then to be born again, to emerge renewed, to bear the world's weight for another while as long as courage lasted.

Very ironic: the hospital room is a kind of womb where people go to be reborn. But what kind of rebirth? Certainly not a spiritual rebirth! Rather, a kind of mechanical thing—in and out, mechanically, of the hospital rooms. The passage which follows is where Faulkner is so good with the particular sounds of the hospital:

> He could hear them up and down the corridor—the tinkle of the bells, the immediate sibilance of rubber heels and starched skirts, the querulous murmur of voices about nothing. He knew it well: and now still another nurse came down the hall, already looking full at him, slowing as she passed, looking at him, her head turning as she went on like an owl's head, her eyes quite wide and filled with something beyond just curiosity and not at all shrinking or horror, going on.

Quite a picture! With it, Faulkner puts *you* in the man's position. Harry sees the nurse looking at him and then, you suddenly realize: that's *me* she's looking at! The nurse is looking right at *me! I've* done this horrible thing! Harry watches the door of the operating room:

> Again the door went inward on its rubber tires and returned, clapped silently to with that iron finality and that illusion of iron impregnability which was so false since even from here he could see how it swung in its frame by one side only, so that a child, a breath, could move it. "Listen," the officer said. "Just take it easy. They'll fix her up. That was Doc Richardson himself."

Trying to console him, the officer tells Harry some long tale about the doctor they had just glimpsed in the operating room. Then:

> Wilbourne discovered that he really could smell the sea, the black shallow slumbering Sound without surf which the black wind blew over. Up the corridor, beyond an elbow, he could hear the voices of two nurses, two nurses not two patients, two females but not necessarily two women even, then beyond the same elbow one of the little bells tinkled, fretful, peremptory, the two voices murmuring on, then they both laughed, two nurses laughing not two women, the little querulous bell becoming irascible and frenzied, the laughter continuing for half a minute longer above the bell,

then the rubber soles on the linoleum, hissing faint and fast; the bell ceased. It was the sea he smelled; there was the taste of the black beach the wind blew over in it, in his lungs, up near the top of his lungs, going through that again but then he had expected to have to, each fast strong breath growing shallower and shallower as if his heart had at last found a receptacle, a dumping-place, for the black sand it dredged and pumped at: and now he got up too, not going anywhere; he just got up without intending to, the officer at the entrance turning at once, snapping the cigarette backward.

Faulkner identifies Harry with the harbor. It's *low tide* for Harry too. He can't breathe. Charlotte is dying, and he is dying with her because they have been living in this sort of symbiotic relationship. The two of them tried to become a sort of "one-body" by losing each self in the other, and ended by destroying each of them.

The officer comes back:

But Wilbourne made no further move and the officer slowed; he even paused at the light-slashed door and flattened his hat-brim against it, against the crack for a moment. Then he came on. He came on, because Wilbourne saw him; he saw the officer as you see a lamp post which happens to be between you and the street because the rubber-tired door had opened again, outward this time (*The Kliegs are off,* he thought. *They are off. They are off now.*) and the two doctors emerged, the door clashing soundlessly to behind them and oscillating sharply once but opening again before it could have resumed, re-entered immobility, to produce two nurses though he saw them only with that part of vision which still saw the officer because he was watching the faces of the two doctors coming up the corridor and talking to one another in clipped voices through their mouth-pads, their smocks flickering neatly like the skirts of two women, passing him without a glance and he was sitting down again because the officer at his elbow said, "That's right. Take it easy," and he found that he was sitting, the two doctors going on, pinch-waisted like two ladies, the skirts of the smocks snicking behind them, and then one of the nurses passed too, in a face-pad also, not looking at him either, her starched skirts rustling on, he (Wilbourne) sitting on the hard bench, listening: so that for a moment his heart evacuated him, beating strong and slow and steady but remote, leaving him globed in silence, in a round vacuum where only the remembered wind murmured, to listen in, for the rubber soles to sibilate in, the nurse stopping at last beside the bench and now he looked up after a space.

"You can go now," she said.

This is a terrific scene! Think about the noises! These are noises you don't hear in the hospital *rooms*—the noises of feet and skirts flicking, starched coats of doctors, starched skirts of nurses . . . You hear these ominous sounds when you're on the operating table getting ready to be anesthetized! Another indication by Faulkner of the symbiotic relationship between Harry in the corridor and Charlotte in the operating room. On the floor of the operating room, there is only empty space—no beds and things like that to deaden the sound. Rather, wide corridors and people moving around; rubber-tired things going by, rubber-soled shoes, etc. I can tell you, that's where you hear that kind of sound—when you're out flat just before they begin to chop you up! That's what is associated with this particular series of sounds Faulkner is describing. You're on the operating table, you're helpless, full of dope, not yet out, but lying there unable to move even if you wanted to. You're drugged. All you can do is lie there and hear these sounds floating in. You don't sit up and look around. You lie there and hear these sounds and see these faces and wonder when they're going to knock you out completely! That's the kind of atmosphere by sounds Faulkner gets into the situation.

Then, there is a bit where Harry goes and looks at Charlotte's body as they take her out:

> There was no especial shape beneath the sheet now at all and it came onto the stretcher as if it had no weight either. The stretcher whispered into motion again, wheeling sibilantly, sucking through the door again when the officer now stood with his hat in his hand. Then it was gone. He could hear it for a moment longer. Then he could not. The nurse reached her hand to the wall, a button clicked and the hum of the blower stopped. It cut short off as if it had run full-tilt into a wall, blotted out by a tremendous silence which roared down upon him like a wave, a sea, and there was nothing for him to hold to, picking him up, tossing and spinning him and roaring on, leaving him blinking steadily and painfully at his dry granulated lids. "Come," the nurse said. "Doctor Richardson says you can have a drink."

What stands out in that passage? Yes, "the tremendous silence which roared down upon him like a wave, a sea . . ." Faulkner brings in the image of the tidal wave again, but completely a *mental* tidal wave hitting Harry like the *physical* tidal wave which carried away the tall convict and the woman in "Old Man." Harry is completely shattered by this wave, his world has collapsed. They have taken out the body of Charlotte, and he's left with nothing.

Listen! The importance of marking well these Faulkner passages is that we are listening to *a writer who knows how to write,* who knows what to do with words! It's good to have that once in a while! We get this sort of thing with words in the Bible and a few other places, but most of the time we are not in the presence of such power and creativity with words.

Well. To close out. Harry is now in a jail. Again, the element of wind:

> The jail was somewhat like the hospital save that it was of two storeys, square, and there were no oleanders. But the palm was there. It was just outside his window, bigger, more shabby; when he and the officer passed beneath it to enter, with no wind to cause it it had set up a sudden frenzied clashing as though they had startled it, and twice more during the night while he stood, shifting his hands from time to time as that portion of the bars which they clasped grew warm and began to sweat on his palms, it clashed again in that brief sudden inexplicable flurry. Then the tide began to fall in the river and he could smell that too—the sour smell of salt flats where oyster shells and the heads of shrimp rotted, and hemp and old piling. Then dawn began (he had been hearing the shrimp boats putting out for some time) and he could see the draw bridge on which the railroad to New Orleans crossed standing suddenly against the paling sky and he heard the train from New Orleans and watched the approaching smoke then the train itself crawling across the bridge, high and toylike and pink like something bizarre to decorate a cake with, in the flat sun that was already hot. Then the train was gone, the pink smoke. The palm beyond the window began to murmur, dry and steady, and he felt the cool morning breeze from the sea, steady and filled with salt, clean and iodinic in the cell above the smell of creosote and tobacco-spit and old vomit; the sour smell of the flats went away and now there would be a glitter on the tide-chopped water, the gars roiling sluggishly up and then down again among the floating garbage. Then he heard feet on the stairs and the jailer entered with a tin mug of coffee and a piece of factory-made coffee cake. "You want anything else?" he said. "Any meat?"

What has Harry been doing? He stood all night at the window of his jail cell, hanging onto the bars. The tide has gone down, he has gone down. But then the tide comes back in again, the fresh morning breeze with it, and you sense that life is coming back into Harry. You get the sense of this man standing all night at the window of his cell, *dead*. Then he comes back to life with the return of morning. Death and resurrection, in a way. There is an interlude where some bizarre things happen—his trial, a chance to commit suicide which he rejects and instead embraces the monastic life of a penitentiary.

As I said at the beginning, one theme of *The Wild Palms* is, in a way, monastic vocations. Or rather, two of them. The one Harry decides for is certainly not the highest kind, but he does decide for it. And what does he determine? To grieve. His last words are *"between grief and nothing I will take grief"!* He will spend the rest of his life grieving: another death and resurrection motif. Harry seems to recover his own autonomy, his own freedom, which perhaps he had lost with Charlotte because they were so completely submerged in each other, so completely trying to be lost in the other, that they could end up only destroying each other.

This is something Faulkner obviously has in mind: the man-and-woman relationship—which is to say, what it is *to be human*—can never be a completely symbiotic thing. When two people become wholly submerged in each other, it is destruction, not love—which is the counterpoint to the story of the convict and the woman in "Old Man."

So much for *The Wild Palms* as Faulkner's meditation on two men and two women, tidal waves, deaths and resurrections, ending, in whatever one wants to make of it, a sort of monastic vocation in a Mississippi penitentiary.

INDEX

"Prince of Darkness" (Powers), 149
"Prisoner, The" (R. Maritain), 308
Prison Letters of Dietrich Bonhoeffer, 88
Pritchett, V. S., 119, 148
"Problem of Symbolism, The" (Danielou), 332n
Prometheus (Aeschylus), 95
Proclus, 399
"Prophetic Ambiguities: Milton and Camus" (Merton), 252–260
Prophetic Books (Blake), 405, 406, 409, 410, 413, 424, 428, 432
"Prospectus of Writings" (Louisville authors), 381n, 383
Proust, Marcel, 44, 118, 466
"Proverb of Hell" (Blake), 447
Proverbs, 88, 149
Psalter (150 psalms), 19, 30, 327–37
Psychiatry, 365n
Ptolemy, 420
Public Address (Blake), 413
Pugin (the younger), 470, 471
Pythagoras, 100, 419

Quasimodo, Salvatore, xv
Quilliot, Roger, 92n
Quintillian, 437

Rabelais, François, 32, 467
Racine, Jean Baptiste, 145, 146
"Rafael Alberti and His Angels" (Merton), xv, 313n
Rahner, Hugo, 114n
Rahner, Karl, 88
Raids on the Unspeakable (Merton), xvi, 124n, 159n, 371n
Rancé, Abbé Armand-Jean de, 276
Ransom, John Crowe, xii, 462–63
Raphael, 393, 394, 396, 403, 411
Read, Herbert, 468
Real Blake, The (E. J. Ellis), 452
Rebel, The (Camus), 235ff, 298
Reflections on the Painting and Sculpture of the Greeks (Winckelmann), 402, 453
Reinhardt, Ad, xii, 146
Re Joyce (Burgess), 13n
Religious Trends in English Poetry (Fairchild), 479–80
Rembrandt van Rijn, 408, 409, 438
Renegade, The (Camus), 183, 210, 277, 278–81, 285
"Réponse à E d'Astier" (Camus), 234n, 247n
Republic (Plato), 374, 439, 453, 472, 473
Requiem for a Nun (Faulkner), 92, 93, 120, 123, 185
Responsibility of the Artist, The (Maritain), 366n

"Restoration of the Pictures, The" (R. Maritain), 308
Revue des Cours et Conferences (Paris), 422n
Reynolds' Discourses (Blake), 433
Reynolds, Joshua, 396, 402, 403, 403n, 404, 412, 413, 423, 432n, 433, 433n, 440, 440n, 448, 449n, 450, 450n
Rice, Edward, xii
"Richard Brothers" (Gordon), 417n
Richardière, G. Boucher de la, 415n, 452
Richards, I. A., 453, 462
Richardson (Sanskritist), 414
Richardson, Samuel, 395, 402
Rilke, Rainer Maria, xiii, xv, 30–33, 58, 61, 314, 346, 497
Rimbaud, Arthur, 141, 255, 270, 310, 346, 361, 375
Rivera, Diego, 321
Robbe-Grillet, Alain, 141, 142, 144, 145
Robertson, W. Graham, 452
Robinson, Crabb, 395, 410n, 413, 417, 434, 434n, 437n, 438, 438n, 440n, 453
Rockefeller Center Weekly, xii
Roman Missal, 330n
Romans, Letter to the, 19, 331n, 333n, 335n
Romanticism and the Gothic Revival (Addison), 470–71
Romney, George, 397, 399
Roosevelt, Theodore, 306
Rosa, Salvator, 437
Roualt, Georges, 308, 357
Rousseau, Jean Jacques, 400, 402
Rowlandson, Thomas, 413
Rubens, Peter Paul, 393, 396, 403
Ruskin, John, 471
Russell, Archibald, 395n, 453
Russell, Bertrand, 57
Ruysbroek, John, 346

Sacramentum Futuri (Danielou), 332n
Sacred Wood, The (T. S. Eliot), 452
Sadler, T., 410n, 453
Safe Conduct (Pasternak), 58, 69
Salinas, Pedro, 313
Salinger, Jerome D., 101
Sallust, 399
Sanctuary (Faulkner), 123
Sanders, Pharaoh, 383
Santayana, George, 462
Sartoris (Faulkner), 505
Sartre, Jean-Paul, xv, 24, 29, 68, 73, 119, 120, 123, 140, 141, 144, 161, 163, 185, 194, 216, 227, 234, 236, 241, 263, 268, 293, 380, 501
Satan, 4–11, 252–60, 296, 307, 477, 482
Saturday Review, 252n
Saurat, Denis, 398, 398n, 401, 401n, 413, 414, 415, 419, 453